HEGEL'S *AESTHETICS*

Silenus with the Infant Bacchus
(*The Munich Faun commended by Hegel. See p. 202*)
Reproduced by courtesy of Staatliche Antikensammlungen und
Glyptothek, München

AESTHETICS

LECTURES ON FINE ART

BY

G. W. F. HEGEL

―――

Translated by T. M. Knox

―――

VOLUME I

CLARENDON PRESS · OXFORD

Oxford University Press, Walton Street, Oxford OX2 6DP
Oxford New York Toronto
Delhi Bombay Calcutta Madras Karachi
Petaling Jaya Singapore Hong Kong Tokyo
Nairobi Dar es Salaam Cape Town
Melbourne Auckland
and associated companies in
Berlin Ibadan

Oxford is a trade mark of Oxford University Press

Published in the United States
by Oxford University Press, New York

ISBN 0 19 824498 3

© Oxford University Press 1975

First published 1975
Reprinted 1988, 1991

Printed in Great Britain by
Antony Rowe Ltd,
Chippenham

TRANSLATOR'S PREFACE

HEGEL's lectures on Aesthetics have long been regarded as the most attractive of all the lectures which were published after his death, mainly from transcripts made by members of his audience. Their great strength and interest lies not in their main philosophical and historical thesis, but in what constitutes the bulk of these two volumes, namely the examples and illustrations drawn from India, Persia, Egypt, Greece, and the modern world, and in Hegel's comments on this detail. These comments on art, perhaps especially on painting and literature, must be fascinating to a student of art, however much he may wish to dissent from them. Consequently, although Hegel professes to be lecturing on the *philosophy* of Fine Art, and although the lectures have a philosophical background (explicitly expressed here and there, and especially in Part I), it is lovers of art and historians of art whom primarily they ought to interest. (Professional philosophers already have the dry bones of Hegel's philosophy of art in §§ 556–63 of his *Encyclopaedia of the Philosophical Sciences*—Eng. tr. by W. Wallace in *Hegel's Philosophy of Mind*.) If a reader finds points laboured with tedious prolixity, and if he is annoyed by repetitions, he must remember that he has in front of him something composed mainly from transcripts of lectures, and not something which Hegel had himself prepared for publication.

Apart from their philosophical background, the lectures have a historical framework (Symbolic, Classical, and Romantic Art) which may be disputable, especially because Hegel says himself that elements of the later forms appear in the earlier and vice versa. But what is still more difficult is Hegel's main thesis that not only has art a meaning but that we can now state in plain prose what that meaning is. That art has a meaning and that it reveals something transcending our everyday experience may be granted. But what that meaning and revelation is cannot be expressed otherwise than by the work of art itself. By professing to extract the meaning, Hegel is bound to conclude that art in the last resort is superfluous. If, as he thinks, Romantic art has the doctrines of the Christian religion as its content, then these are known

independently of art, and their expression by art is unnecessary
Although Hegel did feel that a new artistic development was
heralded in Germany by Goethe and Schiller, this does not seem
to have shaken his conviction that 'art for us is a thing of the past'.
His attempt, towards the end of vol. i, to show that art is after all
necessary may seem weak. He died in 1831 and, despite the closing
sentence of his Introduction, he had no inkling of the wonderful
efflorescence of European Art in the remainder of the nineteenth
century. If he had written a century later his pessimism might
have been more justifiable.

These lectures were edited by H. G. Hotho and appeared for the
first time in 1835 in three volumes of Hegel's collected works. A
second and revised edition appeared in 1842. Hotho's materials
were some of Hegel's own manuscript notes for his lectures and
transcripts of his lectures in 1823, 1826, and 1828–9. These Hotho
worked into a whole with great skill. He kept as close as possible
to Hegel, he says, but his aim was to produce a continuous text,
and this means that we cannot be sure in detail whether some of
the phraseology is his (rather than Hégel's), or whether incon-
sistencies are due to Hegel's changes of mind after 1823.

In 1931 Georg Lasson began to publish what was to be a completely new edition of the lectures. Owing to his death, the first
volume, *Die Idee und das Ideal* (Leipzig, 1931), had no successor.
It contains what in this translation is the Introduction and Part I.
Lasson's desire was to preserve every possible word of Hegel's;
he was dissatisfied with what he regarded as Hotho's modifications
of Hegel's *ipsissima verba*. His book (referred to below and elsewhere as 'Lasson') is based primarily on a reproduction of the
1826 lectures, supplemented occasionally by those of 1823, and
frequently by extracts from Hotho's printed edition. It does provide some material which Hotho had omitted, and I have included
in footnotes one or two extracts from it. In the main, however, the
impression left on the mind by this book is that Hotho did his
work brilliantly.

Lasson (p. 393) lamented the fact that Glockner had included
Hotho's first edition, and not the second, in his reprint of the
collected works. This determined me to make this translation from
Hotho's second edition. This edition is scarce, but it has now been
reprinted (Berlin and Weimar, 2 vols., 1965), edited by F. Bassenge
who has made some alterations and provided a truly magnificent

index to which I am much indebted. About his text, however, I have some misgivings. He never indicates his departures from the text of Hotho's second edition and sometimes even prints errors in the first edition although they were corrected in the second. And while he does correct some of the misprints in the second edition, he does not correct them all. For an ample bibliography of editions and translations of these lectures, and of studies on them, see *Hegel-Studien* 5 (Bonn, 1969), pp. 379–427.

These lectures were first translated by Ch. Bénard (5 vols., Paris, 1840–52). Although he omits some difficult passages, his version is faithful and often illuminating. I am in debt to it. I cannot say so much for the more recent French translation by S. Jankélévitch (4 vols., Paris, 1944), because while some of Bénard's omissions are made good, there are fresh ones. The translator resorts too often to paraphrase, and in general his version is too free to be faithful to Hegel. English translations began with W. M. Bryant who produced (New York, 1879) a translation of Part II of the lectures, partly from Bénard's French, and partly from Hotho's second edition. His work is not to be despised. In 1905 Bosanquet published a translation of Hegel's Introduction, superseding a partial translation by W. Hastie (1886). This is a model translation of Hegel and it has valuable footnotes. A complete English translation was made for the first time by F. P. B. Osmaston (4 vols., London, 1916–20).

My aim has been to supersede Osmaston's version. He seems to me to have made a large number of mistakes and to have been quite unnecessarily verbose. Moreover there are oddities, e.g. 'modern Platonists' for Neo-Platonists, and when Hegel mentions medieval portraits we do not expect to find them described as 'portraits of middle-aged men', and we may be surprised to read of Ariosto's 'raging Roland' or 'the correspondence of Horace'. However, I live in a glass house, and my own version cannot be beyond cavil. If others have paraphrased too much, I may have paraphrased too little, and some may think that I ought to have preserved more of Hotho's italics than I have. Errors I have doubtless made, but I have not omitted anything, so far as I know. At times my English may be more Hegelian than felicitous, because of my wish to be faithful to Hegel and to be as literal as possible; and where Hegel's enthusiasm leads to mixed metaphors, I have not unmixed them.

All the footnotes, and everything in square brackets in the text, are the translator's.

There are no notes to speak of in either the German texts or the French translations, but Bassenge's index does provide some material for annotation. Osmaston has notes, but all too often they are either unnecessary, or wrong, or unintelligible. My own notes will come in for criticism. I know that some of them must be amateurish where the subject matter is beyond the scope of my scholarship. The personal note audible in a few of them must be put down to my occasional need for some relief. One critic will complain that there are too many notes, while another will complain that there are too few. The former critic must reflect that not everyone can claim (I certainly cannot) to have at his command the range of knowledge evidenced in these lectures, and so, e.g., the notes on Greek and Latin literature, superfluous to a classical scholar, may not be unwelcome to another whose expertise is different. With the latter critic I have much sympathy, for while I have tried to identify all Hegel's references, some have escaped me. Moreover, what is required, and it is no credit to German scholarship that it has not yet been forthcoming, is annotation to place Hegel's discussion in the context of aesthetic discussions by his contemporaries and immediate seniors, and to identify far more of his allusions to German literature than I have been able to do.

Whatever the deficiencies in my notes, they would have been multiplied if I had not had the help of many scholars who have so generously come to my aid. One or two are mentioned in the notes, but I am especially indebted to Mr. Huntington Cairns, Professors B. Ashmole, A. J. Beattie, C. T. Carr, K. J. Dover, E. H. Gombrich, T. B. L. Webster, W. Witte, and T. E. Wright.

My debt is greatest to Professor Witte, not only for notes but also for help in many passages of the translation. For other passages in vol. i I am indebted also to Mr. T. J. Reed of St. John's College, Oxford, who went over several pages with meticulous care and saved me from many mistakes.

All errors and failures in the notes and the translation are to be laid to my charge alone. All these scholars are guiltless.

Hegel's terminology, however forbidding, is precise and rigid in his later published works, though not here. Those who take the trouble to understand it have little difficulty in following his thought. But it does create formidable difficulties for a translator. Some day, perhaps, someone who thinks in English will re-think Hegel's philosophy and its terminology and put it all into English— if indeed it be possible to put into a language framed by and for empiricism what Hegel calls 'speculative', i.e. really philosophical, thinking—but, until that day comes, some attempt must be made to accept and then explain Hegel's terminology and the outlook expressed in it. Therefore the following notes on (*a*) Hegel's fundamental outlook, and (*b*) some of his terms and their translation, may assist a reader unfamiliar with his work. It is unfortunate that his own introductory passages are so often obscure, because many things mentioned in them are clarified by the examples and illustrations which follow.

(*a*) Hegel's philosophy is a form of *idealism*. (Terms often used in the translation are italicized here.) In his view, what is ultimately real (or, in his terminology, what is *actual*) is the self-knowing spirit. This is not to deny *reality* to the world in which we live or to ourselves as *sensuous* beings, but, although these are real, they are not, taken in and by themselves, actual. What is actual is not the real, but the ideal, and Hegel's point might be put, in his own paradoxical manner, by saying that the ideal is more really real than the real. The ideal is the synthesis of concept and reality, or, in art, of meaning and shape. This synthesis is what Hegel calls the *Idea*. 'The Idea existent in sensible form is the Ideal, i.e. beauty, which itself is truth implicit' (G. R. G. Mure: *The Philosophy of Hegel*, London, 1965, p. 185). A deformed man is real, but, being deformed, is not an adequate 'embodiment' or 'realization' or 'existence' of the *Concept* or essential nature of man, and therefore is not 'actual'. Hegel's *Idea* is ultimately derived from the Platonic 'form' or 'idea', but it differs from Plato's by being a combination of concept with reality. It is not just an 'ideal', because, as Hegel would say, it is not so impotent as not also to exist.

The complete correspondence of concept and reality is not to be found anywhere in nature, or even in human beings in so far as they are bodies or sensuous beings. This is because things external to one another cannot completely correspond with concepts or categories which, as thoughts, form a whole internally interconnected. It is when man's mind has risen to self-consciousness as spirit that in spirit and its productions the oppositions between universal and particular, subject and object, ideal and real, divine and human, are ultimately *reconciled* in a concrete unity. Knowledge and fact may, at the intellectual level of natural science, be opposed to one another as universal to particular, but, when the fact known is man's spiritual self, knower and known become a unity in which the difference between the two is not expunged but retained and *mediated* or reconciled.

It is important to notice that the one essential route to man's knowledge of himself as spirit is through his knowledge of what is *other* than his true self, i.e. through knowledge and experience of living in what is opposite to him as man (i.e. in nature) or opposite to him as an individual (i.e. ultimately, in the state), and through being *reflected back* into himself out of this opposite or object. Hegel is fond of this metaphor. The eye does not see itself except through its reflection in a mirror. Consciousness becomes aware of itself by being aware of objects and then by being reflected back into itself from them.

The background of all this is theological (whatever may be thought of Hegel's theology): At first God thinks the thoughts or concepts which, particularized, or given embodiment or shape, are nature and man. In coming to know these concepts, man comes to know his own essence and so to consciousness of himself as self-conscious and self-knowing spirit. This is at the same time a consciousness of being united with God in a concrete unity, not vanished in him as happens, according to Hegel's interpretation, in some Eastern religions.

This logico-theological process is figurated in the characteristics of religion which Hegel regards as peculiarly Christian: God, the infinite spirit, is spirit only because he particularizes or embodies himself in a man (the Incarnation). As man, he endures all the pains of an earthly lot, even unto the 'infinite grief' of the Crucifixion, but he is raised from death in the Resurrection, and then elevated to glory in the Ascension. Before the infinite spirit can commune with itself as spirit it must become embodied or particularized in the finite, endure the pain of self-diremption (the harshness of the finite spirit's death), and then, and only then, rise to being self-conscious and infinite spirit.

From this it follows that the negative, the finite as the opposite and cancellation of the infinite, is a necessary factor or 'moment' in the infinite spirit itself. The Incarnation is necessary. In order to become infinite spirit, which it *implicitly* is from the start, the spirit must *negate* itself, *posit* itself as finite, and then, negating this negation (i.e. as 'infinite negativity') rise through Resurrection and Ascension to a concrete infinity, concrete because achieved through becoming particular and being enriched through it and arising out of it, while still comprehending it in itself.

This vision of the necessity of contradiction (or the negative), and the equal necessity of transcending this bare opposition and reconciling the negative with the positive, is the prerogative of *reason* as distinct from the Understanding. Where this Kantian distinction is clearly implied, *Verstand* and its derivatives are translated by 'Understanding' with a capital letter. Elsewhere *Verstand* is 'intellect' and *verständig* is even translated 'mathematical' in some architectural contexts.

For Hegel, the outlook of the Understanding, or the scientific intellect, is one for which oppositions and contradictions are absolute. The universal (e.g. a natural species) is indifferent to and outside the particulars (the universal 'apple' is an abstraction from and indifferent to all real apples), and this is an essential characteristic of all science. ('Science' here is used in the modern English sense in which 'science' is distinguished from 'arts'. In Hegel's *Wissenschaft* there is no such distinction, but unless the context indicates otherwise, he means by 'science' 'philosophy' or the procedure of reason instead of that of the Understanding.) Reason is not concerned with genera and species in a Linnaean classification, but only with the categories in which the concept or essence of natural life is particularized. These categories Hegel expounds in his *Philosophy of Nature*.

Everything in nature is finite, bounded by something else. But spirit is infinite. This conception of the infinite occurs frequently in these lectures, and it may need some explanation. A straight line prolonged indefinitely is an image of what Hegel calls the 'bad' infinite; the true infinite is better imaged as a circle, i.e. as a line which does not go on indefinitely but returns into itself. The infinite, for Hegel, is not the boundless, but the self-bounded. Spirit as self-conscious, is infinite because in self-consciousness subject and object coincide. Mere consciousness is limited by the objects of which it is conscious and therefore is finite. In *self*-consciousness this limitation vanishes. The stones forming a cairn have a unity in the cairn, but this is only an abstract and finite unity; the stones are indifferent to one another and are unaltered whether they are collected into a cairn or remain scattered on the hillside. The unity of lovers is quite different; it is a concrete and infinite unity because each of them is necessary to the other and is what he is because the other is; the unity of their love is constitutive of their very being.

(b) Hegel prided himself on having taught philosophy to speak German. He tries to use ordinary German words and to avoid technical and Latin terminology. It might seem, therefore, that ordinary German words could be translated directly into ordinary English. But this is not always so. Hegel imposes a technical sense of his own on some ordinary German words (e.g. *das Moment*, or *gesetzt*), but then he uses these words sometimes in his technical sense and sometimes in their ordinary sense. The translator must make up his mind whether one of these words is being used technically or ordinarily and adapt his translation accordingly. The same English word will not always suffice to render the same German word. This must be premissed to the following notes on some of the terms commonly used in these lectures.

Begriff is translated here by 'Concept' in technical passages, but I have often tried to bring out the meaning in English by writing 'essential nature', or even 'nature' or 'essence'. Hegel himself sometimes uses 'essence' as a synonym for 'Concept'. But his idealism must be kept in mind: for him, the essential nature of everything is a concept or thought. Other translators prefer 'notion' in English instead of 'Concept', but that is no more intelligible in English, and moreover it carries the suggestion of being something arbitrary or something not thought out, and this is the reverse of Hegel's meaning. 'Concept' does at least preserve, in its derivation, the idea of gripping together, on which Hegel insists in his use of *Begriff*.

Idee is translated 'Idea', with a capital letter; 'idea' without a capital is *Vorstellung*, i.e. 'whatsoever is the object of the understanding when a man thinks'.

Moment. In the neuter, this means feature, or factor, or element. But, following other translators (of Kant as well as Hegel), I have translated it by 'moment' in passages where I think that Hegel has in mind his technical use of the word to mean a stage essential in the development of the Concept or the Idea. Here the stages follow one another (logically, not temporally) in a necessary order, and the earlier are not left behind but retained in the later. An example is the series 'universal, particular, individual'. The second is the negative of the first; the third negates the second and so is positive (the negation of the negation or what Hegel calls 'infinite —or absolute—negativity') and a return to the first which is now thus given a content, i.e. is enriched by its particular. 'Phasal condition', one of Osmaston's renderings of *Moment*, seems to me to be neither German nor English.

Dasein and *Existenz*. Hegel distinguishes between these in his Logic, but since the distinction could be preserved in English only by circumlocution (and is not preserved in these lectures), I have translated both by 'existence'. It must be remembered, however, that 'existence' or 'existent' here always means an embodiment, something determinate or 'real' as opposed to 'ideal'. When some modern theologians say that 'God is beyond existence' etc., they appear to be using the word in this sense, as well as remembering Plato.

Realität—reality, in much the same sense as 'existence'. In the *Philosophy of Right*, for example, Hegel clearly distinguishes it from *Wirklichkeit*, which there means 'actuality'. But in these lectures this distinction is seldom used, and *Wirklichkeit* has its ordinary German sense of 'reality', and it has been so translated.

Moralität and *Sittlichkeit*. When Hegel is writing technically he distinguishes between these, though both words mean 'morality'. So distinguished, the first is 'morality' as something subjective or personal, i.e. conscientiousness, while the second is 'ethical life', objective and social, i.e. living conscientiously in accordance with custom or established institutions. This distinction is made in these lectures, but only rarely. Almost everywhere Hegel uses *sittlich* to mean what in English is covered by the blanket term 'moral', and it has been so translated.

unmittelbar, frequently used, is generally translated 'immediately' or 'directly'. In any case, this has nothing to do with time but means 'without an intermediary', or 'without the interposition of anything', or what something is at the start before its implicit nature becomes explicit through the negative process already described above.

gesetzt is one of Hegel's favourite words. It ordinarily means 'put' or 'set' or 'laid down', but sometimes I have had to follow other translators by adopting the awkward word 'posited'. Hegel uses it to mean 'given reality', in the sense of 'reality' mentioned above. It is sometimes in a way analogous to the English use of 'cashed' when, e.g., plain sense has to be given to what a metaphor is supposed to convey.

sinnlich—'sensuous' represents Hegel's meaning, but it is unnatural English in many contexts, and therefore 'perceptible' has been used occasionally. 'Sensuous' is opposed to 'intellectual'. A sensuous man, in Hegel's meaning, is simply a man who uses his five senses, or who 'perceives' rather than 'thinks'.

Absolut—in English 'Absolute', with a capital when it is a noun. 'Absolute', 'absolute Idea', 'absolute meaning', 'absolute Concept', all appear in these lectures, and they are best regarded, at least in most contexts, as synonyms for God.

Geist means both 'mind' and spirit'. I have kept 'spirit' almost everywhere, except where the context cries out for 'mind', and where that cannot be misleading. 'Spirit' has the religious overtones to which Hegel attached importance in his use of this word. For him the 'mind' of man is the spirit which is the 'candle of the Lord'.

I am deeply grateful both to the Librarian and Staff of the St. Andrews University Library for answering many queries, and to the Leverhulme Trustees for awarding me an Emeritus Fellowship in 1972 to enable me to complete my work for publication.

T. M. KNOX

Crieff, January 1973

CONTENTS OF VOLUME ONE

CONTENTS

Chapter III. THE DISSOLUTION OF THE CLASSI-
CAL FORM OF ART   502

1. Fate   502

2. Dissolution of the Gods through their Anthropomorphism   503

   (a) Deficiency in Inner Subjectivity   504

   (b) The Transition to Christianity is only a Topic of
      Modern Art   506

   (c) Dissolution of Classical Art in its own Sphere   509

3. Satire   512

   (a) Difference between the Dissolution of Classical Art and
      that of Symbolic Art   512

   (b) Satire   512

   (c) The Roman World as the Soil where Satire Flourishes 514

SECTION III. THE ROMANTIC FORM OF ART   517

INTRODUCTION. Of the Romantic in General   517

1. The Principle of Inner Subjectivity   518

2. The more Detailed Features of the Content and Form of the
   Romantic   519

3. Relation of the Subject-matter to the Mode of Representation 524

4. Division of the Subject   528

Chapter I. THE RELIGIOUS DOMAIN OF
ROMANTIC ART   530

1. The Redemptive History of Christ   534

   (a) Apparent Superfluity of Art   535

   (b) Necessary Emergence of Art   535

   (c) The Details of the External Appearance are Accidental 536

2. Religious Love   539

   (a) Concept of the Absolute as Love   539

   (b) The Heart [or Soul]   540

   (c) Love as the Romantic Ideal   540

3. The Spirit of the Community   543

   (a) Martyrs   544

   (b) Repentance and Conversion   548

   (c) Miracles and Legends   550

CONTENTS OF VOLUME TWO

INTRODUCTION

[1 *Prefatory Remarks*]

THESE lectures are devoted to Aesthetics. Their topic is the spacious *realm of the beautiful*; more precisely, their province is *art*, or, rather, *fine art*.

For this topic, it is true, the word Aesthetics, taken literally, is not wholly satisfactory, since 'Aesthetics' means, more precisely, the science of sensation, of feeling. In this sense it had its origin as a new science, or rather as something which for the first time was to become a philosophical discipline,[1] in the school of Wolff at the period in Germany when works of art were treated with regard to the feelings they were supposed to produce, as, for instance, the feeling of pleasure, admiration, fear, pity, and so on. Because of the unsatisfactoriness, or more accurately, the superficiality of this word, attempts were made after all to frame others, e.g. 'Callistics'. But this too appears inadequate because the science which is meant deals not with the beautiful as such but simply with the beauty of art. We will therefore let the word 'Aesthetics' stand; as a mere name it is a matter of indifference to us, and besides it has meanwhile passed over into common speech. As a name then it may be retained, but the proper expression for our science is *Philosophy of Art* and, more definitely, *Philosophy of Fine Art*.

[2] *Limitation and Defence of Aesthetics*

By adopting this expression we at once exclude the beauty of nature. Such a limitation of our topic may appear to be laid down arbitrarily, on the principle that every science has authority to demarcate its scope at will. But this is not the sense in which we should take the limitation of aesthetics to the beauty of art. In ordinary life we are of course accustomed to speak of a beautiful colour, a beautiful sky, a beautiful river; likewise of beautiful flowers, beautiful animals, and even more of beautiful people. We will not here enter upon the controversy about how far the attribute

[1] In Baumgarten's *Aesthetica*, 1750.

of beauty is justifiably ascribed to these and the like, and how far, in general, natural beauty may be put alongside the beauty of art. But we may assert against this view, even at this stage, that the beauty of art is *higher* than nature. The beauty of art is beauty born *of the spirit and born again*,[1] and the higher the spirit and its productions stand above nature and its phenomena, the higher too is the beauty of art above that of nature. Indeed, considered *formally* [i.e. no matter what it says], even a useless notion that enters a man's head is higher than any product of nature, because in such a notion spirituality and freedom are always present. Of course, considered in its *content*, the sun, for example, appears as an absolutely necessary factor [in the universe] while a false notion vanishes as *accidental* and transitory. But, taken by itself, a natural existent like the sun is indifferent, not free and self-conscious in itself; and if we treat it in its necessary connection with other things, then we are not treating it by itself, and therefore not as beautiful.

Now if we said in general that spirit and its artistic beauty stands *higher* than natural beauty, then of course virtually nothing is settled, because 'higher' is a quite vague expression which describes natural and artistic beauty as still standing side by side in the space of imagination and differing only quantitatively and therefore externally. But what is *higher* about the spirit and its artistic beauty is not something merely relative in comparison with nature. On the contrary, spirit is alone the *true*, comprehending everything in itself, so that everything beautiful is truly beautiful only as sharing in this higher sphere and generated by it. In this sense the beauty of nature appears only as a reflection of the beauty that belongs to spirit, as an imperfect incomplete mode [of beauty], a mode which in its *substance* is contained in the spirit itself.— Besides we shall find that a limitation to fine art arises very naturally, since, however much is said about the beauties of nature (less by the ancients than by us), it has not yet entered anyone's head to concentrate on the *beauty* of natural objects and make a science, a systematic exposition, of these beauties. A treatment from the point of view of *utility* has indeed been made and, for example,

---

[1] This is obscure. Bosanquet, in his translation of Hegel's Introduction (London, 1905) p. 39, suggests an allusion to 'born of water and the spirit', but this must be wrong. Hegel means that we have beauty originated by man's mind and also what is reproduced by his mind in his natural world. See below p. 29, and Part I, ch. III, c *ad init.*, and Part II, ch. III *ad init.*

a scientific account of natural objects useful against diseases has been composed, a *materia medica*, a description of the minerals, chemical products, plants, or animals, which are useful for cures. But the realms of nature have not been classified and examined from the point of view of beauty. In [discussing] natural beauty we feel ourselves too much in a vague sphere, without a *criterion*, and therefore such a classification would provide too little interest for us to undertake it.

These preliminary remarks on beauty in nature and art, on the relation of the two, and the exclusion of the former from the scope of our proper subject, should dispose of the idea that the limitation is due merely to caprice and arbitrariness. The proof of this relation should not come here yet, since its consideration falls within our science itself and is therefore not to be further explained and proved until later [see Part I, ch. II].

But if we now limit ourselves provisionally to the beauty of art, this first step brings us at once up against new difficulties.

[3 *Refutation of Objections*]

The *first* that we may encounter is the doubt whether fine art shows itself *deserving* of a scientific treatment. Beauty and art does indeed pervade all the business of life like a friendly genius and brightly adorns all our surroundings whether inner or outer, mitigating the seriousness of our circumstances and the complexities of the actual world, extinguishing idleness in an entertaining way, and, where there is nothing good to be done, filling the place of evil always better than evil itself. Yet even though art intersperses with its pleasing forms everything from the war-paint of the savages to the splendour of temples with all their riches of adornment, these forms themselves nevertheless seem to fall outside the true ends and aims of life. Even if artistic creations are not detrimental to these serious purposes, if indeed they sometimes even seem to further them, at least by keeping evil away, still, art belongs rather to the indulgence and relaxation of the spirit, whereas substantial interests require its exertion. Thus it may look as if it would be inappropriate and pedantic to propose to treat with scientific seriousness what is not itself of a serious nature. In any case, on this view, art appears as a superfluity, even if the softening of the heart which preoccupation with beauty can produce does not altogether become exactly deleterious as downright effeminacy. From this point of view, granted that the fine arts are a luxury, it has frequently been necessary to defend them in their relation to practical necessities in general, and in particular to morality and piety, and, since it is impossible to prove their harmlessness, at least to give grounds for believing that this luxury of the spirit may afford a greater sum of advantages than disadvantages. With this in view, serious aims have been ascribed to art itself, and it has frequently been recommended as a mediator between reason and sense, between inclination and duty, as a reconciler of these colliding elements in their grim strife and opposition. But it may be maintained that in the case of these aims of art, admittedly more serious, nothing is gained for reason and duty by this attempt at mediation, because by their very nature reason and duty permit of no mixture with anything else; they could not enter into such a transaction, and they demand the same purity which they have in themselves. Besides, it may be argued, art is not by this means made any worthier of scientific discussion, since it always remains a servant on both sides [between which it is supposed to mediate], and along with higher aims it all the same also promotes idleness and frivolity. Indeed, to put it simply, in this service, instead of being an end in itself, it can appear only as a means.—If, finally, art is regarded as a means, then there always remains in the form of the means a disadvantageous aspect, namely that even if art subordinates itself to more serious aims in fact, and produces more serious effects, the means that it uses for this purpose is *deception*. The beautiful [*Schöne*] has its being in pure appearance [*Schein*].[1] But an inherently true end and aim, as is easily recognized, must not be achieved by deception, and even if here and there it may

[1] *Schein* is frequently used in what follows. Hegel is following Kant (*Critique of Judgment*, part i) who held that the beautiful was the pleasing, without our having before us any concept or interest, e.g. in the purpose or utility of the object portrayed, so that what counted was the pure appearance of the object. To put the point in modern terms, if we look at a photograph of a shop, what strikes us is the utility of the shop, or the interest the picture may have for us if we are contemplating a purchase. But a work of art is different from a photograph. Even if it portrays a shop, it is the appearance (*Schein*) which pleases us and is the essential thing, without our having any interest in the shop or what it sells. Consequently, with this Kantian doctrine in mind, I translate *Schein* as a rule by 'pure appearance'. 'Semblance', which other translators use, gives a false impression. Hegel has in mind not only Kant but also Schiller's *Aesthetic Letters* which had a considerable influence on the development of his view of art. See below in [7].

be furthered by this means, this should be only in a limited way; and even in that case deception will be unable to count as the right means. For the means should correspond to the dignity of the end, and not pure appearance and deception but only the truth can create the truth, just as science too has to treat the true interests of the spirit in accordance with the true mode of actuality and the true mode of envisaging it.

In these respects it may look as if fine art is unworthy of scientific treatment because [it is alleged] it remains only a pleasing play, and, even if it pursues more serious ends, it still contradicts their nature; but [the allegation proceeds] in general it is only a servant both of that play and of these ends, and alike for the element of its being and the means of its effectiveness it can avail itself of nothing but deception and pure appearance.

But, *secondly*, it is still more likely to seem that even if fine art in general is a proper object of philosophical reflection, it is yet no appropriate topic for *strictly* scientific treatment. For the beauty of art presents itself to *sense*, feeling, intuition, imagination; it has a different sphere from thought, and the apprehension of its activity and its products demands an organ other than scientific thinking. Further, it is precisely the *freedom* of production and configurations that we enjoy in the beauty of art. In the production as well as in the perception of works of art, it seems as if we escape from every fetter of rule and regularity. In place of the strictness of conformity to law,[1] and the dark inwardness of thought, we seek peace and enlivenment in the forms of art; we exchange the shadow realm of the Idea for bright and vigorous reality. Finally, the source of works of art is the free activity of fancy which in its imaginations is itself more free than nature is. Art has at its command not only the whole wealth of natural formations in their manifold and variegated appearance; but in addition the creative imagination has power to launch out beyond them *inexhaustibly* in productions of its own. In face of this immeasurable fullness of fancy and its free products, it looks as if thought must lose courage to bring them *completely* before itself, to criticize them, and arrange them under its universal formulae.[2]

[1] On Hegel's distinction between regularity (*Regelmässigkeit*) and conformity to law (*Gesetzmässigkeit*), see Part I, ch. II, B.

[2] In this paragraph we have the first occurrence of *Phantasie* and *Einbildungs-kraft*, translated here, and sometimes later, as 'fancy' and 'imagination', and we may be inclined at first to recall Coleridge's distinction between these two

Science on the contrary, the objectors admit, has, in its form, to do with the thinking which abstracts from a mass of details. The result is that, on the one hand, imagination with its whim and caprice, the organ, i.e., of artistic activity and enjoyment, remains excluded from science. On the other hand, they say that while art does brighten and vivify the unillumined and withered dryness of the Concept, does reconcile its abstractions and its conflict with reality, does enrich the Concept with reality, a *purely* intellectual treatment [of art] removes this means of enrichment, destroys it, and carries the Concept back to its simplicity without reality and to its shadowy abstractness. Further, in its content, science is occupied with what is inherently *necessary*. If aesthetics leaves natural beauty aside, we have in this respect apparently not only not gained anything, but rather have removed ourselves still further from the necessary. For the very word 'nature' already gives us the idea of necessity and conformity to law, and so of a state of affairs which, it can be hoped, is nearer to scientific treatment and susceptible of it. But in the sphere of the spirit in general, especially in the imagination, what seems, in comparison with nature, to be peculiarly at home is caprice and the absence of law, and this is automatically incapable of any scientific explanation.

In all these respects, therefore [the argument runs], fine art, alike in its origin, its effect, and its scope, instead of showing itself fitted for scientific endeavour, seems rather in its own right to resist thought's regulating activity and *not* to be suitable for scientific discussion.

These scruples, and others like them, against a truly scientific preoccupation with fine art are derived from common ideas, points of view, and considerations; their more prolix elaboration you can

English words. Although Hegel does distinguish between the two German words when he writes about The Artist in Part I, ch. III, c, he usually treats them as synonyms, and I have generally translated both words by 'imagination'. It is a trick of Hegel's style not to repeat the same word in the same sentence, or, often, in a succeeding one, and in order to avoid repetition, he uses two different words as synonyms, even if they are not exactly synonymous. Until this is realized, a translator may perplex himself unnecessarily to find two different English words, in fact synonymous, to render the two different words used by Hegel synonymously. Frequent examples of this Hegelianism occur in his use of *Inhalt* and *Gehalt*; and the use of 'Poseidon' in one sentence and 'Neptune' in the next is perhaps the *reductio ad absurdum* of this stylistic purism. 'Athene', 'Pallas', and 'Minerva' within two or three lines all mean the same goddess.

read *ad nauseam* in older books, especially French ones,[1] about beauty and the fine arts. And in part they contain facts that are right enough, and, in part too, argumentation is derived from them which at first sight seems plausible as well. Thus, for example, it is a fact that the shapes that beauty takes on are as multifarious as its occurrence is universal. If you like, you can infer from this a universal bent in human nature for the beautiful, and then go on to the further inference that because the ideas of the beautiful are so infinitely various, and, therefore, at first sight, something *particular*, there cannot be any *universal* laws of beauty and taste.

Now before we can turn away from such considerations to our proper subject, our next task must consist in a short introductory discussion of the scruples and doubts that have been raised.

[i] As regards the *worthiness* of art to be treated scientifically, it is of course the case that art can be used as a fleeting play, affording recreation and entertainment, decorating our surroundings, giving pleasantness to the externals of our life, and making other objects stand out by artistic adornment. Thus regarded, art is indeed not independent, not free, but ancillary. But what *we* want to consider is art which is *free* alike in its end and its means. The fact that art in general can serve other ends and be in that case a mere passing amusement is something which it shares equally with thought. For, on the one hand, science may indeed be used as an intellectual servant for finite ends and accidental means, and it then acquires its character not from itself but from other objects and circumstances. Yet, on the other hand, it also cuts itself free from this servitude in order to raise itself, in free independence, to the truth in which it fulfils itself independently and conformably with its own ends alone.

Now, in this its freedom alone is fine art truly art, and it only fulfils its supreme task when it has placed itself in the same sphere as religion and philosophy, and when it is simply one way of bringing to our minds and expressing the *Divine*, the deepest interests of mankind, and the most comprehensive truths of the spirit. In works of art the nations have deposited their richest inner intuitions and ideas, and art is often the key, and in many nations the sole key, to understanding their philosophy and religion. Art shares this vocation with religion and philosophy, but in a special way, namely by displaying even the highest [reality] sensuously,

---

[1] e.g. the works of Batteux, see below, p. 16, note 2.

bringing it thereby nearer to the senses, to feeling, and to nature's mode of appearance. What is thus displayed is the depth of a supra-sensuous world which thought pierces and sets up at first as a *beyond* in contrast with immediate consciousness and present feeling; it is the freedom of intellectual reflection which rescues itself from the *here* and now, called sensuous reality and finitude. But this breach, to which the spirit proceeds, it is also able to heal. It generates out of itself works of fine art as the first reconciling middle term between pure thought and what is merely external, sensuous, and transient, between nature and finite reality and the infinite freedom of conceptual thinking.

[ii] So far as concerns the unworthiness of the *element* of art in general, namely its pure appearance and *deceptions*, this objection would of course have its justification if pure appearance could be claimed as something wrong. But appearance itself is essential to essence. Truth would not be truth if it did not show itself and appear, if it were not truth *for* someone and *for* itself, as well as for the spirit in general too. Consequently, not pure appearance in general, but only the special kind of appearance in which art gives reality to what is inherently true can be the subject of reproof. If in this connection the pure appearance in which art brings its conceptions into existence is to be described as 'deception', this reproof first acquires its meaning in comparison with the pheno-mena of the *external world* and its immediate materiality, as well as in relation to our own world of feeling, i.e. the *inner world of sense*. To both these worlds, in our life of experience, our own phenomenal life, we are accustomed to ascribe the value and name of actuality, reality, and truth, in contrast to art which lacks such reality and truth. But it is precisely this whole sphere of the em-pirical inner and outer world which is not the world of genuine actuality; on the contrary, we must call it, in a stricter sense than we call art, a pure appearance and a harsher deception. Only beyond the immediacy of feeling and external objects is genuine actuality to be found. For the truly actual is only that which has being in and for itself, the substance of nature and spirit, which indeed gives itself presence and existence, but in this existence remains in and for itself and only so is truly actual. It is precisely the dominion of these universal powers[1] which art emphasizes and reveals. In the ordinary external and internal world essentiality

[1] See below, Part I, ch. III, B, II 3(*a*).

does indeed appear too, but in the form of a chaos of accidents, afflicted by the immediacy of the sensuous and by the capriciousness of situations, events, characters, etc. Art liberates the true content of phenomena from the pure appearance and deception of this bad, transitory world, and gives them a higher actuality, born of the spirit. Thus, far from being mere pure appearance, a higher reality and truer existence is to be ascribed to the phenomena of art in comparison with [those of] ordinary reality.

Neither can the representations of art be called a deceptive appearance in comparison with the truer representations of historiography. For the latter has not even immediate existence but only the spiritual pure appearance thereof as the element of its portrayals, and its content remains burdened with the entire contingency of ordinary life and its events, complications, and individualities, whereas the work of art brings before us the eternal powers that govern history without this appendage of the immediate sensuous present and its unstable appearance.

But if the mode in which artistic forms appear is called a deception in comparison with philosophical thinking and with religious and moral principles, of course the form of appearance acquired by a topic in the sphere of *thinking* is the truest reality; but in comparison with the appearance of immediate existence and of historiography, the pure appearance of art has the advantage that it points through and beyond itself, and itself hints at something spiritual of which it is to give us an idea, whereas immediate appearance does not present itself as deceptive but rather as the real and the true, although the truth is in fact contaminated and concealed by the immediacy of sense. The hard shell of nature and the ordinary world make it more difficult for the spirit to penetrate through them to the Idea than works of art do.

But while on the one hand we give this high position to art, it is on the other hand just as necessary to remember that neither in content nor in form is art the highest and absolute mode of bringing to our minds the true interests of the spirit. For precisely on account of its form, art is limited to a specific content. Only one sphere and stage of truth is capable of being represented in the element of art. In order to be a genuine content for art, such truth must in virtue of its own specific character be able to go forth into [the sphere of] sense and remain adequate to itself there. This is the case, for example, with the gods of Greece. On the other hand,

there is a deeper comprehension of truth which is no longer so akin
and friendly to sense as to be capable of appropriate adoption and
expression in this medium. The Christian view of truth is of this
kind, and, above all, the spirit of our world today, or, more particularly, of our religion and the development of our reason, appears as beyond the stage at which art is the supreme mode of our
knowledge of the Absolute. The peculiar nature of artistic production and of works of art no longer fills our highest need. We have
got beyond venerating works of art as divine and worshipping
them. The impression they make is of a more reflective kind, and
what they arouse in us needs a higher touchstone and a different
test. Thought and reflection have spread their wings above fine
art. Those who delight in lamenting and blaming may regard this
phenomenon as a corruption and ascribe it to the predominance
of passions and selfish interests which scare away the seriousness
of art as well as its cheerfulness; or they may accuse the distress of
the present time, the complicated state of civil and political life
which does not permit a heart entangled in petty interests to free
itself to the higher ends of art. This is because intelligence itself
subserves this distress, and its interests, in sciences which are useful for such ends alone, and it allows itself to be seduced into
confining itself to this desert.

However all this may be, it is certainly the case that art no longer
affords that satisfaction of spiritual needs which earlier ages and
nations sought in it, and found in it alone, a satisfaction that, at
least on the part of religion, was most intimately linked with art.
The beautiful days of Greek art, like the golden age of the later
Middle Ages, are gone. The development of reflection in our life
today has made it a need of ours, in relation both to our will and
judgement, to cling to general considerations and to regulate the
particular by them, with the result that universal forms, laws,
duties, rights, maxims, prevail as determining reasons and are the
chief regulator. But for artistic interest and production we demand
in general rather a quality of life in which the universal is not
present in the form of law and maxim, but which gives the impression of being one with the senses and the feelings, just as the
universal and the rational is contained in the imagination by being
brought into unity with a concrete sensuous appearance. Consequently the conditions of our present time are not favourable to
art. It is not, as might be supposed, merely that the practising

artist himself is infected by the loud voice of reflection all around
him and by the opinions and judgements on art that have become
customary everywhere, so that he is misled into introducing more
thoughts into his work; the point is that our whole spiritual culture
is of such a kind that he himself stands within the world of reflection and its relations, and could not by any act of will and decision
abstract himself from it; nor could he by special education or
removal from the relations of life contrive and organize a special
solitude to replace what he has lost.

In all these respects art, considered in its highest vocation, is
and remains for us a thing of the past. Thereby it has lost for us
genuine truth and life, and has rather been transferred into our
ideas instead of maintaining its earlier necessity in reality and
occupying its higher place. What is now aroused in us by works of
art is not just immediate enjoyment but our judgement also, since
we subject to our intellectual consideration (i) the content of art,
and (ii) the work of art's means of presentation, and the appropriateness or inappropriateness of both to one another. The
philosophy of art is therefore a greater need in our day than it was
in days when art by itself as art yielded full satisfaction. Art invites
us to intellectual consideration, and that not for the purpose of
creating art again, but for knowing philosophically what art is.

But as soon as we propose to accept this invitation, we are met
by the suspicion, already touched upon [pp. 3–5], that while art
may well be a suitable subject for philosophical reflection in a
general way, it may not be suitable for strictly systematic and
scientific treatment. But this implies at once the false idea that
a philosophical discussion can also be unscientific. On this point
I can only say in brief that, whatever ideas others may have about
philosophy and philosophizing, my view is that philosophizing is
throughout inseparable from scientific procedure. Philosophy has
to consider an object in its necessity, not merely according to
subjective necessity or external ordering, classification, etc.; it
has to unfold and prove the object, according to the necessity of
its own inner nature. It is only this unfolding which constitutes
the scientific element in the treatment of a subject. But in so far
as the objective necessity of an object lies essentially in its logical
and metaphysical nature, the treatment of art in isolation may,
and indeed must, be exempt from absolute scientific rigour; art
has so many preconditions both in respect of its content and in

respect of its material and its medium,[1] whereby it always simultaneously touches on the accidental; and so it is only in relation to the essential inner progress of its content and means of expression that we may refer to its *necessary* formation.

[iii] But what of the objection that works of fine art are not susceptible of a scientific and intellectual treatment because they have their origin in the heart and unregulated imagination, and, incalculable in number and variety, exercise their effect only on feeling and imagination? This is a perplexity which even now still seems to carry some weight. For the beauty of art does in fact appear in a form which is expressly opposed to thought and which thought is compelled to destroy in order to pursue its own characteristic activity. This idea hangs together with the view that the real in general, the life of nature and spirit, is marred and killed by comprehension; that instead of being brought nearer to us by conceptual thinking, it is all the more removed from us, with the result that, by using thinking as a means of grasping what the live phenomenon is, man defeats his own purpose. At this point we cannot deal with this matter exhaustively; we can only indicate the point of view from which this difficulty or impossibility or unadaptability can be removed.

This much at least will be granted at once, that the spirit is capable of considering itself, and of possessing a consciousness, a *thinking* consciousness, of itself and of everything originating in itself. Thinking is precisely what constitutes the inmost essential nature of spirit. In this thinking consciousness of itself and its products, however much freedom and caprice these may always have, the spirit is acting in accordance with its essential nature, provided that it be genuinely in them. Now art and works of art, by springing from and being created by the spirit, are themselves of a spiritual kind, even if their presentation assumes an appearance of sensuousness and pervades the sensuous with the spirit. In this respect art already lies nearer to the spirit and its thinking than purely external spiritless nature does. In the products of art, the spirit has to do solely with its own. And even if works of art are not thought or the Concept, but a development of the Concept out of itself, a shift of the Concept from its own ground to that of sense, still the power of the thinking spirit lies in being able not only to grasp itself in its proper form as thinking, but to know itself

[1] Colours, sounds, etc., are the element in which art is at home, or its medium.

again just as much when it has surrendered its proper form to feeling and sense, to comprehend itself in its opposite, because it changes into thoughts what has been estranged and so reverts to itself. And in this preoccupation with its opposite the thinking spirit is not false to itself at all as if it were forgetting and abandoning itself thereby, nor is it so powerless as to be unable to grasp what is different from itself; on the contrary, it comprehends both itself and its opposite. For the Concept is the universal which maintains itself in its particularizations, overreaches itself and its opposite, and so it is also the power and activity of cancelling again the estrangement in which it gets involved. Thus the work of art too, in which thought expresses itself, belongs to the sphere of conceptual thinking, and the spirit, by subjecting it to philosophic treatment, is thereby merely satisfying the need of the spirit's inmost nature. For since thinking is the essence and Concept of spirit, the spirit in the last resort is only satisfied when it has permeated all products of its activity with thought too and so only then has made them genuinely its own. But art, far removed, as we shall see more definitely later,[1] from being the highest form of spirit, acquires its real ratification only in philosophy.

Nor does art elude philosophical treatment by lawless caprice, since, as has been already hinted [p. 9 above], its true task is to bring the highest interests of spirit to our minds. From this it follows at once that, so far as *content* is concerned, fine art cannot range in wild unfettered fancy,[2] since these spiritual interests set firm stopping-places to it for its content, no matter how multifarious and inexhaustible its forms and configurations. The same holds good for the forms themselves. They too are not left to pure chance. Not every artistic configuration is capable of expressing and displaying those interests, of absorbing and reproducing them; on the contrary, by a definite content the form appropriate to it is also made definite.

And so, after all, seen from this angle, we are able to orientate ourselves by process of thought in what seemed the impossibly vast mass of works and forms of art. Thus we have now stated, in relation to our science, the content to which we propose to restrict ourselves and we have seen that neither is fine art unworthy of

---

[1] See p. 71 below, and also p. 9 above.
[2] Cf. Kant: *Prolegomena*, § 35: 'The Understanding is our only support in setting bounds to the fantasies of the imagination.'

philosophical treatment, nor is philosophical treatment incapable of descrying the essence of fine art.

[4] Scientific Ways of Treating Beauty and Art

If we now ask about the *kind* of scientific treatment [of art] we meet here again two opposed ways of treating the subject; each appears to exclude the other and not to let us reach any true result.

On the one hand we see the science of art only busying itself with actual works of art from the outside, arranging them into a history of art, setting up discussions about existing works or outlining theories which are to yield general considerations for both criticizing and producing works of art.

On the other hand, we see science abandoning itself on its own account to reflections on the beautiful and producing only something universal, irrelevant to the work of art in its peculiarity, in short, an abstract philosophy of the beautiful.

(1) As for the first mode of treatment, which has the *empirical* for its starting-point, it is the indispensable route for anyone who thinks of becoming a *scholar* in the field of art. And just as, at the present day, everyone, even if not a devotee of physics, still likes to be equipped with the most essential physical facts, so it has been more or less necessary for a cultured man to have some acquaintance with art, and the pretension of proving oneself a dilettante and a connoisseur of art is almost universal.

(*a*) But if acquaintance of this sort with art is to be recognized as real scholarship, it must be of many kinds and of wide range. For the first requirement is a precise acquaintance with the immeasurable realm of individual works of art, ancient and modern, some of which (α) have already perished in reality, or (β) belong to distant lands or continents and which the unkindness of fate has withdrawn from our own inspection. Further, every work of art belongs to its own time, its own people, its own environment, and depends on particular historical and other ideas and purposes; consequently, scholarship in the field of art demands a vast wealth of historical, and indeed very detailed, facts, since the individual nature of the work of art is related to something individual and necessarily requires detailed knowledge for its understanding and explanation. Finally, scholarship demands here not only, as in other fields, a memory of the facts, but also a keen imagination to retain pictures of artistic forms in all their varied details, and especially to have them present to the mind for comparison with other works of art.

(b) Within this primarily historical treatment there arise at once different considerations which must not be lost sight of if we are to derive judgements from them. Now these considerations, as in other sciences which have an empirical basis, form, when extracted and assembled, general criteria and propositions, and, by still further generalization, *theories* of the arts. This is not the place to go through the literature of this kind, and it must therefore be enough to cite just a few works in the most general way. Thus, for example (α) Aristotle's *Poetics*—its theory of tragedy is even now of interest, and (β) more particularly, Horace's *Ars Poetica* and Longinus *On the Sublime* provide, among the classics, a general idea of the manner in which this theorizing has been handled. The general characteristics abstracted by these authors were supposed to count in particular as prescriptions and rules in accordance with which works of art had to be produced, especially in times when poetry and art had deteriorated. Yet the prescriptions which these art-doctors wrote to cure art were even less reliable than those of ordinary doctors for restoring human health.

On these theories of art I will only mention that, although in *single* instances they contain much that is instructive, still their remarks were drawn from a very restricted range of works of art which happened to be accounted genuinely beautiful [at the time] yet which always constituted only a small extent of the sphere of art. On the other hand, such characteristics are in part very trivial reflections which in their *universality* make no advance towards establishing the *particular*, which is principally what is at issue; for example, the Horatian *Epistle* that I have mentioned is full of such reflections and therefore is a book for everybody, but for that reason contains much that is vapid: *omne tulit punctum*, etc.[1] This is just like so many proverbial instructions: 'Dwell in the land and thou shalt be fed',[2] which are right enough thus generally expressed, but which lack the concrete specifications necessary for action.

Another kind of interest consisted not in the express aim of producing genuine works of art directly but in the intention of

---

[1] *Ars Poetica*, 343: 'He gets all applause who has mingled the useful with the pleasant' etc.   [2] Ps. 37: 3.

developing through such theories a judgement on works of art, in short, of developing *taste*. As examples, Home's *Elements of Criticism*,[1] the works of Batteux, and Ramler's *Einleitung in die schönen Wissenschaften*[2] were books much read in their day. Taste in this sense concerns the arrangement and treatment, the aptness and perfection of what belongs to the external appearance of a work of art. Moreover they drew into the principles of taste views which were taken from the old psychology and had been derived from empirical observations of mental capacities and activities, passions and their probable intensification, sequence, etc. But it remains ever the case that every man apprehends works of art or characters, actions, and events according to the measure of his insight and his feelings; and since the development of taste only touched on what was external and meagre, and besides took its prescriptions likewise from only a narrow range of works of art and a limited training of the intellect and the feelings, its scope was unsatisfactory and incapable of grasping the inner [meaning] and truth [of art] and sharpening the eye for detecting these things.

In general, such theories proceed in the same kind of way as the other non-philosophical sciences. What they take as their subject matter is derived from our perception as something really *there*; [but] now a further question arises about the character of this perception, since we need closer specifications which are likewise found in our perception and, drawn thence, are settled in definitions. But thus we find ourselves at once on uncertain and disputed ground. For at first it might seem that the beautiful was a quite simple idea. But it is soon obvious that several sides may be found in it, and so one author emphasizes one and another author another, or, if the same considerations are kept in view, a dispute arises about the question which side is now to be treated as the essential one.

In this regard it is a part of scientific completeness to cite and criticize the different definitions of the beautiful. We will not do this either in historical completeness in order to get to know all the various subtleties of definition, or for the sake of *historical* interest; we will only pick out as an example some of the more recent and

---

[1] 1762. By Henry Home, Lord Kames, 1698–1782.

[2] Charles Batteux (1713–80) was a prolific writer, mostly about classical authors. But Hegel is doubtless referring to *Les Beaux Arts réduits à un même principe* (1746). See also K. W. Ramler, 1725–98. His *Introduction to the Beaux Arts* is his translation of part of Batteux's *Cours de belles-lettres*, amplified and annotated by himself (1762).

more interesting ways of looking at beauty which are aimed more precisely at what is in fact implied in the Idea of the beautiful. To this end we must give pride of place to Goethe's[1] account of the beautiful which [J. H.] Meyer [1760–1832] has embodied in his *Geschichte der bildenden Künste in Griechenland*[2] where without naming Hirt he quotes his view too.

[A. L.] Hirt, one of the greatest genuine connoisseurs in our time, wrote an essay on the beauty of art in *Die Horen*,[3] 1797, pt. 7, in which, after writing about the beautiful in the different arts, he sums up in conclusion that the basis for a just criticism of beauty in art and for the formation of taste is the concept of the *characteristic*; i.e. he lays it down that the beautiful is 'the perfect which is or can be an object of eye, ear, or imagination'. He then further defines the perfect as 'what corresponds with its aim, what nature or art intended to produce in the formation of the object within its genus and species'. It follows then that, in order to form our judgement of beauty, we must direct our observation so far as possible to the individual marks which constitute the essence of a thing [*ein Wesen*], since it is just these marks which constitute its characteristic. By 'character' as a law of art Hirt understands 'that specific individuality whereby forms, movement and gesture, mien and expression, local colour, light and shade, *chiaroscuro*, and bearing are distinguished, and indeed, as the previously envisaged object demands'. This formulation is already more significant than other definitions, for if we go on to ask what 'the characteristic' is, we see at once that it involves (i) a content, as, for example, a specific feeling, situation, occurrence, action, individual, and

[1] Since this is the first of Hegel's many mentions of Goethe in these lectures, it may be as well to recall that Goethe (1749–1832) was Hegel's senior by eleven years and outlived him by a year. Hegel knew him well and often visited him in Weimar. Goethe thought highly of Hegel but wished that he could express himself more clearly. Others have had a similar wish.

[2] 1824–36—History of the *bildenden* arts in Greece. Bosanquet, op. cit., p. 67, tentatively suggests 'formative' as a translation of *bildenden*. But all the arts are 'formative' in one way or another. Hegel refers often to the *bildenden* arts, and he means by them architecture, sculpture, and painting, as distinct from music and poetry. These three arts are collectively referred to in English as the 'visual' arts, and I have therefore used this word to render *bildenden*. E. Panofsky, *Meaning in the Visual Arts* (Peregrine Books, 1970), does not mention Hegel, but the book contains a good deal of material which illuminates Hegel's discussion of these arts.

[3] A periodical conducted by Schiller, 1795–8. Hirt, (1759–1839), who is often mentioned below in Part III, was a professor of archaeology in Berlin, and Hegel was friendly with him.

(ii) the mode and manner in which this content is presented. It is on this manner of presentation that the artistic law of 'the characteristic' depends, since it demands that everything particular in the mode of expression shall serve towards the specific designation of its content and be a link in the expression of that content. The abstract category of 'the characteristic' thus refers to the degree of appropriateness with which the particular detail of the artistic form sets in relief the content it is meant to present. If we wish to explain this conception in a quite popular way, the following is the limitation which it involves. In a dramatic work, for example, an action constitutes the content; the drama is to display how this action happens. Now people do all sorts of things; they join in talk, eat occasionally, sleep, put on their clothes, say this and that, and so on. But whatever of all this does not stand immediately in relation to that specific action (which is the content proper) should be excluded, so that, in that content, nothing remains without significance. In the same way, in a picture, which seizes on only one phase of that action, there could be included— such are the wide ramifications of the éxternal world—a mass of circumstances, persons, situations, and other incidents which have no relation to the specific action in that phase and contribute nothing to its distinctive character. But according to the principle of 'the characteristic', nothing is to enter the work of art except what belongs to the appearance and essentially to the expression of this content alone; nothing is to be otiose or superfluous.

This is a very important principle which may be justified in certain respects. Yet Meyer in the book mentioned above thinks that this view has been superseded without trace and, as he maintains, to the benefit of art, on the ground that this idea would probably have led to something like caricature. This judgement immediately implies the perversity of supposing that such a definition of the beautiful would have to do with *leading* to something. The philosophy of art has no concern with prescriptions for artists; on the contrary, it has to determine what the beautiful is as such, and how it has displayed itself in reality, in works of art, without wishing to provide rules for their production. Now, apart from this, in respect to this criticism, it is of course true that Hirt's definition does cover caricature and the like too, for after all what is caricatured may be a characteristic; only one must say at once on the other side that in caricature the specific character is exaggerated and is, as it were, a superfluity of the characteristic. But the super-fluity is no longer what is strictly required for the characteristic, but a troublesome repetition whereby the 'characteristic' itself may be made unnatural. Moreover, caricature and the like may also be the characterizing of the ugly, which is certainly a distortion. Ugliness for its part is closely related to the subject-matter, so that it may be said that the principle of the characteristic involves as a fundamental feature an acceptance of the ugly and its presentation. On what is to be 'characterized' in the beauty of art, and what is not, on the content of the beautiful, Hirt's defini-tion of course gives us no more precise information. In this respect he provides only a purely formal prescription which yet contains something true, even if in an abstract way.

But now the further question arises of what Meyer opposes to Hirt's artistic principle. What does he prefer? In the first place he deals only with the principle in the works of art of antiquity, which must however contain the definition of the beautiful as such. In this connection he comes to speak of Mengs' and Winckelmann's[1] definition of [beauty as] the ideal and says that he neither rejects this law of beauty nor wholly accepts it; on the other hand he has no hesitation in agreeing with the opinion of an enlightened judge of art (Goethe) since it is definitive and seems to be nearer solving the riddle. Goethe says: 'The supreme principle of antiquity was the *significant*, but the supreme result of a successful *treatment* was the *beautiful*.'[2] If we look more closely at what this expression implies, we again find in it two things: (i) the content, the thing, and (ii) the manner and mode of presentation. In a work of art we begin with what is immediately presented to us and only then ask what its meaning or content is. The former, the external appearance, has no immediate value for us; we assume behind it something inward, a meaning whereby the external appearance is endowed with the spirit. It is to this, its soul, that the external points. For an appearance that means something does not present *itself* to our minds, or what it is *as* external, but something else. Consider, for example, a symbol, and, still more obviously, a fable the meaning of which is constituted by its moral and message.

---

[1] A. R. Mengs, 1728–79. J. J. Winckelmann, 1717–68, frequently mentioned below.

[2] The usual works of reference give no clue to the source of this quotation. Probably it comes from Meyer's book (see p. 17 above).

Indeed any word hints at a meaning and counts for nothing in itself. Similarly the spirit and the soul shine through the human eye, through a man's face, flesh, skin, through his whole figure, and here the meaning is always something wider than what shows itself in the immediate appearance. It is in this way that the work of art is to be significant and not appear exhausted by these lines, curves, surfaces, carvings, hollowings in the stone, these colours, notes, word-sounds, or whatever other material is used; on the contrary, it should disclose an inner life, feeling, soul, a content and spirit, which is just what we call the significance of a work of art.

With this demand for meaningfulness in a work of art, therefore, little is said that goes beyond or is different from Hirt's principle of the 'characteristic'.

According to this view, to sum up, we have characterized as the elements of the beautiful something inward, a content, and something outward which signifies that content; the inner shines in the outer and makes itself known through the outer, since the outer points away from itself to the inner. But we cannot go further into detail.

(c) This earlier manner of theorizing has after all been already violently cast aside in Germany, along with those practical rules, principally owing to the appearance of genuinely living poetry. The right of genius, its works and their effects, have been made to prevail against the presumptions of those legalisms and the watery wastes of theories. From this foundation of a genuine spiritual art, and the sympathy it has received and its widespread influence, there has sprung a receptivity for and freedom to enjoy and recognize great works of art which have long been available, whether those of the modern world or the Middle Ages, or even of wholly foreign peoples in the past, e.g. the Indian. These works, because of their age or foreign nationality, have of course something strange about them for us, but they have a content which outsoars their foreignness and is common to all mankind, and only by the prejudice of theory could they be stamped as products of a barbarous bad taste. This general recognition of works of art which lie outside the circle and forms which were the principal basis for the abstractions of theory has in the first place led to the recognition of a special kind of art—Romantic Art, and it has become necessary to grasp the Concept and nature of the beautiful in a deeper way than was possible for those theories. Bound up with this at the same time is the fact that the Concept, aware of itself as the thinking spirit, has now recognized itself on its side, more deeply, in philosophy, and this has thereby immediately provided an inducement for taking up the essence of art too in a profounder way.

Thus then, simply following the phases of this more general development, the mode of reflecting on art, the theorizing we have been considering, has become out of date, alike in its principles and its achievements. Only the *scholarship* of the history of art has retained its abiding value, and must do so all the more, the more the growth of spiritual receptivity, which I mentioned, has extended people's intellectual horizons in every direction. Its task and vocation consists in the aesthetic appreciation of individual works of art and in a knowledge of the historical circumstances which condition the work of art externally; it is only an appreciation, made with sense and spirit, and supported by the historical facts, which can penetrate into the entire individuality of a work of art. Goethe, for example, has written a great deal in this way about art and works of art. This mode of treating the subject does not aim at theorizing in the strict sense, although it may indeed often concern itself with abstract principles and categories, and may fall into them unintentionally, but if anyone does not let this hinder him but keeps before his eyes only those concrete presentations, it does provide a philosophy of art with tangible examples and authentications, into the historical particular details of which philosophy cannot enter.

This is then the first mode of treating art, the one that starts from particular and existent [works].

(2) From this it is essential to distinguish the opposite side, namely the purely theoretical reflection which labours at understanding the beautiful as such out of itself and fathoming its *Idea*.

We all know that Plato, in a deeper way, began to demand of philosophical inquiry that its objects should be understood not in their particularity, but in their universality, in their genus, in their essential reality, because he maintained that it was not single good actions, true opinions, beautiful human beings or works of art, that were the truth, but goodness, beauty, and truth themselves. Now if in fact the beautiful is to be understood in its essence and its Concept, this is possible only through the conceptual thinking whereby the logico-metaphysical nature of the *Idea in general*, as well as of the particular *Idea of the beautiful*, enters conscious reflection. But this treatment of the beautiful by itself in its Idea may itself turn again into an abstract metaphysics. Even if Plato in this connection be taken as foundation and guide, still the Platonic abstraction, even for the logical Idea of the beautiful, can satisfy us no longer. We must grasp this Idea more concretely, more profoundly, since the emptiness, which clings to the Platonic Idea, no longer satisfies the richer philosophical needs of our spirit today. It is indeed the case that we too must begin, in the philosophy of art, with the Idea of the beautiful, but we ought not to be in the position of clinging simply to Platonic Ideas, to that abstract mode with which philosophizing about art first began.

(3) The philosophical Concept of the beautiful, to indicate its true nature at least in a preliminary way, must contain, reconciled within itself, both the extremes which have been mentioned, because it unites metaphysical universality with the precision of real particularity. Only so is it grasped absolutely in its truth: for, on the one hand, over against the sterility of one-sided reflection, it is in that case fertile, since, in accordance with its own Concept, it has to develop into a totality of specifications, and it itself, like its exposition, contains the necessity of its particularizations and of their progress and transition one into another; on the other hand, the particularizations, to which a transition has been made, carry in themselves the universality and essentiality of the Concept, as the proper particularizations whereof they appear. The previously mentioned modes of treating the subject lack both these characteristics,[1] and for this reason it is only this full Concept which leads to substantial, necessary, and complete principles.

[5] *Concept of the Beauty of Art*

After these preliminary remarks, we now come closer to our proper subject, the philosophy of the beauty of art, and, since we are undertaking to treat it scientifically, we have to make a beginning with its Concept. Only when we have established this Concept can we lay down the division, and therefore the plan, of the whole of this science. For a division, if not undertaken in a purely external

---

[1] i.e. finding particulars in the universal, and the universal diversified in the particulars.

manner, as it is in a non-philosophical inquiry, must find its principle in the Concept of the subject-matter itself.

Confronted with such a requirement, we are at once met with the question 'whence do we derive this Concept?' If we start with the Concept itself of the beauty of art, it at once becomes a *presupposition* and a mere assumption; mere assumptions, however, philosophical method does not allow; on the contrary, what is to pass muster has to have its truth proved, i.e. has to be shown to be necessary.

About this difficulty, which affects the introduction to every philosophical discipline considered independently and by itself, we will come to an understanding in a short space.

In the case of the object of every science, two things come at once into consideration: (i) that there *is* such an object, and (ii) *what* it is.

On the first point little difficulty usually arises in the ordinary [i.e. physical] sciences. Why, it would at once be ridiculous to require astronomy and physics to prove that there are a sun, stars, magnetic phenomena, etc.! In these sciences which have to do with what is present to sensation, the objects are taken from experience of the external world, and instead of *proving* them, it is thought sufficient to *point* to them. Yet even within the non-philosophical disciplines, doubts may arise about the existence of their objects, as, for example, in psychology, the science of mind, there may be a doubt whether there *is* a soul, a spirit, i.e. an explicitly independent subjective entity distinct from what is material; or in theology, a doubt whether there is a God. If, moreover, the objects are of a subjective sort, i.e. present only in the mind and not as things externally perceptible, we know that in mind there is only what its own activity has produced. Hence there arises at once the chance that men may or may not have produced this inner idea or intuition in themselves, and, even if the former is really the case, that they have not made such an idea vanish again, or at least degraded it to a purely subjective idea whose content has no independent reality of its own. Thus, for example, the beautiful has often been regarded as not being absolutely necessary in our ideas but as a purely subjective pleasure, or a merely accidental sense. Our intuitions, observations, and perceptions of the external world are often deceptive and erroneous, but this is even more true of our inner ideas, even if they have in themselves the greatest vividness and could carry us away into passion irresistibly.

Now the doubt whether an object of our inner ideas and general outlook *is* or is *not*, like the question whether subjective consciousness has generated it in itself and whether the manner and mode in which it has brought it before itself was also in correspondence with the object in its essential nature, is precisely what arouses in men the higher scientific need which demands that, even if we have a notion that an object *is* or that there is such an object, nevertheless the object must be exhibited or proved in accordance with its *necessity*.

With this proof, provided it be developed really scientifically, the other question of *what* an object is, is sufficiently answered at the same time. However, to expound this fully would take us too far afield at this point, and only the following indications can be given.

If the necessity of our subject, the beauty of art, is to be exhibited, we would have to prove that art or the beautiful was a result of an antecedent which, considered according to its true Concept, was such as to lead on with scientific necessity to the Concept of fine art. But since we begin with art and wish to treat of *its* Concept and the realization thereof, not of its antecedent in its essential character (the antecedent pursuant to its own Concept), art has for us, as a particular scientific subject-matter, a presupposition which lies outside our consideration and, handled scientifically as a different subject-matter, belongs to a different philosophical discipline. Thus the only course left to us is to take up the Concept of art *lemmatically*,[1] so to say, and this is the case with all particular philosophical sciences if they are to be treated *seriatim*. For it is only the *whole* of philosophy which is knowledge of the universe as in itself that *one* organic totality which develops itself out of its own Concept and which, in its self-relating necessity, withdrawing into itself to form a whole, closes with itself to form *one* world of truth. In the circlet of this scientific necessity each single part is on the one hand a circle returning into itself, while on the other hand it has at the same time a necessary connection with other parts. It has a backward whence it is itself derived, and a forward to which it ever presses itself on, in so far as it is fertile, engendering an 'other' out of itself once more, and issuing

[1] i.e. assume that it has been demonstrated.

it for scientific knowledge. Thus it is not our present aim, but the task of an encyclopedic development of the whole of philosophy and its particular disciplines, to prove the Idea of the beautiful with which we began, i.e. to derive it necessarily from the presuppositions which antecede it in philosophy and out of the womb of which it is born. For us the Concept of the beautiful and art is a presupposition given by the system of philosophy. But since we cannot here expound this system and the connection of art with it, we have not yet got the Concept of the beautiful before us scientifically. What *is* before us is only elements and aspects of it as they occur already in the different ideas of the beautiful and art held by ordinary people, or have formerly been accepted by them. From this point we intend to pass on to a deeper consideration of these views in order to gain the advantage, in the first place, of acquiring a general idea of our subject, as well as, by a brief critique, a preliminary acquaintance with the higher determinations with which we will have to do in the sequel. In this way our final introductory treatment of the subject will present, as it were, an overture to the lectures on the matter at issue and will tend [to provide] a general collection and direction [of our thoughts] to our proper subject.

[6] *Common Ideas of Art*

What we are acquainted with at the start, as a familiar idea of the work of art, falls under the three following heads:

(i) The work of art is no natural product; it is brought about by human activity;

(ii) it is essentially made for man's apprehension, and in particular is drawn more or less from the sensuous field for apprehension by the senses;

(iii) it has an end and aim in itself.

(i) *The Work of Art as a Product of Human Activity*

(*a*) As for the first point, that a work of art is a product of human activity, this view has given rise to the thought that this activity, being the *conscious* production of an external object, can also be *known* and expounded, and learnt and pursued by others. For what one man makes, another, it may seem, could make or imitate too, if only he were first acquainted with the manner of proceeding;

so that, granted universal acquaintance with the rules of artistic production, it would only be a matter of everyone's pleasure to carry out the procedure in the same manner and produce works of art. It is in this way that the rule-providing theories, mentioned above [p. 15], with their prescriptions calculated for practical application, have arisen. But what can be carried out on such directions can only be something formally regular and mechanical. For the mechanical alone is of so external a kind that only a purely empty exercise of will and dexterity is required for receiving it into our ideas and activating it; this exercise does not require to be supplemented by anything concrete, or by anything not prescribed in universal rules. This comes out most vividly when such prescriptions do not limit themselves to the purely external and mechanical, but extend to the significant and spiritual activity of the artist. In this sphere the rules contain only vague generalities, for example that 'the theme should be interesting, every character should speak according to his standing, age, sex, and situation'. But if rules are to satisfy here, then their prescriptions should have been drawn up at the same time with such precision that they could be observed just as they are expressed, without any further spiritual activity of the artist's. Being abstract in content, however, such rules reveal themselves, in their pretence of adequacy to fill the consciousness of the artist, as wholly inadequate, since artistic production is not a formal activity in accordance with given specifications. On the contrary, as spiritual activity it is bound to work from its own resources and bring before the mind's eye a quite other and richer content and more comprehensive individual creations [than formulae can provide]. Therefore, in so far as such rules do actually contain something specific and therefore of practical utility, they may apply in case of need, but still can afford no more than specifications for purely external circumstances.

(b) Thus, as it turns out, the tendency just indicated has been altogether abandoned, and instead of it the opposite one has been adopted to the same extent. For the work of art was no longer regarded as a product of *general* human activity, but as a work of an entirely *specially gifted* spirit which now, however, is supposed to give free play simply and *only* to its own particular gift, as if to a specific natural force; it is to cut itself altogether loose from attention to universally valid laws and from a conscious reflection interfering with its own instinctive-like productive activity. Indeed it is supposed to be protected from such reflection, since its productions could only be contaminated and spoiled by such awareness. From this point of view the work of art has been claimed as a product of *talent* and *genius*, and the natural element in talent and genius has been especially emphasized. In a way, rightly, since talent is specific and genius universal capability, which man has not the power to give to himself purely and simply through his own self-conscious activity. On this topic we shall speak at greater length later [in Part I, ch. III, c].

Here we have only to mention the false aspect of this view, namely that in artistic production all consciousness of the artist's own activity is regarded as not merely superfluous but even deleterious. In that case production by talent and genius appears as only a *state* and, in particular, a state of *inspiration*. To such a state, it is said, genius is excited in part by an object, and in part can transpose itself into it by its own caprice, a process in which, after all, the good services of the champagne bottle are not forgotten. In Germany this notion became prominent at the time of the so-called *Period of Genius* which was introduced by Goethe's first poetical productions and then sustained by Schiller's. In their earliest works[1] these poets began afresh, setting aside all the rules then fabricated; they worked deliberately against these rules and thereby surpassed all other writers. However, I will not go further into the confusions which have been prevalent about the concept of inspiration and genius, and which prevail even today about the omnicompetence of inspiration as such. All that is essential is to state the view that, even if the talent and genius of the artist has in it a natural element, yet this element essentially requires development by thought, reflection on the mode of its productivity, and practice and skill in producing. For, apart from anything else, a main feature of artistic production is external workmanship, since the work of art has a purely technical side which extends into handicraft, especially in architecture and sculpture, less so in painting and music, least of all in poetry. Skill in technique is not helped by any inspiration, but only by reflection, industry, and practice. But such skill the artist is compelled to have in order to master his external material and not be thwarted by its intractability.

[1] For further discussion of these see Part I, ch. III, B II 1(c), as well as sections on Mohammedan Poetry and the end of the Romantic Form of Art.

Now further, the higher the standing of the artist, the more profoundly should he display the depths of the heart and the spirit; these are not known directly but are to be fathomed only by the direction of the artist's own spirit on the inner and outer world. So, once again, it is study whereby the artist brings this content into his consciousness and wins the stuff and content of his conceptions.

Of course, in this respect, one art needs more than another the consciousness and knowledge of such content. Music, for example, which is concerned only with the completely indeterminate movement of the inner spirit and with sounds as if they were feeling without thought, needs to have little or no spiritual material present in consciousness. Therefore musical talent announces itself in most cases very early in youth,[1] when the head is empty and the heart little moved, and it may sometimes attain a very considerable height before spirit and life have experience of themselves. Often enough, after all, we have seen very great virtuosity in musical composition and performance accompanied by remarkable barrenness of spirit and character.

In poetry, on the other hand, it is quite different. In it all depends on the presentation, full of content and thought, of man, of his deeper interests, and of the powers that move him; and therefore the spirit and heart must be richly and deeply educated by life, experience, and reflection before genius can bring into being anything mature, of sterling worth, and complete in itself. The first productions of Goethe and Schiller are of an immaturity, yes even of a crudity and barbarity, that can be terrifying. It is this phenomenon, that in most of these attempts there is an overwhelming mass of elements through and through prosaic, partly cold and flat, which principally tells against the common opinion that inspiration is bound up with the fire and time of youth. It was only in their manhood that these two geniuses, our national poets, the first, we may say, to give poetical works to our country, endowed us with works deep, substantial, the product of true inspiration, and no less perfectly finished in form; just as it was only in old age that Homer was inspired and produced his ever undying songs.

[1] Hegel may be thinking of Mozart. But see below, p. 41. He could have mentioned Mendelssohn but he was blind to contemporary composers as others have been and perhaps are.

(c) A third view concerning the idea of the work of art as a product of human activity refers to the placing of the work of art in relation to the external phenomena of nature. Here the ordinary way of looking at things took easily to the notion that the human art-product ranked below the product of nature; for the work of art has no feeling in itself and is not through and through enlivened, but, regarded as an external object, is dead; but we are accustomed to value the living higher than the dead. That the work of art has no life and movement in itself is readily granted. What is alive in nature is, within and without, an organism purposefully elaborated into all its tiniest parts, while the work of art attains the appearance of life only on its surface; inside it is ordinary stone, or wood and canvas, or, as in poetry, an idea expressed in speech and letters. But this aspect—external existence—is not what makes a work into a product of fine art; a work of art is such only because, originating from the spirit, it now belongs to the territory of the spirit; it has received the baptism of the spiritual and sets forth only what has been formed in harmony with the spirit. Human interest, the spiritual value possessed by an event, an individual character, an action in its complexity and outcome, is grasped in the work of art and blazoned more purely and more transparently than is possible on the ground of other non-artistic things. Therefore the work of art stands higher than any natural product which has not made this journey through the spirit. For example, owing to the feeling and insight whereby a landscape has been represented in a painting, this work of the spirit acquires a higher rank than the mere natural landscape. For everything spiritual is better than any product of nature. Besides, no natural being is able, as art is, to present the divine Ideal.

Now on what the spirit draws from its own inner resources in works of art it confers permanence in their external existence too; on the other hand, the individual living thing in nature is transient, vanishing, changeable in outward appearance, while the work of art persists, even if it is not mere permanence which constitutes its genuine pre-eminence over natural reality, but its having made spiritual inspiration conspicuous.

But nevertheless this higher standing of the work of art is questioned by another idea commonly entertained. For nature and its products, it is said, are a work of God, created by his goodness and wisdom, whereas the art-product is a purely human work, made by human hands according to human insight. In this contrast between natural production as a divine creation and human activity as something merely finite there lies directly the misunderstanding that God does not work in and through men at all, but restricts the sphere of his activity to nature alone. This false opinion must be completely rejected if we are to penetrate to the true nature of art. Indeed, over against this view we must cling to the opposite one, namely that God is more honoured by what the spirit makes than by the productions and formations of nature. For not only is there something divine in man, but it is active in him in a form appropriate to the being of God in a totally different and higher manner than it is in nature. God is spirit, and in man alone does the medium, through which the Divine passes, have the form of conscious and actively self-productive spirit; but in nature this medium is the unconscious, the sensuous, and the external, which stands far below consciousness in worth. Now in art-production God is just as operative as he is in the phenomena of nature; but the Divine, as it discloses itself in the work of art, has been generated out of the spirit, and thus has won a suitable thoroughfare for its existence, whereas just being *there* in the unconscious sensuousness of nature is not a mode of appearance appropriate to the Divine.

(*d*) Now granted that the work of art is made by man as the creation of his spirit, a final question arises, in order to derive a deeper result from the foregoing [discussion], namely, what is man's *need* to produce works of art? On the one hand, this production may be regarded as a mere play of chance and fancies which might just as well be left alone as pursued; for it might be held that there are other and even better means of achieving what art aims at and that man has still higher and more important interests than art has the ability to satisfy. On the other hand, however, art seems to proceed from a higher impulse and to satisfy higher needs, —at times the highest and absolute needs since it is bound up with the most universal views of life and the religious interests of whole epochs and peoples.—This question about the non-contingent but absolute need for art, we cannot yet answer completely, because it is more concrete than an answer could turn out to be at this stage. Therefore we must content ourselves in the meantime with making only the following points.

The universal and absolute need from which art (on its formal side) springs has its origin in the fact that man is a *thinking* consciousness, i.e. that man draws out of himself and puts *before himself* what he is and whatever else is. Things in nature are only *immediate* and *single*, while man as spirit *duplicates* himself, in that (i) he *is* as things in nature are, but (ii) he is just as much *for* himself; he sees himself, represents himself to himself, thinks, and only on the strength of this active placing himself before himself is he spirit. This consciousness of himself man acquires in a two-fold way: *first, theoretically*, in so far as inwardly he must bring himself into his own consciousness, along with whatever moves, stirs, and presses in the human breast; and in general he must see himself, represent himself to himself, fix before himself what thinking finds as his essence, and recognize himself alone alike in what is summoned out of himself and in what is accepted from without. *Secondly*, man brings himself before himself by *practical* activity, since he has the impulse, in whatever is directly given to him, in what is present to him externally, to produce himself and therein equally to recognize himself. This aim he achieves by altering external things whereon he impresses the seal of his inner being and in which he now finds again his own characteristics. Man does this in order, as a free subject, to strip the external world of its inflexible foreignness and to enjoy in the shape of things only an external realization of himself. Even a child's first impulse involves this practical alteration of external things; a boy throws stones into the river and now marvels at the circles drawn in the water as an effect in which he gains an intuition of something that is his own doing. This need runs through the most diversiform phenomena up to that mode of self-production in external things which is present in the work of art. And it is not only with external things that man proceeds in this way, but no less with himself, with his own natural figure which he does not leave as he finds it but deliberately alters. This is the cause of all dressing up and adornment, even if it be barbaric, tasteless, completely disfiguring, or even pernicious like crushing the feet of Chinese ladies, or slitting the ears and lips. For it is only among civilized people that alteration of figure, behaviour, and every sort and mode of external expression proceeds from spiritual development.

The universal need for art, that is to say, is man's rational need to lift the inner and outer world into his spiritual consciousness as an object in which he recognizes again his own self. The need for this spiritual freedom he satisfies, on the one hand, within by making what is within him explicit to himself, but correspondingly by giving outward reality to this his explicit self, and thus in this duplication of himself by bringing what is in him into sight and knowledge for himself and others. This is the free rationality of man in which all acting and knowing, as well as art too, have their basis and necessary origin. The specific need of art, however, in distinction from other action, political and moral, from religious portrayal and scientific knowledge, we shall see later [in the Introduction to Part I].

(ii) *The Work of Art, as being for Apprehension by Man's Senses, is drawn from the Sensuous Sphere*

So far we have considered in the work of art the aspect in which it is made by man. We have now to pass on to its second characteristic, namely that it is produced for apprehension by man's *senses* and therefore is more or less derived from the sensuous sphere.

(*a*) This reflection has given rise to the consideration that fine art is meant to arouse feeling, in particular the feeling that suits us, pleasant feeling. In this regard, the investigation of fine art has been made into an investigation of the feelings, and the question has been raised, 'what feelings should be aroused by art, fear, for example, and pity? But how can these be agreeable, how can the treatment of misfortune afford satisfaction?' Reflection on these lines dates especially from Moses Mendelssohn's times[1] and many such discussions can be found in his writings. Yet such investigation did not get far, because feeling is the indefinite dull region of the spirit; what is felt remains enveloped in the form of the most abstract individual subjectivity, and therefore differences between feelings are also completely abstract, not differences in the thing itself. For example, fear, anxiety, alarm, terror are of course further modifications of one and the same sort of feeling, but in part they are only quantitative intensifications, in part just forms not affecting their content, but indifferent to it. In the case of fear, for example, something is present in which the subject has an interest, but at the same time he sees the approach of the negative which threatens to destroy what he is interested in, and now

---

[1] 1729–86. *Über die Empfindungen* (1755) or *Betrachtungen über das Erhabene u.s.w.* (1757).

he finds directly in himself the interest and the negative, both as contradictory affections of his subjectivity. But such fear cannot by itself condition any content; on the contrary, it is capable of receiving into itself the most varied and opposite contents.[1] Feeling as such is an entirely empty form of subjective affection. Of course this form may be manifold in itself, as hope, grief, joy, pleasure; and, again, in this variety it may encompass different contents, as there is a feeling for justice, moral feeling, sublime religious feeling, and so on. But the fact that such content [e.g. justice] is present in different forms of feeling [e.g. hope or grief] is not enough to bring to light its essential and specific nature. Feeling remains a purely subjective emotional state of mind in which the concrete thing vanishes, contracted into a circle of the greatest abstraction.[2] Consequently the investigation of the feelings which art evokes, or is supposed to evoke, does not get beyond vagueness; it is a study which precisely abstracts from the content proper and its concrete essence and concept. For reflection on *feeling* is satisfied with observing subjective emotional reaction in its particular character, instead of immersing itself in the thing at issue i.e. in the work of art, plumbing its depths, and in addition relinquishing mere subjectivity and its states. But in the case of feeling it is precisely this empty subjectivity which is not only retained but is the chief thing, and this is why men are so fond of having feelings. But this too is why a study of this kind becomes wearisome on account of its indefiniteness and emptiness, and disagreeable by its concentration on tiny subjective peculiarities.

(*b*) But since the work of art is not, as may be supposed, meant merely in general to arouse feelings (for in that case it would have this aim in common, without any specific difference, with oratory, historical writing, religious edification, etc.), but to do so only in so far as it is beautiful, reflection on the beautiful hit upon the idea of looking for a peculiar *feeling* of the beautiful, and finding a specific *sense* of beauty. In this quest it soon appeared that such a sense is no blind instinct, made firmly definite by nature, capable from the start in and by itself of distinguishing beauty. Hence education was demanded for this sense, and the educated sense of

---

[1] 'You can be afraid of all sorts of things, but being afraid does not determine what you are afraid of' (Bosanquet's note, op. cit., p. 98).

[2] This is obscure, but the meaning would seem to be that morality, justice, etc., vanish when contracted into the circle of my private feeling which is abstract or ill defined in comparison with their concreteness.

beauty was called *taste* which, although an educated appreciation and discovery of beauty, was supposed to remain still in the guise of immediate feeling. We have already [p. 16] touched on how abstract theories undertook to educate such a sense of taste and how it itself remained external and one-sided. Criticism at the time of these views was on the one hand deficient in universal principles; on the other hand, as the particular criticism of individual works of art, it aimed less at grounding a more definite judgement—the implements for making one being not yet available—than at advancing rather the education of taste in general. Thus this education likewise got no further than what was rather vague, and it laboured only, by reflection, so to equip feeling, as a sense of beauty, that now it could find beauty wherever and however it existed. Yet the depths of the thing remained a sealed book to taste, since these depths require not only sensing and abstract reflections, but the entirety of reason and the solidity of the spirit, while taste was directed only to the external surface on which feelings play and where one-sided principles may pass as valid. Consequently, however, so-called 'good taste' takes fright at all the deeper effects [of art] and is silent when the thing at issue comes in question and externalities and incidentals vanish. For when great passions and the movements of a profound soul are revealed, there is no longer any question of the finer distinctions of taste and its pedantic preoccupation with individual details. It feels genius striding over such ground, and, retreating before its power, finds the place too hot for itself and knows not what to do with itself.

(c) For this reason the study of works of art has given up keeping in view merely the education of taste and proposing only to exhibit taste. The *connoisseur* has taken the place of the man of taste or the judge of artistic taste. The positive side of connoisseurship, in so far as it concerns a thorough acquaintance with the whole sweep of the individual character of a work of art, we have already [pp. 14 ff.] described as necessary for the study of art. For, on account of its nature, at once material and individual, the work of art issues essentially from particular conditions of the most varied sort, amongst them especially the time and place of its origin, then the specific individuality of the artist, and above all the technical development of his art. Attention to all these aspects is indispensable for a distinct and thorough insight into, and acquaintance with, a work of art, and indeed for the enjoyment of it; with them connoisseurship is principally preoccupied, and what it achieves in its way is to be accepted with gratitude. Now while such scholarship is justly counted as something essential, it still may not be taken as the single and supreme element in the relation which the spirit adopts to a work of art and to art in general. For connoisseurship, and this is its defective side, may stick at acquaintance with purely external aspects, the technical, historical, etc., and perhaps have little notion of the true nature of the work of art, or even know nothing of it at all; indeed it can even disesteem the value of deeper studies in comparison with purely positive, technical, and historical information. Yet connoisseurship, if it be of a genuine kind, does itself strive at least for specific grounds and information, and for an intelligent judgement with which after all is bound up a more precise discrimination of the different, even if partly external, aspects of a work of art and the evaluation of these.

(*d*) After these remarks on the modes of study occasioned by that aspect of the work of art which, as itself a sensuous object, gave it an essential relation to men as sensuous beings, we propose now to treat this aspect in its more essential bearing on art itself, namely (α) in regard to the work of art as an object, and (β) in regard to the subjectivity of the artist, his genius, talent, etc., yet without our entering upon what in this connection can proceed only from the knowledge of art in its universal essence. For here we are not yet really on scientific ground and territory; we are still only in the province of external reflections.

(α) Of course the work of art presents itself to sensuous apprehension. It is there for sensuous feeling, external or internal, for sensuous intuition and ideas, just as nature is, whether the external nature that surrounds us, or our own sensitive nature within. After all, a speech, for example, may be addressed to sensuous ideas and feelings. But nevertheless the work of art, as a sensuous object, is not merely for *sensuous* apprehension; its standing is of such a kind that, though sensuous, it is essentially at the same time for *spiritual* apprehension; the spirit is meant to be affected by it and to find some satisfaction in it.

Now the fact that this is what the work of art is meant to be explains at once how it can in no way be a natural product or have in its natural aspect a natural vitality, whether a natural product is supposed to have a higher or a lower value than a *mere* work of art, as a work of art is often called in a depreciatory sense.

For the sensuous element in a work of art should be there only in so far as it exists for the human spirit, regardless of its existing independently as a sensuous object.

If we examine more closely in what way the sensuous is *there* for man, we find that what is sensuous can be related in various ways to the spirit.

(αα) The poorest mode of apprehension, the least adequate to spirit, is purely sensuous apprehension. It consists, in the first place, of merely looking on, hearing, feeling, etc., just as in hours of spiritual fatigue (indeed for many people at any time) it may be an amusement to wander about without thinking, just to listen here and look round there, and so on. Spirit does not stop at the mere apprehension of the external world by sight and hearing; it makes it into an object for its inner being which then is itself driven, once again in the form of sensuousness, to realize itself in things, and relates itself to them as *desire*. In this appetitive relation to the external world, man, as a sensuous individual, confronts things as being individuals; likewise he does not turn his mind to them as a thinker with universal categories; instead, in accord with individual impulses and interests, he relates himself to the objects, individuals themselves, and maintains himself in them by using and consuming them, and by sacrificing them works his own self-satisfaction. In this negative relation, desire requires for itself not merely the superficial appearance of external things, but the things themselves in their concrete physical existence. With mere pictures of the wood that it might use, or of the animals it might want to eat, desire is not served. Neither can desire let the object persist in its freedom, for its impulse drives it just to cancel this independence and freedom of external things, and to show that they are only there to be destroyed and consumed. But at the same time the person too, caught up in the individual, restricted, and nugatory interests of his desire, is neither free in himself, since he is not determined by the essential universality and rationality of his will, nor free in respect of the external world, for desire remains essentially determined by external things and related to them.

Now this relation of desire is not the one in which man stands to the work of art. He leaves it free as an object to exist on its own account; he relates himself to it without desire, as to an object which is for the contemplative side of spirit alone. Consequently the work of art, though it has sensuous existence, does not require in this respect a sensuously concrete being and a natural life; indeed it ought not to remain on this level, seeing that it is meant to satisfy purely spiritual interests and exclude all desire from itself. Hence it is true that practical desire rates organic and inorganic individual things in nature, which can serve its purpose, higher than works of art which show themselves useless to serve it and are enjoyable only by other forms of the spirit.

(ββ) A second way in which what is externally present can be *for* the spirit is, in contrast to individual sense-perception and practical desire, the purely theoretical relation to *intelligence*. The theoretical study of things is not interested in consuming them in their individuality and satisfying itself and maintaining itself sensuously by means of them, but in coming to know them in their *universality*, finding their inner essence and law, and conceiving them in accordance with their Concept. Therefore theoretical interest lets individual things alone and retreats from them as sensuous individualities, since this sensuous individualism is not what intelligence tries to study. For the rational intelligence does not belong to the individual person as such in the way that desires do, but to him as at the same time inherently universal. Inasmuch as man relates himself to things in accordance with his universality, it is his universal reason which strives to find itself in nature and thereby to re-establish that inner essence of things which sensuous existence, though that essence is its basis, cannot immediately display. This theoretical interest, the satisfaction of which is the work of science, art does not share, however, in this scientific form, nor does it make common cause with the impulses of purely practical desires. Of course science can start from the sensuous in its individuality and possess an idea of how this individual thing comes to be there in its individual colour, shape, size, etc. Yet in that case this isolated sensuous thing has as such no further bearing on the spirit, inasmuch as intelligence goes straight for the universal, the law, the thought and concept of the object; on this account not only does it turn its back on the object in its immediate individuality, but transforms it within; out of something sensuously concrete it makes an abstraction, something thought, and so something essentially other than what that same object was in its sensuous appearance. This the artistic interest, in distinction from science, does not do. Just as the work of art proclaims itself *qua* external object in its sensuous individuality and immediate determinateness in respect of colour, shape, sound, or *qua* a single insight, etc., so the consideration of art accepts it like this too, without going so far beyond the immediate object confronting it as to endeavour to grasp, as science does, the concept of this object as a universal concept.

From the practical interest of desire, the interest of art is distinguished by the fact that it lets its object persist freely and on its own account, while desire converts it to its own use by destroying it. On the other hand, the consideration of art differs in an opposite way from theoretical consideration by scientific intelligence, since it cherishes an interest in the object in its individual existence and does not struggle to change it into its universal thought and concept.

(γγ) Now it follows from this that the sensuous must indeed be present in the work of art, but should appear only as the surface and as a pure appearance of the sensuous. For in the sensuous aspect of a work of art the spirit seeks neither the concrete material stuff, the empirical inner completeness and development of the organism which desire demands, nor the universal and purely ideal thought. What it wants is sensuous presence which indeed should remain sensuous, but liberated from the scaffolding of its purely material nature. Thereby the sensuous aspect of a work of art, in comparison with the immediate existence of things in nature, is elevated to a pure appearance, and the work of art stands in the *middle* between immediate sensuousness and ideal thought. It is *not yet* pure thought, but, despite its sensuousness, is *no longer* a purely material existent either, like stones, plants, and organic life; on the contrary, the sensuous in the work of art is itself something ideal, but which, not being ideal as thought is ideal, is still at the same time there externally as a thing. If spirit leaves the objects free yet without descending into their essential inner being (for if it did so they would altogether cease to exist for it externally as individuals), then this pure appearance of the sensuous presents itself to spirit from without as the shape, the appearance, or the sonority of things. Consequently the sensuous aspect of art is related only to the two theoretical senses of sight and hearing, while smell, taste, and touch remain excluded from the enjoyment of art. For smell, taste, and touch have to do with matter as such and its immediately sensible qualities—smell with material vola-

tility in air, taste with the material liquefaction of objects, touch
with warmth, cold, smoothness, etc. For this reason these senses
cannot have to do with artistic objects, which are meant to maintain themselves in their real independence and allow of no *purely*
sensuous relationship. What is agreeable for these senses is not
the beauty of art. Thus art on its sensuous side deliberately produces only a shadow-world of shapes, sounds, and sights; and
it is quite out of the question to maintain that, in calling works of
art into existence, it is from mere impotence and because of his
limitations that man produces no more than a surface of the
sensuous, mere *schemata*. These sensuous shapes and sounds
appear in art not merely for the sake of themselves and their immediate shape, but with the aim, in this shape, of affording satisfaction to higher spiritual interests, since they have the power to
call forth from all the depths of consciousness a sound and an
echo in the spirit. In this way the sensuous aspect of art is *spiritualized*, since the spirit appears in art as made *sensuous*.

(β) But precisely for this reason an art-product is only there in
so far as it has taken its passage through the spirit and has arisen
from spiritual productive activity. This leads on to the other
question which we have to answer, namely in what way the necessary sensuous side of art is operative in the artist as his subjective
productive activity.—This sort and manner of production contains
in itself, as subjective activity, just the same characteristics which
we found objectively present in the work of art; it must be a
spiritual activity which yet contains at the same time the element
of sensuousness and immediacy. Still, it is neither, on the one
hand, purely mechanical work, a purely unconscious skill in
sensuous manipulation or a formal activity according to fixed rules
to be learnt by heart, nor, on the other hand, is it a scientific
production which passes over from the sensuous to abstract ideas
and thoughts or is active entirely in the element of pure thinking.
In artistic production the spiritual and the sensuous aspects must
be as one. For example, someone might propose to proceed in
poetic composition by first apprehending the proposed theme as
a prosaic thought and then putting it into poetical images, rhyme,
and so forth, so that now the image would simply be hung on to
the abstract reflections as an ornament and decoration. But such
a procedure could only produce bad poetry, because in it there
would be operative as *separate* activities what in artistic production

has validity only as an undivided unity. This genuine mode of production constitutes the activity of artistic imagination.

This activity is the rational element which exists as spirit only in so far as it actively drives itself forth into consciousness, yet what it bears within itself it places before itself only in sensuous form. Thus this activity has a spiritual content which yet it configurates sensuously because only in this sensuous guise can it gain knowledge of the content. This can be compared with the characteristic mentality of a man experienced in life, or even of a man of quick wit and ingenuity, who, although he knows perfectly well what matters in life, what in substance holds men together, what moves them, what power dominates them, nevertheless has neither himself grasped this knowledge in general rules nor expounded it to others in general reflections. What fills his mind he just makes clear to himself and others in particular cases always, real or invented, in adequate examples, and so forth; for in his ideas anything and everything is shaped into concrete pictures, determined in time and space, to which there may not be wanting names and all sorts of other external' circumstances. Yet such a kind of imagination rests rather on the recollection of situations lived through, of experiences enjoyed, instead of being creative itself. Recollection preserves and renews the individuality and the external fashion of the occurrence of such experiences, with all their accompanying circumstances, but does not allow the universal to emerge on its own account. But the productive fancy of an artist is the fancy of a great spirit and heart, the apprehension and creation of ideas and shapes, and indeed the exhibition of the profoundest and most universal human interests in pictorial and completely definite sensuous form.

Now from this it follows at once that, on one side, imagination rests of course on natural gifts and talent in general, because its productive activity requires sensuousness [as a medium]. We do indeed speak of 'scientific' talent too, but the sciences presuppose only the universal capacity for thinking, and thinking, instead of proceeding in a natural way, like imagination, precisely abstracts from all natural activity, and so we are righter to say that there is no specifically scientific talent, in the sense of a *merely* natural gift. On the other hand, imagination has at the same time a sort of instinct-like productiveness, in that the essential figurativeness and sensuousness of the work of art must be present in the artist as a natural gift and natural impulse, and, as an unconscious operation, must belong to the natural side of man too. Of course natural capacity is not the *whole* of talent and genius, since the production of art is also of a spiritual, self-conscious kind, yet its spirituality must somehow have in itself an element of natural picturing and shaping. Consequently almost anyone can get up to a certain point in an art, but to get beyond this point, where art proper only now begins, an inborn, higher talent for art is indispensable.

As a natural gift, this talent declares itself after all in most cases in early youth,[1] and it shows itself in the driving restlessness to shape a specific sensuous material at once in a lively and active way and to seize this mode of expression and communication as the only one, or as the most important and appropriate one. And after all an early technical facility, which up to a certain point is effortless, is a sign of inborn talent. For a sculptor everything turns into shapes, and from early years he lays hold of clay in order to model it. In short, whatever ideas such talented men have, whatever rouses and moves them inwardly, turns at once into figure, drawing, melody, or poem.

(γ) Thirdly, and lastly, the subject-matter of art is in a certain respect also drawn from the sensuous, from nature; or, in any case, even if the subject is of a spiritual kind, it can still only be grasped by displaying spiritual things, like human relationships, in the shape of phenomena possessed of external reality.

(iii) *The Aim of Art*

Now the question arises of what interest or *end* man sets before himself when he produces such subject-matter in the form of works of art. This was the third point which we adduced [p. 25] with regard to the work of art, and its closer discussion will lead us on at last to the true concept of art itself.

If in this matter we cast a glance at what is commonly thought, one of the most prevalent ideas which may occur to us is

(*a*) the principle of the imitation of nature. According to this view, imitation, as facility in copying natural forms just as they are, in a way that corresponds to them completely, is supposed to constitute the essential end and aim of art, and the success of this

---

[1] Hegel either changed his mind on this subject or did not make himself clear. See p. 28 above and the section on Talent and Genius below.

portrayal in correspondence with nature is supposed to afford complete satisfaction.

(α) This definition contains, prima facie, only the purely formal aim that whatever exists already in the external world, and the manner in which it exists there, is now to be made over again as a copy, as well as a man can do with the means at his disposal. But this repetition can be seen at once to be

(αα) *a superfluous* labour, since what pictures, theatrical productions, etc., display imitatively—animals, natural scenes, human affairs—we already possess otherwise in our gardens or in our own houses or in matters within our narrower or wider circle of acquaintance. And, looked at more closely, this superfluous labour may even be regarded as a presumptuous game

(ββ) which falls far short of nature. For art is restricted in its means of portrayal, and can only produce one-sided deceptions, for example a pure appearance of reality for *one* sense only, and, in fact, if it abides by the formal aim of *mere* imitation, it provides not the reality of life but only a pretence of life. After all, the Turks, as Mahommedans, do not, as is well known, tolerate any pictures or copies of men, etc. James Bruce in his journey to Abyssinia[1] showed paintings of a fish to a Turk; at first the Turk was astonished, but quickly enough he found an answer: 'If this fish shall rise up against you on the last day and say: "You have indeed given me a body but no living soul", how will you then justify yourself against this accusation?' The prophet too, as is recorded in the Sunna,[2] said to the two women, Ommi Habiba and Ommi Selma, who had told him about pictures in Ethiopian churches: 'These pictures will accuse their authors on the day of judgment.'

Even so, there are doubtless examples of completely deceptive copying. The grapes painted by Zeuxis have from antiquity onward been styled a triumph of art and also of the principle of the imitation of nature, because living doves are supposed to have pecked at them. To this ancient example we could add the modern one of Büttner's monkey[3] which ate away a painting of a cock-

---

[1] *Travels to Discover the Source of the Nile* (3rd edn., London, 1813, vol. vi, pp. 526–7). Hegel quotes from memory, and usually inaccurately, but here he has given the gist of the story accurately enough for his purpose.

[2] The Sunna is a body of traditions incorporating the history of Mahomet's life and so is a sort of supplement to the Koran.

[3] For Zeuxis see, e.g., Pliny, *Natural History*, xxxv. 36. (J. F.) Blumenbach (1752–1840) told a story of an old fellow-student of Linnaeus (1707–78) called

chafer in Rösel's *Insektbelustigungen* [Amusements of Insects] and was pardoned by his master because it had proved the excellence of the pictures in this book, although it had thus destroyed the most beautiful copy of this expensive work. But in such examples and others it must at least occur to us at once that, instead of praising works of art because they have deceived *even* doves and monkeys, we should just precisely censure those who think of exalting a work of art by predicating so miserable an effect as this as its highest and supreme quality. In sum, however, it must be said that, by mere imitation, art cannot stand in competition with nature, and, if it tries, it looks like a worm trying to crawl after an elephant.

(γγ) If we have regard to the continual, though comparative, failure of the copy compared with the original in nature, then there remains over as an aim nothing but taking pleasure in the conjuring trick of producing something *like* nature. And of course a man may enjoy himself in now producing over again by his own work, skill, and assiduity what otherwise is there already. But this enjoyment and admiration become in themselves the more frigid and cold, the more the copy is like the natural original, or they may even by perverted into tedium and repugnance. There are portraits which, as has been wittily said, are 'disgustingly like', and Kant,[1] in relation to this pleasure in imitation as such, cites another example, namely that we soon get tired of a man who can imitate to perfection the warbling of the nightingale (and there are such men); as soon as it is discovered that it is a man who is producing the notes, we are at once weary of the song. We then recognize in it nothing but a trick, neither the free production of nature, nor a work of art, since from the free productive power of man we expect something quite different from such music which interests us only when, as is the case with the nightingale's warbling, it gushes forth purposeless from the bird's own life, like the voice of human feeling. In general this delight in imitative skill can always be but restricted, and it befits man better to take delight in what he produces out of himself. In this sense the discovery of any insignificant technical product has higher value, and man can be prouder of having invented the hammer, the nail, etc., than of

Büttner [? C. W., 1716–1801, professor in Göttingen] who put all his money into books and acquired a copy of Rösel's book with coloured plates, 'the most beautiful thing he had ever seen' etc. (Lasson, p. 30). A. J. Rösel, 1705–59, published his book in parts, 1746–55.

[1] *Critique of Judgment*, part i, § 42.

manufacturing tricks of imitation. For this enthusiasm for copying merely as copying is to be respected as little as the trick of the man who had learnt to throw lentils through a small opening without missing. He displayed this dexterity before Alexander, but Alexander gave him a bushel of lentils as a reward for this useless and worthless art.[1]

(β) Now further, since the principle of imitation is purely formal, *objective beauty* itself disappears when this principle is made the end of art. For if it is, then there is no longer a question of the character of *what* is supposed to be imitated, but only of the correctness of the imitation. The object and content of the beautiful is regarded as a matter of complete indifference. Even if, apart from this, we speak of a difference between beauty and ugliness in relation to animals, men, localities, actions, or characters, yet according to that principle this remains a difference which does not properly belong to art, to which we have left nothing but imitation pure and simple. So that the above-mentioned lack of a criterion for the endless forms of nature leaves us, so far as the choice of objects and their beauty and ugliness are concerned, with mere subjective taste as the last word, and such taste will not be bound by rules, and is not open to dispute. And indeed if, in choosing objects for representation, we start from what people find beautiful or ugly and therefore worthy of artistic representation, i.e. from their taste, then all spheres of natural objects stand open to us, and none of them is likely to lack an admirer. For among us, e.g., it may not be every husband who finds his wife beautiful but he did before they were married, to the exclusion of all others too, and the fact that the subjective taste for this beauty has no fixed rule may be considered a good thing for both parties. If finally we look beyond single individuals and their capricious taste to the taste of *nations*, this too is of the greatest variety and contrariety. How often do we hear it said that a European beauty would not please a Chinese, or a Hottentot either, since the Chinese has inherently a totally different conception of beauty from the negro's, and his again from a European's, and so on. Indeed, if we examine the works of art of these non-European peoples, their images of the gods, for example, which have sprung from their fancy as sublime and worthy of veneration, they may present themselves to us as the most hideous idols; and while their music may sound in our

[1] The source of this story I have been unable to trace.

ears as the most detestable noise, they on their side will regard our sculptures, pictures, and music, as meaningless or ugly.

(γ) But even if we abstract from an objective principle for art, and if beauty is to be based on subjective and individual taste, we soon nevertheless find on the side of art itself that the imitation of nature, which indeed appeared to be a universal principle and one confirmed by high authority, is not to be adopted, at least in this general and wholly abstract form. For if we look at the different arts, it will be granted at once that, even if painting and sculpture portray objects that appear to be like natural ones or whose type is essentially drawn from nature, on the other hand works of architecture, which is also one of the fine arts, can as little be called imitations of nature as poetical works can, in so far as the latter are not confined, e.g., to mere description. In any case, if we still wanted to uphold this principle in relation to these latter arts, we would at least find ourselves compelled to take a long circuitous route, because we would have to attach various conditions to the proposition and reduce the so-called 'truth' of imitation to probability at least. But with probability we would again encounter a great difficulty, namely in settling what is probable and what is not, and, apart from this, we would not wish or be able to exclude from poetry all purely arbitrary and completely fanciful inventions.

The aim of art must therefore lie in something still other than the purely mechanical imitation of what is there, which in every case can bring to birth only technical *tricks*, not *works*, of art. It is true that it is an essential element in a work of art to have a natural shape as its basis because what it portrays it displays in the form of an external and therefore also natural phenomenon. In painting, e.g., it is an important study to get to know and copy with precision the colours in their relation to one another, the effects of light, reflections, etc., as well as the forms and shapes of objects down to the last detail. It is in this respect, after all, that chiefly in recent times the principle of the imitation of nature, and of naturalism generally, has raised its head again in order to bring back to the vigour and distinctness of nature an art which had relapsed into feebleness and nebulosity; or, on the other hand, to assert the regular, immediate, and explicitly fixed sequences of nature against the manufactured and purely arbitrary conventionalism, really just as inartistic as unnatural, into which art had strayed. But whatever is right enough from one point of view in this endeavour, still the naturalism demanded is as such not the substantial and primary basis of art, and, even if external appearance in its naturalness constitutes one essential characteristic of art, still neither is the given natural world the *rule* nor is the mere imitation of external phenomena, as external, the *aim* of art.

(*b*) Therefore the further question arises: what, then, is the *content* of art, and why is this content to be portrayed? In this matter our consciousness confronts us with the common opinion that the task and aim of art is to bring home to our sense, our feeling, and our inspiration everything which has a place in the human spirit. That familiar saying '*nihil humani a me alienum puto*'[1] art is supposed to make real in us.

Its aim therefore is supposed to consist in awakening and vivifying our slumbering feelings, inclinations, and passions of every kind, in filling the heart, in forcing the human being, educated or not, to go through the whole gamut of feelings which the human heart in its inmost and secret recesses can bear, experience, and produce, through what can move and stir the human breast in its depths and manifold possibilities and aspects, and to deliver to feeling and contemplation for its enjoyment whatever the spirit possesses of the essential and lofty in its thinking and in the Idea—the splendour of the noble, eternal, and true: moreover to make misfortune and misery, evil and guilt intelligible, to make men intimately acquainted with all that is horrible and shocking, as well as with all that is pleasurable and felicitous; and, finally, to let fancy loose in the idle plays of imagination and plunge it into the seductive magic of sensuously bewitching visions and feelings. According to this view, this universal wealth of subject-matter art is, on the one hand, to embrace in order to complete the natural experience of our external existence, and, on the other hand, to arouse those passions in general so that the experiences of life do not leave us unmoved and so that we might now acquire a receptivity for all phenomena. But [on this view] such a stimulus is not given in this field by actual experience itself, but only through the pure appearance of it, since art deceptively substitutes its productions for reality. The possibility of this deception through the pure appearance of art rests on the fact that, for man, all reality must come through the medium of perception and ideas, and only

---

[1] Terence: *Heauton Timorumenos*, I. i. 25. 'I count nothing human indifferent to me.' As usual, Hegel quotes inaccurately.

through this medium does it penetrate the heart and the will. Now here it is a matter of indifference whether a man's attention is claimed by immediate external reality or whether this happens in another way, namely through pictures, symbols, and ideas containing in themselves and portraying the material of reality. We can envisage things which are not real as if they *were* real. Therefore it remains all the same for our feelings whether it is external reality, or only the appearance of it, whereby a situation, a relation, or, in general, a circumstance of life, is brought home to us, in order to make us respond appropriately to the essence of such a matter, whether by grief or rejoicing, whether by being touched or agitated, or whether by making us go through the gamut of the feelings and passions of wrath, hatred, pity, anxiety, fear, love, reverence and admiration, honour and fame.

This arousing of all feelings in us, this drawing of the heart through all the circumstances of life, this actualizing of all these inner movements by means of a purely deceptive externally presented object is above all what is regarded, on the view we have been considering, as the proper and supreme power of art.

But now since, on this view, art is supposed to have the vocation of imposing on the heart and the imagination good and bad alike, strengthening man to the noblest ideals and yet enervating him to the most sensuous and selfish feelings of pleasure, art is given a purely formal task; and without any explicitly fixed aim would thus provide only the empty form for every possible kind of content and worth.

(c) In fact art does have also this formal side, namely its ability to adorn and bring before perception and feeling every possible material, just as the thinking of ratiocination can work on every possible object and mode of action and equip them with reasons and justifications. But confronted by such a multiple variety of content, we are at once forced to notice that the different feelings and ideas, which art is supposed to arouse or confirm, counteract one another, contradict and reciprocally cancel one another. Indeed, in this respect, the more art inspires to contradictory [emotions] the more it increases the contradictory character of feelings and passions and makes us stagger about like Bacchantes or even goes on, like ratiocination, to sophistry and scepticism. This variety of material itself compels us, therefore, not to stop at so formal a definition [of the aim of art], since rationality penetrates this jumbled diversity and demands to see, and know to be attained, even out of elements so contradictory, a higher and inherently more universal end. It is claimed indeed similarly that the final end of the state and the social life of men is that *all* human capacities and *all* individual powers be developed and given expression in every way and in every direction. But against so formal a view the question arises soon enough: into what *unity* are these manifold formations to be brought together, what *single* aim must they have as their fundamental concept and final end? As with the Concept of the state, so too with the Concept of art there arises the need (*a*) for a *common* end for its particular aspects, but (*b*) also for a higher *substantial* end. As such a substantial end, the first thing that occurs to reflection is the view that art has the capacity and the vocation to mitigate the ferocity of desires.

(α) In respect of this first idea, we have only to discover in what feature peculiar to art there lies the capacity to cancel rudeness and to bridle and educate impulses, inclinations, and passions. Rudeness in general is grounded in a direct selfishness of the impulses which make straight away precisely and exclusively for the satisfaction of their concupiscence. But desire is all the ruder and imperious the more, as single and restricted, it engrosses the *whole man*, so that he loses the power to tear himself free, as a universal being, from this determinateness and become aware of himself as universal. And if the man says in such a case, as may be supposed, 'The passion is stronger than *I*', then for consciousness the abstract 'I' *is* separated from the particular passion, but only in a purely formal way, since all that is pronounced with this cleavage is that, in face of the power of the passion, the 'I' as a universal is of no account whatever. Thus the ferocity of passion consists in the unity of the 'I' as universal with the restricted object of his desire, so that the man has no longer any will beyond this single passion. Now such rudeness and untamed force of passion is *prima facie* mitigated by art, in that it gives a man an idea of what he feels and achieves in such a situation. And even if art restricts itself to setting up pictures of passions for contemplation, even if indeed it were to flatter them, still there is here already a power of mitigation, since thereby a man is at least made *aware* of what otherwise he only immediately *is*. For then the man contemplates his impulses and inclinations, and while previously they carried him reflectionless away, he now sees them outside himself and already begins to be free from them because they confront him as something objective.

For this reason it may often be the case with an artist that, over-taken by grief, he mitigates and weakens for himself the intensity of his own feeling by representing it in art. Tears, even, provide some comfort; at first entirely sunk and concentrated in grief, a man may then in this direct way utter this purely inward feeling. But still more of an alleviation is the expression of one's inner state in words, pictures, sounds, and shapes. For this reason it was a good old custom at deaths and funerals to appoint wailing women in order that by its expression grief might be contemplated. Even by expressions of condolence the burden of a man's misfortune is brought before his mind; if it is much spoken about he has to reflect on it, and this alleviates his grief. And so to cry one's eyes out and to speak out has ever been regarded as a means of freeing oneself from the oppressive burden of care or at least of relieving the heart. The mitigation of the power of passions therefore has its universal ground in the fact that man is released from his im-mediate imprisonment in a feeling and becomes conscious of it as something external to him, to which he must now relate himself in an ideal way. Art by means of its representations, while remain-ing within the sensuous sphere, liberates man at the same time from the power of sensuousness. Of course we may often hear favourite phraseology about man's duty to remain in immediate unity with nature; but such unity, in its abstraction, is purely and simply rudeness and ferocity, and by dissolving this unity for man, art lifts him with gentle hands out of and above imprisonment in nature. For man's preoccupation with artistic objects remains purely contemplative, and thereby it educates, even if at first only an attention to artistic portrayals in general, later on an attention to their meaning and to a comparison with other subjects, and it opens the mind to a general consideration of them and the points of view therein involved.

(β) Now on this there follows quite logically the second charac-teristic that has been attributed to art as its essential aim, namely the *purification* of the passions, instruction, and *moral* improve-ment. For the theory that art was to curb rudeness and educate the passions, remained quite formal and general, so that it has become again a matter of what *specific* sort of education this is and what is its essential aim.

(αα) It is true that the doctrine of the purification of passion still suffers the same deficiency as the previous doctrine of the mitigation of desires, yet it does at least emphasize more closely the fact that artistic representations needed a criterion for assessing their worth or unworthiness. This criterion [on this view] is just their effectiveness in separating pure from impure in the passions. This effectiveness therefore requires a content which can exercise this purifying force, and, in so far as producing such an effect is supposed to constitute the substantial aim of art, the purifying content will have to be brought into consciousness in accordance with its *universality* and *essentiality*.

(ββ) From this latter point of view, the aim of art has been pronounced to be that it should *instruct*. On this view, on the one hand, the special character of art consists in the movement of feelings and in the satisfaction lying in this movement, lying even in fear, in pity, in grievous emotion and agitation, i.e. in the satisfying enlistment of feelings and passions, and to that extent in a gusto, a pleasure, and delight in artistic subjects, in their representation and effect. But, on the other hand, this aim of art is supposed to have its higher criterion only in its instructiveness, in *fabula docet*,[1] and so in the useful influence which the work of art may exert on the individual. In this respect the Horatian aphorism *Et prodesse volunt et delectare poetae*[2] contains, concentrated in a few words, what later has been elaborated in an infinite degree, diluted, and made into a view of art reduced to the uttermost extreme of shallowness.—Now in connection with such instruction we must ask at once whether it is supposed to be contained in the work of art directly or indirectly, explicitly or implicitly. If, in general, what is at issue is a universal and non-contingent aim, then this end and aim, in view of the essentially spiritual nature of art, can itself only be a spiritual one, and moreover one which is not contingent but absolute. This aim in relation to teaching could only consist in bringing into consciousness, by means of the work of art, an absolutely essential spiritual content. From this point of view we must assert that the more highly art is ranked the more it has to adopt such a content into itself and find only in the essence of that content the criterion of whether what is expressed is appropriate or not. Art has in fact been the first *instructress* of peoples.

---

[1] See below, Part II, ch. III, A 1.
[2] *Ars poetica*, 333. 'Poets wish alike to benefit and to please.'

If, however, the aim of instruction is treated as an aim in such a way that the universal nature of the content represented is supposed to emerge and be explained directly and explicitly as an abstract proposition, prosaic reflection, or general doctrine, and not to be contained implicitly and only indirectly in the concrete form of a work of art, then by this separation the sensuous pictorial form, which is precisely what alone makes a work of art a work of art, becomes a useless appendage, a veil and a pure appearance, expressly pronounced to be a mere veil and a mere pure appearance. But thereby the nature of the work of art itself is distorted. For the work of art should put before our eyes a content, not in its universality as such, but one whose universality has been absolutely individualized and sensuously particularized. If the work of art does not proceed from this principle but emphasizes the universality with the aim of [providing] abstract instruction, then the pictorial and sensuous element is only an external and superfluous adornment, and the work of art is broken up internally, form and content no longer appear as coalesced. In that event the sensuously individual and the spiritually universal have become external to one another.

Now, further, if the aim of art is restricted to this usefulness for instruction, the other side, pleasure, entertainment, and delight, is pronounced explicitly to be inessential, and ought to have its substance only in the utility of the doctrine on which it is attendant. But what is implied here at the same time is that art does not carry its vocation, end, and aim in itself, but that its essence lies in something else to which it serves as a means. In that event art is only one amongst several means which are proved useful for and applied to the end of instruction. But this brings us to the boundary at which art is supposed to cease to be an end in itself, because it is reduced either to a mere entertaining game or a mere means of instruction.

(γγ) This boundary is most sharply marked if in turn a question is raised about a supreme aim and end for the sake of which passions are to be purified and men instructed. As this aim, *moral* betterment has often been adduced in recent times, and the end of art has been placed in the function of preparing inclinations and impulses for moral perfection and of leading them to this final end. This idea unites instruction with purification, inasmuch as art, by affording an insight into genuinely moral goodness and so by instruction, at the same time incites to purification and only so is to accomplish the betterment of mankind as its utility and its highest aim.

Now as regards art in relation to moral betterment, the same must be said, in the first place, about the aim of art as instruction. It is readily granted that art may not take immorality and the intention of promoting it as its principle. But it is one thing to make immorality the express aim of the presentation, and another not to take morality as that aim. From every genuine work of art a good moral may be drawn, yet of course all depends on interpretation and on *who* draws the moral.[1] We can hear the most immoral presentations defended on the ground that one must be acquainted with evil and sins in order to act morally; conversely, it has been said that the portrayal of Mary Magdalene, the beautiful sinner who afterwards repented, has seduced many into sin, because art makes repentance look so beautiful, and sinning must come before repentance. But the doctrine of moral betterment, carried through logically, is not content with holding that a moral may be pointed from a work of art; on the contrary, it would want the moral instruction to shine forth clearly as the substantial aim of the work of art, and indeed would expressly permit the presentation of none but moral subjects, moral characters, actions, and events. For art can choose its subjects, and is thus distinct from history or the sciences, which have their material given to them.

In order, in this aspect of the matter, to be able to form a thorough estimate of the view that the aim of art is moral, we must first ask what specific standpoint of morality this view professes. If we keep more clearly in view the standpoint of the 'moral' as we have to take it in the best sense of the word today, it is soon obvious that its concept does not immediately coincide with what apart from it we generally call virtue, conventional life, respectability, etc. From this point of view a conventionally virtuous man is not *ipso facto moral*, because to be moral needs *reflection*, the specific consciousness of what accords with duty, and action on this preceding consciousness. Duty itself is the law of the will, a law which man nevertheless freely lays down out of himself,

---

[1] e.g., for one reader the moral of Goethe's *Elective Affinities* is approval of marriage, while for another reader it is disapproval (G. H. Lewes, *Life of Goethe*, bk. VII, ch. iv). In a work of art, as in life, the greater a man's character the more are different interpretations put on it by different people.

and then he ough to determine himself to this duty for the sake of duty and its fulfilment, by doing good solely from the conviction he has won that it is the good.[1] But this law, the duty chosen for duty's sake as a guide out of free conviction and inner conscience, and then carried out, is by itself the abstract universal of the will and this has its direct opposite in nature, in sensuous impulses, selfish interests, passions, and everything grouped together under the name of feeling and emotion. In this opposition one side is regarded as *cancelling* the other, and since both are present in the subject as opposites, he has a choice, since his decision is made from within, between following either the one or the other. But such a decision is a *moral* one, from the standpoint we are considering, and so is the action carried out in accordance with it, but only if it is done, on the one hand, from a free conviction of duty, and, on the other hand, by the conquest not only of the particular will, natural impulses, inclinations, passions, etc., but also of noble feelings and higher impulses. For the modern moralistic view starts from the fixed opposition between the will in its spiritual universality and the will in its sensuous natural particularity; and it consists not in the complete reconciliation of these opposed sides, but in their reciprocal battle against one another, which involves the demand that impulses in their conflict with duty must give way to it.[2]

Now this opposition does not arise for consciousness in the restricted sphere of moral action alone; it emerges in a thoroughgoing cleavage and opposition between what is *absolute* and what is external reality and existence. Taken quite abstractly, it is the opposition of universal and particular, when each is fixed over against the other on its own account in the same way; more concretely, it appears in nature as the opposition of the abstract law to the abundance of individual phenomena, each explicitly with its own character; in the spirit it appears as the contrast between the sensuous and the spiritual in man, as the battle of spirit against flesh, of duty for duty's sake, of the cold command against particular interest, warmth of heart, sensuous inclinations and impulses,

---

[1] With this Kantian passage compare my article 'Hegel's attitude to Kant's Ethics' (*Kant-Studien*, 1957–8, 70 ff.).

[2] Here Hegel's interpretation of Kant, like Schiller's, is based on a measure of misunderstanding. See, e.g., translation of Hegel's *Philosophy of Right* (Oxford, 1942), § 124, of his *Early Theological Writings* (Chicago, 1948), p. 211, and H. J. Paton: *The Categorical Imperative* (London, n.d.), pp. 48 and 84.

against the individual disposition in general; as the harsh opposition between inner freedom and the necessity of external nature, further as the contradiction between the dead inherently empty concept, and the full concreteness of life, between theory or subjective thinking, and objective existence and experience.

These are oppositions which have not been invented at all by the subtlety of reflection or the pedantry of philosophy; in numerous forms they have always preoccupied and troubled the human consciousness, even if it is modern culture that has first worked them out most sharply and driven them up to the peak of harshest contradiction. Spiritual culture, the modern intellect, produces this opposition in man which makes him an amphibious animal, because he now has to live in two worlds which contradict one another. The result is that now consciousness wanders about in this contradiction, and, driven from one side to the other, cannot find satisfaction for itself in either the one or the other. For on the one side we see man imprisoned in the common world of reality and earthly temporality, borne down by need and poverty, hard pressed by nature, enmeshed in matter,' sensuous ends and their enjoyment, mastered and carried away by natural impulses and passions. On the other side, he lifts himself to eternal ideas, to a realm of thought and freedom, gives to himself, as *will*, universal laws and prescriptions, strips the world of its enlivened and flowering reality and dissolves it into abstractions, since the spirit now upholds its right and dignity only by mishandling nature and denying its right, and so retaliates on nature the distress and violence which it has suffered from it itself. But for modern culture and its intellect this discordance in life and consciousness involves the demand that such a contradiction be resolved. Yet the intellect cannot cut itself free from the rigidity of these oppositions; therefore the solution remains for consciousness a mere *ought*, and the present and reality move only in the unrest of a hither and thither which seeks a reconciliation without finding one. Thus the question then arises whether such a universal and thoroughgoing opposition, which cannot get beyond a mere ought and a postulated solution, is in general the absolute truth and supreme end. If general culture has run into such a contradiction, it becomes the task of philosophy to supersede the oppositions, i.e. to show that neither the one alternative in its abstraction, nor the other in the like one-sidedness, possesses truth, but that they are both self-dissolving; that truth lies only in the reconciliation and mediation of both, and that this mediation is no mere demand, but what is absolutely accomplished and is ever self-accomplishing. This insight coincides immediately with the ingenuous faith and will which does have precisely this dissolved opposition steadily present to its view, and in action makes it its end and achieves it. Philosophy affords a reflective insight into the essence of the opposition only in so far as it shows how truth is just the dissolving of opposition and, at that, not in the sense, as may be supposed, that the opposition and its two sides *do not exist at all*, but that they exist reconciled.

Now since the ultimate end, moral betterment, has pointed to a higher standpoint, we will have to vindicate this higher standpoint for art too. Thereby the false position, already noticed, is at once abandoned, the position, namely, that art has to serve as a means to moral purposes, and the moral end of the world in general, by instructing and improving, and thus has its substantial aim, not in itself, but in something else. If on this account we now continue to speak of a final end and aim, we must in the first place get rid of the perverse idea which, in the question about an end, clings to the accessory meaning of the question, namely that it is one about utility. The perversity lies here in this, that in that case the work of art is supposed to have a bearing on something else which is set before our minds as the essential thing or as what ought to be, so that then the work of art would have validity only as a useful tool for realizing this end which is independently valid on its own account outside the sphere of art. Against this we must maintain that art's vocation is to unveil the *truth* in the form of sensuous artistic configuration, to set forth the reconciled opposition just mentioned, and so to have its end and aim in itself, in this very setting forth and unveiling. For other ends, like instruction, purification, bettering, financial gain, struggling for fame and honour, have nothing to do with the work of art as such, and do not determine its nature.

[7] *Historical Deduction of the True Concept of Art*

Now, starting from this point of view in which consideration of the matter by the Understanding's abstract reflection is dissolved, we must proceed to grasp the concept of art in its inner necessity, as after all it was from this view too that the true reverence and understanding of art arose historically. For that opposition on which we touched, asserted itself not only in the abstract reflection of general culture, but even in philosophy as such, and only now, when philosophy has thoroughly understood how to overcome this opposition, has it grasped its own essence and therefore at the same time the essence of nature and art.

So this point of view is not only the reawakening of philosophy in general, but also the reawakening of the science of art; indeed it is this reawakening alone that aesthetics proper, as a science, has really to thank for its genuine origin, and art for its higher estimation.

I will therefore touch briefly on the history of the transition which I have in mind, partly for the sake of the history itself, partly because in this way there are more closely indicated the views which are important and on which as a foundation we will build further. This foundation in its most general character consists in recognizing that the beauty of art is one of the means which dissolve and reduce to unity the above-mentioned opposition and contradiction between the abstractly self-concentrated spirit and nature—both the nature of external phenomena and that of inner subjective feeling and emotion.

(i) *The Kantian Philosophy*

It is the *Kantian* philosophy which has not only felt the need for this point of union, but has also clearly recognized it and brought it before our minds. In general, as the foundation alike of intelligence and will, Kant took self-related rationality, freedom, self-consciousness finding and knowing itself as inherently infinite. This recognition of the absoluteness of reason in itself, which has occasioned philosophy's turning-point in modern times, this absolute starting-point, must be recognized, and, even if we pronounce Kant's philosophy to be inadequate, this feature in it is not to be refuted. But since Kant fell back again into the fixed opposition between subjective thinking and objective things, between the abstract universality and the sensuous individuality of the will, he it was above all who emphasized as supreme the afore-mentioned opposition in the moral life, since besides he exalted the practical side of the spirit above the theoretical. Having accepted this fixity of opposition recognized by the thinking of the Understanding, he was left with no alternative but to express the unity purely in the form of subjective Ideas of Reason, for which no adequate reality could be demonstrated, and therefore as postulates, which indeed are to be deduced from the practical reason, but whose essential inner character remained unknowable by thinking and whose practical fulfilment remained a mere ought steadily deferred to infinity. And so Kant had indeed brought the reconciled contradiction before our minds, but yet could neither develop its true essence scientifically nor demonstrate it as what is truly and alone actual. It is true that Kant did press on still further in so far as he found the required unity in what he called the *intuitive understanding*; but even here he stopped again at the opposition of the subjective to objectivity, so that while he does affirm the abstract dissolution of the opposition between concept and reality, universal and particular, understanding and sense, and therefore the Idea, he makes this dissolution and reconciliation itself into a purely *subjective* one again, not one absolutely true and actual.

In this connection his *Critique of the Power of Judgment*, in which he deals with the aesthetic and teleological powers of judgement, is instructive and remarkable. The beautiful objects of nature and art, the purposeful products of nature, through which Kant comes nearer to the concept of the organic and living, he treats only from the point of view of a reflection which judges them subjectively. And indeed Kant defines the power of judgement in general as 'the ability to think the particular as contained under the universal',[1] and he calls the power of judgement *reflective* 'when it has only the particular given to it and has to find the universal under which it comes'. To this end it needs a law, a principle, which it has to give to itself, and as this law Kant propounds 'purposiveness' or teleology. In the concept of freedom in the *Critique of Practical Reason*, the accomplishment of the end does not get beyond a mere ought, but, in the *teleological* judgement of living things, Kant comes to the point of so regarding the living organism that in it the concept, the universal, contains the particular too, and, as an end, it determines the particular and external, the disposition of the limbs, not from without but from within, and in such a way that the particular corresponds to the end of its own accord. Yet, once again, with such a judgement the

[1] These quotations from the *Critique of Judgment* are from § iv of the Introduction.

objective nature of the object is not supposed to be known; all that is expressed is a subjective mode of reflection. Similarly, Kant interprets the *aesthetic* judgement as proceeding neither from the Understanding as such, as the capacity for concepts, nor from sensuous intuition and its manifold variety as such, but from the free play of Understanding and imagination. In this concord of the faculties of knowledge, the object becomes related to the subject and his feeling of pleasure and complacency.

(*a*) Now, in the *first* place, this complacency is to be devoid of all interest, i.e. to be *without any relation* to our *appetitive faculty*. If we have an interest, curiosity for example, or a sensuous interest on behalf of our sensuous need, a desire for possession and use, then the objects are not important to us on their own account, but only because of our need. In that event what exists has a value only in respect of such a need, and the situation is such that, on the one side, there is the object, and, on the other, a determinate need distinct from it, to which we yet relate it. If, for example, I consume an object for the sake of nourishment, this interest resides solely in me and is foreign to the object itself. Now the situation with the beautiful, Kant maintains,[1] is not of this kind. The aesthetic judgement lets the external existent subsist free and independent, and it proceeds from a pleasure to which the object on its own account corresponds, in that the pleasure permits the object to have its end in itself. This, as we saw already above [pp. 36 ff.], is an important consideration.

(*b*) *Secondly*, the beautiful, Kant says,[2] should be that which is put before us without a concept, i.e. without a category of the Understanding, as an object of *universal* pleasure. To estimate the beautiful requires a cultured spirit; the uneducated man has no judgement of the beautiful, since this judgement claims universal validity. True, the universal is as such *prima facie* an abstraction; but what is absolutely true carries in itself the demand for, and the characteristic of, universal validity. In this sense the beautiful too ought to be universally recognized, although the mere concepts of the Understanding are not competent to judge it. The good or the right, for example, in individual actions is subsumed under universal concepts, and the action counts as good if it can correspond with these concepts. The beautiful, on the other hand, is to invoke a universal pleasure directly without any such relation

<hr>

[1] *Critique of Judgment*, book I, § 2.   [2] Ibid., book I, § 6.

[or correspondence]. This only means that, in considering the beautiful, we are unaware of the concept and subsumption under it, and that the separation between the individual object and the universal concept, which elsewhere is present in judgement, is impermissible here.

(c) *Thirdly*, the beautiful is to have the form of *purposiveness*[1] in so far as the purposiveness is perceived in the object without any presentation of a purpose. At bottom this repeats what we have just discussed. Any natural product, a plant, for example, or an animal, is purposefully organized, and in this purposiveness it is so directly there for us that we have no idea of its purpose explicitly separate and distinct from its present reality. In this way the beautiful too is to appear to us as purposiveness. In finite purposiveness, end and means remain external to one another, since the end stands in no inner essential relation to the material of its realization.[2] In this case the idea of the end is explicitly distinguished from the object in which the end appears as realized. The beautiful, on the other hand, exists as purposeful in itself, without means and end showing themselves separated as different aspects of it. The purpose of the limbs, for example, of an organism is the life which exists as actual in the limbs themselves; separated they cease to be limbs. For in a living thing purpose and the material for its realization are so directly united that it exists only in so far as its purpose dwells in it. Looked at from this side, the beautiful should not wear purposiveness as an external form; on the contrary, the purposeful correspondence of inner and outer should be the immanent nature of the beautiful object.

(d) *Fourthly*, and lastly, Kant in treating of the beautiful holds firmly that it is recognized, without a concept, as the object of a *necessary* delight.[3] Necessity is an abstract category and it indicates an inner essential relation of two sides; if and because the

---

[1] Throughout this passage Hegel is dealing with Kant and indicating his connection between artistic and teleological judgement. *Zweck* I have to translate as 'purpose' instead of 'end', and *Zweckmässigkeit* as 'purposiveness'. Bosanquet translates the latter by 'teleology', but he does sometimes translate *Zweck* by 'purpose'. This first sentence is a quotation from Kant, op. cit., § 17 *ad fin.*

[2] We make (finite) things for a purpose, e.g. a knife for cutting, but there is no essential relation between means and end. Cutting can be done with a razor. But in an organism limbs and life, means and end, are related essentially.

[3] *Critique of Judgment*, § 22 *ad fin.*

one is, so also the other is. The one in its specific character contains the other at the same time, as, for example, cause is meaningless without effect. Such a necessity of giving pleasure the beautiful has in itself without any relation whatever to concepts, i.e. to the categories of the Understanding. So, for example, regularity,[1] which is produced according to a category of the Understanding, does please us, although Kant requires for pleasure still more than the unity and equality belonging to such a category of the Understanding.

Now what we find in all these Kantian propositions is an inseparability of what in all other cases is presupposed in our consciousness as distinct. This cleavage finds itself cancelled in the beautiful, where universal and particular, end and means, concept and object, perfectly interpenetrate one another. Thus Kant sees the beauty of *art* after all as a correspondence in which the particular itself accords with the concept. Particulars as such are *prima facie* accidental, alike to one another and to the universal; and precisely this accidental element—sense, feeling, emotion, inclination—is now not simply, in the beauty of art, *subsumed* under universal categories of the Understanding, and *dominated* by the concept of freedom in its abstract universality, but is so bound up with the universal that it is inwardly and absolutely adequate to it. Therefore thought is incarnate in the beauty of art, and the material is not determined by thought externally, but exists freely on its own account—in that the natural, the sensuous, the heart, etc., have in themselves proportion, purpose, and harmony; and intuition and feeling are elevated to spiritual universality, just as thought not only renounces its hostility to nature but is enlivened thereby; feeling, pleasure, and enjoyment are justified and sanctified; so that nature and freedom, sense and concept, find their right and satisfaction all in one. But this apparently perfect reconciliation is still supposed by Kant at the last to be only subjective in respect of the judgement and the production [of art], and not itself to be absolutely true and actual.

These we may take to be the chief results of Kant's *Critique of Judgment* in so far as they can interest us here. His *Critique* constitutes the starting point for the true comprehension of the beauty of art, yet only by overcoming Kant's deficiencies could this comprehension assert itself as the higher grasp of the true

[1] See below, Part I, ch. II, B 1(a).

unity of necessity and freedom, particular and universal, sense and reason.

(ii) Schiller, Winckelmann, Schelling

Therefore it has to be admitted that the artistic sense of a profound and philosophic mind has demanded, and expressed, totality and reconciliation (earlier than philosophy as such had recognized them) as against that abstract endlessness of ratiocination, that duty for duty's sake, that formless intellectualism, which apprehends nature and actuality, sense and feeling, as just a barrier, just contradicting it and hostile. It is *Schiller* [1759–1805] who must be given great credit for breaking through the Kantian subjectivity and abstraction of thinking and for venturing on an attempt to get beyond this by intellectually grasping the unity and reconciliation as the truth and by actualizing them in artistic production. For Schiller in his aesthetic writings has not merely taken good note of art and its interest, without any regard for its relation to philosophy proper, but he has also compared his interest in the beauty of art with philosophical principles, and only by starting from them and with their aid did he penetrate into the deeper nature and concept of the beautiful. Even so, one feels that at one period of his work he busied himself with thought more even than was advantageous for the naïve beauty of his works of art. Deliberate concentration on abstract reflections and even an interest in the philosophical Concept is noticeable in many of his poems. For this he has been reproached, and especially blamed and depreciated in comparison with Goethe's objectivity and his invariable naïveté, steadily undisturbed by the Concept. But in this respect Schiller, as a poet, only paid the debt of his time, and what was to blame was a perplexity which turned out only to the honour of this sublime soul and profound mind and only to the advantage of science and knowledge.

At the same period this same scientific impulse withdrew Goethe too from his proper sphere—poetry. Yet, just as Schiller immersed himself in the consideration of the inner depths of the *spirit*, so Goethe pursued his own proper genius into the *natural* side of art, into external nature, to the organisms of plants and animals, to crystals, the formation of clouds, and colours. To this scientific research Goethe brought his great genius which in these subjects had altogether thrown to the winds the outlook of the mere

Understanding with its error, just as Schiller, on the other side, had succeeded in asserting, against the Understanding's treatment of willing and thinking, the Idea of the free totality of beauty. A number of Schiller's writings is devoted to this insight into the nature of art, especially his *Letters on Aesthetic Education.*[1]

In these *Letters* the chief point from which Schiller starts is that every individual man bears within himself the capacity for ideal manhood. This genuine man, he holds, is represented by the State which he takes to be the objective, universal, and as it were canonical, form in which the diversity of individual persons aims at collecting and combining itself into a unity. Now he thought that there were two ways of presenting how man, living in time, might correspond with man in the Idea: on the one hand, the State, as the genus of ethics, law, and intelligence, might cancel individuality; on the other hand, the individual might raise himself to the genus, and the man of time ennoble himself into the man of the Idea. Reason, he thinks, demands unity as such, what accords with the genus, while nature demands multiplicity and individuality; and both these legislatures make equal claims on man. Now in the conflict of these opposite sides, aesthetic education is precisely to actualize the demand for their mediation and reconciliation, since, according to Schiller, it proceeds by so developing inclination, sensuousness, impulse, and heart that they become rational in themselves; and in this way reason too, freedom, and spirituality emerge from their abstraction and, united with the natural element, now rationalized, acquire flesh and blood in it. The beautiful is thus pronounced to be the mutual formation of the rational and the sensuous, and this formation to be the genuinely actual. In general this view of Schiller's can be recognized already in his *Anmut und Würde* [*Grace and Dignity*, 1793], as well as in his poems, because he makes the praise of women his special subject matter, for in their character he recognized and emphasized just that spontaneously present unification of spirit and nature.

This *unity* of universal and particular, freedom and necessity, spirit and nature, which Schiller grasped scientifically as the principle and essence of art and which he laboured unremittingly to call into actual life by art and aesthetic education, has now, as

[1] First published in his periodical, *Die Horen*, later in a collection of his prose writings (Leipzig, 1801, part 3).

the *Idea itself*, been made the principle of knowledge and existence, and the Idea has become recognized as that which alone is true and actual. Thereby philosophy has attained, with Schelling,[1] its absolute standpoint; and while art had already begun to assert its proper nature and dignity in relation to the highest interests of mankind, it was now that the *concept* of art, and the place of art in philosophy was discovered, and art has been accepted, even if in one aspect in a distorted way (which this is not the place to discuss), still in its high and genuine vocation. Likewise Winckelmann[2] at an earlier date was inspired by his insight into the ideals of the Greeks in a way whereby he opened up a new sense for considering art; he rescued it from ways of regarding it as serving common ends or merely imitating nature, and has powerfully encouraged the discovery of the Idea of art in works of art and the history of art. For Winckelmann is to be regarded as one of the men who, in the field of art, have opened up for the spirit a new organ and totally new modes of treatment. Still, on the theory and philosophical knowledge of art his view has had less influence.

To touch briefly on the course of the further development of the subject, alongside the reawakening of the philosophical Idea, A. W. and Friedrich von Schlegel,[3] greedy for novelty in the search for the distinctive and extraordinary, appropriated from the philosophical Idea as much as their completely non-philosophical, but essentially critical natures were capable of accepting. For neither of them can claim a reputation for speculative thought. Nevertheless, it was they who, with their critical talent, put themselves near the standpoint of the Idea, and with great freedom of speech and boldness of innovation, even if with miserable philosophical ingredients, directed a spirited polemic against the views of their predecessors. And thus in different branches of art they did introduce a new standard of judgement and new considerations which were higher than those they attacked. But since their criticism was not accompanied by a thoroughly philosophical knowledge of their standard, this standard retained a somewhat indefinite and vacillating character, so that they sometimes achieved too much, sometimes too little. It must also be put to their credit that they brought to light again and lovingly exalted things that were antiquated and

---

[1] 1775–1854. See his *System of Transcendental Idealism* (1800).
[2] His *History of Art in Antiquity* appeared in 1764.
[3] 1769–1845 and 1772–1829 respectively.

too little valued at the time, as, for instance, the older Italian and Dutch painting, the *Nibelungenlied*, etc., and that they endeavoured with enthusiasm to learn and teach things little known, like Indian poetry and mythology. But however high their credit is for this, they set too high a value on these epochs, and sometimes fell into the error of admiring the mediocre, e.g. Holberg's[1] comedies, of ascribing universal worth to what was only relatively valuable, or even having the audacity to show themselves enthused by a perverse tendency and a subordinate standpoint, as if it were something supreme.

(iii) *Irony*

From this tendency, and especially from the convictions and doctrines of F. von Schlegel, there was further developed in diverse shapes the so-called 'irony'.[2] This had its deeper root, in one of its aspects, in Fichte's philosophy, in so far as the principles of this philosophy were applied to art. F. von Schlegel, like Schelling, started from Fichte's standpoint, Schelling to go beyond it altogether, Schlegel to develop it in his own way and to tear himself loose from it. Now so far as concerns the closer connection of Fichte's propositions with one tendency of irony, we need in this respect emphasize only the following points about this irony, namely that [*first*] Fichte sets up the *ego* as the absolute principle of all knowing, reason, and cognition, and at that the *ego* that remains throughout abstract and formal. *Secondly*, this *ego* is therefore in itself just simple, and, on the one hand, every particularity, every characteristic, every content is negated in it, since everything is submerged in this abstract freedom and unity, while, on the other hand, every content which is to have value for the *ego* is only put and recognized by the *ego* itself. Whatever is, is only by the instrumentality of the *ego*, and what exists by my instrumentality I can equally well annihilate again.

Now if we stop at these absolutely empty forms which originate from the absoluteness of the abstract *ego*, nothing is treated *in and for itself* and as valuable in itself, but only as produced by the subjectivity of the *ego*. But in that case the *ego* can remain lord and master of everything, and in no sphere of morals, law, things

---

[1] Baron L. Holberg, 1684–1754, Danish dramatist and historian.
[2] See *Philosophy of Right*, § 140(f), Eng. tr. (Oxford, 1942), pp. 101–3, 258. Also see below, p. 69, note, and index, s.v.

human and divine, profane and sacred, is there anything that would not first have to be laid down by the *ego*, and that therefore could not equally well be destroyed by it. Consequently everything genuinely and independently real becomes only a show, not true and genuine on its own account or through itself, but a mere appearance due to the *ego* in whose power and caprice and at whose free disposal it remains. To admit or cancel it depends wholly on the pleasure of the *ego*, already absolute in itself simply as *ego*.

Now *thirdly*, the *ego* is a *living*, active individual, and its life consists in making its individuality real in its own eyes and in those of others, in expressing itself, and bringing itself into appearance. For every man, by living, tries to realize himself and does realize himself. Now in relation to beauty and art, this acquires the meaning of living as an artist and forming one's life *artistically*. But on this principle, I live as an artist when all my action and my expression in general, in connection with any content whatever, remains for me a mere show and assumes a shape which is wholly in my power. In that case I am not really in *earnest* either with this content or, generally, with its expression and actualization. For genuine earnestness enters only by means of a substantial interest, something of intrinsic worth like truth, ethical life, etc.,—by means of a content which counts as such for me as essential, so that I only become essential myself in my own eyes in so far as I have immersed myself in such a content and have brought myself into conformity with it in all my knowing and acting. When the *ego* that sets up and dissolves everything out of its own caprice is the artist, to whom no content of consciousness appears as absolute and independently real but only as a self-made and destructible show, such earnestness can find no place, since validity is ascribed only to the formalism of the *ego*.

True, in the eyes of others the appearance which I present to them may be regarded seriously, in that they take me to be really concerned with the matter in hand, but in that case they are simply deceived, poor limited creatures, without the faculty and ability to apprehend and reach the loftiness of my standpoint. Therefore this shows me that not everyone is so free (i.e. formally free)[1] as to see in everything which otherwise has value, dignity, and sanctity for mankind just a product of his own power of caprice, whereby

---

[1] i.e. not even merely capricious enough.

he is at liberty either to grant validity to such things, to determine himself and fill his life by means of them, or the reverse. Moreover this virtuosity of an ironical artistic life apprehends itself as a divine creative genius for which anything and everything is only an unsubstantial creature, to which the creator, knowing himself to be disengaged and free from everything, is not bound, because he is just as able to destroy it as to create it. In that case, he who has reached this standpoint of divine genius looks down from his high rank on all other men, for they are pronounced dull and limited, inasmuch as law, morals, etc., still count for them as fixed, essential, and obligatory. So then the individual, who lives in this way as an artist, does give himself relations to others: he lives with friends, mistresses, etc.; but, by his being a genius, this relation to his own specific reality, his particular actions, as well as to what is absolute and universal, is at the same time null; his attitude to it all is ironical.

These three points comprise the general meaning of the divine irony of genius, as this concentration of the *ego* into itself, for which all bonds are snapped and which can live only in the bliss of self-enjoyment. This irony was invented by Friedrich von Schlegel, and many others have babbled about it or are now babbling about it again.

The next form of this negativity of irony is, on the one hand, the vanity of everything factual, moral, and of intrinsic worth, the nullity of everything objective and absolutely valid. If the *ego* remains at this standpoint, everything appears to it as null and vain, except its own subjectivity which therefore becomes hollow and empty and itself mere vanity.[1] But, on the other hand, the *ego* may, contrariwise, fail to find satisfaction in this self-enjoyment and instead become inadequate to itself, so that it now feels a craving for the solid and the substantial, for specific and essential interests. Out of this comes misfortune, and the contradiction that, on the one hand, the subject does want to penetrate into truth and longs for objectivity, but, on the other hand, cannot renounce his isolation and withdrawal into himself or tear himself free from this unsatisfied abstract inwardness. Now he is attacked by the yearning which also we have seen proceeding from Fichtean philosophy. The dissatisfaction of this quiescence and impotence—which may not do or touch anything for fear of losing its inner harmony and

[1] *Eitelkeit*. Hegel is playing on its two meanings, vacuity and conceit.

which, even if pure in itself, is still unreal and empty despite its desire for reality and what is absolute—is the source of yearning and a *morbid* beautiful soul. For a *truly* beautiful soul acts and is actual. That longing, however, is only the empty vain subject's sense of nullity, and he lacks the strength to escape from this vanity and fill himself with a content of substance.

But in so far as irony has been made into a form of art, it has not stopped at giving artistic form merely to the personal life and particular individuality of the ironical artist; apart from the artistic work presented in his own actions, etc., the artist was supposed to produce external works of art also as the product of his imagination. The principle of these productions, which can emerge for the most part only in poetry, is now over again to represent the Divine as the ironical. But the ironical, as the individuality of genius, lies in the self-destruction of the noble, great, and excellent; and so the objective art-formations too will have to display only the principle of absolute subjectivity, by showing forth what has worth and dignity for mankind as null in its self-destruction. This then implies that not only is there to be no seriousness about law, morals, and truth, but that there is nothing in what is lofty and best, since, in its appearance in individuals, characters, and actions, it contradicts and destroys itself and so is ironical about itself.

This form, taken abstractly, borders nearly on the principle of the comic; yet in this kinship the comic must be essentially distinguished from the ironic. For the comic must be restricted to showing that what destroys itself is something inherently null, a false and contradictory phenomenon, a whim, e.g., an oddity, a particular caprice in comparison with a mighty passion, or even a *supposedly* tenable principle and firm maxim. But it is a totally different thing if what is in fact moral and true, any inherently substantial content, displays itself in an individual, and by his agency, as null. In such an event the individual is null in character and contemptible, and his weakness and lack of character is brought into his portrayals also. Therefore in this difference between the ironic and the comic what is essentially at issue is the content of what is destroyed. There *are* bad, useless people who cannot stick to their fixed and important aim but abandon it again and let it be destroyed in themselves. Irony loves this irony of loss of character. For true character implies, on the one hand, essentially worthy aims, and, on the other hand, a firm grip of such aims, so that the whole being of its individuality would be lost if the aims had to be given up and abandoned. This fixity and substantiality constitutes the keynote of character. Cato can live only as a Roman and a republican. But if irony is taken as the keynote of the representation, then the most inartistic of all principles is taken to be the principle of the work of art. For the result is to produce, in part, commonplace figures, in part, figures worthless and without bearing, since the substance of their being proves in them to be a nullity; in part, finally, there appear attached to them those yearnings and unresolved contradictions of the heart [which we mentioned above]. Such representations can awaken no genuine interest. For this reason, after all, on the part of irony there are steady complaints about the public's deficiency in profound sensibility, artistic insight, and genius, because it does not understand this loftiness of irony; i.e. the public does not enjoy this mediocrity and what is partly wishy-washy, partly characterless. And it is a good thing that these worthless yearning natures do not please; it is a comfort that this insincerity and hypocrisy are not to people's liking, and that on the contrary people want full and genuine interests as well as characters which remain true to their important intrinsic worth.

As an historical remark it may be added that it was especially Solger and Ludwig Tieck[1] who adopted irony as the supreme principle of art.

Of Solger this is not the place to speak at the length he deserves, and I must confine myself to a few observations. Solger was not content, like the others, with superficial philosophical culture; on the contrary; his genuinely speculative inmost need impelled him to plumb the depths of the philosophical Idea. In this process he came to the dialectical moment of the Idea, to the point which I call 'infinite absolute negativity', to the activity of the Idea in so negating itself as infinite and universal as to become finitude and particularity, and in nevertheless cancelling this negation in turn and so re-establishing the universal and infinite in the finite and particular. To this negativity Solger firmly clung, and of course it is

---

[1] K. W. F. Solger, 1780–1819. See *Philosophy of Right* (Eng. tr. cit., pp. 101–2). Tieck, 1773–1853. See below, section on *The Ancient Epigram*. Hegel dealt at some length with Solger and Tieck in a review of Solger's posthumous writings in 1828.

one element in the speculative Idea, yet interpreted as this purely dialectical unrest and dissolution of both infinite and finite, only *one element*, and not, as Solger will have it, the *whole* Idea. Unfortunately Solger's life was broken off too soon for him to have been able to reach the concrete development of the philosophical Idea. So he got no further than this aspect of negativity which has an affinity with the ironic dissolution of the determinate and the inherently substantial alike, and in which he also saw the principle of artistic activity. Yet in his actual life, having regard to the firmness, seriousness, and stoutness of his character, he was neither himself an ironic artist of the kind depicted above, nor was his profound sense for genuine works of art, nurtured by his persistent study of art, in this respect of an ironical nature. So much in justification of Solger, who in his life, philosophy, and art deserves to be distinguished from the previously mentioned apostles of irony.

As regards Ludwig Tieck, his culture too dates from that period in which Jena was for some time the cultural centre. Tieck and others of these distinguished people are indeed very familiar with such expressions as 'irony', but without telling us what they mean. So Tieck does always demand irony; yet when he goes on himself to judge works of art, while it is true that his recognition and description of their greatness is excellent, if we hope to find here the best opportunity of showing what the irony is in such a work as, e.g., *Romeo and Juliet*, we are deceived. We hear no more about irony.[1]

[8] *Division of the Subject*

After the foregoing introductory remarks it is now time to pass on to the study of our subject itself. But the introduction, where we still are, can in this respect do no more than sketch for our apprehension a conspectus of the entire course of our subsequent

[1] The term 'Romantic Irony' seems to be derived from F. von Schlegel and it is generally understood to mean that the writer, while still creative and emotional, should remain aloof and self-critical. What Hegel says of Tieck is correct. In Tieck's critical essays, especially on Shakespeare, he seldom, if ever, has anything to say about irony. Hegel may have in mind the preface to volume 6 of Tieck's collected Works; it appeared in 1828 and mentions Solger. (I owe this note to Professor James Trainer.) For a full treatment of Romantic Irony and Hegel's attitude to it, see O. Pöggeler, *Hegels Kritik der Romantik* (Bonn, 1956).

scientific studies. But since we have spoken of art as itself proceeding from the absolute Idea, and have even pronounced its end to be the sensuous presentation of the Absolute itself, we must proceed, even in this conspectus, by showing, at least in general, how the particular parts of the subject emerge from the conception of artistic beauty as the presentation of the Absolute. Therefore we must attempt, in the most general way, to awaken an idea of this conception.

It has already been said that the content of art is the Idea, while its form is the configuration of sensuous material. Now art has to harmonize these two sides and bring them into a free reconciled totality. The *first* point here is the demand that the content which is to come into artistic representation should be in itself qualified for such representation. For otherwise we obtain only a bad combination, because in that case a content ill-adapted to figurativeness and external presentation is made to adopt this form, or, in other words, material explicitly prosaic is expected to find a really appropriate mode of presentation in the form antagonistic to its nature.

The *second* demand, derived from the first, requires of the content of art that it be not anything abstract in itself, but concrete, though not concrete in the sense in which the sensuous is concrete when it is contrasted with everything spiritual and intellectual and these are taken to be simple and abstract. For everything genuine in spirit and nature alike is inherently concrete and, despite its universality, has nevertheless subjectivity and particularity in itself. If we say, for example, of God that he is simply *one*, the supreme being as such, we have thereby only enunciated a dead abstraction of the sub-rational Understanding. Such a God, not apprehended himself in his concrete truth, will provide no content for art, especially not for visual art. Therefore the Jews and the Turks have not been able by art to represent their God, who does not even amount to such an abstraction of the Understanding, in the positive way that the Christians have. For in Christianity God is set forth in his truth, and therefore as thoroughly concrete in himself, as person, as subject, and, more closely defined, as spirit. What he is as spirit is made explicit for religious apprehension as a Trinity of Persons, which yet at the same time is self-aware as *one*. Here we have essentiality or universality, and particularization, together with their reconciled unity, and only such unity is the concrete. Now since a content, in order to be true at all, must be of this concrete kind, art too demands similar concreteness, because the purely abstract universal has not in itself the determinate character of advancing to particularization and phenomenal manifestation and to unity with itself in these.

Now, *thirdly*, if a sensuous form and shape is to correspond with a genuine and therefore concrete content, it must likewise be something individual, in itself completely concrete and single. The fact that the concrete accrues to both sides of art, i.e. to both content and its presentation, is precisely the point in which both can coincide and correspond with one another; just as, for instance, the natural shape of the human body is such a sensuously concrete thing, capable of displaying spirit, which is concrete in itself, and of showing itself in conformity with it. Therefore, after all, we must put out of our minds the idea that it is purely a matter of chance that to serve as such a genuine shape an actual phenomenon of the external world is selected. For art does not seize upon this form either because it just finds it there or because there is no other; on the contrary, the concrete content itself involves the factor of external, actual, and indeed even sensuous manifestation. But then in return this sensuous concrete thing, which bears the stamp of an essentially spiritual content, is also essentially *for* our inner [apprehension]; the external shape, whereby the content is made visible and imaginable, has the purpose of existing solely for our mind and spirit. For this reason alone are content and artistic form fashioned in conformity with one another. The *purely* sensuously concrete—external nature as such—does not have this purpose for the sole reason of its origin. The variegated richly coloured plumage of birds shines even when unseen, their song dies away unheard; the torch-thistle, which blooms for only one night, withers in the wilds of the southern forests without having been admired, and these forests, jungles themselves of the most beautiful and luxuriant vegetation, with the most sweet-smelling and aromatic perfumes, rot and decay equally unenjoyed. But the work of art is not so naïvely self-centred; it is essentially a question, an address to the responsive breast, a call to the mind and the spirit.

Although illustration by art is not in this respect a matter of chance, it is, on the other hand, not the highest way of apprehending the spiritually concrete. The higher way, in contrast to representation by means of the sensuously concrete, is thinking, which in a relative sense is indeed abstract, but it must be concrete, not one-sided, if it is to be true and rational. How far a specific content has its appropriate form in sensuous artistic representation, or whether, owing to its own nature, it essentially demands a higher, more spiritual, form, is a question of the distinction which appears at once, for example, in a comparison between the Greek gods and God as conceived by Christian ideas. The Greek god is not abstract but individual, closely related to the natural [human] form. The Christian God too is indeed a concrete personality, but is *pure* spirituality and is to be known as *spirit* and in spirit. His medium of existence is therefore essentially inner knowledge and not the external natural form through which he can be represented only imperfectly and not in the whole profundity of his nature.

But since art has the task of presenting the Idea to immediate perception in a sensuous shape and not in the form of thinking and pure spirituality as such, and, since this presenting has its value and dignity in the correspondence and unity of both sides, i.e. the Idea and its outward shape, it follows that the loftiness and excellence of art in attaining a reality adequate to its Concept will depend on the degree of inwardness and unity in which Idea and shape appear fused into one.

In this point of higher truth, as the spirituality which the artistic formation has achieved in conformity with the Concept of spirit, there lies the basis for the division of the philosophy of art. For, before reaching the true Concept of its absolute essence, the spirit has to go through a course of stages, a series grounded in this Concept itself; and to this course of the content which the spirit gives to itself there corresponds a course, immediately connected therewith, of configurations of art, in the form of which the spirit, as artist, gives itself a consciousness of itself.

This course within the spirit of art has itself in turn, in accordance with its own nature, two sides. *First*, this development is itself a spiritual and universal one, since the sequence of definite conceptions of the world, as the definite but comprehensive consciousness of nature, man, and God, gives itself artistic shape.[1]

---

[1] i.e. the art expressive of one world-view differs from that which expresses another: Greek art as a whole differs from Christian art as a whole. The sequence of different religions gives rise to a sequence of different art-forms.

Secondly, this inner development of art has to give itself immediate existence and sensuous being, and the specific modes of the sensuous being of art are themselves a totality of necessary differences in art, i.e. the *particular arts*. Artistic configuration and its differences are, on the one hand, as spiritual, of a more universal kind and not bound to *one* material [e.g. stone or paint], and sensuous existence is itself differentiated in numerous ways; but since this existence, like spirit, has the Concept implicitly for its inner soul, a specific sensuous material does thereby, on the other hand, acquire a closer relation and a secret harmony with the spiritual differences and forms of artistic configuration.

However, in its completeness our science is divided into three main sections:

First, we acquire a *universal* part. This has for its content and subject both the universal Idea of artistic beauty as the Ideal, and also the nearer relation of the Ideal to nature on the one hand and to subjective artistic production on the other.

Secondly, there is developed out of the conception of artistic beauty a *particular* part, because the essential differences contained in this conception unfold into a sequence of particular forms of artistic configuration.

Thirdly, there is a *final* part which has to consider the individualization of artistic beauty, since art advances to the sensuous realization of its creations and rounds itself off in a system of single arts and their genera and species.

(i) *The Idea of the Beauty of Art or the Ideal*

In the first place, so far as the first and second parts are concerned, we must at once, if what follows is to be made intelligible, recall again that the Idea as the beauty of art is not the Idea as such, in the way that a metaphysical logic has to apprehend it as the Absolute, but the Idea as shaped forward into reality and as having advanced to immediate unity and correspondence with this reality. For the *Idea as such* is indeed the absolute truth itself, but the truth only in its not yet objectified universality, while the Idea as the *beauty of art* is the Idea with the nearer qualification of being both essentially individual reality and also an individual configuration of reality destined essentially to embody and reveal the Idea. Accordingly there is here expressed the demand that the Idea and its configuration as a concrete reality shall be made completely adequate to one another. Taken thus, the Idea as reality, shaped in accordance with the Concept of the Idea, is the *Ideal*.

The problem of such correspondence might in the first instance be understood quite formally in the sense that any Idea at all might serve, if only the actual shape, no matter which, represented precisely this specific Idea. But in that case the demanded *truth* of the Ideal is confused with mere *correctness* which consists in the expression of some meaning or other in an appropriate way and therefore the direct rediscovery of its sense in the shape produced. The Ideal is not to be thus understood. For any content can be represented quite adequately, judged by the standard of its own essence, without being allowed to claim the artistic beauty of the Ideal. Indeed, in comparison with ideal beauty, the representation will even appear defective. In this regard it may be remarked in advance, what can only be proved later, namely that the defectiveness of a work of art is not always to be regarded as due, as may be supposed, to the artist's lack of skill; on the contrary, defectiveness of *form* results from defectiveness of *content*. So, for example, the Chinese, Indians, and Egyptians, in their artistic shapes, images of gods, and idols, never get beyond formlessness or a bad and untrue definiteness of form. They could not master true beauty because their mythological ideas, the content and thought of their works of art, were still indeterminate, or determined badly, and so did not consist of the content which is absolute in itself. Works of art are all the more excellent in expressing true beauty, the deeper is the inner truth of their content and thought. And in this connection we are not merely to think, as others may, of any greater or lesser skill with which natural forms as they exist in the external world are apprehended and imitated. For, in certain stages of art-consciousness and presentation, the abandonment and distortion of natural formations is not unintentional lack of technical skill or practice, but intentional alteration which proceeds from and is demanded by what is in the artist's mind. Thus, from this point of view, there is imperfect art which in technical and other respects may be quite perfect in its *specific* sphere, and yet it is clearly defective in comparison with the concept of art itself and the Ideal.

Only in the highest art are Idea and presentation truly in conformity with one another, in the sense that the shape given to the

Idea is in itself the absolutely true shape, because the content of the Idea which that shape expresses is itself the true and genuine content. Associated with this, as has already been indicated, is the fact that the Idea must be determined in and through itself as a concrete totality, and therefore possess in itself the principle and measure of its particularization and determinacy in external appearance. For example, the Christian imagination will be able to represent God in human form and its expression of *spirit*, only because God himself is here completely known in himself as *spirit*. Determinacy is, as it were, the bridge to appearance. Where this determinacy is not a totality emanating from the Idea itself, where the Idea is not presented as self-determining and self-particularizing, the Idea remains abstract and has its determinacy, and therefore the principle for its particular and solely appropriate mode of appearance, not in itself, but outside itself. On this account, then, the still abstract Idea has its shape also external to itself, not settled by itself. On the other hand, the inherently concrete Idea carries within itself the principle of its mode of appearance and is therefore its own free configurator. Thus the truly concrete Idea alone produces its true configuration, and this correspondence of the two is the Ideal.

(ii) *Development of the Ideal into the Particular Forms of the Beauty of Art*

But because the Idea is in this way a concrete unity, this unity can enter the art-consciousness only through the unfolding and then the reconciliation of the particularizations of the Idea, and, through this development, artistic beauty acquires a *totality of particular stages and forms*. Therefore, after studying artistic beauty in itself and on its own account, we must see how beauty as a whole decomposes into its particular determinations. This gives, as the *second* part of our study, the doctrine of the *forms of art*. These forms find their origin in the different ways of grasping the Idea as content, whereby a difference in the configuration in which the Idea appears is conditioned. Thus the forms of art are nothing but the different relations of meaning and shape, relations which proceed from the Idea itself and therefore provide the true basis for the division of this sphere. For division must always be implicit in the concept, the particularization and division of which is in question.

We have here to consider *three* relations of the Idea to its configuration.

(*a*) *First*, art begins when the Idea, still in its indeterminacy and obscurity, or in bad and untrue determinacy, is made the content of artistic shapes. Being indeterminate, it does not yet possess in itself that individuality which the Ideal demands; its abstraction and one-sidedness leave its shape externally defective and arbitrary. The first form of art is therefore rather a *mere search* for portrayal than a capacity for true presentation; the Idea has not found the form even in itself and therefore remains struggling and striving after it. We may call this form, in general terms, the *symbolic* form of art. In it the abstract Idea has its shape outside itself in the natural sensuous material from which the process of shaping starts[1] and with which, in its appearance, this process is linked. Perceived natural objects are, on the one hand, primarily left as they are, yet at the same time the substantial Idea is imposed on them as their meaning so that they now acquire a vocation to express it and so are to be interpreted as if the Idea itself were present in them. A corollary of this is the fact that natural objects have in them an aspect according to which they are capable of representing a universal meaning. But since a complete correspondence is not yet possible, this relation can concern only an *abstract* characteristic, as when, for example, in a lion strength is meant.

On the other hand, the abstractness of this relation brings home to consciousness even so the foreignness of the Idea to natural phenomena, and the Idea, which has no other reality to express it, launches out in all these shapes, seeks itself in them in their unrest and extravagance, but yet does not find them adequate to itself. So now the Idea exaggerates natural shapes and the phenomena of reality itself into indefiniteness and extravagance; it staggers round in them, it bubbles and ferments in them, does violence to them, distorts and stretches them unnaturally, and tries to elevate their phenomenal appearance to the Idea by the diffuseness, immensity, and splendour of the formations employed. For the Idea is here still more or less indeterminate and unshapable, while the natural objects are thoroughly determinate in their shape.

[1] An unknown block of stone may symbolize the Divine, but it does not represent it. Its natural shape has no connection with the Divine and is therefore external to it and not an embodiment of it. When shaping begins, the shapes produced are symbols, perhaps, but in themselves are fantastic and monstrous.

In the incompatibility of the two sides to one another, the relation of the Idea to the objective world therefore becomes a *negative* one, since the Idea, as something inward, is itself unsatisfied by such externality, and, as the inner universal substance thereof, it persists *sublime* above all this multiplicity of shapes which do not correspond with it. In the light of this sublimity, the natural phenomena and human forms and events are accepted, it is true, and left as they are, but yet they are recognized at the same time as incompatible with their meaning which is raised far above all mundane content.

These aspects constitute in general the character of the early artistic pantheism of the East, which on the one hand ascribes absolute meaning to even the most worthless objects, and, on the other, violently coerces the phenomena to express its view of the world whereby it becomes bizarre, grotesque, and tasteless, or turns the infinite but abstract freedom of the substance [i.e. the one Lord] disdainfully against all phenomena as being null and evanescent. By this means the meaning cannot be completely pictured in the expression and, despite all striving and endeavour, the incompatibility of Idea and shape still remains unconquered.— This may be taken to be the first form of art, the symbolic form with its quest, its fermentation, its mysteriousness, and its sublimity.

(*b*) In the *second* form of art which we will call the *classical*, the double defect of the symbolic form is extinguished. The symbolic shape is imperfect because, (i) in it the Idea is presented to consciousness only as indeterminate or determined *abstractly*, and, (ii) for this reason the correspondence of meaning and shape is always defective and must itself remain purely abstract. The classical art-form clears up this double defect; it is the free and adequate embodiment of the Idea in the shape peculiarly appropriate to the Idea itself in its essential nature. With this shape, therefore, the Idea is able to come into free and complete harmony. Thus the classical art-form is the first to afford the production and vision of the completed Ideal and to present it as actualized in fact.

Nevertheless, the conformity of concept and reality in classical art must not be taken in the purely *formal* sense of a correspondence between a content and its external configuration, any more than this could be the case with the Ideal itself. Otherwise every portrayal of nature, every cast of features, every neighbourhood, flower, scene, etc., which constitutes the end and content of the representation, would at once be classical on the strength of such congruity between content and form. On the contrary, in classical art the peculiarity of the content consists in its being itself the concrete Idea, and as such the concretely spiritual, for it is the spiritual alone which is the truly inner [self]. Consequently, to suit such a content we must try to find out what in nature belongs to the spiritual in and for itself. The *original* Concept[1] itself it must be which *invented* the shape for concrete spirit, so that now the *subjective* Concept—here the spirit of art—has merely *found* this shape and made it, as a natural shaped existent, appropriate to free individual spirituality. This shape, which the Idea as spiritual— indeed as individually determinate spirituality—assumes when it is to proceed out into a temporal manifestation, is the human form. Of course personification and anthropomorphism have often been maligned as a degradation of the spiritual, but in so far as art's task is to bring the spiritual before our eyes in a sensuous manner, it must get involved in this anthropomorphism, since spirit appears sensuously in a satisfying way only in its body. The transmigration of souls is in this respect an abstract idea,[2] and physiology should have made it one of its chief propositions that life in its develop- ment had necessarily to proceed to the human form as the one and only sensuous appearance appropriate to spirit.

But the human body in its forms counts in classical art no longer as a merely sensuous existent, but only as the existence and natural shape of the spirit, and it must therefore be exempt from all the deficiency of the purely sensuous and from the contingent fini- tude of the phenomenal world. While in this way the shape is purified in order to express in itself a content adequate to itself, on the other hand, if the correspondence of meaning and shape is to be perfect, the spirituality, which is the content, must be of such a kind that it can express itself completely in the natural human form, without towering beyond and above this expression in

[1] Bosanquet (op. cit., p. 185) seems to be right in suggesting that 'original Concept' means 'God', and that he *invented* man as an expression of spirit; art *finds* him as appropriate to express the individual spirit. Hegel is fond of the play on words between *erfinden* (invent) and *finden* (find).

[2] Bosanquet points out that the idea is abstract because it represents the soul as independent of an appropriate body—the human soul as capable of existing in a beast's body (op. cit., p. 186).

sensuous and bodily terms. Therefore here the spirit is at once determined as particular and human, not as purely absolute and eternal, since in this latter sense it can proclaim and express itself only as spirituality.

This last point in its turn is the defect which brings about the dissolution of the classical art-form and demands a transition to a higher form, the *third*, namely the *romantic*.

(c) The romantic form of art cancels again the completed unification of the Idea and its reality, and reverts, even if in a higher way, to that difference and opposition of the two sides which in symbolic art remained unconquered. The classical form of art has attained the pinnacle of what illustration by art could achieve, and if there is something defective in it, the defect is just art itself and the restrictedness of the sphere of art. This restrictedness lies in the fact that art in general takes as its subject-matter the spirit (i.e. the *universal*, infinite and concrete in its nature) in a *sensuously* concrete form, and classical art presents the complete unification of spiritual and sensuous existence as the *correspondence* of the two. But in this blending of the two, spirit is not in fact represented in its *true nature*. For spirit is the infinite subjectivity of the Idea, which as absolute inwardness cannot freely and truly shape itself outwardly on condition of remaining moulded into a bodily existence as the one appropriate to it.[1]

Abandoning this [classical] principle, the romantic form of art cancels the undivided unity of classical art because it has won a content which goes beyond and above the classical form of art and its mode of expression. This content—to recall familiar ideas— coincides with what Christianity asserts of God as a spirit, in distinction from the Greek religion which is the essential and most appropriate content for classical art. In classical art the concrete content is *implicitly* the unity of the divine nature with the human, a unity which, just because it is only immediate and implicit, is adequately manifested also in an immediate and sensuous way. The Greek god is the object of naïve intuition and sensuous imagination, and therefore his shape is the bodily shape of man. The range of his power and his being is individual and particular.

---

[1] In other words, thought is 'inwardness' in the sense that thoughts are not outside one another in the way that the parts of a body are. This is why the spirit cannot find an adequate embodiment in things but only in thoughts, or at least only in the inner life.

Contrasted with the individual he is a substance and power with which the individual's inner being is only implicitly at one but without itself possessing this oneness as inward subjective knowledge. Now the higher state is the *knowledge* of that *implicit* unity which is the content of the classical art-form and is capable of perfect presentation in bodily shape. But this elevation of the implicit into self-conscious knowledge introduces a tremendous difference. It is the infinite difference which, for example, separates man from animals. Man is an animal, but even in his animal functions, he is not confined to the implicit, as the animal is; he becomes conscious of them, recognizes them, and lifts them, as, for instance, the process of digestion, into self-conscious science. In this way man breaks the barrier of his implicit and immediate character, so that precisely because he *knows* that he is an animal, he ceases to be an animal and attains knowledge of himself as spirit.

Now if in this way what was implicit at the previous stage, the unity of divine and human nature, is raised from an *immediate* to a *known* unity, the *true* element for the realization of this content is no longer the sensuous immediate existence of the spiritual in the bodily form of man, but instead the *inwardness of self-consciousness*. Now Christianity brings God before our imagination as spirit, not as an individual, particular spirit, but as absolute in spirit and in truth. For this reason it retreats from the sensuousness of imagination into spiritual inwardness and makes this, and not the body, the medium and the existence of truth's content. Thus the unity of divine and human nature is a known unity, one to be realized only by *spiritual* knowing and *in spirit*. The new content, thus won, is on this account not tied to sensuous presentation, as if that corresponded to it, but is freed from this immediate existence which must be set down as negative, overcome, and reflected into the spiritual unity. In this way romantic art is the self-transcendence of art but within its own sphere and in the form of art itself.

We may, therefore, in short, adhere to the view that at this third stage the subject-matter of art is *free concrete spirituality*, which is to be manifested as *spirituality* to the spiritually inward. In conformity with this subject-matter, art cannot work for sensuous intuition. Instead it must, on the one hand, work for the inwardness which coalesces with its object simply as if with itself, for subjective inner depth, for reflective emotion, for feeling which, as spiritual, strives for freedom in itself and seeks and finds its reconciliation only in the inner spirit. This *inner* world constitutes the content of the romantic sphere and must therefore be represented as this inwardness and in the pure appearance of this depth of feeling. Inwardness celebrates its triumph over the external and manifests its victory in and on the external itself, whereby what is apparent to the senses alone sinks into worthlessness.

On the other hand, however, this romantic form too, like all art, needs an external medium for its expression. Now since spirituality has withdrawn into itself out of the external world and immediate unity therewith, the sensuous externality of shape is for this reason accepted and represented, as in symbolic art, as something inessential and transient; and the same is true of the subjective finite spirit and will, right down to the particularity and caprice of individuality, character, action, etc., of incident, plot, etc. The aspect of external existence is consigned to contingency and abandoned to the adventures devised by an imagination whose caprice can mirror what is present to it, *exactly as it is*, just as readily as it can jumble the shapes of the external world and distort them grotesquely. For this external medium has its essence and meaning no longer, as in classical art, in itself and its own sphere, but in the heart which finds its manifestation in itself instead of in the external world and *its* form of reality, and this reconciliation with itself it can preserve or regain in every chance, in every accident that takes independent shape, in all misfortune and grief, and indeed even in crime.

Thereby the separation of Idea and shape, their indifference and inadequacy to each other, come to the fore again, as in symbolic art, but with this essential difference, that, in romantic art, the Idea, the deficiency of which in the symbol brought with it deficiency of shape, now has to appear *perfected* in itself as spirit and heart. Because of this higher perfection, it is not susceptible of an adequate union with the external, since its true reality and manifestation it can seek and achieve only within itself.

This we take to be the general character of the symbolic, classical, and romantic forms of art, as the three relations of the Idea to its shape in the sphere of art. They consist in the striving for, the attainment, and the transcendence of the Ideal as the true Idea of beauty.

(iii) *The System of the Individual Arts*

Now the *third* part of our subject, in contradistinction from the two just described, presupposes the concept of the Ideal and also the three general forms of art, since it is only the realization of these in specific sensuous materials. Therefore we now no longer have to do with the inner development of artistic beauty in its general fundamental characteristics. Instead we have to consider how these characteristics pass into existence, are distinguished from one another externally, and actualize every feature in the conception of beauty independently and explicitly as a *work of art* and not merely as a *general form*. But since it is the differences immanent in the Idea of beauty, and proper to it, that art transfers into external existence, it follows that in this Part III the general forms of art must likewise be the fundamental principle for the articulation and determination of the individual arts; in other words, the kinds of art have the same essential distinctions in themselves which we came to recognize in the general forms of art. Now the *external* objectivity into which these forms are introduced through a sensuous and therefore *particular* material, makes these forms *fall apart* from one another independently, to become distinct ways of their realization, i.e. the particular arts. For each form finds its specific character also in a specific external material, and its adequate realization in the mode of portrayal which that material requires. But, on the other hand, these art-forms, universal as they are despite their determinateness, break the bounds of a *particular* realization through a *specific* kind of art and achieve their existence equally through the other arts, even if in a subordinate way. Therefore the particular arts belong, on the one hand, specifically to *one* of the general forms of art and they shape its adequate external artistic actuality, and, on the other hand, in their own individual way of shaping externality, they present the totality of the forms of art.[1]

---

[1] The forms of art are the symbolic, classical, and romantic. The kinds of art are sculpture, painting, etc. There is a sense in which one kind of art (e.g. sculpture) is the adequate mode in which one form of art (e.g. the classical) is actualized. But no form of art is wholly actualized in one kind of art alone; it requires the others, even if they take a subordinate place. Thus while one kind of art may belong *par excellence* to one form of art, it also appears to some extent in the other forms and may be said to present them all. This whole section on the kinds of art is not easily intelligible except in the light of Hegel's full discussion in Part III of these lectures.

In general terms, that is to say, in Part III of our subject we have to deal with the beauty of art as it unfolds itself, in the arts and their productions, into a world of actualized beauty. The content of this world is the beautiful, and the true beautiful, as we saw, is spirituality given shape, the Ideal, and, more precisely, absolute spirit, the truth itself. This region of divine truth, artistically represented for contemplation and feeling, forms the centre of the whole world of art. It is the independent, free, and divine shape which has completely mastered the externality of form and material and wears it only as a manifestation of itself. Still, since the beautiful develops itself in this region as *objective* reality and therefore distinguishes within itself its single aspects and factors, granting them independent particularity, it follows that this centre now arrays its extremes, realized in their appropriate actuality, as contrasted with itself. One of these extremes therefore forms a still *spiritless objectivity*, the merely natural environment of God. Here the external as such takes shape as something having its spiritual end and content not in itself but in another.

The other extreme is the Divine as inward, as something known, as the variously particularized *subjective* existence of the Deity: the truth as it is effective and living in the sense, heart, and spirit of individual persons, not remaining poured out into its external shape, but returning into the subjective individual inner life. Thereby the Divine as such is at the same time distinguished from its pure manifestation as *Deity*, and thereby enters itself into the particularity characteristic of all individual subjective knowledge, emotion, perception, and feeling. In the analogous sphere of religion, with which art at its highest stage is immediately connected, we conceive this same difference as follows. *First*, earthly natural life in its finitude confronts us on one side; but then, *secondly*, our consciousness makes *God* its object wherein the difference of objectivity and subjectivity falls away, until, *thirdly*, and lastly, we advance from God as such to worship by the *community*, i.e. to God as living and present in subjective consciousness. These three fundamental differences arise also in the world of art in independent development.

(*a*) The *first* of the particular arts, the one with which we have to begin in accordance with this fundamental characterization of them, is *architecture* as a fine art. Its task consists in so manipulating external inorganic nature that, as an external world conformable to art, it becomes cognate to spirit. Its material is matter itself in its immediate externality as a mechanical heavy mass, and its forms remain the forms of inorganic nature, set in order according to relations of the abstract Understanding, i.e. relations of symmetry. In this material and in these forms the Ideal, as concrete spirituality, cannot be realized. Hence the reality presented in them remains opposed to the Idea, because it is something external not penetrated by the Idea or only in an abstract relation to it. Therefore the fundamental type of the art of building is the *symbolic* form of art. For architecture is the first to open the way for the adequate actuality of the god, and in his service it slaves away with objective nature in order to work it free from the jungle of finitude and the monstrosity of chance. Thereby it levels a place for the god, forms his external environment, and builds for him his temple as the place for the inner composure of the spirit and its direction on its absolute objects. It raises an enclosure for the assembly of the congregation, as protection against the threat of storm, against rain, tempest, and wild animals, and it reveals in an artistic way, even if in an external one, the wish to assemble. This meaning it can build into its material and the forms thereof with greater or lesser effect, in proportion as the determinate character of the content for which it undertakes its work is more significant or insignificant, more concrete or abstract, more profoundly plumbing its own depths, or more obscure and superficial. Indeed in this respect architecture may itself attempt to go so far as to fashion in its forms and material an adequate artistic existence for that content; but in that event it has already stepped beyond its own sphere and is swinging over to sculpture, the stage above it. For its limitation lies precisely in retaining the spiritual, as something inner, over against its own external forms and thus pointing to what has soul only as to something distinct from these.

(b) But by architecture, after all, the inorganic external world has been purified, set in order symmetrically, and made akin to spirit, and the god's temple, the house of his community, stands there ready. Then into this temple, *secondly*, the god enters himself as the lightning-flash of individuality striking and permeating the inert mass, and the infinite, and no longer merely symmetrical, form of spirit itself concentrates and gives shape to something corporeal. This is the task of *sculpture*.

In so far as in sculpture the spiritual inner life, at which architecture can only hint, makes itself at home in the sensuous shape and its external material, and in so far as these two sides are so mutually formed that neither preponderates, sculpture acquires the *classical* art-form as its fundamental type. Therefore, no expression is left to the sensuous which is not an expression of spirit itself, just as, conversely, for sculpture no spiritual content can be perfectly represented unless it can be fully and adequately presented to view in bodily form. For through sculpture the spirit should stand before us in blissful tranquillity in its bodily form and in immediate unity therewith, and the form should be brought to life by the content of spiritual individuality. So the external sensuous material is no longer processed either according to its mechanical quality alone, as a mass possessing weight, or in forms of the inorganic world, or as indifferent to colour, etc., but in the ideal forms of the human figure and in all three spatial dimensions too. In this last respect we must claim for sculpture that in it the inward and the spiritual come into appearance for the first time in their eternal peace and essential self-sufficiency. To this peace and unity with itself only that external shape corresponds which itself persists in this unity and peace. This is shape according to its *abstract spatiality*.[1] The spirit which sculpture presents is spirit compact in itself, not variously splintered into the play of accidents and passions. Consequently sculpture does not abandon spirit's external form to this variety of appearance, but picks up therein only this one aspect, abstract spatiality in the totality of its dimensions.

(*c*) Now when architecture has built its temple and the hand of sculpture has set up within it the statues of the god, this sensuously present god is confronted, *thirdly*, in the wide halls of his house, by the *community*. The community is the spiritual reflection into itself of this sensuous existent, and is animating subjectivity and inwardness. With these, therefore, it comes about that the determining principle, alike for the content of art and for the material that represents it outwardly, is particularization and individualization and their requisite subjective apprehension. The compact unity in itself which the god has in sculpture disperses into the plurality of the inner lives of individuals whose unity is not

---

[1] i.e. shape taken simply as an object occupying space (Bosanquet, op. cit., p. 199).

sensuous but purely ideal.[1] And so only here is God himself truly spirit, spirit in his community, God as this to-and-fro, as this exchange of his inherent unity with his actualization in subjective knowing and its individualization as well as in the universality and union of the multitude. In the community God is released alike from the abstraction of undeveloped self-identity and from his sculptural representation as immediately immersed in a bodily medium; and he is raised to spirituality and knowledge, i.e. to spirit's mirror-image which essentially appears as inward and as subjectivity. Consequently the higher content is now the spiritual, the spiritual as absolute. But at the same time, owing to the dispersal mentioned just now, the spiritual appears here as *particular* spirituality, an individual mind. And it is not the self-sufficient peace of the god in himself, but appearance as such, being *for* another, that manifestation of the self, which comes to the fore here as the chief thing; so now what becomes on its own account an object of artistic representation is the most manifold subjectivity in its living movement and activity as human passion, action, and adventure, and, in general, the wide range of human feeling, willing, and neglect.

Now in conformity with this content the sensuous element in art has likewise to show itself particularized in itself and appropriate to subjective inwardness. Material for this is afforded by colour, musical sound, and finally sound as the mere indication of inner intuitions and ideas. And as modes of realizing the content in question by means of these materials we have painting, music, and poetry. Here the sensuous medium appears as particularized in itself and posited throughout as ideal. Thus it best corresponds with the generally spiritual content of art, and the connection of spiritual meaning with sensuous material grows into a deeper intimacy than was possible in architecture and sculpture. Nevertheless this is a more inner unity which lies entirely on the subjective side, and which, in so far as form and content have to particularize themselves and posit themselves as ideal, can only come about at the expense of the objective universality of the content and its fusion with the immediately sensuous element.

Now in these arts form and content raise themselves to ideality,

[1] The unity of the members of a church is not visible, but exists in their common belief and in the recognition of their community (Bosanquet, op. cit., p. 200).

and thus, since they leave behind symbolic architecture and the classical idea of sculpture, they acquire their type from the *romantic* form of art on whose mode of configuration they are adapted to impress themselves in the most appropriate manner. But they are a totality of arts, because the romantic is in itself the most concrete form of art.

The inner articulation of this *third sphere* of the individual arts may be established as follows:

(α) The *first* art, standing next to sculpture, is *painting*. It uses as material for its content, and its content's configuration, visibility as such, in so far as this is at the same time particularized, i.e. developed into colour. True, the material of architecture and sculpture is likewise visible and coloured, but it is not, as in painting, the making visible as such; it is not the simple light which, differentiating itself in its contrast with darkness, and in combination therewith, becomes colour.[1] This quality of visibility inherently subjectivized and posited as ideal, needs neither the abstract mechanical difference of mass operative in heavy matter, as in architecture, nor the totality of sensuous spatiality which sculpture retains, even if concentrated and in organic shapes. On the contrary, the visibility and the making visible which belong to painting have their differences in a more ideal way, i.e. in the particular colours, and they free art from the *complete* sensuous spatiality of material things by being restricted to the dimensions of a *plane* surface.

On the other hand, the content too attains the widest particularization. Whatever can find room in the human breast as feeling, idea, and purpose, whatever it is capable of shaping into act, all this multiplex material can constitute the variegated content of painting. The whole realm of particularity from the highest ingredients of spirit right down to the most isolated natural objects finds its place here. For even finite nature in its particular scenes and phenomena can come on the stage in painting, if only some allusion to an element of spirit allies it more closely with thought and feeling.

(β) The *second* art through which the romantic form is actualized is, as contrasted with painting, *music*. Its material, though still sensuous, proceeds to still deeper subjectivity and particularization.

---

[1] An obvious reference to Goethe's theory of colour, one of Hegel's favourite topics.

I mean that music's positing of the sensuous as ideal is to be sought in the fact that it cancels, and idealizes into the individual singularity of one point, the indifferent self-externality of space, the total appearance of which is accepted by painting and deliberately simulated. But as this negativity, the point is concrete in itself and an active cancellation within the material by being a movement and tremor of the material body in itself in its relation to itself. This incipient ideality of matter, which appears no longer as spatial but as temporal ideality, is sound: the sensuous set down as negated with its abstract visibility changed into audibility, since sound releases the Ideal, as it were, from its entanglement in matter.[1]

Now this earliest inwardness and ensouling of matter affords the material for the still indefinite inwardness and soul of the spirit, and in its tones makes the whole gamut of the heart's feelings and passions resound and die away. In this manner, just as sculpture stands as the centre between architecture and the arts of romantic subjectivity, so music forms the centre of the romantic arts and makes the point of transition between the abstract spatial sensuousness of painting and the abstract spirituality of poetry. Like architecture, music has in itself, as an antithesis to feeling and inwardness, a relation of quantity conformable to the mathematical intellect; it also has as its basis a fixed conformity to law on the part of the notes and their combination and succession.

(γ) Finally, as for the *third*, most spiritual presentation of romantic art, we must look for it in *poetry*. Its characteristic peculiarity lies in the power with which it subjects to spirit and its ideas the sensuous element from which music and painting began to make art free. For sound, the last external material which poetry keeps, is in poetry no longer the feeling of sonority itself, but a *sign*, by itself void of significance, a sign of the idea which has become concrete in itself, and not merely of indefinite feeling and its nuances and gradations. Sound in this way becomes a *word* as a voice inherently articulated, the meaning of which is to indicate ideas and thoughts. The inherently negative point to which music had moved forward now comes forth as the completely

---

[1] For this section on sound and music, see Hegel's *Philosophy of Nature*, i.e. *Enc. of the Phil. Sciences* §§ 300–2. Eng. tr. by A. V. Miller (Oxford, 1970), pp. 136–47, by M. J. Petry (London, 1970), vol. 2, pp. 69–82. Also the whole section on music in part iii.

concrete point, as the point of the spirit, as the self-conscious individual who out of his own resources unites the infinite *space* of his ideas with the *time* of sound. Yet this sensuous element, which in music was still immediately one with inwardness, is here cut free from the content of consciousness, while spirit determines this content on its own account and in itself and makes it into ideas. To express these it uses sound indeed, but only as a sign in itself without value or content. The sound, therefore, may just as well be a mere letter, since the audible, like the visible, has sunk into being a mere indication of spirit. Therefore the proper element of poetical representation is the poetical *imagination* and the illustration of spirit itself, and since this element is common to all the art-forms, poetry runs through them all and develops itself independently in each of them. Poetry is the universal art of the spirit which has become free in itself and which is not tied down for its realization to external sensuous material; instead, it launches out exclusively in the inner space and the inner time of ideas and feelings. Yet, precisely, at this highest stage, art now transcends itself, in that it forsakes the element of a reconciled embodiment of the spirit in sensuous form and passes over from the poetry of the imagination to the prose of thought.

This we may take to be the articulated totality of the particular arts: the external art of architecture, the objective art of sculpture, and the subjective art of painting, music, and poetry. Of course many other classifications have been attempted, since the work of art presents such a wealth of aspects that, as has often happened, now this one and now that can be made the basis of classification. Consider, for example, the sensuous material. In that case architecture is the crystallization, sculpture the organic configuration, of matter in its sensuous and spatial totality; painting is the coloured surface and line; while, in music, space as such passes over into the inherently filled point of time; until, finally, in poetry the external material is altogether degraded as worthless. Alternatively, these differences have been considered in their totally abstract aspect of space and time. But such abstract characteristics of the work of art may of course, like its material, be consistently pursued in their special features, but they cannot be carried through as the final basis of classification, because any such aspect derives its origin from a higher principle and therefore has to be subordinate thereto.

As this higher principle we have found the art-forms of the symbolical, the classical, and the romantic, which are themselves the universal moments of the Idea of beauty.

The concrete form of their relation to the individual arts is of such a kind that the several arts constitute the real existence of the art-forms. *Symbolic art* attains its most appropriate actuality and greatest application in *architecture*, where it holds sway in accordance with its whole conception and is not yet degraded to be the inorganic nature, as it were, dealt with by another art. For the *classical form*, on the other hand, *sculpture* is its unqualified realization, while it takes architecture only as something surrounding it, and it cannot yet develop painting and music as absolute forms for its content. Finally, the *romantic* art-form masters painting and music, and poetic representation likewise, as modes of expression in a way that is substantive and unqualified. But poetry is adequate to all forms of the beautiful and extends over all of them, because its proper element is beautiful imagination, and imagination is indispensable for every beautiful production, no matter to what form of art it belongs.

Now, therefore, what the particular arts realize in individual works of art is, according to the Concept of art, only the universal forms of the self-unfolding Idea of beauty. It is as the external actualization of this Idea that the wide Pantheon of art is rising. Its architect and builder is the self-comprehending spirit of beauty, but to complete it will need the history of the world in its development through thousands of years.

PART I

THE IDEA OF ARTISTIC BEAUTY, OR THE IDEAL

INTRODUCTION

POSITION OF ART IN RELATION TO THE FINITE WORLD AND TO RELIGION AND PHILOSOPHY

Since we are now moving out of the Introduction and entering upon the scientific treatment of our subject, our first task is to indicate briefly the general place of artistic beauty in the realm of reality as a whole and of aesthetics in relation to other philosophical disciplines. Our object is to settle the point from which a true science of the beautiful must start.

To this end, therefore, it might seem useful to begin by giving an account of the various attempts to grasp the beautiful in thought, and by dissecting and assessing these attempts. But, for one thing, this has already been done in the Introduction, and, for another, it cannot possibly be the business of a truly scientific study *merely* to investigate what others have done, rightly or wrongly, or merely to learn from them. On the other hand, it may be better to say a prefatory word once again on the fact that many are of opinion that the beautiful as such, just because it is the beautiful, cannot be grasped in concepts and therefore remains for thought a topic which is not conceivable. To this allegation it may be briefly retorted here that, even if today everything true is pronounced to be beyond conception while only phenomena in their finitude, and temporal events in their accidentality, are conceivable, it is just precisely the true alone which is *conceivable*, because it has the absolute *Concept* and, more closely stated, the Idea as its foundation. But beauty is only a specific way of expressing and representing the true, and therefore stands open throughout in every respect to conceptual thinking, so long as that thinking is actually equipped with the power of the Concept. True, in modern times, *no* concept has come worse off than *the Concept* itself, the Concept implicit and explicit for itself; for by 'concept' people have commonly understood an abstract determinacy and one-sidedness of our ideas or of the thinking of the Understanding, with which, naturally, neither the totality of the true nor the inherently concrete beautiful can be brought thoughtfully into consciousness. For beauty, as was said already [Introduction, 8] and as is to be expounded further later [ch. I, 1(*a*)] is no such abstraction of the Understanding but the inherently concrete absolute Concept and, more specifically, the absolute Idea in its appearance in a way adequate to itself.

If we wish to indicate briefly what the *absolute Idea* is in its genuine actuality, we must say that it is *spirit*, not, as may be supposed, spirit in its restrictedness and involvement with the finite, but the universal infinite and *absolute* spirit which out of itself determines what is genuinely the true. If we ask our ordinary consciousness only, the idea of spirit that presses on us is certainly that it stands over against nature, to which in that case we ascribe a like dignity. But in thus putting nature and spirit alongside one another and relating them to one another as equally essential realms, spirit is being considered only in its finitude and restriction, not in its infinity and truth. That is to say, nature does not stand over against spirit, either as possessing the same value or as spirit's limitation; on the contrary, it acquires the standing of having been posited by spirit, and this makes it a product, deprived of the power of limiting and restricting. At the same time, absolute spirit is to be understood only as absolute activity and therefore as absolutely self-differentiating within. Now this other, as spirit's self-differentiation, is precisely nature, and spirit is the bounty which gives to this opposite of itself the whole fullness of its own being. Nature, therefore, we have to conceive as itself carrying the absolute Idea implicitly, but nature is the Idea in the form of having been posited by absolute spirit as the opposite of spirit. In this sense we call nature a creation. But its truth is therefore the creator itself, spirit as ideality and negativity; as such, spirit particularizes itself within and negates itself, yet this particularization and negation of itself, as having been brought about *by itself*, it nevertheless cancels, and instead of having a limitation and restriction therein it binds itself together with its opposite in free universality. This ideality and infinite negativity constitutes the profound concept of the *subjectivity* of spirit.

But, as subjectivity, spirit is, to begin with, only *implicitly* the truth of nature, since it has not yet made its true Concept explicit to itself. Thus at this stage nature stands over against spirit, not as spirit's opposite, set down by spirit itself, in which spirit reverts into itself, but as a restricting otherness, not overcome. Spirit as subjective, existent in knowing and willing, remains related to this otherness as to an object just found, and it can form only the opposite of nature. In this sphere [of spirit's mere subjectivity] there falls the finitude of both theoretical and practical spirit, restriction in knowing, and the mere 'ought' in the pursuit of realising the good. Here too, as in nature, spirit's appearance is inadequate to its true essence; and we still get the confusing spectacle of skills, passions, aims, views, and talents, running after and flying away from one another, working for and against one another, at cross purposes, while their willing and striving, their opining and thinking, are advanced or deranged by an intermixture of the greatest diversity of sorts of chance. This is the standpoint of the spirit which is purely finite, temporal, contradictory, and therefore transient, unsatisfied, and unblessed. For the satisfactions afforded in this sphere are themselves in their finite shape always still restricted and curtailed, relative and isolated. Therefore discernment, consciousness, willing, and thinking lift themselves above them, and seek and find their true universality, unity, and satisfaction elsewhere—in the infinite and the true. This unity and satisfaction to which the driving rationality of the spirit raises the material of its finitude is then and only then the true unveiling of what the world of appearance is in its essential nature. Spirit apprehends finitude itself as its own negative and thereby wins its infinity. This truth of finite spirit is the absolute spirit.

But in this form spirit becomes actual only as absolute negativity; it puts its finitude into itself and cancels it. Thereby, in its highest realm, it explicitly makes itself the object of its knowing and willing. The Absolute itself becomes the *object* of the spirit, in that the spirit reaches the stage of *consciousness* and *distinguishes* itself within itself as *knowing* and, over against this, as the absolute object of knowledge. From the earlier standpoint of the finitude of spirit, which knows of the Absolute as an infinite object *standing over against it*, spirit is therefore characterized as the *finite,* distinguished therefrom. But, looked at in a higher speculative way, it is the *absolute spirit itself* which, in order explicitly to be knowledge of itself, makes distinctions *within* itself, and thereby establishes the finitude of spirit, within which it becomes the absolute object of the knowledge of itself. Thus it is absolute spirit in its community,[1] the actual Absolute as spirit and self-knowledge.

This is the point at which we have to begin in the philosophy of art. For the beauty of art is neither the Idea as conceived in *Logic*, i.e. absolute thought as it is developed in the pure element of thinking, nor yet, on the other hand, the Idea as it appears in *Nature*; on the contrary, it belongs to the sphere of *spirit*, though without stopping at the knowledge and deeds of the *finite* spirit. The realm of fine art is the realm of the *absolute spirit*. That this is the case we can only indicate here; the scientific *proof* devolves on the preceding philosophical disciplines, namely logic, the content of which is the absolute Idea as such, and the philosophy of nature as the philosophy of the finite spheres of the spirit. For it is the task of these sciences to show how the Idea in logic has, in accordance with its own Concept, to transpose itself into natural existence and then, out of this externality, into spirit; and finally to free itself from the finitude of spirit again to become spirit in its eternity and truth.[2]

From this point of view, which pertains to art in its highest and true dignity, it is at once clear that art belongs to the same province as religion and philosophy. In all the spheres of absolute spirit, spirit liberates itself from the cramping barriers of its existence in externality, by opening for itself a way out of the contingent affairs of its worldly existence, and the finite content of its aims and interests there, into the consideration and completion of its being in and for itself.

This position of art in the entire sphere of natural and spiritual life we can expound more concretely in the following way, with a view to understanding it better.

If we glance over the whole field of our existence, we find already in our ordinary way of looking at things an awareness of the

1 See below, Part II, ch. I.
2 Hegel is referring to the three parts of his *Encyclopaedia of the Philosophical Sciences*. The first part (Logic) and the third (Mind, Art, Religion, Philosophy) have been translated by W. Wallace. The second part (Nature) has appeared in two translations, one by A. V. Miller and the other by M. J. Petry, both in 1970.

greatest multiplicity of interests and their satisfaction. First, the wide system of physical needs for which the great spheres of business work in their broad operation and connection, e.g. trade, shipping, and technologies; then higher is the world of jurisprudence, law, family life, class divisions, the whole comprehensive scope of the State; next the need of religion which every heart feels and which finds its contentment in the life of the church; finally, the variously divided and complicated activity of science, the entirety of observation and knowledge, which comprehends everything. Now among these spheres artistic activity also arises, an interest in beauty and a spiritual satisfaction in artistic creations. Hence a question is raised about the inner necessity of such a need in connection with the other realms of life and the world. Initially we find these spheres simply present as such. But, according to the demands of science, the matter at issue is insight into their essential inner connection and their reciprocal necessity. For they do not stand only, as might be supposed, in a relation of mere utility to one another; on the contrary they complement one another, because in one sphere there are higher modes of activity than there are in the other. Consequently the subordinate one presses on above itself, and now, by the deeper satisfaction of wider-ranging interests, what in an earlier province can find no termination is supplemented. This alone provides the necessity of an inner connection.

If we recall what we have already established about the Concept of the beautiful and art, we find two things: first, a content, an aim, a meaning; and secondly the expression, appearance, and realization of this content. But, thirdly, both aspects are so penetrated by one another that the external, the particular, appears exclusively as a presentation of the inner. In the work of art nothing is there except what has an essential relation to the content and is an expression of it. What we called the content, the meaning, is something in itself simple (the thing itself reduced to its simplest yet most comprehensive characteristics) in distinction from execution. So, for example, the content of a book may be indicated in a few words or sentences,[1] and nothing else should be found in the book beyond the universal aspect of its content which has already

[1] Perhaps Hegel was never asked by a publisher to summarize the content of one of his books in a 'few sentences'. The 'few sentences' are apt to be either unintelligible or misleading, or both.

been stated. This simple thing, this theme, as it were, which forms the basis for the execution of the work, is the abstract; the concrete comes only with the execution.

But the two sides of this opposition have not been given the character of remaining indifferent and external to one another— in the way that for instance the external appearance of a mathematical figure (triangle, ellipse), i.e. its specific size, colour, etc., is indifferent to the figure itself which is the inherently simple content. On the contrary, the meaning, abstract in form by being the content pure and simple, is destined in itself to be actually expressed and thereby to be made concrete. Accordingly there essentially enters an *ought*. Whatever validity a content may have in itself, we are still not satisfied with this abstract validity and crave for something further. At first this is only an unsatisfied need, and for the conscious subject it is something inadequate which strives to go beyond itself and advance to satisfaction. In this sense we may say that the content is at first *subjective*, something purely inward, with the objective standing over against it, so that now this gives rise to a demand that the subjective be objectified. Such an opposition between the subjective and the objective contrasted with it, as well as the fact that it ought to be transcended, is simply a universal characteristic running through everything. Even our physical life, and still more the world of our spiritual aims and interests, rests on the demand to carry through into objectivity what at first was there only subjectively and inwardly, and then alone to find itself satisfied in this complete existence. Now since the content of our interests and aims is present at first only in the one-sided form of subjectivity, and the one-sidedness is a restriction, this deficiency shows itself at the same time as an unrest, a grief, as something *negative*. This, as negative, has to cancel itself, and therefore, in order to remedy this felt deficiency, struggles to overcome the restriction which is known and thought. And this does not mean at all that the other side, the objective, just quits the subjective; on the contrary it means that they have a more specific connection —i.e. this defect in the *subjective* itself, and felt by itself, is a deficiency and a negation *in* the subjective which it struggles to negate again. In itself, that is to say, the individual in his essential nature is the *totality*, not the inner alone, but equally the realization of this inner through and in the outer. If now he exists one-sidedly *only* in one form, he therefore falls at once into the contradiction of being, in essence, the whole, but in his existence, only one side. Only by the cancellation of such a negation in itself does life become affirmative. To go through this process of opposition, contradiction, and the resolution of the contradiction is the higher privilege of living beings; what from the beginning is and remains *only* affirmative is and remains without life. Life proceeds to negation and its grief, and it only becomes affirmative in its own eyes by obliterating the opposition and the contradiction. It is true that if it remains in mere contradiction without resolving it, then on contradiction it is wrecked.

These we may take to be the points, considered in their abstraction, which we require at this stage.

Now the highest content which the subject can comprise in himself is what we can point-blank call *freedom*. Freedom is the highest destiny of the spirit. In the first place, on its purely formal side, it consists in this, that in what confronts the subject there is nothing alien and it is not a limitation or a barrier; on the contrary, the subject finds himself in it. Even under this formal definition of freedom, all distress and every misfortune has vanished, the subject is reconciled with the world, satisfied in it, and every opposition and contradiction is resolved. But, looked at more closely, freedom has the rational in general as its content: for example, morality in action, truth in thinking. But since freedom at first is only subjective and not effectively achieved, the subject is confronted by the unfree, by the purely objective as the necessity of nature, and at once there arises the demand that this opposition be reconciled.

On the other side a similar opposition is found within the subjective sphere itself. On the one hand, whatever is universal and independent, the universal laws of the right, the good, the true, etc., all belong to freedom; while, on the other hand, there are the impulses of mankind, feelings, inclinations, passions, and everything comprised in the concrete heart of man as an individual. This opposition too goes on to a battle, a contradiction, and in this strife there then arise all longings, the deepest grief, torment, and loss of satisfaction altogether. Animals live in peace with themselves and their surroundings, but in the spiritual nature of man duality and inner conflict burgeon, and in their contradiction he is tossed about. For in the inner as such, in pure thought, in the world of laws and their universality man cannot hold out; he needs also sensuous existence, feeling, the heart, emotion, etc. The opposition, which therefore arises, philosophy *thinks* as it is in its thoroughgoing universality, and proceeds to the cancellation of the same in a similarly *universal* way; but man in the immediacy of life presses on for an *immediate* satisfaction. Such a satisfaction through the resolving of that opposition we find most readily in the system of sensuous needs. Hunger, thirst, weariness; eating, drinking, satiety, sleep, etc., are in this sphere examples of such a contradiction and its resolution. Yet in this natural sphere of human existence the content of its satisfactions is of a finite and restricted kind; the satisfaction is not absolute, and so a new want arises continually and restlessly: eating, satiety, sleeping, are no help; hunger and weariness begin again on the morrow.

Consequently, man strives further in the realm of spirit to obtain satisfaction and freedom in knowing and willing, in learning and actions. The ignorant man is not free, because what confronts him is an alien world, something outside him and in the offing, on which he depends, without his having made this foreign world for himself and therefore without being at home in it by himself as in something his own. The impulse of curiosity, the pressure for knowledge, from the lowest level up to the highest rung of philosophical insight arises only from the struggle to cancel this situation of unfreedom and to make the world one's own in one's ideas and thought. Freedom in action issues in the opposite way, from the fact that the rationality of the will wins actualization. This rationality the will actualizes in the life of the state. In a state which is really articulated rationally all the laws and organizations are nothing but a realization of freedom in its essential characteristics. When this is the case, the individual's reason finds in these institutions only the actuality of his own essence, and if he obeys these laws, he coincides, not with something alien to himself, but simply with what is his own. Caprice, of course, is often equally called 'freedom'; but caprice is only non-rational freedom, choice and self-determination issuing not from the rationality of the will but from fortuitous impulses and their dependence on sense and the external world.

Now man's physical needs, as well as his knowing and willing, do indeed get a satisfaction in the world and do resolve in a free way the antithesis of subjective and objective, of inner freedom and externally existent necessity. But nevertheless the content of this freedom and satisfaction remains *restricted*, and thus this freedom and self-satisfaction retain too an aspect of *finitude*. But where there is finitude, opposition and contradiction always break out again afresh, and satisfaction does not get beyond being relative. In law and its actualization, for example, my rationality, my will and its freedom, are indeed recognized; I count as a person and am respected as such; I have property and it is meant to remain mine; if it is endangered, the court sees justice done to me. But this recognition and freedom are always solely confined to single relative matters and their single objects: this house, this sum of money, this specific right, this specific law, etc., this single action and reality. What confronts consciousness here is single circumstances which indeed bear on one another and make up a totality of relations, but only under purely relative categories and innumerable conditions, and, dominated by these, satisfaction may as easily be momentary as permanent.

Now, at a higher level, the life of the state, as a whole, does form a perfect totality in itself: monarch, government, law-courts, the military, organization of civil society, and associations, etc., rights and duties, aims and their satisfaction, the prescribed modes of action, duty-performance, whereby this political whole brings about and retains its stable reality—this entire organism is rounded off and completely perfected in a genuine state. But the *principle* itself, the actualization of which is the life of the state and wherein man seeks his satisfaction, is still once again *one-sided* and inherently abstract, no matter in how many ways it may be articulated without and within. It is only the rational freedom of the *will* which is explicit here; it is only in the *state*—and once again only this *individual* state—and therefore again in a *particular* sphere of existence and the isolated reality of this sphere, that freedom is actual. Thus man feels too that the rights and obligations in these regions and their mundane and, once more, *finite* mode of existence are insufficient; he feels that both in their objective character, and also in their relation to the subject, they need a still higher confirmation and sanction.

What man seeks in this situation, ensnared here as he is in finitude on every side, is the region of a higher, more substantial, truth, in which all oppositions and contradictions in the finite can find their final resolution, and freedom its full satisfaction. This is the region of absolute, not finite, truth. The highest truth,

truth as such, is the resolution of the highest opposition and contradiction. In it validity and power are swept away from the opposition between freedom and necessity, between spirit and nature, between knowledge and its object, between law and impulse, from opposition and contradiction as such, whatever forms they may take. Their validity and power *as* opposition and contradiction is gone. Absolute truth proves that neither freedom by itself, as subjective, sundered from necessity, is absolutely a true thing nor, by parity of reasoning, is truthfulness to be ascribed to necessity isolated and taken by itself. The ordinary consciousness, on the other hand, cannot extricate itself from this opposition and either remains despairingly in contradiction or else casts it aside and helps itself in some other way. But philosophy enters into the heart of the self-contradictory characteristics, knows them in their essential nature, i.e. as in their one-sidedness not absolute but self-dissolving, and it sets them in the harmony and unity which is truth. To grasp this Concept of truth is the task of philosophy.

Now philosophy recognizes the Concept in everything, and only thereby is it conceptual and genuine thinking. Nevertheless the Concept, truth implicit, is one thing, and the existence which does or does not correspond with truth, is another. In finite reality the determinate characteristics of truth appear as outside one another, as a separation of what in its truth is inseparable. So, for example, the living being is an individual, but, by being subject, it comes into an opposition with an environment of inorganic nature. Now of course the Concept contains these two sides, but as reconciled; whereas finite existence drives them asunder and is therefore a reality inadequate to the Concept and to truth. In this sense the Concept is indeed everywhere; but the point of importance is whether the Concept is *truly* actual even in this unity in which the separate sides and their opposition persist in no *real* independence and fixity over against one another but count still as only *ideal* factors reconciled into a free harmony. The only actuality of this supreme unity is the region of truth, freedom, and satisfaction. In this sphere, in this enjoyment of truth, life as feeling is bliss, as thinking is knowledge, and we may describe it in general as the life of religion. For religion is the universal sphere in which the *one* concrete totality comes home to the consciousness of man as his own essence and as the essence of nature. And this one genuine actuality alone evinces itself to him as the supreme power over the particular and the finite, whereby everything otherwise separated and opposed is brought back to a higher and absolute unity.

Now, owing to its preoccupation with truth as the absolute object of consciousness, art too belongs to the absolute sphere of the spirit, and therefore, in its content, art stands on one and the same ground with religion (in the stricter sense of the word) and philosophy. For, after all, philosophy has no other object but God and so is essentially rational theology and, as the servant of truth, a continual divine service.

Owing to this sameness of content the three realms of absolute spirit differ only in the *forms* in which they bring home to consciousness their object, the Absolute.

The differences between these forms are implied in the nature of absolute spirit itself. The spirit in its truth is absolute. Therefore it is not an essence lying in abstraction beyond the objective world. On the contrary, it is present within objectivity in the finite spirit's recollection or inwardization of the essence of all things—i.e. the finite apprehends itself in its own essence and so itself becomes essential and absolute. Now the *first* form [art] of this apprehension is an immediate and therefore *sensuous* knowing, a knowing, in the form and shape of the sensuous and objective itself, in which the Absolute is presented to contemplation and feeling. Then the *second* form [religion] is *pictorial* thinking, while the *third* and last [philosophy] is the *free* thinking of absolute spirit.

(*a*) Now the form of *sensuous intuition* is that of art, so that it is art which sets truth before our minds in the mode of sensuous configuration, a sensuous configuration which in this its appearance has itself a loftier, deeper sense and meaning, yet without having the aim of making the Concept as such in its universality comprehensible by way of the sensuous medium; for it is precisely the *unity* of the Concept with the individual appearance which is the essence of the beautiful and its production by art. Now of course this unity achieved in art is achieved not only in sensuous externality but also in the sphere of imagination, especially in poetry; but still in this too, the most[1] spiritual of the arts, the union of meaning with its individual configuration is present, even if for the imaginative consciousness, and every content is grasped in

---

[1] The superlative is the reading of Hotho's 1st edn.

an immediate way and brought home to the imagination. In general, we must state at once that while art has truth, i.e. the spirit, as its proper subject-matter, it cannot provide a vision of the same by means of particular natural objects as such, i.e. by means of the sun, for example, the moon, the earth, stars, etc. Such things are visible existents, it is true, but they are isolated and, taken by themselves, cannot provide a vision of the spiritual.

Now in giving art this absolute position we are expressly rejecting the above-mentioned [Introduction, 6(iii)] idea which assumes that art is useful for some varied ulterior subject-matter or other interests foreign to itself. On the other hand, *religion* makes use of art often enough to bring religious truth home to people's feelings or to symbolize it for the imagination, and in that event of course art stands in the service of a sphere different from itself. Yet when art is present in its supreme perfection, then precisely in its figurative mode it contains the kind of exposition most essential to and most in correspondence with the content of truth. Thus, for example, in the case of the Greeks, art was the highest form in which the people represented the gods to themselves and gave themselves some awareness of truth. This is why the poets and artists became for the Greeks the creators of their gods, i.e. the artists gave the nation a definite idea of the behaviour, life, and effectiveness of the Divine, or, in other words, the definite content of religion. And it was not as if these ideas and doctrines were already there, *in advance* of poetry, in an abstract mode of consciousness as general religious propositions and categories of thought, and then later were only clothed in imagery by artists and given an external adornment in poetry; on the contrary, the mode of artistic production was such that what fermented in these poets they could work out *only* in this form of art and poetry. At other levels of the religious consciousness, where the religious content is less amenable to artistic representation, art has in this respect a more restricted field of play.

This is the original true standing of art as the first and immediate satisfaction of absolute spirit.

But just as art has its 'before' in nature and the finite spheres of life, so too it has an 'after', i.e. a region which in turn transcends art's way of apprehending and representing the Absolute. For art has still a limit in itself and therefore passes over into higher forms of consciousness. This limitation determines, after all, the position which we are accustomed to assign to art in our contemporary life. For us art counts no longer as the highest mode in which truth fashions an existence for itself. In general it was early in history that thought passed judgement against art as a mode of illustrating the idea of the Divine; this happened with the Jews and Mohammedans, for example, and indeed even with the Greeks, for Plato opposed the gods of Homer and Hesiod starkly enough. With the advance of civilization a time generally comes in the case of every people when art points beyond itself. For example, the historical elements in Christianity, the Incarnation of Christ, his life and death, have given to art, especially painting, all sorts of opportunities for development, and the Church itself has nursed art or let it alone; but when the urge for knowledge and research, and the need for inner spirituality, instigated the Reformation, religious ideas were drawn away from their wrapping in the element of sense and brought back to the inwardness of heart and thinking. Thus the '*after*' of art consists in the fact that there dwells in the spirit the need to satisfy itself solely in its own inner self as the true form for truth to take. Art in its beginnings still leaves over something mysterious, a secret foreboding and a longing, because its creations have not completely set forth their full content for imaginative vision. But if the perfect content has been perfectly revealed in artistic shapes, then the more far-seeing spirit rejects this objective manifestation and turns back into its inner self. This is the case in our own time. We may well hope that art will always rise higher and come to perfection, but the form of art has ceased to be the supreme need of the spirit. No matter how excellent we find the statues of the Greek gods, no matter how we see God the Father, Christ, and Mary so estimably and perfectly portrayed: it is no help; we bow the knee no longer [before these artistic portrayals].

(*b*) Now the next sphere, which transcends the realm of art, is religion. *Religion* has pictorial thinking as its form of consciousness, for the Absolute has removed from the objectivity of art into the inwardness of the subject and is now given to pictorial thinking in a subjective way, so that mind and feeling, the inner subjective life in general, becomes the chief factor. This advance from art to religion may be described by saying that for the religious consciousness art is only *one* aspect. If, that is to say, the work of art presents truth, the spirit, as an object in a sensuous mode and adopts this form of the Absolute as the adequate one, then religion adds to this the worship given by the inner self in its relation to the absolute object. For worship does not belong to art as such. Worship only arises from the fact that now by the subject's agency the heart is permeated with what art makes objective as externally perceptible, and the subject so identifies himself with this content that it is its *inner* presence in ideas and depth of feeling which becomes the essential element for the existence of the Absolute. Worship is the community's cult in its purest, most inward, most subjective form—a cult in which objectivity is, as it were, consumed and digested, while the objective content, now stripped of its objectivity, has become a possession of mind and feeling.

(c) Finally, the *third* form of absolute spirit is *philosophy*. For in religion God, to begin with, is an external object for consciousness, since we must first be taught what God is and how he has revealed and still reveals himself; next, religion does work in the element of the inner life, and stirs and animates the community. But the inwardness of the heart's worship and our pictorial thinking is not the highest form of inwardness. As this purest form of knowledge we must recognize untrammelled *thinking* in which philosophy brings to our minds the same content [as in religion] and thereby attains that most spiritual worship in which thinking makes its own and knows conceptually what otherwise is only the content of subjective feeling or pictorial thinking. In this way the two sides, art and religion, are united in philosophy: the *objectivity* of art, which here has indeed lost its external sensuousness but therefore has exchanged it for the highest form of the objective, the form of thought, and the *subjectivity* of religion which has been purified into the subjectivity of *thinking*. For thinking on one side is the most inward, closest, subjectivity—while true thought, the Idea, is at the same time the most real and most objective universality which only in thinking can apprehend itself in the form of its own self.

With this indication of the difference between art, religion, and philosophy we must here be content.

The sensuous mode of consciousness is the earlier one for man, and so, after all, the earlier stages of religion were a religion of art and its sensuous representation. Only in the religion of the spirit is God now known as spirit in a higher way, more correspondent with thought; this at the same time makes it plain that the manifestation of truth in a sensuous form is not truly adequate to the spirit.

Division of the Subject

Now that we know the position which art has in the domain of spirit and which the philosophy of art has amongst the particular philosophical disciplines, we have first of all to consider in this general section the *general Idea* of artistic beauty.

In order to reach this Idea in its completeness we must once more go through three stages:

the *first* is concerned with the Concept of the beautiful as such;

the *second* with the beauty of nature, the deficiencies of which will make it evident that the Ideal necessarily has the form of *artistic* beauty;

the *third* stage has as its topic for consideration the Ideal in its actualization by being artistically represented in the work of art.

Chapter I

CONCEPT OF THE BEAUTIFUL AS SUCH

1. *The Idea*

We called the beautiful the Idea of the beautiful. This means that the beautiful itself must be grasped as Idea, in particular as Idea in a determinate form, i.e. as Ideal. Now the Idea as such is nothing but the Concept, the real existence of the Concept, and the unity of the two. For the Concept as such is not yet the Idea, although 'Concept' and 'Idea' are often used without being distinguished. But it is only when it is present in its real existence and placed in unity therewith that the Concept is the Idea. Yet this unity ought not to be represented, as might be supposed, as a mere neutralization of Concept and Reality, as if both lost their peculiar and special qualities, in the way in which caustic potash and acid interact to form a salt, and, combining, neutralize their contrasting properties.[1] On the contrary, in this unity the Concept is predominant. For, in accordance with its own nature, it *is* this identity implicitly already, and therefore generates reality out of itself as its own; therefore, since this reality is its own self-development, it sacrifices nothing of itself in it, but therein simply realizes itself, the Concept, and therefore remains one with itself in its objectivity. This unity of Concept and Reality is the abstract definition of the Idea.

However often use is made of the word 'Idea' in theories of art, still vice versa extremely excellent connoisseurs of art have shown themselves particularly hostile to this expression. The latest and most interesting example of this is the polemic of [Karl F.] von Rumohr in his *Italienische Forschungen*.[2] It starts from the practical interest in art and never touches at all on what we call the Idea. For von Rumohr, unacquainted with what recent philosophy calls 'Idea', confuses the Idea with an indeterminate idea and the

---

[1] This translation I owe to Dr. David Traill.

[2] *Italian Studies* (3 vols., Berlin and Stettin, 1827–31). Since Hegel did not lecture on Aesthetics after 1828 he may have used only the first volume. Below he quotes no other. Rumohr lived from 1785 to 1843.

abstract characterless ideal of familiar theories and schools of art—
an ideal the very opposite of natural forms, completely delineated
and determinate in their truth; and he contrasts these forms, to
their advantage, with the Idea and the abstract ideal which the
artist is supposed to construct for himself out of his own resources.
To produce works of art according to these abstractions is of course
wrong—and just as unsatisfactory as when a thinker thinks in
vague ideas and in his thinking does not get beyond a purely vague
subject-matter. But from such a reproof what *we* mean by the
word 'Idea' is in every respect free, for the Idea is completely
concrete in itself, a totality of characteristics, and beautiful only
as immediately one with the objectivity adequate to itself.

According to what he says in his book (i, pp. 145–6) von Rumohr
has found 'that beauty, as understood in the most general way and,
if you like, in terms of the modern intellect, comprises all those
properties of things which stir the sense of sight satisfyingly or
through it attune the soul and rejoice the spirit'. These properties
are further to be divided into three kinds 'of which the first works
only on mere seeing, the second only on man's own presupposedly
innate sense for spatial relationships, and the third in the first
place on the understanding and then, and then only, through
knowledge, on feeling'. This third most important point is supposed (p. 144) to depend on forms 'which quite independently of
what pleases the senses and of the beauty of proportion, awaken
a certain ethical and spiritual pleasure, which proceeds partly from
the enjoyment derived from the ideas' (but query: the ethical and
spiritual ideas) 'thus aroused, and partly also precisely from the
pleasure which the mere activity of an unmistakable knowing
unfailingly brings with it'.

These are the chief points which this serious connoisseur lays
down for his part in relation to the beautiful. For a certain level
of culture they may suffice, but for philosophy they cannot possibly
be satisfying. For in essentials his treatment of the matter amounts
simply to this, that the sense or spirit of sight, and the understanding too, is *rejoiced*, that feeling is excited, and that a delight has
been aroused. The whole thing revolves round this awakening of
joy. But Kant[1] has already made an end of this reduction of

[1] *The Critique of Judgment* is never far from Hegel's mind throughout this
whole section. Many of his topics come from Kant. It would be superfluous to
give precise references in view of the excellent indexes in the translation of the
Critique of Aesthetic Judgment by J. C. Meredith (Oxford, 1911).

beauty's effect to feeling, to the agreeable, and the pleasant, by going far beyond the *feeling* of the beautiful.

If we turn back from this polemic to the Idea that was left unimpugned thereby, we find in the Idea, as we saw, the concrete unity of Concept and objectivity.

(*a*) Now, as regards the nature of the Concept as such, it is not in itself an abstract unity at all over against the differences of reality; as Concept it is already the unity of specific differences and therefore a concrete totality. So, for example, ideas like man, blue, etc., are *prima facie* not to be called 'concepts', but abstractly universal ideas, which only become the Concept when it is clear in them that they comprise different aspects in a unity, since this inherently determinate unity constitutes the Concept: for example, the idea 'blue' as a colour has the unity, the specific unity, of light and dark for its Concept,[1] and the idea 'man' comprises the oppositions of sense and reason, body and spirit; though man is not just put together out of these two sides as constituent parts indifferent to one another; in accordance with his Concept he contains them in a concrete and mediated unity.

But the Concept is so much the absolute unity of its specifications that these do not remain independent and they cannot be realized by separating themselves from one another so as to become independent individuals, or otherwise they would abandon their unity. In this way the Concept contains all its specifications in the form of this its *ideal* unity and universality, which constitutes its *subjectivity* in distinction from real and objective existence. So, for example, gold has a specific weight, a determinate colour, a particular relation to acids of various kinds. These are different specifications, and yet they are all together in one. For each tiniest little particle of gold contains them in inseparable unity. In our minds they stand apart from one another, but in themselves, by their own nature, they are there in unseparated unity. The same identity and lack of independence belongs to the differences which the true Concept has in itself. A closer example is afforded by our own ideas, by the self-conscious *ego* as such. For what we call 'soul' and, more precisely, *ego* is the Concept itself in its free existence. The *ego* contains a mass of the most different ideas and thoughts, it is a world of ideas; yet this infinitely varied content, by being in the *ego*, remains entirely immaterial and without body and, as it

---

[1] Another allusion to Goethe's theory of colours.

were, compressed in this ideal unity, as the pure, perfectly transparent shining of the *ego* into itself. This is the way in which the Concept contains its different determinations in an ideal unity.

The more precise determinations which belong to the Concept in virtue of its own nature are the universal, the particular, and the individual. Each of these determinations, taken by itself, is a purely one-sided abstraction. But they are not present in the Concept in this one-sidedness, because it is their ideal *unity*. Consequently the Concept is the *universal*, which on the one hand negates itself by its own activity into particularization and determinacy, but on the other hand once again cancels this particularity which is the negative of the universal. For the universal does not meet in the *particular* with something absolutely *other*; the particulars are only particular aspects of the universal itself, and therefore the universal restores in the particular its unity with itself as universal. In this returning into itself the Concept is infinite negativity; not a negation of something other than itself, but self-determination in which it remains purely and simply a self-relating affirmative unity. Thus it is true *individuality* as universality closing only with itself in its particularizations. As the supreme example of this nature of the Concept, we can reckon what was briefly touched upon above [in the Introduction to this Part] as the essence of spirit.

Owing to this infinity in itself the Concept is already implicitly a totality. For in the being of its other it is still a unity with itself and therefore is the freedom for which all negation is only self-determination and not an alien restriction imposed by something else. But by being this totality the Concept already contains everything that reality as such brings into appearance and that the Idea brings back into a mediated unity. Those who suppose that they have in the Idea something totally other than the Concept, something particular in contrast with it, do not know the nature of either the Idea or the Concept. But at the same time the Concept is distinguished from the Idea by being particularization only *in abstracto*, since determinacy, as it exists in the Concept, remains caught in the unity and ideal universality which is the Concept's element.

But, that being so, the Concept remains one-sided and it is afflicted with the defect that, although itself implicitly totality, it allows only to the side of unity and universality the right of free development. But because this one-sidedness is incommensurate with the Concept's own essence, the Concept cancels it in accordance with its own Concept. It negates itself as this ideal unity and universality and now releases to real independent objectivity what this unity shut in within itself as ideal subjectivity. By its own activity the Concept posits itself as *objectivity*.

(b) Objectivity, taken by itself, is therefore nothing but the *reality* of the Concept, but the Concept in the form of independent particularization and the *real* distinguishing of all the factors of which the Concept as subjective was the *ideal* unity.

But, since it is only the Concept which has to give itself existence and reality in objectivity, objectivity will have to bring the *Concept* to actuality in objectivity itself. Yet the Concept is the mediated ideal unity of its particular factors. Therefore, although the difference of the particulars is *real*, their *ideal* conceptually adequate unity must all the same be restored within them; they are particularized in *reality* but their unity, mediated into *ideality*, must also exist in them. This is the power of the Concept which does not abandon or lose its universality in the dispersed objective world, but reveals this its unity precisely through and in reality. For it is its own Concept to preserve in its opposite this unity with itself. Only so is the Concept the actual and true totality.

(c) This totality is the *Idea*, i.e. it is not only the ideal unity and subjectivity of the Concept, but likewise its objectivity—the objectivity which does not stand over against the Concept as something merely opposed to it but, on the contrary, the objectivity in which the Concept relates itself to itself. On both sides, subjective and objective, of the Concept, the Idea is a whole, but at the same time it is the eternally completing and completed correspondence and mediated unity of these totalities. Only so is the Idea truth and all truth.

2. *The Idea in Existence*

Everything existent, therefore, has truth only in so far as it is an existence of the Idea. For the Idea is alone the genuinely actual. Appearance, in other words, is not true simply because it has an inner or outer existence, or because it is reality as such, but only because this reality corresponds with the Concept. Only in that event has existence actuality and truth. And truth not at all in the *subjective* sense that there is an accordance between some existent and *my* ideas, but in the *objective* meaning that the *ego* or an external object, an action, an event, a situation in its reality is itself a realization of the Concept. If this identity is not established, then the existent is only an appearance in which, not the total Concept, but only one abstract side of it is objectified; and that side, if it establishes itself in itself independently against the totality and unity, may fade away into opposition to the true Concept. Thus it is only the reality which is adequate to the Concept which is a true reality, true indeed because in it the Idea itself brings itself into existence.

3. *The Idea of the Beautiful*

Now we said that beauty is Idea, so beauty and truth are in one way the same. Beauty, namely, must be true in itself. But, looked at more closely, the true is nevertheless distinct from the beautiful. That is to say, what is *true* is the Idea, the Idea as it is in accordance with its inherent character and universal principle, and as it is grasped as such in thought. In that case what is *there* for thinking is not the Idea's sensuous and external existence, but only the *universal Idea* in this existence. But the Idea should realize itself externally and win a specific and present existence as the objectivity of nature and spirit. The true as such *exists* also. Now when truth in this its external existence is present to consciousness immediately, and when the Concept remains immediately in unity with its external appearance, the Idea is not only true but beautiful. Therefore the beautiful is characterized as the pure appearance of the Idea to sense. For the sensuous and the objective as such preserve in beauty no independence in themselves; they have to sacrifice the immediacy of their being, since this being is only the existence and objectivity of the Concept; and it is posited as a reality which presents the Concept as in unity with its objectivity and thus also presents the Idea itself in this objective existent which has worth only as a pure appearance of the Concept.

(*a*) For this reason, after all, it is impossible for the Understanding to comprehend beauty, because, instead of penetrating to this unity, the Understanding clings fast to the differences exclusively in their independent separation, by regarding reality as something quite different from ideality, the sensuous as quite different from the Concept, the objective as quite different from the subjective, and thinks that such oppositions cannot be [reconciled and] unified. Thus the Understanding steadily remains in the field of the finite, the one-sided, and the untrue. The beautiful, on the other hand, is in itself *infinite* and free. For even if there can be a question too of a particular content, and therefore, once more, of a restricted one, still this content must appear in its existence as a totality infinite in itself and as *freedom*, because the beautiful throughout is the Concept. And the Concept does not set itself against its objectivity by opposing to it a one-sided finitude and abstraction; on the contrary, it closes together with what confronts it and on the strength of this unity and perfection is infinite in itself. In the same way, the Concept ensouls the real existence which embodies it, and therefore is free and at home with itself in this objectivity. For the Concept does not allow external existence in the sphere of beauty to follow its own laws independently; on the contrary, it settles out of itself its phenomenal articulation and shape, and this, as the correspondence of the Concept with itself in its outward existence, is precisely what constitutes the essence of beauty. But the bond and the power which keeps this correspondence in being is subjectivity, unity, soul, individuality.

(*b*) Therefore if we consider beauty in relation to the *subjective* spirit, it is not present either to the unfree intelligence which persists in its finitude or to the finitude of the will.

As finite intelligences, we sense inner and outer objects, we observe them, we become aware of them through our senses, we have them brought before our contemplation and ideas, and, indeed, before the abstractions of our thinking understanding which confers on them the abstract form of universality. The finitude and unfreedom of this attitude lies in presupposing things to be independent. Therefore we direct our attention to things, we let them alone, we make our ideas, etc., a prisoner to belief in things, since we are convinced that objects are rightly understood only when our relation to them is passive, and when we restrict our whole activity to the formality of noticing them and putting a negative restraint on our imaginations, preconceived opinions, and prejudices. With this one-sided freedom of objects there is immediately posited the unfreedom of subjective comprehension. For in the case of this latter the content is *given*, and instead of subjective self-determination there enters the mere acceptance and adoption of what is there, objectively present just as it is. Truth in that case is to be gained only by the subjugation of subjectivity. The same thing is true, though in an opposite way, with finite

willing. Here interests, aims, and intentions lie in the *subject* who wills to assert them in face of the being and properties of things. For he can only carry out his decisions by annihilating objects, or at least altering them, moulding them, forming them, cancelling their qualities, or making them work upon one another, e.g. water on fire, fire on iron, iron on wood, and so on. Thus now it is things which are deprived of their independence, since the subject brings them into his service and treats and handles them as *useful*, i.e. as objects with their essential nature and end not in themselves but in the subject, so that what constitutes their proper essence is their relation (i.e. their service) to the aims of the subject. Subject and object have exchanged their roles. The objects have become unfree, the subjects free.

But, as a matter of fact, in both these relations, both sides are finite and one-sided, and their freedom is a purely supposititious freedom.

In the field of *theory* the subject is finite and unfree because the independence of things is presupposed; the same is true in the field of *practice*, owing to the one-sidedness, struggle, and inner contradiction between aims and the impulses and passions aroused from outside, and owing also to the never wholly eliminated resistance of the objects. For the separation and opposition of the two sides, object and subject, is the presupposition in this matter and is regarded as its true essence.

The same finitude and unfreedom affects the *object* in both theoretical and practical matters. In the *theoretical* sphere, the object's independence, although presupposed, is only an apparent freedom. For objectivity as such just *is*, without any awareness of its Concept as subjective unity and universality within itself. Its Concept is outside it. Therefore, every object, its Concept being outside it, exists as mere particularity which with its many-sidedness is turned outwards and in its infinitely varied relations appears at the mercy of origination and alteration by others, subject to their power, and to destruction by them. In *practical* matters this dependence is expressly posited as such, and the resistance of things to the will remains relative, not possessing in itself the power of ultimate independence.

(c) But the consideration and the existence of objects as *beautiful* is the unification of both points of view, since it cancels the one-sidedness of both in respect of the subject and its object alike, and therefore their finitude and unfreedom.

For, in its *theoretical* relation, the object now is not just taken as being merely an existent individual thing which therefore has its subjective Concept outside its objectivity, and in its particular reality scatters and disperses into external relations in many ways in the most varied directions; on the contrary, the *beautiful* thing in its existence makes its own Concept appear as realized and displays in itself subjective unity and life. Thereby the object has bent its outward tendency back into itself, has suppressed dependence on something else, and, under our consideration, has exchanged its unfree finitude for free infinity.

But the self in relation to the object likewise ceases to be the abstraction of both noticing, sensuously perceiving, and observing, and also of dissolving individual perceptions and observations into abstract thoughts. In this [beautiful] object the self becomes concrete in itself since it makes explicit the unity of Concept and reality, the unification, in their concreteness, of the aspects hitherto separated, and therefore abstract, in the self and its object.

In the matter of *practice*, as we have seen at greater length already [in the Introduction, 6(ii)], desire likewise withdraws when the beautiful is under consideration, and the subject cancels his aims in relation to the object and treats it as independent, an end in itself. Therefore there is dissolved the purely finite standing of the object in which it served purposes external to it as a useful means of fulfilling them, and either, unfree, armed itself against their fulfilment or else was compelled to accept the alien purpose as its own. At the same time the unfree situation of the active agent has disappeared because his consciousness is no longer differentiated into subjective intentions, etc., and their sphere and the means to their achievement; his relation to the fulfilment of his subjective intentions is no longer the finite one of the mere 'ought'; he has gone beyond it and what now confronts him is the perfectly realized Concept and end.

Thus the contemplation of beauty is of a liberal kind; it leaves objects alone as being inherently free and infinite; there is no wish to possess them or take advantage of them as useful for fulfilling finite needs and intentions. So the object, as beautiful, appears neither as forced and compelled by us, nor fought and overcome by other external things.

For, in virtue of the essence of beauty, what must appear in the beautiful object is the Concept with its soul and end, as well as its external determinacy, many-sidedness, and, in general, its reality created by itself and not by something else, since, as we saw just now, the object has truth only as the immanent unity and correspondence of the specific existent and its genuine essence and Concept. Now further, since the Concept itself is the concrete, its reality too appears as just a complete creation, the parts of which are nevertheless revealed as ideally ensouled and unified. For the harmony of the Concept with its appearance is a perfect interpenetration. Consequently the external form and shape does not remain separate from the external material, nor is it stamped on it mechanically for some other purposes; it appears as the form immanent in the reality and corresponding with the nature of that reality, the form giving itself an outward shape.

But, finally, however much the particular aspects, parts, and members of the beautiful object harmonize with one another to form an ideal unity and make this unity appear, nevertheless this harmony must only be so visible in them that they still preserve an appearance of independent freedom over against one another; i.e. they must not, as in the Concept as such, have a *purely* ideal unity, they must also present the aspect of independent reality. In the beautiful object there must be both (i) *necessity*, established by the Concept, in the coherence of its particular aspects, and (ii) the appearance of their *freedom*, freedom for themselves and not *merely* for the unity of the parts on view. Necessity as such is the relation of aspects so essentially interlinked with one another that if one is there, the other is immediately there also. Such necessity should not be missing in beautiful objects, but it must not emerge in the form of necessity itself; on the contrary, it must be hidden behind an appearance of undesigned contingency. For otherwise the particular real parts lose their standing as existing on the strength of their own reality too, and they appear only in the service of their ideal unity, to which they remain abstractly subordinate.

Owing to this freedom and infinity, which are inherent in the Concept of beauty, as well as in the beautiful object and its subjective contemplation, the sphere of the beautiful is withdrawn from the relativity of finite affairs and raised into the absolute realm of the Idea and its truth.

Chapter II

THE BEAUTY OF NATURE

The beautiful is the Idea as the immediate unity of the Concept with its reality, the Idea, however, only in so far as this its unity is present immediately in sensuous and real appearance.

Now the first existence of the Idea is *nature*, and beauty begins as the beauty of nature.

A. NATURAL BEAUTY AS SUCH

1. *The Idea as Life*

In the world of nature we must at once make a distinction in respect of the manner in which the Concept, in order to be as Idea, wins existence in its realization.

(*a*) *First*, the Concept immediately sinks itself so completely in objectivity that it does not itself appear as subjective ideal unity; on the contrary, it has altogether passed over soullessly into the material world perceived by the senses. Purely mechanical and physical separate and particular bodies are of this kind. A metal, for example, is in itself a manifold of mechanical and physical qualities; but every tiny part of it possesses them in the same way. Such a body lacks the complete articulation which it would have if each of its different parts had a particular material existence of its own, nor can it have the negative ideal unity of these parts which would declare itself as their animation. The different parts are only an abstract multiplicity and their unity is only the insignificant one of the uniformity of the same qualities.

This is the Concept's first mode of existence. Its distinctions[1] have no independent existence, and its ideal unity does not emerge as ideal; on this account, then, such separated bodies are in themselves defective and abstract existents.

(*b*) *Secondly*, on the other hand, higher natural objects set free the distinctions of the Concept, so that now each one of them outside the others is there for itself independently. Here alone appears the true nature of objectivity. For objectivity is precisely

[1] i.e. universal, particular, individual. See above, p. 109.

this independent dispersal of the Concept's distinctions. Now at this stage the Concept asserts itself in this way: since it is the totality of its determinacies which makes itself real, the particular bodies, though each possesses an independent existence of its own, close together into one and the same system. One example of this kind of thing is the solar system. The sun, comets, moons, and planets appear, on the one hand, as heavenly bodies independent and different from one another; but, on the other hand, they are what they are only because of the determinate place they occupy in a total system of bodies. Their specific kind of movement, as well as their physical properties, can be derived only from their situation in this system. This interconnection constitutes their inner unity which relates the particular existents to one another and holds them together.

Yet at this purely *implicit* unity of the independently existing particular bodies the Concept cannot stop. For it has to make real not only its distinctions but also its self-relating unity. This unity now distinguishes itself from the mutual externality of the objective particular bodies and acquires for itself at this stage, in contrast to this mutual externality, a real, bodily, independent existence. For example, in the solar system the sun exists as this unity of the system, over against the real differences within it.— But the existence of the ideal unity in this way is itself still of a defective kind, for, on the one hand, it becomes real only as the relation together of the particular independent bodies and their bearing on one another, and, on the other hand, as *one* body in the system, a body which represents the unity as such, it stands over against the real differences. If we wish to consider the sun as the soul of the entire system, it has itself still an independent persistence outside the members of the system which are the unfolding of this soul. The sun itself is only *one* moment of the Concept, the moment of unity in distinction from the Concept's real particularization, and consequently a unity which remains purely *implicit* and therefore abstract. For the sun, in virtue of its physical quality, is the purely identical, the giver of light, the light-body as such, but it is also only this abstract identity. For light is simple undifferentiated shining in itself.—So in the solar system we do find the Concept itself become real, with the totality of its distinctions made explicit, since each body makes *one* particular factor appear, but even here the Concept still remains sunk in its real existence; it does not come forth as the ideality and the inner independence thereof. The decisive form of its existence remains the independent mutual externality of its different factors.

But what the true existence of the Concept requires is that the *real differences* (namely the reality of the independent differences and their equally independently objectified unity as such) be themselves brought back into unity; i.e. that such a whole of natural differences should on the one hand make the Concept explicit as a real mutual externality of its specific determinations, and yet on the other hand set down as cancelled in every particular thing its self-enclosed independence; and now make the ideality, in which the differences are turned back into subjective unity, emerge in them as their universal animating soul. In that event, they are no longer merely *parts* hanging together and related to one another, but *members*; i.e. they are no longer sundered, existing independently, but they have genuine existence only in their ideal unity. Only in such an organic articulation does there dwell in the members the ideal unity of the Concept which is their support and their immanent soul. The Concept remains no longer sunk in reality but emerges into existence in it as the inner identity and universality which constitute its own essence.

(c) This *third* mode of natural appearance alone is an existence of the Idea, the Idea in natural form as *Life*. Dead, inorganic nature is not adequate to the Idea, and only the living organism is an actuality of the Idea. For in life, in the *first* place, the reality of the Concept's distinctions is present as real; *secondly*, however, there is the negation of these as merely real distinctions, in that the ideal subjectivity of the Concept subdues this reality to itself; *thirdly*, there is the soulful *qua* the affirmative appearance of the Concept in its corporeality, i.e. *qua* infinite form which has the power to maintain itself, as form, in its content.

(α) If we examine our ordinary view about life, what it implies is (a) the idea of the body, and (b) the idea of the soul. To the two we ascribe different qualities of their own. This *distinction* between soul and body is of great importance for the philosophical treatment of the subject too, and we must take it up here likewise. But knowledge's equally important interest in this matter concerns the *unity* of soul and body which has always posed the greatest difficulties to thoughtful study. It is on account of this unity that life is precisely a first appearance of the Idea in nature. Therefore we must not take the identity of soul and body as a mere *connection*, but in a deeper way, i.e. we must regard the body and its members as the existence of the systematic articulation of the Concept itself. In the members of the living organism the Concept gives to its determinations an external being in nature, as is already the case, at a lower level, in the solar system. Now within this real existence the Concept rises nevertheless into the ideal unity of all these determinations, and this ideal unity is the soul. The soul is the substantial unity and all-pervasive universality which at the same time is simple relation to itself and subjective self-awareness. It is in this higher sense that the unity of soul and body must be taken. Both, that is to say, are not different things which come into connection with one another, but one and the same totality of the same determinations. And just as the Idea as such can only be understood as the Concept aware of itself in its objective reality, which implies both the difference and the unity of Concept and reality, so life too is to be known only as the unity of soul with its body. The subjective as well as the substantial unity of the soul within the body itself is displayed, for example, as feeling.

Feeling in the living organism does not belong independently to one particular part alone, but is this ideal unity of the entire organism itself. It permeates every member, is all over the organism in hundreds and hundreds of places, and yet in the same organism there are not many thousands of feelers; there is only one, *one* self that feels. Since life in organic nature contains this difference between the real existence of the members and the soul simply aware of itself in them, and yet no less contains this difference as a mediated unity, the organic is a higher sphere than inorganic nature. For only the living thing is Idea, and only the Idea is the truth. Of course even in the organic sphere this truth can be disturbed in that the body does not completely bring to fruition its ideality and its possession of soul, as, for instance, in illness. In that event the Concept does not rule as the sole power; other powers share the rule. But then such an existent is a bad and crippled life, which still lives only because the incompatibility of Concept and reality is not absolutely thorough but only relative. For if the correspondence of the two were no longer present at all, if the body altogether lacked genuine articulation and its true ideality, then life would at once change into death which sunders into independence what the possession of soul holds together in undivided unity.

(β) When we said (i) that the soul is the totality of the Concept, as the inherently subjective ideal unity, and (ii) that the articulated body is this same totality, but as the exposition and sensuously perceived separatedness of all the particular members, and that both (i) and (ii) were posited in the living thing as in *unity*, there is here, to be sure, a contradiction. For the ideal unity is not only *not* the perceived separatedness in which every particular member has an independent existence and a separate peculiarity of its own; on the contrary, it is the direct opposite of such external reality. But to say that opposites are to be identical is precisely contradiction itself. Yet whoever claims that nothing exists which carries in itself a contradiction in the form of an identity of opposites is at the same time requiring that nothing living shall exist. For the power of life, and still more the might of the spirit, consists precisely in positing contradiction in itself, enduring it, and overcoming it. This positing and resolving of the contradiction between the ideal unity and the real separatedness of the members constitutes the constant process of life, and life *is* only by being a *process*.

The process of life comprises a double activity: on the one hand, that of bringing steadily into existence perceptibly the real differences of all the members and specific characteristics of the organism, but, on the other hand, that of asserting in them their universal ideality (which is their animation) if they try to persist in independent severance from one another and isolate themselves in fixed differences from one another. This is the idealism of life. For philosophy is not at all the only example of idealism; nature, as life, already makes a matter of fact what idealist philosophy brings to completion in its own spiritual field.—But only these two activities in one—the constant transfer of the specific characteristics of the organism into realities, and the putting of these real existents ideally into their subjective unity—constitute the complete process of life, the detailed forms of which we cannot consider here. Through this unity of double activity all the members of the organism are constantly upheld and constantly brought to the ideality of their animation. After all, the members display this ideality forthwith in the fact that their animated unity is not indifferent to them, but on the contrary is the substance in which and through which alone they can preserve their particular individuality. This is precisely what constitutes the essential difference between the part of a whole and the member of an organism.

The particular parts of a house, for example, the individual stones, windows, etc., remain the same, whether they together form a house or not; their association is indifferent to them and the Concept remains for them a purely external form which does not live in the real parts in order to raise them to the ideality of a subjective unity. The members of an organism, on the other hand, do likewise possess external reality, yet so strongly is the Concept their own indwelling essence that it is not impressed on them as a form merely uniting them externally; on the contrary, it is their sole sustainer. For this reason the members do not have the sort of reality possessed by the stones of a building or the planets, moons, comets in the planetary system; what they do have is an existence posited as ideal within the organism, despite all their reality. For example, a hand, if severed, loses its independent subsistence; it does not remain what it was in the organism; its mobility, agility, shape, colour, etc., are changed; indeed it decomposes and perishes altogether. It was sustained in existence only as a member of an organism, and had reality only as continually brought back into the ideal unity. Herein consists the higher mode of reality within the living organism; the real, the positive, is continually posited negatively and as ideal, while this ideality is at once precisely the maintenance of the real differences and the element in which they are sustained.

(γ) The reality which the Idea gains as natural life is on this account a reality that *appears*. Appearance, that is to say, means simply that there is some reality which, instead of having its being immediately in itself, is posited negatively in its outer existence at the same time. But the negating of the members that are immediately there externally is not just a negative relation, like the activity of idealization; on the contrary, affirmative being *for self* [or independence] is present in this negation at the same time. Hitherto we have considered particular realities in their complete particularization as the affirmative. But in life this independence is negated, and only the ideal unity within the living organism acquires the power of affirmative relation to self. The soul is to be understood as this ideality which in its negating is also affirmative. Therefore when it is the soul which appears in the body, this appearance is at the same time affirmative. The soul does indeed

display itself as the power against the independent particularization
of the members, and yet it also creates it by containing as inward
and ideal what is imprinted externally on the members and forms
[of the body]. Thus it is this positive inner itself which appears
in the outer; the outer which remains purely external would be
nothing but an abstraction and one-sidedness. But in the living
organism we have an outer in which the inner appears, since the
outer displays itself in itself as this inner which is its Concept.
To this Concept again there belongs the reality in which the Concept appears as Concept. But since in objectivity the Concept as
such is the self-related subjectivity that in its reality is still confronted by itself, life exists only as a living *being*, as an individual
subject. Life alone has found this negative point of unity: the
point is negative because subjective self-awareness can only emerge
through positing the real differences as *merely* real, but therewith
at the same time the subjective affirmative unity of self-awareness
is linked.—To emphasize this aspect of subjectivity is of great
importance. Life is only now actual as individual living subject.

If we ask further by what indications the Idea of life in actual
living individuals can be known, the answer is as follows: Life
must *first* be real as a totality of a bodily organism, but, *secondly*,
as an organism which does not appear as something stubborn, but
as an inherent continual process of idealizing, in which the living
soul displays itself. *Thirdly*, this totality is not determined from
without and alterable; it shapes itself outwardly from within; it is
in process, and therein is continually related to itself as a subjective
unity and an end in itself.

This inherently free independence of subjective life shows itself
principally in *spontaneous* movement. The inanimate bodies of
inorganic nature have their fixed position in space; they are one
with their place, bound to it, or moved from it only by an external
force. For their movement does not proceed from themselves, and
when it is forced on them it appears in consequence as resulting
from an alien influence against which they struggle and react in
order to cancel it. And, even if the movement of the planets, etc.,
does not appear as an external propulsion and as foreign to the
bodies themselves, nevertheless it is tied to a fixed law and its
abstract necessity. But the living animal in its free spontaneous
movement negates by its own means this attachment to a determinate place and is the progressive liberation from physical unity

with such determinacy. Similarly in its movement it is the cancellation, even if only relative, of the abstraction involved in determinate modes of movement, its path, speed, etc. Looked at more closely, however, the animal has in its organism by its very nature a physical position in space, and its life is spontaneous movement within this reality itself, as the circulation of the blood, movement of the limbs, etc.

Movement, however, is not the only expression of life. The free-sounding of the animal voice, which inorganic bodies do not have because they rustle and clang only when impelled from outside, is already a higher expression of ensouled subjectivity. But idealizing activity is displayed in the most impressive manner in the fact that, on the one hand, the living individual separates himself off from the rest of reality, and yet, on the other hand, he equally makes the external world something *for himself*: partly contemplatively, through seeing, etc., partly practically by subjecting external things to himself, using them, assimilating them in the process of eating, and so, by means of what is his opposite, he continually reproduces himself as an individual, and indeed, in stronger organisms, by more definitely separated intervals of needing and consuming, of satisfaction and satiety [i.e. by mealtimes].

All these are activities in which the essential nature of life comes into appearance in ensouled individuals. Now this ideality is not at all only *our* reflection on life; it is *objectively* present in the living subject himself, whose existence, therefore, we may style an 'objective idealism'. The soul, as this ideality, makes *itself* appear, since it steadily degrades into an appearance the *purely* external reality of the body and therefore appears itself objectively in body.

2. *Life in Nature as Beautiful*

Now as the physically objective Idea, life in nature is *beautiful* because truth, the Idea in its earliest natural form as life, is immediately present there in individual and adequate actuality. Yet, because of this purely sensuous immediacy, the living beauty of nature is produced neither *for* nor *out* of *itself* as *beautiful* and for the sake of a beautiful appearance. The beauty of nature is beautiful only for another, i.e. for *us*, for the mind which apprehends beauty. Hence arises the question in what way and by what means life in its immediate existence appears as beautiful.

(a) If we consider the living thing first in its practical self-production and self-maintenance, the first thing that strikes us is *capricious* movement. This, regarded just as movement, is nothing other than the purely abstract freedom of changing place from time to time, in which the animal proves itself to be wholly capricious and its movement haphazard. On the other hand, music and dancing also involve movement; yet this movement is not just haphazard and capricious, but in itself regular, definite, concrete, and measured—even if we abstract altogether from the meaning of which it is the beautiful expression. If we look further at animal movement and regard it as the realization of an inner purpose, still this purpose is haphazard throughout and wholly restricted because it is only an impulse that has been aroused. But if we go further still and judge the movement as a purposeful act and the working together of all parts of the animal, then this mode of considering the movement proceeds solely from the activity of *our* intellect.—The same is the case if we reflect on how the animal satisfies its needs, nourishes itself, on how it gets its food, consumes and digests it, and, in general, how it accomplishes everything necessary for its self-preservation. For here too either we merely look on from the outside at single desires and their capricious and accidental satisfactions—in which case, we may add, the inner activity of the organism does not become perceptible at all, or all these activities and their modes of expression become an object for the intellect, which struggles to understand the purposefulness in them, and the correspondence between the inner purposes of the animal and the organs realizing them.

Neither the sensuous perception of single accidental desires, capricious satisfactions and movements, nor the intellectual consideration of the purposefulness of the organism makes animal life into the beauty of nature for us; on the contrary, beauty has respect to the appearance of an individual shape in its rest, as well as in its movement, regardless alike of its purposefulness in the satisfaction of needs, and of the entire separatedness and accidental nature of its spontaneous movements. But beauty can devolve only on the *shape*, because this alone is the external appearance in which the objective idealism of life becomes for us an object of our perception and sensuous consideration. *Thinking* apprehends this idealism in its *Concept* and makes this Concept explicit in its universality, but the consideration of *beauty* concentrates on the reality in which the Concept *appears*. And this reality is the external shape of the articulated organism, which for us is as much something purely apparent as it is something existent, since the merely real multiplicity of the particular members in the *ensouled* totality of the shape must be posited as purely apparent.

(*b*) According to the Concept of life already explained, there now arise the following points explanatory of the sort of pure appearance involved: The shape is spatially spread out, limited, figured, different in forms, colour, movement, etc., and is a manifold of such differences. But if the organism is to manifest itself as ensouled, then obviously it does not have its true existence in this manifold. This is because the different parts and their modes of appearance, which are present to us as sensuously perceptible, close together at the same time into a whole and therefore appear as an *individual* which is a unit and has these particular differences, even if as different, yet as all harmonious.

(α) But this unity must display itself in the *first* place as an *unintended* identity and therefore must not assert itself as abstract purposefulness. The parts must neither come before our eyes merely as means to a specific end and as in service to it, nor may they abandon their distinction from one another in construction and shape.

(β) On the contrary, the members, in the *second* place, acquire in our eyes an appearance of accident, i.e. the specific character of one is not posited in the other also. None of them has this or that shape because the other has it, as for example is the case in a regular system. In this latter some abstract principle of determination determines the shape, size, etc., of all the parts. For example, in a building the windows are of equal size or at least stand in one and the same row; similarly, in a regiment the regulars have one and the same uniform. Here the particular parts of clothing, their cut, colour, etc., are not accidental to one another, but one has its specific form on account of the other. Neither the difference of forms nor their proper independence gets its due here. But it is totally different in the organic and living individual. There each part is different, the nose from the forehead, the mouth from the cheeks, the breast from the neck, the arms from the legs, and so on. Now since in our eyes each member does not have the shape of another, but a form of its own which is not absolutely determined by another member, the members appear as independent in themselves, and therefore free and accidental to one another. For their material interconnection has nothing to do with their form as such.

(γ) But *thirdly*, for our contemplation an inner connection must nevertheless become visible in this independence of the members, although the unity may not remain abstract and external, as it does in mere regularity, but must recall and preserve the individual particularizations instead of obliterating them. This identity is not perceptible and immediately present to our view, like the difference of the members, and it remains, therefore, a secret *inner* necessity and correspondence. But if *purely* inner, and not outwardly visible too, it would be understood by thinking alone, and altogether beyond the scope of perception. Yet in that case it would lack the look of the beautiful, and by looking at the living thing we would not see the Idea as really appearing before us. Therefore the unity must also emerge into externality, although, because it is the ideally soul-giving thing, it may not remain purely physical and spatial. The unity appears in the individual as the universal ideality of its members which constitutes the up-holding and carrying foundation, the substratum of the living subject. This subjective unity emerges in the living organic being as feeling. In feeling and its expression, the soul manifests itself as *soul*. This is because for the soul the mere juxtaposition of the members has no truth, and for the soul's subjective ideality the multiplicity of spatial forms does not exist. It is true that the soul presupposes the variety, characteristic formation, and organic articulation of the bodily parts; but while the soul as feeling, and its expression, emerges in these, its omnipresent inner unity appears precisely as the annulment of mere independent realities, which now no longer present themselves only but their possession of soul as feeling.

(c) But at first the expression of soul-laden feeling affords neither the impression of a necessary interconnection of the particular members with one another nor the vision of the neces-sary identity of *real* articulation with the *subjective* unity of feeling as such.

(α) If, however, it is the shape, purely as shape, which is to bring this inner correspondence and its necessity into appearance, then for us the connection may seem to be the *habitual* juxta-position of the members, producing a certain type and repeated examples of this type. Habit, however, is itself a purely *subjective* necessity over again. By this criterion we may, for example, find animals ugly because they display an organism which deviates from our customary observations or contradicts them. For this reason we call animal organisms bizarre, if the way their organs are connected falls outside what we have already often seen previously and what therefore has become familiar: an example is a fish whose disproportionately large body ends in a short tail and whose eyes are together on one side of the head. In the case of plants we have long been accustomed to deviations of all sorts, although cacti, for example, with their prickles and the even straighter growth of their angled stems may seem remarkable.[1] Anyone widely versed and knowledgeable in natural history will, in this connection, have the most precise knowledge of the individual parts, as well as carrying in his memory the greatest number of types and their congruity, so that hardly anything unfamiliar comes before his notice.

(β) A deeper examination of this correspondence between the parts of an organism may, secondly, equip a man with the insight and skill that enable him to tell at once from one single member the *whole* shape to which it must belong. In this regard Cuvier,[2] for example, was famous, because by seeing a single bone—whether fossil or not—he could identify the animal species to which the individual bone belonged and was to be allocated. *Ex ungue leonem*[3] is valid here in the strict sense of the word; from a claw or a thigh-bone the conformation of the teeth can be inferred, from the teeth, vice versa, the shape of the hip-bone or the form of the spinal column. But, in such inference, knowledge of the type is no longer a matter of habit alone; there already enter, as guide, reflections and individual categories of thought. Cuvier, for example, in his identifications had before his mind a concrete specification and decisive property which was asserted in all the particular and different parts and therefore could be recognized

---

[1] The translation of this sentence I owe to Professor J. H. Burnett who thinks that Hegel is really referring to *euphorbiae* and not cacti. Professor H. G. Callan informs me that the description of the fish fits a Dover sole.

[2] Georges, Baron de Cuvier, 1769–1832: *Recherches sur les Ossemens Fossiles de Quadrupèdes* (Paris, 1812), vol. i, pp. 58 ff. Hegel quotes this at length in *Philosophy of Nature*, § 370, Addition.

[3] The origin of this familiar phrase seems to be Plutarch, *De Def. Or.*, 2, where he quotes it from Alcaeus.

again in them. Such a specific character, for example, is the property of being carnivorous which then constitutes the law for the organization of all the parts. A carnivorous animal, for example, requires different teeth, jaw-bone, etc.; if it goes hunting it must grip its prey and therefore needs claws—hoofs are insufficient. Here then *one* specific characteristic is the guide for the necessary shape and interconnection of all the members of the organism. Similar universal characteristics are of course also within the scope of the plain man's ideas, as for instance the strength of the lion or the eagle, and so forth. Now this way of considering the organism we may certainly call *beautiful* and ingenious because, as *consideration*, it teaches us to recognize a unity of configuration and its forms, although this unity is not uniformly repeated but is compatible with the members retaining at the same time their full differentiation. Nevertheless it is not *perception* which prevails in this method but a universal guiding *thought*. From this point of view we will therefore not say that we find the *object* beautiful, but that what we will call beauty lies in our *subjective* consideration of the object. And, looked at more closely, these reflections start from a single restricted aspect as a guiding principle, namely from the manner of animal nourishment, from the characteristic, for example, of being carnivorous or herbivorous, etc. But by such a characteristic it is not the connection of the whole, of the Concept, of the soul itself that is brought before our eyes.

(γ) If therefore within this natural sphere we were to bring the inner total unity of life to our ken, this could be achieved only by thinking and comprehending; for in nature the soul *as such* cannot make itself recognizable, because subjective unity in its ideality has not yet become explicit to itself. But if we now apprehend the soul, in accordance with its Concept, by thinking, we have two things: the perception of the shape, and the intellectual concept of the soul as soul. But in the perception of beauty this ought not to be the case; the object should neither float before our eyes as a thought, nor create, in the interest of thought, a difference from and an opposition to perception. Therefore there is nothing left but that the object shall be present for *sense* in general and that as the genuine mode of considering beauty in nature, we consequently get a *sensuous* perception of natural forms. 'Sense' is this wonderful word which is used in two opposite meanings. On the one hand it means the organ of immediate apprehension, but on the other hand we mean by it the sense, the significance, the thought, the universal underlying the thing. And so sense is connected on the one hand with the immediate external aspect of existence, and on the other hand with its inner essence. Now a *sensuous* consideration does not cut the two sides apart at all; in one direction it contains the opposite one too, and in sensuous immediate perception it at the same time apprehends the essence and the Concept. But since it carries these very determinations in a still unseparated unity, it does not bring the Concept as such into consciousness but stops at foreshadowing it. If, for example, three natural realms are identified, the mineral, the vegetable, the animal, then in this series of stages we see foreshadowed an inwardly necessary articulation in accordance with the Concept, without abiding by the mere idea of an external purposefulness. Even in the multiplicity of products within these realms, sensuous observation divines a rationally ordered advance, in the different geological formations, and in the series of vegetable and animal species.[1] Similarly, the individual animal organism—this insect with its subdivision into head, breast, belly, and extremities—is envisaged as an inherently rational articulation, and in the five senses, although at first sight they may seem to be just an accidental plurality, there is likewise found a correspondence with the Concept. Of this sort was Goethe's observation and demonstration of the inner rationality of nature and its phenomena. With great insight he set to work in a simple way to examine objects as they were presented to the senses, but at the same time he had a complete divination of their connection in accordance with the Concept. History too can be so understood and related that through single events and individuals their essential meaning and necessary connection can secretly shine.

3. *Ways of Considering Life in Nature*

Consequently, to sum up, nature in general, as displaying to sense the concrete Concept and the Idea, is to be called beautiful; this is because when we look at natural forms that accord with the Concept, such a correspondence with the Concept is foreshadowed;

[1] Hegel lived at a time before the theory of evolution had been scientifically established, and it was his rule, in discussing nature, to abide by what the scientists told him. But this is one of the passages which show how he foresaw that a rational explanation of the facts demanded an evolutionary theory. See, e.g., R. G. Collingwood, *The Idea of Nature* (Oxford, 1945), pp. 122 ff.

and when we examine them with our senses the inner necessity and the harmony of the whole articulation is revealed to them at the same time. The perception of nature as beautiful goes no further than this foreshadowing of the Concept. But the consequence is that this apprehension of nature, for which the parts, although appearing to have arisen in free independence from one another, yet make visible their harmony in shape, delineation, movement, etc., remains purely indeterminate and abstract. The inner unity remains *inward*; for perception it does not emerge in a concretely ideal form, and consideration acquiesces in the universality of some sort of a necessary animating harmony.

(*a*) Thus at this point we have primarily before us as the beauty of nature only the inherently ensouled harmony within the conceptually appropriate objectivity of natural productions. With this harmony the matter is immediately identical; the form dwells directly in the matter as its true essence and configurating power. This provides the general characterization for beauty at this stage. So, for example, the natural crystal amazes us by its regular shape, produced not by any external, mechanical, influence, but by an inner vocation and free force of its own, free on the part of the object itself. For an activity external to an object could as such of course be equally free, but in the crystal the formative activity is not foreign to the thing; it is an activating form which belongs to this mineral on the strength of its own nature. It is the free force of the matter itself which by immanent activity gives itself its form and does not acquire its specific character passively from without. And so the matter remains free and at home with itself in its realized form as its own form. In a still higher, more concrete, way a similar activity of immanent formation is displayed in the living organism and its outline, shape of limbs, and above all in its movement and the expression of feelings. For here it is the inner activity itself which emerges vitally.

(*b*) Yet even in this indeterminacy of natural beauty as inner animation, we make essential distinctions:

(α) In the light of our idea of life as well as of the foreshadowing of life's true Concept and the customary types of its corresponding appearance, we make distinctions according to which we call animals beautiful or ugly; for example, the sloth displeases because of its drowsy inactivity; it drags itself painfully along and its whole manner of life displays its incapacity for quick movement and activity. For activity and mobility are precisely what manifest the higher ideality of life. Similarly we cannot find beautiful the amphibia, many sorts of fish, crocodiles, toads, numerous kinds of insect, etc.; but hybrids especially, which build the transition from one specific form to another and intermix their shapes, may well astonish us, but they appear unbeautiful, as, for instance the duck-bill which is a mixture of a bird and a quadruped. This attitude of ours too may seem at first to be mere familiarity, because we have in our minds a fixed type for animal genera. But still in the familiarity there is not inactive the inkling that the construction of a bird, for example, belongs to it necessarily and that, because of its essence, it cannot assume forms proper to other genera without producing hybrids. Therefore these mixtures prove to be odd and contradictory. To the sphere of living natural beauty there belong neither the one-sided restrictedness of organization, which appears deficient and meaningless and points only to limited needs in the external world, nor such mixtures and transitions which, though not so one-sided in themselves, yet cannot hold fast to the specific characteristics of different species.

(β) In another sense we talk further about the beauty of nature when we have before our minds no organic living creation, for example if we look at a landscape. Here we have no organic articulation of parts as determined by the Concept and animated into its ideal unity, but on the one hand only a rich variety of objects and the external linkage of different configurations, organic or inorganic: the contours of hills, the windings of rivers, groups of trees, huts, houses, towns, palaces, roads, ships, sky and sea, valleys and chasms; on the other hand, within this variety there appears a pleasing or impressive external harmony which interests us.

(γ) Finally, the beauty of nature gains a special relation to us because it arouses emotional moods and because of its harmony with them. A relationship like this is produced, for example, by the stillness of a moonlit night, the peace of a glen through which a burn meanders, the sublimity of the immeasurable and troubled sea, the restful immensity of the starry heaven. Here significance does not belong to the objects as such, but must be sought in the emotional mood which they arouse. Similarly we call animals beautiful if they betray an expression of soul which chimes in with human qualities such as courage, strength, cunning, good nature, etc. This is an expression which, on the one hand, does of course belong to the animals as we see them and displays one aspect of their life, but, on the other hand, it belongs to our ideas and our own emotions.

(c) But however far even animal life, as the summit[1] of natural beauty, expresses possession of soul, nevertheless every animal life is throughout restricted and tied down to entirely specific qualities. The sphere of its existence is narrow and its interests are dominated by the natural needs of nourishment and sex, etc. Its soul-life, as what is inner and what gains expression in its outward shape, is poor, abstract, and worthless. Further, this inner does not emerge into appearance as *inner*; the living thing in nature does not reveal its soul on itself, for the thing in nature is just this, that its soul remains purely inward, i.e. does not express itself as something ideal. The soul of the animal, that is to say, is, as we have just indicated, not *present to itself* as this ideal unity; if it were, then it would also *manifest* itself to others in this self-awareness. Only the self-conscious *ego* is the simple ideal which, as ideal in its own eyes, knows itself as this simple unity and therefore gives itself a reality which is no mere external, sensuous, and bodily reality, but itself one of an ideal kind. Here alone has reality the form of the Concept itself; the Concept has itself over against itself, has *itself* for its object and in it confronts itself. But animal life is only *implicitly* this unity, in which reality as corporeal has a form different from the ideal unity of the soul. But the self-conscious *ego* is itself *explicitly* this unity, the aspects of which have the like ideality as their element. As this conscious concrete unity, the *ego* manifests itself too to others. But the animal through its form enables our observation only to surmise a soul, since it has itself no more than a cloudy appearance of a soul as the breath and fragrance which is diffused over the whole, brings the members into unity, and reveals in the animal's whole mode of living only the beginning of a particular character. This is the primary deficiency in the beauty of nature, even when considered in its highest configuration, a deficiency which will lead us on to the necessity of the *Ideal* as the beauty of *art*. But before we come

---

[1] Hegel had no liking for mountains, for example. (See his Diary of his Journey to the Bernese Oberland—in, e.g., *Dok. zu H's Entwicklung*, hrsg. J. Hoffmeister, Stuttgart, 1936.)

to the Ideal, there are two points [B and C below] which are the first consequences of this deficiency in all natural beauty. We said that the soul appears in the shape of animals only in a cloudy way as the connection of the parts of the organism, as a unifying point of a possession of soul which lacks any filling of substantial worth. Only an indeterminate and wholly abstract possession of soul emerges. This abstract appearance we now have to consider separately and briefly.

B. THE EXTERNAL BEAUTY OF THE ABSTRACT FORM AND THE ABSTRACT UNITY OF THE SENSUOUS MATERIAL

In nature there is an external reality which externally is determined, but its inner being does not get beyond indeterminacy and abstraction instead of attaining concrete inwardness as unity of soul. Consequently neither as being explicitly inward in an ideal form nor as ideal content, does this inwardness win an existence adequate to itself; on the contrary it appears in the external real objects as a unity determining them externally. The concrete unity of the inner would consist in this, that, on the one hand, the possession of soul would be in and for itself full of content, and, on the other hand, the external reality would be permeated by this its inner, and so make the real outward shape an obvious manifestation of the inner. But such a concrete unity beauty has not attained at this stage, but has this unity as the Ideal still lying ahead of it. Therefore concrete unity can now not yet enter the outward shape, but can only be *analysed*, i.e. the different aspects of the unity can only be considered as sundered and separated. Thus at first the configurating form and the external reality presented to sense fall apart from one another as different from one another, and we have *two* different aspects to consider here. But (*a*) in this separation and (*b*) in its abstraction, the inner unity is itself for the external reality an external unity, and therefore it does not appear in the external as the simply immanent form of the total inner Concept, but as ideality and determinacy dominating from the outside.

These are the matters whose more detailed explanation is our business now.

1. Beauty of Abstract Form

This is the first matter on which we have to touch. The form of natural beauty, as an abstract form, is on the one hand determinate and therefore restricted; on the other hand it contains a unity and an abstract relation to itself. But, regarded more closely, it regulates the external manifold in accordance with this its determinacy and unity which, however, does not become immanent inwardness and a soul-bearing shape, but remains an external determinacy and a unity imposed on the external.—This sort of form is what is called regularity and symmetry, then conformity to law, and finally harmony.

(a) Regularity and Symmetry

(α) Regularity[1] as such is in general sameness in something external and, more precisely, the same repetition of one and the same specific shape which affords the determining unity for the form of objects. On account of its initial abstraction such a unity is poles apart from the rational totality of the concrete Concept, with the result that its beauty is a beauty of the abstract Understanding; for the Understanding has for its principle abstract sameness and identity, not determined in itself. So, for example, among lines the straight line is the most regular, because it has only *one* direction, abstractly continually the same. Similarly, the cube is a completely regular figure. On all sides it has surfaces of the same size, equal lines and angles, which as right angles cannot be altered in size as obtuse or acute angles can.

(β) *Symmetry* hangs together with regularity; i.e. form cannot

---

[1] Hegel's distinction between *Regelmässigkeit* (regularity) and *Gesetzmässigkeit* (conformity to law) is not at first sight obvious and it rests on conceptions of rule and law expounded elsewhere in his works. Rule as uniformity is explicitly distinguished from law in the *Science of Logic* (*Ww.* v, 198–9. Eng. tr. by A. V. Miller, pp. 724–5). Rule is wholly a matter of undifferenced uniformity, but law involves a synthesis of differences. 'The essence of law consists in an inseparable unity, a necessary inner connection, of distinct determinations. . . . According to the law of planetary motion, the squares of the periods of revolution vary as the cubes of the distances, so the law must be grasped as an inner necessary unity of distinct determinations' (*Enc.* § 422, *Zusatz.* Cf. the sections on Mechanism in the *Science of Logic* and the *Philosophy of Nature.*) For quality and quantity, and measure as their synthesis, see *Enc.*, esp. § 108. Since Hegel goes on to quote Hogarth's *Analysis of Beauty* (1753), it is interesting to notice that ch. 3 of that work is headed 'Of Uniformity, Regularity, or Symmetry'. With this whole section it is instructive to compare Kant's *Critique of Judgment*, § 22, where the conceptions discussed here in (*a*), (*b*), and (*c*) all appear.

rest in that extreme abstraction of sameness of character. With sameness unlikeness is associated, and difference breaks in to interrupt empty identity. This is what brings symmetry in. Symmetry consists in this, that a form, abstractly the same, does not simply repeat itself, but is brought into connection with another form of the same kind which, considered by itself, is likewise determinate and self-same, but compared with the first one is unlike it. As a result of this connection, there must come into existence a new sameness and unity which is still further determinate and has a greater inner diversity. We have a sight of a symmetrical arrangement if, for instance, on one side of a house there are three windows of equal size and equidistant from one another, then there are added three or four higher than the first group with greater or lesser intervals between them, and then finally three higher once again, the same in size and distance as the first group. Therefore, mere uniformity and the repetition of one and the same determinate character does not constitute symmetry. Symmetry requires also difference in size, position, shape, colour, sounds, and other characteristics, but which then must be brought together again in a uniform way. Symmetry is provided only by the uniform connection of characteristics that are unlike one another.

Now both forms, regularity and symmetry, as purely external unity and arrangement, fall principally into the category of *size*. For the characteristic which is posited externally and is not purely immanent, is a quantitative one, whereas quality makes a specific thing what it is, so that with the alteration of its qualitative character it becomes a totally different thing. But size and its alteration as mere size is a characteristic indifferent to quality unless it asserts itself as measure. Measure, that is to say, is quantity in so far as it determines itself again qualitatively, so that the specific quality is bound up with a quantitative determination. Regularity and symmetry are chiefly restricted to determinations of size and their uniformity and arrangement in things that are unlike.

If we ask further where this ordering of sizes has acquired its right place, we find shapes, in the organic as well as in the inorganic world, which are regular and symmetrical in their size and form. Our own organism, for example, is, in part at least, regular and symmetrical. We have two eyes, two arms, two legs, equal hip-bones, shoulder blades, etc. On the other hand we know that other parts are irregular, like the heart, the lungs, the liver, the intestines, etc. The question here is: what is the basis of this difference? The place where regularity of size, shape, position, etc., manifests itself is, in the organism, its external side as such. The regular and symmetrical character appears, in accordance with its nature, where the object, conformably with its determinate character, is what is external to itself and manifests no subjective animation. The reality which remains in this externality is tied up with the abstract external unity already mentioned. On the other hand, in ensouled life, and higher still in the free world of the spirit, mere regularity recedes before living subjective unity. Now of course nature in general, contrary to spirit, is existence external to itself, yet regularity prevails in it only where externality as such remains the predominant thing.

(αα) In more detail, if we go briefly through the chief stages, minerals (crystals, for example) as inanimate productions have regularity and symmetry as their basic form. Their shape, as has already been said, is indeed immanent in them, and not determined by a purely external influence; the form they acquire in accordance with their nature elaborates in secret activity their inner and outer structure. But this activity is not yet the total activity of the concrete idealizing Concept which posits the subsistence of the independent parts as something negative and thereby ensouls them as in animal life; on the contrary, the unity and determinacy of the form [of minerals] persists in the abstract one-sidedness of the Understanding, and therefore, as a unity in what is self-external, attains mere regularity and symmetry, forms in which abstractions alone are active as determinants.

(ββ) The plant, however, stands higher than the crystal. It has already developed to the beginning of an articulation and it consumes material in its continually active process of nourishment. But even the plant has not a really ensouled life, since, although it is organically articulated, its activity is always drawn out into externality. It is fixedly rooted without the possibility of independent movement and change of place, it grows steadily, and its unbroken assimilation and nourishment is not the peaceful maintenance of an organism complete in itself, but a continual new production of itself outwards. The animal grows too, but it stops at a definite point of size, and it reproduces itself as the self-maintenance of one and the same individual. But the plant grows without ceasing; only when it withers does the increase of its branches, leaves, etc., cease. And what is produced in this growth is always a new example of the same entire organism. For every branch is a new plant and not at all, as in the animal organism, just a single member. With this continual multiplication of itself into numerous individual plants, the plant lacks ensouled subjectivity and its ideal unity of feeling. On the whole, however inner its digestive process, however active its assimilation of nourishment, however far it is self-determining through its Concept which is becoming free and is active in matter, still in its whole existence and process of life it remains continually caught in externality without subjective independence and unity, and its self-preservation is being incessantly externalized. This character of steadily pushing itself over itself outwards makes regularity and symmetry, as unity in self-externality, into a chief feature in the construction of plants. True, regularity here does not dominate so strictly as it does in the mineral realm and is not formed in such abstract lines and angles, but it still remains preponderant. The stem usually rises rectilineally, the coronae of the higher plants are circular, the leaves approach crystalline forms, and the blooms in number of petals, position, and shape bear, in accordance with their fundamental type, the stamp of a regular and symmetrical character.

(γγ) Finally, in the animal living organism there enters the essential difference of a double mode of the formation of the members. For in the animal body, especially at higher stages, the organism is, on the one hand, a self-related organism, more inner and self-enclosed, which, as it were, returns into itself like a sphere; on the other hand, it is an external organism, as an external process and a process against externality. The nobler viscera are the inner ones—liver, heart, lungs, etc., and life as such is bound up with them. They are not determined by mere types of regularity. But in the members which are in continual relation with the external world, there prevails in the animal organism too a symmetrical arrangement. To this category there belong the members and organs which are active externally, whether theoretically or practically. The purely theoretical process is managed by the tools of the senses of seeing and hearing; what we see or hear we leave as it is. On the other hand, the organs of smell and taste are already the beginnings of a practical relation. For we can smell only what is in the process of wasting away, and we can taste only by destroying. Now of course we have only one nose but it is divided into two nostrils and it is formed regularly in both its halves. The same is true of lips, teeth, etc. But regular throughout in their position, formation, etc., are eyes and ears, and also legs and arms, i.e. the members controlling change of place, and the mastery and practical alteration of external objects.

Thus even in the organic field regularity has its right in accordance with the Concept, but only in the members which provide tools for the immediate relation to the external world and are not active in connection with the relation of the organism to itself as the subjectivity of life returning into itself. These then are the chief characteristics of the regular and symmetrical forms and their domination in shaping natural phenomena.

(b) Conformity to Law

Now, however, in more detail, from the rather abstract form of regularity we must distinguish conformity to law, since it stands at a higher stage and constitutes the transition to the freedom of life, both natural and spiritual. Yet, regarded by itself, conformity to law is certainly not the subjective total unity and freedom itself, though it is already a totality of essential differences which do not simply present themselves as differences and opposites but in their totality display unity and connection. A unity like this, with its dominance and conformity to law, although still asserting itself in the sphere of quantity, is no longer to be referred back to extrinsic and purely calculable differences of size alone; it already permits the entrance of a *qualitative* relation between the different aspects. Thus in their relation what is manifested is neither the abstract repetition of one and the same characteristic nor a uniform interchange of like and unlike, but the association of aspects essentially different. Now if we see these differences associated in their completeness, we are satisfied. In this satisfaction there lies the rational element, the fact that sense is gratified only by the totality, and indeed by the totality of differences demanded by the essence of the thing. Yet once again the connection remains as a secret bond which for the spectator is partly something to which he is accustomed, partly the foreshadowing of something deeper.

A few examples will easily clarify in more detail the transition from regularity to conformity with law: e.g., parallel lines of the same length are abstractly regular.[1] But a further step is the simple equality of ratios of unlike magnitudes, as occurs, e.g., in similar triangles. The inclination of the angles, the ratio of the sides, are the same, but the sizes are different.[2] The circle likewise does not have the regularity of the straight line, but nevertheless still falls under the category of abstract equality, since all the radii have the same length. Thus the circle is still just a curved line of little interest. On the other hand, an ellipse and a parabola have less regularity and can be understood only by their law. So, e.g., the *radii vectores* of the ellipse are unequal, but they conform to law, and similarly the major and minor axes are essentially different, and the *foci* do not fall into the centre as they do in a circle.[3] Thus here there appear qualitative differences, grounded in the law of this line, and their interconnection constitutes the law. But if we divide the ellipse along its major and minor axes, we have four equal parts; thus here too, on the whole, equality prevails. Of higher freedom, with inner conformity to law, is the oval. It conforms to law, but it has not been possible to discover the law and to calculate it mathematically. It is not an ellipse; the upper curve differs from the lower one. Yet even this freer natural

---

[1] Parallel lines of equal length are uniform both in length and in the distance between them, and therefore are simply regular. But lines drawn in a parabola parallel to its axis are not of equal length, and this fact is incidental to the laws of the parabola, so that such parallels have their length determined by law and therefore they are not simply regular. Hegel seems to have the geometry of conics in mind. (I owe the material of this note to Dr. M. J. Petry.)

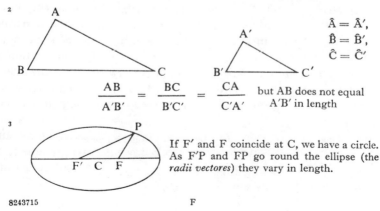

[2] $\hat{A} = \hat{A}'$, $\hat{B} = \hat{B}'$, $\hat{C} = \hat{C}'$

$$\frac{AB}{A'B'} = \frac{BC}{B'C'} = \frac{CA}{C'A'}$$ but AB does not equal A'B' in length

[3] If F' and F coincide at C, we have a circle. As F'P and FP go round the ellipse (the *radii vectores*) they vary in length.

line, if we bisect it along its major axis, still provides two equal halves.[1]

The final supersession of the purely regular in the case of conformity to law occurs in lines similar to ovals, which nevertheless, when divided along their major axis, provide unequal sections, in that one side is not repeated on the other, but waves otherwise. An example of this kind is the so-called 'waving' line which Hogarth[2] has called the line of beauty. Thus, for example, the lines of the arm wave differently on one side from the other. Here is conformity to law without mere regularity. This kind of conformity to law determines the forms of the higher living organisms in a great variety of ways.

Now conformity to law is the essential quality which settles differences and their unity, but, on the one hand, it *only* dominates abstractly and does not let individuality come in any way into free movement; and, on the other hand, it lacks the higher freedom of subjectivity and therefore cannot bring into appearance the animation and ideality thereof.

(c) Harmony

Therefore at this stage harmony stands higher than mere conformity to law, i.e. harmony is a relation of qualitative differences, and indeed of a totality of such differences, a totality grounded in the essence of the thing itself. This relation advances beyond conformity to law, which has in itself the aspect of regularity, and rises above equality and repetition. But at the same time the qualitative differences assert themselves not merely as differences and their opposition and contradiction, but as a congruous unity which has set forth all its proper factors while yet containing them as a whole inherently one. This congruity is harmony. It consists, on the one hand, in the ensemble of essential elements, and, on the other hand, in the dissolution of their bare opposition, so that in this way their association and inner connection is manifested as their unity. In this sense we speak of harmony of shape, colours, notes, etc. So, for example, blue, yellow, green, and red are the

---

[1] It is possible to have ovals (e.g. the oval of Cassini) which are symmetrical about the greater axis, and so are ellipses. But Hegel is obviously taking the oval as egg-shaped. I owe this note and notes 2 and 3 on p. 139 to Professor E. T. Copson and Professor W. N. Everitt.

[2] Op. cit., ch. 7, 'the waving line . . . is more productive of beauty than any of the former', i.e. straight or circular lines, etc.

necessary differences of colour belonging to the essence of colour itself. In them we have not just unlikenesses put together regularly into an external unity, as in symmetry, but direct opposites, like yellow and blue, and their neutralization and concrete identity. Now the beauty of their harmony consists in avoiding their sharp difference and opposition which as such is to be obliterated, so that in their differences their unison is manifested. For they belong together, since colour is not one-sided, but an essential totality. The demand of such a totality can go so far, as Goethe says, that even if the eye has before it only *one* colour as its object, it nevertheless subjectively sees the others equally. Among notes, the tonic, mediant, and dominant, e.g., are such essential differences, which in their difference harmonize unitedly into one whole. It is similarly the case with harmony of [the human] figure, its position, rest, movement, etc. Here no difference may come forward one-sidedly by itself, or otherwise the harmony is disturbed.

But even harmony as such is not yet free ideal subjectivity and soul. In the latter, unity is not just an association and an accord but the positing of differences negatively, whereby alone their ideal unity is established. To such ideality harmony cannot attain. For example, every melody, although it has harmony as its basis, has a higher and more free subjectivity in itself and expresses that. Mere harmony does not in general manifest either subjective animation as such or spirituality, although it is the highest stage of abstract form and already approaches free subjectivity.

These kinds of abstract form provide the first determinant of abstract unity.

2. Beauty as Abstract Unity of the Sensuous Material

The second aspect of abstract unity does not now concern form and shape, but the material, the sensuously perceptible as such. Here unity enters as the concord, entirely undifferentiated in itself, of the determinate sensuous material. This is the sole unity of which the material, taken by itself as sensuously perceptible stuff, is susceptible. In this connection the abstract *purity* of the stuff, in shape, colour, note, etc., is the essential thing at this stage. Absolutely straight lines which go on undifferentiated, swerving neither hither nor thither, polished surfaces, and the like, satisfy us by their fixed determinacy and their uniform homogeneity. The purity of the sky, the clarity of the air, a mirror-like lake, smooth seas, delight us from this point of view. The same is true with the purity of musical notes. The pure sound of the voice, merely as a pure note, is infinitely pleasing and impressive, while an impure voice makes the organ of production resound as well and does not afford the sound in its relation to itself; and an impure note deviates from the note's determinate character. In a similar way speech too has pure notes like the vowels a, e, i, o, u, and mixed notes like ä, ü, ö. Popular dialects especially have impure sounds, mediants like *oa*.[1] A further point about the purity of notes is that the vowels should be associated with such consonants as do not blur the purity of the vowel sounds. The northern languages frequently weaken the vowel sounds with their consonants, whereas Italian preserves the purity of the vowel sounds and for that reason is so singable.

A similar effect is produced by pure, inherently simple, unmixed colours, a pure red, for example, or a pure blue, which is rare because red usually passes over into pink or orange and blue into green. Violet too may indeed be pure, [not in itself] but only externally, i.e. [in the sense of not being] smudged, because it is not in itself simple and is not one of the colour differences determined by the essence of colour. It is these fundamental colours which sensation easily recognizes in their purity, although when juxtaposed they are more difficult to bring into harmony, because their difference sticks out more glaringly. The subdued, variously mixed, colours are less agreeable, even if they harmonize more easily, since the energy of opposition is missing in them. Green is indeed a colour of blue and yellow mixed, but it is a simple neutralization of their opposition, and in its genuine purity as this obliteration of the opposition is precisely more pleasant and less fatiguing than blue and yellow in their fixed difference.

These are the most important points in connection with the abstract unity of form and the simplicity and purity of the sensuously perceived material. But both of these are, owing to their abstraction, lifeless, and afford no truly actual unity; because for such unity we require ideal subjectivity which natural beauty always lacks, even in its perfect appearance. Now this essential deficiency leads us to the necessity of the Ideal, which is not to be found in nature, and in comparison with it the beauty of nature appears as subordinate.

---

[1] i.e. o without an umlaut in German, but sounded as oa instead of plain o.

C. DEFICIENCY OF NATURAL BEAUTY

Our topic proper is the beauty of art as the one reality adequate to the Idea of beauty. Up to this point the beauty of nature has counted as the primary existence of beauty, and now therefore the question is how it differs from the beauty of art.

We could talk abstractly and say that the Ideal is beauty perfect in itself, while nature is beauty imperfect. But such bare adjectives are no use, because the problem is to define precisely what constitutes this perfection of artistic beauty and the imperfection of merely natural beauty. We must therefore pose our question thus: why is nature necessarily imperfect in its beauty, and what is the origin of this imperfection? Only when this is answered will the necessity and the essence of the Ideal be revealed to us in more detail.

Since hitherto we have risen so far as animal life and have seen how beauty can be manifested there, the next thing before us is to fix our eyes more definitely on this feature of subjectivity and individuality in the living organism.

We spoke [in ch. I, 1] of the beautiful as Idea in the same sense as we speak of the good and the true as Idea, in the sense, that is to say, that the Idea is the purely substantial and universal, the absolute matter (not sensuously perceptible at all), the substratum of the world. More specifically, however, as we have seen already [at the beginning of this Chapter], the Idea is not only substance and *universality*, but precisely the unity of the Concept with its *reality*, the Concept rebuilt as Concept within its objective realization. It was Plato, as we mentioned in the Introduction, who emphasized the Idea as alone the truth and the universal, and indeed as the inherently concrete universal. Yet the Platonic Idea is itself not yet the genuinely concrete; for, although, apprehended in its Concept and universality, it does count as the truth, still, taken in this universality, it is not yet actualized and, in its actuality, the truth explicit to itself. It gets no further than [truth] merely implicit. But just as the Concept without its objectivity is not genuinely Concept, so too the Idea is not genuinely Idea without and outside its actuality. Therefore the Idea must go forth into actuality, and it acquires actuality only through the actual subjectivity which inherently corresponds with the Concept and through subjectivity's ideal being for itself. So, for example, the species is actual only as a free concrete individual; *life* exists only as a single living thing, the *good* is actualized by individual men, and all *truth* exists only as knowing consciousness, as spirit confronting itself as spirit. For only concrete individuality is true and actual; abstract universality and particularity are not. This self-knowing, this subjectivity, is therefore what we have to adhere to as essential. But subjectivity lies in the negative unity wherein differences in their real subsistence simultaneously evince themselves posited as ideal. Thus the unity of the Idea and its actuality is the *negative* unity of the Idea as such and its *reality*, as the positing and superseding of the difference between both these sides. Only in this activity is it affirmatively self-knowing, self-relating, infinite unity and subjectivity. Therefore we have to grasp the Idea of beauty too in its actual existence as essentially concrete subjectivity, and thus as individuality, since it is Idea only as actual and has actuality only in concrete individuality.

Now here at once we must distinguish between two forms of individuality, the immediate natural one and the spiritual one. In both forms the Idea gives itself existence, and so in both forms their substantial content, the Idea, and, in our sphere of study, the Idea of beauty, is the same. In this connection it has to be maintained that the beauty of nature has the same content as the Ideal. But, on the other hand, the aforesaid twofold character of the form in which the Idea acquires actuality, the difference between natural and spiritual individuality, introduces an essential difference into the content itself which appears in the one form or in the other. For the question is which form is really correspondent with the Idea; and only in the form genuinely adequate to itself does the Idea make explicit the entire genuine totality of its content.

This is the special point which we have to consider now because under this difference between the forms of individuality there falls the difference between the beauty of nature and the Ideal.

In the first place, so far as *immediate* individuality is concerned, it belongs to nature as such as well as to the spirit, for (α) spirit has its external existence in *body*, and (β) even in *spiritual* relations it at first gains an existence only in immediate reality. We may therefore consider immediate individuality here in three respects.

1. The Inner in Immediacy as only the Inner

(a) We have seen already [on p. 124] that the animal organism attains its being for self only through a steady internal process in opposition to an inorganic nature which it devours, digests, and assimilates; it changes the outer into the inner and thereby alone makes its 'insideness' actual. At the same time we found that this steady process of life is a system of activities which is actualized into a system of organs through which those activities proceed. This complete system has as its sole aim the self-preservation of the living thing through this process, and animal life therefore subsists only in the life of appetite, the course and the satisfaction of which is realized in the system of organs mentioned above. In this way the living thing is articulated purposefully; all its members serve only as means to the one end of self-preservation. Life is immanent in them; they are tied to life and life to them. Now the result of this process is the animal as ensouled, as having a feeling of itself, whereby it acquires enjoyment of itself as an individual. If we compare the animal in this respect with the plant, it has already been indicated [in the passage on Symmetry] that the plant lacks precisely this feeling of itself, this soulfulness, for it continually produces in itself new individuals without concentrating them to the negative point which constitutes the individual self. But what we now see before us in the life of an animal organism is not this *point of unity* of life, but only the *variety* of organs. The living thing still lacks freedom, owing to its inability to bring itself into appearance *as* an individual point, i.e. as a subject, in contrast to the display of its members in external reality. The real seat of the activities of organic life remains veiled from our vision; we see only the external outlines of the animal's shape, and this again is covered throughout by feathers, scales, hair, pelt, prickles, or shells. Such covering does belong to the animal kingdom, but in animals it has forms drawn from the kingdom of plants. Here at once lies one chief deficiency in the beauty of animal life. What is visible to us in the organism is not the soul; what is turned outwards and appears everywhere is not the inner life, but forms drawn from a lower stage than that of life proper. The animal is living only *within* its covering, i.e. this 'insideness' is not itself real in the form of an inner consciousness and therefore this life is not visible over all the animal. Because the inside remains *just* an inside, the outside too appears *only* as an outside and not completely penetrated in every part by the soul.

(*b*) The *human* body, on the contrary, stands in this respect at a higher stage, since in it there is everywhere and always represented the fact that man is an ensouled and feeling unit. The skin is not hidden by plant-like unliving coverings; the pulsation of the blood shows itself over the entire surface; the beating heart of life is as it were present everywhere over the body and comes out into appearance externally as the body's own animation, as *turgor vitae*,[1] as this swelling life. Similarly the skin proves to be sensitive everywhere, and displays the *morbidezza* [delicacy], the tints of colour in flesh and veins, which are the artist's cross. But however far the human, in distinction from the animal, body makes its life appear outwardly, still nevertheless the poverty of nature equally finds expression on this surface by the non-uniformity of the skin, in indentations, wrinkles, pores, small hairs, little veins, etc. The skin itself, which permits the inner life to shine through it, is an external covering for self-preservation, merely a purposeful means in the service of the natural needs. Yet the tremendous advantage which the appearance of the human body continues to enjoy consists in its sensitivity which, even if not altogether actual feeling, does at least demonstrate the possibility of that in general. But at the same time here again the deficiency arises that this feeling, as inwardly concentrated in itself, does not achieve presence in every one of the body's members; on the contrary, in the body itself part of the organs and their shape is devoted to purely animal functions, while another part more nearly adopts the expression of the soul's life, of feelings and passions. From this point of view the soul with its inner life here too does not shine through the entire reality of the bodily form.

(*c*) In a higher way still, the same deficiency makes itself evident likewise in the *spiritual* world and its organizations if we consider it in its immediate life. The greater and the richer this spiritual world's productions are, the more does the *one* aim, which animates this whole and constitutes its inner soul, require co-operative

---

[1] Dr. M. J. Petry informs me that this is a conception originating in the antiquated physiology of J. F. Blumenbach (1735–1840). The power of 'intumescence' is supposed to be a condition displayed in a healthy body by the uniform tensing and expanding of pulpy parts. Blumenbach's pupil E. B. G. Hebenstreit (1735–1803) wrote *Doctrinae physiologicae de turgore vitali brevis expositio* (Leipzig, 1795), to which the curious may be referred.

means. Now in immediate reality these means of course manifest themselves as purposeful organs, and what happens and is produced comes into being only by means of the will; every point in such an organization (e.g. in a state or a family), i.e. every single individual, *wills*, and he manifests himself indeed in connection with the other members of the same organization; but the *one* inner soul of this association (the freedom and reason of the one aim) does not come forward into reality as this one free and total inner animation, and does not make itself obvious in every part.

The same is the case with particular actions and events which, in a similar way, are in themselves an organic whole. The inner, from which they spring, does not come out into the superficial and external form of their immediate actualization. What appears is only a *real* totality, but whose innermost comprehensive animation remains in the background, as inner.

Finally, the single individual gives us in this respect the same impression. The spiritual individual is a totality in himself, held together on the strength of a spiritual centre. In his immediate reality he appears only fragmentarily in life, action, inaction, wishing and urging, and yet his character can be known only from the whole series of his actions and sufferings. In this series, which constitutes his reality, the concentrated point of unity is not visible and graspable as a comprehensive centre.

2. *The Dependence of Immediate Individual Existence*

The next important point which arises from this is the following. With the immediacy of the individual the Idea enters actual existence. But, at the same time, owing to this same immediacy, the Idea becomes interwoven with the complexity of the external world, with the conditioned character of external circumstances, with the relative character of means and ends; in short, it is drawn into the entire finitude of appearance. For the immediate individual is primarily a self-encircled unit, but consequently, for the same reason, he is shut off from others and negatively related to them; and on account of his immediate isolation in which he has only a conditioned existence, he is forced, by the power of the totality which is not actual within him, into relation with others and into the most multiplex dependence on others. In this immediacy the Idea has realized all its sides *separately* and therefore it remains only the *inner* power which relates the individual existents to one another, natural and spiritual alike. This relation is itself external to them and appears too in them as an *external necessity* involving the most diverse reciprocal dependences and determination by others. The immediacy of existence is from this point of view a system of necessary connections between apparently independent individuals and powers, a system in which every individual is used as a means in the service of ends foreign to himself or else he needs as a means to his own ends just what is external to himself. And since here the Idea as such realizes itself only on the ground of the external, what appears at the same time let loose is the unruly play of caprice and chance, and the whole misery of distress. This is the realm of unfreedom in which the *immediate* individual lives.

(*a*) The individual *animal*, for example, is at once tied down to a specific natural element, air, water, or land, and this determines its whole mode of life, kind of nourishment, and therefore its entire plight. This provides the great differences between animal species. Of course there do also emerge other species, intermediate ones, such as natatorial birds, mammals that live in water, amphibia, and transitional stages [in the classificatory scheme]. But these are only mixtures, not higher and comprehensive mediations [between stages in the classification]. Besides, in its self-preservation the animal remains steadily in subjection to external nature, e.g. to cold, drought, lack of food. Under nature's domination it may fail, owing to the parsimoniousness of its environment, to achieve fullness of form; it may lose the bloom of its beauty; it may be emaciated, and simply give the impression of this universal want. Whether it preserves or loses any share of beauty vouchsafed to it is at the mercy of external conditions.

(*b*) The *human* organism in its bodily existence is still subject, even if not to the same extent, to a similar dependence on the external powers of nature. It is exposed to the same chance, unsatisfied natural needs, destructive illnesses, and to every kind of want and misery.

(*c*) If we go higher up, i.e. to the immediate actuality of *spiritual* interests, we find that this dependence really only appears here in the most complete relativity. Here is revealed the whole breadth of prose in human existence. This is the sort of thing already present in the contrast between the purely physical vital aims and the higher aims of spirit, in that both of these can reciprocally hinder, disturb, and extinguish one another. Consequently, the individual man, in order to preserve his individuality, must frequently make himself a means to others, must subserve their limited aims, and must likewise reduce others to mere means in order to satisfy his own interests. Therefore the individual as he appears in this world of prose and everyday is not active out of the entirety of his own self and his resources, and he is intelligible not from himself, but from something else. For the individual man stands in dependence on external influences, laws, political institutions, civil relationships, which he just finds confronting him, and he must bow to them whether he has them as his own inner being or not. Furthermore, the individual subject is not in the eyes of others such an entirety in himself, but comes before them only according to the nearest isolated interest which they take in his actions, wishes, and opinions. Men's primary interest is simply what is related to their own intentions and aims.

Even the great actions and events in which a community cooperates are in this field of relative phenomena confessedly only a manifold of individual efforts. This or that man makes his own contribution with this or that aim in view; the aim miscarries, or it is achieved, and at the end, in fortunate circumstances, something is accomplished which, compared with the whole, is of a very subordinate kind. What most men execute is, in this connection, compared with the greatness of the whole event and the total aim to which they make their contribution, only a trifle. Indeed even those who stand at the head of affairs and feel the whole thing as their own, and are themselves conscious of the fact, appear entangled in many-sided particular circumstances, conditions, obstacles, and relative matters. In all these respects the individual in this sphere does not preserve the look of independent and total life and freedom which lies at the root of the essence of beauty. True, even immediate human affairs and their events and organizations do not lack a system and a totality of activities; but the whole thing appears only as a mass of individual details; occupations and activities are sundered and split into infinitely many parts, so that to individuals only a particle of the whole can accrue; and no matter how far individuals may contribute to the whole with their own aims and accomplish what is in line with their own individual interest, still the independence and freedom of their will remains more or less formal, determined by external circumstances and chances, and hindered by natural obstacles.

This is the prose of the world, as it appears to the consciousness both of the individual himself and of others:—a world of finitude and mutability, of entanglement in the relative, of the pressure of necessity from which the individual is in no position to withdraw. For every isolated living thing remains caught in the contradiction of being itself in its own eyes this shut-in unit and yet of being nevertheless dependent on something else, and the struggle to resolve this contradiction does not get beyond an attempt and the continuation of this eternal war.

3. *The Restrictedness of Immediate Individual Existence*

But now thirdly, the immediate individual whether in the natural or the spiritual world is not only generally dependent on circumstances, but also lacks absolute independence because of being *restricted*, or rather because of being inherently *particularized.*

(*a*) Every single animal belongs to a determinate and therefore restricted and fixed species, beyond the limits of which it cannot step. Before our mind's eye there does float a general picture of life and its organization; but in the actual world of nature this universal organic species bursts asunder into a realm of particulars, each of which has its limited type of form and its particular stage of development. Further, within this unsurmountable barrier what is expressed in every single individual, in a contingent and particular way, is only the above-mentioned element of chance in the conditions and externals of life, as well as of dependence on these. From this point of view too the vision of independence and freedom, requisite for genuine beauty, is dimmed.

(*b*) Now it is true that the spirit finds the whole Concept of natural life completely actualized in its own bodily organism, so that, in comparison with this, the animal species may appear as imperfect in their life, and indeed, at lower stages, as scarcely living at all. Nevertheless, the human organism too is split likewise, even in a lesser degree, split into racial differences and their gradation of beautiful formations. Apart from these—of course more general—differences, contingency next enters here again nearer at hand in the shape of firmly established family idioms and their intermixture as specific modes of life, expression, and behaviour;

and to this differentiation which introduces the trait of an inherently unfree particularity, there are then added the special characteristics of the mode of occupation in the finite circles of living activity, in trade, for example, and calling; to which, finally, are annexed all the idiosyncrasies of special character and temperament, with, consequentially, all sorts of weaknesses and troubles. Poverty, care, wrath, coldness and indifference, the rage of passions, concentration on one-sided aims, inconstancy, schizophrenia, dependence on external nature, the whole finitude of human existence as such, become specified into the accident of quite singular physiognomies and their abiding expression. So there are worn faces on which all the passions have left the imprint of their destructive fury; others afford only the impression of inner coldness and superficiality; others again are so singular that the general type of features has almost entirely disappeared. There is no end to the haphazardness of human shapes. Children, therefore, are on the whole at the most beautiful age because in them all singularities slumber, as it were, quietly enclosed in germ, because no restricted passion has yet tormented their breast, and none of the manifold human interests has engraved for ever on these changing features an expression of its exigency. But although the child's liveliness appears as the possibility of anything, there are nevertheless lacking in this innocence all the same the deeper features of the spirit which is driven to realize itself within and to spread itself in substantial directions and aims.

(c) This defectiveness of immediate existence, whether physical or spiritual, is essentially to be regarded as *finitude*, more precisely as a finitude which does not correspond with its inner essence, and through this lack of correspondence just proclaims its finitude. For the Concept, and, more concretely still, the Idea, is inherently *infinite* and *free*. Although animal life, as life, is Idea, it does not itself display the infinity and freedom which only appear when the Concept so completely pervades its appropriate reality that therein it has only itself, with nothing but itself emerging there. In that event alone is the Concept genuinely free and infinite individuality. But natural life does not get beyond feeling, which remains *in itself*, without completely permeating the entire reality; besides, it is immediately conditioned in itself, restricted, and dependent, because it has no self-wrought freedom, but is determined by something else. The like lot falls to the immediate finite realization of the spirit, in its knowing and willing, its adventures, actions, and fates.

For although even here more substantial concentrations are formed, they are still only concentrations which have truth in and for themselves just as little as particular individualities have; they only display truth in their bearing on one another through the whole. This whole, taken as such, does correspond with its Concept, yet without manifesting itself in its totality, so that in this way it remains something purely inner and therefore is present only to the inwardness of intellectual reflection, instead of visibly entering external reality as the full expression of itself and summoning back the innumerable individualities out of their dispersal in order to concentrate them into *one* expression and *one* shape.

This is the reason why spirit cannot, in the finitude of existence and its restrictedness and external necessity, find over again the immediate vision and enjoyment of its true freedom, and it is compelled to satisfy the need for this freedom, therefore, on other and higher ground. This ground is art, and art's actuality is the Ideal.

Thus it is from the deficiencies of immediate reality that the necessity of the beauty of art is derived. The task of art must therefore be firmly established in art's having a calling to display the appearance of life, and especially of spiritual animation (in its freedom, externally too) and to make the external correspond with its Concept. Only so is the truth lifted out of its temporal setting, out of its straying away into a series of finites. At the same time it has won an external appearance through which the poverty of nature and prose no longer peeps; it has won an existence worthy of the truth, an existence which for its part stands there in free independence since it has its vocation in itself, and does not find it inserted there by something else.

Chapter III

THE BEAUTY OF ART OR THE IDEAL

In relation to the beauty of art we have three chief aspects to consider:

First, the Ideal as such

Secondly, the work of art as the determinateness of the Ideal

Thirdly, the creative subjectivity of the artist.

A. THE IDEAL AS SUCH

1. *Beautiful Individuality*

The most general thing which can be said in a merely formal way about the ideal of art, on the lines of our previous considerations, comes to this, that, on the one hand, the true has existence and truth only as it unfolds into external reality; but, on the other hand, the externally separated parts, into which it unfolds, it can so combine and retain in unity that now every part of its unfolding makes this soul, this totality, appear in each part. If we take the human form as the nearest illustration of this, it is, as we saw earlier, a totality of organs into which the Concept is dispersed, and it manifests in each member only some particular activity and partial emotion. But if we ask in which particular organ the whole soul appears as soul, we will at once name the eye; for in the eye the soul is concentrated and the soul does not merely see through it but is also seen in it. Now as the pulsating heart shows itself all over the surface of the human, in contrast to the animal, body, so in the same sense it is to be asserted of art that it has to convert every shape in all points of its visible surface into an eye, which is the seat of the soul and brings the spirit into appearance.—Or, as Plato cries out to the star in his familiar distich: 'When thou lookest on the stars, my star, oh! would I were the heavens and could see thee with a thousand eyes',[1] so, conversely, art makes every one of its productions into a thousand-eyed Argus, whereby

[1] Diogenes Laertius, *Plato*, 23 § 29. Hegel's quotations are nearly always inexact. His 'thousand' for Plato's 'many' seems to me to be an improvement, if it be not sacrilege to say so. But Hegel's 'when' is an unnecessary addition of his own.

the inner soul and spirit is seen at every point. And it is not only the bodily form, the look of the eyes, the countenance and posture, but also actions and events, speech and tones of voice, and the series of their course through all conditions of appearance that art has everywhere to make into an eye, in which the free soul is revealed in its inner infinity.

(a) With this demand for thoroughgoing possession of soul there arises at once the further question *what* this soul is, the eyes of which all points in the phenomenal world are to become. More precisely still, the question is what sort of soul it is that by its nature shows itself qualified to gain its true manifestation through art. For people[1] speak even of a specific 'soul' of metals, minerals, stars, animals, numerously particularized human characters and their expressions, using the word 'soul' in an ordinary sense. But, for things in nature, such as stones, plants, etc., the word 'soul', in the meaning given to it above, can only be used metaphorically. The soul of merely natural things is explicitly finite and transitory, and should be called 'specific nature' rather than 'soul'. For this reason, the determinate individuality of such things is completely revealed already in their finite existence. It can display only some sort of restrictedness. Elevation to infinite independence and freedom is nothing but an appearance which can indeed be imparted to this sphere; but if this really happens, the appearance is always produced from the outside by art without this infinity's being grounded in the things themselves. In the same way the sentient soul too, as natural life, is a subjective but purely inner individuality, present in reality only implicitly, without knowing itself as a return into itself and by that means as inherently infinite. Its content therefore remains itself restricted. Its manifestation achieves, for one thing, only a formal life, unrest, mutability, concupiscence, and the anxiety and fear incident to this dependent life, and, for another thing, only the expression of an inwardness inherently finite.

The animation and life of *spirit* alone is free infinity; as such, the spirit in real existence is self-aware as something inner, because in its manifestation it reverts into itself and remains at home with itself. To spirit alone, therefore, is it given to impress the stamp of its own infinity and free return into itself upon its external manifestation, even though through this manifestation it is

---

[1] A hit at Schelling and other philosophers of nature.

involved in restriction. Now spirit is only free and infinite when it actually comprehends its universality and raises to universality the ends it sets before itself; but, for this reason, it is capable by its own nature, if it has *not* grasped this freedom, of existing as restricted content, stunted character, and a mind crippled and superficial. In a content of such null worth the infinite manifestation of spirit again remains only formal, for in that case we have nothing but the abstract form of self-conscious spirit, and its content contradicts the infinity of spirit in its freedom. It is only by virtue of a genuine and inherently substantial content that restricted and mutable existence acquires independence and substantiality, so that then both determinacy and inherent solidity, content that is both substantial and restrictedly exclusive, are actual in one and the same thing; and hereby existence gains the possibility of being manifested in the restrictedness of its own content as at the same time universality and as the soul which is alone with itself.—In short, art has the function of grasping and displaying existence, in its appearance, as *true*, i.e. in its suitability to the content which is adequate to itself, the content which is both implicit and explicit. Thus the truth of art cannot be mere correctness, to which the so-called imitation of nature is restricted; on the contrary, the outer must harmonize with an inner which is harmonious in itself, and, just on that account, can reveal itself as itself in the outer.

(*b*) Now since art brings back into this harmony with its true Concept what is contaminated in other existents by chance and externality, it casts aside everything in appearance which does not correspond with the Concept and only by this purification does it produce the Ideal. This may be given out to be flattery by art, as, for example, it is said depreciatingly of portrait painters that they flatter. But even the portrait-painter, who has least of all to do with the Ideal of art, *must* flatter, in the sense that all the externals in shape and expression, in form, colour, features, the purely natural side of imperfect existence, little hairs, pores, little scars, warts, all these he must let go, and grasp and reproduce the subject in his universal character and enduring personality. It is one thing for the artist simply to imitate the face of the sitter, its surface and external form, confronting him in repose, and quite another to be able to portray the true features which express the inmost soul of the subject. For it is throughout necessary for the Ideal that the outer form should explicitly correspond with the soul. So, for example, in our own time what has become the fashion, namely what are called *tableaux vivants*,[1] imitate famous masterpieces deliberately and agreeably, and the accessories, costume, etc., they reproduce accurately; but often enough we see ordinary faces substituted for the spiritual expression of the subjects and this produces an inappropriate effect. Raphael's Madonnas, on the other hand, show us forms of expression, cheeks, eyes, nose, mouth, which, as forms, are appropriate to the radiance, joy, piety, and also the humility of a mother's love. Of course someone might wish to maintain that all women are capable of this feeling, but not every cast of countenance affords a satisfactory and complete expression of this depth of soul.

(c) Now the nature of the artistic Ideal is to be sought in this reconveyance of external existence into the spiritual realm, so that the external appearance, by being adequate to the spirit, is the revelation thereof. Yet this is a reconveyance into the inner realm which at the same time does not proceed to the universal in its abstract form, i.e. to the *extreme* which *thinking* is, but remains in the *centre* where the purely external and the purely internal coincide. Accordingly, the Ideal is actuality, withdrawn from the profusion of details and accidents, in so far as the inner appears itself in this externality, lifted above and opposed to universality, as living individuality. For the individual subjective life which has a substantive content in itself and at the same time makes this content appear on itself externally, stands in this centre. In this centre the substantiality of the content cannot emerge explicitly in its universality in an abstract way; it remains still enclosed in individuality and therefore appears intertwined with a determinate existent, which now, for its part, freed from mere finitude and its conditions, comes together with the inwardness of the soul into a free harmony. Schiller in his poem *Das Ideal und das Leben*[2] [The Ideal and Life] contrasts actuality and its griefs and battles with the 'still shadow-land of beauty'. Such a realm of shadows is the Ideal; the *spirits* appearing in it are dead to immediate existence, cut off from the indigence of natural life, freed

---

[1] i.e. beautiful women set in a frame, to imitate some artist's picture. See, e.g., *O.E.D.* s.v. *tableau*, and L. V. Fildes, *Luke Fildes R.A.* (London, 1968) p. 84.

[2] This poem of Schiller's third period appeared first in 1795 in *Die Horen*.

from the bonds of dependence on external influences and all the perversions and convulsions inseparable from the finitude of the phenomenal world. But all the same the Ideal treads into the sensuous and the natural form thereof, yet it still at the same time draws this, like the sphere of the external, back into itself, since art can bring back the apparatus,[1] required by external appearance for its self-preservation, to the limits within which the external can be the manifestation of spiritual freedom. Only by this process does the Ideal exist in externality, self-enclosed, free, self-reliant, as sensuously blessed in itself, enjoying and delighting in its own self. The ring of this bliss resounds throughout the entire appearance of the Ideal, for however far the external form may extend, the soul of the Ideal never loses itself in it. And precisely as a result of this alone is the Ideal genuinely beautiful, since the beautiful exists only as a total though subjective unity; wherefore too the subject who manifests the Ideal must appear collected together in himself again into a higher totality and independence out of the divisions in the life of other individuals and their aims and efforts.

(α) In this respect, amongst the fundamental characteristics of the Ideal we may put at the top this serene peace and bliss, this self-enjoyment in its own achievedness and satisfaction. The ideal work of art confronts us like a blessed god. For the blessed gods [of Greek art], that is to say, there is no final seriousness in distress, in anger, in the interests involved in finite spheres and aims, and this positive withdrawal into themselves, along with the negation of everything particular, gives them the characteristic of serenity and tranquillity. In this sense Schiller's phrase holds good: 'Life is serious, art cheerful.'[2] Often enough, it is true, pedants have poked fun at this, on the ground that art in general, and especially Schiller's own poetry, is of a most serious kind; and after all in fact ideal art does not lack seriousness—but even in the seriousness cheerfulness or serenity remains its inherent and essential character. This force of individuality, this triumph of concrete freedom concentrated in itself, is what we recognize especially in the works of art of antiquity[3] in the cheerful and serene peace of their shapes. And this results not at all from a mere satisfaction gained without

---

[1] The 'apparatus' is explained below, p. 265.

[2] The last line of Schiller's preface to *Wallenstein* (1799).

[3] i.e. Greece. It is of the gods of Olympus and some Homeric and tragic heroes that Hegel is thinking throughout this passage. See the section on sculpture in Vol. II.

struggle, but on the contrary, only when a deeper breach has rent the subject's inner life and his whole existence. For even if the heroes of tragedy for example, are so portrayed that they succumb to fate, still the heart of the hero recoils into simple unity with itself, when it says: 'It is so.'[1] The subject in this case still always remains true to himself; he surrenders what he has been robbed of, yet the ends he pursues are not just taken from him; he renounces them and thereby does not lose *himself*. Man, the slave of destiny, may lose his life, but not his freedom. It is this self-reliance which even in grief enables him to preserve and manifest the cheerfulness and serenity of tranquillity.

(β) It is true that in romantic art the distraction and dissonance of the heart goes further and, in general, the oppositions displayed in it are deepened and their disunion may be maintained. So, for example, in portraying the Passion, painting sometimes persists in expressing the derision in the expressions of the military tormentors with the horrible grimaces and grins on their faces; and with this retention of disunion, especially in sketches of vice, sin, and evil, the serenity of the Ideal is then lost, for even if the distraction does not remain so fixedly as this, still something, if not ugly every time, at least not beautiful often comes into view. In another school of painting, the older Flemish one, there is displayed an inner reconciliation of the heart in its honesty and truthfulness to itself as well as in its faith and unshakeable confidence, but this firmness does not achieve the serenity and satisfaction of the Ideal. Even in romantic art, however, although suffering and grief affect the heart and subjective inner feeling more deeply there than is the case with the ancients,[2] there do come into view a spiritual inwardness, a joy in submission, a bliss in grief and rapture in suffering, even a delight in agony. Even in the solemnly religious music of Italy this pleasure and transfiguration of grief resounds through the expression of lament. This expression in romantic art generally is 'smiling through tears'. Tears belong to grief, smiles to cheerfulness, and so smiling in weeping denotes this inherent tranquillity amidst agony and suffering. Of course smiling here ought not to be a mere sentimental emotion, a frivolous and self-conceited attitude of the man to misfortunes and his minor personal feelings; on

---

[1] Cf. Hegel's impression of Swiss mountains—see above, p. 132, note (*Dokumente*, p. 236).
[2] i.e. the Greeks and Romans. Cf. our own use of 'Classics'.

the contrary, it must appear as the calmness and freedom of beauty despite all grief—as it is said of Chimena in the *Romances of the Cid*: 'How beautiful she was in tears.'[1] On the other hand, a man's lack of self-control is either ugly and repugnant, or else ludicrous. Children, e.g., burst into tears on the most trifling occasions, and this makes us smile. On the other hand, tears in the eyes of an austere man who keeps a stiff upper lip under the stress of deep feeling convey a totally different impression of emotion.

But laughter and tears may fall apart in abstraction from one another and in this abstraction they have been used inappropriately as a motif for art, as for instance in the laughter chorus of [C. M. F. E.] von Weber's *Der Freischütz* [1821]. Laughing as such is an outburst which yet ought not to remain unrestrained if the Ideal is not to be lost. The same abstraction occurs in the similar laughter in a duet from Weber's *Oberon* [1826] during which one may be anxious and distressed for the throat and lungs of the prima donna! How differently moving, on the other hand, is the inextinguishable laughter of the gods in Homer, which springs from the blessed tranquillity of the gods and is only cheerfulness and not abstract boisterousness. Neither, on the other side, should tears, as unrestrained grief, enter the ideal work of art, as when, for example, such abstract inconsolability is to be heard in Weber's *Der Freischütz*, to mention it again. In music in general, song is this joy and pleasure in self-awareness, like the lark's singing in the freedom of the air. Shrieking, whether of grief or mirth, is not music at all. Even in suffering, the sweet tone of lament must sound through the griefs and alleviate them, so that it seems to us worth while so to suffer as to understand this lament. This is the sweet melody, the song in all art.

(γ) In this fundamental principle the modern doctrine of irony too has its justification in a certain respect, except that irony, on the one hand, is often bare of any true seriousness and likes to delight especially in villains, and, on the other hand, ends in mere heartfelt longing instead of in acting and doing. Novalis,[2] for example, one of the nobler spirits who took up this position, was driven into a void with no specific interests, into this dread of

---

[1] The quotation is from Herder's poetic version of the *Romances of the Cid*, I. 6.

[2] G. F. P. von Hardenberg, 1772–1801. He died of a physical decline, i.e. tuberculosis.

reality, and was wound down as it were into a spiritual decline. This is a longing which will not let itself go in actual action and production, because it is frightened of being polluted by contact with finitude, although all the same it has a sense of the deficiency of this abstraction. True, irony implies the absolute negativity in which the subject is related to himself in the annihilation of everything specific and one-sided; but since this annihilation, as was indicated above in our consideration of this doctrine, affects not only, as in comedy, what is inherently null which manifests itself in its hollowness, but equally everything inherently excellent and solid, it follows that irony as this art of annihilating everything everywhere, like that heart-felt longing, acquires, at the same time, in comparison with the true Ideal, the aspect of inner inartistic lack of restraint. For the Ideal requires an inherently substantive content which, it is true, by displaying itself in the form and shape of the outer as well, comes to particularity and therefore to restrictedness, though it so contains the restrictedness in itself that everything *purely* external in it is extinguished and annihilated. Only on account of this negation of pure externality is the specific form and shape of the Ideal a manifestation of that substantive content in an appearance according with artistic vision and imagination.

2. *The Relation of the Ideal to Nature*

Now the pictorial and external side, which is just as necessary to the Ideal as the inherently solid content, and the manner of their interpenetration, brings us to the relation between nature and the ideal artistic representation. For this external element and its configuration has an association with what in general terms we call 'nature'. In this connection the old, ever-recurring dispute whether art should portray external objects just as they are or whether it should glorify natural phenomena and transfigure them is not yet settled. The right of nature and the right of the beautiful, the Ideal and truth to nature—in such *prima facie* vague words we can hear argument going on unceasingly. For 'the work of art should of course be natural', but 'there is also an ordinary ugly nature, and this should not be reproduced', 'but on the other hand'—and so it goes on without any end or definite result.

In modern times the opposition of Ideal and nature has been raised again and made of importance, especially by Winckelmann.

His enthusiasm, as I have already indicated earlier, was kindled by the works of antiquity and their ideal forms, and he did not rest until he had gained an insight into their excellence and reintroduced to the world a recognition and a study of these masterpieces of art. But out of this recognition there has arisen a mania for ideal representation in which people believed they had found beauty, but it lapsed into flatness, lifelessness, and superficiality without character. It was this emptiness of the Ideal, especially in painting, that von Rumohr had in view in his polemic against the Idea and the Ideal, to which I have referred already.

Now it is the task of theory to resolve this opposition. Interest in the practical side of art-production, however, we may here again leave entirely on one side, for whatever principles are implanted in mediocre minds and their talents, the result is always the same: what they produce, whether according to a perverse theory or the best one, is always but mediocre and feeble. Besides, art in general and painting in particular, influenced by other stimuli, has moved away from this mania for so-called ideals, and in its progress, owing to a freshening of interest in the older Italian and German painting, as well as in the later Dutch school, has at least made an attempt to acquire livelier forms and a fuller content.

But we have had more than enough, not only of these abstract ideals, but also, on the other hand, of the favourite 'naturalness' of art. In the theatre, for example, everyone has got sick and tired of commonplace domestic stories and their true-to-life presentation. A father's moans about his wife and his sons and daughters, about income and expenditure, dependence on Ministers, intrigues of valets and secretaries, and then the wife's trouble with maids in the kitchen, the sentimental love-affairs of daughters in the parlour—all this worry and bother everyone gets better and truer in his own home.[1]

In this opposition between the Ideal and nature, people, so it seems, have had one art more than another in view, painting especially, for its sphere is precisely particular visible objects. We will therefore pose the question of this opposition in more general terms as follows: Is art to be poetry or prose? For the truly poetical element in art is just what we have called the Ideal. If it is a matter of the mere word 'Ideal', we can readily abandon it. But in that

---

[1] This is a quotation from the last two stanzas of Schiller's satirical poem *Shakespeares Schatten* (Shakespeare's Ghost), which he calls a 'parody'.

case the question is: What is poetry and what is prose in art? Albeit, too, adherence to what is inherently poetical may lead to aberrations in relation to specific arts, and has already done so: for what expressly belongs to poetry, especially, as may be supposed, to lyric poetry, has also been represented in painting, while after all such a subject is certainly of a *poetic* kind. The present (1828) art exhibition, e.g., contains several paintings (all out of one and the same school, the one called Düsseldorf)[1] which have all borrowed subjects from poetry, particularly from that side of poetry which is only portrayable as feeling. If you look at these pictures oftener and more closely, they will soon enough appear as sugary and dull.

In the opposition between nature and art there are the following general points:

(a) The purely formal ideality of the work of art. Poetry in general, as the very word indicates, is something made, produced by a man who has taken it into his imagination, pondered it, and issued it by his own activity out of his imagination.

(α) Here the subject-matter may be quite indifferent to us or may interest us, apart from the artistic presentation, only incidentally, for example, or momentarily. In this way Dutch painting,[2] for example, has recreated, in thousands and thousands of effects, the existent and fleeting appearance of nature as something generated afresh by man. Velvet, metallic lustre, light, horses, servants, old women, peasants blowing smoke from cutty pipes, the glitter of wine in a transparent glass, chaps in dirty jackets playing with old cards—these and hundreds of other things are brought before our eyes in these pictures, things that we scarcely bother about in our daily life, for even if we play cards, drink wine, and chat about this and that, we are still engrossed by quite different interests. But what at once claims our attention in matter of this kind, when art displays it to us, is precisely this pure shining and appearing of objects as something produced by the *spirit* which transforms in its inmost being the external and sensuous side of all this material. For instead of real wool and silk, instead of real hair, glass, flesh,

---

[1] This school, founded by Wilhelm Schadow, concentrated on religious and medieval subjects. Its most important member was Peter von Cornelius (1783–1867), head of the Düsseldorf Academy of Art from 1819 to 1825, and subsequently at Munich and Berlin.

[2] Hegel studied Dutch paintings in Amsterdam (*Briefe*, Hamburg, 1953, ii, p. 362).

and metal, we see only colours; instead of all the dimensions requisite for appearance in nature, we have just a surface, and yet we get the same impression which reality affords.

(β) In contrast to the prosaic reality confronting us, this pure appearance, produced by the spirit, is therefore the marvel of ideality, a mockery, if you like, and an ironical attitude to what exists in nature and externally. For think what arrangements nature and man must make in ordinary life, what countless means of the most varied kind they must use, in order to produce things like those depicted; what resistance the material exerts here, e.g. a metal, when it is to be worked upon! On the other hand, the imagination, out of which art creates, is a pliant, simple element which easily and flexibly draws from its inner being everything on which nature, and man in his natural existence, have to work hard. Even so the objects represented and the ordinary man are not of an inexhaustible richness, but have their limitations: precious stones, gold, plants, animals, etc., have in themselves only this bounded existence. But man as creative artist is a whole world of matter which he filches from nature and, in the comprehensive range of his ideas and intuitions, has accumulated a treasure which he now freely disgorges in a simple manner without the far-flung conditions and arrangements of the real world.

In this ideality, art is the middle term between purely objective indigent existence and purely inner ideas. It furnishes us with the things themselves, but out of the inner life of mind; it does not provide them for some use or other but confines interest to the abstraction of the ideal appearance for purely contemplative inspection.

(γ) Now, consequently, through this ideality, art at the same time *exalts* these otherwise worthless objects which, despite their insignificant content, it fixes and makes ends in themselves; it directs our attention to what otherwise we would pass by without any notice. The same result art achieves in respect of time, and here too is ideal. What in nature slips past, art ties down to permanence: a quickly vanishing smile, a sudden roguish expression in the mouth, a glance, a fleeting ray of light, as well as spiritual traits in human life, incidents and events that come and go, are there and are then forgotten—anything and everything art wrests from momentary existence, and in this respect too conquers nature.

But in this formal ideality of art it is not the subject-matter which principally makes a claim on us but the satisfaction which comes from what the *spirit* has produced. The artistic presentation must appear here as natural, yet it is not the natural there as such but that making, precisely the extinction of the sensuous material and external conditions, which is the poetic and the ideal in a formal sense. We delight in a manifestation which must appear as if nature had produced it, while without natural means it has been produced by the spirit; works of art enchant us, not because they are so natural, but because they have been *made* so natural.

(*b*) Yet another interest, which goes deeper, arises from the fact that the subject-matter is not just represented in the forms in which it is presented to us in its immediate existence; grasped now by the spirit, it is enlarged within those forms and otherwise changed. What exists in nature is just a single thing, individualized indeed in all its parts and aspects. On the other hand, our imaginative mentality has in itself the character of universality, and what it produces acquires already thereby the stamp of universality in contrast to the individual things in nature. In this respect our imagination has the advantage that it is of wider range and therefore is capable of grasping the inner life, stressing it, and making it more visibly explicit. Now the work of art is of course not just a universal idea, but its specific materialization; but since it has been produced by spirit and its imaginative power, it must be permeated by this character of universality, even though this character has a visible liveliness. This affords the higher ideality of the poetic in contrast to the formal ideality of mere making. Now here it is the task of the work of art to grasp the object in its universality and to let go, in its external appearance, everything that would remain purely external and indifferent for the expression of the content. The artist therefore does not adopt everything in the forms or modes of expression which he finds outside him in the external world and because he finds it there; on the contrary, if he is to create genuine poetry, he grasps only those characteristics which are right and appropriate to the essence of the matter in hand. If he takes, as a model, nature and its productions, everything just presented to him, it is not because nature has made it so and so, but because it has made it *right*; but this 'rightness' means something higher than just being *there*.

In the case of the human form, for instance, the artist does not proceed, as may be supposed, like a restorer of old paintings who even in the newly painted places reproduces the cracks which, owing to the splitting of the varnish and the paint, have covered all the other older parts of the canvas with a sort of network. On the contrary, the portrait painter will omit folds of skin and, still more, freckles, pimples, pock-marks, warts, etc., and the famous Denner,[1] in his so-called 'truth to nature', is not to be taken as an example. Similarly, muscles and veins are indicated indeed, but they should not appear in the distinctness and completeness which they have in reality. For in all this there is little or nothing of the spirit, and the expression of the spiritual is the essential thing in the human form. Consequently I cannot find it so thoroughly disadvantageous that, in our day, fewer nude statues, for example, are made than was the case in antiquity. On the other hand, the cut of our clothes today is inartistic and prosaic in comparison with the more ideal drapery of the ancients. Both sorts of clothing have in common the purpose of covering the body. But the clothing portrayed in the art of antiquity is a more or less explicitly form-less surface and is perhaps only determined by the fact that it needs a fastening on to the body, to the shoulder, for example. In other respects the drapery remains plastic and simply hangs down freely in accordance with its own immanent weight or is settled by the position of the body or the pose and movement of the limbs. What constitutes the ideal in clothing is the determining principle displayed when the outer wholly and entirely subserves the changeable expression of spirit appearing in the body, with the result that the particular form of the drapery, the fall of the folds, their hanging and lifting is entirely regulated from within, and is adapted to precisely this pose or movement momentarily only. In our modern dress, on the other hand, the whole of the material is fashioned once for all, cut and sewn to fit the shape of the limbs, so that the dress's freedom to fall exists no longer, or hardly at all. After all, the character of the folds is determined by the stitching, and, in

---

[1] Balthasar Denner, 1685–1749, German portrait painter. See above, pp. 45, 155. Hegel would not have approved of Cromwell's instructions to Lely. In his lectures in 1826 Hegel made his point at greater length: 'What the artist must produce is an appearance of the spirit. A portrait must be an expression of individual and spiritual character. This nobler element in a man, which the artist introduces into the portrait, is not ordinarily obvious in a man's features. Therefore, if the artist is to bring out the sitter's character, he must have seen him in several situations and actions, in short been well acquainted with him, got to know his manner, heard him speak, and noticed his sort of feelings' (Lasson, pp. 225–6).

general, the cut and fall of the garment is produced technically and mechanically by the tailor. True, the build of the limbs regulates the form of the clothes generally, but in being formed to suit the body the clothes are precisely only a poor imitation or a disfiguration of human limbs according to the conventional fashion and accidental whim of the day; once the cut is complete it remains always the same, without appearing determined by pose and movement. As, for example, sleeves and trousers remain the same, however we may move our arms and legs. The folds do at most move variously, but always according to the fixed seams, as for example the breeches on the statue of Scharnhorst.[1] Thus, to sum up, our manner of dress, as outer covering, is insufficiently marked out by our inner life to appear conversely as shaped from within; instead, in an untruthful imitation of our natural form, it is done with and unalterable once it has been cut.

Something similar to what we have just seen in relation to the human form and its clothing holds good too of a mass of other externals and needs in human life which in themselves are necessary and common to all men, yet without their being connected with the essential characteristics and interests which constitute the proper universal element, proper on account of its content, in human existence—however variously all these physical conditions, as e.g. eating, drinking, sleeping, dressing, etc., may be externally interwoven with the actions proceeding from our spirit.

Things of this sort may of course be adopted as topics of artistic representation in poetry, and in this connection it is granted that Homer, for example, has the greatest conformity to nature. Yet he too, despite all ἐνάργεια, all clarity for our vision, has to restrict himself to mentioning such things only in general terms, and it would not occur to anyone to demand that in this matter all the details afforded by what confronts us in real life should have been related and described; as, e.g., even in the description of the body of Achilles, the lofty brow, the well-formed nose, the long strong legs may of course be mentioned without bringing into the picture the detail of the actual existence of these members, point by point, the position and relation of each part to the other, the colour, etc., which would alone be the real truth to nature. But, this apart, in poetry the manner of expression is always the universal idea in distinction from natural singularity; instead of the thing, the poet

---

[1] He died in 1813. The reference is to a marble statue by C. D. Rauch, 1822.

always gives only the name, the word, in which the singular rises to a universality, because the word is the product of our ideas, and therefore carries in itself the character of the universal. Now indeed it is permissible to say that in our ideas and speech it is 'natural' to use the name, the word, as this infinite abbreviation for natural existents, but in that case this naturalness would always be the precise opposite of nature proper, and its cancellation. Thus the question arises what sort of naturalness is meant when it is contrasted with poetry, for 'nature' as such is a vague and empty word. Poetry should continually emphasize the energetic, the essential, the significant, and this essential expressiveness is precisely the Ideal and not what is merely at hand; to recite all the details of the latter in the case of some event or some scene would of necessity be dull, spiritless, wearisome, and intolerable.

In relation to this kind of universality, however, one art proves to be more ideal, while another is more adjusted to the wide range of the externally perceptible. Sculpture, for example, is more abstract in its productions than painting is, while in poetry the epic, in respect of external life, falls behind the actual performance of a dramatic work, although, on the other hand, it is superior to drama in the fullness of what it can manifest. The epic poet brings before us concrete pictures drawn from a vision of what has happened, while the dramatist has to content himself with the inner motives of action, of their operation on the will, and of its inner reaction to them.

(c) Now further, since it is the *spirit* which gives reality, in the form of external appearance, to the inner world of its own absolute content and its fullness of interest, the question arises here too about the meaning of the opposition between Ideal and nature. In this connection 'natural' cannot be used in the strict sense of the word, for as the external configuration of spirit it has no value in simply existing immediately as the life of animals, the natural landscape, etc.; on the contrary, in accordance with its specific character of being the *spirit* which gives *itself* a body, it appears here only as an expression of spirit, and so already as idealized. For this assumption into spirit, this forming and shaping on the part of spirit, means precisely idealizing. It is said of the dead that their face assumes once again the lineaments of their childhood; the corporeal fixed expression of passions, habits, and strivings, the look characteristic of all willing and doing, has then flown away, and the indeterminacy of the child's features has come back. In life, however, the features and the whole form derive the character of their expression from within; as, after all, the different peoples, classes, etc., display in their outward form the difference of their spiritual tendencies and activities. In all such respects, the external, as penetrated and brought about by spirit, is already idealized in contrast to nature as such. Now here alone is the properly significant point of the question about the natural and the Ideal. For, on the one hand, some maintain that the natural forms with which spirit is clothed are already in their actual appearance—an appearance not recreated by art—so perfect, so beautiful, and so excellent in themselves that there cannot be still another beauty evincing itself as higher and, in distinction from what is there confronting us, as ideal, since art is not even capable of reaching altogether what is already met with in nature. On the other hand, there is a demand that there should be found for art independently, in contrast to reality, forms and representations of another and more ideal kind. In this respect especially the above-mentioned polemics of von Rumohr are important. While others, with the 'Ideal' on their lips, look down on vulgarity and speak of it contemptuously, he speaks of the Idea and the Ideal with similar superiority and contempt.

But in fact there is in the world of spirit something vulgarly natural both within and without. It is vulgar externally just because the inner side is vulgar, and in its action and all its external manifestations the latter brings into appearance only the aims of envy, jealousy, avarice in trifles and in the sensuous sphere. Even this vulgarity art can take as its material, and has done so. But in that case either there remains, as was said above [in the Introduction, 6(iii)], the representation as such, the cleverness of production, as the sole essential interest, and in that case it would be useless to expect a cultivated man to show sympathy with the whole work of art, i.e. with a topic of this kind, or else the artist must make something further and deeper out of it through his treatment of the subject. It is especially the so-called *genre* painting which has not despised such topics and which has been carried by the Dutch to the pitch of perfection. Now what has led the Dutch to this *genre*? What is it that is expressed in these little pictures which prove to have the highest power of attraction? They cannot be called pictures of vulgarity and then be just set aside altogether and discarded. For, if we look at it more closely, the proper subject-matter of these paintings is not so vulgar as is usually supposed.

The Dutch have selected the content of their artistic representations out of their own experience, out of their own life in the present, and to have actualized this present once more through art too is not to be made a reproach to them. What the contemporary world has brought before our vision and our spirit must also belong to that world if it is to claim our whole interest. In order to ascertain what engrossed the interest of the Dutch at the time of these paintings, we must ask about Dutch history. The Dutch themselves have made the greatest part of the land on which they dwell and live; it has continually to be defended against the storms of the sea, and it has to be maintained. By resolution, endurance, and courage, townsmen and countrymen alike threw off the Spanish dominion of Philip II, son of Charles V (that mighty King of the World), and by fighting won for themselves freedom in political life and in religious life too in the religion of freedom. This citizenship, this love of enterprise, in small things as in great, in their own land as on the high seas, this painstaking as well as cleanly and neat well-being, this joy and exuberance in their own sense that for all this they have their own activity to thank, all this is what constitutes the general content of their pictures. This is no vulgar material and stuff which, it is true, is not to be approached by a man of high society who turns up his nose at it, convinced of the superiority of courts and their appendages. Fired by a sense of such vigorous nationality, Rembrandt painted his famous Night Watch, now in Amsterdam, Van Dyck so many of his portraits, Wouwerman[1] his cavalry scenes, and even in this category are those rustic carousels, jovialities, and convivial merriments.

To cite a contrast, we have, for example, good *genre* paintings in our exhibition this year too [1828], but in skill of representation they fall far below the Dutch pictures of the same kind, and even in content they cannot rise to freedom and joyfulness like that of the Dutch. For example, we see a woman going into an inn to scold her husband. Here we have nothing but a scene of snarling and vicious people. On the other hand, with the Dutch in their taverns, at weddings and dances, at feasting and drinking,

[1] Philips Wouwerman, 1619–68. Rembrandt, 1606–69. A. van Dyck, 1559–1641.

everything goes on merrily and jovially, even if matters come to quarrels and blows; wives and girls join in and a feeling of freedom and gaiety animates one and all. This spiritual cheerfulness in a justified pleasure, which enters even pictures of animals and which is revealed as satisfaction and delight—this freshly awakened spiritual freedom and vitality in conception and execution—constitutes the higher soul of pictures of this kind.

In the like sense the beggar boys of Murillo (in the Central Gallery at Munich) are excellent too. Abstractly considered, the subject-matter here too is drawn from 'vulgar nature': the mother picks lice out of the head of one of the boys while he quietly munches his bread;[1] on a similar picture two other boys, ragged and poor, are eating melon and grapes.[2] But in this poverty and semi-nakedness what precisely shines forth within and without is nothing but complete absence of care and concern—a Dervish could not have less—in the full feeling of their well-being and delight in life. This freedom from care for external things and the inner freedom made visible outwardly is what the Concept of the Ideal requires. In Paris there is a portrait of a boy by Raphael:[3] his head lies at rest, leaning on an arm, and he gazes out into the wide and open distance with such bliss of carefree satisfaction that one can scarcely tear oneself away from gazing at this picture of spiritual and joyous well-being. The same satisfaction is afforded by those boys of Murillo. We see that they have no wider interests and aims, yet not at all because of stupidity; rather do they squat on the ground content and serene, almost like the gods of Olympus; they do nothing, they say nothing; but they are people all of one piece without any surliness or discontent; and since they possess this foundation of all excellence, we have the idea that anything may come of these youths. These are totally different modes of treatment from those we see in that quarrelsome choleric woman, or in the peasant who ties up his whip, or the postillion who sleeps on straw.

But such *genre* pictures must be small and appear, even in the whole impression they give to our vision, as something insignifi-

---

[1] No. 1308, *Toilette familière*. B. E. Murillo, 1618–82. Osmaston has the mother 'scolding' the boy.

[2] No. 1304, *Les Enfants à la Grappe*. Osmaston is wrong to say that Ruskin depreciated these pictures. See C. and W. edition, vii, pp. 494–5.

[3] No. 385, *Portrait d'un jeune homme*. Hegel visited the Louvre in September 1827 (*Briefe*, edn. cit., iii. 186–7).

cant which we have got beyond, so far as the external subject-matter and the content of the painting goes. It would be intolerable to see such things worked out life-size and therefore claiming that we should really be satisfied with them and their like in their entirety.

In this way what is generally called 'vulgarity' must be interpreted if it is to have the right of entry into art.

Now of course there are higher, more ideal, materials for art than the representation of such joy and bourgeois excellence in what are always inherently insignificant details. For men have more serious interests and aims which enter in through the unfolding and deepening of spirit and in which men must remain in harmony with themselves. The higher art will be that which has as its task the representation of this higher content. Now this at once gives rise to the question of whence are to be drawn the forms for this material engendered by spirit. Some entertain the opinion that, just as the artist first carries in himself these lofty ideas which he must create for himself, so he must also shape from his own resources correspondingly lofty forms for them, such as, for example, the figures of the Greek gods, Christ, the Apostles, saints, and so on. Against this view it is von Rumohr above all who has entered the field, in that he recognizes that art is on the wrong road when artists go in the direction of finding their forms arbitrarily instead of finding them in nature, and he has adduced as examples in support of his contention the masterpieces of Italian and Netherlands painting. In this connection his criticism is that (op. cit., i, p. 105) 'the aesthetics of the last sixty years has struggled to prove that the aim, or even the chief aim, of art is to improve on creation in its individual formations, to produce forms unrelated to anything real, forms which should counterfeit creation into something more beautiful, and therefore, as it were, should hold the human race blameless for nature's failure to make itself more beautiful'. Therefore (p. 63) he advises the artist 'to give up the titanic intention of "adorning" natural forms, of "transfiguring" them, or however else writers on art may describe such arrogance on the part of the human spirit'. For he is convinced that, for even the highest spiritual matters, satisfactory external forms are already before our eyes in the world confronting us, and he therefore maintains (p. 83) 'that the artistic representation, even where its subject-matter is thinkable and most spiritual, never rests on arbitrarily fixed symbols, but throughout on a nature-given significance of organic forms'. In saying this, von Rumohr has especially in view the ideal forms of antiquity as expounded by Winckelmann. But it is the eternal merit of Winckelmann to have emphasized and classified these forms, although he may have slipped into errors in relation to some particular features; as, for instance, von Rumohr (p. 115, note) seems to think that the lengthening of the belly, which Winckelmann (*Geschichte der Kunst des Altertums*, book 5, ch. 4, § 2) distinguishes as a feature in Greek ideal forms, is really derived from Roman statuary. Continuing his criticism, von Rumohr, in his polemic against the Ideal, now demands that the artist should utterly and entirely devote himself to the study of natural form, for here alone is beauty proper really brought to light. For, he says (p. 144), 'the most important beauty rests on a symbolism of forms given in nature and not grounded on human caprice. Thereby these forms in specific combinations develop into features and signs which, when we see them, necessarily recall to us specific ideas and concepts or make known to us more specifically feelings that are slumbering in us.' And so, it appears (p. 105), 'a secret spiritual trait, perhaps what is called the "Idea", links the artist after all with allied natural phenomena; in these he learns little by little to recognize his own intention ever more clearly and through them is enabled to express it'.

Of course, in ideal art, there can be no question of symbols settled arbitrarily, and, if it has happened that the ideal forms of antiquity have been copied, by setting aside the genuine natural form, into false and empty abstractions, then von Rumohr was right enough to oppose this in the strongest way.

But concerning this opposition between nature and the artistic ideal, the chief point to make is the following.

The existing natural forms of the spiritual content are in fact to be regarded as symbolic in the general sense that they have no immediate value in themselves; on the contrary, they are an appearance of the inner and spiritual life which they express. This already, in their reality outside art, constitutes their ideality in distinction from nature as such, which does not display anything spiritual. Now in art, at its higher stage, the inner content of spirit is to acquire its external form. This content is there in the real spirit of man, and so, like man's inner experience in general, it has already present there its external form in which it is expressed.

However readily this point may be granted, still, from the philosophical point of view, it is superfluous altogether to ask whether in existent reality there are such beautiful and expressive shapes and countenances which art can use immediately as a portrait for representing e.g. Jupiter (his majesty, repose, and power), Juno, Venus, Peter, Christ, John, Mary, etc. Of course you can argue for and against, but it remains a purely empirical question which, as empirical, cannot be settled. For the only way to decide it would be actually to exhibit these existing beauties, and for the Greek gods, for example, this might be a matter of some difficulty, and even at the present day one man might see perfect beauties, let us say, where another, a thousand times cleverer, did not. Apart from this, however, beauty of form as such does not always afford what we have called the Ideal, because the Ideal requires also individuality of content and therefore also of form. For example, a face altogether regular in form and beautiful may nevertheless be cold and expressionless. But the ideal figures of the Greek gods are individuals which within their universality do not lack determinate characteristics of their own. Now the vitality of the Ideal rests precisely on the fact that this specific spiritual fundamental meaning which is to be represented is completely elaborated through every particular aspect of external appearance, through posture, attitude, movement, facial expressions, form and shape of limbs, etc. The result is that nothing empty and insignificant remains, but everything evinces itself as penetrated by that meaning. For example, what we have seen of Greek sculpture in recent years as actually attributed to Phidias[1] inspires us principally owing to this kind of all-pervasive vitality. The Ideal is still preserved in its strictness and has not passed over into grace, charm, exuberance, and gracefulness, but keeps every form in steady relation to the general meaning which was to be given bodily shape. This supreme vitality is the distinguishing mark of great artists.

Such a fundamental meaning has to be called 'abstract' in itself in contrast to the rich detail of the phenomenal real world. This is especially true of sculpture and painting which bring out only one feature, without proceeding to the many-sided development in which Homer, for example, could sketch the character of Achilles as at once harsh and cruel, kind and friendly, and endowed with so many other qualities of soul. Now in the real world

[1] i.e. the Elgin marbles.

confronting us such a meaning may indeed also find its expression; as, for example, there is hardly any face which could not give us the impression of piety, worship, serenity, etc.; but these features also express besides in thousands of ways as well what either is quite unsuited to portray the fundamental meaning to be impressed on them or else is in no nearer relation to it. Thus a portrait at once announces itself as a portrait by its very detail. In Flemish and old German pictures, for example, we often find the man who gave the commission portrayed along with his family, wife, sons and daughters. They are all supposed to appear sunk in devotion, and piety actually shines out of all their eyes; but nevertheless we see in the men valiant warriors, it may be, men of vigorous action, well versed in life and the passion for achievement, and in the women we see wives of a similar vigorous excellence. If we compare the expressions in these pictures, which are famous for their true-to-life likenesses, with Mary or the saints and Apostles beside her, then on *their* faces we read only *one* expression, and on this one expression the whole formation is concentrated, the build of the bones, the muscles, the traits of movement or rest. It is only the appropriateness of the whole formation which marks the difference between the Ideal proper and the portrait.

Now one might suppose that the artist should select here and there the best forms in the world confronting him and collect them together, or even as has happened, hunt through collections of etchings and wood-cuts for faces, postures, etc. in an endeavour to find the genuine forms for his topic. But with this collecting, and choosing, nothing is achieved, for the artist must act creatively and, in his own imagination and with knowledge of the corresponding forms, with profound sense and serious feeling, give form and shape throughout and from a single casting to the meaning which animates him.

B. THE DETERMINACY OF THE IDEAL

The Ideal as such, which hitherto we have considered in accordance with its general Concept, was relatively easy to grasp. But the beauty of art, by being Idea, cannot stop at its purely general Concept; even in virtue of this Concept it has determinacy and particularity in itself and therefore must advance out of itself into actual determinacy. Consequently, from this point of view, the question arises in what way, despite exit into externality and finitude and therefore the non-Ideal, the Ideal can still maintain itself, and, conversely, in what way finite existence can assume the Ideality of artistic beauty.

In this connection we have the following points to review:

First, the *determinacy* as such of the Ideal;

Secondly, this determinacy in so far as it develops itself through its particularity to *differentiation* in itself and to the resolution of this difference, a process which in general terms we may call *action*;

Thirdly, the *external* determinacy of the Ideal.

I. IDEAL DETERMINACY AS SUCH

1. *The Divine as Unity and Universality*

We have seen already [in the Introduction, 8(iii)] that art has above all to make the Divine the centre of its representations. But the Divine, explicitly regarded as unity and universality, is essentially only present to thinking and, as in itself imageless, is not susceptible of being imaged and shaped by imagination; for which reason, after all, the Jews and Mahometans are forbidden to sketch a picture of God in order to bring him nearer to the vision which looks around in the sensuous field. For visual art, which always requires the most concrete vitality of form, there is therefore no room here, and the lyric alone, in rising towards God, can strike the note of praise of his power and his glory.

2. *The Divine as a Group of Gods*

Nevertheless, on the other hand, however far unity and universality are the characteristics of the Divine, the Divine is nevertheless essentially determinate in itself, and since it therefore disencumbers itself of abstractness, it resigns itself to pictorial representation and visualization. If now it is seized in its determinate form and displayed pictorially by imagination, there at once enters a multiplicity of determinations, and here alone is the beginning of the proper sphere of ideal art.

For *first*, the one divine substance is split and broken up into a multitude of independent and self-reposing gods, as in the polytheistic vision of Greek art; and, even for Christian ideas, God appears, over against his purely inherent spiritual unity, as an actual man immediately involved with the earthly and worldly sphere. *Secondly*, the Divine is present and active in its determinate appearance and actuality generally in man's senses and heart, his will and achievement; and therefore in this sphere men filled with the spirit of God, saints, martyrs, holy and pious men in general, become an equally appropriate subject for ideal art too. But, *thirdly*, with this principle of the division of the Divine and its specific and therefore also mundane existence, there appears the detail of real human life. For the whole human heart with everything whereby it is moved in its innermost being, everything which is powerful in it—every feeling and passion, every deeper interest in the soul—this concrete life forms the living stuff of art, and the Ideal is its representation and expression.

On the other hand, the Divine, as in itself *pure* spirit, is an object of intellectual reflection alone. But the spirit *embodied* in activity, because it always reverberates only in the human breast, belongs to art. Yet thereupon there at once come to light here particular interests and actions, determinate characters and their momentary circumstances and situations—in short, involvements with the external world; and it is therefore necessary to describe, at first in general terms, wherein the Ideal lies in relation to this field of determinacy.

3. *Repose of the Ideal*

In view of what we have already expounded above, the supreme purity of the Ideal will here too be able to consist only in the fact that the gods, Christ, Apostles, saints, penitents, and the devout are set before us in their blessed repose and satisfaction; therein they are untouched by the world with the distress and exigency of its manifold complications, struggles, and oppositions. In this sense it is especially sculpture and painting which have found forms in an ideal way for individual gods, as well as for Christ as Saviour of the world, for individual Apostles and saints. Here what is inherently true at the heart of existence comes into the work of art only as related to itself in its *own* existence, and not dragged out of itself into finite affairs. This self-sufficiency is not indeed lacking in particular character, but the particularization which is dispersed in the sphere of the external and the finite is purified here into simple determinacy, so that the traces of an external influence and relation appear altogether expunged. This inactive, eternal repose in oneself, or this rest—as in the case of Hercules, for example—constitutes the Ideal as such even in the field of determinacy. Therefore, if the gods are represented as involved also in mundane affairs, they must still retain their eternal and inviolable majesty. For Jupiter, Juno, Apollo, Mars, for example, are indeed determinate but fixed authorities and powers which preserve their own independent freedom, even when their activity is directed outwards. And so then, within the determinacy of the Ideal, not only may an individual particular character appear, but spiritual freedom must in itself show itself as a totality and, in this reposing on itself, as the potentiality for anything.

Now further, in this connection, the Ideal proves effective in the sphere of the mundane and the human in the sense that any more substantial content which preoccupies mankind has power to master the purely particular element in subjective life. I mean that in this way the particular element in feeling and acting is wrested from contingency, and the concrete particular is represented in greater correspondence with its proper inner truth; just as, in short, what we call noble, excellent, and perfect in the human soul is nothing but the fact that the true substance of the spiritual, moral, and divine declares its mastery in the subject, and man therefore places his living activity, will-power, interests, passions, etc. in this substantial element alone in order to give satisfaction therein to his true inner needs.

But however far, in the Ideal, spirit's determinacy and its external appearance appears simply resumed into itself, still there is at the same time immediately bound up with spirit's particularization, turned out from within into external existence, the principle of *development*, and therefore, in this relation to externality, the difference and struggle of oppositions. This leads us to a more detailed consideration of the inherently differentiated and progressive determinacy of the Ideal, which we may formulate in general terms as *Action*.

II. ACTION

Characteristic of the Ideal's determinacy as such are rather the friendly innocence of an angelic and heavenly bliss, inactive repose, the sublimity of an independent and self-reliant power, the excellence and perfection of what is in itself substantial. Yet the inner and spiritual element exists nevertheless only as active movement and development. But development is nothing without one-sidedness and separation. Spirit, complete and whole, spreading itself out in its particularizations, abandons its repose *vis à vis* itself and enters the oppositions of this chaotic universe, where in this rift it can now no longer escape the misfortune and calamity of the finite realm.

Even the immortal gods of polytheism do not dwell in perpetual peace. They get into cliques and into struggles with conflicting passions and interests and they must submit to fate. Even the God of the Christians was not exempt from passing to the humiliation of suffering, yes, to the ignominy of death, nor was he spared the grief of soul in which he had to cry: 'My God, my God, why hast thou forsaken me?' His mother suffers a similar agonizing pain, and human life as such is a life of strife, struggles, and sorrows. For greatness and force are truly measured only by the greatness and force of the opposition out of which the spirit brings itself back to unity with itself again. The intensity and depth of subjectivity come all the more to light, the more endlessly and tremendously is it divided against itself, and the more lacerating are the contradictions in which it still has to remain firm in itself. In this development alone is preserved the might of the Idea and the Ideal, for might consists only in maintaining oneself within the negative of oneself.

But owing to such a development, the particularization of the Ideal involves a relation with externality, and therefore surrenders to a world which, instead of displaying in itself the ideal free correspondence of the Concept with its reality, manifests rather an existence which just is not what it ought to be; for this reason we must in considering this relation examine how far the determinate characteristics, into which the Ideal enters, either immediately contain ideality explicitly or are more or less capable of doing so.

In this matter three principal points claim our closer attention:

(i) the *general* state of the world, which is the precondition of the individual action and its character,

(ii) the *particular* character of the situation, the determinacy of which introduces into that substantial unity the difference and strain which is the instigator of action—the situation and its conflicts,

(iii) the apprehension of the situation by the subject, and his reaction whereby the struggle involved in difference and the dissolution of difference appear—*action* proper.

1. *The General State of the World*

It is characteristic of the living subject, in whom ideal subjectivity is enshrined, to act, and in general to bestir and realize himself, because this ideal has to carry out and bring to fruition what is implicit in it. To this end it requires a surrounding world as the general ground for its realizations. When we speak in this connection of the 'state' of something, we understand by it the general way and manner in which the *substantial* element is present which, as the truly essential element within spiritual actuality, holds together all its manifestations. In this sense we can speak, for example, of a 'state' of education, of the sciences, of the religious sense, or even of finances, administration of justice, family life, and other ways of life. But in that case all these aspects are in fact only forms of one and the same spirit and content which makes itself explicit and actual in them.—Now here, because we are discussing more precisely the state of the world of *spiritual* reality, we must take it up from the side of the *will*. For it is through the will that the spirit as such enters upon existence, and the immediate substantial bonds of reality are displayed in the specific manner in which the will's guides, i.e. the concepts of ethics and law, and, in short, what, in general terms, we may call justice, are activated.

Now the question is of what character such a general 'state' must have in order to evince itself as correspondent to the individuality of the Ideal.

(a) *Individual Independence—The Heroic Age*

Arising from the foregoing discussion we can first make the following points in this matter:

(α) The Ideal is inherent unity, a unity of its content, not merely a formal external unity but an immanent one. This inherently harmonious and substantial self-reliance we have already described above as the Ideal's self-enjoyment, repose, and bliss. At the stage we have now reached we will bring out this characteristic as independence, and require [for artistic representation] that the general state of the world shall appear in the form of independence so as to be able to assume the shape of the Ideal.

But 'independence' is an ambiguous expression.

(αα) For ordinarily what is inherently substantial is, on account of this substantiality and effectiveness, called simply the 'independent', and it is usual to describe it as the inherently Divine and absolute. But if it is retained solely in its universality and substance, it is on that account not in itself subjective and therefore it at once finds its fixed opposite in the particularity of concrete individuality. Yet in this opposition—as in any opposition—true independence is lost.

(ββ) Conversely, independence is ordinarily ascribed to the individual who is self-reliant, even if only formally, in the fixity of his subjective character. But every subject who lacks the true content of life, because these powers and substances exist on their own account outside him and remain something foreign to his inner and outer being, falls just the same into an opposition against what is truly substantial and thereby loses the state of concrete independence and freedom.

True independence consists solely in the unity and interpenetration of individuality and universality. The universal wins concrete reality only through the individual, just as the individual and particular subject finds only in the universal the impregnable basis and genuine content of his actual being.

(γγ) Here therefore in connection with the general state of the world we must consider the form of independence only in the sense that substantial universality in this state must, in order to be independent, have in itself the shape of subjectivity. The first mode which can occur to us in which this identity can appear is that of thought. For thinking is on the one hand subjective, but on the other hand it has the universal as a product of its true activity, and so it is both—universality and subjectivity—in a free unity. But the universal element in thinking does not belong to the beauty of art, and, besides, in the case of thinking, the rest of the particular individual in his natural character and shape, as well as in his practical action and accomplishment, is not in necessary concord with the universality of thoughts. On the contrary, a difference enters, or at least may enter, between the subject in his concrete reality and the subject as thinker. The same cleavage affects the content of the universal itself. If, namely, the genuine and the true begins already to be distinguished in the thinking subject from the rest of his reality, then the content of the universal, as explicitly universal, has already separated itself in objective appearance from the rest of existence and acquired against it a fixity and power of subsistence. But in the Ideal it is precisely particular individuality which should remain in inseparable concord with the substantial, and, just as freedom and the independence of subjectivity belong to the Ideal, in the same way the surrounding world of situations and circumstances should not possess any essential objectivity independent of the subjective and individual. The ideal individual must be self-contained; what is objective must still be his own and it must not be separated from the individuality of men and move and complete itself independently, because otherwise the individual retreats, as something purely subordinate, from the world as it exists already independent and cut and dried.

Thus in this regard the universal must indeed be actual in the individual as his own, his very own; not his own, however, in so far as he has *thoughts*, but his own as his *character* and heart. In other words, we are claiming for the unity of the universal and the individual, over against the mediation and distinctions of thinking, the form of immediacy, and the independence which we demand acquires the shape of *immediate* independence. But at once contingency is bound up with this. For if the universal and decisive element in human life is immediately present in the independence of individuals only as their subjective feeling, mentality, state of character, and should it gain no other form of existence, then it is just at once for this reason remitted to the contingency of will and accomplishment. In that case it remains only the peculiar characteristic of precisely these individuals and their mental attitude, and as their particular property it lacks the power and necessity of asserting itself on its own account; on the contrary, instead of actualizing itself ever anew in a universal way firmly fixed by its own effort, it appears simply as the resolution and performance, and equally the arbitrary neglect, of the purely self-dependent subject with his feelings, projects, force, ability, cunning, and dexterity.

In short, this sort of contingency constitutes at this point the characteristic feature of the state of affairs which we required as the ground and the total manner of the Ideal's appearance [in art].

(β) In order to bring out more clearly the specific form of such an actual state of affairs, we will cast a glance at the opposite mode of existence.

(αα) This mode is present where the essence of ethical life, i.e. justice and its rational freedom, has already been worked out and preserved in the form of a *legal* regime, so that now, alike in itself and in the external world, this regime exists as an inflexible necessity, independent of particular individuals and their personal mentality and character. This is the case in the life of the *state* when political life comes into appearance according to the essential nature of the state; for not every combination of individuals into a social community, not every patriarchal union, is to be called a state. In the state proper, that is to say, laws, customs, rights are valid by constituting the universal and rational characteristics of freedom, and, moreover, by being present in this their universality and abstraction, no longer conditioned by accidental whims and particular personal peculiarities. When regulations and laws have been brought to our minds in their universality, they are also actual externally as this universal which goes its explicitly orderly way and has public power and might over individuals if they undertake to oppose and violate the law by their caprice.

(ββ) Such a situation presupposes an actual cleavage between the universals of the legislative intellect and immediate life, if we understand by 'life' that unity in which everything substantial and essential in ethical life and justice has won actuality only in individuals as their feeling and disposition, and is administered solely by means of these. In the fully developed state, law and justice, and even religion and science (or at least provision for education in religion and science) are a matter for the public authority and are directed and pursued thereby.

(γγ) Therefore the position of separate individuals in the state is that they must attach themselves to this regime and its real stability, and subordinate themselves to it, since no longer are they with their character and heart the sole mode of existence of the ethical powers. On the contrary, as happens in genuine states, the whole details of their mental attitude, their subjective opinions and feelings, have to be ruled by this legislative order and brought into harmony with it. This attachment to the objective rationality of the state which has no dependence on subjective caprice may either be pure subjection, because rights, laws and institutions, by being mighty and valid, have the power of compulsion, or it can arise from the free recognition and appreciation of the rationality of what exists, so that the subject finds himself over again in the objective world. But even in that case separate individuals are and always remain only incidental, and outside the reality of the state they have no substantiality in themselves. For substantiality is no longer merely the *particular* property of this or that *individual*, but is stamped upon him on its own account and in a *universal* and *necessary* way in all his aspects down to the tiniest detail. Therefore whatever individuals may achieve in the interest and progress of the whole by way of right, moral, or legal actions, nevertheless their willing and achievement remains always, like themselves, when compared with the whole, insignificant and nothing but an example. For their actions are always only a quite partial actualization of a single case; but this is not the actualization of a universal as it would be if this action, this case, were thereby made into a law or brought into appearance as law. If this is looked at conversely, it does not matter in the least whether individuals as individuals want law and justice to prevail or not; law and justice prevails in and by itself, and even if they did not want it to, nevertheless it would. Of course it does interest the universal and public authority that all individuals should evince their compliance with it, but separate individuals do not arouse this interest on the ground that law and morals receive their validity precisely by the consent of this individual or that; law and morals do not require this individualized consent; punishment validates them if they are transgressed.

The subordinate position of the individual subject is shown finally, in developed states, in the fact that each individual acquires only an entirely specific and always restricted share in the whole. In the genuine state, I mean, work for the universal [i.e. for the general weal], like activity in business, trade, etc., in civil society, is subdivided in the most varied possible way, so that now the entire state does not appear as the concrete action of *one* individual, nor can it be entrusted to one individual's caprice, force, spirit, courage, power, and insight. On the contrary, the innumerable businesses and activities of political life must be assigned to an equally innumerable mass of agents. The punishment of a crime, for example, is no longer a matter of individual heroism and the virtue of a single person; on the contrary, it is split up into its different factors, the investigation and estimation of the facts of the case, judgement, and execution of the judge's sentence; indeed each of these chief factors has its own more specialized differences, and it falls to individuals to carry out only one side of them. The administration of the law therefore does not lie in the hands of *one* individual but results from many-sided co-operation in a stable organization. Besides, each individual has general guides prescribed to him as a standard for his conduct, and what he achieves in accordance with these rules is subject over again to the judgement and control of higher officials.

(γ) In all these matters the public authorities in a legally ordered state do not themselves appear as individuals; the universal as such rules in its universality, in which the life of the individual appears as uplifted or as incidental and unimportant. Thus in such a state of affairs the independence we required is not to be found. Therefore, for the free configuration of individuality we have required the opposite state of affairs, in which the authority of the ethical order rests on individuals alone, who, by their private will and the outstanding greatness and effectiveness of their character, place themselves at the head of the real world in which they live. In that event justice remains *their* very own decision, and if by their action they transgress what is moral absolutely, there is no public authority with powers to call them to account and punish them, but only the right of that inner necessity which is vitally individualized in particular characters, external contingencies and circumstances etc., and is actual only in this form. Herein lies the distinction between punishment and revenge. Legal punishment makes the universal and established law prevail against crime, and it operates according to universal norms through the organs of the public authority, through courts and judges who, as persons, are only incidental. Revenge likewise can be just in itself, but it rests on the *subjectivity* of those who take charge of the affair and out of the right in their own breast and temper wreak revenge for the wrong on the guilty party. The revenge of Orestes, for example, became just, but he had pursued it only in accordance with his private virtue, not with legal judgement and the universal law.

In short, in the state of affairs which we claimed for artistic representation, morals and justice should throughout keep an individual shape in the sense that they depend exclusively on individuals and reach life and actuality only in and through them. Thus, to allude to a further point, in organized states the external existence of the people is secured, their property protected, and it is only their subjective disposition and judgement that they really have on their own account and by their own resources. But when there is still no state the security of life and property depends entirely on the personal strength and valour of each individual who has to provide for his own existence and the preservation of what belongs and is due to him.

Such a state of affairs is the one we are accustomed to ascribe to the *Heroic Age*. Which of these situations, however,—the civilized and developed life of the state, or an heroic age—is the better, this is not the place to explain; here our only concern is with the Ideal of art, and for *art* the cleavage between universal and individual must not yet come on the scene in the way described above, no matter how necessary this difference is for other ways in which spiritual existence is actualized. For art and its Ideal is precisely the universal in so far as the universal is *configurated* for our vision and therefore is still *immediately* one with particular individuals and their life.

(αα) This occurs in the so-called Heroic Age which appears as a time in which virtue, in the Greek sense of ἀρετή, is the basis of actions. In this connection we must clearly distinguish ἀρετή from what the Romans called *virtus*. The Romans already had their city and their legal institutions, and, in contrast to the state as the universal end, personality had to be sacrificed. To be just a Roman, to visualize in his own personal energies only the Roman state, the fatherland and its grandeur and power, this is the seriousness and dignity of Roman virtue. Heroes, on the other hand, are individuals who undertake and accomplish the entirety of an action, actuated by the independence of their character and caprice; and in their case, therefore, it appears as the effect of individual disposition when they carry out what is right and moral. But this immediate unity of the substantial with the individuality of inclination, impulses, and will is inherent in Greek virtue, so that individuality is a law to itself, without being subjected to an independently subsisting law, judgement, and tribunal. Thus, for example, the Greek heroes appear in a pre-legal era, or become themselves the founders of states, so that right and order, law and morals, proceed from them and are actualized as their own individual work which remains linked with them. In this way Hercules was extolled by the ancient Greeks and stands for them as an ideal of original heroic virtue. His free independent virtue, whereby, actuated by his personal and private will, he put an end to wrong and fought against human and animal monsters, was not an effect of the general state of affairs in his day but belonged to him exclusively and personally. Incidentally, he was not exactly a moral hero, as the story of his relations with the fifty daughters of Thespius in a single night shows,[1] nor, if we recall the Augean stables, was he even genteel; he appears in general as a picture of this completely independent force and strength of the right and the just, for the actualization of which he underwent countless hardships and labours by his own free choice and personal caprice. True, he accomplished part of his deeds in the service and at the command of Eurystheus, but this dependence is only a purely abstract connection, no completely legal and firm bond which would have deprived him of the power of acting independently and on his own account as an individual.

The Homeric heroes are of a similar type. Of course they too have an overlord in common, but their bond with him is likewise no previously established legal relation which would have compelled their subjection; of their own free will they follow Agamemnon who is no monarch in the modern sense of the word; and so every hero proffers his own advice, the enraged Achilles asserts his independence by separating himself from his allegiance, and, in general, every one of them comes and goes, fights and rests, just as he pleases. In like independence, not bound to any order settled once and for all, not as mere tiny constituents of such an order, there appear the heroes of the older Arabic poetry, and even the *Shahnameh*[2] of Firdausi provides us with similar characters. In the Christian west, feudalism and chivalry are the basis for free groups of heroes and self-reliant individuals. Of this sort are the heroes of the Round Table and the circle of heroes of which Charlemagne was the centre.[3] Like Agamemnon, Charlemagne was surrounded by free heroic characters, and therefore he was equally powerless to hold them together, because he had continually to draw his vassals into council, and he is forced to be a spectator while they follow their own passions all the same; and swagger as he may, like

---

[1] Pausanias, ix. 27, 5 (where Thestius is the father's name). But Apollodorus (ii. 4, 10) says that Thespius provided a different daughter for each of fifty nights.

[2] *The Book of Kings*. Firdausi = Abul Karim Mansur, c. 940–1020. Hegel used the translation by J. von Görres (see *Ww.*, Glockner edn., xx, p. 437).

[3] Cf. section on the Romantic Epic in Part III below.

Jupiter on Olympus, they can leave him and his undertakings in the lurch and go off on adventures of their own.

Further, the complete exemplar of this sort of thing we find in the Cid.[1] He too is a partner in a group, an adherent of a king, and has to perform his duties as a vassal; but over against this bond there stands the law of honour as the dominating mood of his individual personality, and the Castilian [the Cid] fights for its untarnished lustre, dignity, and fame. And so here too only with the counsel and assent of his vassals can the king pronounce judgement, make decisions, or wage war; if they object, they do not fight in his service and they do not submit to a majority of votes at all; each stands there by himself and draws from his own resources his will and his power to act. A similar brilliant picture of independent self-reliance is afforded by the Saracen heroes who reveal themselves to us in almost a more inflexible form. Even *Reynard the Fox*[2] brings to life for us a glimpse of a similar state of affairs. The lion is indeed lord and king, but the wolf and the bear, etc., likewise sit in council with him; Reynard and the others carry on as they like; if there is an outcry the rascal gets out of it by cunning and lying, or manages to find some particular interest of the king and queen, and puts it to his own use because he is clever enough to wheedle his masters into whatsoever he likes.

(ββ) But just as, in the Heroic Age, the subject remains directly connected with his entire willing, acting, and achieving, so he also takes undivided responsibility for whatever consequences arise from his actions. On the other hand, when *we* act or judge actions, we insist that we can only impute an action to an individual if he has known and recognized the nature of his action and the circumstances in which it has been done. If the actual circumstances are of a different kind, and the objective sphere of his action has characteristics different from those present to the mind of the agent, a man nowadays does not accept responsibility for the whole range of what he has done; he repudiates that part of his act which, through ignorance or misconstruction of the circumstances, has turned out differently from what he had willed, and he enters to his own account only what he knew, and, on the strength of this

---

[1] i.e. Rodrigo Diaz, the 'Lord Conqueror', Spanish national hero. He died in 1099, and his career has been a favourite literary theme since the twelfth century.

[2] In 1794 Goethe published *Reineke Fuchs*, his version of thirteenth-century fables, and it is to this that Hegel is referring.

knowledge, what he did on purpose and intentionally. But the heroic character does not make this distinction; instead he is answerable for the entirety of his act with his whole personality. Oedipus, for example, on his way to the oracle, meets a man, quarrels with him, and kills him. In the days of quarrels like this, his act was no crime; the man had shown violence against him. But the man was his father. Oedipus marries a queen; the wife is his mother. In ignorance he has contracted an incestuous marriage. Yet he passes judgement on himself for the whole of these crimes and punishes himself as guilty of parricide and incest, although killing his father and mounting the marriage bed with his mother was neither within his knowledge nor his intention. The independent solidity and totality of the heroic character repudiates any division of guilt and knows nothing of this opposition between subjective intentions and the objective deed and its consequences, while nowadays, owing to the complexity and ramification of action, everyone has recourse to everyone else and shuffles guilt off himself so far as possible. Our view in this matter is more *moral*, in that in the moral sphere the subjective aspect, i.e. knowledge of the circumstances, conviction of the good, and the inner intention, constitute for us a chief element in the action. But in the Heroic Age, in which the individual is essentially a unity, and the objective action, by being his own production, is and remains his own, the subject claims that what has been done, has been entirely done by him alone and that what has happened is completely his own responsibility.

Neither does the heroic individual separate himself from the ethical whole to which he belongs; on the contrary, he has a consciousness of himself only as in substantial unity with this whole. *We*, on the other hand, according to our views nowadays, separate ourselves, as persons with our personal aims and relationships, from the aims of such a community; the individual does what he does as a person, actuated explicitly by his personality, and thus is answerable only for his own action, but not for the doings of the substantial whole to which he belongs. Therefore we make a distinction, for example, between person and family. Of such a separation the Heroic Age knows nothing. There the guilt of the ancestor descends to his posterity, and a whole generation suffers on account of the original criminal; the fate of guilt and transgression is continually inherited. In our eyes this condemnation appears to be unjust by being an irrational submission to a blind destiny. Just as, with us, the deeds of ancestors do not ennoble their sons and posterity, so the crimes and punishments of our forebears do not dishonour their descendants and still less can they besmirch their private character; indeed, according to our attitude today, even the confiscation of a family's property is a punishment transgressing the principle of deeper subjective freedom. But in the plastic totality of antiquity the individual is not isolated in himself; he is a member of his family, his clan. Therefore the character, action, and fate of the family is every member's own affair, and, far from repudiating the deeds and fate of his forebears, each member on the contrary voluntarily adopts them as his own; they live in him, and so he *is* what his fathers were, suffered, or transgressed. In our view this counts as a hardship, but this [modern] responsibility for oneself alone and the greater subjective independence thus gained is, from another point of view, only the abstract independence of the person, whereas the heroic individual is more ideal because he is not content with his inherent formal unity and infinity but remains united in steadfast immediate identity with the whole substantiality of the spiritual relations which he is bringing into living actuality. In that identity the substantial is immediately individual and therefore the individual is in himself substantial.

(γγ) Now here we can find at once a reason why the ideal artistic figures are transferred to the age of myths, or, in general, to the bygone days of the past, as the best ground for their actualization. I mean that if the artistic subjects are drawn from the present, then their own special form, as it actually confronts us, is firmly fixed in our minds in all its aspects, and thus the changes in it, which the poet cannot renounce, easily acquire the look of something purely manufactured and premeditated. The past, on the other hand, belongs only to memory, and memory automatically succeeds in clothing characters, events, and actions in the garment of universality, whereby the particular external and accidental details are obscured. To the actual existence of an action or a character there belong many insignificant interposing circumstances and conditions, manifold single happenings and deeds, while in memory's picture all these casual details are obliterated. In this liberation from the accidents of the external world the artist in his mode of artistic composition has a freer hand with the particular and individual features if the deeds, histories, and characters belong to ancient times. True, he also has historical recollections from which he must elaborate his topic into the shape of the universal; but the picture of the past, as has been said already, has, as a picture, the advantage of greater universality, while the manifold threads which tie up conditions and relations with their whole environment of finitude provide his hand at once with the means and the checks to prevent the obliteration of the individuality required by the work of art. In this way, looked at more closely, an Heroic Age retains the advantage over a later and more civilized state of affairs, in that the separate character and the individual as such does not yet in those days find the substantial, the moral, the right, contrasted with himself as necessitated by law, and thus far the poet is immediately confronted with what the Ideal demands.

Shakespeare, for example, has drawn much material for his tragedies out of chronicles or old romances which tell of a state of affairs not yet unfolded into a completely established organization, but where the life of the individual in his decision and achievement is still predominant and remains the determining factor. Shakespeare's strictly historical dramas, on the other hand, have, as a chief ingredient, purely external historical matter and so they are further away from the ideal mode of representation, although even here the situations and actions are borne and promoted by the harsh independence and self-will of the characters. It is true that their independence remains again only a mostly *formal* self-reliance, whereas in the independence of the heroic characters what must be an essential keynote is the *content* too which they have made it their aim to actualize.

This last point, after all, in relation to the general ground of the Ideal, refutes the idea that the *Idyllic* is especially suited to the Ideal because in the idyllic situation the cleavage between the legal and necessary, on the one hand, and living individuality on the other, is entirely absent. But however simple and primitive such idyllic situations may be, and however far removed they may intentionally be kept from the developed prose of spiritual existence, still their very simplicity has from another point of view too little interest, so far as their *real* content is concerned, for them to be able to count as the most proper ground and basis of the Ideal. For this ground lacks the most important *motifs* of the heroic character, i.e. country, morality, family, etc., and their development; instead, the whole kernel of its material is altogether confined to the loss of a sheep or a girl's falling in love. So the idyllic counts often enough only as a refuge and diversion of the heart, with which is conjoined, as in Gessner,[1] for example, a mawkishness and sentimental flabbiness. Idyllic situations at the present day, furthermore, have the defect that this simplicity, this domestic and rural element, in the feeling of love, or the comfort of a good coffee in the open air, etc., is likewise of negligible interest, since this country-parson life, etc., is just abstracted from all further connection with deeper entanglements in worthier and richer aims and circumstances. Therefore in this connection too we must marvel at the genius of Goethe (who, in *Hermann und Dorothea*,[2] concentrates himself on a sphere like this) because he picks out of the life of the present a narrowly enclosed particular experience, yet at the same time, as the background and atmosphere in which this circle moves, he reveals the great interests of the French Revolution and his own country, and brings this quite restricted material into relation with the widest and most potent world events.

But in general, there are not excluded from the Ideal the evil and the bad, war, battles, revenge; they were often the substance and ground of the heroic and mythical age, a substance that appeared in a harsher and wilder form the further those times were removed from a thoroughly developed legal and ethical order. In the adventures of chivalry, for example, in which the knights-errant moved about to redress evils and wrongs, the heroes often enough were themselves guilty of truculence and unruliness, and in a similar way the religious heroism of the martyrs presupposes a similar condition of barbarity and savagery. Yet, on the whole, the Christian ideal, which has its place in the inwardness and depth of our inner being, is more indifferent to external circumstances.

Now just as the more ideal state of the world corresponds especially with certain specific periods, so for the personalities which art chooses to bring on the scene there it selects especially

[1] Swiss author and painter, 1730–88. His 'idyllic prose pastorals' had an extraordinary vogue in their day.

[2] For a good account and criticism of this 'idyllic epic' (1796–7), which has as its subject French *emigrés* in a village on the right bank of the Rhine, see, e.g., G. H. Lewes, *Life and Works of Goethe* (2nd edn., 1864), book vi, ch. 4.

one specific class, the class of Princes. And it does so not, as may be supposed, because it is aristocratic and loves the gentry, but because of the perfect freedom of will and production which is realized in the idea of royalty. So we see in Greek tragedy, for example, the chorus as the general background on which the specific action is to take place, a background, void of individuality, for the dispositions, ideas, and modes of feeling of the characters. Then out of this background there arise the individual characters who play an active role, and they belong to the rulers of the people, the royal families. On the other hand, in the figures drawn from the lower classes, if they undertake to act within their restricted circumstances, what we see is subjection everywhere; for in civilized states indeed they are as a matter of fact in every way dependent, straitened, and, with their passions and interests, fall continually under the pressure and compulsion of the necessity outside them. For behind them stands the invincible might of the civil order against which they cannot hold their own, and they remain subject even to the whim of their superiors where these have legal authority. On this restriction by existing circumstances all independence is wrecked. Therefore the situations and characters drawn from these spheres are more appropriate for comedy and the comical in general. For, in comedy, individuals have the right to spread themselves however they wish and can. In their willing and fancying and in their idea of themselves, they may claim an independence which is immediately annihilated by themselves and by their inner and outer dependence. But, above all, this assumed self-reliance founders on external conditions and the distorted attitude of individuals to them. The power of these conditions is on a totally different level for the lower classes from what it is for rulers and princes. On the other hand, Don Cesar in Schiller's *Braut von Messina* [1803] can rightly exclaim: 'There is no higher judge over me', and when he is to be punished, he must pronounce judgement on himself and execute it. For he is not subject to any external necessity of right and law, and even in respect of punishment he is dependent on himself alone.[1] True, Shakespeare's characters do not all belong to the princely class and remain partly on historical and no longer on mythical ground, but they are therefore transferred to the times of the civil wars in which the

---

[1] Act IV, ll. 2636 ff. He has killed his brother and executes judgement on himself by suicide.

bonds of law and order are relaxed or broken, and therefore they acquire again the required independence and self-reliance.

(b) Prosaic States of Affairs in the Present

If we look now at all these points, made above, in relation to the state of affairs in the world of today, with its civilized, legal, moral, and political conditions, we see that nowadays the scope for ideal configuration is only of a very limited kind. For the regions in which free scope is left for the independence of particular decisions are[1] small in number and range. A father's care of his household, and his honesty, the ideals of decent men and good women, are the chief material here, where their willing and acting is restricted to spheres in which the human being, as an individual subject, still operates freely, i.e. is what he is, and does what he does, in accordance with his individual choice. Yet even in these ideals there is a deficiency of deeper content and so the really most important thing remains only the subjective side, the *disposition*. The more objective content is given by the otherwise already existing fixed circumstances, and so what must remain the most essential interest is the way and manner in which this content appears in individuals and their inner subjective life, their morality, etc. On the other hand, it would be inappropriate to set up, for our time too, ideal figures, e.g. of judges or monarchs. If an administrator of justice behaves and acts as his office and duty demands, he is simply carrying out the specific responsibility prescribed to him by *jus* and *lex* in accordance with the juridical order. Whatever else such public officials then introduce from their own personality —clemency in behaviour, sagacity, etc.—is not the chief thing and the substance of the matter, but something incidental and rather indifferent. So too, monarchs in our day, unlike the heroes of the mythical ages, are no longer the concrete heads of the whole, but a more or less abstract centre of institutions already independently developed and established by law and the constitution. The most important acts of government the monarchs of our time have renounced; they no longer pronounce judgement themselves; finance, civil organization and security, is no longer their special business; war and peace are determined by general international relations which no longer are within their single power or

---

[1] *ist* must be an error for *sind*.

conducted by them as individuals. And, even if in all these matters the final, supreme, decision is theirs, still what is really decreed is not so much a matter of their personal will; it has already been settled independently, so that the supremacy of the monarch's own subjective will in respect of universal and public affairs is only of a formal kind.[1] Likewise, today even a General or a Field Marshal has indeed great power; the most essential ends and interests are put into his hands, and his discretion, courage, determination, and spirit have to decide the most important matters; but still what is to be ascribed to his subjective character as his own personal share in this decision is only small in scope. For one thing, the ends are given to him and have their origin, not in his own individual self, but in matters outside the province of his power. For another thing, he does not by himself create the means for achieving these ends; on the contrary, they are provided for him; they are not subject to him or at his beck and call as a *person*; their position is quite different from that accruing to the personality of *this* military individual.

To sum up, then, in the world of today the individual subject may of course act of himself in this or that matter, but still every individual, wherever he may twist or turn, belongs to an established social order and does not appear himself as the independent, total, and at the same time individual living embodiment of this society, but only as a restricted member of it. He acts, therefore, also as only involved in it, and interest in such a figure, like the content of its aims and activity, is unendingly particular.[2] For, at the end of the day, this interest is always confined to seeing what happens to this individual, whether he happily achieves his aim, what hindrances and obstacles he encounters, what accidental or necessary complications obstruct or occasion the outcome, etc. And even if now too the modern person is in his own eyes, as subject, infinite in his heart and character, and if right, law, moral principles, etc., do appear in his acting and suffering, still the existence of the right in this individual is just as restricted as the individual himself; and he is not, as he was in the Heroic Age proper, the embodiment of the right, the moral, and the legal as such. The individual is now no longer the vehicle and sole actualization of these powers as was the case in the Heroic Age.

---

[1] Cf. *Philosophy of Right*, § 280, Addition.
[2] i.e. not universal but only trivial.

(c) The Reconstitution of Individual Independence

But the interest in and need for such an actual individual totality and living independence we will not and cannot sacrifice, however much we may recognize as salutary and rational the essential character and development of the institutions in civilized civil and political life. In this connection we can marvel at the youthful poetic genius of Schiller and Goethe, at their attempt to win back again within the circumstances existing in modern times the lost independence of the [heroic] figures. But how do we see Schiller carrying out this attempt in his earliest works? Only by a revolt against the whole of civil society itself. Karl Moor,[1] injured by the existing order and by those who misused their authority in it, leaves the sphere of legality, and, having the audacity to burst the bonds that constrain him, and so creating for and by himself a new heroic situation, he makes himself the restorer of right and the independent avenger of wrong, injury, and oppression. Yet how tiny and isolated must this private revenge turn out to be, owing to the insufficiency of the requisite means, and, on the other hand, it can only lead to crime, for it incorporates the wrong which it intends to destroy. For Karl Moor this is a misfortune, a failure, and, even if this is tragic, it is still only boys who can be seduced by this robber ideal. So too the individuals in *Kabale und Liebe*[2] are tormented by oppressive and vexatious circumstances with their tiny details and passions, and only in *Fiesco* and *Don Carlos*[3] do the chief characters appear nobler, in that they make their own a more substantial matter, the liberation of their country or the freedom of religious conviction, and so, because of their aims, became heroes. In a higher way still, Wallenstein[4] puts himself at the head of his army to become the regulator of the political situation. The power of this situation on which even his own means, the army, is dependent, he knows perfectly well, and therefore is for a long time reduced to swithering between will and duty. Scarcely had he made his decision before he saw the means, of which he thought he was sure, slipping through his fingers, and his tool broken. For what in the last resort is binding on the captains and the generals is not gratitude for what he has done to deserve their thanks owing to their appointment and promotion, nor his fame

---

[1] In *The Robbers*, Schiller's first play, 1781.
[2] *Intrigue and Love*, 1784.   [3] 1783, 1787 respectively.
[4] Schiller's three dramas on Wallenstein were issued in 1799.

as commander in the field, but their duty to the universally recognized power and government, the oath they have sworn to the monarch of the state, the Emperor of Austria.[1] Thus in the end he finds himself alone; he is not so much fought and conquered by an opposing external power as denuded of all means of achieving his end. Forsaken by the army, he is lost.

A similar, even if opposite, starting-point Goethe takes in *Götz*.[2] The time of Götz and Franz von Sickingen is the interesting period in which chivalry with the independence of noble individuals was passing away before a newly arising objective order and legal system. Goethe's great insight is revealed by his choosing as his first subject this contact and collision between the medieval heroic age and the legality of modern life. For Götz and Sickingen are still heroes who, with their personality, their courage, and their upright, straightforward good sense, propose to regulate the states of affairs in their narrower or wider scope by their own independent efforts; but the new order of things brings Götz himself into wrong and destroys him. For chivalry and the feudal system in the Middle Ages are the only proper ground for this sort of independence. Now, however, the legal order has been more completely developed in its prosaic form and has become the predominant authority, and thus the adventurous independence of knights-errant is out of relation to the modern world and if it still proposes to maintain itself as the sole legitimacy and as the righter of wrong and helper of the oppressed in the sense that chivalry did, then it falls into the ridiculousness of which Cervantes gave us such a spectacle in his *Don Quixote*.

But by alluding to such an opposition between different world views and to action within this clash, we have already touched on what we have indicated above in general terms as the more detailed determinacy and differentiation of the general state of world affairs, i.e. as the *situation* as such.

2. *The Situation*

The ideal world situation which, in distinction from prosaic actuality, art is called upon to present, constitutes, in accordance

---

[1] So they murdered Wallenstein.
[2] Goethe wrote *Götz von Berlichingen* in 1771, but he rewrote it and did not publish it until 1773. Götz lived from 1480 to 1562, and Sickingen, who appears in the play, from 1481 to 1523.

with the foregoing discussion, only spiritual existence in general and therefore only the *possibility* of individual configuration, but not this configuration itself. Consequently what we had before us just now was only the general basis and ground on which the living individuals of art can appear. True, it is impregnated with individuality and rests on the independence of that, but as a *universal* situation it does not yet display the active movement of individuals in their living agency, just as the temple which art erects is not yet the individual representation of the god himself but contains only the germ for it. Therefore we have to regard that world situation primarily as something still unmoved in itself, as a harmony of the powers ruling it, and thus far as a substantial uniformly valid existence which yet cannot be understood at all as a so-called state of innocence. For it is a state in which in its fullness and power of ethical life the monster of disunion still only slumbered, because for *our* examination only the aspect of its substantial unity exhibited itself, and therefore too individuality was present only in its universal guise in which, instead of asserting its determinacy, it disappears again without trace and without essential hindrance. But, for individuality, determinacy is indispensable, and if the Ideal is to confront us as a *determinate* shape, it is necessary for it not to remain simply in its universality; it must express the universal in a particular way and thereby alone give it existence and appearance. In this connection, art has thus not at all to sketch only a *universal* world situation but has to proceed out of this vague idea to pictures of definite characters and actions.

So far as individuals are concerned, the general situation is therefore indeed the stage presented to them, but it opens out into specialized situations, and, with this particularization, into collisions and complications which give the individuals opportunities to show what they are and display themselves as possessed of a determinate shape. On the other hand, so far as the world-situation is concerned, this self-revelation of individuals appears indeed as the development of that situation's universality into a living particularization and individualization, but to a determinate condition in which at the same time the universal powers maintain themselves as in control. For the determinate Ideal, considered in its essential aspect, has the eternal world-ruling powers for its substantial content. Yet the mode of existence which can be gained in the form of mere 'being in a state' is unworthy of this content. Being in a 'state', I mean, has, for one thing, habit as its form, but habit does not correspond with the spiritual self-conscious nature of these deepest interests; for another thing, it was the arbitrariness and caprice of individuals through whose independent activity we were to see these interests come to life; but once again neither are inessential accident and caprice correspondent to the substantial universality which constitutes the very nature of what is inherently genuine. We have therefore to look for both a more specific and also a more worthy artistic manifestation for the concrete content of the Ideal.

This new configuration the universal powers can acquire in their *existence* only because they appear in their essential distinction and movement in general, and, more especially, in their opposition to one another. Now in the particularity into which the universal passes over in this way, there are two factors to be noticed: (i) the substance as a group of universal powers through the particularization of which the substance is divided into its independent parts; (ii) the individuals who come on the scene as the activating realization of these powers and provide them with an individual shape.

But the difference and opposition into which thereby the primarily inner harmonious world-situation is placed with its individuals is—considered in relation to this world situation—the emergence of the essential content of that situation; while, conversely, the substantial universal, inherent in it, advances to particularity and individuality because this universal brings *itself* into existence, since while it does give itself the appearance of accident, disunion, and division, it wipes this appearance out again just because it is *itself* that appears in it.

But, further, the separation of these powers and their self-actualization in individuals can occur only under specific circumstances and states of affairs, under which and as which their entire manifestation reaches existence, or which are the stimulus to this actualization. Taken by themselves, such circumstances are without interest, and they acquire their meaning only in their relation to human beings through whose self-consciousness the content of those spiritual powers is to be activated. On this account the external circumstances are to be viewed essentially only in this relation, for they gain importance only through what they are for the *spirit*, namely through the way they are comprehended by individuals; thereby they provide the opportunity for bringing into existence the inner spiritual need, the aims, dispositions, and, in general, the specific essence of individuals in their various forms. As this closer opportunity, the specific circumstances and states of affairs form the *situation* which is the more particular presupposition for the proper self-expression and activation of everything at first still lying hidden and undeveloped in the general world situation. Therefore, before treating of action proper we must first settle the real nature of the situation.

The situation in general is (α) the state of affairs as such, particularized so as to have a determinate character, and, in this determinacy, it is (β) at the same time the stimulus for the specific expression of the content which has to be revealed in existence by means of artistic representation. From this latter point of view especially, the situation affords a wide field for treatment by art, since from time immemorial the most important part of art has been the discovery of interesting situations, i.e. those that make visible the profound and important interests and the true content of spirit. In this connection, our demands on the different arts are different: sculpture, for example, in respect of the inner variety of situations, is restricted; painting and music have a wider and freer scope; but poetry is the most inexhaustible.

But since here we are not yet treading the ground of the particular arts, we have at this stage to draw attention only to the most general points and we can subdivide them on the following scale:

(*a*) Before the situation has developed to determinacy in itself, it still retains the form of universality, and therefore of indeterminacy, so that at first we have before us the situation, as it were, of absence of situation. For the form of indeterminacy is itself only *one* form contrasted with another, i.e. determinacy, and thus evinces itself as a one-sidedness and a determinacy.

(*b*) But the situation emerges from this universality into particularization and enters a proper determinacy which yet at first is harmless, for it still provides no opportunity for opposition and its necessary resolution.

(*c*) Finally, division and its determinacy constitute the essence of the situation, which therefore becomes a collision leading to reactions, and forming in this respect our starting-point and the transition to action proper.

For the situation as such is the middle stage between the universal, inherently unmoved, state of the world and the concrete action, inherently opened out into action and reaction, on which account the situation has to display in itself the character of both extremes and lead us from one to the other.

(a) Absence of Situation

The form for the general state of the world, as the Ideal of art is to bring it into appearance, is both individual and inherently essential independence. Now independence, regarded as such and explicitly established, appears to us *prima facie* as nothing but secure resting on its own resources in motionless tranquillity. Therefore the specific figure does not issue from itself into relation with something else; it remains the inner and outer self-sufficiency of unity with itself. This affords the absence of situation in which we see, for example, old temple sculptures at the beginnings of art. Their character of profound impassive seriousness, of the most peaceful, even motionless but grandiose, sublimity, has been imitated in later times too in a similar fashion. The Egyptian and the oldest Greek sculpture, for example, affords a vision of this kind of absence of situation. Further, in Christian visual art, God the Father, or Christ, is portrayed in a similar way, especially in busts. As after all, in general, the fixed substantiality of the Divine, apprehended as a specific particular god or as the inherently absolute personality, is suited to such a mode of representation, although medieval pictures too betray a similar lack of specific situations on which the character of the individual could be stamped, and they attempt only to express the entirety of the specific character in its inflexibility.

(b) The Specific Situation in its Harmlessness

But since the situation as such lies in the field of determinacy, the second thing is departure from this stillness and blessed tranquillity or from the exclusive severity and power of personal independence. The situationless figures, unmoved therefore within and without, have to be set in motion and to give up their bare simplicity. But the next advance to a more special manifestation in a particular expression is the situation, specific indeed, but not yet essentially differentiated in itself or pregnant with collisions.

This first individualized expression remains therefore of such a kind that it has no further sequel, for it does not set itself in hostile opposition to something else and therefore cannot call up any reaction; it is finished and perfect in itself on the strength of its own naïveté. To this sort of thing there belong those situations which on the whole are to be considered as play, in so far as nothing is presented or done in them which has any real seriousness in it; for seriousness in acting or doing springs in general only from oppositions and contradictions which press onwards to the cancellation and conquest of one side or the other. Therefore these situations are neither themselves actions nor do they provide the stimulating occasion for action; on the contrary they are partly specific but inherently quite simple states of affairs, and partly a deed without any inherently essential and serious aim which may proceed from conflicts or could lead to them.

(α) The first point in this connection is the transition from the tranquillity of absence of situation to movement and expression, whether as purely mechanical movement or as the original arousing and satisfaction of some inner need. While the Egyptians, for example, in their sculptures represented the gods with legs closed together, unmoved head, and tightly closed arms, the Greeks release the arms and legs from the body and give to the body a walking position and, in general, one moved in many ways. Repose, sitting, a tranquil gaze, are simple situations like this in which the Greeks, for example, apprehend their gods—situations which do give a determinate appearance to the independent divine shape, yet one which does not enter into further relations and oppositions, but remains self-enclosed and has its warrant in itself. Situations of this simplest kind belong principally to sculpture, and the Greeks above all have been inexhaustible in inventing such naïve situations. Here too they display their great insight, for precisely through the insignificance of the specific situation the loftiness and independence of their ideal figures is all the more marked, and, through the harmlessness and unimportance of what is done or left undone, this insignificance brings all the nearer to our vision the blessed peaceful stillness and immutability of the eternal gods. In that case the situation indicates the particular character of a god or hero only in general, without placing him in relation to other gods, still less into a hostile connection and dissension with them.

(β) The situation goes further towards determinacy when it

indicates a particular end, the realization of which is complete in itself, or some deed which is related to something else and expresses the inherently independent content within such a determinate state of affairs. Even here we have expressions in which the tranquillity and serene blessedness of the figures is untroubled but which themselves appear only as a consequence and a specific mode of this serenity. In such devices too the Greeks were extremely ingenious and rich. It is part of the naïveté of these situations that the activity they contain does not appear simply as the beginning of a deed out of which further complications and oppositions would have to arise; on the contrary, the whole determinate situation is manifestly complete and finished in this activity. In this way, for example, we interpret the situation of the Belvedere Apollo:[1] he is conscious of victory after slaying the serpent Python with his arrow, and strides forward in wrathful majesty. This situation no longer has the grandiose simplicity of the earlier Greek sculpture which revealed the tranquillity and innocence of the gods by means of less significant expressions: instead we have, for example, Venus arising from the bath,[2] conscious of her power, quietly looking into the distance; fauns[3] and satyrs in playful situations which, as situations, neither are meant nor wish to be anything beyond, e.g. the satyr who holds the young Bacchus in his arms and handles the child with laughter and infinite sweetness and grace;[4] Eros in the most varied similar naïve activities[5]—all these are examples of this kind of situation.

On the other hand, if the deed becomes more concrete, such a more complicated situation is less appropriate for the sculptural representation of the Greek gods, at least as independent powers, because in that case the pure universality of the individual god

---

[1] Well reproduced in, e.g., G. Richter, *Handbook of Greek Art* (London, 1959), p. 146.

[2] Possibly Praxiteles, *Aphrodite in Cnidos* (G. Rodenwaldt, *Die Kunst der Antike* (Berlin, 1927), p. 394).

[3] See, e.g., ibid., p. 484.

[4] Hegel refers four times to this figure. It was a favourite subject in antiquity. There are several replicas of what was probably an original fourth-century bronze by Lysippus. Hegel's later references show that he was referring to a figure in Munich. As No. 238 it is described and discussed by A. Furtwängler in his *Beschreibung der Glyptothek . . . zu München*, 1900. Its head is an eighteenth- or early nineteenth-century copy of another replica in the Vatican. Hegel did not know this, but his remarks, here and later, apply reasonably well to the Vatican replica also.

[5] See, e.g., Rodenwaldt, op. cit., p. 481, and G. Richter, op. cit., p. 165.

cannot shine through the accumulated detail of his specific deed to the same extent. For example, the Mercury of Pigalle,[1] set up [in 1760] in Sans Souci [by Frederick the Great] as a gift of Louis XV, is just fixing on his winged sandals. This is an entirely harmless occupation. On the other hand, Thorwaldsen's[2] Mercury has a situation almost too complicated for sculpture: i.e. while going on playing his flute, Mercury watches Marsyas, looking at him craftily and seeking a chance to kill him, while maliciously he snatches at the dagger he has concealed. Conversely, to mention still another modern work of art, Rudolf Schadow's *Girl binding on her Sandals*[3] is of course caught in the same simple occupation as Mercury's, but here the harmlessness has not the like interest linked with it as when a god is represented in such naïveté. When a girl fastens her sandals, or spins, there is nothing revealed but precisely this fastening or spinning, and this in itself is meaningless and unimportant.

(γ) Now, thirdly, the implication of the foregoing is that the specific situation as such can be treated as a merely external more or less definite stimulus which provides no more than the occasion for further expressions more closely or loosely connected with it. Many lyric poems, for example, have such an occasional situation. A particular mood and feeling is a situation which can be known and grasped poetically, and which, in relation too to external circumstances, festivals, victories, etc., incites to this or that more comprehensive or more restricted expression and configuration of feelings and ideas. In the highest sense of the word, Pindar's *Odes*, for example, are such *pièces d'occasion*. Goethe too has taken many lyrical situations of this kind as material; indeed in a wider sense we could even describe his *Werther* [1774] as a poetic *pièce d'occasion*, since through *Werther* Goethe has converted into a work of art his own inner distraction and torment of heart, the experiences of his own breast; just as any lyric poet disburdens his heart and expresses what he is affected by in his personal life. Thereby what at first is firmly retained only inwardly is released and becomes an external object from which the man has freed

---

[1] Now in the Louvre. J. B. Pigalle, 1714–85.

[2] A. B. Thorwaldsen, 1768–1844. This marble statue (1818) is in the Thorwaldsen Museum in Copenhagen. Mercury is lulling Argus to sleep by playing his flute, and duly kills him. Hegel or Hotho confuses this with the story of Apollo and Marsyas.

[3] R. Schadow, 1786–1822. This marble statue (1817) is in Munich.

himself, as tears make it easier when grief weeps itself out. Goethe says himself[1] that by writing *Werther* he was freed from the inner affliction and distress which he sketches. But the situation represented here does not belong to this stage because it is developed and comprises the most profound oppositions.

Now in such lyric situations there may of course be obvious some objective state of affairs and an activity in relation to the external world, but, all the same, the mentality as such, in its inner mood, may withdraw into itself from all external connection whatever and take its starting-point from the inwardness of its states and feelings.

(c) Collision

All the situations hitherto considered, are, as has already been touched upon, neither actions themselves nor, in general, stimuli to action proper. Their determinate character remains more or less a purely occasional state of affairs or an action insignificant in itself in which a substantial content is so expressed that its determinate character is now revealed as a harmless play[2] which cannot be taken seriously. The seriousness and importance of the situation in its special character can only begin when its definiteness comes into prominence as an essential difference and, by being in opposition to something else, is the basis of a collision.

In this respect the collision has its basis in a transgression, which cannot remain as such but must be superseded; it is an alteration of the state of affairs which was otherwise harmonious and is itself to be altered. Nevertheless the collision is still not an *action*; on the contrary, it contains only the beginnings of an action and its presuppositions, and therefore, by being merely a stimulus to action, it retains the character of situation. Nevertheless, the opposition, in which the collision is disclosed, may be the result of an earlier action. For example, the trilogies of Greek tragedy are continuations, in the sense that out of the end of the first drama a collision arises for the second, which demands its resolution in the third.

---

[1] *Dichtung und Wahrheit*, book xii (1811 ff.).

[2] Hegel's use of 'play' here and elsewhere is derived especially from Schiller, see his *Aesthetic Letters*, 15, especially 'With the perfect, man is merely serious, but with beauty he plays', and 'Man should only play with beauty, and should play with beauty alone'. Cf. p. 157, note 2.

Now since collision as such requires a solution which follows on the battle of opposites, a situation pregnant with collision is above all the subject-matter of dramatic art, the privilege of which is to represent beauty in its most complete and profound development; while sculpture, for example, is in no position to give complete configuration to an action which reveals the great spiritual powers in their conflict and reconciliation; and even painting, despite its wider scope, can never bring before our eyes more than one feature of the action.

But these serious situations bring with them a difficulty of their own already present in their nature. They rest on transgressions and give rise to circumstances which cannot subsist but necessitate a transforming remedy. But the beauty of the Ideal lies precisely in the Ideal's undisturbed unity, tranquillity, and perfection in itself. Collision disturbs this harmony, and sets the Ideal, inherently a unity, in dissonance and opposition. Therefore, by the representation of such transgression, the Ideal is itself transgressed, and the task of art can lie here only, on the one hand, in preventing free beauty from perishing in this difference, and, on the other hand, in just presenting[1] this disunion and its conflict, whereby out of it, through resolution of the conflict, harmony appears as a result, and in this way alone becomes conspicuous in its complete essentiality. But on the question of to what limit dissonance may be driven, no general specifications can be laid down, because in this matter each particular art follows its own special character. Our inner ideas, for example, can endure far more dissonance than immediate intuition can. Poetry therefore has the right to proceed, in describing the inner feelings, almost to the extreme torment of despair, and, in describing the external world, to downright ugliness. But in the visual arts, in painting, and still more in sculpture, the external shape stands there fixed and permanent without being superseded and without vanishing again fleetingly, like musical notes. Here it would be a blunder to cling to the ugly when the ugly cannot be resolved. Therefore to the visual arts not everything can be allowed which can perfectly well be permitted to dramatic poetry, since it lets an ugly thing appear just for a moment and then vanish again.

In examining the kinds of collision in more detail we can cite at this stage once again only the most general considerations.

[1] i.e. on the stage, like a pageant.

In this connection we must treat three main aspects:

(i) collisions which arise from purely physical or natural circumstances in so far as these are something negative, evil, and therefore disturbing;

(ii) spiritual collisions which rest on natural bases, which, although inherently positive, still bear in themselves for the spirit the possibility of differences and oppositions;

(iii) disunions which have their ground in spiritual differences and which alone are entitled to appear as the truly interesting oppositions, because they proceed from man's own act.

(α) As for conflicts of the first kind, they can count only as mere occasions for action, because here it is only external nature with its illnesses and other evils and infirmities which produces circumstances disturbing the original harmony of life and with differences as a consequence. In and by themselves such collisions are void of interest and are given a place in art only on account of the disunions which may develop out of a natural misfortune as its consequence. So, for example, in the *Alcestis* of Euripides, which provided the material too for Gluck's *Alceste*,[1] the foundation is the illness of Admetus. The illness as such is no material for genuine art, and it becomes so, even in Euripides, only owing to the individuals for whom this misfortune leads to a further collision. The oracle proclaims: Admetus must die unless a substitute is devoted to the underworld. Alcestis submits to this sacrifice and resolves to die in order to avert death from her husband, the father of her children, the King. In the *Philoctetes* of Sophocles too, it is a physical evil which is the basis of the collision. In their voyage to Troy the Greeks put the patient ashore on Lemnos because of his wounded foot, the result of a snake-bite at Chrysa. Here the physical misfortune is likewise only the most external point of connection and occasion for a further collision. For, according to the oracle, Troy is to fall only when the arrows of Hercules are in the hands of the besiegers. Philoctetes refuses to give them up because he has had to endure the wrong of being marooned for nine years full of agony. Now this refusal, like the wrong of being marooned in which it originated, could have been brought about in all sorts of other ways, and the real interest lies not in the illness and its physical distress but in the conflict which arises as a result of Philoctetes' decision not to give up the arrows.

---

[1] C. W. von Gluck, 1714–87. This opera was first produced in 1767.

The position is similar with the plague in the Greek camp before Troy, which, apart from being already represented as a consequence of earlier transgressions, is also represented as punishment. In general, after all, it pertains to epic poetry rather than dramatic to present disturbances and hindrances by means of a natural misfortune, a storm, a shipwreck, a drought, etc. But, on the whole, art does not represent such an evil as a pure accident, but as a hindrance and misfortune, the necessity of which assumes precisely this shape instead of another.

(β) But in so far as the external power of nature as such is not the essential thing in the interests and oppositions of the spiritual sphere, so, secondly, when it appears linked with spiritual matters, it emerges only as the ground on which collision proper leads to breach and disunion. In this class are all conflicts grounded in natural *birth*. Here in general we can distinguish three cases in more detail:

(αα) First, a *right* linked to nature, as, for example, kinship, right of inheritance, etc., which precisely because it is tied up with nature, immediately permits of a number of natural specifications while the right, the thing at issue, is unique. In this matter the most important example is the right of succession to the throne. If this right is to be the occasion for the sort of collisions in question here, then it must not be explicitly regulated and established yet, because otherwise the conflict at once becomes one of a totally different sort. I mean that if the succession is not yet established by positive laws and their valid organization, then it cannot be regarded as absolutely wrong if it is all one whether the elder or the younger brother or some other relative of the royal house is to rule. Now since ruling is something qualitative, and not quantitative like money and goods which, owing to their nature, can be divided with perfect justice, it follows that dissension and strife are present at once in the case of such unregulated succession. So, for example, when Oedipus leaves the throne without a ruler, his sons, the Theban pair, confront one another with the same rights and claims; the brothers adjust the matter by arranging to rule in alternate years, but Eteocles broke the agreement and Polynices returned to Thebes to fight for his right.[1] The enmity of brothers as such is a collision which crops up in every period of

[1] See, e.g., Apollodorus III. v ff. (with Sir J. G. Frazer's notes in the Loeb edition).

art: it begins with Cain who slew Abel. Also in the *Shahnameh*,[1] the earliest Persian hero-book, the starting-point for all sorts of battles is a dissension about succession to the throne. Feridu divided the earth between his three brothers. Salm received Rum and Khavar; Thur's share was Turan and Jin; and Iraj was to rule over the land of Iran. But each makes claims over the territory of the other and the resulting dissensions and wars are without end. In the Christian Middle Ages too the stories of dissensions in families and dynasties are without number. But such discords appear in themselves as accidental; for it is not absolutely necessary for brothers to be at enmity. Special circumstances and loftier causes must be added, as for example the hateful birth of the sons of Oedipus, or as too in the *Braut von Messina* an attempt is made [at the end of Act IV] to ascribe the quarrel of the brothers to a loftier fate. In Shakespeare's *Macbeth* the basis is a similar collision. Duncan is King, Macbeth is his next eldest relative and is therefore strictly heir to the throne even in preference to Duncan's sons. And so the first inducement to Macbeth's crime is the wrong done to him by the King in naming his own son as his successor. This justification of Macbeth, drawn from [Holinshed's] *Chronicles*, is altogether omitted by Shakespeare, because his only aim was to bring out the dreadfulness of Macbeth's passion, in order to make a bow to King James who must have been interested in seeing Macbeth represented as a criminal! Thus, according to Shakespeare's treatment of the subject, there is no reason why Macbeth did not murder Duncan's sons too, but let them escape, and why none of the nobles thought of them. But the whole collision on which *Macbeth* turns is already beyond the situation-stage which was our subject here.

(ββ) Now, secondly, the converse within this sphere consists in this, that differences of birth, which in themselves involve a wrong, are given by custom or law the power of an unsurmountable barrier, so that they appear as a wrong that has become natural, as it were, and they therefore give rise to collisions. Slavery, serfdom, castes, the position of Jews in many states, and, in a certain sense, even the opposition between the birth of nobles and commoners, are to be reckoned in this group. Here the conflict lies in the fact that, while the man has rights, relationships, wishes, aims, and

---

[1] In what follows I have used a modern transliteration of the proper names, instead of Hegel's.

requirements which belong to him by the nature of man, these are stemmed by one or other of the above-mentioned differences of birth as a natural force obstructing them or endangering them. On this sort of collision the following is to be said.

Differences between classes, between rulers and ruled, etc., are of course essential and rational, for they have their basis in the necessary articulation of the whole life of the state, and they are validated everywhere by the specific kind of occupation, turn of mind, disposition, and the whole of spiritual development. But it is another thing if these differences in respect of individuals are to be so determined by *birth* that the individual is from the beginning to be relegated, not by his own doing, but by the accident of nature, to some class or caste irrevocably.

In that event these differences prove to be purely natural and yet they are invested with a supreme determining might. How this fixity and power originated does not matter at present. For the nation may originally have been *one*, and the natural difference between free men and serfs, for example, may only have developed later, or the difference of castes, classes, privileges, etc., may have arisen from differences of nation and race, as has been maintained in relation to the caste system in India. For us here this is of no consequence; the chief point lies only in the fact that such relationships of life, regulating the whole being of man, are supposed to derive their origin from nature and birth. Of course, in the nature of the case, difference of class is to be regarded as justified, but at the same time the individual should not be deprived of his right to align himself of his own free will with this or that class. Aptitude, talent, skill and education alone have to lead to a decision in this matter and to decide it. But if the right of choice is annulled from the very beginning by birth, and if therefore a man is made dependent on nature and its fortuitousness, then within this lack of freedom a conflict may arise between (a) the position assigned to a man by his birth and (b) his different measure of spiritual education and its just demands. This is a melancholy and unfortunate collision, for it rests entirely on a wrong which true free art has not to respect. In our contemporary situation, class differences, a small group excepted, are not tied to birth. The sole exception is the ruling dynasty and the peerage, for higher reasons grounded in the essential nature of the state itself. This apart, birth makes no essential difference in relation to the class which an individual can or wishes to enter. But on this account after all we at once link with the demand for this perfect freedom the further demand that the individual shall, in education, knowledge, skill, and disposition make himself equal to the class to which he aspires. But if birth places an unsurmountable obstacle to the claims which a man, without this restriction, could satisfy by his own spiritual force and activity, then this counts for us not only as a misfortune but essentially as a wrong which he suffers. A purely natural and in itself unjust wall, over which his spirit, talent, feeling, inner and outer education have lifted him, separates him from what he was capable of attaining, and something natural, consolidated by caprice alone into this legal provision, presumes to set insuperable barriers to the inherently justified freedom of the spirit.

Now in the more detailed appreciation of such a collision, the essential points are these:

First, the individual with his spiritual qualities must already have actually overstepped the natural barrier and its power which his wishes and aims are meant to surmount, or otherwise his demand is over again just a folly. If, for example, a lackey with only a lackey's education and skill falls in love with a princess or a lady of high degree, or she with him, such a love affair is only absurd and ridiculous, even if the representation of this passion comprises all the depth and full interest of the glowing heart. For in this instance it is not the difference of birth which really separates the parties, but the whole range of higher interests, broader education, aims in life, and modes of feeling which cuts a lackey off from a woman highly placed in class, means, and social position. If love is the *one* point of union, and does not also draw into itself the remaining scope of what a man has to experience in accordance with his spiritual education and the circumstances of his class, it remains empty and abstract, and touches only the sensuous side of life. To be full and entire, it would have to be connected with the entirety of the rest of the mind, with the full nobility of disposition and interests.

The *second* case, in this context, consists in this, that dependence on birth is imposed as a legally obstructive shackle on the inherently free spirit and its justified aims. This collision too has something unaesthetic in itself which contradicts the Concept of the Ideal, however popular it may be and however readily art may have a notion to make use of it. If, that is to say, differences of birth are made into a definite wrong by positive laws and their validity, as, for example, birth as a pariah, a Jew, etc., it is in a way a perfectly correct view if a man in the freedom of his inner being, rebelling against such an obstacle, regards these laws as dissoluble and knows himself free from them. To fight them seems therefore to be absolutely justified. Now in so far as, owing to the power of existing circumstances, such barriers become unsurmountable and are consolidated into an invincible necessity, this can only afford a situation of misfortune and one inherently false. For the reasonable man must bow to necessity, when he has not the means to subdue its force, i.e. he must not react against it but must bear the inevitable calmly and patiently; the interest and need demolished by such a barrier he must sacrifice, and so what is insuperable he must endure with the still courage of passivity and tolerance. Where battle is of no avail, a reasonable man is quit of it so that he can at least withdraw into the *formal* independence of subjective freedom. In that event the might of wrong has no might at all over him, while he at once experiences his utter dependence if he opposes it. Yet neither this abstraction of a purely formal independence nor this futile snatching at victory is really beautiful.

A *third* case, directly connected with the second, is equally remote from the genuine Ideal. It consists in this, that individuals whose birth has given them a really valid privilege owing to religious regulations, positive laws, or social circumstances, uphold their privilege and wish to insist on it. For in that event independence is there, according to the reality of external and positive law, but, as the subsistence of what is inherently unjust and irrational, it is a false and purely formal independence, and the Concept of the Ideal has vanished. Of course one could suppose that the Ideal is preserved, on the ground that even subjective life goes hand in hand with the universal and the legal, and remains in consistent unity therewith; yet, in this case, on the one hand the universal does not have its force and might in *this* individual, as the Ideal of the heroic requires, but only in the public authority of the positive laws and their administration; on the other hand, what the individual claims is just a wrong and he therefore lacks that substantiality which, as we have seen, likewise is implicit in the Concept of the Ideal. The concern of the ideal individual must be inherently true and justified. What is relevant here is, for example, the legal dominion over slaves and serfs, the right to rob foreigners of their freedom, or to sacrifice them to the gods, and so on.

It is true that such a right can be pursued by individuals innocently, in the belief that they are defending their valid right, as in India, for example, the higher castes take advantage of their privileges, or as Thoas ordered the sacrifice of Orestes,[1] or as in Russia the masters rule their serfs; indeed those in authority may wish to assert rights of this kind as right and legal because of their own interest in them. But in that case their right is only the unrighteous right of barbarism, and they themselves look, in our eyes at least, like barbarians who resolve on and carry out what is absolute injustice. The legality on which the subject relies is to be respected and justified for his time and its spirit and level of civilization, but for us it has through and through been merely laid down without validity or power. Now if the legally privileged individual just uses his right for his own private ends, from a particular passion and selfish intentions, we have before us not just barbarism but a bad character into the bargain.

Through such conflicts attempts have often been made to arouse pity, and even fear as well, according to the law of Aristotle[2] who lays it down that fear and pity are the aim of tragedy; but we entertain neither fear nor awe in the presence of the power of such rights accruing from barbarism and the misfortune of the times, and the pity that we might feel changes at once into repugnance and indignation.

The only true issue of such a conflict can therefore consist solely in the fact that these false rights are not finally asserted, as for example when neither Iphigenia nor Orestes is sacrificed in Aulis and among the Tauri.[3]

(γγ) Now, finally, a last element in collisions which derive their basis from natural conditions is subjective passion when it rests on natural foundations of character and temperament. The best example of this is Othello's jealousy. Ambition, avarice (and love too indeed to some extent) are examples of the same sort.

But these passions lead to collisions of substance only in so far as they induce individuals who are gripped and dominated by the

---

[1] Euripides, *Iphigenia in Tauris*.
[2] What he says is that 'a tragedy is an imitation of an action, serious in itself . . . with incidents arousing pity and fear, wherewith to accomplish the catharsis of such emotions'. *Poetics*, 1449ᵇ 23 ff.
[3] i.e. in the two plays of Euripides about Iphigenia.

exclusive power of such a feeling to turn against what is genuinely moral and absolutely justified in human life, and who consequently fall into a conflict of a profounder kind.

This leads us to consider a *third* chief kind of dissension, namely that which has its proper ground in spiritual forces and their variance, in so far as this opposition is called up by the deed of the man himself.

(γ) It has already been noticed above in relation to purely natural collisions that they form only the connecting point for further oppositions. The same is more or less true of conflicts in the second category also considered just now. In works of art of more profound interest, none of these stops at the antagonism hitherto indicated; they introduce such disturbances and oppositions only as the occasion out of which the absolute spiritual powers of life are presented in their difference from one another and their struggle with one another. But the spiritual realm can only be activated by spirit, and so spiritual differences must also win their actuality by man's act in order to be able to come on the scene in their proper shape.

Thus now we have, on the one hand, a difficulty, an obstacle, a transgression brought about by an actual human deed; on the other hand, a transgression of absolutely justified interests and powers. Only both of these characteristics taken together are the basis of the depth of this final kind of collision.

The chief cases which can occur in this sphere may be distinguished as follows:

(αα) While we are now only just beginning to leave the province of those conflicts which have their foundation in nature, the first case of this new sort still stands in connection with the earlier ones. But if human action is to be the ground of the collision, then the natural result produced by man, otherwise than by man as spirit, consists in the fact that *unknowingly* and unintentionally he has done something which later proves in his own eyes to have been a transgression of ethical powers essentially to be respected. The consciousness of his deed, which he acquires later, then drives him on, through this previously unconscious transgression, into dissension and contradiction with himself, once he imputes the transgression to himself as caused by him. The antagonism between his consciousness and intention in his act and the later consciousness of what the act really was constitutes here the basis of the conflict.

Oedipus and Ajax can count here as examples for us. Oedipus's act, so far as his will and knowledge went, consisted in the fact that he had slain a stranger in a quarrel; but it was what was unknown that was the actual and essential deed, namely the murder of his own father. Ajax, conversely, in a fit of frenzy slaughters the cattle of the Greeks, believing them to be the Greek princes. Then when, with awakened consciousness, he considers what has happened, he is gripped by shame at his deed, and this produces collision. What, in a way like this, a man has unintentionally transgressed must yet be something which essentially and in accordance with his reason he has to honour and regard as sacrosanct. If, on the other hand, this reverence and veneration is a mere opinion and false superstition, then for us at least such a collision can no longer have any deeper interest.

(ββ) But now since, in the kind of conflict we are concerned with at present, a spiritual transgression of spiritual powers is to come about through a man's deed, then, *secondly*, the collision more appropriate to this sphere consists in a transgression which is known and which issues from this knowledge and the intention involved. The starting-point may here too once again be passion, violence, folly, etc. The Trojan war, for example, has its beginning in the abduction of Helen; next, Agamemnon proceeds to sacrifice Iphigenia [his daughter] and thereby commits a transgression against her mother [Clytemnestra his wife] because he kills the dearest fruits of her womb; Clytemnestra therefore slays her husband; Orestes, because she has murdered his father, the King, takes revenge by the death of his mother. Similarly, in *Hamlet* the father is treacherously sent to his grave, and Hamlet's mother defames the shades of the dead by an almost immediate marriage with the murderer.

Even in the case of these collisions the chief point is still that what is fought against is something absolutely ethical, sacrosanct, and genuine which the man has roused against himself by his act. Were this not so, then for us, in so far as we have a consciousness of the genuinely ethical and sacrosanct, such a conflict would be without value and substance, as, for instance, in the familiar episode in the *Mahabharata*, Nala and Damayanti. King Nala had married Damayanti, the prince's daughter, who had had the privilege of choosing of her own accord amongst her suitors. The other claimants hover as genii in the air. Nala alone stands on the earth, and Damayanti had the good taste to select him. Now on this account the genii are angered and they keep a watch on King Nala. But for many years afterwards they could bring nothing against him, because he was not guilty of any offence. But at last they win power over him because he commits a great crime by making water and treading on the ground thus urine-infected. According to Indian ideas this is a serious offence which cannot escape punishment. Hereafter the genii have him in their power; one instils into him the desire for play; the other provokes his brother to be his opponent; and Nala must at last, losing his throne, wander unarmed with Damayanti into misery. At length he has to endure even separation from her, until in the end, after numerous adventures, he is raised once more to his former good fortune. The real conflict, on which the whole thing turns, is only for the ancient Indians an essential transgression of something sacrosanct. In our eyes it is nothing but an absurdity.[1]

(γγ) But, *thirdly*, the transgression need not be direct, i.e. it is not necessary for the deed as such, taken by itself, to be productive of collision; it only becomes such owing to the known relations and circumstances within which it is done and which work against it and contradict it. Romeo and Juliet, for example, love one another; in love as such no transgression is inherent; but they know that their families live in hatred and enmity with one another, that the parents will never consent to their marriage, and

---

[1] Hegel's authority for this story may be W. von Humboldt's *Über die unter den Namen Bhagavad-Gita bekannte Episode des Mahabharata* (Berlin, 1826), reviewed by him in 1827, *Ww.* xvi, pp. 361 ff. But the review, which provides ample evidence for the thoroughness with which Hegel studied Indian religion, quotes so many other works, including translations, German, English, and French, that one cannot be sure. In any event, he has not got the story quite right. Professor R. C. Zaehner has kindly told me that this passage ought to read as follows:
'Consider the familiar episode in *Mahabharata*, Nala and Damayanti, the prince's daughter, who had the privilege of choosing of her own accord amongst the local chieftains. The gods also appear in the shape of Nala as suitors; but since only Nala stands firmly on the ground, sweating and thereby proving that he is a mortal, Damayanti selects him. The gods are well pleased by this, but Kali, an evil genius, is angered and keeps watch on him. But for many years afterwards he could bring nothing against him, because he was not guilty of any offence. But at last he succeeds in entering into him because he commits the technical offence of making water without purifying himself afterwards. Kali then incites him to accept his brother's invitation to a game of dice. He is defeated and loses his throne and everything. He is forced to wander unarmed with Damayanti, whom he deserts, until in the end after numerous adventures he is re-united with her and raised once more to his former good fortune.'

they get into a collision owing to this presupposed ground of antagonism.

In relation to the specific situation, as contrasted with the general state of the world, these most general remarks may suffice. If one wished to consider, and go through, all its aspects, shades, and nuances, and assess every possible kind of situation, then this chapter alone would provide an occasion for discussions of endless prolixity. For the invention of different situations has an inexhaustible wealth of possibilities, and then the essential question always is of their applicability to a specific art, depending on its genus and species. To fairy-tales, for example, much is allowed which would be forbidden to another mode of treatment and representation. But in general the invention of the situation is after all an important point which commonly presents great difficulty to artists. In particular we hear today the frequent complaint about the difficulty of finding the right material from which the situations and circumstances are to be drawn. In this connection, at first sight it may seem to suit the dignity of a poet better to be original and to invent situations by himself. Yet this sort of originality is not an essential matter. For the situation does not in itself constitute what is spiritual, or the artistic form proper; it affects only the external material in which and on which a character and temperament is to be unfolded and represented. Only by elaborating this external starting-point into actions and characters is genuine artistic activity evinced. Therefore we cannot thank the poet at all for having manufactured this inherently unpoetic aspect by himself; he must remain entitled to create always anew from what is already there, from history, saga, myths, chronicles, indeed even from materials and situations previously elaborated artistically; as, in painting, the external element in the situation is drawn from legends of the saints and often enough repeated in a similar way. In the case of such representation the strictly artistic production lies far deeper than in inventing specific situations.

The same is true too of the wealth of circumstances and complications that have been presented to us. In this connection modern art has often enough been praised on the ground that, in comparison with antiquity, it displays an infinitely more fruitful imagination, and in fact in the works of art of the Middle Ages too and the modern world there is the maximum variety and diversity of situations, incidents, events, and fates. But with this external abundance nothing is achieved. In spite of it, we have only a few excellent dramas and epic poems. For the chief thing is not the external march and turn of events, as if these, as events and histories, exhausted the stuff of the work of art, but the ethical and spiritual configuration and the great movements of temperament and character which are disclosed and unveiled through the process of this configuration.

If we glance now at the point from which we must proceed further, we see that, on the one hand, the external and inner specific circumstances, states of affairs, and relations become the situation only through the heart, the passion, which views them and maintains itself in them. On the other hand, as we saw, the situation in its specific character is differentiated into oppositions, hindrances, complications, and *transgressions*, so that the heart, moved by circumstances, feels itself induced to react of necessity against what disturbs it and what is a barrier against its aims and passions. In this sense the action proper only begins when the opposition contained in the situation appears on the scene. But since the colliding action *transgresses* an opposing aspect, in this difference it calls up against itself the power lying over against it which has been assailed, and therefore, with action, reaction is immediately linked. At this point only has the Ideal entered into full determinacy and movement. For now there stand in battle against one another two interests, wrested from their harmony, and in reciprocal contradiction they necessarily demand a resolution of their discord. Now this movement, taken as a whole, belongs no more to the province of the situation and its conflicts, but leads to the consideration of what we have described above as 'the action proper'.

3. *Action*

In the series of stages which we have followed up to this point, action is the *third*, succeeding the general state of the world as the *first* and the specific situation as the *second*.

We have found already that, in its external relation to the situation, the action presupposes circumstances leading to collisions, to action and reaction. Now in view of these presuppositions, we cannot settle with precision where the action must have its beginning. For what from one point of view appears as a beginning, may from another prove to be the result of earlier complications which would serve thus far as the real beginning. Yet these themselves are once again only an effect of previous collisions, and so forth. For example, in the House of Agamemnon, Iphigenia among the Tauri[1] propitiates the guilt and misfortune of the House. Here the beginning may be taken to be Iphigenia's rescue by Diana who brought her to the Tauri; but this circumstance is only the result of events elsewhere, namely the sacrifice at Aulis, which again is conditioned by the transgression suffered by Menelaus, from whom Paris raped Helen, and so on and so on until we come to Leda's famous egg. So also the material treated in the *Iphigenia in Tauris* contains once again as a presupposition the murder of Agamemnon and the whole sequence of crimes in the House of Tantalus. The same sort of thing occurs in the story of the Theban House.[2] Now if an action with this whole series of its presuppositions is to be represented, it may be supposed that only poetry could discharge this task. Yet, according to the saying,[3] to go through the whole gamut like this has become somewhat wearisome; it is regarded as a matter for prose, and instead of prose's prolixity, it has been demanded of poetry as a law that it shall take the listener at once *in medias res*. Now the fact that art is not interested in making a beginning with the external original start of the specific action has a deeper reason, namely that such a start has a beginning only in relation to the natural, external, course of events, and the connection of the action with this start affects only the empirical unity of its appearance, but can be quite a matter of indifference to the proper content of the action itself. The like external unity is also present still, when it is only one and the same individual who is to provide the connecting thread of different events. The totality of the circumstances of life, deeds, fates, is of course what shapes the individual, but his proper nature, the true kernel of his disposition and capacity, is revealed without all these, in *one* great situation and action, in the course of

    [1] i.e. in the Crimea; Euripides again.
    [2] At Aulis the Greeks sacrificed to Apollo before embarking for Troy. Leda was loved by Zeus in the form of a swan. One of her children by him was Helen. Tantalus was a remote ancestor of Agamemnon. The Theban House is that of Oedipus and Antigone.
    [3] K. F. Wander's *Deutsches Sprichwörter-Lexikon* quotes *Er fangt seine Geschichte bei Adam an* (he begins his history with Adam). But Hegel is quoting Horace: *Ars Poetica*, ii. 147–8, where Horace speaks of not telling of the Trojan war *ab ovo*, but always hurrying *in medias res*.

which he is unveiled as he is, whereas previously he was known maybe only by his name and external appearance.

In other words the start of the action is not to be sought in that empirical beginning; what must be envisaged is only those circumstances which, grasped by the individual heart and its needs, give rise precisely to the specific collision, the strife and resolution of which constitute the particular action. Homer, for example, in the Iliad, begins at once without hesitation with his matter in hand on which everything turns, the wrath of Achilles; he does not begin first, as might be expected, by relating the previous events or the life story of Achilles, but gives us forthwith the special conflict, and indeed in such a way that a great interest forms the background of his picture.

Now the presentation of the action, as in itself a total movement of action, reaction, and resolution of their struggle, belongs especially to poetry, for it is given to the other arts to seize only one feature in the course of the action and its occurrence. True, from one point of view, they seem, owing to the wealth of their means, to outclass poetry in this connection, since they have at their command not only the entire external shape but also expression through gestures, the shape's relation to surrounding shapes, and its reflection besides in other objects grouped around it. But all these are means of expression which cannot compare with the clarity of speech. Action is the clearest revelation of the individual, of his temperament as well as his aims; what a man is at bottom and in his inmost being comes into actuality only by his action, and action, because of its spiritual origin, wins its greatest clarity and definiteness in spiritual expression also, i.e. in speech alone.

When we speak of action in general terms, our usual idea is that its variety is quite incalculable. But for art the range of actions suitable for representation is on the whole restricted. For it has to traverse only that range of actions which is necessitated by the Idea.

In this connection, in so far as art has to undertake the representation of action, we must emphasize three principal points derived as follows: the situation and its conflict are the general stimulus; but the movement itself, the differentiation of the Ideal in its activity, arises only through the reaction. Now this movement contains:

(*a*) the universal powers forming the essential content and end for which the action is done;

(b) the activation of these powers through the action of individuals;

(c) these two aspects have to be united into what here in general we will call *character*.

(a) The Universal Powers over Action

(α) However far in our consideration of action we stand at the Ideal's stage of determinacy and difference, still, in the truly beautiful [drama] each side of the opposition which the conflicts disclose must still bear the stamp of the Ideal on themselves and therefore may not lack rationality and justification. Interests of an ideal kind must fight one another, so that power comes on the scene against power. These interests are the essential needs of the human heart, the inherently necessary aims of action, justified and rational in themselves, and precisely therefore the universal, eternal, powers of spiritual existence; not the absolutely Divine itself, but the sons of an absolute Idea and therefore dominant and valid; children of the one universal truth, although only determinate particular factors thereof. Owing to their determinateness they can of course come into opposition to one another, but, despite their difference, they must have essential truth in themselves in order to appear as the determinate Ideal. These are the great themes of art, the eternal religious and ethical relationships; family, country, state, church, fame, friendship, class, dignity, and, in the romantic world, especially honour and love, etc. In the degree of their validity these powers are different, but all are inherently rational. At the same time these are the powers over the human heart, which man, because he is man, has to recognize; he has to accept their power and give them actualization. Yet they should not appear merely as rights in a positive legislative order. For (a), as we saw in dealing with collisions, the form of positive legislation contradicts the Concept and the shape of the Ideal, and (b) the content of positive rights may constitute what is absolutely unjust, no matter how far it has assumed the form of law. But the relationships just mentioned are not something merely fixed externally; they are the absolutely substantial forces which, because they involve the true content of the Divine and the human, remain now precisely also as the impetus in action and what is finally the steadily self-realizing.

Of this kind, for example, are the interests and aims which fight

in the *Antigone* of Sophocles. Creon, the King, had issued, as head
of the state, the strict command that the son of Oedipus, who had
risen against Thebes as an enemy of his country, was to be refused
the honour of burial. This command contains an essential justification, provision for the welfare of the entire city. But Antigone is
animated by an equally ethical power, her holy love for her brother,
whom she cannot leave unburied, a prey of the birds. Not to fulfil
the duty of burial would be against family piety, and therefore she
transgresses Creon's command.

(β) Now collisions may be introduced in the most varied ways;
but the necessity of the reaction must not be occasioned at all by
something bizarre or repugnant, but by something rational and
justified in itself. So, for example, in the familiar German poem
of Hartmann von der Aue—*Der arme Heinrich*[1]—the collision is
repulsive. The hero is afflicted by leprosy, an incurable disease,
and in search of help he turns to the monks of Salerno. They require that someone must of his own free will sacrifice himself for
him, for the necessary remedy can be prepared only out of a
human heart. A poor girl, who loves the knight, willingly decides
on death and travels with him to Italy. This is throughout barbaric,
and the quiet love and touching devotion of the girl can therefore
not achieve its full affect. True, in the case of the Greeks the wrong
of human sacrifice comes on the scene as a collision too, as in the
story of Iphigenia, for example, who at one time is to be sacrificed
and at another is herself to sacrifice her brother; but (*a*) this
conflict hangs together with other matters inherently justified, and
(*b*) the rational element, as was remarked above, lies in the fact
that both Iphigenia and Orestes are saved and the force of that
unrighteous collision is broken—which, it is true, is the case in
the afore-mentioned poem of Hartmann von der Aue, where
Heinrich, refusing at last to accept the sacrifice, is freed from
his disease by God's help, and now the girl is rewarded for her
true love.

To the above-mentioned affirmative powers there are at once
annexed others opposed to them, the powers, namely, of the negative, the bad and the evil in general. Yet the purely negative should
not find its place in the ideal presentation of an action as the essential basis of the necessary reaction. The existence of the negative

---

[1] *Poor Henry*, late twelfth and early thirteenth century. The poem is the basis
of Longfellow's *Golden Legend*.

in reality may well correspond with the essence and nature of the negative; but if the inner conception and aim of the agent is null in itself, the inner ugliness, already there, still less permits of true beauty in that conception's real existence. The sophistry of passion may, through skilfulness, strength, and energy of character, make the attempt to introduce positive aspects into the negative, but then, in spite of this, we have only the vision of a whited sepulchre. For the purely negative is in itself dull and flat and therefore either leaves us empty or else repels us, whether it be used as the motive of an action or simply as a means for producing the reaction of another motive. The gruesome and unlucky, the harshness of power, the pitilessness of predominance, may be held together and endured by the imagination if they are elevated and carried by an intrinsically worthy greatness of character and aim; but evil as such, envy, cowardice, and baseness are and remain purely repugnant. Thus the devil in himself is a bad figure, aesthetically impracticable; for he is nothing but the father of lies and therefore an extremely prosaic person.[1] So too the Furies of hatred, and so many later allegories of a similar kind, are indeed powers, but without affirmative independence and stability, and are unsuitable for ideal representation; nevertheless in this matter a great difference must be laid down between what is allowed and forbidden to the particular arts and the way and manner in which they do, or do not, bring their object immediately home to our vision. But evil is in general inherently cold and worthless, because nothing comes of it except what is purely negative, just destruction and misfortune, whereas genuine art should give us a view of an inner harmony.

Especially despicable is baseness, because it has its source in envy and hatred of what is noble, and it does not shrink from perverting something inherently justified into a means for its own bad or shameful passion. The great poets and artists of antiquity therefore do not give us the spectacle of wickedness and depravity. Shakespeare, on the other hand, in *Lear*, for example, brings evil before us in its entire dreadfulness. Lear in old age divides his kingdom between his daughters and, in doing so, is so mad as to trust the false and flattering words [of Goneril and Regan]

---

[1] See Hegel's *Philosophy of Religion* (*Ww.* xii, 261): 'Milton's devil is, in his fully characteristic energy, better than many an angel.' He adds that there is something affirmative about Milton's devil.

and to misjudge the speechless and loyal Cordelia. This is already madness and craziness, and so the most outrageous ingratitude and worthlessness of the elder daughters and their husbands bring him to actual insanity. In a different way again the heroes of French tragedy[1] often put on fine airs and puff themselves up in a monstrous way with the greatest and noblest motives, and make a great display of their honour and dignity, but at the same time they destroy again our idea of these motives as a result of what they actually are and accomplish. But in most recent times what has especially become the fashion is the inner unstable distraction which runs through all the most repugnant dissonances and has produced a temper of atrocity and a grotesqueness of irony in which Theodor Hoffmann,[2] for example, has delighted.

(γ) Thus the genuine content of the ideal action must be supplied solely by the inherently affirmative and substantive powers. Yet when these driving forces come to be represented, they may not appear in their universality as such, although within the reality of the action they are the essential moments of the Idea; they must be configurated as independent *individuals*. If this does not happen, they remain universal thoughts or abstract ideas, and these do not belong to the domain of art. However little they may derive their origin from mere caprices of imagination, they must still proceed to determinacy and achievedness and therefore appear as inherently individualized. Yet this determinate character must not extend to the detail of external existence nor contract into subjective inwardness, because otherwise the individuality of the universal powers would of necessity be driven into all the complications of finite existence. Therefore, from this point of view, the determinacy of their individuality is not to be taken too seriously.

As the clearest example of such appearance and domination of the universal powers in their independent configuration the Greek gods may be cited. However they may come on the scene, they are always blessed and serene. As individual and particular gods, they do engage in battle, but in the last resort there is no seriousness in this strife because they have not concentrated themselves on some specific end with the whole consistent energy of their character and passion, and, in fighting for this end, found their

---

[1] Possibly a reference to Corneille. The urbane rhetoric of the *siècle d'or* conceals emotions that are less than civilized.

[2] E. T. A. Hoffmann, 1776–1822.

defeat at last. They meddle with this and that, make their own some specific interest in concrete cases, but all the same they let the business stand as it was, and wander back in blessedness to the heights of Olympus. So in Homer we see the gods in battle and war against one another; this is in virtue of their determinate character, but they still remain universal beings and determinate characters. The Trojan battle, for example, begins to rage; the heroes come on the scene individually, one after another; now the individuals are lost in the general hubbub and scuffle; no longer are there special particular characters which can be distinguished; a universal pressure and spirit roars and fights—and now it is the universal powers, the gods themselves, who enter the fray. But they always draw back again out of such imbroglio and difference into their independence and peace. For the individuality of their figures does of course lead them into the sphere of chance and accident, still, because what preponderates in them is the divine universal element, their individual aspect is only an external figure rather than something penetrating the figure through and through into genuinely inner subjectivity. Their determinate character is an outward shape only more or less closely adapted to their divinity. But this independence and untroubled peace gives them precisely the plastic individuality which spares them concern and distress in connection with what is determinate. Consequently, even in their action in the concrete real world, there is no fixed consistency in Homer's gods, although they do continually enter upon diversified and varied activities, since only the material and interest of temporal human affairs can give them anything to do. Likewise we find in the Greek gods further peculiarities of their own which cannot always be referred back to the universal essence of each specific god. Mercury, for example, is the slayer of Argus, Apollo of the lizard, Jupiter has countless love affairs and hangs Juno on an anvil,[1] etc. These and so many other stories are just appendages which cling to the gods in their natural aspect through symbolism and allegory, and their origin we will have to indicate in more detail later.

In modern art too there is a treatment of specific and yet inherently universal powers. But for the most part this amounts only to cold and frosty allegories of hatred, for example, envy,

---

[1] Two anvils, according to Iliad, xv. 18 ff. The anvils were tied to her feet when she was hung from Olympus.

jealousy, or, in general, of virtues and vices, faith, hope, love, fidelity, etc., in which we cannot believe. For in our view it is concrete individuality alone in which, in artistic representations, we feel a deeper interest, so that we want to see these abstractions before us not on their own account but only as features and aspects of the entirety of an individual human character. Likewise angels have none of that universality and independence in themselves as Mars, e.g., Venus, Apollo, etc. have or as Oceanus and Helios have; they are there indeed for our imagination, but as particular servants of the one substantial divine essence, which is not split into independent individuals like those in the circle of the Greek gods. Therefore we do not have the vision of many self-dependent objective powers, which could come to be represented explicitly as divine individuals; on the contrary, we find their essential content actualized either objectively in the one God or, in a particular and subjective way, in human characters and actions. But the ideal representation of the gods has its origin precisely in their being made independent and individualized.

(b) The Individual Agents

In the case of the ideal gods that we have just discussed, it is not difficult for art to preserve the required ideality. Yet so soon as it is a question of coming to concrete action, a special difficulty arises for presentation. The gods, I mean, and the universal powers in general, are indeed the moving force and stimulus, but, in the real world, individual action proper is not to be assigned to them; action belongs to men. Therefore we have two separate sides: on the one there stand those universal powers in their self-reposing and therefore more abstract substantiality; on the other the human individuals on whom devolve the resolution, the final decision on action, and its actual accomplishment. True, the eternal dominant forces are immanent in man's self; they make up the substantial side of his character; but in so far as they are apprehended themselves in their divinity as individuals, and therefore as exclusive, they come at once into an external relation with human beings. This now produces the essential difficulty. For in this relation between gods and men there is a direct contradiction. On the one hand in their content the gods are the personality, the individual passion, the decision and will of man; but on the other hand the gods are viewed and stressed as existing absolutely, not only independent of the individual subject but as the forces driving and determining him; the result is that the same specific things are represented now in independent divine individuality and now as the most intimate possession of the human breast. Therefore the free independence of the gods as well as the freedom of the individual agents is jeopardized. Above all, if the power of command is attributed to the gods, then human independence suffers as a result, while we have stipulated this independence as absolutely and essentially demanded by the Ideal of art. This is the same relation which comes into question also in our Christian religious ideas. It is said, for example, that the Spirit of God leads us to God. But in that case the human heart may appear as the purely passive ground on which the Spirit of God operates and the human will in its freedom is destroyed, since the divine decree of this operation remains for him as it were a sort of fate in which his own self does not participate at all.

(α) Now if this relation is so put that the man in his activity is contrasted externally with the god who is what is substantial, then the *rapport* between the two is wholly prosaic. For the god commands and man has but to obey. From this external relation between gods and men even great poets have not been able to free themselves. In Sophocles, e.g., after Philoctetes has frustrated the deception of Odysseus, he abides by his decision not to go with him to the Grecian camp, until at last Heracles appears as a *deus ex machina* and orders him to give in to the wish of Neoptolemus. The content of this apparition is sufficiently motivated, and it is itself awaited, but the denoument itself always remains foreign and external. In his noblest tragedies Sophocles does not use this kind of presentation through which, if it goes one step further, the gods become dead machines, and individuals mere instruments of an alien caprice.

Likewise, in the epic especially, interventions of the gods appear as a denial of human freedom. Hermes, e.g., escorts Priam to Achilles [*Iliad*, xxiv]; Apollo strikes Patroclus between the shoulders and puts an end to his life [ibid., xvi]. In a similar way mythological traits are often so used as to appear in individuals as an external thing. Achilles, e.g., is dipped by his mother in the Styx, and thereby made invulnerable and unconquerable except in his ankle. If we look at this in an intellectual way, then all the bravery vanishes and the whole heroism of Achilles becomes a purely physical quality instead of a spiritual trait of character. But such a kind of representation may be allowed to epic long before it can be allowed to drama, because in epic the side of inwardness which concerns the intention involved in carrying out one's aims falls into the background, and a wider scope is allowed to the external in general. That purely intellectual reflection which ascribes to the poet the absurdity that his heroes are not heroes at all must therefore be advanced with the greatest caution, for even in such traits, as we shall see presently [in (β)], the poetic relation between gods and men is preserved. On the other hand, the prosaic judgement is valid at once if the powers besides being set up as independent, are inherently without substance and belong only to fantastic caprice and the bizarrerie of a false originality.

(β) The genuinely ideal relationship consists in the identity of gods and men, an identity which must still gleam through when the universal powers are, as independent and free, contrasted with the individual agents and their passions. The character attributed to the gods, I mean, must at once evince itself in individuals as their own inner life, so that while the ruling powers appear explicitly as individualized, this which is external to man is immanent in him as his spirit and character. Therefore it remains the business of the artist to harmonize the difference of these two sides and to link them by a fine thread; he makes conspicuous the beginnings of the action in man's inner spirit, but, even so, emphasizes the universal and substantial which rules there, and brings it before our eyes as explicitly individualized. Man's heart must reveal itself in the gods who are the independent universal forms of what rules and drives its inner being. Only in that case are the gods at the same time the gods of his own breast. If we hear from antiquity that e.g. Venus or Eros has captivated the heart, then of course Venus and Eros are *prima facie* powers external to the man, but love is all the same a stimulus and a passion which belong to the human breast as such and constitute its own centre. The Eumenides[1] are often spoken of in the same sense. At first we imagine the avenging maidens as Furies who pursue the transgressor from without. But this pursuit is equally the inner fury which permeates the transgressor's breast. Sophocles uses this too in the sense of the man's own inner being, as, e.g., in the *Oedipus Coloneus* (l. 1434), the Furies are called the Erinyes

[1] A propitiatory name for the Furies in the play of Aeschylus.

[Furies] of Oedipus himself and signify a father's curse, the power of his offended heart over his sons.[1] Therefore it is both right and wrong to interpret the gods in general as always either purely external to man or purely powers dwelling in him. For they are both. In Homer, therefore, the action of gods and men goes continually criss-cross; the gods seem to bring about what is alien to man and yet actually accomplish only what constitutes the substance of his inner heart. In the Iliad, e.g., when Achilles in a quarrel is about to draw his sword against Agamemnon, Athene comes up behind him, and, visible to him alone, grasps his flaxen hair. Hera, concerned equally for Achilles and Agamemnon, sends Athene from Olympus, and her appearance seems to be quite independent of the heart of Achilles. But on the other hand, it is easy to imagine that Athene's sudden appearance, the prudence that checks the wrath of the hero, is of an inward kind, and that the whole thing is an event which happened in the heart of Achilles. Indeed Homer himself indicates this a few lines earlier (*Iliad*, i. 190 ff.) when he describes how Achilles took counsel with himself:

ἢ ὅ γε φάσγανον ὀξὺ ἐρυσσάμενος παρὰ μηροῦ,
τοὺς μὲν ἀναστήσειεν, ὁ δ᾽ Ἀτρείδην ἐναρίζοι
ἦε χόλον παύσειεν, ἐρητύσειέ τε θυμόν.[2]

This inner interruption of wrath, this check, which is a power foreign to the wrath, the epic poet is fully justified in representing as an external event because Achilles at first appears to be entirely full of wrath alone. In a similar way we find Minerva in the Odyssey [iii *et al.*] as the escort of Telemachus. This escort is more difficult to interpret as at the same time within the heart of Telemachus, although even here the connection of outer and inner is not lacking. What in general constitutes the serenity of the Homeric gods and the irony in the worship of them is the fact that their independence and their seriousness is dissolved again just in so far as they evince themselves as the human heart's own powers and therefore leave men alone by themselves in them.

However, we need not look so far afield for a complete example of the transformation of such purely external divine machinery

---

[1] Oedipus pronounces on his sons, Eteocles and Polynices, the curse that each shall die by the other's hand.
[2] 'Whether to draw his sword and slay Agamemnon or to give up his wrath and restrain his temper' is the substance of the meaning of the Greek.

into something subjective, into freedom and ethical beauty. In his *Iphigenia among the Tauri* [1779] Goethe has produced the most marvellous and beautiful things possible in this connection. In Euripides [in the play with the same title], Orestes and Iphigenia take away the image of Diana. This is just a theft. Thoas comes along and issues a command to pursue them and take the effigy of the goddess from them; then at the end Athene appears in a completely prosaic way and orders Thoas to hold his hand, on the ground that she has already commended Orestes to Poseidon and in deference to her, he has conveyed him far into the sea. Thoas obeys forthwith by replying to the admonition of the goddess (ll. [1475] ff.): 'Queen Athene, whoever hears the words of the gods and does not obey, is out of his mind . . . for how can it be good to strive against the powerful gods?'[1]

We see in this matter nothing but a dry external command of Athene, and an equally empty mere obedience on the part of Thoas. In Goethe, on the other hand, Iphigenia becomes a goddess and relies on the truth in herself, in the human breast. In this sense she goes to Thoas and says [Act v, scene iii]: 'Has only a *man* the right to a deed unheard of? Does he then alone clasp the impossible to his powerful heroic heart?'

What in Euripides Athene brings about by order, the reversal of the attitude of Thoas, Goethe's Iphigenia tries to achieve, and does achieve in fact, through the deep feelings and ideas which she puts before him: 'In my heart a bold enterprise uncertainly stirs. I will not escape great reproof or serious evil if it miscarries; but still I place it on your knees. If you are true, as you are praised for being, then show it through your support, and glorify the truth through me.' And when Thoas replies: 'Thou thinkest that the crude Scythian, the barbarian, will hear the voice of truth and humanity which Atreus in Greece did not discern?', she answers in tenderest purest faith: 'Born under whatever sky, everyone hears it through whose bosom the source of life flows pure and unhindered.'

Now she calls on his magnanimity and clemency, trusting on the height of his dignity; she touches him, conquers him, and in a humanly beautiful way wrings from him permission to return to her own folk. For this is all that is necessary. She does not need

[1] Hegel cites lines 1442 ff., but that is Athene's speech. I have translated the Greek directly and not Hegel's translation. Thoas was the King of the Tauri.

the image of the goddess and can go away without cunning and treachery, since Goethe explains with infinite beauty, in a human reconciling way, the ambiguous[1] oracle 'Bringst thou the sister, who stays against her will in a shrine on the coasts of the Tauri, back to Greece, then the curse will be lifted' as meaning that the pure and holy Iphigenia, the sister, is the divine image and protectress of the House. 'Beautiful and sublime in my eyes is the counsel of the goddess', says Orestes to Thoas and Iphigenia, 'like a holy image[2] unto which a secret oracle has bound the city's unalterable fortune, Diana took thee away, protectress of thy House, and preserved thee in a holy stillness, to be a blessing to thy brother and thy kin. Just when rescue seemed nowhere to be found in the wide world thou givest us all once more.'

In this healing, reconciling way, Iphigenia has already revealed herself to Orestes through the purity and ethical beauty of her deep-feeling heart. In his torn heart he no longer cherishes any belief in peace, and recognizing her does drive him into frenzy, but the pure love of his sister nevertheless heals him from all the torment of his inner furies: 'In thine arms the evil gripped me with all its claws for the last time and shook me horribly to the very marrow; then it vanished like a snake into its hole. Now through thee I enjoy anew the broad light of day.'

In this, as in every other respect, we cannot marvel enough at the deep beauty of the drama.

Now things are worse with the Christian materials than with those of antiquity. In the legends of the saints and generally on the ground of Christian ideas, the appearance of Christ, Mary, other saints, etc., is of course present in the universal faith; but alongside it imagination has built up for itself in related spheres all kinds of fantastic beings like witches, spectres, ghostly apparitions, and more of the like. If in their treatment they appear as powers foreign to man, and man, with no stability in himself, obeys their magic, treachery, and the power of their delusiveness, the whole representation may be given over to every folly and the whole caprice of chance. In this matter in particular, the artist must go straight for the fact that freedom and independence of

---

[1] *Iphigenia*, scene vi, and so the following quotations. The ambiguity led Orestes to apply the words to the goddess Diana, whereas Iphigenia was meant.
[2] i.e. the Palladium of Troy, given by Zeus to Priam, and carried off by Aeneas to Italy.

decision are continually reserved for man. Of this Shakespeare has afforded the finest examples. In *Macbeth*, for instance, the witches appear as external powers determining Macbeth's fate in advance. Yet what they declare is his most secret and private wish which comes home to him and is revealed to him in this only apparently external way. Finer and deeper still, the appearance of the ghost in *Hamlet* is treated as just an objective form of Hamlet's inner presentiment. With his dim feeling that something dreadful must have happened, we see Hamlet come on the scene; now his father's ghost appears to him and reveals to him the whole crime. After this monitory disclosure we expect that Hamlet will at once punish the deed by force and we regard his revenge as completely justified. But he hesitates and hesitates. Shakespeare has been reproved for this inactivity and has been blamed on the ground that the play to some extent never recovers from this flaw. But Hamlet's nature is weak in practice; his beautiful heart is indrawn; it is hard for him to decide to escape from this inner harmony; he is melancholy, meditative, hypochondriacal, and pensive, therefore with no inclination for a rash act. After all, Goethe clung to the idea that what Shakespeare wished to sketch was a great deed imposed on a soul that had not grown enough for its execution. And he finds the whole piece worked out in accordance with this interpretation: 'Here is an oak tree,' he says, 'planted in a costly jar which should only have had lovely flowers blooming in it; the roots expand; the jar is destroyed.'[1] But Shakespeare in relation to the appearance of the ghost brings out a still deeper trait: Hamlet hesitates because he does not blindly believe in the ghost:

> The spirit that I have seen
> May be the devil; and the devil hath power
> To assume a pleasing shape; yea and perhaps,
> Out of my weakness and my melancholy
> (As he is very potent with such spirits)
> Abuses me to damn me; I'll have grounds
> More relative than this. The play's the thing,
> Wherein I'll catch the conscience of the King.[2]

Here we see that the apparition does not command a helpless Hamlet; Hamlet doubts, and, by arrangements of his own, will get certainty for himself, before he embarks on action.

[1] *Wilhelm Meisters Lehrjahre*, iv. 13.
[2] Act II, scene ii, *ad fin*. Hegel quotes the English.

(γ) Now, lastly, the universal powers which not only come on the scene explicitly in their independence but are equally alive in the human breast and move the human heart in its inmost being, can be described in Greek by the word πάθος,[1] păthos. To translate this word is difficult, because 'passion' always carries with it the concomitant concept of something trifling and low, for we demand that a man should not fall into a passion. 'Pathos' therefore we take here in a higher and more general sense without this overtone of something blameworthy, froward, etc. So, e.g., the holy sisterly love of Antigone is a 'pathos' in the Greek meaning of the word. 'Pathos' in this sense is an inherently justified power over the heart, an essential content of rationality and freedom of will. Orestes, e.g., kills his mother, not at all from an inner movement of heart, such as we would call 'passion'; on the contrary, the 'pathos' which drives him to the deed is well considered and wholly deliberate. From this point of view we cannot say that the gods have 'pathos'. They are only the universal content of what drives human individuals to decision and action. But the gods themselves abide as such in their peace and absence of passion, and, if it comes to dissension and strife among them, there is really no seriousness about it, or their strife has a universal symbolic significance as a universal war of the gods. 'Pathos', therefore, we must restrict to human action and understand by it the essential rational content which is present in man's self and fills and penetrates his whole heart.

(αα) Now 'pathos' forms the proper centre, the true domain, of art; the representation of it is what is chiefly effective in the work of art as well as in the spectator. For 'pathos' touches a chord which resounds in every human breast; everyone knows and recognizes the valuable and rational element inherent in the content of a true 'pathos'. 'Pathos' moves us because in and for itself it is the mighty power in human existence. In this regard, what is external, the natural environment and its *mise en scène*, should appear only as a subordinate accessory, something to

---

[1] This means anything that befalls one, whether good or bad. Thus simply to transliterate the word as Hegel does may give a wrong impression in English where our păthos, with a long a, has nothing to do with Hegel's păthos. It is used frequently in what follows, and I have put it into inverted commas. Sometimes it simply means a strong passion, e.g. of love or hate. See *L. and S.*, s.v. But Hegel means by it a 'passionate absorption in fulfilling a one-sided ethical purpose' (Mure, *The Philosophy of Hegel*, London, 1965, p. 192).

buttress the effect of the 'pathos'. Therefore nature must essentially be used as symbolic and must let the 'pathos' re-echo from itself, for the 'pathos' is the proper subject of the representation. Landscape painting, e.g., is in itself a slighter kind of painting than historical painting, but, even where it appears on its own account, it must strike the note of a universal feeling and have the form of a 'pathos'.—In this sense it has been said that art as such must touch us; but, if this principle is to hold good, the essential question is how this experience of being touched may be produced by art. Being touched is, in general, being moved sympathetically as a feeling, and people, especially nowadays, are, or some of them are, easily touched. The man who sheds tears sows tears, and they grow easily enough. But in art what should move us is only the inherently genuine 'pathos'.

(ββ) Therefore neither in comedy nor in tragedy may the 'pathos' be mere folly and subjective caprice. In Shakespeare, e.g., Timon is a misanthrope for purely external reasons; his friends have taken his dinners, squandered his property, and when he now needs money for himself, they desert him. This makes him a passionate misanthrope. This is intelligible and natural, but not a 'pathos' inherently justified. Still more in Schiller's early work, *Der Menschenfeind*,[1] is similar hatred just a modern whim. For in this instance the misanthrope is besides a reflective, judicious, extremely honourable man, magnanimous to his peasants whom he has released from serfdom, and full of love for his daughter who is both beautiful and lovable. In a similar way Quinctius Heymeran von Flaming, in August La Fontaine's novel,[2] torments himself with the capriciousness of the human race, and so on. Above all, however, the latest poetry has screwed itself up to endless fantasticalness and mendacity which is supposed to make an effect by its bizarre character, but it meets with no response in any sound heart, because in such refinements of reflection on what is true in human life, everything of genuine worth is evaporated.[3]

But conversely, whatever rests on doctrine and conviction, and

---

[1] *The Misanthrope*—first published in his periodical *Thalia* (Leipzig, 1791); later in a collection of his prose writings (Leipzig, 1802, part 4).

[2] A. H. J. La Fontaine, 1758–1831. *The Life and Deeds of Count Q. H. von Flaming* was published in 1795–6.

[3] It is not possible to say to what poets Hegel is referring, even if any of them have survived. When he speaks of 'genuinely living poetry' (p. 20 above) he may have had Goethe and Schiller in mind.

insight into their truth, in so far as this *knowledge* is a chief requirement, is no genuine 'pathos' for artistic representation. To this class belong *scientific* facts and truths. For science requires a special kind of education, a repeated study and manifold knowledge of the specific science and its value; but an interest in this sort of study is not a universal moving power in the human breast; it is restricted always to a certain number of individuals.[1] There is the same difficulty in the treatment of purely *religious* doctrines, if, that is to say, they are to be unfolded in their inmost character. The universal content of religion, belief in God, etc., is of course an interest of every deeper mind; yet, granted this faith, it is not the concern of art to proceed to the exposition of religious dogmas or to a special insight into their truth, and art must therefore beware of entering upon such expositions. On the other hand, we credit the human heart with every 'pathos', with all the motivations by ethical powers which are of interest for action. Religion affects the disposition, the heaven of the heart, the universal consolation and elevation of the individual in himself, rather than action proper as such. For the Divine in religion as *action* is morality and the particular powers of the moral realm. But these powers affect, not the pure heaven of religion, but, in contrast, the world and what is strictly human. In antiquity the essence of this worldliness was the character of the gods who therefore, even in connection with action, could enter together completely into the representation of action.

If therefore we ask about the scope of the 'pathos' that belongs to this discussion, the number of such substantial determinants of the will is slight, their scope small. Opera,[2] in particular, will and must keep to a restricted circle of them, and we hear the laments and joys, the fortune and misfortune of love, fame, honour, heroism, friendship, maternal love, love of children, of spouses, etc., continually, over and over again.

(γγ) Now such a 'pathos' essentially demands representation and graphic amplification. And at that it must be a soul inherently rich which puts into its 'pathos' the wealth of its inner being and does not merely concentrate itself in itself and remain intensive,

---

[1] It is a pity that this sentence, so incontestably true, has been so unpalatable to those who have been busy at enlarging and multiplying universities in this country in recent years.

[2] Mozart and especially Rossini were Hegel's favourites.

but expresses itself extensively and rises to a fully developed form. This inner concentration or outer development makes a great difference, and individuals of particular nationalities are in this respect too essentially different. Nations with more developed reflective powers are more eloquent in the expression of their passion. The Greeks, e.g., were accustomed to unfold in its depth the 'pathos' which animates individuals without thereby getting into cold reflections or blethers. The French too in this respect are 'pathetic' and their eloquent description of passion is not always pure verbiage, as we Germans with our emotional reserve often suppose, because the varied expression of feeling seems to us to be a wrong done to it. In this sense there was a period in our German poetry when especially the young spirits, bored by the French rhetorical torrent, yearned for nature and now came to a vigour which expressed itself mainly in interjections alone. Yet with 'Och!' and 'O!' or with the curse of anger, with storming and beating about hither and thither, nothing is to be effected. The vigour of mere interjections is a poor vigour and the mode of expression of a soul uncultured still. The individual spirit, in which the 'pathos' is presented, must be one which is full and capable of spreading and expressing itself.

In this matter too Goethe and Schiller provide a striking contrast. Goethe is less 'pathetic' than Schiller and has a rather intensive manner of presentation; in his lyrics especially he remains more self-reserved; his songs, as is appropriate to song, make us notice their intention, without fully explaining it. Schiller, on the contrary, likes to unfold his 'pathos' at length with great clarity and liveliness of expression. In a similar way Claudius[1] in *Wandsbecker Bothe* (i, p. 153) contrasts Voltaire with Shakespeare: 'the one is what the other brings into *appearance*. M. Arouet *says*: "I weep", and Shakespeare weeps'. But what art has to do with is precisely saying and bringing into appearance, not with actual natural fact. If Shakespeare only wept, while Voltaire brings weeping into *appearance*, then Shakespeare is the poorer poet.

In short, in order to be concrete in itself, as ideal art requires, the 'pathos' must come into representation as the 'pathos' of a rich and total spirit. This leads us on to the third aspect of action—to the more detailed treatment of *character*.

[1] M. Claudius, 1740–1815. *The Wandsbeck Messenger* was published under the pseudonym 'Asmus'.

(c) *Character*

We started from the *universal* and substantial powers of action. They need for their practical proof and actualization human *individuality* in which they appear as the moving 'pathos'. But the universal element in these powers must close up in particular individuals into a totality and singularity in itself. This totality is man in his concrete spirituality and its subjectivity, is the human total individuality as character. The gods become human 'pathos', and 'pathos' in concrete activity is the human character.

Therefore character is the proper centre of the ideal artistic representation, because it unifies in itself the aspects previously considered, unifies them as factors in its own totality. For the Idea as Ideal, i.e. shaped for sensuous imagination and intuition, and acting and completing itself in its manifestation, is in its determinacy self-related subjective individuality. But the truly *free* individuality, as the Ideal requires it, has to evince itself, not only as universality, but no less as concrete particularity and as the completely unified mediation and interpenetration of both these sides which *for themselves* are as a unity. This constitutes the totality of character, the ideal of which consists in the rich powerfulness of subjectivity welding itself into one.

In this matter we have to consider character under three aspects:

(α) as total individuality, as the richness of character;

(β) this totality must at once appear as particularity, and the character, therefore, as *determinate*;

(γ) the character (as in itself one) closes together with this determinacy (as with itself) in its subjective independence and has thereby to maintain itself as an inherently *fixed* character.

These abstract categories we will now explain and bring nearer to our apprehension.

(α) Since the 'pathos' is unfolded within a concrete individual, it appears in its determinacy no longer as the entire and sole interest of the representation but becomes itself only one aspect, even if a chief one, of the character in action. For man does not, as may be supposed, carry in himself only *one* god as his 'pathos'; the human emotional life is great and wide; to a true man many gods belong; and he shuts up in his heart all the powers which are dispersed in the circle of the gods; the whole of Olympus is assembled in his breast. In this sense someone in antiquity said: 'O man, out of thine own passions thou hast created the gods.'[1] And in fact, the more civilized the Greeks became, the more gods they had, and their earlier gods were feebler, not configurated into individuality and specific character.

In this wealth of emotional life, therefore, character must show itself too. What precisely constitutes the interest that we take in a character is the fact that such a totality comes out strongly in it and nevertheless in this fullness it remains itself, a subject entire in himself. If the character is not depicted in this roundness and subjectivity and is abstractly at the mercy of only a *single* passion, then it seems beside itself, or crazy, weak, and impotent. For the weakness and powerlessness of individuals consists precisely in this, that the constituents of those eternal powers do not come into appearance in them as their very own self, as predicates inhering in them *qua* the subject of the predicates.

In Homer, e.g., every hero is a whole range of qualities and characteristics, full of life. Achilles is the most youthful hero, but his youthful force does not lack the other genuinely human qualities, and Homer unveils this many-sidedness to us in the most varied situations. Achilles loves his mother, Thetis; he weeps for Briseis because she is snatched from him, and his mortified honour drives him to the quarrel with Agamemnon, which is the point of departure for all the further events in the Iliad. In addition he is the truest friend of Patroclus and Antilochus, at the same time the most glowing fiery youth, swift of foot, brave, but full of respect for the aged. The faithful Phoenix, his trusted attendant, is at his feet, and, at the funeral of Patroclus, he gives to old Nestor the highest respect and honour. But, even so, Achilles also shows himself irascible, irritable, revengeful, and full of the harshest cruelty to the enemy, as when he binds the slain Hector to his chariot, drives on, and so drags the corpse three times round the walls of Troy. And yet he is mollified when old Priam comes to him in his tent; he bethinks himself of his own old father at home and gives to the weeping King the hand which had slain his son. Of Achilles we may say: here is a man; the many-sidedness of noble human nature develops its whole richness in this one individual. And the same is true of the other Homeric characters—Odysseus, Diomedes, Ajax, Agamemnon, Hector,

---

[1] This familiar quotation I cannot identify. Statius, iii. 661, says 'First in the world fear made the gods', but I think that Hegel has something Greek in mind.

Andromache; each of them is a whole, a world in itself; each is a complete living human being and not at all only the allegorical abstraction of some isolated trait of character. How pale and trumpery in comparison, even if they are powerful individualities, are the horny Siegfried, Hagen of Troy, and even Volker the minstrel![1]

It is such many-sidedness alone that gives living interest to character. At the same time this fullness must appear as *concentrated* in *one* person and not as diffusion, freakishness, and mere diverse excitability—as children, e.g., take up everything and make something of it for a moment, but are without character; character, on the contrary, must enter the most varied elements of the human heart, be in them, be itself completely filled by them, and yet at the same time must not stand still in them but rather, in this totality of interests, aims, qualities, traits of character, preserve the subjectivity which is mustered and held together in itself.

For the presentation of *such* total characters epic poetry above all is suited, dramatic and lyric poetry less so.

(β) But at this totality *as such* art cannot yet stop. For we have to do with the Ideal in its determinacy, and therefore the more specific demand for particularity and individuality of character presses on here. Action, especially in its conflict and reaction, should be presented within fixed and determinate limits. Consequently the heroes of drama are for the most part simpler in themselves than those of epic. Their firmer definition comes out through the particular 'pathos' which is made the essential and conspicuous trait of character and which leads to specific aims, decisions, and actions. But if the restriction is then carried so far that an individual is pared down to a mere inherently abstract

---

[1] Characters in the *Nibelungenlied.* My references to this work, which Hegel often mentions in the sequel, are drawn from the English translation by A. T. Hatto (Penguin Books, 1972), in which there are appendixes discussing such points raised by Hegel as the authorship and geography of the poem. After bathing in dragon's blood, Siegfried became 'horny' and invulnerable except at a spot between his shoulder blades. Volker was a nobleman, called 'minstrel' because he was a competent amateur. Hegel writes Hagen 'of Troy', in conformity with the practice of medieval German writers who liked to trace the ancestry of their heroes back to Trojans or Greeks. Hagen is actually described, however, as 'Lord of Troneck', and the location of this place has been disputed. Trondheim has been suggested, but although Hagen is more devoted to Brunhild of Iceland than to Chriemhild of Burgundy, he was a Burgundian vassal and perhaps unlikely to have his fief at such a distance. Lasson, however (p. 323), reads 'Hagen von Tronje'.

form of a specific 'pathos' like love, honour, etc., then all vitality and subjective life is lost, and the presentation becomes, as with the French, often in this respect trumpery and poor. In the particularized character there must therefore be *one* chief aspect which is dominant, but, within this determinacy, complete vitality and fullness must remain preserved, so that the individual has an opportunity to turn in many directions, to engage in a variety of situations, and to unfold in diverse expressions the wealth of a developed inner life. Despite their inherently simple 'pathos', the characters in the tragedies of Sophocles are examples of this quality of life. In their plastic self-sufficiency they may be compared to the figures of sculpture. After all, in spite of its determinateness, sculpture may express a many-sidedness of character. In contrast to the tempestuous passion which concentrates with all its force on one point alone, sculpture presents in its stillness and speechlessness the forceful neutrality which quietly locks up all powers within itself; yet this undisturbed unity nevertheless does not stop at abstract determinateness but in its beauty foreshadows the birthplace of everything as the immediate possibility of entering into the most diverse sorts of relation. We see in the genuine figures of sculpture a peaceful depth which has in itself the ability to actualize all powers out of itself. Even more than from sculpture we must require from painting, music, and poetry the inner multiplicity of character, and this requirement has been fulfilled by genuine artists at all times. For example, in Shakespeare's *Romeo and Juliet*, Romeo has love as his chief 'pathos'; yet we see him in the most diverse relations to his parents, to friends and his page, in honour-squabbles and his duel with Tybalt, in his piety and trust in the Friar, and, even on the edge of the grave, in talk with the apothecary from whom he buys the deadly poison, and all the time he is dignified and noble and deeply moved. Similarly in Juliet there is comprised a totality of relations to her father, her mother, her nurse, to Count Paris, and the Friar. And yet she is just as deeply sunk in herself as in each of these situations, and her whole character is penetrated and borne by only one feeling, the passion of her love which is as deep and wide and 'boundless as the sea', so that she may rightly say 'the more I give to thee, the more I have, for both are infinite' [Act II, scene ii].

Therefore, even if it be only *one* 'pathos' which is represented, still, because it is a wealth in itself, it must be developed. This is the case even in lyric poetry where yet the 'pathos' cannot come into action in concrete affairs. Even here the 'pathos' must be displayed as the inner situation of a full and developed heart which can disclose itself in every aspect of situations and circumstances. Lively eloquence, an imagination which fastens on everything, brings the past into the present, can use the whole exterior surroundings as a symbolic expression of the inner life and does not shun deep objective thoughts but in their exposition betrays a noble spirit which is far-reaching, comprehensive, clear and estimable—this richness of the character which expresses its inner world is in its right place even in lyric. Considered by the *Understanding*, such many-sidedness within a dominant determining 'pathos' may, it is true, appear to be illogical. Achilles, e.g., in his noble heroic character, the man whose youthful force of beauty is his fundamental trait, has a tender heart in relation to father and friend; now how is it possible, one may ask, for him to drag Hector round the walls in his cruel thirst for revenge? Similarly illogical are Shakespeare's clowns, almost always clever and full of gifted humour; so one may say: How can such clever individuals come to such a pass that they behave so clownishly? The Understanding, that is, will emphasize abstractly only one side of the character and stamp it on the whole man as what alone rules him. What is opposed to such dominance of a one-sidedness appears to the Understanding as simply illogical. But in the light of the *rationality* of what is inherently total and therefore living, this illogicality is precisely what is logical and right. For man is this: not only the bearer of the contradiction of his multiple nature but the sustainer[1] of it, remaining therein equal and true to himself.

(γ) But it follows that the character must combine his particularity with his subjectivity; he must be a determinate figure and in this determinacy possess the force and firmness of *one* 'pathos' which remains true to itself. If the man is not thus *one* in himself, the different aspects of his diverse characteristics fall apart and in that case are senseless and meaningless. Being in unity with oneself constitutes in art precisely the infinite and divine aspect of individuality. From this point of view, firmness and decision are an important determinant for the ideal presentation of character.

[1] The bearer (*tragen*) and sustainer (*ertragen*) are inadequate translations of the German words. But they cannot be reproduced in English. The French have *porter* and *supporter*.

As has already been touched upon above, this ideal presentation appears when the universality of the powers is pervaded by the particularity of the individual and, in this unification, becomes a subjectivity and individuality which is fully unified in itself and self-related.

Still, by making this demand, we must attack many productions, especially of more modern art.

In Corneille's *Cid* [1636], e.g., the collision of love and honour plays a brilliant part. Such a 'pathos' in different characters can of course lead to conflicts; but when it is introduced as an inner opposition in one and the same character, this provides an opportunity for splendid rhetoric and affecting monologues, but the diremption of one and the same heart, which is tossed hither and thither out of the abstraction of honour into that of love, and *vice versa*, is inherently contrary to solid decisiveness and unity of character.

It is equally contrary to individual decision if a chief character in whom the power of a 'pathos' stirs and works is himself determined and talked over by a subordinate figure, and now can shift the blame from himself on to another—as, e.g., Phèdre in Racine's [play, 1677] is talked over by Oenone. A genuine character acts out of himself and does not allow a stranger to look into his conscience and make decisions. But if he has acted out of his own resources, he will also take on himself the blame for his act and answer for it.

Another type of instability of character has been developed, especially in recent German productions, into an inner weakness of sensibility which has ruled long enough in Germany. As the nearest famous example [Goethe's] *Werther* [1774] is to be cited, a thoroughly morbid character without the force to lift himself above the selfishness of his love. What makes him interesting is the passion and beauty of his feeling, his close relationship to nature along with the development and tenderness of his heart. More recently, this weakness, with ever increasing deepening into the empty subjectivity of the character's own personality, has assumed numerous other forms. For example, we may include here the 'beautiful soul' of Jacobi's *Woldemar*.[1] In this novel there is

[1] F. H. Jacobi, 1743–1819. The novel was published at Flensburg in 1779. See Hegel's *Philosophy of Right*, § 140, and the reference there to his *Phenomenology*.

displayed in the fullest measure the imposture of the heart's splendour, the self-deceptive delusion of its own virtue and excellence. There is an elevation and divinity of soul which in every way comes into a perverse relation with actuality, and the weakness which cannot endure and elaborate the genuine content of the existing world it conceals from itself by the superiority in which it spurns everything as unworthy of itself. After all, to the truly moral interests and sterling aims of life such a beautiful soul is not open; on the contrary, it spins its own web in itself and lives and weaves solely within the scope of its most subjective religious and moral hatchings. With this inner enthusiasm for its own unbounded excellence, which it makes so much of in its own eyes, there is then at once bound up an infinite irritability towards everyone else who at every moment is supposed to find out, understand, and admire this solitary beauty; if others cannot do this, then at once its whole heart is moved to its depths and infinitely injured. Then forthwith it is all up with the whole of mankind, all friendship, all love. Inability to endure pedantry and rudeness, trifling circumstances and blunders which a greater and stronger character overlooks and by which he is uninjured, is beyond all imagination, and it is just the most trifling matter which brings such a beautiful heart to the depths of despair. Then, therefore, mournfulness, worry, grief, bad temper, sickness, melancholy, and misery have no end. Thence there springs a torture of reflections on self and others, a convulsiveness and even a harshness and cruelty of soul, in which at the last the whole miserableness and weakness of the inner life of this beautiful soul is exposed.—We cannot have any heart for this oddity of heart. For it is a property of a genuine character to have spirit and force to will and take hold of something actual. Interest in such subjective characters who always remain shut into themselves is an empty interest, however much they hug the notion that their nature is higher and purer, one that has engendered in itself the Divine (which for others is entirely clothed in the recesses of the heart) and exposed it entirely in undress.

In another form this deficiency in inner substantial solidity of character is also developed when these remarkable higher splendours of heart are hypostatized in a perverse way and treated as independent powers. This is the province of magic, magnetism, demons, the superior apparitions of clairvoyance, the disease of somnambulism, etc. The living and responsible individual in regard to these dark powers is put into relation with something which on the one hand is within himself, but on the other hand is a beyond, alien to his inner life, by which he is determined and ruled. In these unknown forces there is supposed to lie an indecipherable truth of dreadfulness which cannot be grasped or understood. From the sphere of art, however, these dark powers are precisely to be banned, for in art nothing is dark; everything is clear and transparent. With these visionary notions nothing is expressed except a sickness of spirit; poetry runs over into nebulousness, unsubstantiality, and emptiness, of which examples are provided in Hoffmann and in Heinrich von Kleist's[1] *Prince of Homburg*. The truly ideal character has for its content and 'pathos' nothing supernatural and ghost-ridden but only true interests in which he is at one with himself. Clairvoyance especially has become trivial and vulgar in recent poetry. In Schiller's *Wilhelm Tell* [1804, Act II, scene i], on the other hand, when old Attinghausen, on the point of death, proclaims the fate of his country, prophecy of this sort is used in a fitting place. But to have to exchange health of character for sickness of spirit in order to produce collisions and arouse interest is always unfortunate; for this reason too insanity is to be made use of only with great caution.

To these perversities which are opposed to unity and firmness of character we may as well annex the more modern principle of irony.[2] This false theory has seduced poets into bringing into characters a variety which does not come together into a unity, so that every character destroys itself as character. [On this theory] if an individual comes forward at first in a determinate way, this determinacy is at once to pass over into its opposite, and his character is therefore to display nothing but the nullity of its determinacy and itself. By irony this is regarded as the real height of art, on the assumption that the spectator must not be gripped by an inherently affirmative interest, but has to stand above it, as irony itself is away above everything.

In this sense it has been proposed, after all, to explain characters

---

[1] 1777–1811. The drama was written in 1809–10, but not produced until 1821.

[2] See above, Introduction 7(iii), and notes there. Also *Philosophy of Right*, § 140 (f).

in Shakespeare. Lady Macbeth, e.g., is supposed [by Tieck (Lasson, p. 331)] to be a loving spouse with a soft heart, although she not only finds room for the thought of murder, but also carries it out [by her husband's hand]. But Shakespeare excels, precisely owing to the decisiveness and tautness of his characters, even in the purely formal greatness and firmness of evil. Hamlet indeed is indecisive in himself, yet he was not doubtful about *what* he was to do, but only *how*. Yet nowadays they make even Shakespeare's characters ghostly, and suppose that we must find interesting, precisely on their own account, nullity and indecision in changing and hesitating, and trash of this sort. But the Ideal consists in this, that the Idea is *actual*, and to this actuality man belongs as subject and therefore as a firm unity in himself.

At this point this may suffice in relation to the individual's fullness of character in art. The important thing is an inherently specific essential 'pathos' in a rich and full breast whose inner individual world is penetrated by the 'pathos' in such a way that this penetration, and not the 'pathos' alone as such, is represented. But all the same the 'pathos' in the human breast must not so destroy itself in itself as thereby to exhibit itself as unsubstantial and null.

III. THE EXTERNAL DETERMINACY OF THE IDEAL

In connection with the determinacy of the Ideal, we treated it *first* in general terms, namely how and why the Ideal as such has to clothe itself with the form of the particular. *Secondly*, we found that the Ideal must be moved in itself and advance therefore to that difference in itself, the totality of which is displayed as action. Yet through action the Ideal goes out into the external world, and the question arises, *thirdly*, how this final aspect of concrete reality is to be configured in a way compatible with art. For the Ideal is the Idea identified with its *reality*. Hitherto we have pursued this reality only so far as human individuality and its character. But man has also a concrete *external* existence, out of which indeed, as subject, he withdraws himself and becomes self-enclosed, yet in this subjective unity with himself he still remains related to externality all the same. To man's actual existence there belongs a surrounding world, just as the statues of a god have a temple. This is the reason why we must now mention the manifold threads which link the Ideal to externality and are drawn through it.

Thus we now enter upon an almost unreviewable breadth of circumstances and entanglement in external and relative matters. For, in the first place, nature presses on us at once from outside, in locality, time, climate; and in this respect, at our every step, wherever we go, a new and always specific picture already confronts us. Further, man avails himself of external nature for his needs and purposes; and there come into consideration the manner and way that he uses it, his skill in inventing and equipping himself with tools and housing, with weapons, seats, carriages, his way of preparing food and eating it, the whole wide sphere of the comfort and luxury of life, etc. And, besides, man lives also in a concrete actual world of spiritual relations, which all equally are given an external existence, so that there also belong to the surrounding actual world of human life the different modes of command and obedience, of family, relatives, possession, country and town life, religious worship, the waging of war, civil and political conditions, sociability, in short the whole variety of customs and usages in all situations and actions.

In all these respects, the Ideal immediately encroaches on ordinary external reality, on the daily life of the actual world, and therefore on the common prose of life. For this reason, if one keeps in view the modern nebulous idea of the Ideal, it may look as if art must cut off all connection with this world of relative things, since the aspect of externality is supposed to be something purely indifferent, and even, in comparison with the spirit and its inwardness, vulgar and worthless. From this point of view, art is regarded as a spiritual power which is to lift us above the whole sphere of needs, distress, and dependence, and to free us from the intelligence and wit which people are accustomed to squander on this field. Furthermore, this is supposed to be a field, mostly purely conventional, a field of mere accidents, because it is tied down in time, place, and custom, and these, it is thought, art must disdain to harbour. Yet this semblance of ideality is partly only a superior abstraction made by that modern subjective outlook which lacks courage to commit itself to externality, and partly a sort of power which the subject assumes in order by his own effort to put himself outside and beyond this sphere, if he has not already been absolutely raised above it by birth, class, and situation. As a means for this putting oneself outside and beyond, there remains nothing over in that case except withdrawal into the inner world of feelings which the individual does not leave, and now in this unreality regards himself as a sapient being who just looks longingly to heaven and therefore thinks he may disdain everything on earth. But the genuine Ideal does not stop at the indeterminate and the purely inward; on the contrary; it must also go out in its totality into a specific contemplation of the external world in all its aspects. For, the human being, this entire centre of the Ideal, *lives*; he is essentially now and here, he is the present, he is individual infinity, and to life there belongs the opposition of an environment of external nature in general, and therefore a connection with it and an activity in it. Now since this activity is to be apprehended, not only as such, but in its determinate appearance, by art, it has to enter existence on and in material of this [mundane] kind.

But, just as a man is in himself a subjective totality and therefore separates himself from what is external to him, so the external world too is a whole, rounded and logically interconnected in itself. Yet in this exclusion from one another both worlds stand in essential relationship and constitute concrete reality only in virtue of this interconnection, and the representation of this reality affords the content of the Ideal. Hence arises the question mentioned above: in what form and shape can externality be represented by art in an ideal way within such a totality?

In this connection too we have once more to distinguish three aspects in the work of art.

First, it is the whole of abstract externality as such—space, time, shape, colour—which needs a form compatible with art.

Secondly, the external comes on the scene in its concrete reality, as we have just sketched it, and it demands in the work of art an harmonization with the subjectivity of man's inner being which has been placed in such an environment.

Thirdly, the work of art exists for contemplation's delight—for a public which has a claim to find itself again in the *objet d'art* in accordance with its genuine belief, feeling, imagination, and to be able to come into concord with the represented objects.

1. *Abstract Externality as such*

When the Ideal is drawn out of its bare essentiality into external existence, it at once acquires a double sort of reality. For one thing, the work of art gives to the content of the Ideal in general the concrete shape of reality, since it displays that content as a specific state of affairs, a particular situation, as character, event, action, and indeed in the form of what is at the same time external fact; for another thing, this appearance, already total in itself, art transfers into a specific *sensuous* material, and thereby creates a new world of art, visible to the eye and audible to the ear. In both these respects art reveals the most remote corners of externality, in which the inherently total unity of the Ideal cannot, in its concrete sprituality, come into appearance any more. In this connection the work of art has also a double external aspect: i.e. (*a*) it remains an external object as such and therefore (*b*) in its configuration as such can also assume only an external unity. Here there returns again the same relation which we already had an opportunity to discuss in connection with the beauty of nature, and so too the same characteristics come into prominence once again, and here in relation to art. In other words, the mode of con- figuration of the external is, on the one hand, regularity, symmetry, and conformity to law, and, on the other hand, unity as the sim- plicity and purity of the sensuous material which art employs as the external element for the existence of its productions.

(*a*) *First*, as regards regularity and symmetry, these, as a mere lifeless geometrical unity, cannot possibly exhaust the nature of a work of art, even on its external side; they have their place only in what is inherently lifeless, in time, spatial forms, etc. In this sphere they therefore appear as a sign of mastery and deliberation even in the most external things. We see them, therefore, asserting themselves in works of art in two ways. Retained in their abstrac- tion, they destroy the quality of life; the ideal work of art must therefore, even on its external side, rise above the purely sym- metrical. Yet, in this matter, as in musical tunes, for example, regularity is not wholly superseded at all. It is only reduced to being simply a foundation. But, conversely, this restraint and regulation of the unruly and unrestrained is again the sole funda- mental characteristic which certain arts can adopt in line with the material for their representation. In that event, regularity is the sole ideal in the art.

Its[1] principal application, from this point of view, is in archi- tecture, because the aim of an architectonic work of art is to give

[1] i.e. the application of both regularity and symmetry.

artistic shape to the external, inherently inorganic, environment of spirit. What therefore dominates in architecture is the straight line, the right angle, the circle, similarity in pillars, windows, arches, columns, and vaults. For the architectural work of art is not just an end in itself; it is something external for something else to which it serves as an adornment, dwelling-place, etc. A building awaits the sculptural figure of a god or else the group of people who take up their home there. Consequently such a work of art should not essentially draw attention to itself. In this connection regularity and symmetry are pre-eminently appropriate as the decisive law for the external shape, since the intellect takes in a thoroughly regular shape at a glance and is not required to preoccupy itself with it for long. Naturally there is no question here of the symbolic relation which architectural forms also assume in relation to the spiritual content for which they provide surroundings or an external locality.

The same thing is valid too for that strict kind of gardening which can count as a modified application of architectural forms to actual nature. In gardens, as in buildings, man is the chief thing. Now of course there is another kind of gardening which makes variety and its lack of regularity into a rule; but regularity is to be preferred. For if we look at the variously complex mazes and shrubberies continually diversified in their twistings and windings, the bridges over stagnant water, the surprise of gothic chapels, temples, Chinese pagodas, hermitages, urns, pyres, mounds, statues—despite all their claims to independence we have soon had more than enough; and if we look a second time, we at once feel disgust. It is quite different with natural regions and their beauty; they are not there for the purpose of use and gratification, and may come before us on their own account as an object of consideration and enjoyment. On the other hand, regularity in gardens ought not to surprise us but to enable man, as is to be demanded, to appear as the chief person in the external environment of nature.

Even in painting there is a place for regularity and symmetry in the arrangement of the whole, in the grouping of figures, their placing, movement, drapery, etc. Yet since, in painting, the spiritual quality of life can penetrate external appearance in a far profounder way than it can in architecture, only a narrower scope is left for the abstract unity of the symmetrical, and we find rigid uniformity and its rule for the most part only in the beginnings of art, while later the freer lines,[1] which approach the form of the organic, serve as the fundamental type.

On the other hand, in music and poetry regularity and symmetry are once again important determinants. In the duration of their sounds these arts have an element of pure externality as such which is incapable of any other more concrete kind of configuration. Things together in space can comfortably be seen at a glance; but in time one moment has gone already when the next is there, and in this disappearance and reappearance the moments of time go on into infinity. This indeterminacy has to be given shape by the regularity of the musical beat which produces a determinateness and continuously recurring pattern and thereby checks the march to infinity. The beat of music has a magical power to which we are so susceptible that often, in hearing music, we beat time to it without being aware of the fact. This recurrence of equal time intervals is not something belonging objectively to the notes and their duration. To the note as such, and to time, to be divided and repeated in this regular way is a matter of indifference. The beat therefore appears as something purely created by the subject [the composer], so that now in listening we acquire the immediate certainty of having in this regularization of time something purely subjective and indeed the basis of the pure self-identity which the subject inherently possesses as his self-identity and unity and their recurrence in all the difference and most varied many-sidedness of experience. Therefore the beat resounds in the depths of our soul and takes hold of us in virtue of this inner subjectivity, a subjectivity at first abstractly self-identical. From this point of view it is not the spiritual content, not the concrete soul of feeling, which speaks to us in the musical notes; neither is it the note as note that moves us in our inmost being; on the contrary, it is this abstract unity, introduced into time by the subject, which echoes the like unity of the subject. The same is true of the metre and rhyme of poetry. Here too, regularity and symmetry are the systematic rule, and throughout are necessary to this external side of poetry. The sensuous element is thereby at once drawn out of its sensuous sphere and shows in itself already that here what is at issue is something other than the pronouncements of the

[1] i.e. as distinct from the rigidity of geometrical shapes.

ordinary consciousness which treats the duration of the notes arbitrarily and with indifference.

A similar, even if not so strictly determined, regularity now rises still further and is mingled, although in a quite external way, with the properly living content. In an epic and a drama, e.g., which has its specific divisions, cantos, acts, etc., it is important to give these separate parts an approximate equality of length; the same equality is important in individual groupings in paintings, although in this case there should be no appearance of a compulsion in respect of the essential subject-matter or of a conspicuous domination by mere regularity.

Regularity and symmetry as the abstract unity and determinacy of what is inherently external, alike in space and time, govern principally only the quantitative, the determinacy of size. What no longer belongs to this externality as its proper element therefore discards the domination of purely quantitative relations and is determined by deeper relations and their unity. Thus the more that art fights its way out of externality as such, the less is its mode of configuration ruled by regularity, to which it ascribes only a restricted and subordinate sphere.

Having mentioned symmetry, we must at this point mention harmony once more. It is no longer related to the purely quantitative but to essentially qualitative differences which do not persist as mere opposites over against one another but are to be brought into concord. In music, e.g., the relation of the tonic to the mediant and dominant is not purely quantitative; on the contrary, these are essentially different notes which at the same time coalesce into a unity without letting their specific character cry out as a sharp opposition and contradiction. Discords, on the other hand, need resolution. The case is similar with the harmony of colours. Here likewise what art demands is that in a painting the colours shall neither appear as a varied and arbitrary confusion nor so that their oppositions are simply dissolved, but that they are harmonized into the concord of a total and unitary impression. Thus, looked at more closely, harmony requires a totality of differences which in the nature of the case belong to a determinate sphere: colour, e.g., has a determinate range of colours as the so-called fundamental colours which are derived from the basic nature of colour as such and are not accidental mixtures. Such a totality in its concord constitutes harmony. In a painting, e.g., the totality of the fundamental colours, yellow, blue, green, and red must be present as well as their harmony, and the old masters, even unconsciously, have attended to this completeness and observed its law. Now since harmony begins to disengage itself from the pure externality of determinate existence, it is thereby also enabled to adopt and express in itself a wider and more spiritual content. The old masters gave the fundamental colours in their purity to the dress of important people, while mixed colours were given to their retinue. Mary, e.g., generally wears a blue mantle, because the gentle peace of blue corresponds to inner serenity and gentleness; more seldom she has a conspicuous red gown.

(b) The *second* feature of externality, as we saw, affects the sensuous material as such, which art uses for its representations. Here unity consists in the simple determinacy and uniformity of the material in itself which may not deviate into indefinite variety and mere mixture, or, in general, into unclarity. This requirement too is related only to space (to the clarity of outlines, for example, to the precision of straight lines, circles, etc.) and to the fixed determinacy of time, e.g. the strict maintenance of the beat, and, further, to the purity of determinate notes and colours. In painting, e.g., the colours ought not to be blurred or greyish, but clear, definite, and inherently simple. Their pure simplicity on this sensuous side constitutes the beauty of colour, and the simplest colours in this connection are the most effective: pure yellow, e.g., which does not pass over into green, red which has not a dash of blue or yellow, etc. Of course it is difficult in that case to maintain these colours in harmony at the same time in their fixed simplicity. But these inherently simple colours are the foundation which should not be entirely shaded down, and, even if mixtures cannot be dispensed with, still the colours must not appear as a murky confusion, but as clear and simple in themselves, or otherwise instead of the luminous clarity of colour there is nothing but a smudge.

The like demand is to be raised too in connection with the sound of notes. In the case of strings, e.g., whether of metal or catgut, it is the vibration of this material which produces the sound, and specifically the vibration of a string of definite tension and length; if the tension is slackened or if the string struck is not of the right length, the note no longer possesses this simple determinateness and rings false, since it passes over into other notes.

The same thing happens if, instead of that pure vibrating and quivering, we hear as well the mechanical grating and scraping as a noise intermixed with the sound of the note as such. Similarly, the note produced by the human voice must develop pure and free out of the throat and the chest, without allowing any humming interference, or, as is the case with hoarseness, without allowing some hindrance, not overcome, to disturb our listening. This freedom from any foreign admixture, this clarity and purity in their fixed unwavering determinateness, is in this purely sensuous connection the beauty of the note, which distinguishes it from rustling, screeching, etc. The same sort of thing can be said about speech too, especially about the vowels. A language which has a, e, i, o, u, definite and pure is, like Italian, melodious and singable. Diphthongs, on the other hand, have always a mixed note. In writing, the sounds of speech are reduced to a few regularly similar signs and appear in their simple determinate character; but, in speaking, this determinate character is all too often blurred, so that now especially dialects like the South-German, Swabian, Swiss, have sounds that are so blurred that they cannot possibly be written down. But this is not, as may be supposed, a deficiency in the written language, but arises rather from the dullness of the people.

For the present this is enough about this external side of the work of art, the side which, as mere externality, is only capable of an external and abstract unity.

But the next point is that it is the spiritual concrete *individuality* of the Ideal which enters externality in order to display *itself* there, so that the external must be penetrated by this inwardness and totality which it has the function of expressing. For this purpose mere regularity, symmetry, and harmony, or the simple determinacy of the sensuous material, are found to be inadequate. This leads us on to the second aspect of the external determinacy of the Ideal.

2. *Correspondence of the Concrete Ideal with its External Reality*

The general law which in this connection we can assert consists in this, that man in his worldly environment must be domesticated and at home, that the individual must appear as having his abode, and therefore as being free, in nature and all external relations, so that both sides, (i) the subjective inner totality of character and the character's circumstances and activity and (ii) the objective totality of external existence, do not fall apart as disparate and indifferent to one another, but show that they harmonize and belong together. For external objectivity, in so far as it is the actuality of the Ideal, must give up its purely objective independence and inflexibility in order to evince itself as identical with that [subjectivity] of which it is the external existence.

In this matter we have to state three different ways of looking at such harmony:

First, the unity of the two may remain purely implicit and appear only as a secret inner bond linking man with his external environment.

Secondly, however, since concrete spirituality and its individuality serves as the starting-point and essential content of the Ideal, the harmony with external existence has also to be displayed as originating from human activity and as produced thereby.

Thirdly, and lastly, this world produced by the human spirit is itself again a totality; in its existence this totality forms an objective whole with which individuals, moving on this ground, must stand in essential connection.

(*a*) Now in relation to the first point we may start from the fact that since the environment of the Ideal does not yet appear here as established by human activity, it is still in the first place what is in general external to man, i.e. the external world of *nature*. Its representation in the ideal work of art is therefore the first thing to talk about.

Here too we can emphasize three aspects:

(α) In the first place, as soon as external nature is presented in its external formation, it is in every direction a reality formed in a *specific* way. Now if it is actually to be given the due which it has to claim in respect of the representation, then the representation must be drawn up in complete fidelity to nature, although we have seen earlier what differences must be respected even here between immediate nature and art. But on the whole it is precisely characteristic of the great masters to be truly, genuinely, and completely tied down in regard to the external natural environment. For nature is not merely earth and sky in general, and man does not hover in the air; he feels and acts in a specific locality of brooks, rivers, sea, hills, mountains, plains, woods, gorges, etc. Although Homer, e.g., may not give us modern portrayals of nature, he is so true in his descriptions and lists, and gives us such an accurate picture of the Scamander, the Simoeis, the coasts and bays of the sea, that even now the same country has been found by geographers to correspond with his description. On the other hand, the crudely sensational poems of fairground entertainers, both in characters and descriptions, are poor, empty, and wholly nebulous. The Mastersingers[1] also, when they put old Bible stories into verse and locate them in Jerusalem, e.g., provide nothing but names. The same is true in the *Heldenbuch*:[2] Ortnit rides in the pine-forest, fights with the dragon, without any human surroundings, specific locality, etc., so that in this respect we get as good as nothing for our vision. Even in the *Nibelungenlied* there is nothing different: we hear indeed of Worms, the Rhine, the Danube, but here too we get no further than what is poor and vague. But it is perfect determinacy which constitutes the aspect of individuality and reality which, without it, is just an abstraction, and that contradicts the very conception of external reality.

(β) Now with this requirement of determinacy and fidelity to nature there is immediately linked a certain fullness of detail whereby we acquire a picture, a vision even, of this external aspect of nature. It is true that there is an essential distinction between the different arts according to the medium in which they are expressed. The fullness and detailing of external fact lies further away from sculpture because of the peace and universality of its figures, and it has externals, not as environment and locality, but only as drapery, coiffure, weapons, seat, and the like. Yet many figures of ancient sculpture are specifically distinguishable only by conventions of drapery, the dressing of the hair, and further similar marks. But this is not the place for discussing this conventionality, because it is not to be attributed to the natural as such; it cancels precisely the aspect of accident in such matters and is the way and means of their becoming permanent and more universal.

Opposed here to sculpture, the lyric displays predominantly the inner heart only and therefore when it takes up the external world does not need to pursue it to such definite perceptibleness. Epic,

---

[1] The musical and poetic guilds which flourished in German cities from the fourteenth to the sixteenth century. Wagner's opera provides a faithful representation of guild practices.

[2] *Book of the Heroes*, a collection of heroic and popular epics of the Middle High German period, c. 1225. Ortnit is the eponymous hero of one of them.

on the other hand, says *what* is there, *where* and *how* deeds have been done, and therefore, of all kinds of poetry, needs the greatest breadth and definiteness of the external locality. So too painting by its nature enters especially in this respect upon detail more than any other art does. But in no art should this definiteness go astray into the prose of actual nature and its direct imitation, nor should it overtower in partiality and importance the fullness of detail devoted to the presentation of the spiritual side of individuals and events. In general it should not make itself exclusively independent, because here the external should achieve appearance only in connection with the inner.

(γ) This is the point of importance here. Namely, for an individual to come on the scene as actual, two things, as we saw [in the preamble], are required: (i) he himself in his subjective character, and (ii) his external environment. Now for this externality to appear as *his*, it is essential that between these two things there shall prevail an essential harmony which may be more or less inward and into which of course a great deal of contingency enters too, yet without the loss of the fundamental identity. In the whole spiritual disposition of epic heroes, e.g., in their mode of life, mentality, feeling, and accomplishment, there must be made perceptible a secret harmony, a note of concord between the two which closes them into a whole. The Arab, e.g., is one with his natural surroundings and is only to be understood along with his sky, his stars, his hot deserts, his tents, and his horses. For he is at home only in such a climate, zone, and locality. Similarly Ossian's heroes (according to Macpherson's invention or his modern revision) are extremely subjective and turned inward, but in their gloom and melancholy they appear throughout tied to their moors where the wind whispers through the thistles, to their clouds, mists, hills, and dark glens. The face of this whole locality alone makes us really completely clear about the inner life of the figures living and moving on this ground with their sadness, grief, sorrows, battles, and misty apparitions, for they are entirely involved in this environment and only there are they at home.

From this point of view we can now for the first time observe that historical material has the great advantage of containing, immediately developed, even indeed into detail, such a harmony of the subjective and objective sides. *A priori* this harmony can be drawn from the imagination only with difficulty, and yet we should always have an inkling of it, however little it can be developed conceptually in most parts of a subject-matter. Of course we are accustomed to rate a free production of the imagination higher than the manipulation of material already available, but the imagination cannot go so far as to provide the required harmony so firmly and definitely as it already lies before us in actual reality where national traits themselves proceed from this harmony. This is the general principle for the purely implicit unity of subjectivity with its external natural environment.

(b) A second kind of harmony does not stop at this purely implicit unity but is expressly produced by human activity and skilfulness, in that man converts external things to his own use and puts himself in correspondence with them as a result of the satisfaction which he has thus acquired. In contrast to that first concord, which only concerned more general matters, this aspect is related to the particular, to special needs and their satisfaction through the special use of natural objects. This sphere of need and satisfaction is one of absolutely infinite variety, but natural things are still infinitely more many-sided and acquire a greater simplicity only because man introduces into them his spiritual characteristics and impregnates the external world with his will. Thereby he humanizes his environment, by showing how it is capable of satisfying him and how it cannot preserve any power of independence against him. Only by means of this effectual activity is he no longer merely in general, but also in particular and in detail, actually aware of himself and at home in his environment.

Now the fundamental conception to be stressed in relation to art for this whole sphere lies briefly in the following: Man, on the particular and finite side of his needs, wishes, and aims, stands primarily not only in a *general* relation to external nature, but more precisely in a relation of *dependence*. This relativity and lack of freedom is repugnant to the ideal, and man can become an object for art only if he is first freed from this labour and distress, and has cast off this *dependence*. The act of conciliating the two sides, furthermore, may take a double starting-point, in that, *first*, nature for its part supplies man in a friendly way with what he needs, and instead of putting an obstacle in the way of his interests and aims, rather presents them to him itself and welcomes them in every way. But, *secondly*, man has needs and wishes which nature is in no position to satisfy directly. In these cases he must work out his necessary satisfaction by his own activity; he must take possession of things in nature, arrange them, form them, strip off every hindrance by his own self-won skilfulness, and in such a way that the external world is changed into a means whereby he can realize himself in accordance with all his aims. Now the purest relationship is to be found where both these aspects come together, when spiritual skilfulness is so far linked with the friendliness of nature that the fully accomplished harmony has come throughout into appearance instead of the harshness and dependence of struggle.

From the ideal ground of art the distress of life must be banished. In so far as possession and affluence afford a situation in which poverty and labour vanish, not merely momentarily but entirely, they are therefore not only not unaesthetic, but they rather coincide with the Ideal; although it would only betray an untrue abstraction to set aside altogether, in modes of representation which are compelled to take notice of concrete reality, the relation of man to those needs. This sphere of needs belongs of course to finitude, but art cannot dispense with the finite; it must not treat it as something purely bad; it has to reconcile and link it with what is genuine and true, for even the best actions and dispositions, taken in their *determinate* character and regarded in their abstract content, are restricted and therefore finite. The fact that I must keep myself alive, eat and drink, have a house and clothing, need a bed, a chair, and so many appurtenances of other kinds, is of course a necessity for the externals of life; but the inner life is so greatly involved with these things that man gives clothing and weapons even to his gods, and envisages them in manifold needs and their satisfaction. Still, as we have said, this satisfaction must in that case appear as assured. In the case of knights errant, e.g., the removal of external distress in the chance of their adventures occurs only as reliance on chance, just as savages rely on nature simply as it is. Both are unsatisfactory for art. For the genuine ideal consists not only in man's being in general lifted above the grim seriousness of dependence on these external circumstances, but in his standing in the midst of a superfluity which permits him to play freely and cheerfully with the means put at his disposal by nature.

Within these general considerations the following two points may now be more precisely distinguished from one another:

(α) The first concerns the use of natural things for purely

contemplative satisfaction. Under this head comes every adornment and decoration which man bestows on himself, in general all the splendour with which he surrounds himself. By so bedecking himself and his environment he shows that the costliest things supplied by nature and the most beautiful things that catch the eye—gold, jewels, pearls, ivory, expensive robes—these rarest and most resplendent things, have no interest for him in themselves and should not count as merely natural, but have to show themselves on *him* or as belonging to *his* environment, to what he loves and venerates, to his monarchs, his temples, his gods. To this end he chooses especially what in itself as external already appears as beautiful, pure bright colours, the lustre of metals, fragrant woods, marble, etc. Poets, especially oriental ones, do not fail to use such wealth; it plays its part too in the *Nibelungenlied*; and art in general does not stop at mere descriptions of this magnificence but equips its actual works with the same wealth, where this is possible and in place. There was no sparing of gold and ivory on the statue of Pallas Athene at Athens and the statue of Zeus at Olympia; the temples of the gods, churches, images of the saints, royal palaces, afford amongst nearly all peoples an example of splendour and magnificence. From time immemorial nations have delighted to have their own wealth before their eyes on their divinities, just as in the case of the splendour of their monarchs, they were delighted that such things were there and drawn from amongst themselves.

It is true that such delight can be disturbed by so-called moral conceptions when one reflects how many poor Athenians could have been fed from the mantle of Pallas Athene and how many slaves could have been ransomed; and in times of great national distress, even in antiquity, such wealth has been devoted to useful ends, and the same thing has happened now amongst us with the treasures of monasteries and churches. Further, such miserable considerations may be applied not only to single works of art, but to the whole of art itself; what sums, it may be asked, has a State not expended on an Academy of Arts, or for the purchase of old and modern works of art, and the establishment of galleries, theatres, museums? But however many moral and touching emotions may be excited in this connection, this is possible only by calling to mind again the distress and poverty which art precisely demands shall be set aside, so that it can but redound to the fame and supreme honour of every people to devote its treasures to a sphere which, within reality itself, rises luxuriously above all the distress of reality.

(β) But man has not merely to bedeck himself and the environment in which he lives; he must also use external things *practically*, for his practical needs and ends. In this area there only now begin all man's work and trouble, and his dependence on the prose of life, and the chief question here, therefore, is how far even this sphere can be represented compatibly with the demands of art.

(αα) The first way in which art has tried to dismiss this whole sphere is the idea of a so-called Golden Age or even of an idyllic life. Under such conditions on the one hand nature satisfies without trouble to man every need that may stir within him, while on the other hand in his innocence he is content with what meadows, woods, flocks, a little garden and a hut can afford him by way of nourishment, housing, and other amenities, because all the passions of ambition or avarice, impulses which appear contrary to the higher nobility of human nature, are still altogether quiescent. Of course at a first glance such a state of affairs has a touch of the ideal, and certain restricted spheres of art may be content with this kind of presentation. But if we probe it more deeply, such a life will soon bore us. Gessner's writings, e.g., are little read nowadays, and if we do read them we cannot be at home in them. For a restricted mode of life of this kind presupposes an insufficient development of spirit also. A full and entire human life requires higher urgings, and this closest association with nature and its immediate products cannot satisfy it any longer. Man may not pass his life in such an idyllic poverty of spirit; he must work. What he has an urge for, he must struggle to obtain by his own activity. In this sense even physical needs stir up a broad and variegated range of activities and give to man a feeling of inner power, and, out of this feeling, deeper interests and powers can then also be developed. But at the same time even here the harmony of inner and outer must still remain the fundamental thing, and nothing is more offensive in art than when physical distress is displayed exaggerated to an extreme. Dante, e.g., by only a few strokes of the pen touchingly presents to us Ugolino's death from starvation [*Hell*, Canto xxxiii]. When Gerstenberg, on the other hand, in his tragedy of the same name[1] gives a prolix description of every degree of horror, of how first his three sons

---

[1] *Ugolino*, by H. W. von Gerstenberg (1737–1823).

and finally Ugolino himself perish from hunger, this is material entirely at variance, from this point of view, with artistic representation.

(ββ)¹ Yet the situation opposed to the idyllic, namely that of universal culture, all the same provides, in an opposite way, many hindrances to art. In this situation the long and complicated connection between needs and work, interests and their satisfaction, is completely developed in all its ramifications, and every individual, losing his independence, is tied down in an endless series of dependences on others. His own requirements are either not at all, or only to a very small extent, his own work, and, apart from this, every one of his activities proceeds not in an individual living way but more and more purely mechanically according to universal norms. Therefore there now enters into the midst of this industrial civilization, with its mutual exploitation and with people elbowing other people aside, the harshest cruelty of poverty on the one hand; on the other hand, if distress is to be removed [i.e. if the standard of living is to be raised], this can only happen by the wealth of individuals who are freed from working to satisfy their needs and can now devote themselves to higher interests. In that event of course, in this superfluity, the constant reflection of endless dependence is removed, and man is all the more withdrawn from all the accidents of business as he is no longer stuck in the sordidness of gain. But for this reason the individual is not at home even in his immediate environment, because it does not appear as his own work. What he surrounds himself with here has not been brought about by himself; it has been taken from the supply of what was already available, produced by others, and indeed in a most mechanical and therefore formal way, and acquired by him only through a long chain of efforts and needs foreign to himself.

(γγ) Therefore what is most fitted for ideal art proves to be a *third* situation which stands midway between the idyllic and golden ages and the perfectly developed universal mediations of civil society. This is a state of society which we have already learnt to recognize as the Heroic or, preferably, the ideal Age. The Heroic Ages are no longer restricted to that idyllic poverty in spiritual interests; they go beyond it to deeper passions and aims; but the nearest

---

¹ The section on Civil Society in Hegel's *Philosophy of Right* should be compared with this whole passage. By this state of 'universal culture' he means precisely what he described there as 'civil society'. See § 187.

environment of individuals, the satisfaction of their immediate needs, is still their own doing. Their food is still simple and therefore more ideal, as for instance honey, milk, wine; while coffee, brandy, etc., at once call to our mind the thousand intermediaries which their preparation requires. So too the heroes kill and roast their own food; they break in the horse they wish to ride; the utensils they need they more or less make for themselves; plough, weapons for defence, shield, helmet, breastplate, sword, spear, are their own work, or they are familiar with their fabrication. In such a mode of life man has the feeling, in everything he uses and everything he surrounds himself with, that he has produced it from his own resources, and therefore in external things has to do with what is his own and not with alienated objects lying outside his own sphere wherein he is master. In that event of course the activity of collecting and forming his material must not appear as painful drudgery but as easy, satisfying work which puts no hindrance and no failure in his way.

Such a form of life we find, e.g., in Homer. Agamemnon's sceptre is a family staff, hewn by his ancestor himself, and inherited by his descendants [*Iliad*, ii]. Odysseus carpentered himself his huge marriage bed [*Odyssey*, xxiii]; and even if the famous armour of Achilles was not his own work, still here too the manifold complexity of activities is cut short because it is Hephaestus who made it at the request of Thetis [*Iliad*, xviii]. In brief, everywhere there peeps out a new joy in fresh discoveries, the exuberance of possession, the capture of delight; everything is domestic, in everything the man has present before his eyes the power of his arm, the skill of his hand, the cleverness of his own spirit, or a result of his courage and bravery. In this way alone have the means of satisfaction not been degraded to a purely external matter; we see their living origin itself and the living consciousness of the value which man puts on them because in them he has things not dead or killed by custom, but his own closest productions. Thus here everything is idyllic, but not in that limited mode where earth, rivers, sea, trees, cattle, etc., provide man with his sustenance, and where consequently he is visible, in the main, only in his restriction to this environment and its enjoyment. On the contrary, within this original mode of life deeper interests arise in relation to which the whole external world is there only as an accessory, as the ground and means for higher ends, yet as a ground and an environment over which that harmony and independence is diffused and comes into appearance only because each and everything produced and used by human hands is at the same time prepared and enjoyed by the very man who needs it.

But to apply such a mode of representation to materials drawn from later completely civilized times always involves great difficulty and danger. Yet Goethe, in this connection, has given us a complete masterpiece in *Hermann und Dorothea*. I will cite only a few small points by way of comparison. Voss,[1] in his well-known *Luise*, sketches, in an idyllic way, life and activity in a quiet and restricted, though independent, circle. The village parson, the tobacco pipe, the dressing gown, the easy chair, and then the coffee-pot play a great part. Now coffee and sugar are products which could not have originated in such a circle, and they point at once to a totally different context, to a strange world with its manifold interconnections of trade and factories, in short to the world of modern industry. That circle of country life is therefore not wholly self-enclosed. On the other hand, in the beautiful picture of Hermann and Dorothea we did not need to require such a self-containment, for, as has already been indicated on another occasion, in this poem—which indeed maintains an idyllic tone throughout—an extremely dignified and important part is played by the great interests of the age, the battles of the French Revolution, the defence of our country. The narrower circle of family life in a country village therefore does not keep itself at all so self-enclosed that the world deeply involved in most powerful affairs is just ignored, as it is by the village pastor in Voss's *Luise*; on the contrary, owing to the association with those greater world-commotions within which the idyllic characters and events are portrayed, we see the scene transferred into the broader scope of a fuller and richer life; and the apothecary who lives only in the context of local affairs, restricting and conditioning him everywhere, is represented as a narrow-minded philistine, as good-natured but peevish. Still, in respect of the nearest environment of the characters, the note that we required above is struck throughout. So, e.g., to recall just this one thing, the host does not drink coffee, as you might expect, with his guests, the parson and the apothecary: 'With care the gammer brought clear, excellent wine in a cut-glass

---

[1] J. H. Voss, 1751–1826. *Luise* (1795) has been called a source of Goethe's *H. u. D.*, which appeared a year later and may have been stimulated by it.

flask on a shining pewter plate, along with greenish rummers, the proper goblets for Rhine wine.' In the cool of the day they drink a local growth, 1783, in the local glasses which alone are suitable for Rhine wine; 'the flow of the Rhine and its lovely bank'[1] is thus equally brought before our imagination and soon we are led into the vineyard behind the owner's house, so that here nothing takes us out of the proper sphere of a mode of life agreeable in itself and productive of its needs within itself.

(c) Apart from these first two sorts of external environment, there is still a *third* mode in concrete connection with which every individual has to live. This consists of the general *spiritual* relationships of religion, law, morality, the sort and kind of political organization, the constitution, law-courts, family, public and private life, sociability, etc. For the ideal character must come on the scene satisfied not only in his physical needs but in his spiritual interests also. It is true that the substantial, divine, and inherently necessary element in these relationships is, in its essential nature, simply one and the same; but in the objective world it assumes manifold shapes of different kinds and enters the sphere of the contingency of the particular, the conventional, and what is valid only for specific times and peoples. In this form all the interests of spiritual life come to have an external reality which confronts the individual as custom, usage, and habit, and, at the same time, by being a self-enclosed subject, he enters into connection not only with external nature but also with this totality which is related to him and belongs to him still more nearly. On the whole, we can claim for this sphere the same living harmony, with the indication of which we were concerned just now, and here we will therefore pass over its more detailed consideration, the chief points of which will be cited immediately in another context.

3. *The Externality of the Ideal* [*Work of Art*] *in relation to the Public*

Art by being the representation of the Ideal must introduce it in all the previously mentioned relations to external reality, and associate the inner subjectivity of character closely with the external world. But however far the work of art may form a world inherently harmonious and complete, still, as an actual single

[1] Both quotations are from the first canto of *H. u. D.*, *ad fin.*

object, it exists not for *itself*, but for *us*, for a public which sees and enjoys the work of art. The actors, for example, in the performance of a drama do not speak merely to one another, but to us, and they should be intelligible in both these respects. And so every work of art is a dialogue with everyone who confronts it. Now the truly ideal [work of art] is indeed intelligible to everyone in the universal interests and passions of its gods and men; yet since it brings its individuals before our eyes within a specific external world of customs, usages, and other particular details, there arises the new demand that this external world shall come into correspondence not only with the characters represented but equally with *us* too. Just as the characters in the work of art are at home in their external surroundings, we require also for ourselves the same harmony with them and their environment. Now to whatever age a work of art belongs, it always carries details in itself which separate it from the characteristics proper to other peoples and other centuries. Poets, painters, sculptors, composers choose materials above all from past times whose civilization, morals, usages, constitution, and religion are different from the whole civilization contemporary with themselves. Such a step backward into the past has, as has already been remarked [in the section on The Heroic Age], the great advantage that this departure from the present and its immediacy brings about automatically, owing to our memory, that generalization of material with which art cannot dispense. Yet the artist belongs to his own time, lives in its customs, outlooks, and ideas. The Homeric poems, e.g., whether Homer actually lived as the single author of the Iliad and the Odyssey or not, are yet separated by four centuries at least from the time of the Trojan war; and a twice greater period separated the great Grecian tragedians from the days of the ancient heroes from which they transferred the content of their poetry into their own time. The same is true about the *Nibelungenlied* and the poet who could put together into one organic whole the different sagas which this poem contains.

Now of course the artist is quite at home with the universal 'pathos', human and divine, but the variously conditioning external form of the ancient period itself, the characters and actions of which he presents, has changed essentially and become foreign to him. Further, the poet creates for a public, and primarily for his own people and age, which may demand ability to understand

and be at home in the work of art. True, the genuine, immortal works of art remain enjoyable by all ages and nations, but even so for their thorough understanding by foreign peoples and in other centuries there is involved a wide apparatus of geographical, historical, and even philosophical, notes, facts, and knowledge.

Now, given this clash between different ages, the question arises of how a work of art has to be framed in respect of the external aspects of locality, customs, usages, religious, political, social, moral conditions: namely whether the artist should forget his own time and keep his eye only on the past and its actual existence, so that his work is a true picture of what has gone; or whether he is not only entitled but in duty bound to take account solely of his own nation and contemporaries, and fashion his work according to ideas which coincide with the particular circumstances of his own time. These opposite requirements may be put in this way: the material should be handled either objectively, appropriately to its content and its period, or subjectively, i.e. assimilated entirely to the custom and culture of the present. To cling to either of these in their opposition leads to an equally false extreme which we will touch upon briefly so that thereby we can ascertain the genuine mode of representation.

Therefore in this connection we have three points to study:

(i)   the subjective stress on the contemporary civilization,

(ii) purely objective fidelity in relation to the past,

(iii) true objectivity in the representation and adoption of foreign materials distant in time and nationality.

(a) The purely *subjective* interpretation in its extreme one-sidedness goes so far as to cancel the objective form of the past altogether and put in its place simply the way that the present appears.

(α) On the one hand this may arise from ignorance of the past, or also from the naïveté of not feeling, or not becoming conscious of, the contradiction between the topic and such a way of making it the artist's own; thus the basis of such a manner of representation is lack of culture. We find this sort of naïveté most strongly marked in Hans Sachs,[1] who with fresh perceptibility, it is true, and joyful heart, has made into Nürnbergers, in the strictest sense of the word, our Lord God, God the Father, Adam, Eve, and the

---

[1] 1494–1576, leader of the guild of Mastersingers in Nürnberg, and author of numerous songs, poems, and dramas.

Patriarchs. God the Father, for example, once has a kindergarten and school for Abel and Cain and Adam's other children in manner and tone just like a schoolmaster in Sachs's day; he catechizes them on the Ten Commandments and the Lord's Prayer; Abel learns everything really piously and well, but Cain behaves and answers like a bad and impious boy; when he is to repeat the Ten Commandments, he turns them all upside down: thou shalt steal, thou shalt not honour thy father and mother, and so on. So too in southern Germany they have represented the story of the Passion in a similar way (this was banned, but it has been renewed again):[1] Pilate appears as an official, boorish, coarse, arrogant; the soldiers, entirely in keeping with the vulgarity of our time, offer to Christ *in extremis* a pinch of tobacco; he disdains it and they force snuff into his nose; and the whole audience have their joke at this, while being perfectly pious and devout at the same time; indeed the more devout they are in this exhibition, the more does the inwardness of religious ideas become livelier for them in this immediate presence, in their own world, of this external portrayal of the Passion.

Of course in this sort of transformation and perversion of the past into our own views and the shape of our world there is some justification, and there may seem something great in Hans Sachs's audacity in being so familiar with God and these ancient ideas and, with all piety, assimilating them to the ideas of a narrow-minded bourgeoisie. But nevertheless it is an outrage on the heart, and a cultural and spiritual deprivation, not merely to deny to the subject matter in any connection the right to its own objectivity, but even to bring it into a form wholly opposed thereto, with the result that nothing then appears but a burlesque contradiction.

(β) On the other hand, the same subjective outlook of the artist may proceed from pride in his own culture, because he treats the views of his own age and its own moral and social conventions as the only ones valid and acceptable, and therefore his audience cannot be expected to bear any subject-matter until it has assumed the form of that same culture. This sort of thing was exemplified in the so-called classical good taste of the French. What was to

---

[1] Some liturgical dramas did include elements of rough comedy, but I have been unable to discover to which of them Hegel is referring. The mention of tobacco may date it later than Sachs. Oberammergau started in 1634, but I am not implying that it is to that that Hegel is referring.

please had to be frenchified; what had a different nationality and especially a medieval form was called tasteless and barbaric, and was rejected with complete contempt. Therefore Voltaire was wrong to say[1] that the French had improved on the works of antiquity; they have only nationalized them, and in this transformation they treated everything foreign and distinctive with infinite disgust, all the more so as their taste demanded a completely courtly social culture, a regularity and conventional universality of sentiment and its representation. The like abstraction involved in cultural delicacy they carry over too into the language used in their poetry. No poet might use the word *cochon* or speak of spoons and forks and a thousand other things. Hence the prolix definitions and circumlocutions: e.g. instead of 'spoon' or 'fork', 'an instrument wherewith liquid or solid food is brought to the mouth', and more of the same kind. But just because of this their taste remained extremely narrow; for art, instead of smoothing and flattening its content out into such polished generalities, particularizes it rather into living individuality. This is why the French have been least able to come to terms with Shakespeare, and when they put him on the stage cut out every time precisely those passages that are our favourites. Similarly Voltaire makes fun of Pindar because he could say ἄριστον μὲν ὕδωρ.[2] And so, after all, in French dramatic works, Chinese, Americans, or Greek and Roman heroes must speak and behave exactly like French courtiers. Achilles, e.g., in *Iphigénie en Aulide*[3] is through and through a French prince, and if his name were not there no one would discover an Achilles in him. On the stage indeed his clothing was Greek, and he was equipped with helmet and breastplate; but at the same time his hair was curled and powdered; his hips were broadened by pockets, and he had red spurs fastened to his shoes with coloured ribbons. In Louis XIV's time Racine's *Esther* [1689] was popular chiefly because, when Ahasuerus came on the scene, he looked like Louis XIV himself entering the great hall of audience; true, Ahasuerus had oriental trappings, but he was powdered from head to foot and had an ermine royal robe, and

---

[1] *Siècle de Louis XIV*, ch. xxxii. The context is drama and a pane gyric on Racine.

[2] 'Water is best', the first line of Pindar's first Ode. The meaning is probably that water is the most translucent of liquids. In his *Ode sur le carosse de l'Impératrice de Russie*, Voltaire describes Pindar as verbose and unintelligible.

[3] Racine's Play, 1674.

behind him a great crowd of curled and powdered chamberlains, *en habit français*, with wigs, feathered bonnets on their arm, vests and hose of *drap d'or*, silk stockings and red heels on their shoes. What only the Court and specially privileged persons could get, was seen on the stage by the other classes—the entry of the King, brought into verse.

On the like principle, historiography in France has been pursued not for its own sake or on account of its subject-matter, but to serve the interest of the time, in order, we may suppose, to give good lessons to the government or to make it detested. Similarly, many dramas contain allusions to contemporary events, either expressly in their whole content or only incidentally, or, if similar allusive passages occur in older pieces, they are deliberately emphasized and received with the greatest enthusiasm.

(γ) As a third mode of this subjective outlook we may cite abstraction from all proper and genuine artistic content drawn from the past and the present, so that what is put before the public is merely its own casual subjectivity, i.e. the man in the street in his ordinary present activity and concerns. Thus this subjectivity then means nothing else but the characteristic mode of everyday consciousness in our prosaic life. In that, of course, everyone is at once at home; and only someone who approaches such a work with the demands of art cannot be at home in it, since art should precisely free us from this sort of subjectivity. Kotzebue,[1] e.g., has only had such a great effect in his day by such representations because 'our misery and distress, the pocketing of silver spoons, the risk of the pillory' and, further, 'parsons, trade councillors, lieutenants, secretaries, or majors of hussars'[2] were brought before the eyes and ears of the public, and now everyone was confronted with his own domesticity or with that of an acquaintance or relative, etc., or, in general, experienced where the shoe pinched in his own particular circumstances and special ends. Such subjectivity inherently fails to rise to the feeling and imagination of what constitutes the genuine content of the work of art, even if it can reduce interest in its subject-matters to the ordinary demands of the heart and to so-called moral commonplaces and reflections. In all these three

---

[1] A. F. F. Kotzebue, 1761–1819, dramatist. His murder resulted in the suppression of student clubs. See my note on pp. 299–300 of my translation of the *Philosophy of Right*.

[2] The quotations are not from Kotzebue but from Schiller's *Shakespeares Schatten*.

aspects the representation of external circumstances in a one-sided way is subjective and cannot do justice at all to their actual objective form.

(b) The second mode of interpretation, on the other hand, is the opposite of the first, in that it tries to reproduce the characters and events of the past so far as possible in their actual locality and in the particular characteristics of their customs and other external details. In this matter it is we Germans especially who have led the way. For, unlike the French, we are in general the most careful recorders of all that is peculiar to other nations, and therefore require in art also faithfulness to time, place, usages, clothes, weapons, etc. Neither have we any lack of patience in putting ourselves to the painful trouble of engaging in the scholarly study of the modes of thought and perception of foreign countries and of centuries long past, in order to be at home with their particular characters. And this interpretation and understanding of the spirit of other nations from each and every point of view makes us in art too not only tolerant of foreign oddities but even all too scrupulous in our demand for the most exact accuracy in such trivial external matters. True, the French appear likewise versatile and active, but, however supremely cultivated and practical they may be, they have all the less patience for calm and knowledgeable interpretation. With them the first thing is always to judge. We, on the other hand, especially in foreign works of art, allow the value of every faithful picture: exotic plants, products of nature, no matter from what realm, utensils of every kind and shape, dogs and cats, even disgusting objects, all are acceptable to us; and so we can make friends with the most foreign ways of looking at things, with sacrifices, legends of the saints and their numerous absurdities, as well as with other anomalous ideas. Thus what may seem to us to be the most important thing in the representation of characters in action is to make them come on the scene in their speech, costume, etc., for their own sake, and as they actually lived, in their mutual relation or opposition, in accordance with the character of their period or nation.

In recent times, especially since Friedrich von Schlegel's work, the idea has arisen that the objectivity of a work of art should be established by this sort of fidelity. It followed that objectivity had to be the chief consideration and that even our subjective interest had to be confined mainly to delight in this fidelity and its vivacity.

When such a demand is raised, what is expressed in it is that we should not bring with us any interest of a higher sort in regard to the essential basis of the represented material or any closer interest involved in our contemporary culture and purposes. It is very much in this way after all that in Germany, as a result of Herder's[1] instigation, attention began to be paid to folk-song again in a more general way, and all sorts and kinds of songs in the national style of peoples and tribes at a primitive stage of culture—Iroquois, modern Greek, Lappish, Turkish, Tartar, Mongolian, etc.—have been composed, and it was taken to be great genius to think oneself into foreign customs and the insights of foreign peoples, and make poetry entirely out of them. But even if the poet himself works his way completely into such foreign oddities and sympathizes with them, they can yet be only something outside the ken of the public which is supposed to enjoy them.

But, in general, if this view is maintained one-sidedly, it rests in the purely formal characteristic of historical exactitude and fidelity, because it abstracts from the subject-matter and its substantial importance, as well as from modern culture and the content of our present-day outlook and contemporary sentiment. Yet there should be no abstraction from either of these; both sides demand their equal satisfaction, and they have to bring into harmony with them the third demand, i.e. that for historical fidelity, in a totally different way from what we have seen hitherto. This brings us to a consideration of the true objectivity and subjectivity to which the work of art has to do justice.

(c) What can be said in general on this point consists primarily in this, that neither of the aspects considered just now may be emphasized one-sidedly at the expense and to the detriment of the other; but that purely historical exactitude in external matters, locality, morals, usages, institutions, constitute that subordinate part of the work of art, which must give way to the interest of a genuine content that even the culture of the present-day regards as imperishable.

In this matter we may likewise contrast in the true sort of representation the following relatively defective modes of treatment:

(α) First, the representation of the special features of a period

[1] J. G. von Herder, 1744–1803. See, e.g., 'Über Ossian und die Lieder alter Völker' in *Von deutscher Art und Kunst*, 1773.

may be entirely faithful, correct, vivid and intelligible throughout even to the modern public, yet without escaping from the ordinary language of prose and becoming poetic in itself. Goethe's *Götz von Berlichingen*, e.g., provides us here with striking samples. We only need to open the beginning which brings us into an inn at Schwarzenberg in Franconia:

> Metzler and Sievers [two Swabian peasants, leaders in the peasants' rebellion] at table; two grooms [from Bamberg] at the fire; inn-keeper:
> Sievers: Hänsel, another glass of brandy, and good Christian measure.
> Innkeeper: Thou never gettest thy fill.
> Metzler, *sotto voce* to Sievers: Tell that once again about Berlichingen. The Bambergers there are so angry that they are nearly black in the face.

The same sort of thing is in the third Act:

> Enter Georg with a rhone [a gutter taking rain from the roof]:
> There is lead for thee. If thou hittest with only half of it, no one will be able to tell His Majesty: 'Lord, we have come off badly'.
> Lerse (cuts off a bit): A fine bit.
> Georg: The rain may look for another way. I am not frightened for it. A brave knight and a proper rain never lack a path.
> Lerse pours [the lead]: Hold the gunner's ladle. (He goes to the window.) There's an imperial chap prowling around with a musket. They think we have shot our bolt. He shall have a taste of the bullet, warm from the pan. (He loads.)
> Georg puts the ladle down: Let me see.
> Lerse shoots: There lies the game.

All this is sketched most vividly and intelligibly in the character of the situation and the grooms, but nevertheless these scenes are extremely trivial and inherently prosaic since they take for content and form purely ordinary objective occurrences and their mode of appearance which of course is familiar to everybody. The same thing is found too in many of Goethe's other youthful productions which were directed especially against everything that previously counted as a rule, and they created their chief effect through the nearness into which they brought everything home to us owing to the maximum comprehensibility of the vision and feeling expressed. But the nearness was too great and the inner content of the material in part so slight that, just for this reason, they were trivial. This triviality we really notice above all, in the case of dramatic works, only during the play's performance because, so soon as we enter the theatre, numerous arrangements —the lights, elegantly dressed people—put us in the mood to want to find something other than two peasants, two grooms, and yet another glass of schnapps. *Götz*, after all, has had its special attraction for a reader; on the stage it has not been able to have a long run.

(β) On the other hand, the history of an earlier mythology, foreign historical political conditions and customs, may become familiar to us and assimilated, because, owing to the general culture of our time, we have acquired a varied acquaintance with the past too. For example, acquaintance with the art and mythology, the literature, the religion, the customs, of antiquity is the starting-point of our education today; from his schooldays every boy knows about Greek gods, heroes, and historical characters; therefore, because the figures and interests of the Greek world have become ours in imagination, we can take pleasure in them too on the ground of imagination, and there is no saying why we should not be able to get so far with Indian or Egyptian or Scandinavian mythology too. Besides, in the religious ideas of these peoples the universal element, God, is present too. But the specific element, the *particular* Greek or Indian divinities have no longer any *truth* for us; we no longer believe in them and they give us pleasure only for our imagination. But therefore they always remain foreign to our real deeper consciousness, and nothing is so empty and cold as when in opera we hear, e.g., 'O ye gods' or 'O Jupiter' or even 'O Isis and Osiris',[1] not to speak of the addition of wretched oracular utterances—and seldom does an opera get along without an oracle —nowadays replaced in tragedy by insanity and clairvoyance.

It is just the same with other historical material—customs, laws, etc. True, this historical material *is*, but it *has been*, and if it has no longer any connection with our contemporary life, it is not *ours*, no matter how well and how precisely we know it; but our interest in what is over and done with does not arise from the pure and simple reason that it did once exist as present. History is only ours when it belongs to the nation to which we belong, or when we can look on the present in general as a consequence of a chain of events in which the characters or deeds represented form an essential link. After all, the mere connection with the same land

[1] Sarastro's first aria in *The Magic Flute* (1791).

and people as ours does not suffice in the last resort; the past even of one's own people must stand in closer connection with our present situation, life, and existence.

In the *Nibelungenlied*, for example, we are geographically on our own soil, but the Burgundians and King Etzel[1] are so cut off from all the features of our present culture and its national interests that, even without erudition, we can find ourselves far more at home with the Homeric poems. So Klopstock[2] has been induced by a patriotic urge to substitute Scandinavian gods for Greek mythology; but Wotan, Valhalla, and Freya have remained mere names which belong less to our imagination than Jupiter and Olympus, and they speak less to our heart.

In this connection we must make clear that works of art are not to be composed for study or for the learned, but must be immediately intelligible and enjoyable in themselves without this circuitous route of far-fetched and far-off facts. For art does not exist for a small enclosed circle of a few eminent *savants* but for the nation at large and as a whole. But what is valid for the work of art as such is equally applicable to the external aspect of the historical reality there represented. We too belong to our time and our people, and this reality must be clear and apprehensible for us without wide learning, so that we can become at home in it and are not compelled to remain confronted by it as by a foreign and unintelligible world.

(γ) Now in this way we have approached the true artistic mode of portraying objectivity and assimilating materials drawn from past epochs.

(αα) The first point that we may adduce here affects the genuine national poetry which, amongst all peoples, has, from time immemorial, been of such a kind that its external, historical, side has of itself belonged already to the nation and not remained foreign to it. This is the case with the Indian epics, the Homeric poems, and the dramatic poetry of the Greeks. Sophocles did not allow Philoctetes, Antigone, Ajax, Orestes, Oedipus, and his choragi and choruses to speak as they would have done in their own day. The same sort of thing is true of the Spanish in their romances of the Cid; Tasso in his *Jerusalem Delivered* chanted the universal cause of Catholic Christianity; Camoens, the Portuguese poet, depicted

---

[1] i.e. Attila, King of the Huns, resident in Vienna at the time of the poem.
[2] F. G. Klopstock, 1724–1803. The reference is to his *Odes*.

the discovery of the sea-route to the East Indies round the Cape of Good Hope and the infinitely important deeds of the heroic seamen, and these deeds were those of his nation; Shakespeare dramatized the tragic history of his country, and Voltaire himself wrote his *Henriade*. Even we Germans have at last got away from the attempt to work up into national epic poems remote stories which no longer have any national interest for us. Bodmer's *Noachide*[1] and Klopstock's *Messiah* are out of fashion, just as, after all, there is no longer any validity in the view that the honour of a nation requires it to have its Homer, and, into the bargain, its Pindar, Sophocles, and Anacreon. Those Bible stories[2] do come nearer to our imagination because of our familiarity with the Old and New Testaments, but the historical element in these obsolete modes of life still always remains for us an alien affair of erudition; actually it confronts us as merely the familiar element in the prosaic threads of events and characters which, in the process of composition, are only thrust into a new phraseology, so that in this respect we get nothing but the feeling of something purely artificial.

(ββ) But art cannot restrict itself to native material alone. In fact, the more that particular peoples have come into contact with one another, by so much the more has art continually drawn its subject-matter from all nations and centuries. Nevertheless, it is not to be regarded as a mark of great genius, as may be supposed, when the poet wholly familiarizes himself with periods not his own. On the contrary, the historical aspect must be so put on one side in the representation that it becomes only an insignificant accessory to what is human and universal. In such a way, the Middle Ages, e.g., did borrow material from antiquity, but they introduced into it the contents of their own epoch, and it is true that they went to the opposite extreme and left nothing over [from the past] but the mere names of Alexander, or Aeneas, or Octavian, the Emperor [Augustus].

The most fundamental thing is and remains immediate-intelligibility; and actually all nations have insisted on what was to please them in a work of art, for they wanted to be at home in it, living and present in it. Calderón dramatized his Zenobia and Semiramis within this independent nationality, and Shakespeare understood how to imprint an English national character on the

---

[1] J. J. Bodmer, 1698–1783. His biblical epic, *Noah*, appeared in 1750.
[2] i.e. in Bodmer and Klopstock.

most variegated materials, although, far more deeply than the Spaniards, he could preserve in its essential basic traits the historical character of foreign nations, e.g. the Romans. Even the Greek tragedians had their eye on the contemporary character of their time and the city to which they belonged. Oedipus at Colonus, e.g., has not only a closer relation to Athens because Colonus is near Athens but also for the reason that, dying at Colonus, Oedipus was to be a safeguard for Athens. In other connections the *Eumenides* of Aeschylus too has a closer domestic interest for the Athenians owing to the judgement of the Areopagus. On the other hand, despite the numerous ways in which it has been used, and always anew since the Renaissance of arts and sciences, Greek mythology will not be perfectly at home amongst modern peoples, and it has remained cold more or less even in the visual arts, and still more in poetry, despite poetry's wide scope. For example, it would not now occur to anyone to make a poem to Venus or Jupiter or Athene. Sculpture indeed cannot yet ever subsist without the Greek gods, but its productions are therefore for the most part accessible and intelligible only to connoisseurs, scholars, and the narrow circle of the most cultivated people. In a similar sense, Goethe has given himself a great deal of trouble[1] to explain to painters, and to bring closer to their warm consideration and imitation, the *Eikones*[2] of Philostratus, but he had little success; ancient subjects of that kind in their ancient present and actuality remain always something foreign to the modern public, as to the painters too. On the other hand, in a far deeper spirit Goethe has succeeded, in the later years of his free inner inspiration, in bringing the East into our contemporary poetry by his *West-östliche Divan* [1819] and assimilating it to our contemporary vision. In this assimilation he has known perfectly well that he is a westerner and a German, and so, while striking throughout the eastern keynote in respect of the oriental character of situations and affairs, at the same time he has given its fullest due to our contemporary consciousness and its own individuality. In this way the artist is of course allowed to borrow his materials from distant climes, past ages, and foreign peoples, and even by and large to preserve the

[1] In his essay *Philostrats Gemälde* (1818).
[2] Two sets of descriptions in prose of pictures which the author purports to have seen. There was more than one Philostratus. This one may have flourished about A.D. 210.

historical form of their mythology, customs, and institutions; but at the same time he must use these forms only as frames for his pictures, while on the other hand their inner meaning he must adapt to the essential deeper consciousness of his contemporary world in a way in which the most marvellous example hitherto is always there before us in Goethe's *Iphigenie*.

In relation to such a transformation the individual arts once again have a different position. Lyric, e.g., requires in love songs the minimum of external, historical surroundings sketched with precision, since for it the chief thing is feeling, the movement of the heart. Of Laura herself, e.g., in Petrarch's Sonnets, we have in this respect only very little information, hardly more than the name, which could equally well be another; of the locality, etc., we are told only in the most general terms—the fountain of Vaucluse, and the like. Epic, on the other hand, demands the maximum of detail, which, if only it is clear and intelligible, most readily gives us pleasure, after all, in the matter of those external historical facts. But these externalities are the most dangerous reef for dramatic art, especially in theatrical performances where everything is spoken to us directly or comes in a lively way before our perception and vision, so that we are ready at once to find ourselves acquainted and familiar with what is there. Therefore here the representation of historical external actuality must remain as subordinate as possible and a mere frame; there must, as it were, be retained the same relation which we find in love poems where, even though we can completely sympathize with the feelings expressed and the manner of their expression, the name of the beloved is not that of our own beloved. Here it does not matter at all if pedants deplore the inaccuracy of manners, feelings, level of culture. In Shakespeare's historical pieces, e.g., there is plenty which remains strange to us and can be of little interest. In reading them we are satisfied indeed, but not in the theatre. Critics and connoisseurs think of course that such historical splendours should be represented on their own account, and then they vituperate about the bad and corrupt taste of the public if it makes known its boredom with such things; but the work of art and its immediate enjoyment is not for connoisseurs and pedants but for the public, and the critics need not ride the high horse; after all, they too belong to the same public and they themselves can take no *serious* interest in the exactitude of historical details. Knowing this, the English, e.g., nowadays produce on the stage only those scenes from Shakespeare which are absolutely excellent and self-explanatory, for they have not got the pedantry of our aesthetic experts who insist that all these now strange external circumstances in which the public can no longer take any part should nevertheless be brought before its eyes. Therefore, if foreign dramatic works are staged, every people has the right to ask for remodellings. Even the most excellent piece *requires* remodelling from this point of view. It could of course be said that what is really excellent must be excellent for all time, but the work of art has also a temporal, perishable side, and this it is which requires alteration. For the beautiful appears for others, and those for whom it has been brought into appearance must be able to be at home in this external side of its appearance.

Now in this assimilation of historical material we find the basis and exculpation of everything which has customarily been called *anachronism* in art, and has generally been reckoned a great defect in artists. Anachronisms occur primarily in merely external things. If Falstaff, e.g., talks of pistols,[1] this is a matter of indifference. It is worse when Orpheus stands there[2] with a violin in his hand because the contradiction appears all too sharply between mythical days and such a modern instrument, which everyone knows had not been invented at so early a period. Therefore nowadays astonishing care is taken in the theatre with such things, and the producers have kept carefully to historical truth in costume and scenery—as e.g. a great deal of trouble has been taken in this matter with the procession in the *Maid of Orleans*,[3] a trouble in most cases just wasted, because it concerns only what is relative and unimportant.

The more important kind of anachronism does not consist in dress and other similar externals, but in the fact that in a work of art the characters, in their manner of speech, the expression of their feelings and ideas, the reflections they advance, their accomplishments, could not possibly be in conformity with the period, level of civilization, religion, and view of the world which they are representing. To this kind of anachronism the category of naturalness is usually applied, and the view is that it is unnatural if the characters represented do not speak and act as they would have

---

[1] e.g. *1 Henry IV*, Act v, scene iii.
[2] Presumably in Gluck's opera, *Orfeo*, 1762.　　　　[3] Schiller's play, 1802.

I. THE IDEA OF ARTISTIC BEAUTY

acted and spoken in the period they are representing. But the demand for such naturalness, if it be maintained one-sidedly, leads at once to perversities. For when the artist sketches the human heart with its emotions and its inherently substantial passions, he should still, while always preserving individuality, not so sketch them as they occur in the ordinary daily life of today, for he ought to bring every 'pathos' to light in an appearance which absolutely corresponds with it. He is alone an artist because he knows what is true and brings it in its true form before our contemplation and feeling. Therefore, to express this, he has to take into account in each case the culture of his time, its speech, etc. At the time of the Trojan war the kind of expression and the whole mode of life had a level of development quite different from what we find in the Iliad. Similarly the mass of the people and the preeminent figures in the Greek royal families did not have that polished sort of outlook and speech which we have to marvel at in Aeschylus or in the perfect beauty of Sophocles. Such a transgression of so-called naturalness is, for art, a *necessary* anachronism. The inner substance of what is represented remains the same, but the development of culture makes necessary a metamorphosis in its expression and form. True, it is a quite different matter if insights and ideas of a *later* development of the religious and moral consciousness are carried over into a period or nation whose whole earlier outlook contradicts such newer ideas. Thus the Christian religion brought in its train moral categories which were foreign throughout to the Greeks. For example, the inner reflection of conscience in deciding what is good or bad, remorse, and penitence belong only to the moral development of modern times; the heroic character knows nothing of the illogicality of penitence —what he has done, he has done. Orestes[1] has no penitence for his mother's murder; the Furies arising from his deed do pursue him, but the Eumenides are at the same time represented as universal powers and not as the gnawing of his purely subjective conscience. This essential kernel of a period and a people must be within the poet's ken, and only if he inserts into this innermost central core something opposite and contradictory is he guilty of an anachronism of a higher kind. In this respect, that is, the artist must be required to familiarize himself with the spirit of past ages

---

[1] Here the reference again is to the *Oresteia*, the trilogy of Aeschylus. But see above, p. 227, note, and the relevant passage.

and foreign peoples; for this substantial element, if it is of a genuine sort, remains clear to all ages; but to propose to reproduce with complete accuracy of detail the purely external appearance of the rust of antiquity is only a puerile pedantry undertaken for what is itself only an external end. Of course, even in this matter, a general exactitude is to be desired, but it must not be robbed of its right to hover between *Dichtung und Wahrheit.*[1]

(γγ) All this said, we have now penetrated to the true mode of appropriating what is strange and external in a past period, and to the true objectivity of the work of art. The work of art must disclose to us the higher interests of our spirit and will, what is in itself human and powerful, the true depths of the heart. The chief thing essentially at issue is that these things shall gleam through all external appearances and that their keynote shall resound through all other things in our restless life. Thus true objectivity unveils for us the 'pathos', the substantive content of a situation, and the rich, powerful individuality in which the fundamental factors of the spirit are alive and brought to reality and expression. In that case for such material there can in general be required only a determinate reality, something appropriately and intelligibly circumscribed. When such material is found and unfolded in conformity with the principle of the Ideal, a work of art is absolutely objective, whether the external details are historically accurate or not. In that event the work of art speaks to our true self and becomes our own property. For even if the material with its superficial form is taken from ages past long, long ago, its abiding basis is that human element of the spirit which as such is what truly abides and is powerful, and its effect can never fail, since *this* objective basis constitutes the content and fulfilment of our own inner life. On the other hand, the purely historical external material is the transient side, and to this, in the case of works of art lying far away from us, we must try to reconcile ourselves, and we must be able to disregard it even in works of art of our own time. So the Psalms of David with their brilliant celebration of the Lord in the goodness and wrath of his omnipotence, like the deep grief of the Prophets, is appropriate and still present to us today, in spite of Babylon and Zion, and even a moral theme like what Sarastro sings in the *Magic Flute* will

---

[1] *Poetry and Truth*, the title of Goethe's autobiography (1811).

give pleasure to everyone, Egyptians included, because of the inner kernel and spirit of its melodies.

Confronted with such objectivity in a work of art, the individual must therefore give up the false demand of wishing to have himself before him in it with his purely subjective characteristics and idiosyncrasies. When *Wilhelm Tell*[1] was first produced in Weimar, not a single Swiss was satisfied with it; similarly, many a man seeks in vain in the most beautiful love-songs for his own feelings and therefore declares that the description is false, just as others, whose knowledge of love is drawn from romances alone, do not now suppose themselves to be actually in love until they encounter in and around themselves the very same feelings and situations [as those described in the romances].

C. THE ARTIST

In this First Part we have treated *first* the general *Idea* of the beautiful, *secondly* its inadequate existence in nature, in order to press on, *thirdly*, to the Ideal as the adequate actuality of the beautiful. The Ideal we developed *first*, once again in accordance with its *general* nature, which led us, *secondly*, to the *specific* mode of representing it. But since the work of art springs from the spirit, it needs a subjective productive activity as its cause, and as a product thereof it is there for others, i.e. for the contemplation and feeling of the public. This activity is the imagination of the artist. Therefore we have now still, in conclusion, to deal with the *third* aspect of the Ideal, i.e. to discuss how the work of art belongs to the subjective inner consciousness, though as its product it is not yet *born* into actuality, but is shaped only by creative subjectivity, by the genius and talent of the artist. Yet strictly we need to mention this aspect only to say of it that it is to be excluded from the area of scientific discussion, or at least that it permits of a few generalities only—although a question often raised is: whence does the artist derive his gift and his ability to conceive and execute his work, how does he create a work of art? We might just as well ask for a recipe or prescription for managing this, or for the circumstances and situations in which a man must place himself in order to produce the like. Thus [Ippolito] Cardinal d'Este asked Ariosto about his *Orlando Furioso*: 'Master Ludovico, where have you got

---

[1] Schiller's play, 1804.

all this damned stuff from?' Raphael, asked a similar question, answered in a well-known letter[1] that he was striving after a certain *'idea'*.

The finer details we can treat under three heads, since *first*, we establish the Concept of artistic genius and inspiration, *secondly*, we discuss the objectivity of this creative activity, and *thirdly*, we try to discover the character of true originality.

1. *Imagination (Phantasie), Genius, and Inspiration*

When a question is asked about 'genius', more precise definition is at once required, because 'genius' is an entirely general expression used not only of artists but of great kings and military commanders, as well as of the heroes of science. Here once again we may distinguish three aspects for the sake of greater precision.

(*a*) First, when we come to the general capacity for artistic production, then, as soon as there is talk of 'capacity', 'fancy' (*Phantasie*) is said to be the most prominent artistic ability. Yet in that case we must immediately take care not to confuse fancy with the purely passive imagination (*Einbildungskraft*). Fancy is creative.[2]

(α) Now in the *first* place this creative activity involves the gift and the sense for grasping reality and its configurations which, attentively heard or seen, impress on the spirit the greatest multiplicity of pictures of what is *there*; this activity also presupposes a retentive memory of the variegated world of these manifold pictures. In this respect, therefore, the artist is not relegated to what he has manufactured by his own imagination but has to abandon the superficial 'ideal' (so-called) and enter reality itself. To embark on art and poetry with an ideal is always very suspect, for the artist has to create out of the abundance of life and not out of the abundance of abstract generalities, since, while the medium of philosophy's production is thought, art's is actual external configurations. Therefore the artist must live and become at home in this medium. He must have seen much, heard much, and retained much, just as in general great individuals are almost always signalized by a great memory. For what interests a man he engraves

---

[1] to Baldassare Castiglione. He was asked where he had found such a beautiful model for his Galatea.

[2] For the terminology used in this paragraph and not elsewhere, see p. 5, note 2.

on his memory, and a most profound spirit spreads the field of his interests over countless topics. Goethe, e.g., began like this and throughout his life has widened more and more the scope of his observations. This gift and this interest in a specific grasp of the actual world in its real shape, together with a firm retention of what has been seen, is thus the *first* requirement of an artist. On the other hand, bound up with precise knowledge of the external form there must be equal familiarity with man's inner life, with the passions of his heart, and all the aims of the human soul. To this double knowledge there must be added an acquaintance with the way in which the inner life of the spirit expresses itself in the real world and shines through the externality thereof.

(β) But *secondly* imagination does not stop at this mere assimilation of external and internal reality, because what the ideal work of art properly provides is not only the appearance of the inner spirit in the *reality* of external forms; on the contrary, it is the absolute truth and rationality of the *actual* world which should attain external appearance. This rationality of the specific topic he has chosen must not only be present in the artist's consciousness and move him; on the contrary, he must have pondered its essentiality and truth in its whole range and whole depth. For without reflection a man does not bring home to his mind what is in him, and so we notice in every great work of art that its material in all its aspects has been long and deeply weighed and thought over. From the facile readiness of fancy no solid work proceeds. Yet this is not to say that the artist must grasp in a *philosophical* form the true essence of all things which is the general foundation in religion, as well as in philosophy and art. For him philosophy is not necessary, and if he thinks in a philosophical manner he is working at an enterprise which, so far as the form of knowing is concerned, is the precise opposite of art. For the task of imagination consists solely in giving us a consciousness of that inner rationality, not in the form of general propositions and ideas, but in concrete configuration and individual reality. What therefore lives and ferments in him the artist must portray to himself in the forms and appearances whose likeness and shape he has adopted, since he can so subdue them to his purpose that they now on their side too become capable of adopting what is inherently true and expressing it completely.

In order to achieve the interpenetration of the rational content and the external shape, the artist has to call in aid (i) the watchful circumspection of the intellect, and (ii) the depth of the heart and its animating feelings. It is therefore an absurdity to suppose that poems like the Homeric came to the poet in sleep. Without circumspection, discrimination, and criticism the artist cannot master any subject-matter which he is to configurate, and it is silly to believe that the genuine artist does not know what he is doing. Equally necessary for him is a concentration of his emotional life.

(γ) Through this feeling, I mean, which penetrates and animates the whole, the artist has his material and its configuration as his very own self, as the inmost property of himself as a subjective being. For the pictorial illustration estranges every subject-matter by giving it an external form, and feeling alone brings it into subjective unity with the inner self. In accord with this point of view, the artist must not only have looked around at much in the world and made himself acquainted with its outer and inner manifestations, but he must have drawn much, and much that is great, into his own soul; his heart must have been deeply gripped and moved thereby; he must have done and lived through much before he can develop the true depths of life into concrete manifestations. Consequently genius does burst forth in youth, as was the case with Goethe and Schiller, but only middle or old age can bring to perfection the genuine maturity of the work of art.[1]

(b) Now this productive activity of imagination whereby the artist takes what is absolutely rational in itself and works it out, as his very own creation, by giving it an external form, is what is called genius, talent, etc.

(α) The elements of genius we have therefore already considered just now. Genius is the *general* ability for the true production of a work of art, as well as the energy to elaborate and complete it. But, even so, this capacity and energy exists only as subjective, since spiritual production is possible only for a self-conscious subject who makes such creation his aim. However, it has been common for people to go into more detail and make a specific difference between 'genius' and 'talent'. And in fact the two are not immediately identical, although their identity is necessary for

[1] One of Hegel's more hazardous generalizations—Mozart, Keats, etc., come to mind.

perfect artistic creation. Art, I mean, in so far as in general it individualizes and has to issue in the objective appearance of its productions, now demands also for the particular kinds of this accomplishment different particular capacities. One such may be described as talent, as, e.g., when one man may have a talent for perfect violin-playing and another for singing, and so on. But a mere talent can only attain to excellence in one such entirely separate side of art, and, if it is to be perfect in itself, it still requires always over again the capacity for art in general, and the inspiration, which genius alone confers. Talent without genius therefore does not get far beyond an external skill.

(β) Now further, it is commonly said, talent and genius must be innate. Here too this is right enough in a way, although in another it is equally false. For man as man is also born to religion, e.g., to thinking, to science, i.e. as man he has the capacity to acquire a consciousness of God and to come to intellectual reflection. Nothing is needed for this but birth as such and education, training, and industry. With art the thing is different; it requires a *specific* aptitude, in which a natural element plays an essential part too. Just as beauty itself is the Idea made real in the sensuous and actual world, and the work of art takes what is spiritual and sets it out into the immediacy of existence for apprehension by eye and ear, so too the artist must fashion his work not in the exclusively spiritual form of thought but within the sphere of intuition and feeling and, more precisely, in connection with sensuous material and in a sensuous medium. Therefore this artistic creation, like art throughout, includes in itself the aspect of immediacy and naturalness, and this aspect it is which the subject cannot generate in himself but must find in himself as immediately given. This alone is the sense in which we may say that genius and talent must be inborn.[1]

Similarly the different arts too are more or less national, connected with the natural side of a people. The Italians, e.g., have song and melody almost by nature, while although the cultivation of music and opera has been urgently pursued with great success amongst northern peoples, they have no more been completely at home there than orange trees. What the Greeks have as their

---

[1] With this remark compare: 'Anyone can make verses like F. von Schlegel, but to get beyond this and produce real art needs an inborn talent' (Lasson, p. 69).

own is the most beautiful elaboration of epic poetry and, above all, the perfection of sculpture, whereas the Romans had no really independent art but had to transplant it from Greece on to their own soil. Therefore the art most universally spread is poetry because in it the sensuous material and its formation makes the fewest demands. Yet, within poetry, folk-song is in the highest degree national and tied up with the natural side of a people's life, and on this account folk-song belongs to periods of lesser spiritual development and preserves to the maximum the simplicity of a natural existence. Goethe has produced works of art in all forms and sorts of poetry, but it is his earliest songs which are the most intimate and unpremeditated. In them there is the minimum of cultural elaboration. Modern Greeks, e.g., are even now a people of poetry and songs. Bravery of today or yesterday, a death and its particular circumstances, a burial, every adventure, every single oppression by the Turks—each and every episode they bring at once into song; and there are plenty of examples that often, on the day of the battle, songs are sung at once about the newly-won victory. Fauriel has published a collection of modern Greek songs,[1] taken partly from the lips of women, nurses, and schoolgirls, who could not be more surprised that he was astonished by their songs.

In this way art and its specific mode of production hangs together with the specific nationality of peoples. Thus improvisers are especially at home in Italy and their talent is marvellous. Even today an Italian improvises dramas in five acts, and nothing there is memorized; everything springs from his knowledge of human passions and situations and from deep immediate inspiration. An impecunious improviser, after poetizing for a long time, at last went round with a miserable hat to collect from the audience; but he was still so full of enthusiasm and fever that he could not stop declaiming, and he gesticulated so long, waving his arms and hands, that at the end all his beggings were scattered.

(γ) Now the *third* characteristic of genius, for all that genius does include a natural gift as one of its elements, is facility in producing ideas from within and in the external technical dexterity required in the several arts. In this connection a lot is talked, for example in the case of a poet, about the fetters of metre and rhyme,

---

[1] C. Fauriel, 1772–1844: *Chants populaires de Grèce moderne*, 1824–5. In 1827 Hegel met him at dinner in Paris.

or, in the case of a painter, about the manifold difficulties which draughtsmanship, knowledge of colours, light and shade, put in the way of invention and execution. Of course all the arts require lengthy study, constant industry, a skill developed in many ways; but the greater and more abundant the talent and genius, the less it knows of laboriousness in the acquisition of the skills necessary for production. For the genuine artist has a *natural* impulse and an immediate need to give form at once to everything that he feels and imagines. This process of formation is *his* way of feeling and seeing, and he finds it in himself without labour as the instrument proper and suited to him. A composer, e.g., can declare only in melodies what moves and stirs him most deeply. What he feels, immediately becomes melody, just as to a painter it becomes form and colour, or to a poet the poetry of the imagination, clothing its structure in euphonious words. And this gift for formation the artist does not possess merely as *theoretical* idea, imagination, and feeling, but also immediately as *practical* feeling, i.e., as a gift for actual execution. Both are bound together in the genuine artist. What lives in his imagination comes to him, therefore, as it were to his finger-tips, just as it comes to our lips to speak out our thoughts, or as our inmost thoughts, ideas, and feelings appear directly on ourselves in our posture and gestures. From time immemorial the true genius has easily mastered the external side of technical execution, and has also so far mastered the poorest and apparently most intractable material that it has been compelled to assimilate and display the inner shapes devised by imagination. What in this way lies in him immediately, the artist must indeed work over until his proficiency with it is complete, but yet the possibility of immediate execution must all the same be there in him as a natural gift; otherwise a purely learnt proficiency never produces a living work of art. Both sides, the inner production and its external realization, go hand in hand in accordance with the essential nature of art.

(*c*) Now the activity of imagination and technical execution, considered in itself as the fundamental condition of the artist, is what is generally called, in the *third* place, 'inspiration'.

(α) In this matter the first question raised is about the manner of its origin, in regard to which the most varied ideas are in circulation:

(αα) Since genius in general involves the closest connection between the spiritual and the natural, it has been believed that inspiration can be produced primarily through *sensuous* stimulus. But the heat of the blood achieves nothing by itself; champagne produces no poetry, as Marmontel, e.g., tells how in a cellar in Champagne he had six thousand bottles confronting him and yet nothing poetic flowed out of them for him.[1] So too the finest genius may often enough lie on the grass morning and evening, enjoying a fresh breeze and gazing up into the sky, but of tender inspiration not a breath reaches him.

(ββ) On the other hand, neither can inspiration be summoned by a spiritual *intention* to produce. A man who simply resolves to be inspired in order to write a poem, paint a picture, or compose a tune, without already carrying in himself some theme as a living stimulus and must just hunt around here and there for some material, then, no matter what his talent, cannot, on the strength of this mere intention, form a beautiful conception or produce a solid work of art. Neither a purely sensuous stimulus nor mere will and decision procures genuine inspiration, and to make use of such means proves only that the heart and the imagination have not yet fastened on any true interest. But if the artistic urge is of the right kind, this interest has already in advance been concentrated on a specific object and theme and kept firmly to it.

(γγ) Thus true inspiration takes fire on some specific material which the imagination seizes with a view to expressing it artistically; moreover inspiration is the state of the artist in his active process of forming both his subjective inner conception and his objective execution of the work of art, because for this double activity inspiration is necessary. Thus the question is raised again: In what way must such a material come to the artist? In this connection too there are all sorts of views. How often have we not heard the demand that the artist shall create his material solely out of his own self! Of course this can be the case when, e.g., the poet 'sings like the bird that dwells in the bough'.[2] His own joy is then the incentive which from within can offer itself at the same time as material and theme for external expression, since it drives him on to the artistic enjoyment of his own cheerfulness. In that case

---

[1] In book ii of his memoirs, Marmontel says that his imagination was warmed when he was in congenial feminine company and surrounded by 50,000 bottles of champagne. He does not say whether he was influenced by them or by the lady. Hegel's remark may be a confused recollection of this passage.

[2] This quotation and the next are from Goethe's ballad *Der Sänger*, 1783.

too is 'the song which comes straight from the heart a reward which rewards richly'. Yet, on the other side, the greatest works of art have often owed their creation to some quite external stimulus. Pindar's *Odes*, e.g., were frequently commissioned; similarly the aim of buildings and the subject of paintings has countless times been prescribed to artists, who yet have been able to acquire the necessary inspiration for executing their commission. Indeed there is even frequently noticeable a complaint of artists that they lack topics on which they could work. Such external material and the impulse it gives to production is here the factor of the natural and the immediate which belongs to the essence of talent and which therefore has likewise to raise its head in connection with the beginning of inspiration. From this point of view, the sort of position that the artist is in is that he enters, with a *natural* talent, into relation with an available *given* material; he finds himself solicited by an external incentive, by an event (or, as in Shakespeare's case for example, by sagas, old ballads, tales, chronicles), to give form to this material and to express himself in general on *that*. Thus the occasion for production may come entirely from without, and the one important requirement is just that the artist shall lay hold of an essential interest and make the subject-matter become alive in itself. In that event the inspiration of genius arises automatically. And a genuinely living artist finds precisely through this aliveness a thousand occasions for his activity and inspiration—occasions which others pass by without being touched by them.

(β) If we ask further wherein artistic inspiration consists, it is nothing but being completely filled with the theme, being entirely present in the theme, and not resting until the theme has been stamped and polished into artistic shape.

(γ) But if the artist has made the subject-matter into something entirely his own, he must on the other hand be able to forget his own personality and its accidental particular characteristics and immerse himself, for his part, entirely in his material, so that, as subject, he is only as it were the form for the formation of the theme which has taken hold of him. An inspiration in which the subject gives himself airs and emphasizes himself as subject, instead of being the instrument and the living activation of the theme itself, is a poor inspiration.—This point brings us on to the so-called 'objectivity' of artistic productions.

2. Objectivity of the Representation

(a) In the ordinary sense of the word, 'objectivity' is taken to mean that in the work of art every subject-matter must assume the form of an otherwise already existent reality and confront us in this familiar external shape. If we wanted to be content with objectivity of that kind, then we could call even Kotzebue an 'objective' poet. In his case it is commonplace reality that we find over and over again throughout. But the aim of art is precisely to strip off the matter of everyday life and its mode of appearance, and by spiritual activity from within bring out only what is absolutely rational and give to it its true external configuration. Therefore the artist should not make straight for purely external reality if the full substance of the subject-matter is not there. For although the treatment of what is otherwise already there may indeed rise to be in itself of supreme vitality, and, as we saw earlier in some examples from Goethe's youthful works, may exercise great attraction on the strength of its inner animation, nevertheless if it lacks genuine substance, then it cannot reach the true beauty of art.

(b) Therefore a second type of art does not aim at the external as such; on the contrary, the artist has seized his theme with the deep inwardness of his heart. But this inwardness remains so very reserved and concentrated that it cannot struggle out to conscious clarity and reach true deployment. The eloquence of the 'pathos' is restricted to indicating and alluding to the 'pathos' through external phenomena with which it is in harmony, without having the strength and cultivation to develop the full nature of what the 'pathos' contains. Folk-songs in particular belong to this manner of representation. Externally simple, they point to a wider deep feeling which lies at their roots, but which cannot be clearly expressed; for at this stage art itself has not developed so far as to bring its content to light openly and transparently and must be satisfied by means of externals to make the content guessable by the mind's foreboding. The heart is driven and pressed in upon itself, and, in order to be intelligible to itself, is mirrored only in purely finite external circumstances and phenomena, which of course are expressive, even if their echo in mind and feeling is only quite slight. Even Goethe has produced extremely excellent songs in this manner. The *Shepherd's Lament*, e.g., is one of the most beautiful of this kind: the heart broken with grief and longing is dumb and reserved, making itself known in plain external traits, and yet the most concentrated depth of feeling resounds throughout, though unexpressed. In the *Erl-King* and in so many others the same tone prevails. Nevertheless this tone may sink to the barbarism of an obtuseness which does not bring the essence of the thing and the situation into consciousness, and which simply stops at externals, partly crude, partly tasteless. As, e.g., praise has been given, on the ground that they are extremely touching, to the words of the drummer in *The Boy's Magic Horn*:[1] 'O gallows, thou noble house' or 'Adieu, corporal'. When, on the other hand, Goethe sings: 'The nosegay I have plucked, may it greet thee many thousand times, I have often bowed before it, och! a thousand times, and I have pressed it to my heart how many thousands of times',[2] here the depth of feeling is indicated in a quite different way which brings before our eyes nothing trivial or in itself repugnant. But what in general this whole sort of objectivity lacks is the actual clear manifestation of feeling and passion which in genuine art should not remain in that reserved profundity which only resounds weakly through the external; on the contrary, feeling must completely either disclose itself on its own account or shine clearly and thoroughly through the external material in which it has enshrined itself. Schiller, e.g., is present with his whole soul in his 'pathos', but with a great soul which familiarizes itself with the essence of the thing in hand, the depths of which it can at the same time express most freely and brilliantly in the fullness of the wealth and harmony [of his verse].

(*c*) In this connection, keeping to the essential nature of the Ideal, we may affirm as follows what true objectivity is, even here as regards subjective expression: from the genuine subject-matter which inspires the artist, nothing is to be held back in his subjective inner heart; everything must be completely unfolded and indeed in a way in which the universal soul and substance of the chosen subject-matter appears emphasized just as much as its individual configuration appears completely polished in itself and permeated by that soul and substance in accord with the whole representation. For what is supreme and most excellent is not, as

---

[1] A collection of folk-songs made by L. J. von Arnim and C. Brentano, published 1805–8. The drummer has been condemned to death, and he speaks to his former companions as he is being led out of prison to the place of execution.
[2] This is from the poem *Blumengruss*, c. 1810.

may be supposed, the inexpressible[1]—for if so the poet would be still far deeper than his work discloses. On the contrary, his works are the best part and the truth of the artist; what he is [in his works], that he *is*; but what remains buried in his heart, that *is* he not.

3. Manner, Style, and Originality

But however far an objectivity in the sense indicated just now must be demanded of the artist, his production is nevertheless the work of *his* inspiration. For, as subject, he has entirely identified himself with his topic, and fashioned its embodiment in art out of the inner life of *his* heart and *his* imagination. This identity of the artist subjectively with the true objectivity of his production is the third chief point which we still have to consider briefly, because in this identity we see united what hitherto we have separated as genius and objectivity. We can describe this unity as the essence of genuine originality.

Yet before we push on to give body to this conception, we have still to keep in view two points, and their one-sidedness is to be superseded if true originality is to be able to appear. These are (*a*) subjective manner, and (*b*) style.

(*a*) Mere manner [i.e. mannerism] must be essentially distinguished from originality. For manner concerns the particular and therefore accidental idiosyncrasies of the artist, and these, instead of the topic itself and its ideal representation, come out and assert themselves in the production of the work of art.

(α) Manner, then, in this sense [of mannerism] does not concern the general kinds of art which in and for themselves require different modes of representation, as, e.g., the landscape painter has to view his subjects in a way different from that of the historical painter, the epic poet differently from the lyric or dramatic one; on the contrary, 'manner' is a conception appropriate only to *this* personality and the accidental idiosyncrasy of his accomplishment, and this may go so far as to be in direct contradiction with the true nature of the Ideal. Looked at in this way, manner is the worst thing to which the artist can submit because in it he indulges simply in his own restricted and personal whims. But art as such cancels the mere accidentality of the topic as well as of its external

---

[1] This is a hit at F. von Schlegel who had maintained the contrary in his *Prosaische Jugendschriften* (ed. by Minor), vol. ii, p. 364.

appearance and therefore demands of the artist that he shall extinguish in himself the accidental particular characteristics of his own subjective idiosyncrasy.

(β) Therefore, secondly, manner after all may perhaps not be directly opposed to the true artistic representation, but its sphere is confined rather to the external aspects of the work of art. In the main it has its place in painting and music, because these arts provide for treatment and execution the widest scope for external matters. A special mode of representation belonging to a particular artist and his disciples and school, and developed by frequent repetition into a habit, constitutes 'manner' here, and this provides us with an opportunity to consider it in two aspects.

(αα) The first aspect concerns treatment. In painting, e.g., the atmospheric tone, the foliage, the distribution of light and shade, the whole tone of colour as a whole, permit of an infinite variety. Especially in the sort of colour and illumination we therefore find the greatest difference between painters, and their most individual modes of treatment. For example, there may even be a tone of colour which in general we do not perceive in nature, because, although it occurs, we have not noticed it. But it has struck this or that artist; he has made it his own and has now become accustomed to see and reproduce everything in this kind of colouring and illumination. As with colouring, his procedure may be equally individual with the objects themselves, their grouping, position, and movement. Especially in the Netherlands painters we commonly meet with this aspect of manner: van der Neer's [1603–77] night pieces, e.g., and his treatment of moonlight, van Goyen's [1596–1656] sandhills in so many of his landscapes, the continually recurring sheen of satin and other silken materials in so many pictures by other masters belong to this category.

(ββ) Secondly, manner extends to the execution of the work of art, the handling of the brush, the laying on of the paint, the blending of colours, etc.

(γγ) But since such a specific kind of treatment and representation, owing to its constantly returning anew, is generalized into a habit and becomes second nature to the artist, there is a serious risk that, the more specialized the manner is, the more easily does it degenerate into a soulless and therefore cold repetition and fabrication, in which the artist is no longer present with full sensibility and entire inspiration. In that event art sinks to mere manual skill and professional dexterity, and the manner, not in itself objectionable, may become something jejune and lifeless.

(γ) Thus the more genuine manner must rid itself of this restricted idiosyncrasy, and so broaden itself within that these specialized modes of treatment cannot mortify into a pure matter of habit; for the genuine artist clings in a more general way to the nature of the things in hand and can make his own this more general mode of treatment in the way that its essence implies. In this sense we can speak of 'manner' in Goethe, e.g., because of his knack in rounding off not only his convivial poems, but also other more serious elements, with a happy turn of phrase in order to supersede or remove the seriousness of the reflection or situation. Horace too in his *Epistles* adopts this manner. This is a turning of the conversation and social conviviality in general which, in order not to go into the matter more deeply, stops, breaks off, and adroitly changes the deeper topic into something cheerful. This way of treating the thing is indeed manner too and it belongs to the subject's handling of his topic, but to a subjective procedure which is of a more general kind and so within the intended kind of representation works all the time in a necessary way. From this final level of manner we can pass on to the consideration of style.

(b) 'Le style c'est l'homme même' is a familiar French saying.[1] Here style as such means the idiosyncrasy of the artist, completely ascertainable in his mode of expression, the way he turns his phrases, etc. On the other hand, von Rumohr (op. cit., i, p. 87) tries to explain the word 'style' as a 'self-accommodation, developed into a habit, into the inner demands of the material in which the sculptor actually shapes his forms and the painter makes them appear', and in this connection he provides us with extremely important remarks about the mode of representation which the specific sensuous material, e.g. of sculpture, permits or forbids. Yet we need not restrict the word 'style' simply to this aspect of the sensuous element; we can extend it to characteristics and rules of artistic representation arising from the nature of a species of art within which a work is executed. Thus in music we distinguish the style of church music from that of opera, and, in painting, the historical style from that of genre. 'Style', so interpreted, is applicable to a mode of representation which complies with the conditions of its material as well as corresponding throughout with the

---

[1] From *Discours sur le Style*, by G. L. L. de Buffon, 1707-88.

demands of definite species of art and the laws originating in their essence. In this wider meaning of the word, consequently, defectiveness of style is either the artist's inability to make his own such an inherently necessary mode of representation, or else his subjective caprice which gives free play to his own whims instead of to conformity with rules, and sets up in their place a bad mannerism of his own. It follows that, as von Rumohr has already noticed, it is inadmissible to carry over the stylistic rules of one species of art into those of the others, as Mengs, e.g., did in his well-known group of the Muses in the Villa Albani, where he 'treated and executed the coloured forms of his Apollo on the principle of sculpture'.[1] Similarly we see in many of Dürer's[2] pictures that he has made the style of the woodcut entirely his own and has had it in mind in his painting too, especially in the drapery.

(c) Now, lastly, originality does not consist in merely following the rules of style, but in the subjective inspiration which, instead of succumbing to a mere mannerism, grasps an absolutely rational material, and from within, by the subjective activity of the artist, gives it external form both in the essence and conception of a definite species of art and also appropriately to the general nature of the Ideal.

(α) Thus originality is identical with true objectivity and links together the subjective and factual sides of the representation in such a way that the two sides are no longer opposed or strangers to one another. Therefore, in one respect, it is the most personal inner life of the artist, yet on the other hand it reveals nothing but the nature of the object, so that the special character of the artist's work appears only as the special character of the thing itself and proceeds therefrom, just as the thing does from his productive subjective activity.

(β) Therefore originality is above all to be entirely distinguished from the caprice of mere fancies. For people are commonly accustomed to understand by 'originality' only the production of peculiarities, proper precisely only to the individual, which would never enter anyone else's head. But in that case this is only a bad idiosyncrasy. No one, e.g., in this meaning of the word is more 'original' than the English; i.e. every one of them resorts to some

---

[1] The reference seems to be to the ceiling *Mount Parnassus*. The villa is in Rome. Apollo is the leader of the Muses. The quotation is from von Rumohr.
[2] A. Dürer, 1471–1528.

specific folly, which no reasonable man will imitate, and in the consciousness of his folly calls himself 'original'.

Connected with this, after all, is what is especially famous today, namely, originality of wit and humour. Here the artist starts from his own subjective life and continually comes back to it, so that the proper topic of his production is treated only as an external occasion for giving free play to witticisms, jokes, fancies, and the extravagances of his most subjective mood. But, since this is so, the topic and this subjective side fall apart from one another, and the material is treated capriciously throughout, so that the idiosyncrasy, yes the idiosyncrasy, of the artist may be conspicuous as the chief thing. Such a humour may be full of spirit and deep feeling and commonly appears as extremely impressive, but on the whole it is easier than is supposed. For steadily to interrupt the rational course of the thing, to begin, proceed, and end capriciously, and to throw into mutual confusion a series of witticisms and feelings, and thereby to produce fantastic caricatures, is easier than to develop from oneself and round off an inherently solid whole, stamped with the true Ideal. But the present-day humour likes to present the unpleasantness of an ill-bred talent, and all the same wobbles after all from true humour into banality and drivel. True humour we have seldom had; but nowadays the flattest trivialities with only a pretence of humour and its external colour are supposed to be ingenious and deep. Shakespeare, on the contrary, had great and deep humour, and yet, even in him, trivialities are not lacking. Similarly, Jean Paul's[1] humour often surprises us by its depth of wit and beauty of feeling, but equally often, in an opposite way, by its grotesquely combining things which have no real connection with one another, and the relations into which his humour brings them together are almost indecipherable. Even the greatest humourist has not relations of this kind present in his memory and so after all we often observe that even Jean Paul's interconnections are not the product of the power of genius but are brought together externally. Thus in order always to have new material, Jean Paul looked into books of the most varied kind, botanical, legal, philosophical, descriptive of travel, noted at once what struck him and wrote down the passing fancies it suggested; when it was a matter of actual composition, he brought together the most heterogeneous material—Brazilian plants and the old Supreme

[1] J. P. F. Richter, 1763–1825.

Court of the Empire.[1] This is then given special praise as originality or as humour by which anything and everything is excused. But such caprice is precisely what true originality excludes.

This gives us an opportunity after all to allude once more to the irony which likes to pass itself off as the highest originality, especially when it treats nothing seriously and carries on the business of joking merely for the sake of joking. In another aspect it brings together in its representations a mass of external details, the inmost meaning of which the poet keeps to himself. Then the cunning and loftiness of this procedure is supposed to consist in enlarging the imagination on the ground that precisely in these collocations and external details there lie concealed the 'poetry of poetry' and everything most profound and excellent, which, purely and simply because of its depth, cannot be expressed. So, e.g., in F. von Schlegel's poems at the time when he imagined himself a poet, what is unsaid is given out as the best thing of all; yet this 'poetry of poetry' proved itself to be precisely the flattest prose.

(γ) The true work of art must be freed from this perverse originality, for it evinces its genuine originality only by appearing as the *one* personal creation of *one* spirit which gathers and compiles nothing from without, but produces the whole topic from its own resources by a single cast, in one tone, with strict interconnection of its parts, just as the thing itself has united them in itself. If on the other hand we find scenes and motives brought together not by themselves but purely from outside, then the inner necessity of their unification is not there, and they appear as linked accidentally by a third and alien subjective activity [i.e. that of the artist]. So we marvel at Goethe's *Götz*, especially for its great originality, and of course, as we have said above already, in this work Goethe, greatly daring, has given the lie to, and trodden underfoot, whatever at that time was firmly held in aesthetic theories as a law of art. Yet the execution of the play is not of true originality. For in this early work we still see the poverty of Goethe's own material, because many traits and whole scenes, instead of being worked out from the great topic itself, appear here and there to have been scraped up out of the interests of the time in which the play was written, and inserted into it in an external way. For example, the scene [Act I, scene ii] of Götz with Brother Martin, which hints at Luther, contains only ideas drawn by

[1] At Wetzlar; see *Hegel's Political Writings* (Oxford, 1964), p. 170.

Goethe from the things which in his own period in Germany began to make people pity the monks again [Martin bewails his lot and theirs]: they might not drink any wine, must sleep off their meals, and therefore are subject to all sorts of desires, and must above all have taken the three intolerable vows of poverty, chastity, and obedience. On the other hand, Brother Martin is enthusiastic for Götz's life as a knight: let Götz recall how, when he was laden with the booty of his enemies, 'I struck him from his horse before he could shoot and then I ran him down, horse and all'; and then how Götz goes to his castle and finds his wife. Martin drinks Elizabeth's health and wipes his eyes.—But with these mundane thoughts Luther did not begin; as a pious monk he drew from Augustine a totally different depth of religious insight and conviction. Similarly there follow in the next scene pedagogical notions contemporary with Goethe which Basedow[1] in particular had instigated. For example, it was said in his time that children learnt a lot of unintelligible stuff, while the right method was to teach them facts by sight and experience. Now Karl speaks to his father entirely from memory, just as was customary in Goethe's youth: 'Jaxthausen is a village and a castle on the Jaxt, belonging to the Lords of Berlichingen for two centuries by inheritance', yet when Götz asks him: 'Knowest thou the Lord of Berlichingen?', the boy stares him in the face and not having been explicitly taught, does not know who his own father is. Götz asserts that he was acquainted with every path, road, and ford before he knew the names of any river, village, and town. These are alien appendages not affecting the matter itself; while when the thing at issue could have been treated in its proper depth, e.g. in the conversation of Götz and Weislingen [ibid.], nothing appears except cold and prosaic reflections on the times.

A similar collection of individual traits which do not arise from the subject-matter we find over again even in Goethe's *Wahlverwandschaften* [*Elective Affinities*, 1809]: the parks, the *tableaux vivants*, and the swingings of the pendulum, the feel of metals, the headaches, the whole picture, derived from chemistry, of chemical affinities are of this kind. In a novel, set in a specific prosaic time, it is true that this sort of thing is more permissible, especially when, as in Goethe's case, it is used so skilfully and gracefully, and, besides, a work of art cannot entirely free itself

---

[1] J. B. Basedow, 1723–90.

from the culture of its time; but it is one thing to mirror this culture itself, and another to search outside and collect materials together independent of the proper subject of the representation. The genuine originality of the artist, as of the work of art, lies solely in his being animated by the rationality of the inherently true content of the subject-matter. If the artist has made this objective rationality entirely his own, without mixing it and corrupting it either from within or without with particular details foreign to it, then alone in the topic to which he has given form does he give *himself* in his truest subjective character, a character that will be but the living corridor for a work of art perfect in itself. For in all true poetry, in thinking and action, genuine freedom makes what is substantial prevail as an inherent power; and this power at the same time is so completely the very own power of subjective thinking and willing itself that, in the perfect reconciliation of both, no separation between them can remain over any longer. So the originality of art does indeed consume that accidental idiosyncrasy of the artist, but it absorbs it only so that the artist can wholly follow the pull and impetus of his inspired genius, filled as it is with his subject alone, and can display his own self, instead of fantasy and empty caprice, in the work he has completed in accordance with its truth. To have no manner has from time immemorial been the one grand manner, and in this sense alone are Homer, Sophocles, Raphael, Shakespeare, to be called 'original'.

PART II

DEVELOPMENT OF THE IDEAL INTO THE PARTICULAR FORMS OF ART

INTRODUCTION

What up to this point we have dealt with, in Part I, concerned the actuality of the Idea of the beautiful as the Ideal of art, but [no matter] under how many aspects we also developed the Concept of the ideal work of art, still all our distinctions bore only on the ideal work of art in *general*. But, like the Idea, the Idea of the beautiful is a totality of essential differences which must issue as such and be actualized. Their actualization we may call on the whole the *particular forms* of art, as the development of what is implicit in the Concept of the Ideal and comes into existence through art. Yet if we speak of these art forms as different species of the Ideal, we may not take 'species' in the ordinary sense of the word, as if here the particular forms came from without to the Idea as their universal genus and had become modifications of it: on the contrary, 'species' should mean nothing here but the distinctive and therefore more concrete determinations of the Idea of the beautiful and the Ideal of art itself. The general character of [artistic] representation, i.e., is here made determinate not from without but in itself through its own Concept, so that it is this Concept which is spread out into a totality of particular modes of artistic formation.

Now, in more detail, the forms of art, as the actualizing and unfolding of the beautiful, find their origin in the Idea itself, in the sense that through them the Idea presses on to representation and reality, and whenever it is explicit to itself either only in its abstract determinacy or else in its concrete totality, it also brings itself into appearance in another real formation. This is because the Idea as such is only truly Idea as developing itself explicitly by its own activity; and since as Ideal it is immediate appearance, and indeed with its appearance is the identical Idea of the beautiful, so also at

L

every particular stage on which the Ideal treads the road of its unfolding there is immediately linked with every *inner* determinacy another *real* configuration. It is therefore all one whether we regard the advance in this development as an inner advance of the Idea in itself or of the shape in which it gives itself existence. Each of these two sides is immediately bound up with the other. The consummation of the Idea as content appears therefore simultaneously as also the consummation of form; and conversely the deficiencies of the artistic shape correspondingly prove to be a deficiency of the Idea which constitutes the inner meaning of the external appearance and in that appearance becomes real to itself. Thus if in this Part we encounter art-forms at first which are still inadequate in comparison with the true Ideal, this is not the sort of case in which people ordinarily speak of unsuccessful works of art which either express nothing or lack the capacity to achieve what they are supposed to represent; on the contrary, the specific shape which every content of the Idea gives to itself in the particular forms of art is always adequate to that content, and the deficiency or consummation lies only in the relatively untrue or true determinateness in which and as which the Idea is explicit to itself. This is because the content must be true and concrete in itself before it can find its truly beautiful shape.

In this connection, as we saw already in the general division of the subject [on pp. 76–81], we have three chief art-forms to consider:

(i) The *Symbolic*. In this the Idea still *seeks* its genuine expression in art, because in itself it is still abstract and indeterminate and therefore does not have its adequate manifestation on and in itself, but finds itself confronted by what is external to itself, external things in nature and human affairs. Now since it has only an immediate inkling of its own abstractions in this objective world or drives itself with its undetermined universals into a concrete existence, it corrupts and falsifies the shapes that it finds confronting it. This is because it can grasp them only arbitrarily, and therefore, instead of coming to a complete identification, it comes only to an accord, and even to a still abstract harmony, between meaning and shape; in this neither completed nor to be completed mutual formation, meaning and shape present, equally with their affinity, their mutual externality, foreignness, and incompatibility.

(ii) But, secondly, the Idea, in accordance with its essential nature, does not stop at the abstraction and indeterminacy of universal thoughts but is in itself free infinite subjectivity and apprehends this in its actuality as spirit. Now spirit, as free subject, is determined through and by itself, and in this self-determination, and also in its own nature, has that external shape, adequate to itself, with which it can close as with its absolutely due reality. On this entirely harmonious unity of content and form, the second art-form, the *classical*, is based. Yet if the consummation of this unity is to become actual, spirit, in so far as it is made a topic for art, must not yet be the purely absolute spirit which finds its adequate existence only in spirituality and inwardness, but the spirit which is still particular and therefore burdened with an abstraction. That is to say, the free subject, which classical art configurates outwardly, appears indeed as essentially universal and therefore freed from all the accident and mere particularity of the inner life and the outer world, but at the same time as filled solely with a universality particularized within itself. This is because the external shape is, as such, an external déterminate particular shape, and for complete fusion [with a content] it can only present again in itself a specific and therefore restricted content, while too it is only the inwardly particular spirit which can appear perfectly in an external manifestation and be bound up with that in an inseparable unity.

Here art has reached its own essential nature by bringing the Idea, as spiritual individuality, directly into harmony with its bodily reality in such a perfect way that external existence now for the first time no longer preserves any independence in contrast with the meaning which it is to express, while conversely the inner [meaning], in its shape worked out for our vision, shows there only itself and in it is related to itself affirmatively.[1]

(iii) But, thirdly, when the Idea of the beautiful is comprehended as absolute spirit, and therefore as the spirit which is free in its own eyes, it is no longer completely realized in the external world, since its true determinate being it has only in itself as spirit. It therefore dissolves that classical unification of inwardness and external manifestation and takes flight out of externality back into itself. This provides the fundamental typification of the *romantic*

---

[1] The translation of this paragraph rests on accepting Hotho's text, and rejecting Bassenge's emendation of it.

art-form; the content of this form, on account of its free spirituality, demands more than what representation in the external world and the bodily can supply; in romantic art the shape is externally more or less indifferent, and thus that art reintroduces, in an opposite way from the symbolic, the separation of content and form.

In this way, symbolic art *seeks* that perfect unity of inner meaning and external shape which classical art *finds* in the presentation of substantial individuality to sensuous contemplation, and which romantic art *transcends* in its superior spirituality.

SECTION I

THE SYMBOLIC FORM OF ART

Introduction—The Symbol in general

The symbol, in the meaning of the word used here, constitutes the beginning of art, alike in its essential nature and its historical appearance, and is therefore to be considered only, as it were, as the threshold of art. It belongs especially to the East and only after all sorts of transitions, metamorphoses, and intermediaries does it carry us over into the genuine actuality of the Ideal as the classical form of art. Therefore from the very start we must at once distinguish the symbol in its own independent characteristic form, in which it serves as the decisive type for artistic vision and representation, from that sort of symbolism which is just reduced to a mere external form, explicitly not independent. In this latter mode we do find the symbol recurring in the classical and romantic art-forms, in just the same way as single aspects even in the symbolic may assume the shape of the classical Ideal or present the beginning of romantic art. But, in that event, this interplay of characteristics always affects only subsidiary productions and individual traits, without constituting the proper soul and determining nature of entire works of art.

On the other hand, when the symbol is developed independently in its own proper form, it has in general the character of sublimity, because at first, on the whole, it is only the Idea which is still measureless, and not freely determined in itself, that is to be given shape, and therefore it cannot find in concrete appearance any specific form corresponding completely with this abstraction and universality. But in this non-correspondence the Idea transcends its external existence instead of having blossomed or been perfectly enclosed in it. This flight beyond the determinateness of appearance constitutes the general character of the sublime.

As for what, to begin with, concerns the formal [side of our subject], we have now to explain in purely general terms what is understood by 'symbol'.

Symbol as such is an external existent given or immediately

present to contemplation, which yet is to be understood not simply as it confronts us immediately on its own account, but in a wider and more universal sense. Thus at once there are two distinctions to make in the symbol: (i) the meaning, and (ii) the expression thereof. The first is an idea or topic, no matter what its content, the second is a sensuous existent or a picture of some kind or other.

1. Now the symbol is *prima facie* a *sign*. But in a *mere sign* the connection which meaning and its expression have with one another is only a purely arbitrary linkage. In that case this expression, this sensuous thing or picture, so far from presenting *itself*, brings before our minds a content foreign to it, one with which it does not need to stand in any proper affinity whatever. So in languages, for example, the sounds are a sign of some idea, feeling, etc. But the predominant part of the sounds in a language is linked purely by chance with the ideas expressed thereby, so far as their content is concerned, even if it can be shown, by an historical development, that the original connection was of another character; and the difference between languages consists chiefly in the fact that the same idea is expressed by a difference in sounds. Another example of such signs is afforded by the colours[1] (*les couleurs*) which are used in cockades and flags to express the nationality to which an individual or a ship belongs. Such colours likewise have in themselves no quality in common with their meaning, i.e. with the nation which is represented by them. Therefore, when symbol is taken in *this* sense as a mere sign with such an indifference between meaning and its expression, we may not take account of it in reference to art, since art as such consists precisely in the kinship, relation, and concrete interpenetration of meaning and shape.

2. Therefore it is a different thing when a sign is to be a *symbol*. The lion, for example, is taken as a symbol of magnanimity, the fox of cunning, the circle of eternity, the triangle of the Trinity. But the lion and the fox do possess in themselves the very qualities whose significance they are supposed to express. Similarly the circle does not exhibit the endlessness or the capricious limitation of a straight or other line which does not return into itself, a limitation likewise appropriate enough for some *limited* space of time; and the triangle as a *whole* has the same *number* of sides and angles

---

[1] i.e. a regiment's colours, or the colours that are nailed to the mast.

as that appearing in the idea of God when the determinations which religion apprehends in God are liable to *numeration*.

Therefore in these sorts of symbol the sensuously present things have already in their own existence that meaning, for the representation and expression of which they are used; and, taken in this wider sense, the symbol is no purely arbitrary sign, but a sign which in its externality comprises in itself at the same time the content of the idea which it brings into appearance. Yet nevertheless it is not to bring *itself* before our minds as this concrete individual thing but in itself only that universal quality of meaning [which it signifies].

3. Further, thirdly, we must notice that, although the symbol, unlike the purely external and formal sign, should not be wholly inadequate to its meaning, still conversely in order to remain a symbol it must not be made entirely adequate to that meaning. This is because even if, on the one hand, the content, which is the meaning, and the shape, which is used for the signalization thereof, harmonize in *one* property, still, on the other hand, the symbolic shape contains yet other characteristics of its own utterly independent of that common quality which the symbolic shape signified *once*; just as, similarly, the content does not need to be an abstract one like strength or cunning, but may be a more concrete one which now for its part may contain qualities, again peculiar to itself, different from the first property which constitutes the meaning of its symbol, and, in the same way, still more different from the other peculiar characteristics of this [symbolic] shape. So, for example, the lion is not only strong, the fox not only cunning, but God especially has quite different properties from those which can be comprised in number, a mathematical figure, or an animal shape. Therefore the content remains also indifferent to the shape which portrays it, and the abstract determinacy which it constitutes can equally well be present in infinitely many other existents and configurations. Likewise a concrete content has in it many characteristics which other configurations containing the same characteristic may serve to express. Exactly the same holds good for the external existent in which some meaning or other is expressed symbolically. It too, as a concrete thing, similarly has in it numerous characteristics for which it may serve as a symbol. So, for example, the obviously best symbol for strength is of course the lion, but nevertheless the bull or a horn can serve too, and, conversely, the

bull over again has a mass of other symbolical meanings. But altogether endless is the mass of figures and pictures used as symbols to represent God.

Now it follows from all this that the symbol by its very nature remains essentially ambiguous.

(*a*) In the first place, the look of a symbol as such raises at once the doubt whether a shape is to be taken as a symbol or not, even if we set aside the further ambiguity in respect of the *specific* meaning which a shape is supposed to signify amongst the *several* meanings for which it can often be used as a symbol through associations of a more remote kind.

What we have before us at first sight is, in general, a shape, a picture which gives us only the idea of an immediate existent. A lion, for example, an eagle, the colours, present *themselves* and can count as satisfying in themselves. Hence the question arises whether a lion, whose picture is brought before us, is to express and mean only itself or whether besides it is supposed to portray and signify something still further, the more abstract meaning of mere strength or the more concrete meaning of a hero or a season or agriculture; whether such a picture, as we say, is to be taken literally or at the same time metaphorically, or even perhaps *only* metaphorically.

The latter is the case, e.g., with symbolical expressions in speech, with words like *begreifen*, *schliessen*,[1] and so forth. When these signify spiritual activities [i.e. comprehending or concluding], we have immediately before our minds only their meaning of a spiritual activity without recalling at all at the same time the visible actions of touching or closing. But in the picture of a lion there confronts us not only the meaning which it may have as a symbol, but also this visible shape and existent.

Such dubiety disappears only when each of the two sides, the meaning and its shape, are expressly named and thereby their relation is enunciated at once. But in that case the concrete existent set out before us is no longer a symbol in the strict sense of the word but just an image, and the relation between image and meaning acquires the familiar form of comparison, i.e. simile. In the simile, that is to say, there must float before our minds both, first, the general idea and then its concrete image. Whereas if reflection

---

[1] *Begreifen* is literally to touch or handle; figuratively, to comprehend or understand; *schliessen* is to close, and so to conclude [an argument].

has not yet advanced far enough to take good note of universal ideas independently and so to set them out by themselves, then the related sensuous shape in which a more general meaning is supposed to find its expression is not yet thought to be separate from that meaning; both are still immediately at one. As we shall see later on [in Chapter 3], this constitutes the difference between symbol and comparison. So, for example, Karl Moor cries out[1] at the sight of the setting sun: 'Thus dies a hero.' Here the meaning is expressly separated from what is presented to our eyes and at the same time the meaning is annexed to what is seen. In other cases, indeed, this separation and relation is not so clearly emphasized in similes; on the contrary, the connection remains more immediate; but in that event it must already be clear from the further connection of the narrative, from the context and other circumstances, that the image is not supposed to suffice on its own account but that there is meant by it this or that specific significance which cannot remain uncertain. When, for example, Luther says [in his hymn] 'A safe stronghold our God is still', or when it is said that 'Youth sails the ocean with a thousand masts; quietly on the boat that has been saved old age drives into harbour',[2] there is no doubt about the meaning 'protection' in the case of 'stronghold', 'a world of hopes and plans' in the case of the picture of the ocean and the thousand masts, 'the restricted aim and possession, the small safe piece of ground' in the case of the picture of the boat and the harbour. Similarly, when we read in the Old Testament [Ps. 58: 6]: 'Break their teeth, O God, in their mouth, break out the great teeth of the young lions', we recognize at once that the teeth, the mouth, the great teeth of the young lions, are not meant literally; they are only pictures and sensuous images, to be understood metaphorically, and in their case it is only a matter of what their *meaning* is.

But this dubiety enters in the case of the symbol as such all the more as a picture with a meaning is in the main called a symbol only when this meaning is not, as in comparison, explicitly expressed or is otherwise clear already. No doubt its ambiguity is removed from the symbol, strictly so-called, if, on account of this very uncertainty, the linkage of the sensuous picture with the

[1] In Schiller, *The Robbers*, Act III, scene ii.
[2] Schiller, *Erwartung und Erfüllung* (Expectation and Fulfilment), a 'votive-tablet'.

308 II. I. THE SYMBOLIC FORM OF ART

meaning is made customary, and becomes more or less conventional—as is indispensably requisite in a mere sign; whereas the simile announces itself as something invented for only a momentary purpose, something individual, clear in itself, because it carries its meaning along with itself. Still, even if to those living in such a conventional range of ideas, the specific symbol is clear because they are accustomed to it, it is on the other hand a totally different matter with all others who do not move in the same circle or for whom that range of ideas is something past and gone. To them what is given at first is only the immediate sensuous representation, and for them it remains every time doubtful whether they have to content themselves with what confronts them or whether thereby they are referred to still other ideas and thoughts. If, for example, in Christian churches we see the triangle in a prominent place on the wall, we recognize at once from this that here it is not the sensuous perception of this figure as a mere triangle that is meant, but that we have to do with a meaning of it. In a different place, however, it is equally clear to us that the same figure is not to be taken as a symbol or sign of the Trinity. But other, non-Christian peoples, who lack the same habit and knowledge, may swither in doubt on this matter, and even we ourselves may not in all circumstances determine with the same assurance whether a triangle is to be considered as a triangle proper or as a symbol.

(b) Now it is not at all a matter of encountering this uncertainty in restricted cases; on the contrary, it is a matter of encountering it in quite extended realms of art, in the content of a prodigious material confronting us: the content of almost the whole of Eastern art. Thus when we first enter the world of the old-Persian, Indian, Egyptian shapes and productions, our footing is not really secure; we feel that we are wandering amongst *problems*; in themselves alone these productions say nothing to us; they do not please us or satisfy us by their immediate appearance, but by themselves they encourage us to advance beyond them to their meaning which is something wider and deeper than they are. In the case of other productions, on the contrary, we see at first glance that, like nursery tales, for example, they are meant to be a mere play with images and casual far-fetched connections. This is because children are content with the superficiality of such pictures and with their unintellectual and idle play and staggering juxtapositions. But nations, even in their childhood, demanded more substantial material, and this in fact we do find even in the art-forms of the Indians and Egyptians, although in these enigmatic productions of theirs, the elucidation is only hinted at, and great difficulty is put in the way of a solution. But in such incongruity between meaning and the immediate artistic expression, how much is to be ascribed to the deficiency of art, the turbidity of imagination itself and its lack of ideas? Or how much of it has the character it has because the clearer and more accurate configuration was incapable by itself of expressing the deeper meaning, and because the fantastic and grotesque is just used instead on behalf of a more far-reaching idea? All this is precisely what at first sight may to a very great extent admit of doubt.

Even in the field of classical art a similar uncertainty enters here and there, although the classical element in art consists in its not being symbolical by nature but in its being, in itself and throughout, distinct and clear. In fact the classical ideal is clear because it compasses the true content of art, i.e. substantial subjectivity, and precisely thereby it finds too the true form, which in itself expresses nothing but that genuine content. That is to say, the significance, the meaning, is no other than that which actually lies in the external shape, since both sides correspond perfectly; whereas in the symbol, simile, etc., the image always still presents something other than the meaning alone for which it furnishes the image. But even classical art has an aspect of ambiguity since in the case of the mythological productions of antiquity it may seem doubtful whether we are to stick to the external shapes as such and marvel at them as merely a charming play of a happy fancy—because mythology is indeed in general only an idle invention of fables—or whether we still have to search for a further and deeper meaning. This latter demand may make things specially difficult when the content of these fables affects the life and works of the Divine itself, since the stories reported to us would have to be regarded both as wholly beneath the dignity of the Absolute and as purely inadequate and tasteless inventions. When, for example, we read of the twelve labours of Hercules, or even hear that Zeus has hurled Hephaestus down from Olympus on to the island of Lemnos so that as a result Hephaestus has a limp, we believe that this is to be understood as nothing but a fabulous picture drawn by imagination. Similarly it may appear to us that Jupiter's numerous love-affairs are invented purely arbitrarily. But, conversely, because such stories are told precisely of the supreme divinity, it may all the same be credible that still another, wider meaning, than what the myth provides on the surface, lies concealed under them. In this matter there are therefore especially two opposed ideas which have come into prominence. The *first* takes mythology as purely external stories, beneath God's dignity, even though, when considered in themselves, they may be graceful, delightful, interesting, nay even of great beauty, yet cannot afford any inducement for the further elucidation of deeper meanings. Mythology is therefore on this view to be considered purely *historically*—according to the form in which it is present to us, for the reason that, on the one hand, looked at on its artistic side, it is sufficient in itself in its configurations, pictures, gods and their actions and adventures, and indeed in itself affords the elucidation by making the meanings conspicuous; while, on the other hand, from the point of view of its historical *origin*, it has developed out of historical events, foreign tales and traditions, out of local origins, out of the caprice of priests, artists, and poets. But the *second* point of view will not be content with the purely external side of mythological shapes and tales, but insists that a general deeper sense dwells in them, and that to know this sense nevertheless, by unveiling it, is the proper business of mythology as the scientific treatment of myths. On this view mythology must therefore be interpreted *symbolically*. For 'symbolically' means here only that the myths, as a product of spirit (no matter how bizarre, jocular, grotesque they may look, no matter how much too of the casual external caprices of fancy is intermingled with them) still comprise meanings, i.e. general thoughts about the nature of God, i.e. philosophical theories.

On these lines in recent times Creuzer[1] especially has begun again in his *Symbolik* to study the mythological ideas of the ancients not, in the usual manner, externally and prosaically, nor according to their artistic value; on the contrary, he has sought in them inner rational meanings. In this enterprise he is guided by the presupposition that the myths and legendary tales took their origin in the human spirit. This spirit may indeed make play with its ideas of the gods, but, when the interest of religion enters, it treads on a higher sphere in which reason is the inventor of shapes, even if it too remains saddled with the defect of being unable yet

---

[1] F. Creuzer, 1771–1858, one of Hegel's colleagues at Heidelberg. The reference is to his *Symbolik und Mythologie* (1810–23).

at this first stage to unfold their inner core adequately. This hypothesis is absolutely true: religion has its source in the spirit, which seeks its own truth, has an inkling of it, and brings the same before our minds in some shape or other more closely or more distantly related to this truthful content. But when reason invents the shapes, there arises also the need to know their rationality. This knowledge alone is truly worthy of man. Whoever leaves this aside aquires nothing but a mass of external facts. If on the other hand we dig down for the inner truth of mythological ideas, without in the process rejecting their other side, namely the fortuitousness and caprice of imagination, the locality, etc., we may then justify even the different mythologies. But to justify man in his spiritual images and shapes is a noble preoccupation, nobler than the mere collection of historical external details. Now it is true that Creuzer has been pounced upon with the reproof that, following the example of the Neo-Platonists, he just first reads these wider meanings into the myths and looks in the myths for thoughts whose presence there is a supposition without any historical basis; indeed it can even be proved historically that in order to find these meanings there the investigator must first have dragged them there. For, it is argued, the people, the poets and priests—although on the other side much is said again about the great secret wisdom of the priests!—knew nothing of such thoughts which were incompatible with the whole culture of their age. This latter point is of course entirely correct. The peoples, poets, priests did not in fact have before their minds in this form of universality the universal thoughts lying at the root of their mythological ideas; and only if they had had them in this way could they have then intentionally veiled them in a symbolic form. But that they had such an intention was not maintained even by Creuzer. Yet if the Greeks did not think in their mythology the thoughts that we now see there, it does not follow in the least that their ideas are not *implicitly* symbols and so of necessity to be taken as such—on the ground that the peoples at the time when they composed their myths lived in purely poetical conditions and so brought their inmost and deepest convictions before their minds not in the form of thought but in shapes devised by imagination without separating the universal abstract ideas from the concrete pictures. That this is actually the case is something which here we have essentially to maintain and assume, even if it be granted as possible that, in such a symbolic mode of explanation, purely droll and ingenious deductions may often slip in, as happens with [the quest for] etymologies.

(c) But however firmly we may assent to the view that mythology with its tales of the gods and its vast productions of a persistent poetic imagination contains in itself a rational content and deep religious ideas, yet the question arises in relation to the symbolic form of art whether in that event *all* mythology and art is to be understood symbolically—as Friedrich von Schlegel maintained[1] that in every artistic representation an allegory was to be sought. In that case the symbolical or allegorical is so understood that for every work of art and every mythological shape there serves as a basis a universal thought which, then explicitly emphasized in its universality, is supposed to provide the explanation of what such a work, such an idea, really means. This method of treatment has likewise become very common in recent times. So, for example, in the more recent editions of Dante, where of course manifold allegories occur, attempts have been made to explain every stanza allegorically throughout; and in his editions of the classical poets, Heyne[2] also tries in his notes to explain in terms of abstract categories of the Understanding the universal sense of every metaphor. This is because the Understanding especially runs quickly to symbol and allegory, since it separates picture and meaning and therefore destroys the form of art, a form with which this symbolical explanation, aimed only at extricating the universal as such, has nothing to do.

This extension of symbolism to *every* sphere of mythology and art is by no means what we have in view here in considering the symbolic form of art. For our endeavour does not rise to finding out how far artistic shapes could be interpreted symbolically or allegorically in this sense of the word 'symbol'; instead, we have to ask, conversely, how far the symbolical itself is to be reckoned an art-form. We want to establish the artistic relation between meaning and its shape, in so far as that relation is *symbolical* in distinction from other modes of representation, especially the classical and the romantic. Our task must therefore consist, not in accepting that diffusion of the symbolic over the entire field of art, but conversely expressly limiting the range of what in itself

[1] In the passage cited in the note on p. 291.
[2] C. G. Heyne, 1729–1812. Carlyle wrote an interesting essay on his life and works.

is presented to us as a symbol proper and therefore is to be treated as symbolical. In this sense there has already been advanced [on pp. 76–81] the division of the ideal of art into the forms of the Symbolic, the Classical, and the Romantic.

The symbolic, that is to say, in our meaning of the word at once stops short of the point where, instead of indefinite, general, abstract ideas, it is free individuality which constitutes the content and form of the representation. For the person is what is significant for himself and is his own self-explanation. What he feels, reflects, does, accomplishes, his qualities, his actions, his character, are himself; and the whole range of his spiritual and visible appearance has no other meaning but the person who, in this development and unfolding of himself, brings before our contemplation only himself as master over his entire objective world. Meaning and sensuous representation, inner and outer, matter and form, are in that event no longer distinct from one another; they do not announce themselves, as they do in the strictly symbolic sphere, as merely related but as *one* whole in which the appearance has no other essence, the essence no other appearance, outside or alongside itself. What is to be manifested and what is manifested are lifted into a concrete unity. In this sense the Greek gods, in so far as Greek art represents them as free, inherently and independently self-sufficient individuals, are not to be taken symbolically; they content us in and by themselves. For art the actions of Zeus, Apollo, Athene, belong precisely to these individuals alone, and are meant to display nothing but their power and passion. Now if from such inherently free personalities a general concept is abstracted as their meaning and set beside their particular aspect as an explanation of the entire individual appearance, then what in these figures is in conformity with art is left unnoticed and destroyed. For this reason artists too cannot reconcile themselves to such a mode of interpreting all works of art and their mythological figures. For what we may think is left as an actually symbolic indication or allegory in the Classical and Romantic sort of artistic representation affects incidentals and is in that case expressly degraded to a mere attribute and sign, as e.g. the eagle stands beside Zeus, and Luke the Evangelist is accompanied by an ox; but the Egyptians had in Apis [the bull] a vision of God himself.

But the difficult point in this artistically adequate appearance of free subjectivity lies in distinguishing whether what is represented as person has also actual individuality and subjectivity or whether it carries in itself only the empty semblance of the same as mere personification. In this latter case, that is to say, the personality is nothing but a superficial form which both in particular actions and in the bodily shape does not express its own inner being and thereby permeate the entire externality of its appearance as its own; on the contrary, it has for the meaning of the external reality still another inner being, which is not this personality and subjectivity itself.

This is the chief consideration in relation to the delimitation of symbolic art.

Now, to sum up, our interest in considering symbolism consists in recognizing the inner process of the origin of art, in so far as this can be derived from the Concept of the Ideal in its development up to true art, and so of recognizing the sequence of stages in the symbolic as stages on the way to genuine art. Now, however close the connection between religion and art may be, we still have not to go over the symbols themselves (or religion as comprising ideas which in the wider sense of the word are symbolic or allegorical); we have only to consider that element in them in accordance with which they belong to art as such. The religious element we must hand over to the history of mythology.

Division of the subject

For the more detailed division of the symbolic form of art, the first thing is to settle the boundaries within which the development proceeds.

In general, as has been said already, this whole sphere is on the whole only the threshold of art, since at first we have before us only abstract meanings, not yet in themselves essentially individualized, and the configuration immediately linked with them is just as adequate as inadequate. The first boundary line is therefore the disengaging of the artistic vision and representation in general; while the opposite boundary is provided by art proper to which the symbolic lifts itself as to its truth.

In proposing to discuss the *subjective* aspect of the first origin of symbolic art, we may recall the saying that the artistic intuition as such, like the religious—or rather both together—and even scientific research, have begun in wonder.[1] The man who does *not yet* wonder at anything still lives in obtuseness and stupidity. Nothing interests him and nothing confronts him because he has not yet separated himself on his own account, and cut himself free, from objects and their immediate individual existence. But on the other hand whoever wonders *no longer* regards the whole of the external world as something which he has become clear about, whether in the abstract intellectual mode of a universally human Enlightenment, or in the noble and deeper consciousness of absolute spiritual freedom and universality, and thus he has changed the objects and their existence into a spiritual and self-conscious insight into them. Whereas wonder only occurs when man, torn free from his most immediate first connection with nature and from his most elementary, purely practical, relation to it, that of desire, stands back spiritually from nature and his own singularity and now seeks and sees in things a universal, implicit, and permanent element. In that case for the first time natural objects strike him; they are an 'other' which yet is meant to be for his apprehension and in which he strives to find himself over again as well as thoughts and reason. Here the inkling of something higher and the consciousness of externality are still unseparated and yet at the same time there is present a contradiction between natural things and the spirit, a contradiction in which objects prove themselves to be just as attractive as repulsive, and the sense of this contradiction along with the urge to remove it is precisely what generates wonder.

Now the first product of this situation consists in the fact that man sets nature and objectivity in general over against himself on the one hand as cause, and he reverences it as power; but even so on the other hand he satisfies his need to make external to himself the subjective feeling of something higher, essential, and universal, and to contemplate it as objective. In this unification there is immediately present the fact that the single natural objects—and above all the elemental ones, like the sea, rivers, mountains, stars—are not accepted just as they are in their separation, but, lifted into the realm of our ideas, acquire for our ideas the form of universal and absolute existence.

Now these ideas in their universality and essential implicit character art concentrates again into a picture for contemplation by

[1] e.g. Aristotle, *Metaphysics*, 982$^\mathrm{b}$ 11 ff.

direct consciousness and sets them out for the spirit in the objective form of a picture. This is the beginning of art. The immediate reverence for natural objects—nature worship and fetish worship —is therefore not yet art.

On its *objective* side the beginning of art stands in the closest connection with religion. The earliest works of art are of a mythological kind. In religion it is the Absolute as such, even if in its most abstract and poorest definition, which is brought to men's minds. Now the first self-revelation available for the Absolute is natural phenomena; in their existence man divines the Absolute and therefore makes it perceptible to himself in the form of natural objects. In this endeavour art finds its basic origin. Yet, even in this respect, it has not come on the scene when man merely descries the Absolute directly in the objects actually present, and is satisfied with that mode of divine reality, but only when the mind produces from its own resources both the apprehension of its Absolute in the form of what is external in itself and also the objectivity of this more or less adequate connection [of spirit with nature]. For art appropriates a substantial content grasped through the spirit, a content that does not appear externally, but in an externality which is not only present immediately but is first *produced* by the *spirit* as an existent comprising that content in itself and expressing it. But the first interpreter of religious ideas, one which brings them nearer to us by giving them shape, is art alone, because the prosaic treatment of the objective world only prevails when man, as spiritual self-consciousness, has battled himself free from nature as immediacy and now confronts it with the intellectual freedom which envisages objectivity as a pure externality. Yet this cleavage [between subject and object] is always only a later stage. The first knowledge of truth, on the other hand, proves to be a middle position between the purely spiritless immersion in nature and the spirituality altogether freed therefrom. This middle position in which spirit sets its ideas before our eyes in the shape of natural things just because it has still won no higher form (though in this linkage [of ideas and things] it struggles to make both sides adequate to one another) is, in general, the standpoint of poetry and art in distinction from that of the prosaic intellect. It is for this reason, after all, that the completely prosaic consciousness only arises when the principle of subjective spiritual freedom, [first] in its abstract and [later in its] genuinely concrete form, succeeds in attaining actuality, i.e. in the Roman and then later in the modern Christian world.

The goal, secondly, which the symbolic art-form strives to reach is classical art, and the attainment of this goal marks the dissolution of the symbolic form as such. Classical art, however, though it achieves the true manifestation of art, cannot be the first form of art; it has the multiple intermediate and transitional stages of the symbolic as its presupposition. This is because its appropriate content is spiritual individuality which, by being the content and form of what is absolutely true, can appear in consciousness only after complex mediations and transitions. The beginning is always constituted by what is abstract and indeterminate in its meaning. But spiritual individuality must be absolutely concrete, essentially and inherently; it is the self-determining Concept in its adequate actualization, and this Concept can be grasped only after it has sent ahead, in their one-sided development, the abstract aspects which it reconciles and harmonizes. Once it has done so, the Concept makes an end of these abstractions by its own appearance as a totality at the same time. This is the case in classical art. The classical form puts a stop to the purely symbolizing and sublime preliminary experiments of art, because spiritual individuality now has its shape, its adequate shape, in itself, just as the self-determining Concept generates out of itself the particular existence adequate to it. When this true content and therefore the true form is found for art, then the seeking and striving after both of these, wherein the deficiency of symbolic art precisely consists, ceases immediately.

If we ask, within these boundaries which have been indicated, for a narrower principle of division for symbolic art, then, in so far as symbolic art just struggles towards true meanings and their corresponding mode of configuration, it is in general a battle between the content which still resists true art and the form which is not homogeneous with that content either. For both sides [content and form, meaning and shape], although bound into an identity, still coincide neither with one another nor with the true nature of art, and therefore they struggle none the less to escape from this defective unification. In this respect the whole of symbolic art may be understood as a continuing struggle for compatibility of meaning and shape, and the different levels of this struggle are not so much different kinds of symbolic art as stages and modes of one and the same contradiction [of incompatibility between meaning and shape].

At first, however, this battle is present only implicitly, i.e. the incompatibility between the two sides, set and forced into a unity, has not yet become something confronting the artistic consciousness itself, because this consciousness cannot understand the universal nature of the meaning which it grasps, nor can it interpret the real shape independently in its separate existence. For this reason, instead of setting before its eyes the difference between the two, it starts from their immediate identity. Therefore what forms the *beginning* is the unity of the artistic content and its attempted symbolical expression—an enigmatic unity still undivided and fermenting in this contradictory linkage. This is the proper unconscious original symbolism, the configurations of which are not yet made into symbols.

The *end*, on the other hand, is the disappearance and dissolution of the symbolic, since the hitherto *implicit* battle has now come into the artistic consciousness; and symbolizing therefore becomes a conscious severance of the explicitly clear meaning from its sensuous associated picture; yet in this separation there remains at the same time an express *relation*, but one which instead of appearing as an *immediate* identity, asserts itself only as a mere *comparison* of the two, in which the difference, previously unconscious, comes to the fore just as clearly. This is the sphere of the symbol known as a symbol: the meaning known and envisaged on its own account in its universality, the concrete appearance of which is expressly reduced to a mere *picture* and is compared with the meaning for the purpose of its illustration by art.

In the middle between the beginning and the end just mentioned there stands *sublime* art. Here the meaning, as spiritual explicit universality, is separated for the first time from the concrete existent, and makes that existent known as its negative, external to it, and its servant. In order to express *itself* therein, the meaning cannot allow this existent to subsist independently, but must posit it as the inherently deficient, something to be superseded—although it has for its expression nothing other than precisely this existent which is external to it and null. The splendour of this sublimity of meaning naturally precedes comparison strictly so-called, because the concrete singleness of natural and other phenomena must first be treated negatively, and applied only as decoration and ornament for the unattainable might of the absolute meaning,[1] before there can be set forth that express severance and selective comparison of phenomena which are allied to and yet distinct from the meaning whose picture they are to provide.

These three chief stages which have been indicated are inwardly articulated in more detail in the following way.

A. (α) The first stage is itself neither to be called symbolic proper nor properly to be ranked as art. It only builds the road to both. This is the immediate substantial unity of the Absolute as spiritual meaning with its unseparated sensuous existence in a natural shape.

(β) The second stage forms the transition to symbol proper, in that this first unity begins to be dissolved and now, on the one hand, the universal meanings lift themselves explicitly above the single natural phenomena, yet, on the other hand, thus envisaged in their universality they are all the same to come into consciousness again in the form of concrete natural objects. Next in this double struggle to spiritualize the natural and to make the spiritual perceptible, there is revealed at this stage of the difference between spirit and nature the whole fantastic character and confusion, all the fermentation and wild medley, staggering hither and thither, of symbolic art. This art has indeed an inkling of the inadequacy of its pictures and shapes and yet can call in aid nothing but the distortion of shapes to the point of the boundlessness of a purely quantitative sublimity. At this stage, therefore, we live in a world full of blatant contrivances, incredibilities, and miracles, yet without meeting works of art of genuine beauty.

(γ) By this battle between meanings and their sensuous representation we reach, thirdly, the standpoint of the symbol proper, at which the symbolical work of *art* is first developed in its complete character. Here the forms and shapes are no longer those sensuously present which—as at the first stage—coincide immediately with the Absolute as its existence, without having been produced by art; or—as at the second stage—which can annul their difference from the universality of meanings only through imagination's sprawling extension of particular natural objects and events; on the contrary, what is now brought before our vision as a symbolic shape is a production generated by art. This production is on

---

[1] It appears from the summary of this passage in ch. III, c, below that 'absolute meaning' is a synonym for 'God'.

the one hand to present itself in its own special character, but on the other hand is to manifest not only this isolated object but a wider universal meaning, to be linked therewith and recognized therein. Thus these shapes stand before us as problems, making the demand that we shall conjecture the inner meaning lying in them.

On these more specific forms of the still original symbol we may in general premise that they proceed from the religious world outlooks of entire peoples, and therefore in this connection we will call history too to mind. Yet the lines of division between them cannot be drawn in full strictness, because the individual ways of treatment and configuration, like the art-forms in general, are mixed, so that we find over again in earlier or later ages, even if subordinated and isolated, the form which we regard as the fundamental type for the world-outlook of a single people. But in essence we have to look for the more concrete outlooks and examples for (α) in the ancient Parsi religion, for (β) in the Indian, and for (γ) in the Egyptian.

B. Through the course indicated above, the meaning which hitherto has been more or less obscured owing to its particular sensuous shape has at last wrung its way to freedom and so comes explicitly into consciousness in its clarity. Thereby the strictly symbolic situation is dissolved, and, since the absolute meaning is grasped as the universal all-pervading *substance* of the entire phenomenal world, there now enters the art of substantiality—as the symbolism of sublimity—in the place of purely symbolical and fantastic allusions, disfigurations, and riddles.

In this regard there are especially to be distinguished two points of view which have their basis in the varying relation of substance, as the Absolute and the Divine, to the finitude of appearance. This relation, that is to say, can be double, positive and negative; although in both forms—because it is always the universal substance which has to emerge—what is to come before our vision in things is not their particular shape and meaning but their universal soul and their position relatively to this substance.

(α) At the first stage this relation is so conceived that substance, as the All and One liberated from every particularity, is immanent in the specific appearances as the soul that produces and animates them, and now in this immanence is viewed as *affirmatively* present, and is grasped and presented by the individual who is self-abandoning owing to his ecstatic immersion in this essence that dwells in all these things. This affords the art of sublime pantheism, as we see it already in its beginnings in India, and then developed in the most brilliant way in Mohammedanism and its mystical art, and finally as we find it again in a more profound and subjective way in some phenomena of Christian mysticism.

(β) The *negative* relation, on the other hand, of sublimity strictly so called, we must seek in Hebrew poetry: this poetry of sublimity can celebrate and exalt the imageless Lord of heaven and earth only by using his whole creation as merely an accident of his power, as the messenger of his sovereignty, as the praise and ornament of his greatness, and in this service by positing even the greatest [earthly] splendour as negative. This is because it cannot find an adequate and affirmatively sufficient expression for the power and dominion of the supreme being, and can aquire a positive satisfaction only through the servitude of the creature, who is only adequate to himself and his significance in the feeling and establishment of his own unworthiness.

c. Through this process whereby the meaning, explicitly known in its simplicity, gains independence, its severance from the appearance which at the same time is *established* as inadequate to it, is already implicitly accomplished. Now if, within this actual cleavage, shape and meaning are to be brought into a relation of inner affinity, as symbolic art requires, then this relation lies directly neither in the meaning nor in the shape, but in a *subjective* third thing [the spectator's, or artist's, consciousness] which, in its subjective vision, finds aspects of similarity in both, and in reliance thereon illustrates and explains the independently clear meaning through the cognate individual picture.

But in that case the picture, instead of being as before the sole expression [of the meaning], is only a mere ornament, and therefore there arises a relation not in correspondence with the nature of the beautiful, since picture and meaning are contrasted with one another instead of being moulded into one another—as was the case, even if in a less complete way, in symbolic art strictly so-called. Works of art which make this form their foundation remain therefore of a subordinate kind, and their content cannot be the Absolute itself but some different and restricted situation or occurrence; on this account the forms belonging here are used in the main only occasionally as accessories.

Yet, in more detail, we have to distinguish in this section too three principal stages.

(α) To the first there belongs the mode of representation used in fables, parables, and apologues; in these the separation of shape from meaning, characteristic of this whole sphere, is not yet *expressly* established, and the subjective activity of comparing is not yet emphasized; consequently the presentation of the single concrete appearance, which is to illumine the universal meaning, remains the predominant thing.

(β) At the second stage, on the other hand, the universal meaning comes explicitly into dominion over the explanatory shape which can still only appear as a mere tribute or capriciously chosen picture. To this class there belong allegory, metaphor, simile.

(γ) The third stage, finally, completely reveals the utter sundering of the two sides which hitherto in symbolic art were either united immediately—despite their relative hostility, or, in their independently established cleavage, were yet still related. To the content explicitly known in its prosaic universality the art-form appears thoroughly external, as in *didactic* poetry, while on the other side the explicitly external is treated and represented in its mere externality in so-called *descriptive* poetry. But in this way the symbolic linkage [of shape and meaning] and their relation has vanished and we have to look for a further unification of form and content which truly corresponds to the real nature of art.

Chapter I

UNCONSCIOUS SYMBOLISM

If, to consider the matter in more detail, we now proceed to the stages of development of the symbolic, we have to make a beginning with the beginning of art as it proceeds from the Idea of art itself. This beginning, as we saw in the Introduction to this Section, is the symbolic form of art in its still immediate shape, a shape not yet known and made a mere image and simile—unconscious symbolism. But before this can acquire its strictly symbolical character in itself and for *our* consideration, there must be taken up still more presuppositions determined by the nature of the symbolic itself.

The nearer point of departure may be established in the following way.

The symbol on the one hand has its basis in the immediate unification of the universal and therefore spiritual meaning with the sensuous shape which is just as adequate as inadequate; but as yet there is no consciousness of their incongruity. But, on the other hand, the linkage must already be shaped by imagination and art and not merely apprehended as a purely immediately present actuality of the Divine. This is because the symbolic only arises for art with the detachment of a universal meaning from what is immediately present in nature, although in the existence of the latter the Absolute is envisaged, but *now* envisaged by *imagination* as actually present.

Thus the first presupposition of the symbolical's coming into being is precisely that *immediate* unity of the Absolute with its existence in the phenomenal world, a unity not produced by art but found, without art, in actual natural objects and human activities.

A. IMMEDIATE UNITY OF MEANING AND SHAPE

In this intuited immediate identity of the Divine, the Divine which is brought before consciousness as one with its existence in nature and man, neither is nature as such accepted as it is, nor is the

Absolute explicitly torn free from it and given independence—
so that in consequence there is strictly no question of a difference
between inner and outer, meaning and shape, because the inner
has not yet been explicitly separated as meaning from its immediate actuality in what is present. If therefore we speak here
of meaning, this is *our* reflection which proceeds for us from the
need to regard the [external] form (which affords [to others]
a [mere direct] intuition of the spiritual and the inward) as in
general something external, and, to be in a position to understand
it, we want to look into its heart, its soul and its meaning. But,
therefore, in the case of such general intuitions [of the Divine]
we must make the essential distinction between whether the inner
itself was envisaged as inner and meaning by those peoples who
originally apprehended these intuitions, or whether it is only *we*
who recognize in them a meaning which receives its external
expression in what is intuited.

Now, in other words, in this first unity there is no such difference between soul and body, concept and reality. The bodily
and the sensuous, the natural and the human, is not merely an
expression of a meaning to be distinguished therefrom; on the
contrary, what appears is itself apprehended as the immediate
actuality and presence of the Absolute. The Absolute does not
acquire for itself still another independent existence, but has only
[as its existence] the immediate presence of an object which is
God or the Divine. In Lamaism, for instance, this individual
actual man is immediately known and reverenced as God, just as
in other nature-religions the sun, mountains, rivers, the moon,
single animals, the bull, the monkey, etc., are regarded as immediate divine existents and reverenced as sacred. A similar thing,
even if in a deeper way, still appears in many respects even in the
Christian outlook. In Catholic doctrine, for example, the consecrated bread is the actual flesh, the wine the actual blood of God,
and Christ is immediately present in them; and even in the
Lutheran faith bread and wine are transformed by the believer's
enjoyment into actual flesh and blood. In this mystical identity
there is nothing purely symbolical; the latter only arises in the
Reformed [i.e. Calvinist] doctrine, because here the spiritual is
explicitly severed from the sensuous, and the external object is
taken in that case as a mere pointing to a meaning differentiated
therefrom. In the miracle-working images of the Madonna too the

power of the Divine operates by immediate presence in them and is not, as might be thought, only hinted at symbolically through the images.

But in the most thoroughgoing and widespread way we find the intuition of this wholly immediate unity in the life and religion of the ancient Zend people whose ideas and institutions are preserved for us in the Zend-Avesta.

1. *The Religion of Zoroaster*[1]

The religion of Zoroaster, namely, takes *light* as it exists in nature —the sun, the stars, fire in its luminosity and flames—to be the Absolute, without explicitly separating this divinity from light, as if light were a mere expression and image or symbol. The Divine, the meaning, is not severed from its existence, from the lights. This is because, even if light is taken all the same in the sense of the good, the just, and therefore of what is rich in blessing, upholding and propagating life, then it still is not thought at all to be a mere image of the good; on the contrary, the good is itself light. The same is the case with the opposite of light—the sombre and the dark as the impure, the harmful, the bad, the destructive, and the deadly.

In more detail this view is particularized and articulated in the following way.

(*a*) In the first place, the Divine as inherently pure light and as its opposite, darkness and impurity, is personified and is then called Ormuzd and Ahriman; but this personification remains entirely superficial. Ormuzd is no inherently free imperceptible subject, like the God of the Jews, or truly spiritual and personal, like the God of the Christians who is made known to us as actually personal and self-conscious spirit; on the contrary, Ormuzd, however much he is also called king, great spirit, judge, etc., still remains unseparated from his sensuous existence as light and lights. He is only the universal in all particular existents in which the light, and therefore the Divine and the pure, is actual; he is in them without abstractly withdrawing, out of everything present, into himself as the universal spirit independent of these existents. He remains in the existing particulars and individuals just as the

[1] The transliteration of proper names in the Zend-Avesta differs in different translations. I have preserved many of Hegel's, but see notes on pp. 328 and 329 and note 2 on p. 332, all of which I owe to Professor R. C. Zaehner.

genus remains in the species and individuals. As this universal he indeed acquires precedence over everything particular, and is the first, the supreme, the gold-shining king of kings, the purest and best, but he has his existence solely in everything light and pure, just as Ahriman has his in everything dark, evil, pernicious, and sick.

(b) Therefore this view expands at once into the further idea of a realm of light and darkness and the battle between them. In the realm of Ormuzd it is the Amshaspands as the seven chief lights in heaven who enjoy divine worship first, because they are the essential particular existences of light and therefore, as a pure and great heavenly people, constitute the determinate being of the Divine itself. Each Amshaspand (Ormuzd too is of their company in this) has its days of presiding, blessing, and beneficence. In further specification, the Izeds and Fervers[1] are subordinate to them; like Ormuzd himself they are personified indeed but without more detailed human configuration for contemplation, so that what remains the essential thing for contemplation is neither spiritual nor bodily subjectivity but determinate being as light, brightness, splendour, illumination, radiation, etc.

Similarly there are also treated as an existence of Ormuzd individual natural things which do not themselves exist externally as lights and luminous bodies—animals, plants, the phenomena of the human world whether spiritual or corporeal, individual actions and situations, the entire life of the state, the king, surrounded by seven great men, the division of classes, the cities, the provinces with their governors who as the best and purest people have to serve as a model and protection—in short the whole of reality. For everything which carries in itself and propagates growth, life, maintenance, is a mode in which light and purity and therefore Ormuzd really exist; every single truth, goodness, love, justice, mercy, spirit, bliss, every single living thing, everything beneficent and protective, etc., is regarded by Zoroaster as inherently light and divine. The realm of Ormuzd is what is actually present as pure and luminous, and in this realm there is no difference between the phenomena of nature and those of spirit, just as in Ormuzd himself light and goodness, spiritual and sensuous qualities, immediately coincide. The splendour of a creature is therefore for Zoroaster the sum of spirit, power, and every kind of stirring of

---

[1] These are the spirits or genii of individuals. By 'Izeds' Yazatas may be meant. For 'Fervers' read 'Fravashis'.

life, in so far as, that is to say, they promote the maintenance of everything positive and the banishment of everything in itself evil and harmful. What in animals, men, and plants, is real and good is light, and by the measure and condition of this luminosity the higher or lower splendour of all objects is determined.

The like articulation and gradation occurs also in the realm of Ahriman, except that in this province the spiritually bad and the naturally evil, in short what is destructive and actively negative, acquires actuality and dominion. But the might of Ahriman is not to be extended, and the aim of the whole world is therefore put in annihilating and smashing the realm of Ahriman, so that Ormuzd alone shall be living, present, and dominant in everything.

(c) To this one and only end the whole of human life is consecrated. The task of every individual consists in nothing but his own spiritual and bodily purification, and in the spreading of this blessing and the struggle against Ahriman throughout human and natural situations and activities. Thus, the supreme, most sacred duty is to glorify Ormuzd in his creation, to love and venerate everything which has proceeded from this light and is pure in itself, and to make oneself pleasing to it. Ormuzd is the beginning and end of all veneration. Before everything else the Parsi has therefore to call on Ormuzd in thoughts and words, and to pray to him. After praising him from whom the whole world of the pure emanates, the Parsi must next turn in prayer to particular things according to their level of majesty, dignity, and perfection; for, says the Parsi, so far as they are good and unalloyed, Ormuzd is in them and loves them as his pure sons in whom he takes pleasure as at the beginning of creation, since everything proceeded by his agency new and pure. So prayer is directed first to the Amshaspands as the nearest antitypes of Ormuzd, as the first and most brilliant beings who surround his throne and further his dominion. Prayer to these heavenly spirits is precisely related to their properties and functions, and, if they are stars, to the time of their uprising. The sun is called upon by day, and always in a different way according to whether it is rising, standing at midday, or setting thereafter. From dawn to midday the Parsi asks especially that Ormuzd may be pleased to heighten his splendour, and in the evening he prays that the sun may complete its career through the protection of Ormuzd and all the Izeds. But Mithras is especially venerated; as the fructifier of the earth and the deserts he pours forth nourishment over the whole of nature, and as the mighty struggler against all the Devas[1] of contention, war, disorder, and wreck, he is the author of peace.

Further, the Parsi in his on the whole monotonous prayers of praise emphasizes as it were the ideals, the purest and truest in man, the Fervers as pure spirits of men, no matter where on earth they live or have lived. Especially is prayer made to the pure spirit of Zoroaster, but after him to the governors of classes, cities, and provinces; and the spirits of all men are now already considered to be exactly bound together as members in the living society of light, which one day is to be still more of a unity in Gorotman.[2]

Finally, even animals, hills, trees are not forgotten, but they are called on with eyes fixed on Ormuzd; their goodness, the service they afford to man, is praised, and especially the first and most excellent of its kind is venerated as a determinate being of Ormuzd. Over and above this praying, the Zend-Avesta insists on the actual practice of goodness and of purity in thought, word, and deed. The Parsi in the whole conduct of his inner and outer man should be as the light, as Ormuzd, the Amshaspands, Izeds, Zoroaster and all good men live and work. This is because these live and have lived in the light, and all their deeds are light; therefore every man must have their pattern in view and follow their example. The more a man expresses in his life and accomplishment goodness and the purity of light, the nearer the heavenly spirits come to him. Just as the Izeds with beneficence bless everything, vivify it, make it fruitful and friendly, so the Parsi too seeks to purify nature, to exalt it, above all to spread the light of life and its cheerful fruitfulness. In this spirit he feeds the hungry, cares for the sick, to the thirsty he gives the refreshment of drink, to the traveller shelter and lodging; to the earth he gives pure seeds, he digs tidy canals, plants the deserts with trees and promotes growth wherever he can; he provides for the nourishment and fructifying of what lives, for the pure splendour of fire; he banishes dead and impure animals, arranges marriages; and the holy Sapandomad[3] herself, the Ized of the earth, delights therein and stops the harm which the Daevas and Darwands are actively preparing.

---

[1] 'Daevas' is meant. In Persian, *daeva* is a demon. *Deva* belongs to Indian religion, and is a god there.   [2] The House of Song, i.e. Heaven.
[3] i.e. righteousness.

2. The Non-symbolic Character of Zoroastrianism

What we called the symbolic is still not present at all in these fundamental views. On the one hand, it is true that light is existent naturally, and on the other hand it means the good, the upholder, full of blessing, so that we might say that the actual existence of light is a purely cognate image for this universal meaning which permeates nature and the human world. But, looked at from the point of view of the Parsis themselves, the separation between existence and its meaning is false, because for them the light, precisely as light, is goodness and is so interpreted that, as *light*, it is present and effective in all particular goods, in all living and positive things. The universal and the Divine does pervade the differences of particular mundane reality, but in this its particularized and separated existence there still remains subsistent the substantial and undivided unity of meaning and shape, and the differentiation of this unity has nothing to do with the difference between meaning as meaning and its manifestation, but only with the differentiation of existent objects, as, e.g., the stars, organic life, human dispositions and actions, in which the Divine, as light or darkness, is intuited as present.

In further [Persian] ideas there is of course an advance to some beginnings of symbolism, but these do not afford the proper type of this whole manner of viewing things; they can count only as isolated achievements. So Ormuzd says once, for example, of his darling, Jamshid: 'The holy Ferver of Jamshid, the son of Vivengham,[1] was great before me. His hand took from me a dagger, the edge of which was gold and its point was gold. Therewith Jamshid marked out three hundred parts of the earth. He split up the kingdom of the earth with his gold-plate, with his dagger, and spake: "Let Sapandomad rejoice". With prayer he spake the holy word to the tame cattle, to wild animals, and to men. So his passage was good fortune and blessing for these countries, and in great masses there thronged together men, domestic animals, and beasts of the field'. Now here the dagger and the splitting of the earth is an image whose meaning may be taken to be agriculture. Agriculture is still no explicitly spiritual activity, but neither is it something purely natural; instead it is a universal work of man, proceeding from deliberation, intelligence, and experience, and

[1] Yima, son of Vivanghvan, was originally the Persian 'patriarch of mankind'. He was later called Jamshid.

spreading through all relations of his life. The fact that this splitting of the earth with the dagger may be supposed to hint at agriculture is certainly not expressly said at all in the idea of Jamshid's progress, and nothing is said in connection with this splitting about any fertilizing or about any crops; yet since in this single action there seems at the same time to lie more than this single upturning and loosening of the soil, something symbolically indicated is to be looked for in it. It is similar with later ideas as they occur especially in the subsequent development of Mithras worship, where Mithras is portrayed [e.g. on Roman reliefs] as a stripling in the twilight of the grotto raising the head of the bull on high and plunging a dagger into its neck, while a snake licks its blood and a scorpion gnaws at its genitals. This symbolic representation has been explained, now astronomically and now otherwise. Yet in a more general and deeper way the bull can be taken as the natural principle in general over which man, the spiritual being, carries off the victory, although astronomical associations too may have their part to play here. But that such a revolution, like this victory of spirit over nature, is therein contained, is hinted at too by the name of Mithras, the mediator, especially in a later time when elevation above nature became a need of the peoples.

But symbols like these, as was said above, occur in the views of the ancient Persians only incidentally and do not constitute the all-pervading principle of their total manner of looking at things.

Still less is the *cult* prescribed by the Zend-Avesta of a symbolic kind. Here we do not find any symbolic dances which are supposed to celebrate or imitate the interlaced course of the stars, or other sorts of activities counting only as an allusive image for universal ideas; on the contrary, all actions made into religious duties for the Parsis are activities which concern the actual propagation of purity internally and externally and they appear as a purposeful accomplishment of the universal end, namely the actualization of Ormuzd's dominion in all men and in all natural objects—an end, therefore, not just alluded to in this business itself, but wholly and completely attained.

3. Non-artistic Interpretation and Presentation of Zoroastrianism

Now since what is typical of the symbolic is absent from this whole outlook the character of what is strictly artistic is also

missing. In general, this way of visualizing things may be called
poetic, since in it neither the individual objects in nature nor
individual human attitudes, situations, deeds, actions, are to be
construed in their immediate and therefore accidental and prosaic
lack of significance; on the contrary, they are seen in accordance
with their essential nature, in the light of the Absolute, which is
light; and, conversely, the universal essence too of concrete natural
and human reality is not grasped in its universality, devoid of
existence and shape, but, on the contrary, this universal and that
individuality are visualized and expressed as immediately one.
Such a view may be counted as beautiful, broad, and great, and,
compared with bad and senseless idols, light as this inherently
pure and universal element is of course an adequate image for the
good and the true. But the poetry in this does not get beyond the
universal at all and it never reaches art and works of art. For
neither are the good and the Divine inwardly determinate, nor are
the shape and form of this content generated by the spirit; on the
contrary, as we have seen already, what is really present—the sun,
the stars, actual plants, animals, men, existent fire—is apprehended
as the Absolute's shape which is already in its *immediacy* adequate
thereto. The sensuous representation is not, as art demands,
formed, shaped, and invented by the spirit; on the contrary the
adequate expression of the Divine is found and enunciated directly
in the external existent. True, the individual, on the other hand,
is fixed, independently of its reality, by imagination, as, e.g., in
the Izeds and Fervers, the genii of individual men; but in this
start of separation [between meaning and shape] poetic invention
is of the weakest kind, because the difference remains entirely
formal, so that the genius, Ferver, Ized, does not and is not meant
to acquire any special configuration of its own, but has, for one
thing, only just the same content as any individual, and, for another
thing, only the mere explicitly empty form of subjectivity which
the existent individual already possesses. On this account imagination produces neither another deeper meaning nor the independent form of an inherently richer individuality. And even if,
moreover, we see particular existents gripped together into general
ideas and genera to which a real existence, conformably to the
genus, is given by imagination, still this elevation of multiplicity
to a comprehensive essential unity, as germ and basis for individuals of the same species and genus, is only in a rather vague sense

an activity of imagination and no proper work of poetry and art. So, e.g., the holy fire of Bahram is the essential fire, and amongst the waters, equally, one water precedes all others.[1] Hom [the drink of immortality] counts as the first, purest, and most powerful amongst all trees, the original tree in which the sap of life flows full of immortality. Amongst hills Albordsch,[2] the holy hill, is visualized as the original germ of the whole earth; he stands in radiance; from him proceed the human benefactors who had knowledge of the light and on him rest the sun, moon, and stars. But on the whole the universal is intuited in immediate unity with the present reality of particular things and only here and there are universal ideas illustrated by particular images.

Still more prosaically the cult has as its aim the actual accomplishment and dominion of Ormuzd in all things, and it demands only this appropriateness and purity of every object, without even merely making of it a work of art existing as it were in immediate life, as in Greece the warriors and wrestlers, etc., could present such a work in their trained bodies.

In all these respects and relations the first unity of spiritual universality with sensuous reality constitutes only the groundwork of the symbolic in art, yet without being itself already strictly symbolical and bringing works of art into existence. In order to attain this next objective there must be an advance from our subject hitherto, i.e. from this first unity, to difference and the battle between meaning and shape.

B. FANTASTIC SYMBOLISM

If consciousness does advance out of the immediately intuited identity between the Absolute and its externally perceived exis-

---

[1] The meaning of this obscure passage seems to be the following: Meaning and shape begin to be differentiated when, e.g., the individual as such, taken abstractly apart from the reality of a concrete individual, is imaged as Ferver, the genius of an individual man. But the Ferver does not differ from the individual in either content or form. In content, or general character, the Ferver is just an abstract individual over again and in form he has the same sort of subjectivity as the individual has. Thus the 'poetry' here does not create a deeper meaning than abstract individuality, or a better form than abstract subjectivity. There may seem to be an advance when hills, e.g., are brought together under an idea or genus hill, and then the genus is given a real embodiment in a special hill. But this reality is then just a pattern for the genus. Alburz is *the* hill, Bahram *the* fire or the essence of fire. The universal is not differentiated in the particulars but is simply directly present in them.

[2] i.e. Alburz, a mythical mountain supposed to support the sky.

tence, then what confronts us as the essential point is the cleavage between the hitherto united aspects, i.e. the battle between meaning and shape, which immediately provokes the attempt to heal the breach again by building the separated parts together in a fanciful way.

It is with this attempt alone that there arises the proper need for art. For if the content of ideas is established independently, freed now from its existence and no longer only intuited directly in present reality, then thereby the task is set before spirit of giving for contemplation and perception—in a renewed mode produced by spirit—a richly fanciful shape to universal ideas and in this activity creating artistic productions. Now since in the first sphere, where still we are at present, this task can be discharged symbolically only, it may seem as if we are already standing on the ground of the strictly symbolic. But this is not the case.

The first thing that we encounter is configurations produced by a fermenting imagination which in the unrest of its fantasticalness only indicates the way which can lead to the genuine centre of symbolic art. That is to say that, at the first appearance of the difference and the relation between meaning and the form of representation, both the separation and the linkage are still of a confused kind. This confusion is necessitated by the fact that neither of the different sides has yet become a totality carrying in itself the feature constituting the fundamental character of the other side, whereby alone the really adequate unity and reconciliation can be established. Spirit in its totality, determines, e.g., its external appearance out of its own resources, just as the inherently total and adequate appearance is explicitly only the external existence of the spirit. But, in this first separation of meanings, apprehended by the spirit, from the existing world of appearances, the meanings are not those of the concrete spirit but abstractions, and their expression is likewise unspiritualized and therefore, in its abstraction, only external and sensuous. The pressure for distinction and unification is therefore a frenzy which from sensuous individual details ranges over directly, indefinitely, and wildly to the most general meanings, and for what is inwardly grasped in consciousness can find only the precisely opposite form of sensuous configurations. It is this contradiction which is supposed to produce a genuine unification of the elements which struggle against one another; yet from one side it[1] is driven into the opposite one, and out of this is pushed back again into the first; without rest it is just thrown hither and thither, and in the oscillation and fermentation of this striving for a solution thinks it has already found appeasement. As a result, instead of genuine satisfaction it is precisely only the contradiction itself which passes for the true unification, and thus the most imperfect unity passes for what properly corresponds to art. True beauty, therefore, we may not seek in this field of murky confusion. For in the restless sudden leap from one extreme to the other, on the one hand we find the breadth and might of universal meanings linked to the sensuous taken both in its individuality and in its elementary appearance, linked therefore in a wholly inadequate way; on the other hand, what is most universal, if a start is made from that, is shamelessly shifted, in the converse manner, into the heart of the most sensuous present; and moreover if the sense of this incompatibility comes to mind, imagination here can have no recourse but to distortions, since it drives particular shapes beyond their firmly limited particular character, stretches them, alters them into indefiniteness, and intensifies them beyond all bounds; it tears them apart from one another and therefore in this struggle towards accord brings to light only the very opposite in its lack of reconciliation.

These first, still wildest, attempts of fancy and art we find especially amongst the ancient Indians.[2] Their chief defect, compatibly with the general nature of this stage, consists in this, that they cannot grasp either the meanings themselves in their clarity, or existing reality in its own proper shape and significance. Therefore the Indians have proved themselves incapable of an historical interpretation of persons and events, because an historical treatment requires *sang-froid* in taking up and understanding the past on its own account in its actual shape with its empirical links, grounds, aims, and causes. This prosaic circumspection is at variance with the Indian pressure to refer each and everything back to the sheerly Absolute and Divine, and to contemplate in the commonest and most sensuous things a fancifully created

[1] i.e. the contradiction, which is the subject of this sentence. But Hegel really means that a person caught by the frenzy above-mentioned is tossed to and fro in an endeavour to find unity instead of contradiction.

[2] Hegel's reports of Indian views are based on an exhaustive study of the relevant books and periodicals in English and French, as well as in German. Cf. above, p. 215, note.

presence and actuality of the gods. In their confused intermixture of finite and Absolute, therefore, since the order, intelligibility, and fixity of everyday life and prose remains totally disregarded, they fall, despite all their exuberance and magnificent boldness of conception, into a monstrous extravagance of the fantastic which runs over from what is inmost and deepest into the most commonplace present in order to turn one extreme directly into the other and confuse them.

For the more determinate traits of this continuing intoxication, this crazing and crazedness, we have here to go through not the religious ideas as such, but only the chief features in accordance with which this way of looking at things belongs to art. These chief points are the following.

1. *The Indian Conception of Brahma*

One extreme in the Indian mind is the consciousness of the Absolute as what in itself is purely universal, undifferentiated, and therefore completely indeterminate. Since this extreme abstraction has no particular content and is not visualized as a concrete personality, it affords in no respect a material which intuition could shape in some way or other. For Brahma, as this supreme divinity, is entirely withdrawn from sense and observation, indeed he is not even properly an object for thought. For thinking requires self-consciousness which sets an object before itself in order to find itself therein. All understanding is already an identification of self and object, a reconciliation between two terms which, outside this understanding, are separated; what I do not understand or know remains something foreign to me, different from me. But the Indian way of unifying the human self with Brahma is nothing but the steadily enhanced 'screwing oneself up' to this extreme abstraction itself, wherein not only the entire concrete content but even self-consciousness must perish before man can attain to this abstraction. Therefore the Indian knows no reconciliation and identity with Brahma in the sense of the human spirit's reaching *knowledge* of this unity; on the contrary, the unity consists for the Indian precisely in the fact that consciousness and self-consciousness and therefore all the content of the world and the inner worth of the man's own personality totally disappear. This emptying and annihilation, reaching absolute pointlessness, counts as the highest condition which makes man into the supreme god himself, into Brahma.

This abstraction, which is amongst the harshest things that man can lay on himself, on the one hand as Brahma and, on the other, as the purely theoretical inner cult of dullness and mortification, is no object for imagination and art. Art, we may suppose, acquires here an opportunity of indulging in manifold productions only in the course of sketching the way to this end [of self-annihilation].

2. *Sensuousness, Boundlessness, and the Activity of Personifying*

But, conversely, the Indian outlook nevertheless springs directly out of this super-sensuousness into the wildest sensuousness. Yet since the immediate and therefore peaceful identity of the two sides is superseded and, instead of it, *difference* within the identity has become the fundamental model, this contradiction pushes us, with no mediation, out of the most finite things into the Divine and then back again; and we live amongst configurations arising out of this mutual perverse transposition of one side into the other as in a witches' world where no determinacy of form, when we hope to fix our attention on it, stays firm but suddenly is changed into its opposite or swells and spreads into extravagance.

Now the general ways in which Indian art comes before us are the following.[1]

(*a*) In the first place, imagination places the most tremendous content of the Absolute into what is immediately sensuous and individual so that this individual thing, just as it is, is supposed to represent such a content perfectly in itself and to exist for contemplation as so representing it. In the *Ramayana*, for instance, the friend of Rama, Hanuman, the Prince of Apes, is a chief figure and he accomplishes the boldest deeds. To speak generally, in India the ape is revered as divine, and there is a whole city of apes. In the ape as this individual ape the infinite content of the Absolute is gazed at with wonder and is deified. Similarly the cow Sabala appears likewise in the *Ramayana*, in the episode of Vishwamitra's penances, clothed with boundless might. Furthermore there are families in India in which the Absolute itself vegetates in the form of this actual man, even if an entirely dull and simple one,

---

[1] Here again transliterations vary. I have followed Hegel except where a different spelling has become current in English.

who in his immediate life and presence is venerated as god. The same thing we find in Lamaism too where also a single individual man enjoys supreme adoration as a present god. But in India this veneration is not paid exclusively to one man only; on the contrary, every Brahman counts from the beginning, by his birth in his caste, as Brahma already; he has achieved in a natural way, through his physical birth, the spiritual rebirth which identifies the man with god, so that thus the pinnacle of the supremely Divine itself falls back immediately into the purely commonplace physical reality of existence. For although Brahmans are under the most sacred obligation to read the Vedas and thereby acquire an insight into the depths of the Divine, this duty can be discharged adequately all the same with the greatest lack of spirituality without depriving the Brahman of his divinity. In a similar way one of the most general matters which the Indians portray is procreation and the beginning of life, just as the Greeks specify Eros as the oldest god. Now this procreation, the divine activity, is again taken entirely sensuously in numerous portrayals, and the male and female sexual organs are regarded as supremely holy. So too, even if the Divine enters reality explicitly in its divinity, it is drawn into the midst of everyday life in an entirely trivial way. For example, in the beginning of the *Ramayana* there is a story of how Brahma came to Valmikis, the mythical singer of the [poem] *Ramayana*. Valmikis welcomes him entirely in the ordinary Indian way, compliments him, places a chair for him, brings him water and fruit; Brahma actually sits down and compels his host to sit likewise; they sit for a long time until at last Brahma commands Valmikis to compose the *Ramayana*.

This likewise is still not a properly symbolic conception, for although here, as symbol requires, the figures are drawn from the contemporary world and applied to universal meanings, still there is missing here the other aspect of symbols, i.e. the fact that the particular existents are not supposed actually to *be* the absolute meaning for our vision, but only to indicate it. For Indian imagination the ape, the cow, the individual Brahman, etc., are not a cognate symbol of the Divine; they are treated and represented as the Divine itself, as an existent adequate thereto.

But herein lies the contradiction which drives Indian art on to a second mode of conception. For, on the one hand, the purely invisible, the Absolute as such, the bare meaning, is grasped as the truly Divine, while, on the other hand, individual things in concrete reality are also, in their sensuous existence, directly regarded by imagination as divine manifestations. In part, indeed, they are supposed to express only particular aspects of the Absolute, yet even then the immediate individual thing, represented as an adequate existence of this specific universality, is plainly simply inadequate to this its content; the individual is in contradiction with the content all the more sharply as the meaning is here already seized in its universality and yet, expressly in this universality, is posited immediately by imagination as identical with what is most sensuous and most individual.

(b) The first resolution of this disunion is sought by Indian art, as was already indicated above, in the extravagance of its productions. In order, as sensuous figures themselves, to reach universality, the individual figures are wildly tugged apart from one another into the colossal and grotesque. For the individual figure which is to express not itself and the meaning appropriate to it as a particular phenomenon but a universal meaning lying outside its own, does not satisfy contemplation until it is torn out of itself into monstrosity without aim and measure. For here above all there is the most extravagant exaggeration of size, alike in the spatial figure and in temporal immeasurability, as well as the multiplication of one and the same characteristic, the many heads, the mass of arms, etc., whereby attainment of the breadth and universality of meanings is pursued. The egg, for example, includes the bird. This individual existent is expanded to the immeasurable idea of a world-egg as enveloping the universal life of all things, in which life Brahma, the procreating god, without action of his own, spends a year in creation until by his mere thought the halves of the egg fall apart. Now besides natural objects, human individuals and events are also equally elevated to having the meaning of an actual divine act in such a way that neither the Divine by itself nor the human can be retained apart, but both appear continually entangled hither and thither with one another. To this category there belong particularly the incarnations of the gods, especially of Vishnu, the conserving god, whose deeds provide a main subject-matter of the great epic poems. In these materializations divinity passes over immediately into mundane manifestation. So, for example, Rama is himself the seventh incarnation of Vishnu (Ramchandra). In individual needs, actions, situations, forms and modes of behaviour, the contents of these poems are clearly drawn in part from actual events, from the deeds of ancient kings who were strong enough to found new conditions of order and legality, and we are therefore in the midst of humanity on the firm ground of reality. But then conversely everything is expanded again, stretched into nebulosity, played over into the universal once more, so that we lose again the ground that had scarcely been won and we know not where we are. The same thing meets us in the *Shakuntala*. At the start we have before us the tenderest, most fragrant world of love where everything goes on its appropriate way in a human fashion, but then we are suddenly snatched away from this entirely concrete reality and carried up into the clouds of Indra's heaven where everything is changed and broadened out of its limited sphere into universal meanings of the life of nature in relation to Brahmans and that power over the gods of nature which is granted to man on the strength of his severe penances.

Even this mode of representation cannot be strictly called symbolical. For the determinate shape which the symbolic mode uses is allowed, in symbolism proper, to persist just as it is, because symbolism does not seek to see in the shape the immediate existence of the meaning in its universality, but merely hints at the meaning by reference to the properties of the object that are cognate to the meaning. But Indian art, although severing universality from individual existence, nevertheless demands the immediate unity of both as well, a unity produced by imagination; it must therefore deprive the determinate existent of its limitedness and, in a purely sensuous way, enlarge it into indefiniteness and, in general, transform and disfigure it. In this dissolution of determinacy and in the confusion arising from the fact that the loftiest content is always introduced into things, phenomena, incidents, and deeds which in their limitedness are incapable either of actually having the might of such a content in themselves or of expressing it, we may therefore look for a touch of *sublimity* rather than what is properly symbolical. In the sublime, that is to say, as we shall learn later on [in Chapter 2], the finite appearance expresses the Absolute, which it is supposed to bring before our vision, but only in such a way that the Absolute withdraws from the appearance and the appearance falls short of the content. This is the case with eternity, for example. The idea of eternity becomes sublime if it is to be expressed in temporal terms, since every greatest number is always not yet sufficient and must be increased on and on without end; as it is said of God: 'A thousand years are in thy sight one day.'[1] In this way and the like, Indian art contains many things which begin to strike this note of sublimity. Yet the great difference from sublimity, properly so-called, consists in this, that the Indian imagination in such wild configurations does not succeed in positing negatively the phenomena that it presents, but precisely by that immeasurability and unlimitedness thinks that the difference and contradiction between the Absolute and its configuration has been obliterated and made to vanish.

However little we can allow Indian art in its excess to count as strictly symbolical or sublime, neither is it, strictly speaking, beautiful. For we may concede that, especially in sketching human life as such, it affords us much that is delightful and gentle, many friendly images and delicate feelings, the most brilliant descriptions of nature and the most charming and most chilldike traits of love and naïve innocence, as well as much that is grand and noble; but, so far as the universal fundamental meanings are concerned, the spiritual, on the other hand, still always remains entirely sensuous again; the most commonplace is set on a level with the supreme, determinacy is destroyed, the sublime is just boundlessness, and what belongs to myth gets involved for the most part only in the fantasticalness of a restless inquisitive imagination and an unintelligent talent for configuration.

(c) Finally, the purest manner of portraying universal meanings which we find at this stage is personifying them by using the human form in general. Nevertheless since the meaning here is not yet conceived as free spiritual subjectivity and what is meant instead is either some *abstract* characteristic taken in its universality, or else mere nature, e.g. the life of rivers, hills, stars, and the sun, it is properly below the dignity of the human form to be used as an expression for this sort of subject-matter. For in accordance with their true specific character the human body, as well as the form of human activities and events, express only the concrete spirit and its inner content, and the spirit therefore remains with its whole self in this its real embodiment which thus is no mere symbol or external sign.

It follows [that personification here is unsatisfactory in two ways: for (i)] if the meaning, which the personification is summoned to

1 Hegel's version of Ps. 90: 4.

portray, is to belong to the spiritual sphere as much as to the natural one, then, owing to the *abstractness* of the meaning at this stage, the personification is still superficial and for its clearer elucidation requires manifold figures in addition; and with these it is confused and thereby is itself vitiated. [ii] It is not subjectivity and its shape which is the indicative thing here, but its expressions, deeds, etc., for it is in doing and acting alone that there lies the more determinate particularization which can be brought into relation with the determinate content of the universal meanings. But in that case there enters again the defect that not the subject but only his expression is the significant thing, and there is also the confusion that events and deeds, instead of being the reality and self-actualizing determinate being of the subject, derive their content and their meaning from elsewhere [i.e. from being personified]. A series of such actions may therefore in itself have a sequence and a logicality derived from the content which such a series serves to express, but by personification and humanization this logicality is nevertheless interrupted again and partly superseded, because the imposition of a subject on them [i.e. by personifying them] leads conversely to the caprice of actions and expressions, so that thus the meaningful and the meaningless are turned topsy-turvy in a varied and irregular way, all the more so the less is imagination capable of bringing its meanings and their shapes into a fundamental and fixed interconnection.—But if the purely natural is adopted as the sole subject-matter, the natural for its part does not deserve to be clothed with the human form, and this latter, appropriate only to the expression of spirit, is for its part incapable of portraying the merely natural.

In all these respects this personification cannot be true, because truth in art, like truth in general, requires the harmony of inner and outer, of concept and reality. Greek mythology does personify even the Black Sea and the Scamander; it has its river-gods, nymphs, dryads, and, in general, it makes nature in many ways the content of its anthropomorphic gods. Yet it does not leave personification purely formal and superficial, but shapes out of it individuals whence the purely natural meaning retires, and the human element, which has adopted such natural content into itself, becomes the predominant thing. But Indian art does not get beyond the grotesque intermixture of the natural and the human, so that neither side gets its right, and both are reciprocally vitiated.

To speak generally, these personifications too are not yet properly symbolical, because, on account of their superficiality of form, they do not stand in any essential relation and close affinity with the specific content which they were supposed to express symbolically. But at the same time, in respect of the particular further figures and attributes with which such personifications appear intermingled and which are supposed to express the more specific qualities ascribed to the gods, there begins a striving after symbolical representations, for which personification in that event remains rather only the universal and comprehensive form.

As for the more important views belonging to this context, in the first place mention must be made of Trimurti, the tri-formed divinity. This divinity is composed, *first*, of Brahma, the productive generating activity, the creator of the world, lord of the gods, etc. On the one hand, Trimurti is distinct from Brahma (in the neuter), from the supreme being, and is its first-born; but, on the other hand, he coincides again with this abstract divinity, since in general, in the case of the Indians, differences cannot be retained within fixed limits but are partly confused and partly pass over into one another. Now his shape in detail has much that is symbolical; he is portrayed with four heads and four hands, with sceptre, ring, etc. In colour he is red, which hints at the sun, because these gods always at the same time bear universal natural significances which they personify. The *second* god in Trimurti is Vishnu, the god who preserves, and the *third* is Shiva, who destroys. The symbols for these gods are innumerable. For along with the universality of their meanings they comprise infinitely many single effects, partly in connection with particular phenomena in nature (especially elemental ones, as e.g. Vishnu has the quality of fire—Wilson's Lexicon,[1] s.v. 2) but partly also with spiritual ones; this material then ferments confusedly in various ways and frequently brings the most repulsive shapes into appearance for contemplation.

In this tri-form god it appears at once most clearly that here the spiritual shape cannot yet emerge in its truth, because here the spiritual does not constitute the proper and decisive meaning. This trinity of gods would be spirit if the third god were a concrete unity and a return into itself out of difference and duality. For, according to the true conception, God is spirit as this active

[1] i.e. H. H. Wilson, *A Dictionary in Sanskrit and English* (Calcutta, 1819).

absolute difference and unity which, in general terms, constitutes the essence of spirit. But in Trimurti the third god is not a concrete totality at all; on the contrary, it is itself only *one*, side by side with the two others, and therefore is likewise an abstraction: there is no return into itself, but only a transition into something else, a change, procreation, and destruction. Therefore we must take great care not to try to recover the supreme truth in such first inklings of reason or to recognize the Christian Trinity already in this hint, which in its rhythm does of course contain threefoldness, a fundamental idea in Christianity.

Starting from Brahma and Trimurti Indian imagination proceeds still further fantastically to an infinite number of most multitudinously shaped gods. For those universal meanings, viewed as what is essentially divine, are met again in thousands and thousands of phenomena which now themselves are personified and symbolized as gods; and they put the greatest hindrances in the way of a clear understanding because of the indeterminacy and confusing restlessness of imagination which in its inventions deals with nothing in accordance with its proper nature and overturns each and every thing. For these subordinate gods, with Indra, air and sky, at their head, the more detailed content is provided above all by the universal forces of nature, by the stars, streams, mountains, in the different features of their efficacy, their alteration, their influence whether beneficent or harmful, preservative or destructive.

But one of the chief topics of Indian fancy and art is the origin of the gods and of all things, i.e. theogony and cosmology. For Indian imagination is in general caught in the steady process of introducing into the midst of external appearance whatever is most non-sensuous and, at the same time, conversely, of obliterating again the most natural and sensuous realm by the most extreme abstraction. In a similar way the origin of the gods out of the supreme divinity and the operation and determinate existence of Brahma, Vishnu, and Shiva are represented in particular things, in hills, waters, and human affairs. The same content may then, on the one hand, acquire on its own account a particular shape of the gods, but, on the other hand, these gods pass over again into the universal meanings of the highest gods. Of such theogonies and cosmogonies there is a great number and endless variety. If therefore it is said that *thus* have the Indians represented to themselves the creation of the world, the origin of all things, this can be valid always for one sect only or one specific book, for elsewhere you can always find the same thing stated differently. The fancy of this people in its images and shapes is inexhaustible.

A principal idea running through the stories of origins is the continually recurring description of natural *generation* instead of the idea of a spiritual *creation*. Once we are acquainted with these modes of looking at things, we have the key to many representations which entirely confound our sense of shame, for shamelessness is pushed to an extreme and in its sensuousness proceeds to the incredible. A brilliant example of this manner and mode of treatment is afforded by the famous and familiar episode in the *Ramayana*, the descent of Ganga. The tale is told of the occasion when Rama comes accidentally to the Ganges. The wintry ice-covered Himavan, Prince of Mountains, had two daughters by the slender Mena, namely Ganga, the elder, and the beautiful Uma, the younger. The gods, especially Indra, had begged the father to send Ganga to them in order that they might celebrate the sacred rites, and, since Himavan showed himself ready to accede to their petition, Ganga rose on high to the blessed gods. Now follows the further history of Uma who, after accomplishing many wonderful deeds of humility and penitence, is married to Rudra, i.e. Shiva. From this marriage rugged and barren mountains are engendered. For a century long, without intermission, Shiva lay with Uma in a conjugal embrace, with the result that the gods, alarmed by Shiva's progenitive powers and full of alarm about the child to be born, begged him to turn his seed to the earth. (This passage the English translator [Sir Charles Wilkins] had no mind to translate word for word because it is all too wanting in decency and shame.) Shiva after all heeds the request of the gods; he gives up further procreative activity in order not to destroy the universe, and casts his seed on the earth; from it, fecundated by fire, there comes to birth the white mountain which separates India from Tartary. But Uma falls into anger and fury at this and curses all wedlock. These are in a way horrible and grotesque compositions at variance with our imagination and any intelligence, so that, instead of actually presenting what is to be taken as their real meaning, they only hint at it.

[A. W.] Schlegel has not translated this part of the episode. He only recounts how Ganga descended to earth again. This happened in the following way. An ancestor of Rama, Sagara, had a bad son, but from a second wife had sixty thousand sons who came to the world in a pumpkin, but, in jars with clarified butter, grew up to be strong men. One day Sagara wished to sacrifice a steed, but it was snatched from him by Vishnu in the form of a snake. Thereupon Sagara sends out the sixty thousand. Vishnu's breath, as they approached him after great hardships and much searching, burnt them to ashes. At last after a protracted wait a grandson of Sagara, Ansuman, the resplendent one, son of Asamanja, set forth to rediscover his sixty thousand uncles and the sacrificial horse. He did indeed actually come across the horse, Shiva, and the heap of ashes; but the bird-king Garudas told him that his relatives would never return to life again unless the river of the holy Ganga flowed down from heaven over the heap of ashes. Then the stalwart Ansuman undergoes the strictest penances throughout thirty-two thousand years on the peak of Himavan. In vain. Neither his own mortifications nor those of his son Dwilipa for thirty thousand years help in the slightest. Only in the son of Dwilipa, the excellent Bhagiratha, is the great work successful after a further thousand years of penance. Now Ganga rushes down, but, to prevent her from ruining the earth, Shiva holds his head underneath so that the water flows away into the locks of his hair. Thus then again new penances are required from Bhagiratha in order to free Ganga from these locks so that she can stream on. Finally, she pours forth into six streams; the seventh stream Bhagiratha, after enormous difficulties, diverts to the sixty thousand who mount to heaven, while Bhagiratha himself rules over his people for yet a long time in peace.

Other theogonies, e.g. the Scandinavian and the Greek, are similar to the Indian. In all of them the chief category is generation and being generated; but none of them lets itself go so wildly [as the Indian] and, in the main, with such caprice and inappropriateness of invention in its configurations. The theogony of Hesiod especially is far more perspicuous and definite, so that every time we know where we are and we clearly recognize the meaning, because it is more brightly prominent and shows that the external shape is only its external manifestation. The theogony begins[1] with Chaos, Erebus, Eros, and Gaia; Gaia produces Uranus by herself alone, and then, mated with him, brings forth the mountains, the Black Sea, etc., as well as Cronus, the Cyclopes, and the

[1] *Theogony*, 116 ff.

hundred-handed giants whom, soon after their birth, Uranus shut up in Tartarus. Gaia induces Cronus to unman Uranus; this happens; the blood is caught by the earth and hence grew the Furies and the Giants, while the castrated member is caught by the sea and the Cytherean [i.e. Aphrodite] springs from its foam. All this is clearer and brought more firmly together, and also it does not stop at the circle of gods of mere nature.

3. *View of Purification and Penance*

If we look now for a transitional point to symbol proper, we may already find its first beginnings in Indian imagination also. For however preoccupied Indian fancy may be with the task of screwing sensuous appearance up into a polytheism which no other people has to exhibit in the like boundlessness and mutability, still on the other hand in all sorts of insights and narratives it is always mindful again of that spiritual abstraction of the supreme god, compared with whom the individual, the sensuous, and the phenomenal spheres are apprehended as non-divine, inappropriate, and therefore as something which must be negatived and superseded. For, as was said at the outset, it is just this conversion of one side into the other which constitutes the peculiar type, and the unappeased lack of reconciliation, of the Indian outlook. Indian art therefore, has never been tired of giving shape in the most varied ways to the self-sacrifice of the sensuous and to the force of spiritual abstraction and immersion in one's inner being. To this category there belong the portrayals of protracted penances and profound meditations, of which not only the oldest epic poems, the *Ramayana* and *Mahabharata*, but also many other poetic works of art provide the most important samples. Such penances were indeed often undertaken from ambition or at least for specific ends which are not supposed to lead to the supreme and final unification with Brahma and to the destruction of the mundane and the finite—as, e.g., the end of acquiring the power of a Brahman, etc. Yet, at the same time, there is always implicit the view that penance, and the continued meditation which turns away more and more from everything specific and finite, far surpass birth in a specific caste as well as the dominion of mere nature and the gods of nature. Wherefore Indra in particular, the Prince of Gods, opposes strict penitents and tries to lure them away, or, if no allurement is any use, calls on the higher gods to aid him, because otherwise the whole heaven would get into confusion.

In the portrayal of such penances and their different kinds, stages, and grades Indian art is almost as inventive as it is in its polytheism, and it pursues the business of such invention with great seriousness.

This is the point from which we can extend our inquiry further.

C. SYMBOLISM PROPER

For symbolic art, as well as for fine art also, it is essential that the meaning to which it undertakes to give shape shall not only (as happens in Indian art) emerge from the first immediate unity with its external existence, a unity still basic there prior to all division and differentiation, but shall also become explicitly *free* from the *immediate* sensuous shape. This liberation can only take place in so far as the sensuous and natural is apprehended and envisaged in itself as negative, as what is to be, and has been, superseded.

Yet further it is necessary that the negative, coming into appearance as the passing and self-transcendence of the natural, shall be accepted and shaped as the absolute meaning of things in general, as a factor in the Divine. Yet thereby we have already forsaken Indian art. Indian imagination, it is true, does not lack a vision of the negative; Shiva is the destroyer, and Indra, the procreator, dies; indeed even Time, the annihilator, personified as Kala, the fearsome giant, destroys the whole universe and all the gods, even Trimurti who likewise passes away into Brahma, just as the individual, in his identification with the supreme god, lets himself and his whole knowing and willing dwindle away. But in these views the negative is partly only a changing and altering, partly only the abstraction which sheds the determinate in order to press on to the undetermined and therefore empty universality utterly devoid of all content. Against this, the substance of the Divine remains unaltered, one and the same in changes of form, in transition, advance to polytheism, and elevation from many gods to a single supreme god once more. This is not the one God who in himself, as this one, has the negative as his own determinate character necessarily belonging to his essential nature.[1] In a way similar to

[1] The necessary presence of the finite, i.e. the negative of the infinite, within God himself, is a cardinal point in Hegel's philosophy of Christianity. See, e.g., my *A Layman's Quest* (London, 1969), ch. 6.

the Indian, in the Parsi outlook the bringer of corruption and harmfulness lies *outside* Ormuzd in Ahriman and therefore produces only an opposition and a battle which does not belong to the one god, Ormuzd, as an allotted factor in him.

The further step we now have to take consists in this, that (*a*) the negative is fixed independently by consciousness as the Absolute, but (*b*) is regarded as only *one* factor in the Divine—yet as a factor which does not merely fall outside the true Absolute into another god [like Ahriman], but is so ascribed to the Absolute that the true God appears as the negativing of *himself* and therefore has the negative as his own immanent determinate character.

In virtue of this further idea the Absolute becomes for the first time inherently *concrete*, by having its determinateness within itself and therefore by being a unity in itself, and the factors of this unity reveal themselves to contemplation as the different determinations of one and the same God. This is because what is principally at issue here is the first satisfaction of the need for the determinateness of the absolute meaning in itself. The meanings previously considered remained, on account of their abstraction, purely indeterminate and therefore shapeless, or, if alternatively they advanced to determinacy, either coincided immediately with natural existence or fell into a battle between shapes, a battle which never came to either peace or reconciliation. This double defect is now to be remedied in the following way by the inner process of thought and by the external progress of national convictions.

(i) A closer bond is forged between inner and outer by the fact that every determining of the Absolute is inherently already a beginning of an outward passage into expression. For every determining is inherent differentiation; but the external as such is always determinate and differentiated, and therefore an aspect is present in which the external is more in correspondence with the meaning than was the case at the stages hitherto considered. But the first determinateness and negation of the Absolute in itself cannot be the free self-determination of the *spirit* as spirit, but is itself only the immediate negation. The immediate and therefore natural negation in its most comprehensive mode is *death*. Thus the Absolute now is interpreted as having to enter this negation as a determination accruing to its own essence and to tread the path of extinction and death. Therefore we see the glorification of death and grief arising in the consciousness of peoples as primarily the death of the expiring sensuous sphere; the death of what is natural becomes known as a necessary constituent in the life of the Absolute. Yet the Absolute, on the one hand, in order to experience this factor, i.e. death, must come into being and have a determinate existence, while on the other hand it does not stop at annihilation in death but out of it is restored to a positive unity in itself in an exalted way. Here, therefore, dying is not taken at all as the whole meaning, but only as *one* aspect of it; the Absolute is indeed apprehended as a transcendence of its immediate existence, as a passing and a passing away of that existence, but also, conversely, through this process of the negative, as a return into itself, as a resurrection to a life inherently eternal and divine. This is because death has a double meaning: (*a*) it is precisely the immediate passing away of the natural, (*b*) it is the death of the *purely* natural and therefore the birth of something higher, namely the spiritual realm to which the merely natural dies in the sense that the spirit has this element of death in itself as belonging to its essence.

(ii) But therefore the natural shape in its immediacy and sensuous existence can no longer be interpreted as coinciding with the meaning glimpsed in it, because the meaning of the external itself just consists in its dying in its real existence and transcending itself.

(iii) In the like manner the mere battle between meaning and shape dies away along with that ferment of imagination which produced the fantastic in India. True, the meaning is even now not yet known in that pure unity with itself which is *liberated* from present reality, not yet so known as meaning in its perfectly purified clarity that it could be contrasted with the shape illustrative of it. But, conversely, the individual shape, as this individual animal, or this human personification, or event, or action, cannot bring before contemplation an immediate adequate existence of the Absolute. This inadequate identity is already surpassed just to the same extent that that perfect liberation is not yet attained. In place of both there is set that kind of representation which we have already described above as the strictly symbolic. On the one hand, the symbol *can* come to the fore now, because what is inward, and comprehended as meaning, no longer, as in Indian conceptions, merely comes and goes, now sinking here and there directly into externality, now withdrawing therefrom into the solitude of abstraction; on the contrary, it begins to establish itself explicitly in face of purely natural reality. On the other hand, the symbol *must* now attain configuration. For although the meaning completely pertinent up to this point has for its content the element of the negation of the natural, still the truly inward only now *begins* to wrest its way out of the natural and is therefore still intertwined with the external mode of appearance, with the result that it cannot without an external shape enter our minds on its own account in its clear universality.

To the essential nature of what in general constitutes the fundamental *meaning* in symbolic art there now corresponds the manner of *configuration*, in the sense that the specific natural forms and human actions in the individualized features proper to them are neither to portray and mean themselves alone nor to bring the Divine before the spectator's mind as *immediately* present and perceptible in them. Their specific determinate being in its particular shape is to have only qualities *hinting* at a more comprehensive meaning cognate with them. On this account, it is precisely that universal dialectic of life—birth, growth, passing away, and rebirth out of death—which constitutes in this matter too the adequate content for the strictly symbolic form; this is so because in almost all departments of natural and spiritual life there are phenomena which have this process as the basis of their existence and therefore can be used for illustrating such meanings and for pointing to them. For between the two sides [meaning and expression] there occurs in fact a real affinity. For example, plants spring from their seed, they germinate, grow, blossom, produce fruit, and then the fruit decays and brings forth new seeds. The sun, similarly, stands low in winter, rises high in spring, until in summer it reaches its zenith and now bestows its greatest blessings or wreaks its destructiveness, but then it sinks down again. The different ages in life—childhood, youth, manhood, and old age—also display the same universal process. But above all, to particularize further, specific localities too enter this list of illustrations, for instance the Nile valley. Since the purely fantastic is displaced solely by these more fundamental traits of affinity and by the closer correspondence between meaning and its expression, there enters a circumspect choice between symbolizing shapes in respect of their adequacy or inadequacy; and that restless frenzy is quietened into a more intelligent sobriety.

We see therefore coming forward again a more reconciled unity, as we found it at the first stage, but with the difference that the identity of the meaning with its real existence is no longer an immediate unification but one re-established out of difference and therefore not just met with but *produced* by spirit. The inner life in general begins here to grow towards independence and self-knowledge; it seeks its counterpart in the natural which, on its side, has a like counterpart in the life and fate of the spiritual. The tremendous impulse towards symbolic *art* proceeds here from this urge which seeks to recognize the one side in the other, which seeks to present to our contemplation and imagination the inner meaning through the outward shape and the significance of the outward shapes through the inner meaning, the two being linked. Only when the inner becomes free and yet preserves the impulse to picture to itself, in a real shape, what it is in its essence, and to have this very picture before itself as also an external work, only then does there begin the proper impulse towards art, especially the visual arts. In other words, hereby alone is there present the necessity of giving to the inner by spiritual activity an appearance not merely met with in advance [in nature] but no less devised by spirit.[1] Imagination in that event makes a second shape which does not count by itself as an end but is used only to illustrate a meaning allied to it and therefore is dependent on it.

Now this situation could be so conceived that it might be thought that the meaning is what consciousness starts from and that only then does it look around, in the next place, for an expression of its ideas in analogous shapes. But this is not the way of strictly symbolical art. For its special character consists in the fact that it does not yet penetrate to the comprehension of meanings in and by themselves, independently of every external shape. On the contrary it takes its departure from the present and the present's concrete existence in nature and spirit, and then and only then expands it to [enshrine] universal meanings whose significance is contained likewise in such a real existent for its part, even if only in a rather restricted manner and in a purely approximate way. But at the same time symbolic art seizes on these objects only to

---

[1] Hegel's emphasis on '*vor*gefundene' (met with) and '*er*fundene' (devised) I cannot reproduce in English. 'Second shape', i.e. the one devised by spirit, as distinct from the first one which is just met with in the external world. See p. 2, note.

create out of them by imagination a shape which makes the universality in them something that the mind can contemplate and picture in this particular reality. Therefore, as symbolic, artistic productions have not yet gained a form truly adequate to the spirit, because the spirit here is itself not yet inwardly clear to itself, as it would be if it were the free spirit; nevertheless at least there are configurations which reveal in themselves at once that they are not merely chosen to display *themselves* alone, but that they are meant to hint at meanings that lie deeper and are more comprehensive. The *purely* natural and sensuous object presents *itself*; whereas while the symbolic work of art may bring before our eyes natural phenomena or human forms, it hints at once outside and beyond itself at something else which yet must have an inwardly grounded affinity with the shapes presented and have an essential relationship with them. The connection between the concrete shape and its universal meaning may be of many kinds, now more external and therefore less clear, but now also more fundamental, if, that is to say, the universality to be symbolized constitutes in fact the essential element in the concrete appearance; in that case the comprehensibility of the symbol is made much more easy.

In this connection the most abstract sort of expression is *number*, which yet is only to be used as a clearer allusion when the meaning itself contains a numerical determination. The numbers 7 and 12, for example, occur frequently in Egyptian architecture, because seven is the number of the planets, twelve the number of the months or of the feet by which the waters of the Nile must rise in order to fructify the land. Such a number is in that case regarded as sacred, because it is a numerical determination in the great relations of the elements which are reverenced as the powers governing the whole life of nature. Twelve steps, seven columns, are to this extent symbolical. The like symbolism of numbers extends indeed to still more advanced mythologies. The twelve labours of Hercules, for example, seem also to originate from the twelve months of the year, since Hercules on the one hand comes on the scene as the entirely humanly individualized hero, but on the other hand he still carries in himself a meaning symbolical of nature, and he is a personification of the sun's course.

Then further on there are *spatial* configurations which are more concrete: paths in labyrinths are a symbol for the revolution of the planets, just as dances too in their intricacies have the more secret sense of imitating symbolically the movement of the great elemental bodies.

Then, still further on, *animal* shapes afford symbols; but in the most perfect way the form of the *human* body is a symbol, a form which appears elaborated in a higher and more appropriate way because the spirit at this stage already begins in general to give shape to itself, disengaging itself from the purely natural and rising to its own more independent existence.

This constitutes the general nature of symbol proper and the necessity of art for its presentation. Now in order to review the more concrete conceptions underlying this stage, we must, in connection with this first descent of spirit into itself, leave the East and turn rather to the West.

As a general symbol indicative of this standpoint we may put at the top the picture of the phoenix which sets fire to itself but rises again rejuvenated out of ashes and death in the flames. Herodotus [ii. 73] tells us that he had never seen this bird in Egypt except in pictures, and in fact it is the Egyptians who provide the focus for the symbolical art-form. Yet before we go forward to a more detailed consideration of this, we may mention some other myths which form the transition to that symbolism which is completely worked out in all its aspects. These are the myths of Adonis, his death, Aphrodite's lament for him, the funeral ceremonies, etc., insights with their home on the coast of Syria. Cybele worship in Phrygia has the same meaning, and this reverberates too in the myths of Castor and Pollux, Ceres and Proserpine.

As a meaning, what is here principally emphasized and made explicitly perceptible is the already mentioned factor of the negative, the death of what is natural, as a factor absolutely grounded in the Divine. Hence the funeral ceremonies in connection with the death of the god, the extravagant laments over the loss which, however, is then compensated by rediscovery, resurrection, renewal, so that now ceremonial *festivities* can follow. This universal meaning has over again in this case its more specific natural sense: in winter the sun loses its force, but in spring it, and nature along with it, is rejuvenated again, and then it dies and is reborn. Here, in other words, the Divine, *personified* in a *human* occurrence, has its meaning in the life of nature, which then, on the other hand, is once more a symbol for the essential character of the negative in general alike in spirit and in nature.

But the complete example of the thorough elaboration of symbolic art, both in its special content and in its form, we have to seek in Egypt. Egypt is the country of symbols, the country which sets itself the spiritual task of the self-deciphering of the spirit, without actually attaining to the decipherment. The problems remain unsolved, and the solution which *we* can provide consists therefore only in interpreting the riddles of Egyptian art and its symbolic works as a problem remaining undeciphered by the Egyptians themselves. In this way spirit here still looks for itself in externality, out of which it then struggles again, and it now labours in tireless activity to exhibit for perception, not thought, (*a*) its own essence by its own effort in the phenomena of nature, and (*b*) nature in its being a shape of spirit. For this reason the Egyptians, amongst the peoples hitherto mentioned, are the properly artistic people. But their works remain mysterious and dumb, mute and motionless, because here spirit itself has still not really found its own inner life and still cannot speak the clear and distinct language of spirit. Spirit's unsatisfied urge and pressure to bring this wrestling with itself before perception by means of art in so mute a way, to give shape to the inner life, and to attain knowledge of its own inner life, as of inner life in general, only through external cognate shapes, is characteristic of Egypt. The people of this wonderful country were not only agriculturalists, they were builders; they dug the ground everywhere, excavated canals and lakes; in this instinct for art they not only produced the most prodigious edifices above ground but also with great vigour constructed equally immense buildings, of the most enormous dimensions, in the bowels of the earth. The erection of such monuments, as Herodotus relates,[1] was a principal occupation of the people and a chief accomplishment of its rulers. The buildings of the Indians too were colossal indeed, but we cannot find this endless variety anywhere else but in Egypt.

1. *Egyptian View and Representation of the Dead: Pyramids*

If we consider the Egyptian artistic outlook in its particular aspects, we find here in the first place the inward kept firmly in view on its own account contrasted with the immediacy of existence:

---

[1] Not explicitly, but this is a fair enough inference from all that he does say, in book ii, about the construction of the Pyramids, etc.

the inward indeed as the negative of life, as death—not as the abstract negation which the evil and perishable is, like Ahriman in opposition to Ormuzd, but in even a concrete shape.

(a) The Indian rises only to the emptiest abstraction and therefore the abstraction which is likewise negative in contrast to everything concrete. Such an Indian process of becoming Brahma does not occur in Egypt; on the contrary, the invisible has a deeper meaning for the Egyptians; the dead acquires the content of the living itself. Deprived of immediate existence, the dead still preserves in its separation from life its relation to the living, and in this concrete shape it is made independent and maintained. It is well known that the Egyptians embalmed and worshipped cats, dogs, hawks, ichneumons, bears, wolves,[1] but especially men who had died (Herodotus, ii. 67, 86–90). The honour paid to the dead by the Egyptians is not burial, but their perennial preservation as corpses.

(b) Moreover, the Egyptians go beyond this immediate and even still natural duration of the dead. What is preserved naturally is also interpreted in their *ideas* as enduring. Hérodotus says [ii. 123] of the Egyptians that they were the first to teach the immortality of the human soul. With them, that is, there first emerges in this higher way too the separation between nature and spirit, since it is not merely the natural which acquires independence for itself. The immortality of the soul lies very close to the freedom of the spirit, because [the conception of immortality implies that] the self comprehends itself as withdrawn from the naturalness of existence and as resting on itself; but this self-knowledge is the principle of freedom. Now of course this is not to say that the Egyptians had completely reached the conception of the free spirit, and in examining this faith of theirs we must not think of our manner of conceiving the immortality of the soul; but still they did already have the insight to take good account, both externally and in their ideas, of the body in its existence separated from life. Therefore they have made the transition of mind to its liberation, although they have only reached the threshold of the realm of freedom.—This insight of theirs is broadened into the conception of an independent realm of the dead in contrast to the presence of what is immediately real. In this kingdom of the invisible

---

[1] Herodotus says that all these animals were sacred, but he speaks of embalming only in reference to cats.

a judgement of the dead is held, and Osiris as Amenthes[1] presides over it. The same tribunal is then also present in immediate reality, since among men too the dead are judged, and after the decease of a king, for example, anyone could bring his grievances to that court of judgement.

(c) If we ask further for a *symbolical* art-form to express this idea, we have to look for it in the chief structures built by the Egyptians. Here we have before us a double architecture, one above ground, the other subterranean: labyrinths under the soil, magnificent vast excavations, passages half a mile long, chambers adorned with hieroglyphics, everything worked out with the maximum of care; then above ground there are built in addition those amazing constructions amongst which the Pyramids are to be counted the chief. On the purpose and meaning of the Pyramids all sorts of hypotheses have been tried for centuries, yet it now seems beyond doubt that they are enclosures for the graves of kings or of sacred animals, Apis for example, or cats, the ibis, etc.[2] In this way the Pyramids put before our eyes the simple prototype of symbolical art itself; they are prodigious crystals which conceal in themselves an inner meaning and, as external shapes produced by art, they so envelop that meaning that it is obvious that they are there for this inner meaning separated from pure nature and only in relation to this meaning. But this realm of death and the invisible, which here constitutes the meaning, possesses only one side, and that a formal one, of the true content of art, namely that of being removed from immediate existence; and so this realm is primarily only Hades, not yet a life which, even if liberated from the sensuous as such, is still nevertheless at the same time self-existent and therefore in itself free and living spirit. On this account the shape for such an inner meaning still remains just an external form and veil for the definite content of that meaning.

The Pyramids are such an external environment in which an inner meaning rests concealed.

---

[1] Here Hegel seems to have been misreported. Amenthes is the Egyptian word for Hades, the kingdom of the dead, over which Osiris presides, and this is what Hegel says in his *Philosophy of Religion* (Lasson's edn., *Die Naturreligion*, 1927, p. 216).

[2] Hegel is drawing again on Herodotus ii. For the ibis, a bird, see ch. 76. For Herodotus Apis is a god (chs. 38 and 153) but he is better regarded as the sacred bull.

2. Animal Worship and Animal Masks

Now while in general the inner life should be presented to our vision as something present externally, the Egyptians have fallen into the opposite extreme by worshipping an actual existence of the Divine in living animals like the bull, cats, and many others. The living thing stands higher than inorganic externality, for the living organism has something inner at which its external shape hints, but which yet remains inner and therefore rich in mystery. So here animal worship must be understood as an intuition of a secret inner being which, as life, is a higher power over the purely external. Of course it always remains repugnant to us to see animals, dogs, and cats, instead of what is truly spiritual, regarded as sacred.

This worship, taken by itself, has in it nothing symbolic, because in it the actual living animal, Apis for example, was itself worshipped as an existence of god. But the Egyptians have used the animal form symbolically too. In that event this form is no longer valued on its own account but is debased ·to the expression of something more general. In its most naïve form this is the case with animal masks which occur especially in portrayals of embalming; in this occupation the persons who dissect the corpse and take out the entrails are painted wearing animal masks. Here it is clear at once that such an animal head is supposed not to mean itself but to have a different and more general significance. Moreover, the animal form is used intermingled with the human; we find human figures with lions' heads, and these are taken for shapes of Minerva; hawks' heads occur too, and horns are left on the heads of Ammon. Symbolic connections cannot be missed here. Similarly the hieroglyphic script of the Egyptians is also largely symbolic, since *either* it tries to make us acquainted with the meanings by sketching actual objects which display not themselves but a universal related to them, *or*, more commonly still, in its so-called phonetic element this script indicates the individual letters by illustrating an object the initial letter of which has in speech the same sound as that which is to be expressed.

3. Complete Symbolism—Memnons, Isis and Osiris, the Sphinx

In Egypt, on the whole, almost every shape is a symbol and hieroglyph not signifying itself but hinting at another thing with which it has affinity and therefore relationship. Yet symbols proper are only really complete when this relation is of a more fundamental and deeper kind. In this connection I will mention briefly only the following frequently recurring ideas.

(a) Just as on one side the Egyptian superstition has an inkling, in the animal form, of a secret inwardness, so on the other side we find the human form so represented that it still has the inner element of subjectivity outside itself and therefore cannot unfold itself into free beauty. Especially remarkable are those colossal statues of Memnon which, resting in themselves, motionless, the arms glued to the body, the feet firmly fixed together, numb, stiff, and lifeless, are set up facing the sun in order to await its ray to touch them and give them soul and sound. Herodotus at least relates[1] that statues of Memnon gave a sound automatically at sunrise. Of course higher criticism has cast doubt on this, yet the fact of this sound has lately been established again by Frenchmen and Englishmen; and if the sound is not produced by contrivances of some sort, it may still be explained by assuming that, just as there are minerals which rustle in water, the voice of these stone monuments proceeds from the dew and the cool of the morning and then from the falling of the sun's rays on them, if small rifts arise consequentially and vanish again. But taken as *symbols*, the meaning to be ascribed to these colossi is that they do not have the spiritual soul freely in themselves and therefore, instead of being able to draw animation from within, from what bears proportion and beauty in itself, they require for it light from without which alone liberates the note of the soul from them. The human voice, on the other hand, resounds out of one's own feeling and one's own spirit without any external impulse, just as the height of art in general consists in making the inner give shape to itself out of its own being. But the inner life of the human form is still dumb in Egypt and in its animation it is only a natural factor that is kept in view.

(b) A further type of symbolical presentation is Isis and Osiris. Osiris is begotten, born, and then done to death by Typhon. But Isis looks for the scattered limbs, finds, collects, and buries them. Now this story of the god has, *prima facie*, purely natural significances for its content. On the one hand Osiris is the sun and his

---

[1] No. Hegel's memory is at fault. His authority was probably Tacitus, *Annals*, ii. 61, where one such statue is mentioned.

story is a symbol for the sun's yearly course; on the other hand, he means the rising and falling of the Nile which has to bring fertility to the whole of Egypt. For in Egypt there are often years without rain and it is the Nile alone which waters the country by its floods. In winter it flows shallowly within its bed, but then (Herodotus, ii. 19) from the summer solstice onwards it begins to rise for a hundred days together, bursts its banks, and streams far over the country. Finally the water dries up again owing to the heat and hot winds from the desert, and it returns again into its river-bed. Thereafter the ground is cultivated with little effort, the lushest vegetation burgeons, everything germinates and ripens. Sun and Nile, their weakening and strengthening, are the natural powers over the Egyptian soil, and the Egyptian illustrates them to himself symbolically in the humanly shaped story of Isis and Osiris. After all there belongs to this context too the symbolism of the signs of the zodiac which is connected with the year's course, just as the number of the twelve gods is with the months. But conversely Osiris means humanity itself: he is held sacred as the founder of agriculture, of the demarcation of fields, of property, of laws, and his worship is therefore no less related to human spiritual activities which have the closest affinity with morality and law. So too he is the judge of the dead and wins thereby a meaning entirely detached from the pure life of nature; in this meaning the symbolical begins to disappear, because here the inner and the spiritual becomes itself the content of the human form which thereby begins to portray its own inner being. But this spiritual process adopts the external life of nature again all the same as its inner content and makes that content perceptible in an external way: in temples, e.g., in the number of steps, floors, pillars; in labyrinths in their variety of passages, windings, and chambers. In this way Osiris is just as much natural as spiritual life in the different features of his process and transformations, and the symbolic shapes become symbols for the natural elements, while the natural situations are themselves over again only symbols of spiritual activities and their variation. Therefore it turns out that the human form remains here no mere personification, because here what is natural, although appearing on the one hand as the proper meaning, becomes on the other hand itself only a symbol of spirit, and in general it has to be subordinate in this sphere, where the inward is extricating itself from the vision of nature.

Nevertheless the human bodily form acquires a quite different formation and therefore already reveals the struggle to rise upward to the inner and spiritual life; but this effort here attains its proper aim, the freedom of spirit in itself, in only a defective way. The shapes remain colossal, serious, petrified; legs without freedom and serene distinctness, arms and head closely and firmly affixed to the rest of the body, without grace and living movement. The art of cutting the arms and the feet free and giving movement to the body is ascribed to Daedalus[1] first of all.

Now owing to this alternating symbolism, the symbol in Egypt is at the same time an ensemble of symbols, so that what at one time appears as meaning is also used again as a symbol of a related sphere. In a symbolism which confusedly intertwines meaning and shape, presages a variety of things in fact or alludes to them, and therefore already comes close to that inner subjectivity which alone can develop itself in many directions, the associations are ambiguous, and this is the virtue of these productions, although their explanation is of course made difficult owing to this ambiguity.

In deciphering such a meaning we often, to be sure, go too far today because in fact almost all the shapes present themselves directly as symbols. In the same way in which we try to explain this meaning to ourselves, it might have been clear and intelligible as a meaning to the insight of the Egyptians themselves. But the Egyptian symbols, as we saw at the very beginning, contain implicitly much, explicitly nothing. There are works undertaken with the attempt to make them clear to themselves, yet they do not get beyond the struggle after what is absolutely evident. In this sense we regard the Egyptian works of art as containing riddles, the right solution of which is in part unattained not only by us, but generally by those who posed these riddles to themselves.

(c) The works of Egyptian art in their mysterious symbolism are therefore riddles; the objective riddle *par excellence*. As a symbol for this proper meaning of the Egyptian spirit we may mention the Sphinx. It is, as it were, the symbol of the symbolic itself. In innumerable quantities, set up in rows in hundreds, there are sphinx shapes in Egypt, constructed out of the hardest stone, polished, covered with hieroglyphics, and [one] near Cairo is of

---

[1] Athenian sculptor and architect, who was said to have made statues which could move themselves. He also constructed the Labyrinth in Crete for Minos. See, e.g., Apollodorus, iii. xv. 8; Euripides: *Hecuba*, 836 ff.; *et al.*

such colossal size that the lion's claws alone amount to a man's height. Some of them are recumbent animal bodies out of which as an upper part, the human body struggles; here and there again there is a ram's head, but elsewhere most commonly a female head. Out of the dull strength and power of the animal the human spirit tries to push itself forward, without coming to a perfect portrayal of its own freedom and animated shape, because it must still remain confused and associated with what is other than itself. This pressure for self-conscious spirituality which does not apprehend itself from its own resources in the one reality adequate to itself but only contemplates itself in what is related to it and brings itself into consciousness in precisely what is strange to it, is the symbolic as such which at this peak becomes a riddle.

It is in this sense that the Sphinx in the Greek myth, which we ourselves may interpret again symbolically, appears as a monster asking a riddle. The Sphinx propounded the well-known conundrum: What is it that in the morning goes on four legs, at mid-day on two, and in the evening on three? Oedipus found the simple answer: a man, and he tumbled the Sphinx from the rock.[1] The explanation of the symbol lies in the absolute meaning, in the spirit, just as the famous Greek inscription calls to man: Know thyself. The light of consciousness is the clarity which makes its concrete content shine clearly through the shape belonging and appropriate to itself, and in its [objective] existence reveals itself alone.

[1] According to Apollodorus, III. v. 8, the Sphinx threw herself down after the riddle had been guessed. 'Know thyself' was the inscription on the temple of Apollo at Delphi (Plato, *Protagoras*, 343 B).

Chapter II

SYMBOLISM OF THE SUBLIME

The unenigmatic clarity of the spirit which shapes itself out of its own resources in a way adequate to itself is the aim of symbolic art, but it can only be reached if in the first place the meaning comes into consciousness on its own account, separated from the entire world of appearance. For in the immediately intuited unity of the two [meaning and shape] lay the absence of art in the case of the ancient Parsis; the contradiction between the separation of the two and what was nevertheless demanded, i.e. their immediate linkage, produced the fantastic symbolism of the Indians; while even in Egypt knowledge of the inner life and the absolute meaning was still not free, still not released from the world of appearance, and this provided the reason for the riddles and the obscurity of Egyptian symbolism.

Now the first decisive purification of the absolute [meaning] and its express separation from the sensuous present, i.e. from the empirical individuality of external things, is to be sought in the *sublime*. Sublimity lifts the Absolute above every immediate existent and therefore brings about the liberation which, though abstract at first, is at least the foundation of the spirit. For although the meaning thus elevated is not yet apprehended as concrete spirit, it is nevertheless regarded as the inner life, self-existent and reposing on itself, which by its very nature is incapable of finding its true expression in finite phenomena.

Kant has distinguished the sublime from the beautiful in a very interesting way, and his detailed discussion of this in the first part of the *Critique of Judgment* from § 20 onwards[1] still always retains its interest despite all prolixity and the premissed reduction of all categories to something subjective, to the powers of mind, imagination, reason, etc. In its general principle, this reduction must be recognized as correct to this extent, that sublimity—as Kant says himself—is not contained in anything in nature but only in our

---

[1] Kant's distinction is made in § 23. Thereafter he goes on to deal with the sublime in detail.

minds, in so far as we become conscious of our superiority to the nature within us and therefore to nature without. In this sense Kant's view is that 'the sublime, in the strict sense of the word, cannot be contained in any sensuous form but concerns only Ideas of Reason which, although no adequate representation of them is possible, may be aroused and called to our mind precisely by this inadequacy which does admit of sensuous representation' (*Critique of Judgment*, 1799, p. 77 [§ 23]). The sublime in general is the attempt to express the infinite, without finding in the sphere of phenomena an object which proves adequate for this representation. Precisely because the infinite is set apart from the entire complex of objectivity as explicitly an invisible meaning devoid of shape and is made inner, it remains, in accordance with its infinity, unutterable and sublime above any expression through the finite.

Now the first content which the meaning gains here is this, that in contrast to the totality of appearance it is the inherently substantial *unity* which itself, as a pure thought, can be apprehended only by pure thought. Therefore this substance is now no longer able to have its configuration in something external, and thus far the strictly symbolical character vanishes. But if this inherent unity is to be brought before our vision, this is only possible if, as substance, it is also grasped as the creative power of all things, in which it therefore has its revelation and appearance and to which it thus has a positive relation. But at the same time this essentially expresses the fact of substance's elevation above individual phenomena as such, and above their totality, with the logical result that the positive relation is transposed into the negative one in which the substance is purified from everything apparent and particular and therefore from what fades away in it and is inadequate to it.

This outward shaping which is itself annihilated in turn by what it reveals, so that the revelation of the content is at the same time a supersession of the revelation, is the sublime. This, therefore, differing from Kant, we need not place in the pure subjectivity of the mind and its Ideas of Reason; on the contrary, we must grasp it as grounded in the one absolute substance *qua* the content which is to be represented.

The classification of the art-form of the sublime is likewise derived from the above-indicated double relationship of substance, as meaning, to the phenomenal world.

The character common to the two sides of this relation—i.e. the positive and the negative—lies in this, that the substance is raised above the single phenomenon in which it is to acquire representation, although it can be expressed only in relation to the phenomenal in general, because as substance and essentiality it is in itself without shape and inaccessible to concrete vision.

As the first mode of apprehension, the affirmative one, we may cite pantheistic art as it occurs partly in India and partly in the later freedom and mysticism of the Mohammedan Persian poets, and as we find it again also in the deeper inwardness of thought and sentiment in the Christian west.

In its general character at this stage substance is envisaged as immanent in all its created accidents, which thus are not yet degraded to serving, and merely adorning, the glorification of the Absolute, but are preserved affirmatively through the substance dwelling in them, although in every single thing it is only the One and the Divine which is to be imaged and exalted. Wherefore the poet, who in everything descries and marvels at this One and immerses himself, as well as things, in this contemplation, can preserve a positive relation to the substance to which he links everything.

The second [mode of] apprehension, namely the negative praise of the power and glory of the one God, we encounter as sublimity in the strict sense in Hebrew poetry. It cancels the positive immanence of the Absolute in its created phenomena and puts the *one* substance explicitly apart as the Lord of the world in contrast to whom there stands the entirety of his creatures, and these, in comparison with God, are posited as the inherently powerless and perishable. Now when the power and wisdom of the One is to be represented through the finitude of natural things and human fates, we no longer find here any Indian distortion into the shapelessness of the boundless; on the contrary, the sublimity of God is brought nearer to contemplation by reason of the fact that what exists in the world, with all its splendour, magnificence, and glory, is represented as only a serving accident and a transient show in comparison with God's being and stability.

A. THE PANTHEISM OF ART

Nowadays the word 'pantheism' is at once liable to the crassest misunderstandings. This is because in one way 'everything' means in our modern sense 'all and everything in its purely empirical individuality', e.g. this mull with all its own qualities, with this colour, size so and so, shape, weight, etc., or that house, book, animal, table, chair, oven, cirrus clouds, etc. Now many contemporary theologians accuse philosophy of turning 'everything' into God, but when 'everything' is taken precisely in the sense just mentioned, what they allege about philosophy is as a matter of fact entirely false and their complaint against it is thus quite unjustified. Such an idea of Pantheism can only arise in crazy heads and is not found in any religion, not even amongst the Iroquois and the Eskimos, let alone in any philosophy. The 'everything' in what has been called 'Pantheism' is therefore not this or that individual thing, but rather is 'everything' in the sense of the *All*, i.e. of the one substance which indeed is immanent in individuals, but is abstracted from individuality and its empirical reality, so that what is emphasized and meant is not the individual as such but the universal soul, or, in more popular terms, truth and excellence which also have their presence in this individual being.

This constitutes the proper meaning of 'Pantheism' and under this meaning alone have we to talk of Pantheism here. It belongs primarily to the East which grasps the thought of an absolute unity of the Divine and the thought of all things as comprised in this unity. Now, as unity and All, the Divine can come into consciousness only through the vanishing of the particular individuals in which the Divine is expressed as present. On the one hand, that is to say, the Divine is envisaged here as immanent in the most various objects and indeed, more particularly, as the most excellent and most pre-eminent thing amongst and in the different existents; but, on the other hand, since the One is this thing and another and another again and rolls through all things, the individuals and particulars for this very reason appear as superseded and vanishing; for it is not any and every individual thing which is this One; on the contrary, the One is this totality of individuals which for contemplation coalesce into the totality. For if the One is life, for example, it is also death, and therefore precisely not only life; so that thus life or the sun or the sea do not, as life, sea, or sun, constitute the Divine and the One. Yet at the same time the accidental is not here posited expressly as negative and as a servant, as it is in sublimity proper, but, on the contrary, since the substance in everything particular is this One, the substance becomes *implicitly* something particular and accidental; yet, conversely, this individual thing changes all the same, and imagination does not restrict the substance to a specific existent but advances over each determinacy, abandoning it in order to proceed to another, and thus the individual existent becomes for its part something accidental, away and above which the one substance rises and therefore is sublime.

Such a way of looking at things can, on this account, be expressed artistically only in poetry, not in the visual arts which bring to our vision only as existent and static the determinate and individual thing which is to disappear in face of the substance present in such existents. Where Pantheism is pure, there is no visual art for its representation.

1. *Indian Poetry*

As the first example of such pantheistic poetry we may once again cite the Indian which alongside its fantasticalness has brilliantly developed this aspect also.

The Indians, as we saw, have as their supreme Divinity the most abstract universality and unity, which does thereupon become specified in particular gods, Trimurti, Indra, etc.; but there is no holding fast to the specific; the subordinate gods revert all the same into the higher ones, and these into Brahma. Thus it is already clear that this universal constitutes the one permanent and self-identical foundation of everything. The Indians of course display in their poetry the double struggle (*a*) so to magnify the individual existent that in its sensuousness it may already appear adequate to the universal meaning, and (*b*) conversely, in face of the abstraction of the One, to waive all determinacy in a purely negative way. On the other hand, there appears even in the Indians the purer mode of representation of the above-mentioned Pantheism which emphasizes the immanence of the Divine in the individual who for the eye of contemplation is present and vanishing. In this mode of looking at things we could propose to find once more something of a resemblance to that immediate unity of pure thought and sense which we encountered in the Parsis; but in their case the One and the Excellent, considered on its own account, is itself something natural, i.e. light; whereas in the case of the Indians the One, Brahma, is merely the formless One which, only when transformed into the infinite multiplicity of terrestrial phenomena, provides an opportunity for the pantheistic mode of representation. So it is said, e.g., of Krishna (*Bhagavad Gita*, 7. iv): 'Earth, water and wind, air and fire, spirit, understanding, and self-hood are the eight syllables of my essential power; yet recognise thou in me another and a higher being who vivifies the earth and carries the world: in him all beings have their origin; so know thou, I am the origin of this entire world and also its destruction; beyond me there is nothing higher, to me this All is linked as a chaplet of pearls on a thread; I am the taste in flowing water, the splendour in the sun and the moon, the mystical word in the holy scriptures, in man his manliness, the pure fragrance in the earth, the splendour in flames, in all beings the life, contemplation in the penitent, in living things the force of life, in the wise their wisdom, in the splendid their splendour; whatever natures are genuine, are shining or dark, they are from me, I am not in them, they are in me. Through the illusion of these three properties the whole world is bewitched and mistakes me the unalterable; but even the divine illusion, Maya, is my illusion, hard to transcend; but those who follow me go forth beyond illusion.'[1] Here such a substantial unity is expressed in the most striking way, in respect both of immanence in what is present and also transcendence over everything individual.

In a similar way, Krishna says of himself that amongst all different existents he is always the most excellent (10. xxi): 'Among the stars I am the shining sun, amongst the lunary signs the moon, amongst the sacred books the book of hymns, amongst the senses the inward, Meru amongst the tops of the hills, amongst animals the lion, amongst letters I am the vowel A, amongst seasons of the year the blossoming spring', etc.

But this recitation of the height of excellence, like the mere change of shapes in which what is to be brought before our eyes is

---

[1] Professor R. C. Zaehner translates the closing section of this passage as follows: 'Know too that all states of being whether they be of Nature's constituent purity, energy, or lethargy proceed from me; but I am not in them, they are in me. By these three states of being inhering in the constituents the whole universe is led astray and does not understand that I am far beyond them and that I neither change nor pass away. For all this is my Maya, composed of the constituents, divine, hard to transcend. Whoso shall put his trust in me alone, shall pass beyond this my Maya' (*Concordant Discord*, Oxford 1970, pp. 124, 135). Professor Zaehner points out that at this stage of Indian thought 'Maya' means creative power, not illusion. The 'three properties' are the three 'constituents' through which Nature acts.

always one and the same thing over again, despite the wealth of fancy which seems at first sight to be deployed there, still remains, precisely on account of this similarity of content, extremely monotonous and, on the whole, empty and wearisome.

2. Mohammedan Poetry

Secondly, in a higher and more subjectively free way, oriental Pantheism has been developed in Mohammedanism, especially by the Persians.

Now here a characteristic relation appears, especially on the part of the individual poet:

(*a*) Since the poet longs to descry the Divine in everything and does actually descry it, in face of it he now sacrifices his own personality, but he all the same apprehends the immanence of the Divine in his inner being thus enlarged and freed; and therefore there grows in him that serene inwardness, that free good fortune, that riotous bliss characteristic of the Oriental who, in renouncing his own particularity, immerses himself entirely in the Eternal and the Absolute, and feels and recognizes in everything the picture and presence of the Divine. Such a self-penetration by the Divine and a blissful intoxicated life in God borders on mysticism. In this connection Jalal-ed-Din Rumi [1207–73] is to be praised above all; Rückert[1] has given us most beautiful examples of his work; Rückert's marvellous power of expression enables him to play in the most ingenious and free way with words and rhymes, just as the Persians do. The love of God—with whom man identifies his personality by the most boundless surrender and whom, the One, he now glimpses in all spaces of the universe, to whom he relates each and everything, and to whom he brings everything back— constitutes here the centre which radiates in the widest way in every direction and region.

(*b*) Furthermore, in sublimity, strictly so-called, as will be shown directly, the best objects and most splendid configurations are used only as a mere adornment of God and serve as a procla-mation of the magnificence and glorification of the One, since they are set before our eyes only to celebrate him as the lord of all creation. In Pantheism, on the other hand, the immanence of the Divine in objects exalts mundane, natural, and human existence itself into a more independent glory of its own. The personal life of

[1] F. Rückert, Poet and Orientalist, 1788–1866.

the spirit in natural phenomena and human affairs animates and spiritualizes them in themselves and founds anew a special relation between the subjective feeling, and soul, of the poet and the objects of his song. Filled by this soulful glory, the heart in itself is peaceful, independent, free, self-subsistent, wide, and great; and in this affirmative identity with itself the heart imagines and now makes its own the soul of things until it attains a like peaceful unity with it; it grows into the most blissful and cheerful intimacy with objects in nature and their splendour, with the beloved and the tavern, in short with everything worth praise and love. The western romantic deep feeling of the heart does display a similar absorption in nature's life, but on the whole, especially in the north, it is rather unhappy, unfree, and wistful, or it still remains subjective, shut in upon itself, and therefore becomes self-seeking and sentimental. Such oppressed and troubled deep feeling is expressed especially in the folksongs of barbarian peoples. On the other hand, a free, happy, depth of feeling is characteristic of Orientals, especially the Mohammedan Persians, who openly and cheerfully sacrifice their entire selves to God and to everything praiseworthy, yet in this sacrifice they do precisely retain the free substantiality which they can preserve even in relation to the surrounding world. So we see in the glow of passion the most widespread bliss and parrhesia of feeling through which, in the inexaustible wealth of brilliant and splendid images, there resounds the steady note of joy, beauty, and good fortune. If the Oriental suffers and is unhappy, he accepts this as the unalterable verdict of fate and he therefore remains secure in himself, without oppression, sentimentality, or discontented dejection. In the poems of Hafiz[1] we find complaints and outcries enough about the beloved, filling the glass, etc., but even in grief he remains just as carefree as he is in good fortune. So, e.g., he says once: 'Out of thanks that the presence of thy friend enlightens thee, in woe burn like the candle and be satisfied.'

The candle teaches us to laugh and cry; through the flame it laughs in cheerful splendour, while at the same time it melts away in hot tears; in its burning it spreads cheerful splendour. This is the general character of this whole poetry.

Just to mention a few more detailed pictures, the Persians have

---

[1] Shamsud-Din-Mohammed, c. 1320–89.

much to do with flowers and jewels, but above all with the rose and the nightingale. Especially common with them is the representation of the nightingale as the bridegroom of the rose. This gift of soul to the rose and the love of the nightingale is common, e.g., in Hafiz. 'Out of thanks, O rose, that thou art the queen of beauty', he says, 'beware that thou disdain not the nightingale's love.' He himself speaks of the nightingale of his own heart. Whereas if *we* speak in our poems of roses, nightingales, wine, this occurs in a quite different and more prosaic sense; the rose serves us as an adornment, 'garlanded with roses', etc., or we hear the nightingale and it just arouses our corresponding emotions; we drink wine and call it the banisher of care. But with the Persians the rose is no image or mere adornment, no symbol; on the contrary, it appears to the poet as ensouled, as an affianced beloved, and with his spirit he is engrossed in the soul of the rose.

The same character of brilliant Pantheism is still displayed in the most recent Persian poetry too. von Hammer,[1] e.g., has informed us of a poem sent by the Shah with other gifts to the Emperor Francis in 1819. In 33,000 distichs it recounts the deeds of the Shah who has conferred his own name on the Court poet.

(c) Goethe too, in contrast to his troubled youthful poems and their concentrated feeling, was gripped in his later years by this broad and carefree serenity, and, as an old man, inspired by the breath of the East, and with his soul filled with boundless bliss, turns in the poetic fervour of his heart to this freedom of feeling, a freedom that even in polemics keeps the most beautiful tranquillity. The songs in his *West-östliche Divan*[2] are neither *jeux d'esprit* nor insignificant social gallantries, but are the products of such a free feeling and *abandon*. He calls them himself in a song to Suleika: 'Poetic pearls, which the mighty surge of your passion cast up on my life's deserted shore, tenderly gathered with careful fingers, they are ranged on a necklace of jewels and gold.' 'Take', he calls to his beloved, 'Take them on thy neck, to thy bosom—raindrops of Allah, ripened in a modest shell.'[3]

For such poems there needed a sense self-confident in all storms and of the widest range, a depth and childlikeness of heart and

---

[1] Joseph, Freiherr von Hammer-Purgstall, Orientalist, 1774–1856.
[2] Goethe, who lived to be eighty-three, was sixty-four when he published this in 1813.
[3] The idea is that the pearl is a raindrop that fell into the sea and was 'ripened' in an oyster shell.

'a world of living buds which in their thrusting abundance presaged the nightingale's love and her soul-stirring song'.

3. Christian Mysticism

Now the pantheistic unity, emphasized in relation to the subject who feels *himself* in this unity with God and senses God as this presence in subjective consciousness, is afforded in general by mysticism, developed as it has been in this more subjective way within Christianity too. As an example I will only cite Angelus Silesius, who, with the greatest audacity and depth of intuition and feeling, has expressed in a wonderfully mystical power of representation the substantial existence of God in things and the unification of the self with God and of God with human subjectivity.[1] The strictly Eastern Pantheism, on the other hand, emphasizes rather the contemplation of the one substance in all phenomena and their sacrifice by the subject who thereby acquires the supreme enlargement of consciousness as well as, through entire liberation from the finite, the bliss of absorption into everything that is best and most splendid.

B. THE ART OF THE SUBLIME

But the one substance, grasped as the proper meaning of the entire universe, is in truth only established as substance when it is brought back into itself, as pure inwardness and substantial might, out of its presence and actuality in the vicissitudes of phenomena, and thereby is made *independent* itself over against finitude. Only through this intuition of the being of God as the purely spiritual and imageless, *contrasted* with the mundane and the natural, is spirit completely wrested from nature and sense and released from existence in the finite. Yet conversely the absolute substance remains in a *relation* to the phenomenal world, out of which it is reflected back into itself. This relation now acquires the above-mentioned negative aspect, namely that the entire mundane sphere, despite the fullness, force, and splendour of its phenomena, is expressly established, in relation to the substance, as only the inherently negative, created by God, subjected to his power, and

---

[1] e.g. 'God in my nature is involved, As I in the divine' (*Hours with the Mystics*, by R. A. Vaughan, London, 1895, vol. ii, pp. 5 ff.). Angelus Silesius is probably the pseudonym of Johannes Scheffler, 1624–77.

his servant. The world is therefore indeed regarded as a revelation of God, and he himself is the goodness which, although the created world has in itself no right to subsist and to relate itself to itself, yet permits it to thrive and gives it stability; still, the stability of the finite is without substance, and the creature, held over against God, is what is perishing and powerless, so that in the creator's goodness his *justice* has to be manifested at the same time; and this justice brings into actual appearance also, in the inherently negative, the powerlessness thereof and therefore the substance as that alone which has power.

This relation, when art asserts it as the fundamental one for both its content and its form, affords the art-form of sublimity, strictly so-called. Beauty of the Ideal must of course be distinguished from sublimity. For in the Ideal the inner life pervades external reality, whose inner being the inner life is, in the sense that both sides appear as adequate to one another and therefore precisely as pervading one another. In sublimity, on the contrary, external existence, in which the substance is brought before contemplation, is degraded in comparison with the substance, since this degradation and servitude is the one and only way whereby the *one* God can be illustrated in art; this is because the one God is explicitly without shape and is incapable of expression in his *positive* essence in anything finite and mundane. Sublimity presupposes the meaning in an independence in comparison with which the external must appear as merely subordinate, because the inner does not appear in it but so transcends it that nothing comes into the representation except as this transcendence and superiority.

In the symbol the shape was the chief thing. The shape was supposed to have a meaning, yet without being able to express it perfectly. In contrast to this symbol and its obscure content there is now the meaning as such and its clear intelligibility; and the work of art thus becomes the outpouring of the pure Being as the meaning of all things—but of the Being which establishes the incongruity of shape and meaning, *implicitly* present in the symbol, as the meaning of God himself, a meaning present in the mundane and yet transcending everything mundane [and this is incongruous]; and therefore the Being becomes sublime in the work of art which is to express nothing but this absolutely clear meaning. If therefore symbolic art in general may already be called *sacred* art because it adopts the Divine as the content of its productions, the art of sublimity is *the* sacred art as such which can be called exclusively sacred because it gives honour to God alone.

Here on the whole the content, in its fundamental meaning, is still more restricted than it is in the symbol proper which does not get beyond striving after the spiritual, and in its reciprocal relations [between spirit and nature] affords a wide extension of spirit's transformation in natural productions and nature's transformation in echoes of the spirit.

This sort of sublimity in its first original character we find especially in the outlook of the Jews and in their sacred poetry. For visual art cannot appear here, where it is impossible to sketch any adequate picture of God; only the poetry of ideas, expressed in words, can. In handling this stage in more detail we may set out the following general points.

1. *God as Creator and Lord of the World*

For its most general content this poetry has God, as Lord of the world that serves him, as not incarnate in the external world but withdrawn out of mundane existence into a solitary unity. What in symbolism proper was still bound into one, thus falls apart here into the two sides—the abstract independence of God and the concrete existence of the world.

(*a*) God himself, as this pure independence of the one substance, is necessarily without shape and, taken in this abstraction, cannot be brought nearer to our vision. What therefore imagination can grip at this stage is not what God is in his pure essentiality, since that inhibits representation by art in an appropriate shape. The sole divine topic which is left is therefore the *relation* of God to the world created by him.

(*b*) God is the creator of the universe. This is the purest expression of the sublime itself. For the first time, that is to say, ideas of procreation and the mere natural generation of things by God vanish and give place to the thought of *creation* by spiritual might and activity. 'God said: Let there be light; and there was light'; this Longinus[1] quoted long ago as in every way a striking example of the sublime. The Lord, the one substance, does proceed to manifestation, but the manner of creation is the purest, even bodiless, ethereal manifestation; it is the word, the manifestation of thought as the ideal power, and with its command that

[1] *On the Sublime*, ix. 10, quoting Genesis 1: 3.

the existent shall be, the existent is immediately and actually brought into being in silent obedience.

(c) Yet God does not pass over, as may be supposed, into the created world as into his reality; he remains, on the contrary, withdrawn into himself, though with this opposition no fixed dualism is created. For what is brought forth is his work, which has no independence in contrast with him; on the contrary it is there only as the proof of *his* wisdom, goodness, and justice as such. The One is Lord over all, and natural things are not the presence of God but only powerless accidents which in themselves can only show him, not make him appear.[1] This constitutes the sublime so far as God is concerned.

2. *The Finite World bereft of God*

Since the one God is separated in this way on the one hand from the concrete phenomena of the world and settled in his independence, while the externality of the existent is determined and disdained as the finite on the other hand, it follows that existence both natural and human now acquires the new position of being a representation of the Divine only because its finitude appears on its own surface.

(a) For the first time, therefore, nature and the human form confront us as prosaic and bereft of God. The Greeks tell us that when the heroes of the voyage of the Argonauts made ship through the narrows of the Hellespont, the rocks, which hitherto had clanged shut and then opened again like shears, suddenly stood there for ever rooted to the ground.[2] This is similar to what we find in the sacred poetry of sublimity: in contrast with the infinite Being, the finite becomes fixed in its intelligible determinacy; whereas in the symbolic outlook nothing keeps its right place, since the finite collapses into the Divine, just as the Divine proceeds out of itself into finite existence.

If we turn from, e.g. the ancient Indian poems, to the Old Testament, we find ourselves at once on a totally different ground on which we can feel at home, no matter how strange and different from ours the situations, events, actions, and characters

---

[1] Hegel's contrast between *Scheinen* (show) and *Erscheinen* (appear), a favourite one of his, has no English equivalent.

[2] The Argonauts passed safely through the Symplegades which were fated to come to rest if any ship passed safely through them. See Sir James Frazer's note to the Loeb edition of Apollodorus, I. ix. 22, for references

displayed there may be. Instead of a world of riot and confusion we come into situations and have figures before us which appear perfectly natural, and their firm patriarchal characters in their determinateness and truth are closely connected with us by being perfectly intelligible.

(b) For this outlook which can grasp the natural course of events and assert the laws of nature, *miracle* gets its place for the first time. In India everything is miracle and therefore no longer miraculous. On a ground where an intelligible connection is continually interrupted, where everything is torn from its place and deranged, no miracle can tread. For the miraculous presupposes intelligible consequences and also the ordinary clear consciousness which alone calls a 'miracle' that interruption of this accustomed connection which is wrought by a higher power. Yet miracles in this sense are not a strictly specific expression of sublimity because the normal course of natural phenomena, as well as this interruption, is produced by the will of God and the obedience of nature.

(c) The sublime in the strict sense we must look for, on the contrary, when the whole created world appears entirely as finite, restricted, not bearing or carrying itself, and for this reason can only be regarded as a glorifying accessory for the praise of God.

3. *The Human Individual*

At this stage the human individual seeks his own honour, consolation, and satisfaction in this recognition of the nullity of things and in the exaltation and praise of God.

(a) In this connection the Psalms supply us with classic examples of genuine sublimity set forth for all time as a pattern in which what man has before himself in his religious idea of God is expressed brilliantly with the most powerful elevation of soul. Nothing in the world may lay claim to independence, for everything is and subsists only by God's might and is only there in order, in praise of this might, to serve him and to express its own unsubstantial nullity. While therefore we found in the imagination of substantiality and its pantheism an infinite *enlargement*, here we have to marvel at the force of the *elevation* of the mind which abandons everything in order to declare the exclusive power of God. In this connection Psalm 104 [2 ff.] is of magnificent power. 'Who coverest thyself with light as with a garment; who stretchest out the heavens like a curtain' and so on. Light, heavens, clouds, the wings of the wind are here nothing in and by themselves but only an external vesture, the chariot or the messenger for the service of God. Then, further on, God's wisdom is extolled, which has put everything in order: the springs which burst forth in the depths, the waters that flow between the mountains, and the birds of heaven sitting by the waters and singing under the boughs; grass, wine which delights the heart of man, and the cedars of Lebanon which the Lord hath planted; the sea where creatures swarm, and there are whales which God hath made to play therein. —And what God has created, he also maintains, but [v. 29] 'thou hidest thy face and they are troubled; thou takest away their breath; they die and return to their dust'. The nullity of man is spoken of more expressly in Psalm 90, 'a prayer of Moses, the man of God', when it says [vv. 5–7]: 'Thou carriest men away as with a flood; they are as a sleep, even as grass which in the morning flourisheth and in the evening is cut down and withereth. This is thy wrath for our transgressions, and thine anger that we must so suddenly be carried away'.

(b) Therefore, so far as man is concerned, there are bound up with sublimity at the same time the sense of man's finitude and the insurmountable aloofness of God.

(α) Therefore the idea of *immortality* does not arise originally in this sphere, for this idea involves the presupposition that the individual self, the soul, the human spirit, is something absolute. In sublimity, only the One is imperishable, and in contrast with him everything else is regarded as arising and perishing, but not as free and infinite in itself.

(β) Therefore, further, man views himself in his *unworthiness* before God; his exaltation consists in fear of the Lord, in trembling before his wrath, and we find depicted in a penetrating and affecting way grief over nullity, and the cry of the soul to God in complaint, suffering, and lament from the depths of the heart.

(γ) Whereas if the individual in his finitude holds to himself firmly over against God, then this willed and intended finitude becomes *wickedness*, which, as evil and sin, belongs only to the natural and human, but, like grief and the negative in general, can find no sort of place in the one inherently undifferentiated substance.

(c) Yet, thirdly, within this nullity man nevertheless gains a freer and more independent position. For on the one hand, along with the substantial peace and constancy of God in respect of his will and its commands for men, there arises the *law*; on the other hand, in man's exaltation there lies at the same time the complete and clear distinction between the human and the Divine, the finite and the Absolute, and thereby the judgement of good and evil, and the decision for one or the other, is transferred to the subject himself. Relationship to the Absolute and the adequacy or inadequacy of man thereto has therefore also an aspect accruing to the individual and his own behaviour and action. Thereby in his righteousness and adherence to the law he finds at the same time an *affirmative* relation to God, and has in general to connect the external positive or negative situation of his existence—prosperity, pleasure, satisfaction, or grief, misfortune, oppression—with his inner obedience to or stubbornness against the law, and therein accept well-being and reward or trial and punishment.

Chapter III

CONSCIOUS SYMBOLISM OF THE COMPARATIVE ART-FORM

What has emerged from sublimity as distinct from strictly un-conscious symbolizing consists on the one hand in the *separation* between the meaning, explicitly known in its inwardness, and the concrete appearance divided therefrom; on the other hand in the directly or indirectly emphasized *non-correspondence* of the two, wherein the meaning, as the universal, towers above individual reality and its particularity. In the imagination of Pantheism, how-ever, as in sublimity, the proper content, i.e. the universal sub-stance of all things, could not become explicitly visualized without being related to created existence, even if that created existence were inadequate to its own essence. Yet this relation belonged to the substance itself which in the negativity of its accidents gave proof of its wisdom, goodness, might, and justice. Consequently, in general at least, the relation of meaning and shape is here of a still essential and necessary kind, and the two linked sides have not yet become external to one another in the strict sense of the word 'external'. But since this externality is present *implicitly* in symbolism, it must also be posited [explicitly] and it emerges in the forms which we now have to consider in this final chapter on symbolic art. We can call them *conscious* symbolism, or, more precisely, the *comparative* form of art.

By conscious symbolism, I mean, we are to understand that the meaning is not only explicitly known but is *expressly* posited as different from the external way in which it is represented. In that case, as in sublimity, the meaning, thus explicitly expressed, does not essentially appear in and as the meaning of the shape given to it in such a way. But the relation of the two to one another no longer remains, as it did at the preceding stage, a relation grounded purely in the meaning itself; on the contrary, it becomes a more or less accidental concatenation produced by the subjective activity of the poet, by the immersion of his spirit in an external existent, by his wit and his invention in general. In this activity he may then start at one time rather from something perceived, and out of his own resources imagine for it a cognate spiritual meaning; at another time he may take his starting-point rather from an actual inner idea, or even from only a relatively inner one, in order to represent it by an image, or even merely to put one image in relation to another which has similar characteristics.

From naïve and *unconscious* symbolism this kind of connection is thus distinguished at once by the fact that now the subject kens both the inner essence of the meanings he has adopted as the content of his work and also the nature of the external phenomena which he uses in a comparative way for their better illustration, and he puts the two together *consciously* and intentionally on account of their discovered similarity. But the difference between the present stage and the sublime is to be sought in the fact that, on the one hand, the separation and juxtaposition of meaning and its concrete shape is expressly emphasized in the work of art itself in a lesser or greater degree; while, on the other hand, the sublime relation altogether disappears. For what is taken as content is no longer the Absolute itself but only some determinate and restricted meaning; and within its intended severance from its representation in an image a relation is set up which, involving a *conscious* comparison, does what *unconscious* symbolism aimed at in its own way.

Yet, for the *content* [here], the Absolute, the one Lord, can no longer be taken as the meaning because, simply by the sundering of concrete existence from the concept [or meaning] and by the juxtaposition of the two (even if by way of comparison), finitude is at once established fact for the artistic consciousness in so far as that consciousness lays hold of this [comparative] form as the final and proper one. In sacred poetry, on the contrary, God alone gives meaning to all things which, compared with him, prove to be transient and null. But if the meaning is to find its like image and similitude in what is restricted in itself and finite, then it must itself be of a restricted kind, all the more so as, at the stage now occupying our attention, the image (of course external to its content and chosen by the poet only arbitrarily) is regarded precisely as relatively adequate on account of its similarities to the content. Therefore in the comparative form of art there remains of sublimity only the one trait that each image, instead of giving shape to the meaning and the topic in hand in a reality adequate to them, is to afford *only* an image and similitude of them.

Therefore this sort of symbolizing as a fundamental type of whole works of art remains a subordinate species. For the shape consists only in the description of an immediate perceptible existent or occurrence from which the meaning is to be expressly distinguished. But in works of art which are formed from *one* conception and in their configuration are one undivided whole, such comparison can assert itself, if at all, only incidentally as an adornment and accessory, as is the case, e.g., in genuine products of classical and romantic art.

If therefore we regard this whole stage as a unification of the two previous stages, in that it comprises both that separation between meaning and external reality (which was the basis of the sublime) and also a concrete phenomenon's hinting at a related universal meaning (which we saw emerging in the symbol proper), still this unification is not a higher form of art at all but rather a clear but superficial [mode of] treatment which, limited in its content and more or less prosaic in its form, deserts the mysteriously fermenting depth of the symbol proper, and strays down from the height of sublimity into common consciousness.

Now as concerns the more specific division of this sphere, the distinction involved in comparison presupposes the meaning by itself and relates to it, and in contrast with it, a sensuous or pictorial shape; in this situation it is almost always found that the meaning is taken as the chief thing and the configuration as a mere cloak and externality; yet at the same time a further distinction appears, namely that now the one, now the other of the two sides is selected first and so a beginning is made from that. In this way either the configuration exists as an explicitly external, immediate, natural event or phenomenon, and then a universal meaning is produced from it, or the meaning is procured otherwise independently and only then is a configuration for it selected externally from somewhere or other.

In this connection we may distinguish two chief stages:

(*a*) In the first the concrete phenomenon, whether drawn from nature or from human affairs, events, and actions, constitutes the starting-point, but also the important and essential thing for the representation. It is selected indeed only on account of the more general meaning which it contains and alludes to, and it is only so far explained as the aim of illustrating this meaning in a related single situation or event demands; but the comparison between the universal meaning and the individual case is a *subjective* activity and it is not yet *expressly* revealed, and the whole representation will not be just an embellishment on a work independent without this adornment, but still appears with the pretension of serving on its own account as a whole. The kinds of thing that belong to this context are fable, parable, apologue, proverb, and metamorphoses.

(*b*) At the second stage, on the other hand, the meaning is the first thing in the artist's mind, and its concrete illustration in an image is only something accessory and an accompaniment to it which in itself has no independence at all but appears as entirely subordinate to the meaning, so that now the subjective caprice of comparison, a caprice seeking precisely this and no other image, comes more clearly to light. This mode of representation cannot for the most part amount to independent works of art and must therefore content itself with annexing its forms, as purely incidental, to other artistic productions. As the chief kinds of thing at this stage riddle, allegory, metaphor, image, and simile may be enumerated.

(*c*) Thirdly and lastly, we may by way of appendix make mention of didactic and descriptive poetry. For in these kinds of poetry there are explicitly made independent (*a*) the mere disclosure of the general nature of objects as the poet's mind grasps it in the clarity of his intelligence, and (*b*) the depicting of its concrete appearance. Thus is developed the complete separation of the two sides whose unification and genuine mutual formation alone makes possible the production of genuine works of art.

Now the separation of the two factors in the work of art implies that the different forms which have their place in this whole comparative sphere belong almost always solely to the art of speech, since poetry alone can express such a rendering of independence to both meaning and shape, while it is the task of the visual arts to exhibit in the outward shape as such its inner being.

A. COMPARISONS ORIGINATING FROM THE EXTERNAL OBJECT

With the different kinds of poetry or prose to be allocated to this first stage of the comparative art-form we find ourselves every time in a perplexity, and we have great trouble if we undertake to arrange them in definite chief species. There are subordinate hybrid kinds, I mean, which do not characterize any purely necessary aspect of art. In general, therefore, it is the same in aesthetics as it is in the natural sciences with certain classes of animals or other natural phenomena. In both spheres the difficulty lies in the fact that it is the very Concept of nature and art which partitions itself and posits its differentiations. As the differentiations of the Concept, they are now the differentiations which are also truly adequate to the Concept, and therefore conceivable; but hybrid transitional stages will not fit into these because they are just merely defective forms which leave one chief stage without being able to attain the following one. This is not the fault of the Concept;[1] and if we wished to take, as the basis of division and classification, such hybrids instead of the moments of the Concept of the thing at issue, then what is precisely inadequate to the Concept would be regarded as the adequate mode of its development. The true classification, however, may proceed only out of the true Concept, and hybrid productions can only find their place where the proper explicitly stable forms begin to dissolve and pass over into others. This is the case here in relation to the symbolic form of art, as we have pursued it.

But the kinds indicated belong to the *praeambula* or the symbolic form of art because they are generally imperfect and therefore a mere search for true art; this search does contain the ingredients for a genuine mode of configuration, yet it views them only in their finitude, separation, and mere relation, and so it remains subordinate. Therefore when we speak here of fable, apologue, parable, etc., we have not to discuss these kinds as if they belonged to poetry as their art distinct alike from the visual arts and from music, but only in the relation which they have to the general *forms* of art; their specific character can be elucidated only from this relation, and not from the essential nature of the proper species of *poetic* art, namely, epic, lyric, and dramatic.

We will articulate these kinds of art with more precision by dealing first with fable, then with parable, apologue, and proverb, and finally by considering metamorphoses.

---

[1] but of Nature, Hegel would add. In nature everything is external to everything else, e.g. in parts of space or moments of time. Thus nature is powerless to embody without remainder the determinations or differentiations of the Concept, or categories of thought, since these are not external to one another in the same sense.

1. *Fable*

Since in this chapter we have always spoken so far only of the formal side of the relation between an expressed meaning and its shape, we have now to specify the content which proves fitting for this present mode of configuration.

We have already seen that, in contrast to sublimity, at the present stage there is no longer any question of illustrating the Absolute and One in its undivided might by way of the nullity and insignificance of created things; on the contrary, we are now at the stage of the finitude of consciousness and therefore of the finitude of content too. If conversely we turn our attention to the symbol strictly so-called, one aspect of which the comparative art-form too was to adopt, then the inner element which, as we have already seen in Egyptian symbolism, appears over against the hitherto always immediate shape, i.e. the natural, is the spiritual. Now since that natural element is left and envisaged as independent, so the spiritual too is something determinate and finite, i.e. man and his finite aims; and the natural acquires a relationship, albeit a theoretical one, to these aims by providing signs and revelations with a bearing on man's weal and interest. The phenomena of nature, storm, the flight of birds, character of the entrails, etc., are now therefore taken in a quite different sense from the one they have in the views of the Parsis, Indians, or Egyptians. For them the Divine is made one with the natural in such a way that in nature man wanders to and fro in a world full of gods, and his own activity consists in producing this same identity in his work; the result then is that this activity, so far as it is appropriate to the being of the Divine in nature, appears itself as a revelation and production of the Divine in man. But when man is withdrawn into himself, and, divining his freedom, shuts himself into himself, he becomes an end in himself on his own account in his individuality; he acts, works, and labours according to his own will, he has a selfish life of his own and feels the essentiality of his aims in himself, and to them the natural has an external relation. Consequently nature disperses around him and serves him, so that, in regard to the Divine, he does not win in nature a vision of the Absolute, but treats nature only as a means whereby the gods afford recognition of themselves with a view to the best outcome of his ends; this is because they unveil their will to the human spirit through the medium of nature and so let men elucidate their will. Here, that is to say, there is presupposed an identity of the Absolute and the natural, in which *human* aims are the chief thing. But this sort of symbolism does not yet belong to art; it remains religious. For the *Vates* undertakes this interpretation of natural events only, in the main, for practical ends, in the interest whether of single individuals in relation to particular plans or of the entire people in respect of their common enterprises. Whereas poetry has to recognize and express even practical situations and relations in a more general theoretical form.

But what must be taken into account in this context is a natural phenomenon, an occurrence, containing a particular relation or an issue, which can be taken as a symbol for a universal meaning drawn from the sphere of human activity and doings, for an ethical doctrine, for a prudential maxim: in other words for a meaning which has for its content a reflection on the way in which things go or should go in human affairs, i.e. in matters of the will. Here we no longer have the divine will revealing its inwardness to man by natural events and their religious interpretation. Instead there is an entirely commonplace course of natural occurrences; from its detailed representation there can be abstracted, in a way we can understand, an ethical maxim, a warning, a doctrine, a prudential rule, and it is presented for the sake of this reflection and displayed to contemplation.

This is the setting which we may ascribe here to the fables of Aesop.

(a) Aesop's fables, that is to say, in their original form, are such an interpretation of a natural relation or occurrence between single natural things in general, especially between animals, whose activities spring from the same vital needs which move men as living beings. This relation or occurrence, taken in its more general characteristics, is therefore of such a kind that it can occur in the sphere of human life too, and only by its bearing on this does it acquire significance for man.

In keeping with this definition, the genuine fable of Aesop is the representation of some situation or other in animate and inanimate nature, or of an event in the animal world not devised capriciously, as may be supposed, but taken as it actually is in the world and truly observed; and then it is so recounted that there may be drawn from it a general lesson related to human existence and more particularly to its practical side, to prudence and morality in action. The *first* requirement is consequently to be sought in the fact that the specific case which is to supply the so-called moral shall not be merely fabricated, and especially that it shall not be fabricated in a way contradicting similar phenomena actually existent in nature. *Secondly*, and more particularly, the narrative must report the case not in its universality (which would make it typical of every happening in external reality) but according to its concrete individuality and as an actual event.

This original form of the fable gives to it, *thirdly* and lastly, the maximum of *naïveté*, because the aim of teaching and consequently the emphasis on general and useful meanings appears only as something arising later and not as what was intended from the beginning. Thus the most attractive of what are called Aesop's fables are those which correspond with the above definition and which relate actions—if you like to use that word—or relations and events which (*a*) have animal instinct as their basis, or (*b*) express some other natural relationship, or (*c*) in general, actually occur and are not merely put together by some capricious fancy. But thus it is then easily seen that the *fabula docet* attached to Aesop's fables in their present-day form[1] either makes the representation flat or frequently is out of place so that often it is rather the opposite lesson that can be drawn, or many other better ones.

A few examples may be cited here to illustrate this proper conception of Aesop's fables.

For example, an oak and a reed stand before a stormy wind; the weak reed is only bent, the strong oak breaks. This is something which has occurred often enough in a violent storm; interpreted morally, there is an unbending man of high station contrasted with a man of lower degree who in adverse circumstances can preserve himself by pliancy, while the other is destroyed by his stubbornness and haughtiness.

A similar case is the fable, preserved by Phaedrus,[2] of the

---

[1] i.e. and missing in their original form. But ὁ μῦθος δηλοῖ (*fabula docet*) is in the Greek text. Hegel, however, regarded these words as 'clearly a later addition, and often a very perverse one' (Lasson, p. 46). Aesop for him was originally a teller of tales who did not explicitly ascribe any obvious moral point to them.

[2] Not, as Mr. Osmaston thinks, Plato's dialogue of that name, but the fabulist who, under the early Roman Empire, published five books of fables, some drawn from Aesop. See his Appendix, fable xii, for this story of the swallows.

swallows. With other birds the swallows look on while a plough-man sows flax out of which the cord is woven for bird-snaring. The swallows, with their foresight, fly away; the other birds are incredulous; they remain in their own nests without a care and are caught. Here too it is an actual natural phenomenon which is the basis. It is well known that in autumn swallows migrate to more southerly regions, and therefore are not there when birds are trapped. The like can be said about the fable of the bat which is despised by day and at night-time because it belongs neither to the one nor to the other.

To such prosaic actual events a more general interpretation is given in relation to human affairs, just as even now some pious people can still draw from everything that happens an edifying and useful moral. Yet in this matter it is not necessary for the actual natural phenomenon to leap to the eyes every time. In the fable of the fox and the raven,[1] for instance, the actual fact is not to be recognized at a first glance, although it is not missing altogether; for it is the manner of ravens and crows to begin to caw when they see strange objects, men or animals, moving before them. Similar natural circumstances underlie the fable of the briar which tears the wool off the passer-by or wounds the fox that looks for pro-tection in it; or the fable of the husbandman who warms a snake at his bosom, etc. Other incidents are represented which may also occur among animals; in the first fable of Aesop, e.g., the eagle devours the fox's cubs; later he snatches entrails from a sacrificial pyre and along with them a live coal; and then the coal burns the eagle's nest. [The eaglets fall out and the fox eats them.] Other fables, finally, contain traits drawn from ancient myths, like the fable[2] of the beetle, the eagle, and Zeus, where there is presented

---

[1] The fox sees a raven high up on a tree eating cheese which it has stolen. The fox calls up that it would like to hear the raven's lovely voice. Flattered, the raven caws, drops the cheese from its mouth, and the fox eats it (Phaedrus, i. 13).

[2] For further remarks on this fable (no. 223 in the Tauchnitz edition), see below, p. 447. A hare pursued by an eagle takes refuge with a beetle and begs him to save him. The beetle begs the eagle not to carry off the suppliant, but the eagle hits the beetle and eats the hare, thereby sinning against Zeus the protector of suppliants. The beetle destroys the eagle's eggs until, to protect the next clutch, the eagle lays its eggs on Zeus's lap. The beetle makes a ball of dung and deposits it there also. Zeus shakes it off and the eggs with it. Eventually, so that the race of eagles may not die out, Zeus arranges that eagles shall lay their eggs at a time when there are no beetles.

the circumstance of natural history—I leave aside the question whether this is accurate or not—that eagles and beetles lay their eggs at different times; but there is perceptible too what is obviously the traditional importance of the scarab, which yet appears here already drawn into the sphere of the comic, as has occurred still more in Aristophanes.[1] A complete settlement of the question how many of these fables emanated from Aesop himself may be passed over here anyhow, because it is well known either that only a few of them, including, e.g., this fable of the beetle and the eagle, can be shown to be Aesop's, or that antiquity has been conferred on them generally so that they can be regarded as Aesop's.

Aesop himself is said to have been a misshapen humpbacked slave; his home is transferred to Phrygia, i.e. to the country where the transition is made from immediate symbolism, and attachment to nature, to the country in which man begins to apprehend the spiritual and his own self. In this situation Aesop does not regard animals and nature in general, as the Indians and Egyptians do, as something lofty and divine on their own account; he treats them, on the contrary, with prosaic eyes as something where circumstances serve only to picture human action and suffering. But yet his notions are only witty, without any energy of spirit or depth of insight and substantive vision, without poetry and philosophy. His views and doctrines prove indeed to be ingenious and clever, but there remains only, as it were, a subtle investigation of trifles. Instead of creating free shapes out of a free spirit, this investigation only sees some other applicable side in purely given and available materials, the specific instincts and impulses of animals, petty daily events; this is because Aesop does not dare to recite his doctrines openly but can only make them understood hidden as it were in a riddle which at the same time is always being solved. In the slave, prose begins, and so this entire species is prosaic too.

Nevertheless, almost all peoples and ages have run through these old stories and, however much any nation, generally acquainted with fables in its literature, may boast of possessing more fabulists, still their poems are mostly reproductions of these first notions, only translated into the taste of every age; and what these

---

[1] The beetle has an important part in his play *Peace*.

fabulists have added to the inherited stock of stories is left far behind by these originals.

(b) But we also find amongst Aesop's fables a number which in invention and execution are of great barrenness, but above all are told with the aim of teaching, so that animals or even gods are a mere cloak. Yet these fables are far from doing violence to the nature of animals, as has possibly been the case with modern writers; as e.g. with Pfeffel's[1] fables of one hamster which collected a stock in the autumn, a foresight neglected by another who therefore is to be reduced to beggary and hunger—or of a fox, bloodhound, and lynx, where the story is that they came before Jupiter with their one-sided talents, cunning, keen smell, and sharp sight, in order to acquire an equal distribution of their natural gifts; after they consented to judgement the verdict is: 'The fox is made stupid, the bloodhound is no longer any use for hunting, the Argus lynx acquires a cataract.' That a hamster puts by no produce, that these three other animals fall into an accidental or natural equal division of their qualities, is absolutely contrary to nature and therefore wearisome. Thus better than these fables is the one of the ant and the grasshopper, better than this again is the one of the stag with glorious antlers and thin shanks.

With the sense of such fables in mind, we have after all become accustomed in fables as such so to represent the lesson as the first thing that the occurrence related is itself merely a cloak and therefore an event purely fabricated for the purpose of the lesson. But such cloaks, especially when the incident described cannot possibly have occurred in the life of real animals, i.e. in accordance with their natural character, are extremely wearisome inventions, meaning less than nothing. The ingenuity of a fable consists only in conferring on what already exists otherwise, and has a shape, a still more universal sense beyond what it has directly.

Then further, presupposing that the essence of fable is only to be sought in the fact that animals act and speak instead of men, the question has been raised about what constitutes the attractive thing in this exchange. Yet nothing much attractive can lie in such clothing of men like animals, if it is supposed to be more than or different from something in a comedy played by apes and dogs, where on the contrary the contrast between the nature of animals

---

[1] K. Pfeffel, 1736–1809. See his *Fabeln* . . . (Basle, 1783).

as it appears on the stage and human action remains the sole interest apart from the spectacle of skilfulness in the training of the actors. Breitinger[1] therefore cites the *wonderful* as the proper attraction. But in the original fables the appearance of animals speaking is *not* set forth as something unusual and wonderful; for this reason Lessing[2] thinks that the introduction of animals affords a great advantage for the intelligibility and abbreviation of the exposition owing to our acquaintance with the characteristics of animals, with the cunning of the fox, the magnanimity of the lion, the voracity and brutality of the wolf—so that instead of abstractions, like cunning, magnanimity, etc., a definite picture comes at once before our minds. Yet this advantage alters nothing essential in the trivial circumstance of the mere cloak, and, on the whole, there is just the disadvantage of bringing animals on the scene instead of men, because the animal form in that case always remains a mask which veils the meaning, so far as its intelligibility goes, quite as much as it explains it.

The greatest fable of this kind, consequently, is the old story of Reynard the Fox,[3] but this is not strictly a fable at all.

(*c*) As a third stage we may here append the following way of treating fable, but with it we are already beginning to go beyond the sphere of fable. The ingenuity of a fable lies generally in finding, amongst the manifold phenomena of nature, cases which can serve as a support for general reflections on human action and behaviour, but in which animals and nature are not withdrawn from their own proper mode of existence. For the rest, however, the juxtaposition and relation of the so-called moral and the individual case remains only a matter of caprice and subjective wit and is therefore in itself only a matter of joking. Now it is this aspect which appears explicitly at this third stage. The form of fable is adopted as a joke. In this vein Goethe has composed many charming and ingenious poems. In one, entitled *Der Kläffer* [The Barker], he writes, for example, as follows: 'We ride in all directions on pleasure and on business, but the barking dog always comes behind us and yelps with all his power. So the Pomeranian from our kennel

---

[1] J. J. Breitinger, Swiss writer, 1701–76. See his *Critische Dichtkunst* (Zürich and Leipzig, 1740), ch. 7. Goethe prohibited performing dogs on the Weimar stage.

[2] In his *Abhandlungen über die Fabel*, ii: Von dem Gebrauche der Tiere in der Fabel (On the Use of Animals in Fables).

[3] See above, p. 187, note 2.

constantly accompanies us and the loud sound of his bark proves only that we are riding.[1]

But it is inherent in this class that the natural shapes used are presented in their proper character, as in Aesop's fables, and in their action and doings develop for us human situations, passions, and traits of character which have the closest affinity with those of animals. *Reynard*, just mentioned, is of this kind, but it is rather something of a fairy tale than a fable in the strict sense. The background is provided by an age of disorder and lawlessness, of wickedness, weakness, baseness, force and arrogance, of unbelief in religion, of only apparent rule and justice in secular matters, so that cunning, ingenuity, and selfishness carry off the victory over everything. This is the situation of the Middle Ages, developed as it was especially in Germany. Powerful vassals do show some respect to the King, but, at bottom, every one of them does what he likes, robs, murders, oppresses the weak, betrays the King, can gain the favours of the Queen, so that the whole country keeps together but only just. This is the human background; but it consists here not at all in an abstract proposition, but in a totality of situations and characters, and, on account of its wickedness, it turns out to be appropriate for the animal nature in the form of which it is unfolded. Therefore there is nothing disturbing when we find the human subject-matter quite openly transferred into the animal world, while the cloak does not appear, as might be thought, as a purely individual cognate case, but is released from this singularity and acquires a certain universality whereby it becomes clear to us that 'that's how things go generally in the world'. Now the droll feature lies in this cloak itself; the joke and jest is mingled with the bitter seriousness of the thing, since it brings human meanness before our eyes in the most excellent way in animal meanness and emphasizes even in the purely animal world a mass of the most entertaining traits and most appropriate stories, so that despite all harshness we have before us a joke, not bad and just intended, but one actual and seriously meant.

2. *Parable, Proverb, Apologue*

(a) *Parable*

Parable has with fable the general affinity that it takes up events drawn from the sphere of ordinary life but attributes to them

---

[1] The 'barking dog' is a captious critic of some of Goethe's later work.

a deeper and more general meaning with the aim of making this meaning intelligible and perceptible through this occurrence, an everyday one if considered by itself.

But at the same time parable is distinct from fable by reason of the fact that it looks for such occurrences not in nature and the animal world, but in human action and doings as everyone has them familiarly before his eyes; and the chosen individual case that at first sight appears trivial in its particularity, it enlarges into something of a more general interest by hinting at a deeper meaning.

Consequently, in respect of the *content*, the scope and solid importance of the meanings may be enlarged and deepened, while, in respect of *form*, the subjective activity of deliberate comparison and the presentation of a general lesson begin to come into appearance in a higher degree likewise.

As a parable, still bound up with a purely practical aim, we can regard the means used by Cyrus in order to incite the Persians to revolt (Herodotus, i. 126). He writes to the Persians to the effect that they are to betake themselves, equipped with sickles, to a specified place. There on the first day he made them set to with hard labour to make cultivable a field overgrown with thistles. But on the next day, after they had rested and bathed, he led them to a meadow and feasted them royally on meat and wine. Then when they had risen from the banquet, he asked them which day they had enjoyed most, yesterday or today. They all voted for today which had brought them nothing but good, whereas the day just past had been one of toil and exertion. Thereupon Cyrus exclaimed: 'If you will follow me, good days like today will be multiplied for you; but if you will follow me not, then prepare yourselves for innumerable labours like yesterday's.'

Of a related kind, though of the deepest interest and broadest universality in their meanings, are the parables that we find in the Gospels. The parable of the sower [in all the Synoptics], for example, is a story in itself trivial in content, and it is important only because of the comparison with the doctrine of the Kingdom of Heaven. In these parables the meaning throughout is a religious doctrine to which the human occurrences in which it is represented are related in much the same way as man and animal are related in Aesop's fables, where the former constitutes the meaning of the latter.

Of an equal breadth of content is the familiar story of Boccaccio[1] which Lessing has used in *Nathan* for his parable of the three rings. Here too the story, taken independently, is entirely commonplace, but it points to a matter of the widest scope, the difference and the truth of the three religions, Jewish, Mohammedan, and Christian. Precisely the same is the case, to refer to the most recent publications in this sphere, with Goethe's parables. In the *Cat made into a Pasty*, for example, a bold cook, to show himself a hunter too, went off, but shot a tom-cat instead of a hare; nevertheless he set the cat before the company, dressed with plenty of ingenious herbs—this is to be taken as a reference to Newton. The hash that the mathematician made of the science of physics is, to be sure, always something higher than a cat which a cook futilely substituted for a hare in a pasty!—These parables of Goethe's, like his poems written in the manner of fables, often have a jocular tone through which he wrote his soul free from the annoyances of life.

(b) Proverbs

A middle stage within this sphere is formed by the proverb. Amplified, that is to say, proverbs may be changed now into fables, now into apologues. They adduce an individual case which is drawn for the most part from day-to-day human life, but which is then to be taken in a universal meaning. For example: 'One hand washes the other' [i.e. one good turn deserves another]. Or 'Let everyone sweep the front of his *own* door' [i.e. mind your own business, or 'and then the village will be clean'], 'Who digs a grave for another falls into it himself' [i.e. hoist with his own petard], 'Roast me a sausage and I will slake your thirst' [i.e. one good turn deserves another]. To this class there also belong the aphorisms of which Goethe, to mention him again, has made a number in recent times with infinite grace and often of great depth.

These are not comparisons where the universal meaning and the concrete phenomenon appear outside one another and contrasted with one another. The former is immediately expressed with the latter.

(c) Apologue [or Moral Fable]

The apologue, thirdly, may be regarded as a parable which does not use the individual case merely as a *simile* to illustrate a universal

---

[1] *Decameron*, first day, third story. Lessing's drama *Nathan the Wise* appeared in 1779.

meaning but in this cloak itself brings out and expresses the universal maxim—since the maxim is actually contained in the individual case which yet is recounted as only an individual example. Taken in this sense Goethe's *God and the Bayadere*[1] is to be called an apologue. We find here the Christian story of the repentant Magdalene cloaked in Indian modes of thinking: the Bayadere shows the same humility, the like strength of love and faith; God puts her to the proof, which she completely sustains, and now her exaltation and reconciliation follow.—In the apologue the narrative may be so conducted that its conclusion provides the lesson itself without any mere comparison, as, e.g., in the *Treasure Seeker*: 'Work by day, guests at night, arduous weeks, joyful festivals, Be thy future talisman.'

3. *Metamorphoses*

The third class with which we have to deal, in contrast to fable, parable, proverb, and apologue, is metamorphoses. They are indeed of a symbolic, mythological kind, but at the same time they expressly oppose the natural to the spiritual, since they give to a natural existent, a rock, animal, flower, spring, the meaning of being a degradation and a punishment of spiritual existents, e.g. of Philomela, the Pierides, Narcissus, Arethusa, who through a false step, a passion, a crime, fall into infinite guilt or an endless grief, whereby the freedom of spiritual life is lost to them and they have become mere natural existents.

Thus on the one hand the natural is not treated here purely externally and prosaically as a mere hill, spring, tree, etc., but there is given to it an import belonging to an action or event springing from the spirit. The rock is not just stone but Niobe who weeps for her children.[2] On the other hand this human deed is guilt of some sort and the metamorphosis into a purely natural phenomenon is to be taken as a degradation of the spiritual.

We must therefore clearly distinguish these metamorphoses of

[1] Indian female dancer. This and the *Treasure Seeker* are two of Goethe's Ballads.

[2] For Philomela and the Pierides, see below, pp. 449–51, a further treatment of metamorphoses. Narcissus was punished by Aphrodite for rejecting the love of Echo and was changed into a flower; Arethusa fled from the passion of a river god and was changed into a fountain by Artemis; Niobe boasted so much about her numerous children that Apollo and Artemis slew them all. Niobe was changed into stone and still wept for her children in streams trickling down the rock.

gods and human individuals into natural objects from unconscious symbolism proper. In Egypt (a) the Divine is immediately
intuited in the closed rich mysteriousness of the inwardness of
animal life, and (b) the symbol proper is a natural shape *directly*
coincident with a wider cognate meaning, although this shape is
not to constitute an actual adequate existence of the meaning,
because unconscious symbolism is an outlook not yet liberated
into a spiritual one, whether in form or content. The metamorphoses, on the contrary, make the essential *distinction* between the
natural and the spiritual, and they form in this respect the transition from symbolic mythology to mythology strictly so-called—
mythology, i.e., if we so understand it that it starts in its myths
from a concrete natural existent, the sun, the sea, rivers, trees,
fertility, or the earth, but then expressly segregates this purely
natural element; for it extracts the inner content of the natural
phenomenon and artistically individualizes it, as a spiritualized
power, into gods with a human shape alike in mind and body.
In this way Homer and Hesiod first gave the Greeks their mythology,[1] not as merely significant of the gods, not as an exposition
of moral, physical, theological, or speculative doctrines, but as
mythology pure and simple, the beginning of spiritual religion in
a human configuration.

   In Ovid's *Metamorphoses*, apart from the quite modern treatment of the mythical, the most heterogeneous material is mixed up
together. Apart from those metamorphoses which could be interpreted generally as just one mode of mythical representation, the
specific viewpoint of this form is especially emphasized in those
stories in which such figures [e.g. the wolf or the cat] as are usually
taken to be symbolical or already even to be entirely mythical,
appear transformed into metamorphoses, and what otherwise was
united is brought into the opposition between meaning and shape
and into the transition from one to the other. So, e.g., the Phrygian
and Egyptian symbol of the wolf is so torn adrift [in Greek mytho-
logy] from its indwelling meaning that the meaning is referred
to a previous existence, if not of the sun, then of a king, and the
vulpine existence is represented as a consequence of a deed in that
human existence.[2] So too in the song of the Pierides the Egyptian

---

[1] This is derived from Herodotus, ii. 53.

[2] This is a reference to Lycaon, King of Arcadia, who set human flesh before
Zeus and was changed into a wolf. See a longer treatment of the story, below,
pp. 448–9.

gods, the ram and the cat, are represented as animal shapes in which the mythical Greek gods, Zeus, Aphrodite, etc., have hidden in fear. But the Pierides themselves are punished for daring to enter the lists against the Muses with their singing and are changed into magpies.

On the other hand, on account of the more precise character implicit in the content constituting their meaning, metamorphoses must all the same be distinguished from fable. In the fable the connection between the moral maxim and the natural event is a harmless[1] association which does not present in the natural occurrence the importance of being merely natural in distinction from spirit and so introduces this important distinction only into the meaning [of the fable]. Nevertheless, there are also single fables of Aesop which with slight alteration would become metamorphoses, as e.g. Fable 42[2] of the bat, the thorn, and the gull; their instincts are explained from misfortune in earlier undertakings.

With this we have gone through this first sphere of the comparative art-form, which starts from present reality and the concrete phenomenon, in order to go on from there to a further meaning illustrated therein.

B. COMPARISONS WHICH START FROM THE MEANING

If the separation of meaning and shape is the consciously presupposed form within which the relation of the two is to proceed, then, granted the independence of one side as well as of the other, a beginning can and must be made not only from what exists externally but just as much, conversely, from what is present internally, namely from general ideas, reflections, feelings, or maxims. For this inner element is, like the pictures of external things, something present to our minds and in its independence of

---

[1] In a metamorphosis the connection is harm*ful* because it involves a 'degradation' of the spiritual.

[2] 124 in the Tauchnitz edition. The three decide to go into business together. The bat borrows silver, the thorn contributes clothing and the gull bronze (or a halfpenny). They sail away together; the boat sinks; the three are saved, but they have lost their goods. Thereafter the bat, fearing its creditors, goes out only at night; the gull keeps to the sea-shore, hoping that its bronze (or coin) may be jetsam; the thorn keeps seizing the clothes of passers-by in the hope of recognizing its own clothing.

the external originates with itself. Now if the meaning is in this way the starting-point, then the expression, the reality, appears as the means, drawn from the concrete world for the sake of making the meaning, as the abstract content, definitely picturable, visible, and perceptible.

But, as we saw earlier [in the preamble to this chapter], both sides being mutually indifferent to one another, the connection into which both are brought is not one in which they belong to one another by absolute necessity. Therefore their bearing on one another, not lying objectively in the nature of the case, is something manufactured subjectively which no longer conceals this subjective character but makes it recognizable through the manner of the representation. The *absolute* shape has the connection of content and form, soul and body, as concrete ensoulment, as the unification of both, grounded absolutely in the soul as in the body, in the content as in the form. Here, however, the separatedness of the two sides is the presupposition and therefore their association is (*a*) a purely subjective enlivenment of the meaning through a shape external to it and (*b*) an interpretation of a real existent equally subjective through its bearing on the other ideas, feelings, and thoughts of the spirit. Therefore, as it turns out, what especially appears in these forms is the subjective art of the poet as maker, and in complete works of art, especially in this aspect, what belongs to the meaning and its necessary configuration can be distinguished from what the poet has added as decoration and adornment. These easily recognizable additions, especially images, similes, allegories, and metaphors, are the things for which we can commonly hear him praised to the skies; and part of the praise is supposed to redound to the sharp eyes and astuteness, as it were, which have made him out and noticed his peculiar subjective inventions. Yet the forms that belong here, as has been said already, should only appear in genuine works of art as mere accessories, although we find in older books[1] on poetry that these incidental things in particular are treated as the very ingredients of poetic activity.

But while at first the two sides which are to be connected are of course indifferent to one another, still, for the justification of the subject's relating and comparing, the shape must in its make-up include in a cognate way the same circumstances and properties

---

[1] Hegel probably has Aristotle's *Poetics* in mind, especially 1458-9.

which the meaning has in itself. This is because the apprehension of this similarity is the only basis for associating the meaning with precisely this specific shape and illustrating the former by the latter.

Finally, since a beginning is not made from the concrete phenomenon from which something universal can be abstracted, but conversely from this universal itself which is to be mirrored in an image, it follows that the meaning can now shine out actually as the proper end and dominate the image which is its means of illustration.

As the more detailed sequence in which we can discuss the particular kinds to be mentioned in this sphere, the following may be indicated:

First, as the stage most related to the last one, we have to discuss the riddle.

Secondly, allegory, in which it is especially the domination of the abstract meaning over the external shape that appears.

Thirdly, comparison proper, namely metaphor, image, and simile.

1. *Riddle*

The symbol, strictly so-called, is *inherently* enigmatical because the external existent by means of which a universal meaning is to be brought to our contemplation still remains different from the meaning that it has to represent, and it is therefore open to doubt in what sense the shape has to be taken. But the riddle belongs to conscious symbolism and it is distinguished at once from the symbol, strictly so-called, by reason of the fact that the meaning is clearly and completely known to the inventor of the riddle; and the shape that veils it, through which the meaning is to be guessed, is therefore chosen deliberately for this semi-veiling. Symbols in the strict sense are, both before and after, unsolved problems, while the riddle is absolutely solved, so that Sancho Panza says quite rightly after all: 'I would far rather be given the solution first and the riddle afterwards.'[1]

(*a*) In inventing a riddle, that is to say, the first step from which a start is made is the known sense or meaning of it.

(*b*) But, secondly, individual traits of character and properties

---

[1] The remark is in character, but I am not the only person unable to find it in *Don Quixote*.

drawn from the otherwise known external world and, as in nature and in externality generally, lying there scattered outside one another, are associated together in a disparate and therefore striking way. Therefore they lack a subject embracing them together [as predicates] into a unity and their deliberate concatenation and connection one with another has as such absolutely no sense; although, on the other hand, they do all the same point to a unity in relation to which even the apparently most heterogeneous traits nevertheless acquire sense and meaning again.

(c) This unity, the subject of those scattered predicates, is precisely the simple idea, the word that solves the riddle, and the problem of the riddle is to discover or guess it out of this apparently confused disguise. The riddle in this respect is the conscious wit of symbolism which puts to the test the wit of ingenuity and the flexibility in combining things, and its mode of representation is self-destructive because it leads to the guessing of the riddle.

Riddle therefore belongs especially to the art of speech, though it may find a place in the visual arts too, in architecture, horticulture, and painting. Its appearance in history lies principally in the East, in the intervening and transitional period between more obtuse symbolism and more conscious wisdom and generalization. Whole peoples and periods have delighted in such problems. Even in the Middle Ages in Arabia and Scandinavia, and in the German poetry of the singing contests at the Wartburg, e.g., it plays a great part. In modern times it has sunk down more or less to conversation and mere witticisms and jokes in social gatherings.

To the riddle we may append that infinitely wide field of witty and striking notions which are developed as plays on words, and epigrams in relation to some given situation, event, or topic. Here on the one side we have some indifferent object, on the other side a subjective notion which unexpectedly, with remarkable subtlety, emphasizes one aspect, one relation, which previously did not appear in the topic as it was and sets the topic in a new light as a result of the new significance given to it.

2. Allegory

The opposite of the riddle, in this sphere which begins from the universality of the meaning, is allegory. It too does try to bring the specific qualities of a universal idea nearer to our vision through cognate qualities of sensuously concrete objects; yet it does so not by way of the semi-veiling and the enigmas of the riddle, but precisely with the converse aim of producing the most complete clarity, so that the external thing of which the allegory avails itself must be as transparent as possible for the meaning which is to appear in it.

(a) The first concern of allegory therefore consists in personifying, and therefore conceiving as a *subject*, general abstract situations or qualities belonging to both the human and the natural world, e.g. religion, love, justice, discord, glory, war, peace, spring, summer, autumn, winter, death, fame. But this subjectivity in neither its content nor its external shape is truly in itself a subject or *individual*; on the contrary, it remains the abstraction of a universal idea which acquires only the empty *form* of subjectivity and is to be called a subject only, as it were, in a grammatical sense. An allegorical being, however much it may be given a human shape, does not attain the concrete individuality of a Greek god or of a saint or of some other actual person, because, in order that there may be congruity between subjectivity and the abstract meaning which it has, the allegorical being must make subjectivity so hollow that all specific individuality vanishes from it. It is therefore rightly said of allegory that it is frosty and cold and that, owing to the intellectual abstractness of its meanings, it is even in its invention rather an affair of the intellect than of concrete intuition and the heartfelt depth of imagination. Poets like Virgil are therefore especially concerned with allegorical beings, because they cannot create individual gods like the Homeric ones.

(b) But, secondly, the meanings of allegories are, in their abstractness, at the same time determinate and they are recognizable only owing to this determinacy. The result is that now the expression of such particular characteristics does not lie immediately in the idea which at first is only personified *in general*, and therefore it must enter on its own account alongside the subject as its explanatory predicates. This separation of subject and predicate, universal and particular, is the second aspect of frostiness in allegory. Now the illustration of the determinate qualities to be indicated is drawn from the expressions, effects, consequences which come into appearance through the meaning once it acquires reality in concrete existence, or from the instruments and means of which it avails itself in its actual realization. Battle and war, for example, are indicated by armed forces, side-arms, cannon, drums, colours; seasons by flowers and fruits which flourish above all under the favourable influence of spring, summer, and autumn. Such things, again, may also have purely symbolical bearings, as justice is brought to our ken by scales and blindfolding, death by the hour-glass and scythe. But since the meaning is the dominant thing in allegory and its closer illustration is subordinate to it just as abstractly as the meaning itself is a pure abstraction, the shape of such definite things acquires here only the value of a mere attribute.

(c) In this way allegory is in both aspects bleak; its general personification is empty, the specific externality is only a sign, meaningless if taken by itself; and the centre [the idea personified] which ought to have unified the multiplicity of attributes does not have the force of a subjective unity shaping itself and relating itself to itself in its real existence, but becomes a purely abstract form, and its filling with such particular things, degraded to the position of attributes, remains for it something external. Consequently allegory is not to be taken really seriously with the independence into which it personifies its abstractions and their indication, with the result that to what is independent absolutely the form of an allegorical being should properly not be given. The *Dike* of the Greeks, for example, is not to be called an allegory; she is universal necessity, eternal justice, the universal powerful person, the absolutely substantial basis of the relations of nature and spiritual life, and therefore herself the absolutely independent being whom individuals, gods as well as men, have to follow. F. von Schlegel, as was remarked above, has observed that every work of art must be an allegory. Yet this saying is true only if it is to mean nothing but that every work of art must contain a universal idea and an inherently true meaning. Whereas what *we* have here called allegory is a mode of representation subordinate in both form and content, only imperfectly corresponding to the essence of art. For every human event and imbroglio, every relationship, etc., has some sort of universality in itself which can also be extracted *as* universality; but such abstractions we have otherwise already in our minds, and with them in their prosaic universality and their external indication, to which alone allegory attains, art has nothing to do.

Winckelmann too wrote an immature work on allegory[1] in which

[1] *Versuch einer Allegorie, besonders für die Kunst* (1766).

he assembles a mass of allegories, but for the most part he confuses symbol and allegory.

Amongst the particular arts within which allegorical representations occur, poetry is wrong in taking refuge in such media, whereas sculpture cannot in the main be managed without them. This is specially true of modern sculpture which in many ways admits of being portraiture and so, for the closer indication of the multiple relations in which the represented individual stands, must avail itself of allegorical figures. On Blücher's memorial, erected here in Berlin, we see the genius of fame and victory, but when it comes to the general treatment of the war of liberation, the allegorical is avoided by a series of individual scenes as, e.g., the departure of the army, its march, and its victorious return. But on the whole in portrait-statues sculptors have been content to surround the simple statues with allegories and to multiply them. The ancients, on the other hand, rather availed themselves on sarcophagi, e.g., of general mythological representations of sleep, death, etc.[1]

Allegory in general belongs less to ancient art than to the romantic art of the Middle Ages, even if as allegory it is not properly anything romantic. This frequent occurrence of allegorical treatment in the medieval epoch is to be explained in the following way. On the one side the Middle Ages had for their content particular individuals with their subjective aims of love and honour, with their vows, pilgrimages, and adventures. The variety of these numerous individuals and events provides imagination with a wide scope for inventing and developing accidental and capricious collisions and their resolution. But, on the other side, over against the varied secular adventures, there stands the universal element in the relations and situations of life. This universal is not individualized

[1] This treatment of allegory is made needlessly obscure by the vagueness, and sometimes the ambiguity, of such terms as 'universal idea', 'qualities', 'particular characteristics'. The 'universal idea' is the basic conception (e.g. justice) underlying the allegorical work. But this 'idea' is also called a 'quality'. Justice, e.g., is represented as a woman blindfolded and holding scales. She is not an individual woman, or genuinely a 'subject' or person, but only a generalized allegorical figure, and so is not living but cold. What is to be allegorized, however, has 'particular characteristics' (also unfortunately called 'determinate qualities') and these cannot be 'expressed' (or treated artistically) in the allegorical generalized figure itself, which is completely determined by the 'idea' (or 'quality') allegorized, and so they have to be treated alongside it as its attributes. Blücher's monument, by C. D. Rauch, erected in 1826, consists of a figure of Blücher on a pedestal surrounded by reliefs illustrating some of his campaigns and containing allegorical figures of victory.

into independent gods as it was with the ancients, and therefore it appears readily and naturally explicitly sundered in its universality alongside those particular personalities and their particular shapes and events. Now if the artist has an idea of such universalities, and if he wishes to emphasize their universality as such and not to clothe them in the accidental form just described, there is nothing left to him but the allegorical manner of representation. This happens too in the religious sphere. Mary, Christ, the acts and fates of the Apostles, the saints with their penances and martyrdoms are, it is true, here again quite definite individuals; but Christianity is equally concerned with universal spiritual things which cannot be embodied in the definite character of living and actual persons because they should be represented precisely as *universal* relationships like love, faith, and hope. In general the truths and dogmas of Christianity are independently familiar as religious, and one chief interest even of poetry consists in this, that these doctrines shall appear as *universal* doctrines and that the truth shall be known and believed as universal truth. But in that case the concrete representation must remain subordinate and indeed external to the content, and allegory is the form which satisfies this need in the easiest and most appropriate way. In this sense Dante has much that is allegorical in his *Divine Comedy*. So there, e.g., theology appears fused with the picture of his beloved, Beatrice. But this personification hovers (and this constitutes its beauty) between allegory proper and a transfiguration of his youthful beloved. He saw her for the first time when he was nine years old; she seemed to him to be the daughter, not of a mortal man, but of God; his fiery Italian nature conceived a passion for her which was never again extinguished. When it had awakened in him the genius of poetry, then, after the early death of his dearest love had lost her for him, he put into the chief work of his life this marvellous memorial of, as it were, this inner subjective religion of his heart.

3. *Metaphor, Image, Simile*

After riddle and allegory the third sphere is the figurative in general. The riddle still conceals the explicitly known meaning, and the chief thing was still clothing the meaning in related though heterogeneous and far-fetched ways. Allegory, on the other hand, made the clarity of the meaning so very much the sole dominating end that personification and its attributes appear degraded into purely external signs. Now the figurative unites the clarity of the allegorical with the pleasantry of the riddle. The meaning clearly confronting our minds is illustrated in the shape of some cognate external expression, yet so that thereby no problems arise which have first to be deciphered; what does arise is a figurative expression through which the envisaged meaning shines in perfect clarity and at once makes plain what it is.

(a) Metaphor

The first point concerning metaphor is that it is to be taken as *implicitly* already a simile, because it expresses the meaning, clear in itself, in a similar and comparable phenomenon of concrete reality. But in comparison as such both the sense proper and the image are specifically separated from one another, while this cleavage, though present implicitly, is not yet *posited*, in metaphor. On this account Aristotle[1] distinguished comparison from metaphor long ago by pointing out that in the former an 'as' is added, while it is missing in the latter. The metaphorical expression, that is, names only one side, the image; but in the connection in which the image is used, the meaning proper which is intended is so near the surface that it is immediately given at the same time, as it were without direct separation from the image. When, e.g., we hear 'the springtime of these cheeks' or a 'sea of tears' we are compelled to take this expression not literally but only as an image, the meaning of which the context expressly indicates to us. In symbol and allegory the relation between the sense and the external shape is not so immediate and necessary. In the nine flights of an Egyptian stair and a hundred other things it is only the initiated, the cognoscenti, the scholars who can find a symbolic meaning; and, conversely, they sniff out and find something mystical or symbolical where to look for it is unnecessary, because it is not there. This may have happened many a time with my dear friend Creuzer, as well as with Neo-Platonists and commentators on Dante.

(α) The range, the variety of form, of metaphor is infinite, yet its definition is simple. It is an entirely compressed and abbreviated comparison, in that it does not oppose image and meaning to one

[1] *Poetics,* 1457[b]. This work of Aristotle is in Hegel's mind throughout this section.

another but presents the image alone; the literal sense of the image, however, it extinguishes and it makes the actually intended meaning recognizable at once in the image through the context in which the image occurs, although this meaning is not expressly stated.

But since the sense so figurated is clear only from the context, the meaning expressed in metaphor cannot claim the value of an independent artistic representation but only of an incidental one, so that metaphor therefore can arise in an even enhanced degree only as a mere external adornment of a work of art which itself is independent.

(β) Metaphor has its principal application in linguistic expressions which in this connection we may treat under the following aspects.

(αα) In the first place, every language already contains a mass of metaphors. They arise from the fact that a word which originally signifies only something sensuous is carried over into the spiritual sphere. *Fassen, begreifen,* and many words, to speak generally, which relate to knowing, have in respect of their literal meaning a purely sensuous content, which then is lost and exchanged for a spiritual meaning, the original sense being sensuous, the second spiritual.[1]

(ββ) But gradually the metaphorical element in the use of such a word disappears and by custom the word changes from a metaphorical to a literal expression, because, owing to readiness to grasp in the image only the meaning, image and meaning are no longer distinguished and the image directly affords only the abstract meaning itself instead of a concrete picture. If, for example, we are to take *begreifen* in a spiritual sense, then it does not occur to us at all to think of a perceptible grasping by the hand. In living languages the difference between actual metaphors and words already reduced by usage to literal expressions is easily established; whereas in dead languages this is difficult because mere etymology cannot decide the matter in the last resort. The question does not depend on the first origin of a word or on linguistic development generally; on the contrary, the question above all is whether a word which looks entirely pictorial, depictive, and illustrative has not already, in the life of the language, lost this its first sensuous

---

[1] *Fassen* is originally to 'grasp', and hence to 'apprehend'. *Begreifen* is similar. See p. 306, note.

meaning, and the memory of it, in the course of its use in a spiritual sense and been endowed altogether with a spiritual meaning.

(γγ) This being the case, the invention of new metaphors, expressly first constructed by poetic imagination, is necessary. A principal task of this invention consists, *first*, in transferring, in an illustrative way, the phenomena, activities, and situations of a higher sphere to the content of lower areas and in representing meanings of this more subordinate kind in the shape and picture of the loftier ones. The organic, e.g., is inherently of higher worth than the inorganic, and to present death in the phenomenon of life enhances the expression. So Firdausi says long ago: 'The sharpness of my *sword devours* the lion's brain and *drinks* the dark blood of the stout-hearted one.'

In a more spiritualized degree a similar thing occurs if the natural and sensuous is imaged in the form of spiritual phenomena and therefore is elevated and ennobled. In this sense it is quite common for us to speak of '*laughing* fields', '*angry* flood', or to say with Calderón 'the waves *sigh* under the heavy burden of the ships'. What is solely human is used here as an expression for the natural. Roman poets too use this sort of metaphor, as e.g. Virgil (*Georgics*, iii. 132) says: 'Cum graviter tunsis gemit area frugibus' [when the threshing floor *groans* heavily under the threshing of the corn].

Next, *secondly*, and conversely, something spiritual is also brought nearer to our vision through the picture of natural objects.

Yet such illustrations may easily degenerate into preciousness, into far-fetched or playful conceits, if what is absolutely lifeless appears notwithstanding as personified and such spiritual activities are ascribed to it in all seriousness. It is especially the Italians who have let themselves go in the like hocus-pocus; even Shakespeare is not entirely free from this when, e.g., in Richard II, iv. ii,[1] he makes the king say in taking leave of his spouse:

> For why, the senseless brands will sympathize
> The heavy accent of thy moving tongue,
> And in compassion weep the fire out;
> And some will mourn in ashes, some coal-black,
> For the deposing of a rightful King.

(γ) *Finally*, as for the aim and interest of metaphor, a literal saying is in itself one intelligible expression, metaphor another. So

---

[1] Act V, scene i in our text. Hegel gives a prose translation.

the question arises: why this double expression, or, what is the same thing, why metaphor, which is this duality in itself? The usual answer is that metaphors are used for the sake of a more lively poetic representation, and this vivacity is especially what Heyne commends in metaphor. The liveliness consists in rendering things precise to the visual imagination, in providing a sensuous image to counteract the pure indefiniteness of the saying which is always general. Of course metaphor has a greater vivacity than ordinary literal expressions have; but true life must not be sought in metaphors whether separately or in an array of them; their imagery may indeed incorporate something which happily introduces into the expression both a perceptible clarity and a higher definiteness, but, all the same, when every detailed feature is independently imaged, it makes the whole thing ponderous and suffocates it by the weight of individual detail.

Therefore the sense and aim of metaphorical diction in general, as we have still to explain in more detail in dealing with simile, must be found in the need and power of spirit and heart which are not content with the simple, customary, and plain, but place themselves above it in order to move on to something else, to linger over various things, and to join two things together into one. This conjunction has itself again more than one reason.

(αα) First, the reason of reinforcement; heart and passion, full and moved in themselves, on the one hand make this power manifest by sensuous exaggeration; on the other hand, they strive to express their own stormy passion and their grip on all sorts of ideas by correspondingly transferring them out into all sorts of cognate phenomena and by moving in images of the most varied kinds.

In Calderón's *Devotion at the Cross*, e.g., Julia says, as she sees the newly slain corpse of her brother, Lisardo, and as her lover, Eusebio, his murderer, stands before her: 'Glad would I close my eyes here before the innocent blood which *cries* for vengeance, pouring forth in purple *flowers*; would that thou mightest be forgiven by the tears that flow for thee; wounds are eyes, yes *mouths* that know naught of lies', etc.

Far more passionately still, Eusebio recoils from Julia's glance when she is finally ready to give herself to him, and he cries: 'Flames spark from thine eyes, the breath of thy sigh is *burning*; every word is a *volcano*, every hair a *flash of lightning*, every syllable is *death*, every one of thy caresses *hell*. Such a horror stirs in me from that crucifix upon thy breast, a wondrous symbol.'[1]

This is the movement of the heart which for what is immediately envisaged substitutes another picture, and with this search and discovery of ever new modes of expression for its passion can scarcely ever reach an end.

(ββ) A second reason for metaphor lies in the fact that, when spirit is plunged by its inner emotion into the contemplation of cognate objects, at the same time it still wishes to free itself from their externality, because in the external it seeks *itself* and spiritualizes it; and now by shaping itself and its passion into something beautiful, it evinces its power to bring into representation its elevation above everything external.

(γγ) But even so, thirdly, the metaphorical expression may arise from the purely bacchanalian delight of fancy which cannot put before us either an object in its own appropriate shape or a meaning in its simple absence of imagery, but longs above all for a concrete intuition cognate with both. Or metaphor may arise from the wit of a subjective caprice which, to escape from the commonplace, surrenders to a piquant impulse, not satisfied until it has succeeded in finding related traits in the apparently most heterogeneous material and therefore, to our astonishment, combining things that are poles apart from one another.

In this connection it may be remarked that it is not so much a prosaic and a poetic style as a classical and a modern style that are to be distinguished from one another by the preponderance of either literal or metaphorical expressions. Not only the Greek philosophers, like Plato and Aristotle, or great historians and orators, like Thucydides and Demosthenes, but also the great poets, Homer and Sophocles, on the whole stick almost always to literal expressions, although similes do also occur. Their plastic severity and solidity does not tolerate the sort of blending involved in metaphor or permit them to stray hither and thither away from the homogeneous material and the simple, self-contained, complete cast,[2] in order to gather up so-called 'flowers' of expression here and there. But metaphor is always an interruption of the course of

---

[1] The first quotation is Act I, 805–12; the second is Act II, 1605–12. Hegel quotes the translation by A. W. Schlegel.

[2] Hegel is straying away from the literal and using the metaphor of casting e.g. a bronze statue. Cf. above, pp. 174, 296, *et al.*

ideas and a constant dispersal of them, because it arouses and brings together images which do not immediately belong to the matter in hand and its meaning, and therefore draw the mind away from that to something akin and foreign to it. The Greeks were saved from an all too frequent use of metaphors, in prose by the infinite clarity and suppleness of their language, in poetry by their quiet and fully developed taste.

On the other hand, it is particularly the East, especially the later Mohammedan poetry, which uses figurative expressions and indeed has them of necessity. The same is true of modern poetry also. Shakespeare, e.g., is very metaphorical in his diction; the Spaniards too, who have deviated into the most tasteless excess and agglomeration, love the florid style; Jean Paul also; Goethe, in his uniformly clear vision, less. But Schiller, even in prose, is very rich in images and metaphors; in his case this arises rather from his effort so to express deep concepts as to bring them before our minds without pressing on to the strictly philosophical expression of thought. In his work, then, the inherently rational and speculative unity sees and finds its counterpart in the life of the present world.

(b) *Image*

Between metaphor on one side and simile on the other we may place the image. For it has such a close affinity with metaphor that it is strictly only a metaphor *in extenso* which therefore now acquires in turn a great resemblance to simile, but with this difference, namely that, in the image as such, the meaning is not explicitly separated out and contrasted with the concrete external object expressly compared with it. An image occurs especially when two phenomena or situations (more or less independent when taken by themselves) are unified, so that one situation affords the meaning which is to be made intelligible by the image of the other. In other words, the first thing here, the fundamental characteristic, is thus the independence, the separation, of the different spheres whence the meaning and its image are drawn; and what is common to them (properties, relations, etc.) is not, as in the symbol, the undetermined universal and the substantial itself, but firmly determinate concrete existence on both the one side and the other.

(α) In this connection the image can have for its meaning

a whole series of situations, activities, productions, modes of existence, etc., and it can illustrate the meaning by a similar series drawn from an independent but cognate sphere, without putting the meaning as such in so many words into the image itself. Of this kind Goethe's poem *Mahomet's Song* is an example: the image is that of a spring, issuing from a rock, which in the freshness of youth hurls itself over the crags into the depths, enters the plain reinforced by bubbling springs and brooks, absorbs brother-streams, gives a name to localities, sees cities growing below its feet, until, its heart bubbling over with joy, it carries all these glories, its brothers, its treasures, its children to the creator who awaits it.—It is only the title that shows that what is happily represented in this spacious and brilliant image of a mighty stream is Mohammed's bold appearance, the quick dissemination of his doctrine, and the intended adoption of all people into the one faith. Of a similar kind are many of the *Xenien* of Goethe and Schiller; these are partly scornful, partly playful sayings addressed to authors and the public, e.g. 'In silence we pounded saltpetre, carbon, and sulphur, drilled holes; now enjoy the firework!' 'Some rose as shining balls and others exploded; many too we threw in play to delight the eye.' Many of these epigrams were in fact rockets and they have given annoyance—to the endless delight of the better part of the public which rejoiced when the mob of mediocre and bad authors, who had long made much of themselves and held the floor, were given a capital 'yin on the neb' and a cold douche into the bargain.

(β) Yet in these last examples there already appears a second aspect to be emphasized in respect of images. The content, namely, is here a subject who acts, produces things, lives through situations and now, *not* as subject but only in respect of what he does or effects or what meets him, is represented in an image. Whereas as subject, he is himself introduced without an image and only his literal actions and affairs acquire the form of a metaphorical expression. Here too, as in the case of the image in general, the *entire* meaning is not severed from its cloak; on the contrary, the subject alone is revealed explicitly, while his determinate content at once acquires an imaged shape; and thus the subject is represented as if he himself brought into being the objects and actions in this their imaged existence. To the expressly named subject something metaphorical is ascribed. This mixture of the literal and the metaphorical has often been blamed, but the grounds for this blame are weak.

(γ) In this kind of imagery the Orientals especially display great boldness since they bind together and intertwine into one image existents entirely independent of one another. So Hafiz, for example, says once: 'The course of the world is a bloody dagger, and the drops falling from it are crowns.'[1] And elsewhere: 'The sun's sword pours out in the reddening dawn the blood of the night, over which it has won the victory.' Similarly: 'No one like Hafiz has torn the veil from the cheeks of thought since the locks of the word's betrothed were curled.' The meaning of this image seems to be this: thought is the word's betrothed (as Klopstock, e.g., calls the word the twinbrother of thought) and since the time when this fiancée was adorned in words like curls, no one has been more skilled than Hafiz in making the thought so adorned appear clearly in its unveiled beauty.

(c) *Simile*

From this last kind of imagery we can proceed directly to simile. For in it, since the subject of the image is named, there already begins the independent expression of the meaning without an image. Yet the difference lies in this, that whatever the image presents exclusively in the form of an image (even in its abstraction as a meaning which therefore appears alongside its image and is compared with it) can acquire for itself in the simile an independent mode of expression. Metaphor and image illustrate the meanings *without* expressing them, so that only the context in which metaphors and images occur makes known openly what their literal significance is supposed to be. In simile, on the contrary, both sides, image and meaning, are completely severed—if indeed with greater or lesser completeness, now of the image, now of the meaning; each is presented by itself, and only then, in this separation, are they related to one another on account of the similarities n their content.

In this respect the simile may be called (*a*) a merely idle *repetition*, in that one and the same matter comes into the representation in a double form, indeed in a triple or quadruple form, and (*b*) an

---

[1] The first two quotations from Hafiz (and probably others) are taken from *Hafis' Diwan*, translated by J. von Hammer-Purgstall (1812), part i, pp. 101 ff. (See Hegel's *Berliner Schriften*, ed. by J. Hoffmeister, Hamburg 1956, p. 714.)

often wearisome *superfluity*, since the meaning is explicitly present already and needs no further mode of configuration to make it intelligible. The question therefore presses in the case of comparison more than it does in that of image and metaphor: what essential interest and aim is there in the use of single or multiplied similes? They are neither to be employed on account of mere vivacity (the common opinion) nor for the sake of greater clarity. On the contrary, similes all too often make a poem dull and ponderous, and a mere image or a metaphor can have just as much clarity without having its meaning set beside it in addition.

The proper aim of the simile we must therefore find in the poet's subjective imagination. However clearly he makes himself aware of the subject-matter which he intends to express, however far he has brought this subject home to his mind in its more abstract universality and has expressed it [to himself] in this universality, still he finds himself equally driven to seek a concrete shape for the subject and to make perceptible to himself in a sensuous appearance the meaning already before his mind. From this point of view, the simile, like the image and the metaphor, therefore expresses the boldness of the imagination which, having something confronting it—whether a single perceptible object, a specific situation, or a universal meaning—works on it and evinces its power to bind together things lying poles apart and connected externally, and so to drag into our interest in one topic the most varied material, and, by the labour of the spirit, to chain to the given topic a world of heterogeneous phenomena. This power of imagination in inventing shapes and, by ingenious relations and connections, binding together the most diverse material is what in general lies at the root of simile.

(α) Now, first, the pleasure of comparing can be satisfied solely on its own account, with no aim of displaying anything in this splendour of images except the boldness of fancy. This is as it were the orgy of imagination's power, which especially in the Orientals and in the peace and *dolce far niente* of the south, delights in the wealth and brilliance of its images without any further aim, and it inveigles the listener into abandoning himself to the same *dolce far niente*. But often we are surprised by the wonderful power with which the poet launches out into the most variegated images and betrays a wit of combination which is more *spirituel* than a mere witticism. Even Calderón has many similes of this kind, especially when he sketches great and magnificent pageants and ceremonies, describes the beauty of chargers and their riders, or when in speaking of ships he calls them every time 'birds without pinions, fish without fins'.

(β) But, secondly, looked at more closely, similes are a dwelling on one and the same topic which thereby is made the substantial centre of a series of other ideas remote from it; through their indication or portrayal the greater interest in the topic compared becomes objective.

This dwelling on a topic may have several reasons.

(αα) As the first reason we must cite the heart's absorption in the topic by which it is animated and which grips its depths so firmly that it cannot renounce an enduring interest in it. In this connection we can immediately emphasize once again an essential difference between eastern and western poetry, a difference that we had occasion to touch upon earlier in our treatment of Pantheism. The Oriental in his absorption is less self-seeking, and he therefore neither sighs nor languishes; his aspiration remains a more objective joy in the topic of his comparisons and therefore is more contemplative. With a free heart he looks about him in order to see in everything surrounding him, in everything he knows and loves, an image of what his sense and spirit are preoccupied with and of what engrosses him to the full. Imagination, freed from all concentration on self alone, cured from all sickliness, is satisfied in the comparative presentation of the topic itself, especially when that topic, by a comparison with what is most brilliant and beautiful, is to be praised, extolled, and transfigured. The West, on the other hand, is more subjective, and in complaint and grief sighing more and longing more.

This dwelling [on one topic], secondly, is principally an interest of the feelings, particularly of love which rejoices in the object of its grief and pleasure, and, as it cannot free its inner being from these feelings, is now never tired of portraying their object anew over and over again. Lovers are especially rich in wishes, hopes, and changing fancies. Amongst such fancies we must include similes too; to these love in general has recourse all the more readily because the feeling occupies and permeates the whole soul and makes comparisons on its own account. What preoccupies love is e.g. a single beautiful feature, the mouth, the eye, the hair, of the beloved. Now the human spirit is active and disturbed, and joy and grief especially are not dead and at peace but restless and moved hither and thither in a way which yet brings all other material into relation with the one feeling which the heart makes the centre of its world. Here the interest in comparing lies in the feeling itself which experience forces to realize that there are other objects in nature just as beautiful or as much the cause of pain; consequently the feeling draws the whole of these objects into the circle of what it feels, compares them with that and thereby expands and universalizes it.

But if the topic of the simile is something entirely singular and sensuous and is put into connection with similar sensuous phenomena, then comparisons of this sort, especially when they are multiplied, are due to only a very shallow reflection and a scarcely developed feeling. The result is that the variety which merely circulates in an external material readily seems to us to be dull and cannot be of much interest because it is devoid of spiritual reference. So, e.g., it is said in chapter iv [1–6] of the Song of Solomon: 'Behold, thou art fair, my love; behold, thou art fair; thou hast doves' eyes within thy locks; thy hair is as a flock of goats, that appear from Mount Gilead. Thy teeth are like a flock of sheep that are even shorn, which came up from the washing; whereof every one bear twins, and none is barren among them. Thy lips are like a thread of scarlet, and thy speech is comely: thy temples are like a piece of a pomegranate within thy locks. Thy neck is like the tower of David builded for an armoury, whereon there hang a thousand bucklers, all shields of mighty men. Thy two breasts are like two young roes that are twins, which feed among the lilies. Until the day break, and the shadows flee away [I will, etc.].'

The same naïveté is found in many of the poems called Ossian's, as e.g. it is said:[1] 'Thou art as snow on the heather; thine hair like a mist on Cromla when it curls on the rock and shimmers before the gleam in the west; thine arms are like two pillars in the halls of the mighty Fingal.'

In a similar way, though rhetorically throughout, Ovid makes Polyphemus say: 'Thou art whiter, O Galatea, than the leaf of the snowy privet, more flowery than the meadows, taller than the high alder tree, more gleaming than glass, more playful than the

---

[1] *The Poems of Ossian*, translated by James Macpherson (London, 1785), *Fingal*, canto 1 (vol. i, p. 227). Macpherson imagines Cromla to be a hill on the coast of Ulster (ibid., p. 223, fn.).

tender kid, smoother than shells polished by ocean's endless chafing, more grateful than winter's suns and summer's shade, more glorious than the palm tree and more striking than the tall plane tree' (*Met.* xiii. 789–807), and so it goes on through all nineteen hexameters, rhetorically fine, but, as the sketching of a scarcely interesting feeling, it is itself of slight interest.

In Calderón too there are numerous examples of this kind of comparison, although such dwelling on a topic is fitted rather for lyrical feeling, and it fetters the progress of a drama all too rigidly if it is not appropriately motivated in the nature of the case. So, e.g., Don Juan in the complications of his fate describes at length the beauty of a veiled lady whom he has followed, and he says *inter alia*: 'Although many a time through the dark barriers of that impenetrable veil there broke a hand of most splendid sheen, it was the princess of the lilies and the roses and to it the snow's sheen did homage like a slave, a dark-skinned African.'

It is a very different thing when a more deeply moved heart expresses itself in images and similes revealing inner and spiritual emotional connections, for then the heart either turns itself as it were into an external natural scene or makes such a scene the reflection of a spiritual matter.

In this connection too many images and comparisons occur in the so-called Ossianic poems, although the sphere of the topics used here for similes is poor and usually restricted to clouds, mist, storm, tree, stream, spring, sun, thistle, grass, etc. Thus, e.g., he says: 'Delightful is thy presence O Fingal! It is like the sun on Cromla, when the hunter has bewailed its absence for a whole year long, and now catches sight of it between the clouds.'[1] In another passage we read: 'Did Ossian not hear a voice just now? or is it the voice of the days that are past? Often there comes like the sunset into my soul the remembrance of times past.'[2] Similarly Ossian relates: 'Pleasant are the words of the song, said Cuchulain, and delightful are the stories of times past. They are like the quiet dew of the morning on the hill of the roe-deer, when the sun shimmers faintly on its side and the lake lies motionless and blue in the vale.'[3]

This dwelling on the same feelings and their similes is of such

---

[1] Fingal, canto 6 (*The Poems of Ossian*, vol. i, p. 328).
[2] *Coulath and Cuthona* (ibid., vol. ii, p. 183).
[3] *Fingal*, canto 3 (ibid., vol. i, p. 263).

a kind in these poems that it expresses an old age weary and fatigued in mourning and memories of grief. In general a melancholy and weak feeling readily overflows into comparisons. What such a soul desires, what constitutes its interest, is far off and past, and so, in general, instead of regaining courage it is induced to immerse itself in something else. The many comparisons [in Ossian] therefore correspond as much to this subjective mood as to mainly melancholy ideas and the narrow sphere in which that mood is compelled to dwell.

Conversely, however, in so far as passion, despite its unrest, concentrates itself on one object, it may toss to and fro in a variety of images and comparisons which are only conceits about one and the same object, and it does this in order to find in the surrounding external world a counterpart to its own inner being. Of this kind is, e.g., Juliet's monologue in *Romeo and Juliet* when she turns to the night and cries out [Act III, scene ii]:

> Come night! come Romeo! come, thou day in night!
> For thou wilt lie upon the wings of night
> Whiter than new snow upon a raven's back.—
> Come, gentle night; come, loving, black-brow'd night,
> Give me my Romeo: and, when he shall die,
> Take him and cut him out in little stars,
> And he will make the face of heaven so fine,
> That all the world will be in love with night,
> And pay no worship to the garish sun.

(ββ) Contrasted with these similes, throughout almost lyrical, of a feeling immersing itself in what it feels, there are the epic similes which we find often in Homer, for example. Here the poet, dwelling in his comparison on one specific object, has, on the one hand, the interest of raising us over the as it were *practical* curiosity, expectation, hope, and fear which we cherish in respect of the issue of events connected with single situations and deeds of the heroes, raising us over the connection of cause, effect, and consequence, and riveting our attention on pictures which he sets before us like works of sculpture, peaceful and plastic, designed for *theoretical* consideration. This peace, this withdrawal from a purely practical interest in what he presents to our vision, gains its effect all the more if the object compared is drawn from another field. On the other hand, this dwelling on one topic in similes has the further sense of marking out a specific object as important, as a result of this as it were double sketching, and not letting it just rustle away fleetingly with the stream of the song and its incidents. Thus Homer says, e.g. (*Iliad*, xx. 164–75) of Achilles who, inflamed with ardour for battle, stands up against Aeneas: 'He got up like a ravenous lion which men aimed to slay, the whole city assembled to this end; at first the lion, as if despising them, pranced about but when one of the youths, eager for the fray, hurls a lance at him, he then crouches yawning, foaming at the mouth; in his breast his strong heart groans, he lashes his sides and hips with his tail both left and right, and drives himself to battle. With glaring eyes he waits for battle whether he kills one of the men or perishes himself at the first onslaught. Thus Achilles is urged on by valour and high-hearted spirit to confront the haughty Aeneas.' Similarly Homer says (*Iliad*, iv. 130 ff.) of Pallas when she averted the arrow which Pandarus had launched against Menelaus: 'She forgot him not and repelled the deadly arrow as a mother flicks a fly away from her son when he lies in sweet slumber.' And further on (141–6), when the arrow did nevertheless wound Menelaus: 'As when a woman from Lydia or Caria bedecks ivory with purple to make a bridle for a horse, but it stands in her room and many riders have wished to carry it away; yet it stands as a king's prize; two things, adornment for the horse, fame for the rider: so the blood of Menelaus flowed down his thighs.'

(γ) A third reason for similes, contrasted with the mere riot of fancy as well as with self-deepening feeling or the imagination that dwells on important topics and compares them, is to be emphasized especially in reference to dramatic poetry. Drama has for its subject-matter warring passions, activity, 'pathos', action, accomplishment of what is innerly willed; these it does not present at all, as epic does, in the form of past events, but brings the individuals themselves before us and makes them express their feelings as their own and accomplish their actions before our eyes, so that thus the poet does not intrude as a third person [between actor and spectator]. Now in this connection it looks as if dramatic poetry demands the maximum naturalness in the expression of passions, and as if their impetuousness in grief, terror, or joy cannot, on account of this naturalness, permit of similes. To make the individual agents, in the storm of feeling and in the struggle to act, say much in metaphors, images, or similes is to be regarded as throughout 'unnatural' in the usual sense of the word, and therefore as disturbing. For by comparisons we are carried away from the present situation, and from the individuals who feel and act in it, into something external, foreign, and not immediately belonging to the situation itself; and thereby the tone of conversational interchange in particular meets with an obstructive and burdensome interruption. And after all in Germany, at the time when young spirits tried to free themselves from the shackles of the rhetorical taste of the French, they regarded the Spaniards, Italians, and French as mere craftsmen who put into the mouths of the *dramatis personae* their own subjective imagination, their wit, their conventional behaviour and elegant eloquence, at the very moment when what alone should have dominated was the most violent passion and its natural expression. In many dramas of that time, therefore, in accordance with this principle of naturalness, we find the shriek of feeling, exclamation marks, and hyphens instead of a diction noble, elevated, rich in images, and full of similes. In a similar sense even English critics have often criticized Shakespeare for the multiplied and variegated comparisons which he frequently gives to his characters in the supreme oppression of their grief where the violence of feeling seems to provide the minimum of room for the peace of reflection inherent in every simile. Of course the images and comparisons in Shakespeare are now and then awkward and multiplied; but, on the whole, an essential place and effect must be allowed even in drama for similes.

While feeling dwells on one topic because it is sunk in its object and cannot free itself from it, in the *practical* sphere of action similes have the aim of showing that the individual has not merely immersed himself directly in his specific situation, feeling, or passion, but that as a high and noble being he is superior to them and can cut himself free from them. Passion restricts and chains the soul within, narrows it, and concentrates it within limits, and therefore makes it inarticulate, talking in single syllables, or raging and blustering in vagueness and extravagance. But greatness of mind, force of spirit, lifts itself above such restrictedness and, in beautiful and tranquil peace, hovers above the specific 'pathos' by which it is moved. This liberation of soul is what similes express, in the first place quite formally. It is only a profound composedness and strength of soul which is able to objectify even its grief and its sorrows, to compare itself with something else, and therefore to contemplate itself *theoretically* in strange things confronting it; or in the most frightful mockery of itself to confront itself with even its own annihilation, as if it were an external existent, and yet to be able to remain still calm there and preserve its *sang-froid*. In epic, as we saw, it was the poet who through ondwelling and graphic similes was intent upon communicating to his audience the contemplative calm which art requires. Whereas in drama it is the *dramatis personae* who appear as themselves the poets and artists, since they make their inner life an object to themselves, an object which they remain powerful enough to shape and form and thus to manifest to us the nobility of their disposition and the might of their mind. For here this absorption in something other and external is the liberation of the inner life from a purely practical interest or from the immediacy of feeling into free theoretical shapes, whereby that comparison for the sake of comparison, as we find it at the first stage, recurs in a deeper way because it can now come on the scene only as an overcoming of mere preoccupation [with passion] and as release from passion's power.

In the course of this liberation the following chief points may be distinguished, of which Shakespeare in particular provides the most examples.

(αα) When a heart is to meet with great misfortune whereby it is shaken to its depths, and the grief of this unavoidable fate is now actually present, then it would be the way of an ordinary man directly to scream out his horror, grief, and despair, and thereby to disburden himself. A stronger and nobler spirit suppresses his lamentation as such, imprisons his grief, and therefore in the deep feeling of his very suffering preserves freedom to occupy himself with some far-off idea and in this remote object to express his own fate to himself in an image. In that case the man surmounts his grief; he is not one with it in his entire self but is just as much distinct from it, and therefore he can linger in something else which as a cognate object is related to his feeling. So in Shakespeare's *Henry IV* when old Northumberland asks the messenger who came to tell him of Percy's death 'How doth my son and brother?' and gets no answer, he cries out in the composure of bitterest grief [*2 Henry IV*, Act I, scene i]:

> Thou tremblest; and the whiteness in thy cheek
> Is apter than thy tongue to tell thy errand.

Even such a man, so faint, so spiritless,
So dull, so dead in look, so woe-begone,
Drew Priam's curtain in the dead of night,
And would have told him half his Troy was burnt;
But Priam found the fire ere he his tongue,
And I my Percy's death ere thou report'st it.

But when Richard II has to atone for the youthful frivolity of his days of happiness, it is especially *he* who has a heart that however much it secludes itself in its grief yet retains the force to set it steadily before itself in new comparisons. And this is precisely the touching and childlike aspect in Richard's grief, that he constantly expresses it to himself objectively in felicitous images and retains his suffering all the more profoundly in the play of this self-expression. When Henry demands the crown from him, e.g., he replies[1]:

Here, cousin, seize the crown; . . .
On this side my hand, and on that side yours.
Now is this golden crown like a deep well
That owes two buckets, filling one another,
The emptier ever dancing in the air,
The other down, unseen and full of water:
That bucket down and full of tears am I,
Drinking my griefs, whilst you mount up on high.

(ββ) The other aspect in this context consists in the fact that a character who is already one with his interests, his grief and his fate, tries by comparisons to free himself from this immediate unity and makes the liberation actual and obvious by showing that he is still capable of making similes. In *Henry VIII*, for example, Queen Katharine, forsaken by her spouse, cries out in the deepest sadness [Act III, scene i]:

I am the most unhappy woman living . . .
Shipwreck'd upon a kingdom where no pity,
No friends, no hope; no kindred weep for me;
Almost no grave allow'd me; like the lily,
That once was mistress of the field and flourish'd,
I'll hang my head and perish.

---

[1] *Richard II*, Act IV, scene i. For 'when Henry demands the crown', read 'when he realizes that Henry must have the crown'.

Still more splendidly Brutus in *Julius Caesar* says in his rage against Cassius whom he had striven in vain to spur on [Act IV, scene iii]:

> O Cassius! you are yoked with a lamb,
> That carries anger as the flint bears fire;
> Who, much enforced, shows a hasty spark
> And straight is cold again.

That Brutus can find in this context a transition to a simile proves by itself that he has repressed his anger and begun to make himself free from it.

Shakespeare lifts especially his criminal characters above their evil passion by endowing them with a greatness of spirit alike in crime and in misfortune. Unlike the French, he does not leave them in the abstraction of always just saying to themselves that they intend to be criminals; on the contrary, he gives them this force of imagination which enables them to see themselves not just as themselves but as another shape strange to them. Macbeth, e.g., when his hour has struck utters the famous words [Macbeth Act v, scene v]:

> Out, out, brief candle!
> Life's but a walking shadow; a poor player
> That struts and frets his hour upon the stage
> And then is heard no more: it is a tale
> Told by an idiot, full of sound and fury,
> Signifying nothing.

So too it is in *Henry VIII* with Cardinal Wolsey who, struck down from his greatness, exclaims at the end of his career:

> Farewell! a long farewell to all my greatness!
> This is the state of man: to-day he puts forth
> The tender leaves of hopes; to-morrow blossoms,
> And bears his blushing honours thick upon him;
> The third day comes a frost, a killing frost,
> And, when he thinks, good easy man, full surely
> His greatness is a-ripening, nips his root,
> And then he falls, as I do.[1]

(γγ) In this objectification and comparative expression there lies then at the same time the peace and inherent tranquillity of character by which a man appeases himself in his grief and fall.

---

[1] Act III, scene ii. For 'state' Hegel substitutes 'fate' (*Schicksal*).

So Cleopatra, after putting the deadly asp to her breast, says to Charmian [Antony and Cleopatra Act v, scene ii]:

> Peace, peace!
> Dost thou not see my baby at my breast,
> That sucks the nurse asleep? . . .
> As sweet as balm, as soft as air, as gentle.

The bite of the snake relaxes her limbs so softly that death itself is deceived and regards itself as sleep.—This image can itself be counted as an image for the gentle and tranquillizing nature of these comparisons.

C. DISAPPEARANCE OF THE SYMBOLIC FORM OF ART

Our interpretation of the symbolic form of art in general has been that in it a complete reciprocal interpenetration of meaning and expression could not be thoroughly established. In unconscious symbolism the incompatibility of content and form present there remained *implicit*, whereas in sublimity it appeared as an *open* incompatibility, in that both the absolute meaning (God) and its external reality, the world, were expressly represented in this negative relation. But, conversely, there was all the same dominant in all these forms the other aspect of the symbolic, namely the kinship between meaning and that external shape in which the meaning is brought into appearance; in original symbolism, which does not yet contrast the meaning with its concrete existence, the relationship is one in which the two sides *exclude* one another; it becomes an *essential* tie in sublimity which, in order to express God even in only an inadequate way, required natural phenomena, the events and deeds of God's people; and in the comparative form of art it becomes a subjective and therefore *capricious* bearing of the one on the other. But although this caprice is wholly there especially in metaphor, image, and simile, yet it is as it were even here hidden behind the kinship between the meaning and the image used [to express it]; since caprice embarks on comparison precisely on the basis of the similarity of both [the things compared], the chief aspect of the comparison is not the external thing but precisely the *relation*, brought about by subjective activity, between inner feelings, intuitions, ideas, and their cognate configurations. Yet if it is not the Concept of the thing itself but only caprice which brings together the meaning and the artistic shape, then both are to be posited as wholly external to one another, so that their association is an unrelated attachment to one another and a mere adornment of one side by the other. Therefore, as an appendix, we have here to treat of those subordinate forms of art which proceed from such a complete diremption of the factors belonging to genuine art and, in this absence of relation, expose the self-destruction of the symbolic.

Owing to the general standpoint of this stage, we have on the one side the meaning, cut and dried, explicitly defined but not given outward shape, so that for artistic purposes there is nothing left but to add to it a purely external and capricious adornment; on the other side, externality as such which, instead of being mediated into identity with its essential inner meaning, can be construed and described only as it becomes independent in contrast with this inner element and therefore only in the pure externality of its appearance. This difference between meaning and shape is the formal characteristic of didactic and descriptive poetry, a difference which only the art of poetry can maintain, at least in didactic poetry, because poetry alone can represent meanings in their abstract generality.

But since the essence of art lies not in the dissociation but in the identification of meaning and shape, even at this stage what is conspicuous is not only their complete separation but equally a bearing of each side on the other. Once the character of the symbolic is transcended, however, this bearing can no longer be itself of a symbolic kind. It implies an attempt to cancel the proper character of the symbolic, namely the incompatibility and independence of form and content which all the previously considered forms were incapable of surmounting. But since the *separation* of the two sides which are to be united is presupposed here, this attempt must remain a mere 'ought', and the satisfaction of its demands is reserved for a more perfect form of art, the classical.—We will now cast a brief glance at these final supplementary forms in order to gain a clearer transition to the classical art-form.

1. *Didactic Poetry*

The didactic poem arises when a meaning (even if forming a concrete and consistent whole) is apprehended on its own account as meaning and not given shape as such but only embellished externally with artistic adornment. Didactic poetry is not to be numbered amongst the proper forms of art. For in it we find, on the one hand, the content already cut and dried and developed explicitly as meaning in its therefore prosaic form, and, on the other hand, the artistic shape which yet can only be tacked on to the content in an entirely external way because the content has already been completely characterized prosaically for apprehension; and in its prosaic aspect, i.e. its universal abstract significance, and in no other aspect, the content is to be expressed for intellectual examination and reflection with the aim of instruction. Therefore, given this external relation [between form and content], art can, in the didactic poem, concern itself with nothing but externals such as metre, for example, elevated diction, interspersed episodes, images, similes, subjoined explosions[1] of feeling, faster development, quicker transitions, etc. These do not penetrate the content as such; they stand beside it as an appendage in order by their relative vivacity to enliven the seriousness and dryness of the doctrine and to make life more ágreeable. What has become prosaic in itself is not to be reshaped poetically; it can only be dressed up; just as horticulture, e.g., is for the most part just an external arrangement of a site already given by nature and not in itself beautiful, or as architecture by ornament and external decoration makes pleasant the utility of premises devoted to prosaic circumstances and affairs.

In this way Greek philosophy, e.g., adopted in its beginnings the form of a didactic poem; Hesiod too may be cited as an example; although a really and properly prosaic treatment only makes its appearance in the main when the intellect with its reflections, inferences, classifications, etc., has mastered the topic and on that basis can teach pleasingly and elegantly. Lucretius in relation to the natural philosophy of Epicurus, Virgil with his agricultural instructions, afford examples of such a treatment which, despite all skilfulness, cannot attain a genuine free form of art. In Germany the didactic poem is now no longer popular; but apart from his earlier poem *Les jardins, ou l'art d'embellir les paysages*, and his *L'homme*

---

[1] Hegel's word is *Expectorationen*, expectorations. This may be an allusion to *Expectorationen, ein Kunstwerk und zugleich ein Vorspiel zum Alarkos* (Berlin, 1803). This skit on Schlegel's *Alarcos* was published anonymously, but was by Kotzebue.

des champs, Delille[1] has in this century presented the French with a didactic poem, a compendium of physics, in which magnetism, electricity, etc., are treated *seriatim*.

2. Descriptive Poetry

The second form belonging to this context is the one opposed to the didactic. Its starting point is not drawn from a meaning explicitly cut and dried in consciousness but from the external as such, from natural surroundings, from buildings, etc., from seasons, times of the day, and their external shape. While in the didactic poem the content remains essentially in unshaped universality, here conversely the external material confronts us on its own account in its individuality and external appearance, not penetrated by spiritual meanings; this appearance is now on its side represented, sketched, and described in the way that we ordinarily see it. Such a sensuous content belongs entirely to only one side of true art, namely to the external existence which in art has the right of appearing solely as the reality of *spirit*, of individuality and its actions and events on the stage of a surrounding world, but not of appearing on its own account as mere externality cut adrift from spirit.

3. The Ancient Epigram

Consequently, as it turns out, the didactic and the descriptive cannot be retained in this one-sidedness whereby art would be entirely cancelled, and once more we see external reality brought into relation with what is grasped inwardly as meaning, and the abstract universal with its concrete appearance.

(*a*) In this regard we have already mentioned didactic poetry. It can seldom get along without sketching external situations and individual phenomena, without relating episodically mythological and other examples, etc. But, by this parallelism of the spiritual universal and the external individual, what is established, instead of a completely developed unification, is only an entirely incidental relation which, not to mention its complete failure to take in the total content and its entire artistic form, comprises only single aspects and traits of these.

(*b*) More of such a relativity is found to a great extent in the

---

[1] J Delille, 1738–1813. See *Les Trois Règnes de la Nature* (Paris, 1808).

case of descriptive poetry, seeing that it accompanies its sketches with feelings which can be aroused by the look of a natural landscape, the change in the times of day, the natural divisions of the year, a forest-clad hill, a lake or a murmuring burn, a churchyard, a friendly situated village, or a quiet cosy cottage. As in the didactic poem so too, therefore, in descriptive poetry episodes enter as enlivening decoration, especially the sketching of moving feelings, of sweet melancholy, e.g., or of trifling occurrences drawn from the circle of human life in its less significant spheres. But this connection between spiritual feeling and an external natural phenomenon may even here still be quite external. For the natural locality is presupposed as present on its own account as independent; a man enters it and feels this and that about it, but the external shape and the inner sentiment remain external to one another in the case of moonlight, woods, or valleys. In such a case I am not the interpreter or inspirer of nature; I feel on this occasion only an entirely· indefinite harmony between my inner being, excited by so and so, and the objective world confronting me. In the case of our German countrymén, this is by far the favourite form: namely, sketches of nature and, alongside them, whatever such natural scenes may suggest to an individual in the way of fine feelings and outpourings of heart. This is the general highway which anyone can travel. Even several of Klopstock's *Odes* are tuned to this key.

(*c*) If therefore thirdly we ask for a deeper relation between the two sides in their presupposed separation, we can find it in the epigram of antiquity.

(α) The original essence of the epigram is expressed at once by its name: it is an inscription. Of course here too there stands a topic on one side and, on the other, something said about it; but in the oldest epigrams, of which Herodotus[1] has preserved a few, we do not get the sketch of an object in association with some sentiment or other; we have the thing itself in a double way: (*a*) the external existent and (*b*) then its meaning and explanation; these are pressed together as an epigram with the most salient and most apposite touches. Yet even among the Greeks the later epigram has lost this original character and has proceeded more and more to take account of and to describe sketchy, ingenious, witty, agreeable, and touching notions about individual occurrences,

[1] e.g. vii. 228, the inscriptions at Thermopylae.

works of art, or persons, etc. These set forth not so much the topic itself as the author's clever relations to it.

(β) Now the less the topic itself enters as it were into this sort of representation, the more imperfect does the representation become as a result. In this connection passing mention may be made of more recent art-forms. In Tieck's novels, e.g., the matter in hand often consists of special works of art, or artists, or a specific art-gallery or piece of music, and then some little story or other is tacked on to it. But these specific pictures which the reader has not seen, the music which he has not heard, the poet cannot make visible and audible, and the whole form when it turns on precisely these topics and the like remains in this respect defective. So too in longer romances whole arts and their most beautiful works have been taken as the proper subject-matter, as Heinse[1] took music in his *Hildegard von Hohenthal*. Now if the whole work of art cannot represent its fundamental topic adequately, then in accordance with its basic character it retains an inadequate form.

(γ) The demand springing from the deficiencies that have been cited is simply this, that the external appearance and its meaning, the thing itself and its spiritual interpretation, must not, as was the case just now, be altogether separated from one another; neither should there remain as their unification a linkage which is symbolical or sublime and comparative. The genuine representation is to be sought, therefore, only where the thing itself through and in its external appearance affords the interpretation of its spiritual content, since the spiritual unfolds itself completely in its reality, and the corporeal and external is therefore nothing but the adequate explication of the spiritual and the inward itself.

But in order to consider the perfect fulfilment of this task we must take leave of the symbolical art-form, since the character of the symbolic consists precisely in the ever purely imperfect unification of the soul of the meaning with its corporeal shape.

---

[1] J. J. W., 1749–1803. *H. von H.*, 1796.

SECTION II

THE CLASSICAL FORM OF ART

Introduction—The Classical Type in General

The centre of art is a unification, self-enclosed so as to be a free totality, a unification of the content with its entirely adequate shape. This reality, coinciding with the Concept of the beautiful, towards which the symbolic form of art strove in vain, is first brought into appearance by classical art. We have therefore in our earlier treatment of the Idea of the beautiful already settled in advance the general nature of the classical; the Ideal provides the content and form of classical art which in this adequate mode of configuration achieves what true art is in its essential nature.

But there contributed to this perfection all the particular factors, the development of which we took as the content of the foregoing Section. For classical beauty has for its inner being the free independent meaning, i.e. not a meaning *of* this or that but what means [*Bedeutende*] itself and therefore intimates [*Deutende*] itself. This is spirit, which in general makes itself into an object to itself. In this objectivity of itself it then has the form of *externality* which, as identical with its own inner being, is therefore on its side the meaning of its own self and, in knowing itself, it points to itself. We started, even in the case of the symbolic sphere, from the unity of meaning and its sensuous mode of appearance produced by art, but this unity was only *immediate* and therefore inadequate. For the proper content *either* remained the natural itself in its substance and abstract universality, for which reason, although the isolated natural existent was regarded as the actual determinate being of that universality, it could not represent that universality in a corresponding way; *or else* when what was purely inner and graspable by spirit alone was made the content, it thereby acquired an equally inadequate appearance in something foreign to itself, namely in something immediately individual and sensuous. In general, meaning and shape stood only in a relation of mere affinity and allusiveness, and however nearly they could be brought into connection in certain respects, they all the same

P

in other respects fell apart from one another. This primitive unity was therefore broken: for Indian conceptions the abstractly simple inner and ideal stands on one side, the varied reality of nature and finite human existence on the other; and imagination in the restlessness of its ardour rushed hither and thither from one to the other without being able to bring the Ideal on its own account to pure absolute independence or really to fill it with the available and transformed material of appearance and therein represent it in peaceful unification. The confusion and grotesqueness in the mixture of elements striving against one another did likewise disappear again but only to give place to an equally unsatisfying enigma which instead of solving the problem was only able to pose the task of solving it. For here too there was still absent that freedom and independence of the content which appears only through the inner's coming into consciousness as total in itself and therefore as overlapping the externality which at first is other than and strange to it. This independence in and by itself as the free absolute meaning is the self-consciousness which has the Absolute for its content, spiritual subjectivity for its form. Contrasted with this self-determining, thinking, and willing power, everything else is only relatively and momentarily independent. The sensuous phenomena of nature, the sun, the sky, stars, plants, animals, stones, streams, the sea, have only an abstract relation to themselves, and in the steady process of nature are drawn into connection with other existents, so that only for finite perception can they count as independent. In them the true meaning of the Absolute does not yet emerge. Nature, it is true, emerges, but only in its self-externality; its inner being is not apprehended by itself as inner, but is poured out into the diverse multiplicity of appearance and therefore is not independent. Only in spirit as the concrete free infinite relation to itself is the true absolute meaning really emergent and independent in its external existence.[1]

On the way to this liberation of the meaning from the immediately sensuous and to its achievement of independence in itself,

---

[1] This presupposes Hegel's philosophy of Nature and Spirit. It is in and through embodying itself in something other than itself, e.g. nature, that spirit comes to consciousness of itself and its own inner being as spirit. The inner being of nature is the spirit which it embodies, but nature is not aware of this. Thus it is not only a realm of externality, everything in it being external to everything else, but also self-external, or self-estranged, because it is unaware of its own essence, i.e. the absolute meaning, the Absolute or God, its creator.

we met with the sublimity and sanctification produced by imagination. The absolutely meaningful, that is to say, is primarily the thinking, absolute, non-sensuous One, which, as the Absolute, relates itself to itself, and in this relation posits the other, its creation, i.e. nature and externality in general, as the negative, with no stability in itself. It is the universal absolutely, envisaged as the objective power over the whole of existence, whether this One be brought to consciousness and representation in its expressly negative bias towards its creation or in its positive pantheistic immanence therein. But the double deficiency of this outlook consists for art, *first*, in the fact that this one and universal [Being] which constitutes the fundamental meaning has so far neither reached closer determination and differentiation in itself nor, therefore, the individuality and personality proper in which it could be grasped as spirit and brought before contemplation in an external shape belonging and adequate to the spiritual content in its essential nature. The concrete Idea of spirit, on the other hand, demands that spirit be determined and differentiated in itself, and, making itself objective to itself, shall gain in this duplication an ´external appearance which, although corporeal and present, yet remains wholly penetrated by spirit and therefore, though taken by itself it expresses nothing, it reveals, as its inner being, spirit alone whereof it is the expression and reality. On the part of the objective world there is, *secondly*, bound up with this abstraction of the undifferentiated Absolute the deficiency that now too the real appearance, as what is without inherent substantiality, is incapable of exhibiting the Absolute in a concrete shape in a genuine way.

As a contrast to those hymns and words of praise, triumphs of the abstract universal glorification of God, we have in this transition to a higher art-form to recall what we likewise found in the East, the factor of negativity, i.e. change, grief, and the process through life and death. There it was inner differentiation which appeared, without the collection of differences into the unity and independence of subjectivity. But both sides, the inherently independent unity and its differentiation and definite inner repletion afford only now in their concrete harmonized totality a genuinely free independence.

In this connection we may mention incidentally alongside sublimity another view which likewise began to be developed in the East. Contrasted with the substantiality of the one God, there is an apprehension of the inner freedom, self-subsistence, and independence of the individual person in himself, so far as the East permitted a development in this direction. For a chief form of this outlook we must look to the Arabs who in their deserts, on the infinite sea of their plains, in the clear sky above them, in such natural surroundings have counted only on their own courage and the bravery of their fists, as well as on the means of their self-preservation, namely the camel, the horse, the lance and the sword. Here in distinction from Indian feebleness and loss of self, and from the later Mohammedan pantheistic poetry, there arises the more inflexible independence of personal character, and objects too are allowed to possess their circumscribed and definitely fixed immediate reality. With these beginnings of the independence of individuality there are then bound up at the same time true friendship, hospitality, sublime generosity, but all the same an infinite thirst for revenge, an inextinguishable memory of a hatred which makes room and satisfaction for itself by pitiless passion and absolutely unfeeling cruelty. But what happens on this soil appears as human, within the sphere of human affairs; there are deeds of revenge, relations of love, traits of self-sacrificing generosity from which the fantastic and wonderful have vanished, so that everything is presented fixedly and definitely in accordance with the necessary connection of things.

A similar treatment of real objects as reduced to their fixed proportions and as coming into view in their free and not merely useful forcefulness we found earlier[1] in the case of the Hebrews. Firmer independence of character, and the fierceness of revenge and hatred, are characteristic of the Jewish people in its origin. Yet the difference appears at once that here even the most forceful natural formations are not depicted on their own account but rather on account of the power of God, in relation to which they immediately lose their independence, and even hate and persecution are not directed personally against individuals, but, in the service of God, against whole peoples in a national quest for revenge. For example, the later Psalms and, above all, the Prophets can often wish and pray for the misfortune and downfall of other peoples and they find their chief strength not infrequently in cursing and execrating.

At these points of view just mentioned, the elements of true

---

[1] Not in so many words, but see Section I, ch. II, B, The Art of Sublimity.

beauty and art are of course present, but at first torn asunder from one another, scattered, and set, not in genuine identity, but only in a false relationship. Therefore it is impossible for the purely ideal and abstract unity of the Divine to achieve a plainly adequate artistic appearance in the form of real individuality, while nature and human individuality in both inner and external aspects are either not filled with the Absolute at all or at least not *positively* pervaded by it. This mutual externality of the meaning which is made the essential content and the specific appearance in which this meaning is to be represented appeared, *thirdly* and lastly, in the *comparative* activity of art. In it both sides have become perfectly independent, and the unity holding them together is only the invisible subjective activity that is making the comparison. But thereby precisely the deficiency of such an external relation was presented in a steadily intensified measure, and for genuine artistic representation was proved to be something negative, and therefore something to be superseded. If this cancellation is actually effected, then the meaning can no longer be the inherently *abstract* ideal but the inner self, determined in and through itself, which in this its concrete totality has equally in itself the other side, i.e. the form of a self-contained and specific appearance. In the external existent, as something of its own, it expresses and means itself alone.

1. *Independence of the Classical as Interpenetration of Spirit and its Shape in Nature*

This inherently free totality remaining equal to itself in its opposite which becomes its own self-determination, this inner life which relates itself to itself in its object, is what is absolutely true, free, and independent, displaying in its existence nothing but itself. Now in the realm of art this content is not present in its infinite form (i.e. is not the *thinking* of itself, not the essential, the Absolute, which becomes objective to itself in the form of ideal universality and makes itself explicit to itself) but is present only in immediate natural and sensuous existence. But in so far as the meaning is independent, it must in art produce its shape out of itself and have the principle of its externality in itself. It must therefore revert to the natural, but as dominant over the external which, as one side of the totality of the inner itself, exists no longer as purely natural objectivity but, without independence of its own, is only the expression of spirit. Thus in this interpenetration the natural shape and externality as a whole, transformed by spirit, directly acquires its meaning in itself and points no longer to the meaning as if that were something separated and different from the corporeal appearance. This is that identification of the spiritual and the natural which is adequate to the spirit and which does not rest in the neutralization of the two opposed sides but lifts the spiritual to the higher totality where it maintains itself in its opposite, posits the natural as ideal, and expresses itself in and on the natural. In this sort of unity the essential nature of the classical art-form is grounded.

(*a*) Now here this identity of meaning and corporeality is to be conceived in more detail as follows: within their completely accomplished unity no separation of the sides occurs and therefore the inner does not, as purely inner spirituality, withdraw into itself out of corporeal and concrete reality because in that way a difference between the two, contrasted with one another, could appear. Now since the objective and external, in which spirit becomes visible, is, in accordance with its nature, determinate and particularized throughout at the same time, it follows that the free spirit, which art causes to appear in a reality adequate to it, can in its shape in nature be only spiritual individuality equally determinate and inherently independent. Therefore humanity constitutes the centre and content of true beauty and art; but as the content of art (as has been already explained [in Part I, ch. III, A 1] *in extenso* in connection with the Concept of the Ideal) humanity must appear essentially determined as concrete individuality and its adequate external appearance which in its objectivity is purified from the defect of finitude.

(*b*) From this point of view it is obvious at once that the classical mode of representation cannot, by its very nature, be any longer of a *symbolical* kind, in the stricter sense of the word, even if here and there some symbolic ingredients have their part to play too. Greek mythology, e.g., which, so far as art possesses itself of it, belongs to the classical ideal, is when viewed at its heart not of symbolical beauty but is shaped according to the genuine character of the ideal of art, although some traces of the symbolic still cling to it, as we shall see.

But if we now ask about the specific shape which can enter into this unity with spirit without being a mere indication of its content,

it is clear from the determinate character of classical art, where content and form are meant to be adequate to one another, that even on the side of the shape there is a demand for totality and independence in itself. This is because the free independence of the whole, in which the fundamental characteristic of classical art consists, implies that each of the two sides, the spiritual content and its external appearance, shall be in itself a totality which is the essential nature of the whole. Only in this way, in other words, is each side *implicitly* identical with the other, and therefore their difference is reduced to a difference purely of form between two things that are one and the same, with the result that now the whole appears as free since the two sides are proved adequate to one another, the whole displaying itself in both of them and being one in both. The lack of this free duplication of itself within the same unity precisely carried with it in symbolic art absence of freedom in the content and therefore in the form too. Spirit was not clear to itself and therefore did not show its external reality to itself as its own, posited absolutely through and in spirit. Conversely the shape was indeed intended to be meaningful, but the meaning lay there only partially, only on one side or another of it. Therefore by being external to its inner [meaning] as well, the external existent primarily presented not the meaning it was meant to represent but only *itself*, and if it was to show that it was meant to hint at something further, it would have to be interpreted in a forced way. Now in this distortion it neither remained itself nor became the other, i.e. the meaning, but showed only an enigmatic connection and confusion of foreign material, or fell, as a purely ancillary decoration and external adornment, into the mere glorification of an absolute meaning of all things, until at last it had to succumb to a purely subjective caprice of comparison with a far-fetched and indifferent meaning. If this unfree relation is to be dissolved, the shape must have its meaning already in itself and indeed, more precisely, the meaning of spirit.

This shape is essentially the human form because the external human form is alone capable of revealing the spiritual in a sensuous way. The human expression in face, eyes, posture and air is material and in these is not what spirit is; but within this corporeality itself the human exterior is not only living and natural, as the animal is, but is the bodily presence which in itself mirrors the spirit. Through the eye we look into a man's soul, just as his spiritual character is expressed by his whole demeanour in general. If therefore the bodily presence belongs to spirit as *its* existence, spirit belongs to the body as the body's inner being and is not an inwardness foreign to the external shape, so that the material aspect neither has in itself, nor hints at, some other meaning. The human form does carry in itself much of the general animal type, but the whole difference between the human and the animal body consists solely in this, that the human body in its whole demeanour evinces itself as the dwelling-place of spirit and indeed as the sole possible existence of spirit in nature. Therefore too spirit is immediately present for others in the body alone. But this is not the place to expound the necessity of this connection and the special correspondence of soul and body;[1] here we must presuppose this necessity. Of course in the human form there are dead and ugly things, i.e. determined by other influences and by dependence on them; while this is the case, it is precisely the business of art to expunge the difference between the spiritual and the purely natural, and to make the external bodily presence into a shape, beautiful, through and through developed, ensouled and spiritually living.

It follows that in this mode of representation nothing symbolical remains in regard to the external shape, and every mere search, pressure, confusion, and distortion is cast away. For when the spirit has grasped itself as spirit, it is explicitly complete and clear, and so too its connection with the shape adequate to it on the external side is something absolutely complete and given, which does not first need to be brought into existence by way of a linkage produced by imagination in contrast to what is present. Neither is the classical art-form a purely corporeally and superficially presented personification, since the whole spirit, so far as it is to constitute the content of the work of art, comes out into the bodily form and can identify itself with it perfectly. This is the point of view from which to consider the idea that art has imitated the human form. According to the usual view, however, this adoption and imitation seems accidental, whereas we must maintain that art, once developed to its maturity, must of necessity produce its representations in the form of man's external appearance because only therein does the spirit acquire its adequate existence in sensuous and natural material.

---

[1] Hegel expounds this in his *Encyclopaedia of the Philosophical Sciences*, part iii, § 410. See also the *Zusatz* to that paragraph.

What we have said about the human body and its expression applies also to human feelings, impulses, deeds, events, and actions; this externality too is characterized in classical art not only as alive in the natural way but as spiritual, and the inner side is brought into an adequate identity with the outer.

(c) Now since classical art comprehends free spirituality as determinate individuality and envisages it directly in its bodily appearance, the charge of anthropomorphism has often been raised against it. In the case of the Greeks, e.g., Xenophanes spoke against the mode of picturing the gods by saying that if lions had been sculptors they would have given their gods the shape of lions.[1] Of a similar kind is the witty French saying: 'God made men in his own image, but man has returned the compliment by making God in the image of man.' In relation to the following form of art, the romantic, it is to be remarked in this connection that the content of the classical beauty of art is of course still defective, like the religion of art itself; but so little does the deficiency lie in the anthropomorphic as such that on the contrary it is steadily to be maintained that classical art' is anthropomorphic enough for art, but not enough for higher religion. Christianity has pushed anthropomorphism much further; for, according to Christian doctrine, God is not an individual merely humanly shaped, but an actual single individual, wholly God and wholly an actual man, drawn into all the conditions of existence, and no merely humanly shaped ideal of beauty and art. If our idea of the Absolute were only an idea of an abstract innerly undifferentiated being, then it is true that every sort of configuration vanishes; but for God to be spirit he must appear as man, as an individual subject—not as ideal humanity, but as actual progress into the temporal and complete externality of immediate and natural existence. The Christian view, that is to say, implies an endless movement and drive into an extreme opposition and into an inner reversion to absolute unity only by cancelling this separation. This moment of separation is that in which God becomes man, because, as an actual individual subject, he enters difference as opposed to both unity and substance as such; in this ordinary spatial and temporal existence he experiences the feeling, consciousness, and grief of disunion in order to come, through this opposition and likewise its dissolution, to infinite reconciliation. According to Christian

[1] Fragment 15 (Diels).

ideas, this transition lies in the nature of God himself. In fact, through this process, God is to be apprehended as absolute free spirituality, in which the factor of nature and immediate individuality is present indeed but must equally be transcended. Whereas in classical art while the sensuous is not killed and dead, it is also not resurrected from death to absolute spirit. Therefore classical art and its religion of beauty does not satisfy the depths of the spirit; however concrete it is in itself, it still remains abstract for spirit because it has as its element not that movement and that reconciliation of infinite subjectivity which has been achieved out of opposition, but instead only the untroubled harmony of determinate free individuality in its adequate existence, this peace in that real existence, this happiness, this satisfaction and greatness in itself, this eternal serenity and bliss which even in misfortune and grief do not lose their assured self-repose. The opposition, grounded in the Absolute, classical art has not probed to its depths and reconciled. But, for this reason, classical art knows nothing of the aspect related to this opposition, namely (a) the obduracy of the subject in himself as abstract personality contrasted with the ethical and the Absolute, as sin and evil, and (b) the withdrawal of subjective inwardness into itself, the distraction, the helplessness, the whole series, in short, of disunions which produce in their midst the ugly, the hateful, the repulsive, in both the sensuous and the spiritual spheres. Classical art does not pass beyond the pure ground of the genuine ideal.

2. Greek Art as the Actual Existence of the Classical Ideal

As regards the actualization of classical art in history, it is scarcely necessary to remark that we have to look for it in the Greeks. Classical beauty with its infinite range of content, material, and form is the gift vouchsafed to the Greek people, and we must honour this people for having produced art in its supreme vitality. The Greeks in their immediate real existence lived in the happy milieu of both self-conscious subjective freedom and the ethical substance.[1] They did not persist on the one hand in the unfree Oriental unity which has a religious and political despotism as its consequence; this is because the subject, losing his self, is submerged in the one universal substance, or in some particular

---

[1] i.e. the state. Hegel is using the terminology of his *Philosophy of Right*.

aspect of it, since he has no right and therefore no support in himself as a person. Nor, on the other hand, did the Greeks make the advance to that deepening of subjective life in which the individual subject separates himself from the whole and the universal in order to be independent in his own inner being; and only through a higher return into the inner totality of a purely spiritual world does he attain a reunification with the substantial and essential. On the contrary, in Greek ethical life the individual was independent and free in himself, though without cutting himself adrift from the universal interests present in the actual state and from the affirmative immanence of spiritual freedom in the temporal present. The universal element in ethical life, and the abstract freedom of the person in his inner and outer life, remain, in conformity with the principle of Greek life, in undisturbed harmony with one another, and at the time when this principle asserted itself in the actual present in still undamaged purity there was no question of an independence of the political sphere contrasted with a subjective morality distinct from it; the substance of political life was merged in individuals just as much as they sought this their own freedom only in pursuing the universal aims of the whole.

The beautiful feeling, the sentiment and spirit, of this happy harmony pervades all productions in which Greek freedom has become conscious of itself and portrayed its essence to itself. Therefore the world-view of the Greeks is precisely the milieu in which beauty begins its true life and builds its serene kingdom; the milieu of free vitality which is not only there naturally and immediately but is generated by spiritual vision and transfigured by art; the milieu of a development of reflection and at the same time of that absence of reflection which neither isolates the individual nor can bring back to positive unity and reconciliation his negativity, grief, and misfortune; a milieu which yet, like life in general, is at the same time only a transitional point, even if at this point it attains the summit of beauty and in the form of its plastic individuality is so rich and spiritually concrete that all notes harmonize with it, and, moreover, what for its outlook is the past still occurs as an accessory and a background, even if no longer as something absolute and unconditioned.

In this sense even in its gods the Greek people has brought its spirit into its conscious perception, vision, and representation, and has given them by art an existent embodiment which is perfectly adequate to the true content. On account of this correspondence which lies in the essence of Greek art and of Greek mythology too, art in Greece has become the supreme expression of the Absolute, and Greek religion is the religion of art itself, while the later romantic art, although it is art, yet points already to a higher form of consciousness than art can provide.

3. *Position of the Productive Artist in Classical Art*

Now up to this point, on the one hand we have established as the content of classical art inherently free individuality, and on the other hand we have required the like freedom for the form. This thus implies that the entire blending of both sides, however far it may be represented as an immediacy, still cannot be an original and so a natural unity; clearly it must be an artificial link, forged by the subjective spirit. In so far as the form and content of classical art is freedom, it springs only from the freedom of the spirit which is clear to itself. It follows that the artist now acquires a position different from previous ones. His production, that is to say, is the free deed of the clear-headed man who equally *knows* what he wills and *can* accomplish what he wills, and who, in other words, neither is unclear about the meaning and the substantial content which he intends to shape outwardly for contemplation, nor in the execution of his work does he find himself hindered by any technical incapacity.

If we take a closer look at this altered position of the artist,

(*a*) his freedom is clear in respect of the content because he has not had to seek it with the restless fermentation of the symbolic. Symbolic art remains involved in the labour of first producing its content and making it clear to itself, and this content is itself only the first that comes to hand, i.e. on one side, being or nature in its immediate form, on the other, the inner abstraction of the universal, the One, transformation, change, becoming, rising and setting again. But at the first step success is not to be achieved. Therefore the representations of symbolic art which were intended to be expositions of the content remain themselves only enigmas and problems, and they testify only to a wrestling for clarity and to the struggle of the spirit which continually invents without finding repose and peace. In contrast to this troubled quest, for the classical artist the content must already be there cut and dried, given, so that in its essential nature it is already determined for imagination as settled, as belief personal or national, or as a past event perpetuated by tales and tradition. Now the artist's relation to this objectively established material is freer because he does not enter himself into the process of its generation and parturition, nor does he remain caught in a pressure to obtain genuine meanings for art; on the contrary, an absolute content for art confronts him; he adopts it and freely reproduces it out of his own resources. The Greek artists obtained their material from the national religion in which what was taken over from the East by the Greeks had already begun to be reshaped. Phidias took his Zeus from Homer, and even the tragedians did not invent the fundamental material which they represented. Similarly, the Christian artists too, Dante and Raphael, only gave a shape to what was already present in the creeds and in religious ideas. In one way this is in a similar respect the case with the art of sublimity too, but with the difference that there the relation to the content as the *one* substance prevents subjectivity from coming into its rights and does not allow it any independent self-sufficiency. Conversely, the comparative art-form does proceed from the choice of both the meanings and the images utilized, but this choice remains left to purely subjective caprice and lacks on its part over again the substantial individuality which constitutes the essential nature of classical art and therefore must also belong to the subject who is producing the work of art.

(*b*) But the more the artist has available confronting him an absolute and free content in national faith, myth, and other realities, all the more does he concentrate himself on the task of shaping the external artistic appearance in a way congruent to such content. Now in this matter symbolic art tosses about in a thousand forms without being able to hit upon the plainly adequate one; with an imagination that runs riot without proportion and definition, it gropes around in order to adapt to the meaning sought the shapes that ever remain alien. Here too the classical artist, on the other hand, is self-sufficient and restrained. In classical art, in other words, the content is determinate and the free shape is determined by the content itself and it belongs to it absolutely, so that the artist seems only to execute what is already cut and dried on its own account in essence. While the symbolic artist therefore strives to imagine a shape for the meaning, or a meaning for the shape, the classical artist transmutes the meaning into the shape since he only frees the already available external appearances, as it were, from an accessory which does not belong to them. But in this activity, although the artist's mere caprice is excluded, he does not simply *copy* or adhere to one fixed type, but is at the same time *creative* for the whole. Art which must first seek and invent its true content pays little attention besides to the formal aspect; but where the development of form is made the essential interest and proper task, there with the progress of the representation the content too is unnoticeably and unostentatiously developed, just as in general we have hitherto seen form and content going steadily hand in hand in their advance to perfection. In this respect the classical artist works for a present world of religion; its given materials and mythological ideas he develops cheerfully in the free play of art.

(c) The same applies to the technical side of art. It too must be already cut and dried for the classical artist; the sensuous material in which the artist works must have already been rid of all brittleness and stubbornness and must immediately obey the artist's intentions, so that the content, conformably to the nature of the classical sphere, may shine free and unhindered even through this external corporeality. Classical art therefore requires a high degree of technical skill which has subdued the sensuous material to willing obedience. Such technical perfection, if it is to carry out everything required by the spirit and its conceptions, presupposes the complete development of every craftsmanship in art, and this is achieved especially within a static religion. In other words, a religious outlook, like the Egyptian, e.g., first invents for itself specific external shapes, idols, colossal constructions whose type remains fixed, and now, by the established likeness of forms and figures, provides a considerable field for developing the steadily growing dexterity. This craftsmanship in the production of inferior and grotesque objects must have been there already before the genius of classical beauty transformed mechanical skill into technical perfection. For only when mechanical skill no longer puts any difficulty in the way on its own account can art go freely forward to the elaboration of form, and then the actual exercise of skill develops at the same time continually *pari passu* with the progress of content and form.

4. Division of the Subject

So far as concerns the division of this subject, it is usual in a more general sense to call every perfect work of art 'classical', whatever character it may otherwise have, whether symbolic or romantic. In the sense of the perfection of art we too have of course used the word 'classical', but with this difference, that this perfection was to be grounded in the complete interpenetration of inner free individuality and the external existent in which and as which this individuality appears. It follows that we expressly distinguish the classical art-form and its perfection from the symbolic and the romantic because their beauty in content and form is throughout of another kind. Neither have we anything to do here yet, in connection with 'classical' art in the usual rather indefinite meaning of the word, with the particular kinds of art in which the classical ideal is displayed, e.g. sculpture, epic, definite kinds of lyric poetry, and specific forms of tragedy and comedy. Although these particular kinds of art bear the stamp of classical art, they come into consideration only in the Third Part of these Lectures where the development of the individual arts and their species is discussed. What therefore we have before us here for more detailed treatment is 'classical' art in the sense of the word that we have laid down, and as grounds for the division of the subject we can thus look only for the stages of development which proceed themselves from this conception of the classical ideal. The essential features of this development are the following.

The *first* point to which we must direct our attention is this, that the classical art-form is not to be regarded, like the symbolic, as the direct commencement or the *beginning* of art, but on the contrary as a *result*. For this reason we have in the first place developed it out of the course of symbolic modes of representation which are its presupposition. The chief point on which this advance turned was the concentration of the content into the clarity of inherently self-conscious individuality which cannot use for its expression either the mere natural shape, whether inorganic or animal, or personification and the human shape, compounded with the natural one, though badly; on the contrary, it achieves expression in the vitality of the human body that is completely pervaded by the breath of the spirit. Now just as the essence of freedom consists in being what it is through its own resources, so what at first appeared as mere presuppositions and conditions of art's origin outside the classical sphere must fall into that sphere's own territory, so that the actual appearance of the true content and genuine shape may be produced by overcoming what is negative and inappropriate for the ideal. This process of formation through which classical beauty proper, alike in form and content, engenders itself out of itself is therefore our point of departure and what we have to treat in a *first* chapter.

In the *second* chapter, on the other hand, we have reached through this process the true ideal of the classical art-form. The centre here is formed by the beautiful new artistic world of Greek gods which we must develop and settle alike in its spiritual individuality and the bodily form immediately bound up therewith.

But, *thirdly*, the nature of classical art implies not only the growth of that art's beauty out of its own resources but, on the other hand, its dissolution too, which will conduct us on to a further sphere, i.e. to the romantic form of art. The gods and the human individuals of classical beauty arise but pass away again for the artistic consciousness which (*a*) turns against the relics of the natural aspect within which Greek art has precisely developed to the perfection of beauty, or (*b*) turns away out into a reality, bad, vulgar, godless, in order to bring to light its falsity and negativity. In this dissolution, the artistic activity of which we must take as the topic of the *third* chapter, there are separated the factors which were fused harmoniously into the immediacy of beauty and constituted the truly classical art. The inner then stands by itself on one side, the external existent separated therefrom on the other, and subjectivity, withdrawn into itself because in the previous shapes it can no longer find its adequate reality, has to be filled with the content of a new spiritual world of absolute freedom and infinity and look around for new forms of expression for this deeper content.

Chapter I

THE PROCESS OF SHAPING THE CLASSICAL ART-FORM

One essential factor directly present in the essence of the free spirit is that of self-concentration, coming to self, being self-aware and being determinately present to self, even if, as was indicated earlier, this absorption in the realm of inwardness need not go so far as either to a subjective independence gained by a negative attitude to everything substantial in spirit and stable in nature, or to that absolute reconciliation which constitutes the freedom of truly infinite subjectivity. But with the freedom of spirit, whatever form it may take, there is bound up in general the cancellation of the purely natural *qua* spirit's opposite. The spirit must first withdraw into itself from nature, lift itself above it, and overcome it, before it can prevail in it without hindrance as in an element which cannot withstand it, and transform it into a positive existence of its own freedom. But if we ask about the more specific object which in classical art spirit transcends, thereby acquiring its independence, this object is not nature as such but a nature already itself permeated by spiritual meanings, that is to say, the symbolic form of art; this form made use of immediate natural configurations for the expression of the Absolute, since its artistic consciousness either saw gods present in animals, etc., or struggled in vain and in a false way towards the true unity of the spiritual and the natural. It is by invalidating and transforming this false linkage that the Ideal first produces itself as the Ideal, and therefore has to develop within itself, as a factor belonging to itself, what is to be overcome.

This enables us, in passing, to settle the question whether the Greeks adopted their religion from foreign peoples or not. We have seen already that subordinate stages are necessary as a presupposition of classical art in the nature of the case. So far as these actually appear and are separated in time, they are, in contrast to the higher form which is striving to extricate itself, something present from which the newly developing art proceeds—even if in the matter of Greek mythology this cannot be entirely proved by historical evidence. But the relation of the Greek spirit to these presuppositions is essentially a relation of formation and, first of all, of negative transformation. Were this not the case the ideas and shapes presupposed must have remained the same. Herodotus does say, in the passage [ii. 53] quoted earlier, that Homer and Hesiod gave the Greeks their gods, but he also says expressly of individual gods, that this or that one is Egyptian, etc. Therefore poetical composition does not exclude the reception of material from elsewhere but only points to its essential transformation. For the Greeks already had mythological ideas before the period which Herodotus ascribes to these two earliest poets.

Now if we ask further about the more detailed aspects of this necessary transformation of what does of course belong to the Ideal, though in an unsuitable form at first, we find this transformation represented in a naïve way as the content of mythology itself. The chief deed of the *Greek* gods is to engender and frame themselves out of the past belonging to the history of the origin and progress of their own race. Since the gods are supposed to exist as spiritual individuals in bodily shape, this involves that, on the one side, instead of contemplating its own essence in what is merely living and animal, the spirit regards the living being as unworthy of it, as its misfortune and its death, and, on the other side, overcomes the elemental in nature and its own confused representation therein. But conversely it is equally necessary for the ideal of the classical gods that they should not merely stand contrasted with nature and its elemental powers, like the individual spirit in its abstract finite self-sufficiency, but have the elements of universal natural life in themselves as, conformably with their own essence, a factor constituting the life of the spirit. Just as the gods are in themselves essentially *universal* and in this universality are purely specific individuals, so too their corporeal side must contain in itself the natural at the same time as an essential far-reaching natural force and an activity intertwined with the spiritual.

From this point of view we may divide the process of shaping the classical art-form in the following way:

The *first* chief point concerns the degrading of the animal element and its removal from the sphere of free pure beauty.

The *second*, more important, aspect concerns the elemental powers of nature, presented themselves at first as gods; only through their conquest can the genuine race of gods achieve unquestioned dominion; this concerns the battle and war between the old and the new gods.

But then, *thirdly*, this negative orientation all the same becomes affirmative again after the spirit has won its free right, and elemental nature constitutes a positive aspect of the gods, one permeated by individual spirituality, and the gods are now girt with the animal element, even if only as an attribute and external sign. From these points of view we will now try to emphasize, still briefly, the more specific traits which come under consideration here.

1. *The Degradation of the Animal*

In the case of the Indians and Egyptians, and Asiatics in general, we see the animal kingdom, or at least specific kinds of animals, revered and regarded as sacred because in them the Divine itself was supposed to be visibly present. Therefore the animal form is a chief ingredient of their artistic representations, even if it is used besides only as a symbol and in connection with human forms at a time before the human and only the human came into consciousness as what is alone true. The self-consciousness of spirit is what alone makes respect for the dark and dull inwardness of animal life disappear. This is already the case with the ancient Hebrews since they, as was already remarked above, regarded the whole of nature neither as a symbol nor as a presence of God, and they ascribed to external objects only that force and life which dwells in them in fact. Yet even in their case there is still, as it were accidentally, at least the remains of reverence for life as such, since Moses, e.g., forbids the consumption of animal blood because life is in the blood [Genesis, 9: 4; Leviticus, 17: 11; Deuteronomy, 12: 15 ff.]. But man must strictly be allowed to eat what is available to him. Now the next step that we have to mention in connection with the transition to classical art consists in debasing the high dignity and position of the animal world and making this degradation itself into the content of religious ideas and artistic productions. In this matter there is a variety of topics out of which I will select only the following as an illustration.

(a) *Animal Sacrifices*

Among the Greeks certain animals appear as preferred above others, e.g. the snake occurs in Homer (*Iliad*, ii. 308; xii. 208) as an especially popular genius in the case of sacrifices, and one kind of animal especially is sacrificed to one god, another kind to another; further, the hare crossing the road is noticed, birds in flight either to right or left are watched, entrails are examined for prophetic indications; all this still implies a certain veneration of the animal, for the gods declare themselves in this way and speak to man by omens, but in essence all this is only single revelations—something superstitious of course, yet only purely momentary indications of the Divine. Whereas what is important is the sacrifice of animals and the eating of the sacrifice. Among the Indians on the contrary, the sacred animals were entirely preserved and cherished, while the Egyptians kept them from putrefaction even after their death. To the Greeks sacrifice counted as sacred. In sacrifice a man shows that he wishes to renounce the object consecrated to his gods and cancel the use of it by himself. Now here there is obvious a characteristic trait of the Greeks, namely that with them to slaughter for a 'sacrifice' means at the same time 'to slaughter for a feast' (*Odyssey*, xiv. 414; xxiv. 215), because they destined for the gods only one part of the animals and the inedible part at that, but the flesh they kept for themselves and had a grand feast. In Greece itself a myth has arisen from this. The ancient Greeks sacrificed to the gods with great solemnity, and the animals in their entirety were consumed by the sacrificial flames. Yet this great expense the poorer could not bear. Therefore Prometheus [Hesiod, *Theog.*, 521 ff.] by asking Zeus tried to obtain from him a ruling that their necessary obligation was limited to sacrificing only one part of the animal, while they might keep the rest for their own use. He slaughtered two oxen, burnt the liver of both, but put all the bones into the skin of one of the animals and the flesh into the skin of the other, and then gave Zeus the choice. Zeus, deceived, chose the bones because they made up the bigger package and so left the flesh to men. Therefore when the flesh of the sacrificial animals was eaten, the remains—the portion of the gods—were burnt in the same fire. But Zeus deprived men of fire, because without it their flesh portion was useless to them. But this was little help to him. Prometheus purloined fire and in his joy flew back quicker than he went, and therefore, as the tale goes, men bringing good news run quickly even now. In this way the Greeks have directed their attention to every advance in human culture and reshaped it in myths and so preserved it in their minds.

(b) Hunts

A similar example of a still further debasement of the animal world comes in here, namely the reminiscences of famous hunts ascribed to the heroes and continually commemorated with gratitude. In Greece the killing of animals which appear to be dangerous foes, e.g. the strangling of the Nemean lion by Hercules, his slaying of the Lernaean hydra, and his hunting of the Erymanthian boar, counts as something lofty whereby the heroes fought their way to the rank of gods; whereas the Indians punished with death, as a crime, the killing of certain animals. Of course in exploits of this kind further symbols play their part or lie at their basis, as in the case of Hercules the sun and its course, so that such heroic actions afford also an essential aspect for symbolical exegesis; nevertheless these myths are taken at the same time in their plain meaning as beneficial hunts, and it was thus that they were understood by the Greeks. In a similar connection we must recall here some of Aesop's fables, especially the one mentioned earlier[1] about the beetle. The beetle [scarab], this old Egyptian symbol, in whose balls of dung the Egyptians, or the interpreters of their religious ideas, saw the ball of the world, occurs again in Aesop in relation to Zeus, and with the important point that the eagle does not respect Zeus's protection of the hare. Aristophanes, on the other hand, has degraded the beetle altogether into a joke.

(c) Metamorphoses

Thirdly, the degradation of the animal world is directly expressed in the stories of the numerous metamorphoses which Ovid has painted for us in detail, charmingly, ingeniously, with fine traits of feeling and sentiment, but he has also put them together with much loquacity as purely mythological and childish plays and external events without their great inner dominating spirit, and without recognizing any deeper sense in them. But they do not lack such a deeper meaning and we will therefore at this point make mention of it again. In great part the individual stories are baroque in their material and barbaric, not owing to the corruptness of a civilized environment but, as in the *Nibelungenlied*, owing to the corruptness of a [state of] nature still in the raw; up to Ovid's thirteenth book, subjects older than the Homeric stories,

---

[1] See above, p. 386, note 2.

intermingled besides with cosmogony and foreign elements drawn from Phoenician, Phrygian, and Egyptian symbolism are, to be sure, treated in a human way, yet the uncouth background has even so remained, while the metamorphoses related in tales which belong to a time later than the Trojan War (although they also contain material drawn from fabulous times) clash in a blundering way with the names of Ajax and Aeneas.

(α) In general we may consider metamorphoses as the opposite of the Egyptian contemplation and veneration of animals. Looked at from the ethical and spiritual side, metamorphoses entail essentially a negative tendency against nature, a tendency to make animals and inorganic forms into a presentation of the degradation of man, so that, i.e., while in the case of the Egyptians the gods of elemental nature were raised to animals and given life, here, on the other hand, as was noticed earlier [in Section I, ch. III, A 3], natural forms appear as a punishment for some slighter or more serious fault and monstrous crime, as the existence of something godless and miserable, and as a configuration of grief in which man can no longer hold his own. Therefore they are not to be interpreted as the transmigration of souls in the Egyptian sense, for that is a migration without guilt and it is regarded on the contrary as an elevation when a man becomes a cow.

On the whole, however, no matter how different the natural objects may be into which the spiritual is banished, this cycle of myths does not form a systematic whole. A few examples may clarify my points.

Among the Egyptians the wolf plays a great part; Osiris, e.g., appears [in the form of a wolf] as a helpful protector of his son Horus in the latter's struggle against Typhon, and in a series of Egyptian coins he stands beside Horus. In general the association of the wolf with the sun-god is extremely ancient. In the *Metamorphoses* of Ovid, on the other hand, the transformation of Lycaon into a wolf is represented as punishment for impiety against the gods. After the Giants had been overcome and their bodies crushed, the story goes (*Met.*, i. 150-243), the earth, warmed by the blood of its sons, shed everywhere, animated the warm blood and, so that no trace of the savage stock might remain, brought forth a race of men. Yet this offspring too was contemptuous of the gods and eager for savage deeds and murder. Then Jupiter called the gods together to destroy this mortal race. He related how Lycaon had cunningly laid a trap for him, the lord of lightning and the gods, when the worthlessness of the time had reached his ear and he had desended from Olympus and reached Arcadia. 'I gave a sign', he says, 'that a god had drawn nigh and the people began to pray'. But Lycaon first scoffed at these pious prayers and then cried out: 'I will make trial whether this be a god or a mortal, and the truth will admit of no doubt.' Jupiter proceeds 'He prepares to slay me in a heavy sleep at night; this way of investigating the truth fascinates him. And not yet content with this, he cut the throat of a Molossian hostage with his sword, and he cooked some of the only half-dead limbs and baked others on the fire and set them both before me as a meal. With avenging flame I laid his house in ashes. Terrified, he flies outside and when he reaches the silent fields he howls all around and tries in vain to speak. With rage in his jaws, with avidity for the usual murder, he turns against the cattle and even now rejoices in their blood; his clothes have become hairs, his arms legs; he is a wolf and preserves traces of his former shape.'

The atrocity committed is of similar grávity in the story of Procne who was changed into a swallow (*Met.*, vi. 440-676). When she stood well with her husband Tereus, she asked him to send her to see her sister or to let her sister come to her. He made haste to launch his ship into the sea and with sail and oar quickly reached the shore of the Piraeus. But scarcely does he set eyes on Philomela than he burns with passionate love for her. At their departure Pandion, her father, conjures him to protect her with a father's love and, as soon as may be, send her back to him, her the sweet comfort of his old age; but the journey is hardly over before the barbarian locks her up, pale, trembling, fearing the worst, asking with tears where her sister is; by force he makes her his concubine, a twin-consort with her sister. Full of wrath and casting all shame aside, Philomela threatens to betray the deed herself. Then Tereus draws his sword, grabs her, ties her up, and cuts out her tongue, but he hypocritically tells his wife that her sister is dead. The wailing Procne tears her state-robes from her shoulders and dons mourning clothes, prepares an empty tomb and bewails the fate of her sister, who is not *thus* to be bewailed. What does Philomela do? Imprisoned, deprived of speech and voice, she bethinks her of cunning. With purple threads she works into a white web the story of the crime, and sends the dress secretly to Procne. The wife reads her sister's pitiful communication, she says nothing and does not weep but she lives entirely in the imagination of revenge. It was the time of the festival of Bacchus; driven by the furies of grief, she forces her way to her sister, tears her out of her apartment and carries her off with her. Then in her own house, as she still doubts what horrible revenge she is to take on Tereus, Itys comes to his mother. With wild eyes she looks at him: 'How like his father he is.' She says no more and accomplishes the melancholy deed. The sisters kill the boy and serve him at table to Tereus who gulps down his own blood. Now he asks for his son, and Procne says to him: 'Thou carriest in thyself what thou askest for'; and as he looks around and searches for where the boy is, and asks and calls again, Philomela brings the bloody head for him to see. Thereupon with an awful yell of anguish he shoves away the table, weeps, and calls himself his son's grave; and then pursues the daughters of Pandion with naked steel. But given feathers they float away thence, one to the wood [Philomela, the nightingale] the other to the roof [Procne, the swallow], and Tereus too, made agile by his grief and eagerness for revenge, becomes a bird with a comb of feathers on the crown of his head and a disproportionately protuberant beak; the name of the bird is the hoopoe.

Other metamorphoses, on the other hand, arise from less serious guilt. So Cycnus is changed into a swan; Daphne, the first love of Apollo, becomes a laurel (*Met.*, i. 451-567), Clytie a heliotrope; Narcissus, who in his self-conceit despised girls, is in love with his reflection in a stream,[1] and Byblis (ibid., ix. 454-664) loved her brother Caunus and, when he spurned her, was changed into a spring which even now still bears her name and flows beneath a dark ilex.

However, we must not lose ourselves in further details, and therefore for the sake of the transition to the next point I will

---

[1] Phaethon, who stole the chariot of the sun and burnt the earth, was destroyed by Zeus. Cycnus, his friend, gathered up his remains and was changed into a swan (*Met.*, ii. 367 ff.). Daphne refused Apollo. Clytie followed Apollo's (the sun's) course daily but languished because she did not find favour with him and, pitying her, the gods changed her into a flower that always turned to the sun, i.e. heliotrope. (Ibid., iv. 234–70 tells a slightly different story, and others say that she was changed into a sunflower.) Narcissus tries to embrace his own reflection, thinking it to be a water sprite, and, a victim of love and despair, is changed into a flower which is said to grow beside quiet pools and to be reflected therein (ibid., iii. 339 ff.).

mention no more than the metamorphosis of the Pierides, who according to Ovid (*Met.*, v. 302) were the daughters of Pierus and challenged the Muses to a contest. For us the only important thing is the difference between what the Pierides and what the Muses sang. The former celebrated the battles of the gods (ibid., 319-31) and give false honour to the Giants and disparage the deeds of the great gods: sent up from the bowels of the earth, Typhoeus[1] struck terror into heaven; all the gods fled thence until, worn out, they rest on Egyptian soil. But even here, the Pierides tell, Typhoeus arrives and the high gods hide themselves in delusive shapes. Jupiter, the song says, was the leader of the herd [a ram], whence even now the Libyan Ammon is figured with crumpled horns; Apollo becomes a raven; the scion of Semele [Bacchus] a goat; the sister of Phoebus [Artemis] a cat; Juno a snow-white cow; Venus is concealed in a fish and Mercury in the feathers of the ibis. Thus here the gods suffer ignominy because of their animal shape, and, even if they have not been transformed as punishment for a fault or a crime, still cowardice is cited as the reason for their own self-imposed transformation.

On the other hand, Calliope [Muse of Epic Poetry] hymns the good deeds and stories of Ceres: 'Ceres was the first', she says [ibid., 341], 'to dig up the ground with the curved ploughshare; the first to give fruits and fruitful nourishment to the earth; the first to give us laws, and, in short, we ourselves are the gift of Ceres. Her have I to praise; would I could only sing songs worthy of the goddess! The goddess indeed is worthy of songs.' As she ended, the Pierides ascribed victory in the contest to themselves; but as they tried to speak, Ovid says (ibid., 670), and with loud cries tried to brandish their insolent hands, they saw their nails become feathers, their arms bedecked with down, and each saw the other's mouth grown into a stiff beak; and while they want to bewail their lot they are carried away on outspread wings, and, screamers in the woods, they hover in the air as magpies. And to this day, Ovid adds, they still have their earlier readiness of tongue, their raucous chatter, and their huge delight in babbling.

Thus it turns out that here again the metamorphosis is represented as punishment, and punishment indeed, as is the case with many of these stories, for impiety against the gods.

---

[1] A monster with the heads of a hundred serpents on his hands. Titans, giants, and monsters are often confused in the literature.

(β) As for the further metamorphoses of men and gods into animals that are familiar to us from other sources, there is at their basis no direct transgression on the part of those transformed; Circe, e.g., had the power to bewitch men into animals, but in that case the animal condition appears as no more than a misfortune and a degradation which does not bring honour even to the person who works the transformation for selfish ends. Circe was only a subordinate and obscure goddess; her power appears as mere magic and when Ulysses takes measures to free his bewitched comrades, Mercury helps him [*Odyssey*, x].

Of a similar kind are the numerous shapes which Zeus assumes, as when he changes himself into a bull on account of Europa, approaches Leda as a swan, and impregnates Danae as a shower of gold; his aim is always deception and his intentions are not spiritual but natural and indecorous, and he is incited to them by the constantly well-founded jealousy of Juno. The idea of a universal procreative life of nature which was the chief characteristic in many older mythologies is here recast by fancy into single stories of the profligacy of the father of gods and men, but he achieves his exploits not in his own shape, for the most part not in human shape, but expressly in animal or some other natural shape.

(γ) Finally, associated with these are the hybrid shapes of man and beast which likewise are not excluded from Greek art, but the beast is assumed to be only something degrading and unspiritual. Amongst the Egyptians the goat, Mendes, was revered as god (Herodotus ii. 46—according to Jablonski's view, see F. Creuzer, *Symbolik*, i, p. 477, in the sense of a procreative natural force, especially the sun), and with such abomination that even women, as Pindar indicates,[1] gave themselves to goats. With the Greeks, on the other hand, Pan is the one who arouses awe of the divine presence, and, later, in fauns, satyrs, Pans, the goat shape appears only in a subordinate way in the feet and, in the most beautiful of them, only, if at all, in pointed ears and tiny horns. The rest of the shape is that of the human form, the animal being thrust into the background as a trivial remnant. And yet the fauns did not count with the Greeks as high gods and spiritual powers; their character remained one of sensuous unbounded joviality. They were indeed

---

[1] Fragment 201 (Snell). Hegel probably read this in Strabo, 17. i. 19. Herodotus, loc. cit., encountered this abomination, but he implies that it was very unusual.

represented also with a deeper expression as, e.g. the beautiful faun in München who holds the young Bacchus in his arms and looks on him with a laugh full of supreme love and affection. He is not meant to be the father of Bacchus, but only his foster-father, and now there is ascribed to him that beautiful feeling of joy in the innocence of the child which, as Mary's maternal feeling for Christ, has been raised to such a lofty spiritual topic in romantic art. But with the Greeks this most charming love belongs to the subordinate sphere of fauns in order to indicate that its origin is derived from the animal and natural realm and that therefore it can be allotted to this sphere too.

The Centaurs also are similar hybrid formations in which likewise the natural aspect of sensuousness and concupiscence is predominantly presented, while the spiritual side is pressed into the background. Chiron, of course, [though a Centaur] is of a nobler sort, a clever physician and the tutor of Achilles, but this instruction in his capacity as tutor to a child does not belong to the sphere of the Divine as such but is related to human skill and cleverness.

Thus in classical art the character of the animal form is altered in every respect; here the animal form is used to indicate the evil, the bad, the trivial, the natural, and the unspiritual, whereas formerly it was the expression of the positive and the Absolute.

2. *The Battle between the Old Gods and the New*

The second stage, a higher one, of this debasement of the animal sphere consists in this, that since the genuine gods of classical art have for their inner character free self-consciousness as the self-reposing power of the individual spirit, they can also come into our view only as possessed of knowledge and will, i.e. as spiritual powers. In this way the human shape in which they are represented is not, as might be supposed, a mere form which is tacked on to their content purely externally by imagination, but is implied in the meaning, the content, the inner itself. But the Divine in general is to be apprehended essentially as the unity of the spiritual and the natural; both of these belong to the Absolute and, this being so, it is only the different ways in which this harmony is presented that make up the series of stages in the different art-forms and religions. According to our Christian ideas, God is the creator and lord of nature and the spiritual world and so is of course exempt from immediate existence in nature, because only as withdrawal into himself, as spiritual and absolute self-independence, is he truly God; but the purely finite human spirit is bounded and restricted by its opposite, namely nature. This restriction, therefore, the human spirit in its existence only overcomes, and thereby raises itself to infinity, by grasping nature in thought through theoretical activity, and through practical activity bringing about a harmony between nature and the spiritual Idea, reason, and the good. Now God is this infinite activity, in so far as dominion over nature is his prerogative, and, as this infinite activity, with its knowing and willing, he is explicit to himself.

Conversely, as we saw, in the religions of strictly symbolic art the unity of the inner and the ideal with nature is an *immediate* linkage which therefore had nature as its chief characteristic both in content and form. Thus there were venerated as god's existence and life the sun, the Nile, the sea, the earth, the natural process of coming to be and passing away and of procreation and reproduction, the changing course of the universal life of nature. Yet these natural powers were already personified in symbolic art and thereby put in opposition to the spiritual. Now if, as the classical artform demands, the gods are to be spiritual individuals in harmony with nature, mere personification is insufficient for attaining this result. For if what is personified is a mere universal power and natural agency, personification remains entirely formal without penetrating into the content and cannot in that content bring into existence either the spiritual element or the individuality of that. Therefore the converse necessarily belongs to classical art: for we have just treated the animal world in its debasement, and so now the universal power of nature is degraded for its part, and the spiritual is contrasted with it as something higher. But in that case, instead of personification, it is subjectivity which constitutes the chief characteristic. Yet, on the other hand, in classical art the gods may not cease to be natural powers, because here God cannot yet come into representation as inherently and absolutely free spirituality. But nature can stand in the relation of a merely created and subservient creature to a lord and creator separated from it, only if God is envisaged either, as in the art of sublimity, as inherently abstract and purely ideal domination by the single substance, or, as in Christianity, as concrete spirit raised into the pure element of spiritual existence and personal independence, and so to complete freedom. Neither of these alternatives corresponds with the outlook of classical art. Its god is not *yet* lord of nature because he has not yet got absolute spirituality as his content and form; he is *no longer* lord of nature because the sublime relation between human individuality and god-forsaken natural things has ceased and been modified into beauty in which both sides, the universal and the individual, the spiritual and the natural, are to be given their full rights unrestrictedly for artistic representation. That is to say, in the god of classical art the natural power remains contained, but as a natural power, not in the sense of *universal* all-embracing nature, but as the specific and therefore restricted agency of the sun, the sea, etc., or in short as a *particular* natural power which appears as a spiritual individual and has this spiritual individuality as its own essence.

Now since, as we saw already at the start of this chapter, the classical ideal is not present immediately but can only appear through the process in which the negative side of spirit's shape is transcended, this transformation and upward development of the raw, ugly, wild, baroque, purely natural or fantastic, which has its origin in earlier religious ideas and artistic insights, must be a chief interest in Greek mythology and therefore be portrayed in a specific group of particular meanings.

If we now proceed to a closer consideration of this chief point, I must at once premiss that we have no business here with an historical investigation of the variegated and manifold ideas of Greek mythology. What concerns us in this matter is only the essential factors in this upward development in so far as these prove to be universal factors in artistic configuration and its content; whereas the endless mass of particular myths, narrations, stories, and events related to a locality and a symbolism, which taken together maintain their right in the new gods also and occur incidentally in artistic images, but which are not strictly intrinsic to the central point which we are striving to reach along our route—all this is a breadth of material which we must leave aside here and we can only refer to one or two features by way of example.

On the whole we may compare this route, along which we are proceeding, with the course of the history of sculpture. For since sculpture places the gods in their genuine shape before sense-perception, it forms the proper centre of classical art, even if poetry complements it by describing gods and men in a way distinct from the self-reposing objectivity of sculpture or by presenting the divine and human world in their very activity and movement. Now just as in sculpture the chief feature at its start is the transformation of the formless stone or block of wood fallen from heaven (διοπετής)[1] (as the great goddess[2] from Pessinus in Asia Minor still was when the Romans took it to Rome by a solemn embassy) into a human shape and figure, so we have to begin here too with the formless uncouth natural powers and only indicate the stages by which they rise to individual spirituality and contract into fixed shapes.

In this connection we may distinguish three different aspects as the most important.

The first that claims our attention is oracles in which the knowledge and will of the gods is declared, still formlessly, through natural existents.

The second chief point concerns the universal powers of nature as well as the abstractions of law etc., which lie at the base of the genuine spiritual individual gods as their birthplace and serve as the necessary presupposition of their origin and activity—these powers are the old gods in distinction from the new.

Thirdly and lastly, the absolutely necessary advance to the Ideal is exhibited in the fact that the originally superficial personifications of natural activities and the most abstract spiritual relationships are fought and suppressed as what is in itself subordinate and negative, and by this degradation independent spiritual individuality and its human form and action are enabled to acquire undisputed mastery. This transformation, which forms the proper centre in the history of the origin of the Greek gods, is represented in Greek mythology both naïvely and explicitly in the battle between the old and the new gods, in the downfall of the Titans, and in the victory won by the divine race of Zeus.

(a) Oracles

Now first, there is no need to make any extended mention of oracles here; the essential point of importance rests only on the fact that in classical art natural phenomena are no longer venerated as such, in the way that the Parsis, e.g., worshipped naphtha springs

---

[1] i.e. that fell from Zeus; Euripides, *Iphigenia in Tauris*, 977.

[2] Magna Mater (Cybele) removed by the Romans in 204 B.C. in obedience to a Sibylline oracle. She was worshipped in a block of stone (Livy, xxix. 11–14).

or fire, nor do the gods remain inscrutable secret dumb enigmas, as was the case with the Eygptians; in classical art the gods, as themselves knowing and willing, declare their wisdom to men by way of natural phenomena. So the ancient Hellenes [Pelasgi] asked the oracle at Dodona (Herodotus, ii. 52) whether they should adopt the names of the gods imported from the barbarians, and the oracle replied: use them.

(α) The signs through which the gods revealed themselves were for the most part quite simple: at Dodona the rustling and soughing of the sacred oak, the murmur of the spring, and the tone of the brazen vessel which resounded in the wind. So too at Delos the laurel rustled, and at Delphi too the wind on the brazen tripod was a decisive factor. But apart from such immediate natural sounds, man himself is also the voice of the oracle when he is stupefied and stimulated out of his alert and intelligent presence of mind into a natural state of enthusiasm, as, e.g., Pythia at Delphi, stupefied by vapours, spoke the oracular words, or in the cave of Trophonius[1] the man who consulted the oracle had visions, and from their interpretation the answer was given him.

(β) But there is still another aspect in the external signs. For in the oracles the god is indeed apprehended as the one who *knows*, and to Apollo, therefore, the god of knowledge, the most famous oracle [i.e. the one at Delphi] is dedicated; yet the form in which he declares his will remains something natural and completely vague, a natural voice or word-sounds without any connection. In this obscurity of form the spiritual content is itself dark and therefore needs clarification and explanation.

(γ) The pronouncement of the god is submitted at first purely in the form of something natural. But although the explanation makes the inquirer aware of it in a spiritualized form, it nevertheless remains obscure and ambiguous. For in his knowing and willing the god is concrete universality, and his advice or command, revealed by the oracle, must be of the same kind. But the universal is not one-sided and abstract but, as concrete, contains both one side of the ambiguity and the other. Now since the man stands there as ignorant opposite the god who knows, he accepts the oracle ignorantly too; i.e. its concrete universality is not obvious to him and when he decides to act in accordance with the ambiguous divine saying he can choose only one side of it; every action in

[1] There is a description of this in Pausanias, ix. 39.

particular circumstances is always determinate, and decision must be in accordance with one side of the oracle and exclude the other. But scarcely has he acted and the deed been actually accomplished, a deed therefore which has become his own and for which he must answer, than collision occurs; he suddenly sees turned against him the other side which was also implicit in the oracle, and, against his knowledge and will, he is caught in the toils of that fate of his deed which the gods know though he did not. Conversely again, the gods are *determinate* powers, and their utterance, when it carries in itself this character of determinacy, as, e.g., the command of Apollo which drove Orestes to revenge, produces collision too on account of this determinacy.

Since the form assumed in the oracle by the inner knowledge of the god is the entirely indefinite externality or the abstract inwardness of the saying, and the content itself comprises, owing to its ambiguity, the possibility of discord, it follows that in classical art it is not sculpture but poetry, especially dramatic poetry, in which oracles constitute one aspect of the subject-matter and become of importance. But in classical art they do acquire an essential place because in such art human individuality has not pressed on to the extreme of inwardness at which the subject draws the decision for his action purely from within himself. What we call 'conscience' in our sense of the word has not yet found its place here. The Greek does often act from his own passion, good or bad, but the real 'pathos' which should and does animate him comes from the gods whose content and might is the universal element in such a 'pathos', and the heroes are either immediately full of it or they consult the oracle when the gods are not present in person to command the act.

(*b*) *The Old Gods in Distinction from the New*

In the *oracle* the *content* [of what is declared] lies in the knowing and willing of the gods, while the *form* of its external appearance is what is abstractly external and *natural*. *Now*, on the other hand, the natural with its universal powers and their agencies becomes the *content* out of which independent individuality has first to force its way and it acquires for its first *form* only the formal and superficial personification [of these powers]. The repulse of these purely natural powers, the clash and opposition through which they are vanquished, is just the important point for which we have to thank strictly classical art alone and which on this account we will subject to a closer examination.

(α) The first point to notice in this connection is the fact that now we have not to do, as was the case in the world view of sublimity, or partly even in India, with an explicitly ready-made god, devoid of sensuous appearance, as the beginning of all things; on the contrary, the beginning is provided here by nature-gods and primarily by the more universal powers of nature, Chaos the ancient, Tartarus, Erebus, all these wild subterranean beings, and further by Uranus, Gaia, the Titanic Eros, Cronus, etc. Then from these there first arose the more definite powers, such as Helios, Oceanus, etc., which become the natural basis for the later spiritually individualized gods. Thus there here enters again a theogony and cosmogony invented by imagination and shaped out by art; but its first gods are viewed on the one hand as either still remaining of an indefinite kind or as being enlarged beyond all measure, and, on the other hand, as still carrying in themselves much that is symbolical.

(β) As for the more definite difference within these Titanic powers themselves, they are,

(αα) first, powers of earth and the stars, without spiritual and ethical content, and therefore ungovernable, a raw and savage race, misshapen, like products of Indian or Egyptian fancy, gigantic and formless. With other sorts of natural individuals, e.g. like Brontes and Steropes,[1] the hundred-handed Giants Briareus, Cottus, and Gyges, they stand under the dominion of Uranus first, then of Cronus, this chief Titan, who obviously signifies time: he swallows all his children just as time annihilates everything it has brought to birth. This myth is not lacking in symbolical meaning. For natural life is in fact subjected to time and brings into existence only the ephemeral, just as e.g. the prehistoric age of a people, which is only a nation, a tribe, but does not form a state or pursue aims that are inherently stable, falls a victim to the unhistorical power of time. Only in law, ethical life, and the state is there present something solid which remains as the generations pass, just as the muse gives duration and consolidation to everything which as natural life and actual action is only ephemeral, and in the course of time has passed away.

---

[1] Two of the Cyclopes, children of Earth and Sky, younger than the three Giants.

(ββ) But further there belong to this group of the ancient gods not only natural powers as such but also the first forces that master the elements. Especially important is the earliest working on metal through the power of the still raw elemental nature itself, of air, water, or fire. We may cite here the Corybantes, Telchins (demons of beneficent as well as of evil influence), Pataeci (pygmies, dwarfs skilled in mining work, small men with fat bellies).[1]

As an especially prominent transitional point, however, mention must be made of Prometheus. He is a Titan of a special kind and his story deserves particular notice. With his brother Epimetheus he appears at first as a friend of the new gods; then he appears as a benefactor of men who otherwise have no concern with the relation between the new gods and the Titans; he brings fire to men and therefore the possibility of satisfying their needs, developing technical skills, etc., which yet are no longer something natural and therefore apparently stand in no closer connection with the Titans. For this act Zeus punishes Prometheus, until at last Hercules releases him from his agony. At a first glance there is nothing properly Titanic in all these chief details, indeed we could find an illogicality there, in that Prometheus, like Ceres, is a benefactor of mankind and yet is reckoned amongst the old Titanic powers. Yet on closer inspection the illogicality disappears at once, for a few passages from Plato, e.g., give us a satisfactory explanation.

For example, there is the myth in which the guest of young Socrates tells that in the time of Cronus there was an earthborn race of men and the god himself took care of the whole, but then an opposed revolution took place and the earth was left to itself so that now the beasts became wild, and the men whose nourishment and other requirements previously came to them immediately were left without counsel or aid. In this situation, it is said (*Politicus*, 274), fire was given to men by Prometheus, but the technical skills (τέχναι) by Hephaestus and Athene, his partner in craftsmanship.—Here there is an express difference between fire and what is produced by skill in working on raw materials, and what is ascribed to Prometheus is only the gift of fire.

At greater length Plato relates the myth of Prometheus in the

---

[1] Corybantes were priests of Cybele in Phrygia but were associated with Telchins by Strabo. Telchins were metalworkers, the first inhabitants of Crete. Pataeci were Phoenician deities of strange dwarfish shape (Herodotus, iii. 37). All editions read '*Pätaken*', but that is a mistake.

Protagoras. There (320-3) it is said: Once upon a time there were gods but no mortal creatures. When the appointed time came for their birth, the gods formed them within the earth out of a mixture of earth and fire and the substances compounded of earth and fire. Then when the gods were ready to bring them to light, they charged Prometheus and Epimetheus with the task of equipping them and allotting suitable powers to each. But Epimetheus begs Prometheus to let him make the division himself. 'When I have made it', he said, 'you can review it'. But Epimetheus stupidly used up all the powers on the animals, so that there was nothing left for human beings. So when Prometheus comes to review the scene, he sees the other living things wisely equipped with everything, but men he finds naked, unshod, without clothing or weapons. But already the appointed day had come on which it was necessary for man to come up out of the earth into daylight. Now being at a loss to find help for men, he stole from Hephaestus and Athene both their skill and fire also (for without fire it was impossible for anyone to possess or use this skill) and so he bestows them on men. Now in this way man acquired the necessary skill to keep himself alive but he had no *political* wisdom, for this was still in the hands of Zeus, and Prometheus had no longer the right of entry to the citadel of Zeus around whom stood his frightening sentinels. But he goes stealthily into the dwelling shared by Hephaestus and Athene in which they practised their art, and after stealing the art of working with fire from Hephaestus and the other (the art of weaving) from Athene, he gives these arts to men. And through this gift men had the means of life (εὐπορία τοῦ βίου) but Prometheus, thanks to Epimetheus, later, as is told, suffered punishment for theft.

Plato then goes on in the immediately following passage to relate that men also lacked for their nurture the art of war against beasts, an art which is only one part of politics; therefore they collected together in cities, but there, for want of political skill, they injured one another and scattered again so that Zeus was compelled to give them, with Hermes as his messenger, respect for others and a sense of justice.

In these passages there is specifically emphasized the difference between (*a*) the immediate aims of life, which are related to physical comfort and provision for the satisfaction of primary needs, and (*b*) political organization which makes its aim the spiritual realm, i.e. ethics, law, property rights, freedom, and community.

This ethical and legal life Prometheus had not given to men; he only taught them the cunning to master things in nature and use them as a means to human satisfaction. Fire and the skills that make use of it are nothing ethical in themselves, and the art of weaving has nothing of the sort either; in the first instance they appear solely in the service of selfishness and private utility without having any bearing on the community of human existence and the public side of life. Because Prometheus was not in a position to impart anything more spiritual and ethical to men, he belongs to the Titans and not to the race of new gods. Hephaestus indeed has likewise got fire and the techniques associated with it as the element of his agency, and yet is a newer god; but Zeus hurled him down from Olympus and he has remained the god who limps. Neither, therefore, is it an illogicality when we find Ceres, who, like Prometheus, proved herself a benefactor of the human race, included amongst the new gods. For what Ceres taught was agriculture with which property is connected at once, and, later, marriage, ethics, and law.

(γγ) Now a third group of the ancient gods contains neither personified powers of nature as such in their savagery or cunning nor the primary power over the separate elements of nature in the service of man's lower needs, but is one that already borders on what is inherently ideal, universal, and spiritual. But nevertheless what is lacking to the powers to be included in this group is spiritual individuality and its adequate shape and appearance, so that now, more or less in relation to their agency, they retain a closer bearing on what is necessary and essential in nature. As examples we may refer to the idea of Nemesis, Dike, the Furies, the Eumenides, and the Fates. Here of course the categories of right and justice already obtrude; but instead of being grasped and given shape as the inherently spiritual and substantial element in ethical life, this necessary right either does not go beyond the most general abstraction or else affects the obscure right of the natural element within spiritual relationships, e.g. love of kindred and its right. This does not belong to the spirit which is conscious of itself in its clear freedom, and therefore it does not appear as a legal right but on the contrary in opposition thereto as the irreconcilable right of revenge.

For further detail I will mention only a few ideas. Nemesis, for example, is the power to bring down the lofty, to hurl the all too fortunate man from his height and so to restore equality. But the right of equality is the purely abstract and external right which does prove active in the sphere of spiritual situations and relationships, yet their ethical organization is not made into the content of justice on the basis of equality.

Another important aspect lies in the fact that the old gods are assigned the right of family situations in so far as these rest on nature and therefore are opposed to the public law and right of the community. As the clearest example for this point we may cite the *Eumenides* of Aeschylus. The direful maidens [the Furies or Eumenides] pursue Orestes on account of his mother's murder which Apollo, the new god, ordered him to commit so that Agamemnon, her slain husband and King, might not remain unavenged. The whole drama is therefore moulded into a battle between these divine powers which make their appearance against one another in person. On the one side we have the goddesses of revenge, but they are called here the beneficent, i.e. the Eumenides, and our usual idea of the Furies, into which we convert them, is crude and barbaric. For they have an essential right of persecution and therefore they are not just hateful, wild, and gruesome in the tortures they impose. Yet the right which they assert against Orestes is only the right of the family, rooted in blood-relationship. The most intimate tie between son and mother which Orestes has snapped is the substance which the Furies defend. Apollo [on the other side] opposes to this natural ethical order, felt and grounded physically in blood-relationship, the right of the spouse and prince whose deeper right has been transgressed. *Prima facie* this difference seems external because both parties are defending the ethical order within one and the same sphere, namely the family. Yet here the sterling imagination of Aeschylus, which on this account we must rate more and more highly, has laid bare a clash that is not superficial at all, but is throughout of an essential kind. The relation of children to parents, that is to say, rests on a natural unity, whereas the bond between husband and wife must be taken as a marriage which does not issue merely from purely natural love or from a natural- and blood-relationship; it springs on the contrary from an inclination which is known and therefore from the free ethical life of the self-conscious will. Thus however far marriage is also linked with love and feeling, it is still distinct from the natural feeling of love because, independently of that, it still recognizes definite known obligations even if love be dead. The conception and knowledge of the substantial character of married life is something later and deeper than the natural concord of son and mother, and it constitutes the beginning of the state as the realization of the free and rational will. In a similar way the relation between prince and citizens implies the political connection of the same rights and laws, of self-conscious freedom and spiritual ends. This is the reason why the Eumenides, the old goddesses, are set on punishing Orestes, while Apollo defends clear conscious and self-conscious ethical life, the right of the spouse and prince, in that he rightly retorts to the Eumenides: Were Clytaemnestra's crime not avenged, 'truly would I be without honour and deem as nought the pledges of Hera, goddess of marriage, and Zeus' (*Eumenides*, 206-9).

More interesting still, although entirely transferred into human feeling and action, the same clash appears in the *Antigone*, one of the most sublime and in every respect most excellent works of art of all time. Everything in this tragedy is logical; the public law of the state is set in conflict over against inner family love and duty to a brother; the woman, Antigone, has the family interest as her 'pathos', Creon, the man, has the welfare of the community as his. Polynices, at war with his native city, had fallen before the gates of Thebes, and Creon, the ruler, in a publicly proclaimed law threatened with death anyone who gave this enemy of the city the honour of burial. But this command, which concerned only the public weal, Antigone could not accept; as sister, in the piety of her love for her brother, she fulfils the holy duty of burial. In doing so she appeals to the law of the gods; but the gods whom she worships are the underworld gods of Hades (Sophocles; *Antigone*, 451, ἡ ξύνοικος τῶν κάτω θεῶν Δίκη), the inner gods of feeling, love, and kinship, not the daylight gods of free self-conscious national and political life.

(γ) The third point which we may emphasize in respect of the theogony envisaged by classical art concerns the difference between the old gods in relation to their power and the duration of their dominion. Here we have three aspects to notice.

(αα) The first of these is that the gods originate successively. According to Hesiod, after Chaos came Gaia, Uranus, etc., then Cronus and his race, and finally Zeus with his. Now this series seems on the one hand to be a rise from the more abstract and shapeless natural powers to a more concrete and already more determinate shaping of them; but, on the other hand, it appears as the beginning of the superiority of the spiritual over the natural. So, for example, Aeschylus in the *Eumenides* makes Pythia in the temple at Delphi begin with the words: 'First with this prayer I put first in rank of the gods Gaia who first gave us oracles, and then Themis who as second after her mother had her seat of prophesying in this place' [*Eum.* 1-4]. Pausanias [x. 5. 5], on the other hand, who likewise names Earth as the first giver of oracles [at Delphi], says that Daphnis was then ordained by her to the prophetic office. In another series again, Pindar[1] puts Night first, then he gives the succession to Themis, then to Phoebe until he comes finally to Phoebus. It would be interesting to pursue these specific differences, but this is not the place for that.

(ββ) Further, since the succession has all the same to be counted as an advance to more self-concentrated and richer gods, it appears also in the form of degrading the earlier and more abstract gods within the race of the old gods itself. Cronus, e.g., dethrones Uranus, and the later gods are substituted for them.

(γγ) Therefore the negative relation of re-formation which from the beginning we laid down as the essence of this first stage of the classical art-form now becomes its proper centre; and since personification is here the universal form in which the gods enter our ideas and since the progressive movement [of fancy] presses the gods on towards human and spiritual individuality, even if this enters at first in an indefinite and formless shape, fancy brings to our vision the negative relation of the younger gods to the older as battle and war. But the essential advance is from nature to the spirit which is the true content and proper form for classical art. This advance, and the battles through which we see it being realized, belongs no longer exclusively to the group of the old gods but takes place in the war whereby the new gods establish their enduring dominion over the old.

(c) The Conquest of the Old Gods

The opposition between nature and spirit is necessary absolutely. For the Concept of the spirit, as a genuine totality, is, as we

---

[1] This is a mistake. There is no such genealogy in Pindar, although Hegel cites it as Pindar's again in his *Philosophy of Religion*, *Werke* xii. 106.

saw earlier [in dealing with The Idea in Part I], implicitly only this, namely to divide itself as object in itself and subject in itself in order through this opposition to arise out of nature and then, as its conqueror and as the power over it, to be free and serene in contrast with it. This chief factor in the essence of spirit itself is therefore also a chief factor in the idea of itself which it gives to itself. Looked at historically or in reality this transition is the progressive transformation of man in a state of nature into a system of established rights, i.e. to property, laws, constitution, political life; looked at *sub specie deorum et aeternitatis* this is the idea of the conquest of the natural powers by the spiritually individual gods.

(α) This battle presents an absolute catastrophe and is the essential deed of the gods whereby alone the chief difference between the old gods and the new becomes visible. For this reason we must not refer to the war, which discloses this difference, as if it were some myth with the same value as any other; on the contrary, we must regard it as the myth which marks the turning-point and expresses the creation of the new gods.

(β) The result of this violent strife among the gods is the overthrow of the Titans, the victory exclusively of the new gods who in their assured dominion have thereupon been endowed by imagination with qualities of all kinds. The Titans on the contrary were banished and had to dwell in the heart of the earth or, like Oceanus, linger on the dark edge of the bright and serene world, or endure otherwise all sorts of punishments. Prometheus, for example, is chained to a mountain in Scythia where the eagle insatiably devours his liver which ever grows afresh; similarly Tantalus in the underworld is tormented by an endless unquenched thirst, and Sisyphus has always uselessly to trundle up anew the rock that continually rolls down again. Like the Titanic powers of nature themselves, these punishments are the inherently measureless, the bad infinite,[1] the longing of the 'ought', the unsatiated craving of subjective natural desire which in its continual recurrence never attains the final peace of satisfaction. For the Greek correct sense of the Divine, unlike the modern longing, did not regard egress into the boundless and the vague as what was supreme for men; the Greeks regarded it as a damnation and relegated it to Tartarus.

(γ) If we ask in general what from now on must fall into the

---

[1] Hegel's usual expression for the infinite regarded as a straight line going on indefinitely instead of returning into itself, like a circle.

background for classical art and can no longer be justified in counting as its final form and adequate content, then the first thing is the natural elements. Along with them everything murky, fantastic, unclear, every wild confusion of the natural with the spiritual, of meanings inherently substantial with casual externalities, is banished from the world of the new gods; in that world the creations of an unbounded imagination which have not yet absorbed the proportion observed by the spiritual find room no longer and must rightly flee the pure light of day. For you may dress up as much as you like the great Cabiri,[1] the Corybantes, the representations of procreative force, etc., nevertheless conceptions like these in all their details—to say nothing of old Baubo whom Goethe sets careering over the Blocksberg on a sow[2]—belong more or less to the twilight of consciousness. It is only the spiritual which presses on into the light; what does not manifest itself and make itself clearly self-explanatory is the non-spiritual which sinks back again into night and darkness. But the spiritual manifests itself and, by itself determining its outer form, purifies itself from the caprice of fancy, from overflowing configurations and other sorts of murky symbolical accessories.

Similarly we now find human activity put into the background so far as it is restricted to merely natural needs and their satisfaction. The old right (Themis, Dike, etc.), by not being specified in laws deriving their origin from the self-conscious spirit, loses its unrestricted validity; and equally, but conversely, mere locality, although it still plays a part, is changed into the universal figures of the gods where it still remains as only a trace of the past. For just as in the Trojan war the Greeks fought and conquered as *one* people, so too the Homeric gods, with the battle against the Titans behind them, are an inherently fixed and determinate world of gods which thereafter at last became always more completely determinate and fixed through later poetic and plastic art. This invincible fixed relationship in the content of the Greek gods is alone the spirit; yet it is not the spirit in its abstract inwardness, but only as identical with its external adequate existence, just as in Plato[3]

---

[1] Pelasgic gods of fertility (Herodotus, ii. 51; iii. 37) worshipped in Asia Minor and Samothrace. Hegel is probably alluding to Schelling's *Die Gottheiten von Samothrace* (1815) in which the Cabiri are certainly 'dressed up'. The Corybantes were associated with them by Strabo.

[2] *Faust*, pt. 1, sc. xxi (Witches' Sabbath). Blocksberg is the Brocken.

[3] Hegel seems to have the *Timaeus* in mind.

soul and body, as brought into one nature and all of one piece in this solidity, is the Divine and the eternal.

3. Affirmative Retention of the Negatived Features

Despite the victory of the new gods, however, the old ones now still remain in the classical art-form partly in their original form as considered up to this point, partly retained and venerated in a transformed shape. Only the restricted national God of the Jews can tolerate no other gods beside himself, because he is supposed to be the All *qua* the One, although on account of his determinate character he cannot surmount the restriction of being the God of his own people alone. For he displays his universality as Lord of heaven and earth, but strictly only on the strength of his creation of nature; for the rest, he is the God of Abraham, the God who led the children of Israel out of Egypt, issued laws from Sinai, gave the land of Canaan to the Jews, and through his narrow identification with the Jewish people is quite particularly only the God of this people and therefore, to sum up, does not stand in positive harmony with nature nor does he really appear as absolute spirit withdrawn from his determinacy and objective manifestation into his universality. This is why this harsh national God is so zealous, and why in his jealousy he commands his people to see in other gods only downright false idols. The Greeks, on the other hand, found their gods amongst all peoples and made foreign material their own. For the god of classical art has spiritual and bodily individuality and is therefore not the one and only god but a *particular* divinity which, like everything particular, has a group of particulars around it, or confronting it as its opposite, out of which it emerges and which can retain its own validity and value. This is the same as what happens with the particular spheres of nature. Although the plant kingdom is the truth of geological natural formations, and the animal again the higher truth of vegetation, still the mountains and thalassic[1] land persist as the ground for trees, shrubs, and flowers which in turn do not lose their existence alongside the animal kingdom.

(a) The Mysteries

Now the first form in which we find the Greeks preserving the old gods is the Mysteries. The Greek Mysteries were not secret in

---

[1] *aufgeschwemmte*—Hegel may be thinking of the Nile valley again and this word may mean simply 'flooded', but 'deposited by geological action' is more probable.

the sense that the Greek people were not generally familiar with their subject-matter. On the contrary, most Athenians and many strangers were amongst those initiated into the Eleusinian secrets, only they might not speak of what they had learnt through the initiation. In our time especially, great trouble has been taken to research into the details of the sort of ideas contained in the Mysteries and the sort of acts of divine worship entered upon at their celebration. Yet on the whole no great wisdom or profound knowledge seems to have been hidden in the Mysteries; on the contrary, they only preserved old traditions, the basis of what was later transformed by genuine art, and therefore they had for their contents not the true, the higher, and the better, but the lower and the more trivial. This subject-matter, regarded as holy, was not clearly expressed in the Mysteries but was transmitted only in symbolical outlines. And in fact the character of the undisclosed and the unspoken belongs also to the old gods, to what was telluric, sidereal, and Titanic, for only the spirit is the revealed and the self-revealing. In this respect the symbolical mode of expression constitutes the other side of the secrecy in the Mysteries, because in the symbolical the meaning remains dark and contains something other than what the external, on which it is supposed to be represented, provides directly. So, e.g., the Mysteries of Demeter and Bacchus[1] were spiritually interpreted and acquired therefore a deeper meaning, but this content could not clearly emerge from its form because the form remained external to it. For art, therefore, the Mysteries are of trivial influence, for even if it be said of Aeschylus that he wilfully betrayed something from the Mysteries of Demeter, this only amounted to his having said that Artemis is the daughter of Ceres [i.e. Demeter][2] and this is a trivial piece of wisdom.

(b) Preservation of the Old Gods in Artistic Representation

Secondly, the worship and preservation of the old gods appears more clearly in artistic portrayal itself. At the previous stage, e.g., we spoke of Prometheus as the Titan who was punished. But all

---

[1] i.e. the Eleusinian Mysteries.

[2] This seems to be Hegel's conflation of two passages otherwise unconnected. Herodotus (ii. 156) says that Aeschylus alone of the poets made Artemis the daughter of Ceres. For all others she was the daughter of Leto. Aristotle, *E.N.* 1111[a] 9, presupposes that Aeschylus was accused (before the Areopagus) of betraying the Mysteries (he was acquitted).

the same we find him freed again. For fire, which Prometheus brought down to men, and the eating of meat which he had taught them, are, like the earth and the sun, an essential feature in human existence, a necessary condition for the satisfaction of human needs, and so Prometheus too has his glory preserved. In the *Oedipus Coloneus* of Sophocles it is said (ll. 54 ff.):

χῶρος μὲν ἱερὸς πᾶς ὅδ ἔστ'· ἔχει δέ νιν
σεμνὸς Ποσειδῶν· ἐν δ'ὁ πυρφόρος θεὸς
Τιτὰν Προμηθεύς·

['The whole place is sacred; the holy Poseidon possesses it, and the fire-bringing Prometheus, the Titan, is there too.'] And the Scholiast [on l. 56] adds that 'in the Academy too Prometheus was worshipped, like Hephaestus, along with Athene; and a temple is shown in the grove of the goddess and an old pedestal at the entrance on which there is an image of Prometheus and of Hephaestus too; but Prometheus, as Lysimachides[1] adds, was represented as the first and the elder, holding a sceptre in his hand, Hephaestus as younger and second, and the altar on the pedestal is common to both'. As it turns out, according to the myth, Prometheus did not have to suffer his punishment for ever but was released from his chains by Hercules. In the story of this liberation too some remarkable traits occur, viz.: Prometheus is released from his agony because he tells Zeus of the danger threatening his rule from his thirteenth descendant. This descendant is Hercules to whom Poseidon in the *Birds* of Aristophanes (ll. 1645–8) says that he will do himself an injury if he joins a conspiracy for upsetting the rule of the gods, [for if it succeeds, he will get nothing, whereas if Zeus remains in power then] everything that Zeus leaves behind him at his death will surely be his. And in fact Hercules is the one man who was taken up to Olympus and became a god instead of a mortal man, and he is superior to Prometheus who remained a Titan. The overthrow of the old ruling families is also connected with Hercules and the name of the Heraclidae. The Heraclidae break the power of the old dynasties and royal houses in which a dominating self-will recognizes no law either for its own ends and its unruliness, or in relation to the inhabitants, and therefore perpetrates monstrous cruelties. Hercules himself, not as

---

[1] An historian, quoted by the Scholiast.

a free man but in the service of a ruler, conquers the barbarity of this savage will.

In a similar way, to abide by examples already used, we may here refer to the *Eumenides* of Aeschylus once more. The conflict between Apollo and the Eumenides is to be settled by the verdict of the Areopagus. A court, human on the whole, at the head of which stands Athene herself as the concrete spirit of the people, is to resolve the conflict. The judges give equal votes for condemnation and acquittal, because they honour the Eumenides and Apollo equally, but the white stone of Athene decides the case for Apollo. The Eumenides lift their voices in indignation against this judgement of Athene, but she silences them because she promises them worship and altars in the famous grove at Colonus. What the Eumenides are to do for her people in return is (*Eum.*, ll. 901 ff.) defence against the evil arising from *natural* elements, earth, sky, sea, and winds, protection from unfruitfulness in the crops, from failure of the human seed. But Athene undertakes for herself in Athens the charge of warlike strife and sacred battles.[1]—Similarly Sophocles in his *Antigone* does not make Antigone alone suffer and die; on the contrary, we also see Creon punished by the grievous loss of his wife and [his son] Haemon, who both likewise perish owing to the death of Antigone.

(c) Natural Basis of the New Gods

Thirdly and lastly, not only do the old gods preserve their place alongside the new ones but, what is more important, the natural basis remains in the new gods themselves and it enjoys an enduring veneration since, in conformity with the spiritual individuality of the classical ideal, it reverberates in them.

(α) For this reason people have often been deceived into interpreting the Greek gods in their human shape and form as mere *allegories* of the elements of nature. This they are not. For example, we hear people speaking often enough of Helios as the god of the sun, of Diana as the goddess of the moon, or of Poseidon as the god of the sea. Such separation, however, of the natural element, as content, from the humanly shaped personification, as form, as well as the external connection of the two (i.e. the mere dominion of God over things in nature, a notion to which the Old Testament has accustomed us) is quite inapplicable to Greek ideas, because

[1] Aeschylus only says 'victory in renowned battles in war'.

nowhere in the Greeks do we find the expression ὁ θεὸς τοῦ ἡλίου, τῆς θαλάσσης etc. [the god *of* the sun, of the sea, etc.], while they would certainly have used this expression for this relation if it had been compatible with their outlook. Helios *is* the sun as god.

(β) But in this connection we must at the same time take good note of the fact that the Greeks did not in any way regard the natural as such as divine. On the contrary, they had the distinct idea that the natural is not the divine; and while sometimes this remains unexpressed in [their description of] what their gods are, sometimes it was expressly emphasized about them. Plutarch, e.g., in his essay on Isis and Osiris comes to speak of the different ways of interpreting the myths and the gods. Isis and Osiris belong to the Egyptian outlook and had the elements of nature as their content to a greater extent than the corresponding Greek gods had; this is because they express only the longing and the struggle to advance out of the natural into the spiritual; later[1] they enjoyed great reverence in Rome and constituted one of the chief Mysteries. Nevertheless Plutarch [*Isis and Osiris* § 64] thinks it would be disgraceful to interpret them as sun, earth, or water. Everything that in the sun, earth, etc. is measureless and without order, is defective or superfluous, and this alone must be ascribed to the natural elements; and only the good and orderly is the work of Isis, while intellect, λόγος, is the work of Osiris. As the substance of these gods, therefore, it is not the natural as such which is to be adduced, but the spiritual, the universal, λόγος, intellect, conformity to law.

In virtue of this insight into the spiritual nature of the gods, it turns out that the Greeks nevertheless distinguished the more determinate natural elements from the new gods. Of course we are accustomed to identify e.g. Helios and Selene [sun and moon] with Apollo and Diana, but in Homer they appear distinguished from one another. The same is true about Oceanus [sea] and Poseidon, and others.

(γ) But, thirdly, there remains in the new gods an echo of the powers of nature, the agency of which belongs to the spiritual individuality of the gods themselves. The ground of this positive linkage of the spiritual and the natural in the ideal of classical art we have already expounded earlier [in the passage on the Classical

---

[1] i.e. in the early Roman Empire. The Mysteries are described in the closing chapters of Apuleius, *c.* A.D. 155. Plutarch wrote *c.* A.D. 100.

in General], and therefore we may confine ourselves here to citing a few examples.

(αα) In Poseidon, as in Pontus and Oceanus, lies the might of the sea that streams round the earth, but his power and activity stretches further: he built Troy and was a safeguard of Athens; in general he was worshipped as the founder of cities, because the sea is the element for shipping, trade, and the bond between men. Similarly Apollo, the new god, is the light of knowledge, and the giver of oracles, and yet preserves a reminiscence of Helios as the natural light of the sun. Of course there is a dispute, e.g. between Voss and Creuzer, whether Apollo is to betoken the sun or not, but in fact we may say that he is and is not the sun, because he does not remain restricted to this natural content but is elevated to meaning the spiritual. Indeed it must absolutely amaze us what an essential connection there is between knowledge and illumination, the light of spirit and of nature, in keeping with their fundamental character. Light, that is to say, as a natural element is that which manifests; without our seeing it itself, it makes illuminated and irradiated objects visible. By means of light everything becomes apprehensible by something else. The same character of manifestation is possessed by spirit, by knowing and cognizing, by the free light of consciousness. Apart from the variation of the spheres in which these two manifestations display their activity, the difference between them consists only in the fact that spirit reveals *itself* and remains by itself in what it gives to us or what is made for it, while the light of nature makes apprehensible not itself but, on the contrary, what is other than itself and external to itself; and in this relation it does go out of itself, but unlike spirit does not return into itself and therefore does not win the higher unity of being by itself in the other. Just as light and knowing have a close connection, so we find in Apollo too as a spiritual god the reminiscence once again of the light of the sun. So, e.g., Homer [in *Iliad*, i. 9-10] ascribes the plague in the Grecian camp to Apollo who here is treated as the agency of the sun in the heat of summer. Similarly his death-dealing arrows undoubtedly have a symbolical connection with the sun's rays. It follows that in the external representation there must be more detailed external indications to determine in what meaning the god is principally to be taken.

It is especially when we trace the historical origin of the new gods that, as Creuzer above all has emphasized, we can recognize the natural element which the gods of the classical ideal preserve in themselves. So, e.g., in Jupiter there are indications of the sun; and the twelve labours of Hercules, for example his expedition in which he carried off the apples of the Hesperides, have likewise a relation to the sun and the twelve months. Fundamentally Diana has the office of being the universal mother of nature, e.g. as Diana of the Ephesians, who hovers between the old and the new, she has, as her chief content, nature in general, procreation and nutrition, and this meaning is indicated even in her external form, in her breasts, etc. Whereas in the case of the Greek Artemis, the huntress, who kills beasts, this natural aspect recedes altogether into the background in her humanly beautiful maidenly form and independence, although the half-moon and the arrows still always recall Selene [Selene, moon = Diana = Artemis]. In a similar way the more Aphrodite's origin is traced back to Asia, the more she becomes a natural [or sensual] power; when she comes over into Greece proper, she presents the spiritually more individual aspect of charm, grace, and love, an aspect yet in no way lacking a natural foundation. Ceres in the same way has natural productivity as her starting-point which then leads on to a spiritual content, the relations in which develop out of agriculture, property, etc. The Muses have the murmur of a spring as their natural basis, and Zeus himself is to be taken as a universal power of nature and is worshipped as the Thunderer, although in Homer thunder is a sign of misfortune or approval, an omen, and therefore it acquires a relation to the spiritual and the human. Even Juno has a natural echo of the vault of heaven and the airy region where the gods wander, for it is said, e.g., that Zeus put Hercules to Juno's breast, and from the milk that was spilt the milky way was hurled into being.

(ββ) Now just as in the new gods the universal elements of nature are disparaged but yet retained, the same is true with the animal kingdom as such, which earlier we had to treat only in its degradation. At this point we can give a more positive position to the animal kingdom as well. Yet because the classical gods have been stripped of their symbolic mode of configuration, and now win for their content the spirit which is clear to itself, the symbolical *meaning* of animals must be lost in proportion as the animal *shape* is deprived of the right of mingling with the human in an inappropriate way. This shape therefore occurs as a merely indicative attribute and is placed alongside the human shape of the gods. So we see the eagle beside Jupiter, the peacock beside Juno, the doves accompanying Venus, the dog[-headed] Anubis as the guard of the underworld, etc. Even if, therefore, something symbolical is still retained in the ideal figures of the spiritual gods, nevertheless it is not apparent in its original meaning, and the indication as such of nature, earlier constitutive of the essential content, remains in the background as only a relic and something particular and external which now here and there, on account of its accidental character, looks bizarre because the earlier meaning no longer dwells in it. Further, since the inner essence of these gods is the spiritual and the human, what is external about them now becomes a *human* accident and weakness. In this connection we may refer once again to the manifold love affairs of Jupiter. In their original symbolical meaning they are related, as we saw, to the universal activity of generation, to the life of nature. But since his marriage with Juno is to be regarded as his fixed substantial relationship, Jupiter's love-affairs appear as faithlessness to his spouse; and so they have the shape of casual adventures and exchange their symbolical sense for the character of capriciously invented and morally lax stories.

With this degradation of purely natural powers and the animal kingdom, as well as the abstract universality of spiritual relationships, and with the re-acceptance of these within the higher independence of spiritual individuality permeated by and permeating nature, we have left behind us the proper presupposition of the essence of classical art, namely its necessary origin in history; this is so because along this route the Ideal has by its own effort reached what it is in accordance with its Concept. This conceptually adequate reality of the spiritual gods leads us to the proper ideals of the classical form of art which, contrasted with the old gods, now conquered, display what is immortal, for mortality in general lies in inadequacy between the Concept and its existence.

Chapter II

THE IDEAL OF THE CLASSICAL FORM
OF ART

What the proper essence of the Ideal is we have seen already in our general treatment of the beauty of art. Here we must take it up in the special sense of the *classical* Ideal, the Concept of which is given to us already along with the Concept of the classical form of art. For the classical Ideal, our subject now, consists only in the fact that classical art actually attains and sets forth what constitutes its innermost Concept and essence. At this point it lays hold of the spiritual as its *content*, in so far as the spiritual draws nature and its powers into its own sphere and so is represented otherwise than as pure inwardness or as dominion over nature; but for its *form* it adopts the human shape, deed, and action, through which the spiritual shines clearly in complete freedom, making the sensuous shape its own, not at all as an external thing merely symbolically significant but as a reality which is the adequate existence of spirit.

The more specific division of this chapter may be laid down as follows:

First, we have to consider the *universal* nature of the classical Ideal which has the human for both its content and form and so works both sides in with one another that they come into the most complete correspondence with one another.

Secondly, however, since here the human is entirely immersed in bodily shape and external appearance, it becomes shaped externally in a *specific* way to which only a specific content is adequate. Since as a result we have the Ideal before us at the same time as *particularity*, there is presented to us a range of particular gods and powers over human existence.

Thirdly, particularity does not rest in the abstraction of being only a *single* determinate type, the essential character of which would constitute the entire content and one-sided principle for [artistic] representation; on the contrary, it is all the same a totality [of qualities] in itself and that totality's unity and harmony as an *individual.* Without this filling, particularity would be cold and empty and it would lose the vitality which the Ideal can never lack in any circumstances.

Keeping to these three aspects of universality, particularity, and single individuality, we will now study the Ideal of classical art in more detail.

1. *The Ideal of Classical Art in General*

Questions about the origin of the Greek gods, in so far as the gods afford the proper centre for ideal representation, we have already touched upon, and we have seen that the gods belong to a tradition transformed by art. Only as a result of a double depreciation, on the one hand of the universal powers of nature and their personification, on the other of the animal kingdom and its symbolical meaning and shape, could this transformation occur in order that thereby the spiritual might be won as the true content, and the human mode of appearance as the true form.

(a) *The Ideal as Originated by Free Artistic Creation*

Now since the classical Ideal comes essentially into being only through such a transformation of what went before, the first aspect which we must bring out in this connection is this, that this Ideal is generated by the spirit and therefore has originated in the most inward and personal being of poets and artists who have created it with clear and free deliberateness, consciously aiming at artistic production. But this creation seems to run counter to the fact that Greek mythology rests on older traditions and hints at something foreign and oriental. Although Herodotus, e.g., in the passage already cited above, says that Homer and Hesiod made their gods for the Greeks, he elsewhere brings the same Greek gods into close connection with the Egyptian, etc. For in Book ii. 49 he expressly tells that Melampus brought the name of Dionysus to the Hellenes [from Egypt] and introduced the phallus and the whole sacrificial festival; with one difference, however, because Herodotus thinks that Melampus learnt the worship of Dionysus [not directly from Egypt but] from Cadmus the Tyrian and the Phoenicians who came with Cadmus to Boeotia. In recent times these contradictory assertions have become of interest especially in connection with Creuzer's researches; he tries to discover in Homer, e.g., old Mysteries, and all the sources which converged in Greece, Asiatic, Pelasgic, Dodonian, Thracian, Samothracian, Phrygian, Indian, Buddhistic, Phoenician, Egyptian, Orphic, along with an endless number of domestic traditions associated with specific localities and other details. It is true that at a first glance there is a contradiction between these varied traditional origins and the view that those poets gave names and a shape to the gods. But both tradition and original creation can be wholly united. Tradition comes first, the starting-point which provides ingredients but does not yet bring with them the proper content and the genuine form for the gods. This content those poets took from their own spirit and found the true form for it in the course of their free transformation of this material and they have therefore become in fact the creators of the mythology at which we marvel in Greek art. Nevertheless, on the other hand, the Homeric gods are not for this reason, as might be supposed, a purely subjective invention or a purely artificial production; on the contrary, they have their root in the spirit and faith of the Greek people and its national religious foundations. They are the absolute forces and powers, the supreme height of Greek imagination, the centre of the beautiful in general, granted to the poet by the Muses themselves.

Now in this free creation the artist acquires a position quite different from the one he has in the East.[1] The Indian poets and sages also have material there for them as their starting-point; natural elements, sky, animals, rivers, etc., or the pure abstraction of the formless and empty Brahma; but their inspiration is a destruction of the inward life of subjectivity; the subject [i.e. the artist] is given the hard task of working on what is external to himself and, owing to the intemperance of his imagination which lacks any firm and absolute direction, he cannot create really freely and beautifully, but must continue to produce in an unruly way and range around in his material. He is like a builder who has no clear ground; ancient debris of half-ruined walls, mounds, projecting rocks obstruct him, quite apart from the particular ends which are to dictate the construction of his building, and he can achieve nothing but a wild, unharmonious, fantastic structure. What he produces is not the work of his own imagination freely creating out of his own spiritual resources. Conversely, Hebrew poets give us revelations which the Lord bade them speak, so that here again the creative force is an unconscious inspiration, separate and

[1] Cf. above, Introduction to this Section, 3.

distinct from the individuality and productive spirit of the artist, just as in sublimity generally what comes before contemplation and consciousness is the abstract and the eternal related essentially to something other than and external to itself.

In classical art, on the contrary, the artists and poets are of course also prophets and teachers who proclaim and reveal to man what is absolute and Divine, but,

(α) *first*, the content of their gods is not nature as purely external to the human spirit, or the abstraction of the one Divinity, in which case nothing would be left to them but a superficial formation or a shapeless inwardness; instead, their content is drawn from the human spirit and human existence, and therefore is the human breast's very own, a content with which man can freely associate himself as with himself, since what he produces is the most beautiful manifestation of himself.

(β) *Secondly*, the artists are also *makers*, fashioners of this material and content into a shape freely self-dependent. Accordingly the Greek artists evince themselves as genuinely creative poets. All the varied foreign ingredients they have brought into the melting-pot, yet they have not made a brew out of them like what comes from a witches' cauldron; on the contrary, in the pure fire of the deeper spirit they have consumed everything murky, natural, impure, foreign, and extravagant; they have burnt all this together and made the shape appear purified, with only faint traces of the material out of which it has been formed. Their business in this connection consisted partly in stripping away the formless, symbolic, ugly, and misshapen things which confronted them in the material of the tradition, partly in emphasizing the properly spiritual which they had to individualize and for which they had to seek or invent the corresponding external appearance. Here for the first time it is the human shape and the form of human actions and events (no longer used as mere personification) which, as we saw, enters necessarily as the one adequate reality. These forms too the artist finds in the real world, but nevertheless he has to extinguish the accidental and inappropriate element in them before they can be proved adequate to the spiritual content of man which, seized in its essence, comes to serve as the representation of the eternal powers and gods. This is the free, spiritual, and not merely arbitrary production of the artist.

(γ) Now, *thirdly*, since the gods do not merely stand aloof by themselves but are also active within the concrete reality of nature and human affairs, the business of the poets is directed to recognizing the presence and agency of the gods in this relation to human matters, to interpreting the particular aspect of natural occurrences and human deeds and destinies wherein the divine powers appear as involved, and therefore to sharing the business of the priest and the prophet. At the standpoint of our modern prosaic reflection we explain natural phenomena in accordance with universal laws and forces, the actions of men by their inner intentions and self-conscious aims, but the Greek poets looked for the Divine everywhere, and since they shaped human activities into actions of the gods, they create by this interpretation only the different aspects under which the gods exercise their power. For a mass of such interpretations is afforded by a mass of actions in which one god or another reveals what he is. If we open the Homeric poems, e.g., we find there scarcely any important event which is not more clearly elucidated as proceeding from the will or actual aid of the gods. These interpretations are the product of the insight, the self-wrought faith, the intuition of the poets, since Homer after all often expresses them in his own name, and only occasionally puts them into the mouth of his characters, the priests or the heroes. For example, right at the beginning of the *Iliad* (i. 9-12) he has accounted for the plague in the Greek camp by the indignation of Apollo at Agamemnon's refusal to release Chryseis to her father Chryses, and then later (94-100) makes Calchas announce the same interpretation to the Greeks.

In a similar way, in the last book of the *Odyssey* (xxiv. 41-63) when Hermes has conducted the souls of the suitors to the asphodel meadows and there they find Achilles and the other heroes who fought before Troy, and when finally Agamemnon too approaches them, Homer tells how Agamemnon sketches the death of Achilles: 'All day the Greeks had fought and only when Zeus separated the combatants did they bear the noble corpse to the ships with many tears, wash it and anoint it. Then there burst forth on the sea a divine uproar, and the terrified Achaeans were ready to flock to their hollow ships, had they not been kept back by a man learned in ancient and many things, Nestor, whose counsel earlier had seemed the best.' He explains the phenomenon to them by saying: 'The mother [Thetis] yonder comes forth from the sea with the immortal sea-nymphs in order to meet with her dead son. At this saying the great-hearted Achaeans lost their fear.' Now, that is, they knew where they were: this was something human, the mother, mourning, meets her son, and it was only what they themselves were that struck their eye and ear. Achilles is her son, she herself is full of grief. And so after all Agamemnon, turning to Achilles, continues his sketch with a description of the universal grief: 'But around thee', he says, 'stand the daughters of the Father of the Sea, lamenting and clad in ambrosial garments; the Muses too, all nine, wailed by turns in beautiful song and then indeed no Argives were seen without tears, so moved were they by the clear-toned song.'

But above all in this connection another divine appearance in the Odyssey has every time fascinated and preoccupied me. In his wanderings amongst the Phaeacians, Odysseus was taunted by Euryalus on the occasion of the games because he had declined to take part in the competition for discus-throwing; aroused, he answered with black looks and harsh words. Then he stands up, grasps the quoit that is bigger and heavier than all the others, and flings it far over the mark. One of the Phaeacians marks the place and calls to him: 'Even a blind man can see the stone; it does not lie mingled with the others but far beyond them; in this competition thou hast nothing to fear, no Phaeacian will reach or surpass thy throw.' So he spake, but the much-enduring divine Odysseus was delighted (viii. 159-200) to see in the contest a well-disposed friend. This word, the friendly nod of a Phaeacian, Homer attributes to the friendly appearance of Athene [in the shape of the Phaeacian].

(b) *The New Gods of the Classical Ideal*

Now the further question arises, what are the products of this classical mode of artistic activity, of what sort are the new gods of Greek art?

(α) The most general and at the same time the most perfect idea of their nature is afforded by their concentrated individuality; their individuality has pulled itself together out of the variety of appendages, single actions and events into the one focus of its simple unity with itself.

(αα) What impresses us about these gods is in the first place the spiritual *substantial* individuality which, withdrawn into itself out of the motley show of the particularity of need and the unrest of the finite with its variety of purposes, rests secure on its own universality as on an eternal and clear foundation. Only thereby do the gods appear as the eternal powers whose untroubled dominion comes into view, not in the sphere of the particular, entangled with something other than and external to them, but in their own unalterability and intrinsic worth.

(ββ) Conversely, however, they are not by any means the pure abstraction of spiritual universalities and therefore so called universal ideals; on the contrary, because they are individuals they appear as an ideal which has existence and therefore determinacy in itself, and which, i.e. as spirit, has *character*. Without character no individuality comes on the scene. In this respect, as has already been expounded [on pp. 471–5], even the spiritual gods have as their basis a specific natural power with which a specific ethical substance is fused and which assigns to each god a limited sphere for his more exclusive activity. The manifold aspects and traits which enter on account of this particularity constitute, when reduced to simple unity, the character of the gods.

(γγ) Yet neither, in the true Ideal, may this determinacy terminate in a sharp restriction to *one-sidedness* of character but must equally appear as drawn back again into the universality of the Divine. In this way, since each god bears in himself the determinate attribute of being a divine and therewith universal individual, he is partly a determinate character and partly all in all, and he hovers in the very middle between pure universality and equally abstract particularity. This gives to the genuine ideal figure of classical art infinite security and peace, untroubled bliss and untrammelled freedom.

(β) Now further, by being beauty in classical art, the inherently determinate divine character appears not only spiritually but also externally in its bodily form, i.e. in a shape visible to the eye as well as to the spirit.

(αα) Since this beauty has for its content not only a spiritual personification of the natural and the animal but the spiritual itself in its adequate existence, it may only incidentally assume the *symbolical* form and what is related to the purely natural; its proper expression is the external shape peculiar to spirit, and to spirit alone, in so far as what lies within spirit brings itself into existence in that shape and permeates it completely.

(ββ) On the other hand, classical beauty must not be called 'sublime'. For what alone has the look of the sublime is the abstract universal which never coincides with itself in anything determinate; on the contrary, its attitude to the particular in general, and therefore to every embodiment also, is *purely* negative. But classical beauty carries spiritual individuality right into the midst of what is at the same time its natural existence and unfolds the inner only in the medium of external appearance.

(γγ) On this account, however, the external shape, like the spirit which fashions an existence for itself there, must be freed from every accident of external determinacy, from every dependence on nature, and from morbidity; it must be withdrawn from all finitude, everything transient, all preoccupation with what is purely sensuous; its determinacy, closely allied with the determinate spiritual character of the god, must be purified and elevated into a free harmony with the universal forms of the human shape. Only flawless externality, from which every trait of weakness and relativity has been obliterated and every tiny spot of capricious particularity extinguished, corresponds to the spiritual inwardness which is to immerse itself in it and therein attain an embodiment.

(γ) But while the gods are at the same time reflected back from their determinacy of character into universality, there must be displayed at the same time in their appearance the self-subsistence of spirit as well as its self-repose and self-security in its opposite.

(αα) Therefore in the concrete individuality of the gods as it is conceived in the properly classical Ideal we see all the same this nobility and this loftiness of spirit in which, despite spirit's entire absorption in the bodily and sensuous shape, there is revealed to us its distance from all the deficiency of the finite. Pure inwardness and abstract liberation from every kind of determinacy would lead to sublimity; but since the classical Ideal issues in an existence which is only its own, i.e. the existence of spirit itself, the sublimity of the Ideal too is fused into beauty and has passed over into it, as it were immediately. For the shapes of the gods this necessitates the expression of loftiness, of classical *beautiful* sublimity. An immortal seriousness, an unchangeable peace is enthroned on the brow of the gods and is suffused over their whole shape.

(ββ) In their beauty these gods appear therefore raised above their own corporeality, and thus there arises a divergence between their blessed loftiness, which is a spiritual inwardness, and their beauty, which is external and corporeal. The spirit appears entirely immersed in its external form and yet at the same time immersed thence into itself. It is like the wandering of an immortal god amongst mortal men.

In this connection the Greek gods produce an impression, despite all difference, similar to that made on me by Rauch's[1] bust of Goethe when I first saw it. You too have seen it, this lofty brow, this powerful commanding nose, the free eye, the round chin, the affable and well-formed lips, the intelligent placing of the head with a glance sideways and a little upwards; and at the same time the whole fullness of sensitive friendly humanity, and in addition these finished muscles of the forehead and face, [expressive of the] feelings and passions, and, in all the vitality of the bust, the peace, stillness, and majesty of an elderly man; and now along with this the leanness of the lips which retreat into a toothless mouth, the looseness of the neck and cheeks whereby the bridge of the nose appears still greater and the sides of the forehead still higher.—The power of this fixed shape which at bottom suggests immutability especially, looks, in its loosely hanging mantle, like the raised head and the shape of the Oriental in his wide turban but loose outer garments and shuffling slippers; it is the firm, powerful, and timeless spirit which, in the mask of encircling mortality, is on the point of letting this veil fall away and still lets it just hang freely around itself.

In a similar way the gods too, in virtue of this lofty freedom and spiritual peace, appear as raised above their body so that they feel their shape, their limbs, as if they were a superfluous appendage, amidst all the beauty and perfection of their figures. And yet the whole shape is vitally ensouled, identical with spiritual being, without any division, without that separation between what is inherently fixed and the weaker parts, the spirit neither escaping the body nor emergent from it, but both one solid whole out of which the inwardness of the spirit quietly peeps solely in the wonderful certainty of itself.

(γγ) But since the above-mentioned divergence is present, yet without appearing as a difference and separation between inner spirituality and its external shape, the negative inherent in it is on this account immanent in this undivided *whole* and expressed therein itself. Within the loftiness of the spirit this is the breath and air of affliction which gifted men have felt in the ancient pictures

---

[1] C. D. Rauch, 1777–1857. There are several copies of this bust. Hegel probably refers to the bronze one in Berlin (1822).

of the gods even in their consummate beauty and loveliness. The repose of divine serenity may not be particularized into joy, pleasure, and contentment, and the peace of the eternal must not sink into the laughter of self-satisfaction and comfortable enjoyment. Contentment is the feeling of correspondence between our individual self and the condition of our specific situation whether that be given to us or brought about by us. Napoleon, for example, has never more thoroughly expressed his contentment than when he had achieved some success by which the whole world showed itself discontented. For contentment is only the approval of my own being, acting, and doing, and the extreme of this approval can be recognized in that Philistine feeling to which every successful man must rise! But this feeling and its expression is not the expression of the plastic eternal gods. Free perfect beauty cannot be satisfied in compliance with a specific finite existence; on the contrary, although its individuality, whether of spirit or shape, is characteristic and specific in itself, it still coincides with itself only as being at once free universality and self-reposing spirituality.

This universality is what in the case of the Greek gods some have proposed to accuse of frigidity. However, they are cold only for our modern fervour in the sphere of the finite; regarded by themselves, they have warmth and life; the blissful peace mirrored in their body is essentially an abstraction from the particular, an indifference to the transient, a sacrifice of the external, a renunciation neither sorrowful nor painful, yet all the same a renunciation of the earthly and evanescent, just as their spiritual serenity in its depth looks far away beyond death, the grave, loss, and time, and, precisely because it is deep, contains the negative in itself. But the more that seriousness and spiritual freedom appear in the shapes of the gods, so much the more can we feel a contrast between (a) this loftiness and (b) determinacy and bodily form. The blessed gods mourn as it were over their blessedness or their bodily form. We read in their faces the fate that awaits them, and its development, as the actual emergence of that contradiction between loftiness and particularity, between spirituality and sensuous existence, drags classical art itself to its ruin.

(c) *The Sort of External Representation*

If, thirdly, we now ask about the sort of external portrayal adequate to that concept of the classical Ideal which we have just expounded, the essential points in this matter have already been expounded in more detail in connection with our consideration of the Ideal in general. Here therefore we need say no more than that in the strictly classical Ideal the spiritual individuality of the gods is not apprehended in its bearing on something else nor is it brought, through its particularization, into conflict and battle; on the contrary, it appears before us in its eternal self-repose and in this sorrow of the divine peace. The specific character [of the gods] is therefore not manifested by way of its provoking the gods to particular feelings and passions or compelling them to carry out specific aims. On the contrary, they are brought back out of every collision and complication, indeed out of every relation to what is finite and inherently discordant, into pure absorption in themselves. This most austere repose, not rigid, cold, and dead, but sensitive and immutable, is the highest and most adequate form of portrayal for the classical gods. On this account, if they enter into specific situations, then these may not be circumstances or actions which give an opening to conflicts, but such as, being harmless in themselves, leave the harmlessness of the gods also untouched. Amongst the particular arts, therefore, sculpture is above all adapted to represent the classical Ideal in its simple unity with itself, in which what is to come into appearance is universal divinity rather than particular character. It is especially the older, more austere, sculpture which adheres to this aspect of the Ideal, and only later does sculpture proceed to an increased dramatic liveliness of situations and characters. Poetry, on the other hand, makes the gods act, which means relating themselves negatively to an existent, and thereby introduces them to battle and strife also. When the repose of plastic art remains within the sphere that is uniquely that art's own, it can express that feature of the spirit which is its negative relation to particulars, only in that seriousness of mourning which we have already indicated above [in (b)] in more detail.

2. The Group of Particular Gods

As individuality made visible, portrayed in immediate existence, and therefore specific and particular, the Godhead necessarily becomes a *plurality* of shapes. Polytheism is absolutely essential to the principle of classical art, and it would be a foolish undertaking to propose to shape in plastic beauty the one god of sublimity and pantheism or of that absolute religion[1] which apprehends God as spiritual and purely inner personality, or to suppose that, in the case of the Jews, Mohammedans, or Christians, their original outlook could have produced the classical forms for the content of their religious faith, as happened in the case of the Greeks.

(a) Plurality of Individual Gods

In this plurality the universe of the Divine at this stage bursts asunder into a group of particular gods, each of which is an independent individual and contrasted with the others. But these individuals are not of such a kind as to be taken merely as allegories of universal qualities, e.g. Apollo as god of knowledge, Zeus of dominion; on the contrary, Zeus is knowledge just as much, and Apollo in the *Eumenides*, as we saw, also protects Orestes, the son, the *king's son*, whom he himself had stimulated to vengeance. The group of Greek gods is a plurality of individuals in which each single god, even if endowed with the specific character of a particular person, is still a comprehensive totality, containing also in itself the attribute of another god. For every shape, as Divine, is always also the whole. For this reason alone do the Greek individual gods have a wealth of characteristics, and although their blessedness consists in their universal and spiritual self-repose and in their abstraction from the direct bent towards finitude and towards the dispersive manifold of things and relations, still they have all the same the power to evince themselves as active and effective in various ways. They are neither the abstract particular nor the abstract universal, but the universal which is the source of the particular.

(b) Lack of a Systematic Arrangement

But on account of this kind of individuality Greek polytheism cannot form a *systematically* organized totality in itself. At a first glance it seems imperative to demand of divine Olympus that the many gods assembled there must in their ensemble, if the particularization of that ensemble is to have truth and its content to be classical, also express in themselves the totality of the Idea, exhaust the whole range of the necessary powers of nature and spirit, and be construed from that angle, i.e. be demonstrable as

---

[1] i.e. Christianity. 'Absolute Religion' is the title of the third and last part of Hegel's lectures on the Philosophy of Religion.

necessary. But in that case this demand would at once have to be accompanied by a limitation because those powers of the heart and the absolute spiritual inner life in general, which only become effective in later and higher religion, remained excluded from the sphere of the classical gods, so that, for this reason, the scope of the content whose particular aspects could be brought before contemplation in Greek mythology was already diminished. But, this apart, on the one hand the inherently manifold character of individuality necessarily entails contingency in determining [viz., here, the forms of particular gods], and therefore determining them is not susceptible of the strict arrangement characteristic of the differences within the Concept because this contingency precludes the gods from being immobilized in the abstraction of a *single* determinacy; on the other hand, universality, the element in which the individual gods have their blessed existence, cancels fixed particularity, and the loftiness of the eternal powers rises serenely over the cold seriousness of the finite. In default of this inconsistency, the divine shapes would be implicated in the finite by their restrictedness.

(c) Fundamental Character of the Group of the Gods

However far, therefore, the chief powers of the world, i.e. of the totality of nature and spirit, are portrayed in Greek mythology, this ensemble still cannot come on the scene as a *systematic* whole, because the gods possess both universal divinity and also individuality. Otherwise, instead of being *individual* characters, the gods would be more like allegorical beings, and instead of being *divine* individuals would in the end become restricted abstract characters.

Therefore, if we consider more closely the group of the Greek divinities, i.e. the group of the so-called chief gods in their simple fundamental character as it appears consolidated by sculpture in a portrayal which is most universal and yet sensuously concrete, we do find the essential differences and their totality settled, but in particulars they are also always confused again and the rigour of the execution is tempered to an inconsistency between beauty and individuality. Thus Zeus has in his hands dominion over gods and men, yet without thereby essentially jeopardizing the free independence of the other gods. He is the supreme god, but his power does not absorb the power of the others. He has a connection with the sky, with thunder and lightning, and with the generative life of nature, but still more, and more properly, he is the power over the state and the legal order of things; he is too the obligatoriness of contracts, oaths, and hospitality, and in short he is the bond of the substance of human, practical, and ethical life, and the might of knowing and the spirit. His brothers turn [for dominion] outward to the sea and beneath to the underworld. Apollo appears as the god of knowledge, as the expression and beautiful presentation of the interests of the spirit, as the teacher of the Muses; 'Know thyself' is the inscription on his temple at Delphi, a command which does not relate at all to the weaknesses and deficiencies of the spirit but to its essence and to art and every genuine consciousness. Cunning and eloquence, mediation in general as it appears in those subordinate spheres which, although mixed with immoral elements, are yet within the scope of the perfect spirit—all these are a chief territory of Hermes who also conducts the souls of the dead to the underworld. Power over war is a chief trait of Ares. Hephaestus proves himself skilled in work in technical arts. And the enthusiasm which still carries in itself an element of the natural, the enthusing natural power of wine, as well as the games, dramatic productions, etc. are assigned to Dionysus. The female divinities run through a similar series of characteristics. In Juno the ethical bond of wedlock is a principal characteristic; Ceres has taught and propagated agriculture and therefore endowed man with both the aspects inherent in agriculture: first, provision for the growth of the natural products which satisfy man's most immediate needs, but, secondly, the spiritual element in property, wedlock, law, the beginnings of civilization and an ethical order. So too Athene is moderation, prudence, legality, the might of wisdom, technical skill, and bravery, and in her intelligent and warlike maidenhood embraces the concrete spirit of the people, the free proper substantial spirit of the city of Athens, and displays it objectively as a ruling might to be reverenced as divine. Diana [i.e. Artemis], on the other hand, entirely different from Diana of the Ephesians, has the inflexible independence of maidenly modesty as her essential trait of character; she loves the chase and is in general not the quietly pensive but the austere maiden with aspirations only beyond. Aphrodite with the seductive Amor, who out of the old Titanic Eros has become a boy, points to the human emotion of affection, sexual love, etc.

This is the sort of content possessed by the spiritually shaped individual gods. As for their external portrayal, we may here again mention sculpture as the art which proceeds even to this particularization of the gods. Yet if it expresses individuality in its more specific determinacy, it already passes beyond its original austere loftiness, although it does even then unify the variety and wealth of individuality into *one* determinacy, into what we call character; and it fixes this character, in its simpler clarity, for sense-perception, i.e. fixes it in divine shapes as what is externally most completely and finally determinate. For the imagination of the gods in respect of their external and real existence always remains vague, even if, as poetry, it develops the subject-matter into a mass of stories, utterances, and events connected with the gods. Therefore sculpture is on the one hand more ideal, while on the other hand it individualizes the character of the gods into an entirely specific human form and perfects the anthropomorphism of the classical Ideal. As this presentation of the Ideal in that externality which yet is entirely adequate to the inner essential content, the sculptures of the Greeks are the Ideals in and for themselves, the independent eternal shapes, the centre of plastic classical beauty, the type of which remains the basis even when these shapes enter into specific actions and appear involved in particular events.

3. *The Individuality of the Gods* seriatim

But individuality and its portrayal cannot be content with the ever still more or less abstract particularity of character. The star is exhausted by its simple law and brings this law into appearance; a few specific traits characterize the configuration of the world of rocks; but already in the nature of plants there arises an infinite copiousness of the most diversified forms, transitions, hybrids, and anomalies; animal organisms display a still greater range of difference and of interaction with the surroundings to which they are related; and if, finally, we rise to the spiritual and its appearance, we find a still infinitely wider many-sidedness of inner and outer existence. Now since the classical Ideal does not abide by the individuality that reposes in itself but has to set it in motion, bring it into relation with an opposite and show itself effective thereon, the character of the gods too does not stop at inherently *substantial* determinacy but enters into further particularizations. This self-revealing movement into external existence and the mutability bound up with it provide only the more obvious traits for the individuality of each god as they properly and necessarily do for a living individual. But with this sort of individuality there is bound up at the same time the contingency of the particular traits which are no longer brought back to the universal element in the substantial meaning; therefore this particular aspect of the individual gods becomes something laid down arbitrarily which on this account may only surround them as an external accessory and re-echo within them.

(a) Material for Individualization

Therefore at once the question arises: Whence comes the *material* for this mode of appearance of the gods as individuals, how do they progress in their particularization? For an actual human individual, for his character out of the resources of which he accomplishes his actions, for the events in which he is involved, for the fate in which he is caught, the positive material closer at hand is afforded by external circumstances, the date of his birth, his inborn aptitudes, his parents, education, surroundings, contemporary events, the whole range of relevant inner and outer circumstances. This material is contained in the present world, and, this considered, the biographies of individual men will vary from one another in the most manifold ways every time. But it is otherwise with the free figures of the gods which have no existence in concrete reality but are the product of imagination. But therefore we might believe that the poets and artists, who fashioned the Ideal in general out of their freedom of spirit, derived the material for accidental details purely from the subjective caprice of imagination. Yet this idea is false. For the position we gave to classical art in general was that only through reaction against the presuppositions belonging of necessity to its sphere was it elevated to what it is as genuinely Ideal. From these presuppositions there are spelt out the special particular characteristics which fashion for the gods their more detailed individual life. The chief factors in these presuppositions have already been cited, and here we have only to refer briefly to what was said earlier [on pp. 440–4].

(α) The primary abundant source is supplied by the symbolical nature religions. These serve Greek mythology with the basis which is transformed within it. But since such borrowed traits are here apportioned to the gods now represented as spiritual individuals, they must essentially lose the character of counting as symbols;

for now they may no longer preserve a meaning different from what the individual is himself and what he brings to light. The earlier symbolic content, therefore, now becomes the content of a divine subject himself, and since it does not concern the substantial nature of the god but only his incidental particular character, such material falls to the level of an external story, an act or an event which is ascribed to the will of the gods in this or that particular situation. So there enter here again all the symbolical traditions of earlier sacred literature and they assume, transformed into the actions of a subjective individual, the form of human events and stories which are supposed to have happened to the gods and cannot at all have been merely invented by the poets at will. When Homer,[1] e.g., tells us that the gods went off on a journey to feast for twelve days together amongst the blameless Ethiopians, this as a pure fancy of the poet would be a poor invention. The same is true of the narrative [Hesiod, 453 ff.] of the birth of Zeus. Cronus, it is said, devoured all the children he had begotten, so that now when Rhea, his spouse, was pregnant with Zeus the youngest, she went off to Crete; there she bore her son, but what she gave to Cronus to devour was not the child but a stone swaddled in a skin. Then later Cronus vomited up all his children again, his daughters and Poseidon too. This story, as an artist's invention, would be silly; but the remains of symbolic meanings peep through, which yet, having lost their symbolic character, appear as a purely external event. It is the same with the story of Ceres and Proserpine. Here there is the old symbolic meaning of the dying and the burgeoning of the seed-corn. The myth represents this as follows: Proserpine played with flowers in a valley and plucked the fragrant narcissus which from one root sprouted a hundred blooms. Then the earth heaves. Pluto comes up out of the ground, puts the lamenting maiden into his golden chariot and carries her off to the underworld. Now Ceres in her maternal grief wanders over the earth for a long while in vain. At last Proserpine returns to the upper world, but Zeus has allowed this, subject only to the condition that Proserpine has not yet eaten the food of the gods. But unfortunately she had once eaten a pomegranate in Elysium and therefore could pass only spring and summer in the upper world. Here too the general meaning has not preserved its symbolic shape but is worked up into a human event which only lets the universal

[1] *Iliad*, i. 423 ff.

sense shine from afar through the numerous external details. In the same way the cognomina of the gods often hint at such symbolic bases but these have been stripped of their symbolic form and only serve to give a fuller characterization to the individual god.

(β) Another source of the positive particular characterization of the individual gods is provided by relations to localities. These concern both the origin of ideas about the gods and also the advent and introduction of their service and the different places where their worship was chiefly to be found.

(αα) Therefore although the portrayal of the Ideal and its universal beauty is raised above a particular locality and its special character, and although it has drawn together the external details contained in the universality of the artistic imagination into a total picture wholly in correspondence with the substantial meaning, still, when sculpture brings the individual gods into separated connections and relations, these particular traits and local colours always play their part again in order to manifest something of that individuality, though something more specific only externally. Pausanias, e.g., cites a number of such local ideas, images, pictures, tales, which he had seen, or had had brought to his notice otherwise, in temples, public places, temple treasures, in regions where something important had occurred. On the same lines, similarly, localities and old traditions drawn from abroad run into native ones in the Greek myths, and all of them are more or less given a relation to the history, birth, and foundation of states, especially through colonization. But since this diverse special material in the universality of the gods has lost the meaning it originally had, the consequence is that stories arise which are varied and outrageous and for us remain without sense. So, e.g., Aeschylus in his *Prometheus* presents the wanderings of Io [ll. 788 ff.] in their whole harshness and externality like a stone bas-relief, without alluding to an ethical, historical, or natural meaning. The same is the case with Perseus, Dionysus, etc., but especially with Zeus, his nurses, his infidelities to Hera whom after all he incidentally hung with an anvil on her legs and made her swing between heaven and earth.[1] In Hercules too the most diverse and varied material is brought together, and then in such stories it assumes a thoroughly human look in the form of accidental events, deeds, passions, misfortunes, and other occurrences.

[1] Cf. above, p. 224, note.

(ββ) Apart from this, the eternal powers in classical art are the universal substances in the actual shape of the *human* world and action of the Greeks; therefore many particular remains of this world's original national beginnings, from the Heroic Age and other traditions, cling to the gods even in later days. After all, many traits in the various stories of the gods certainly hint at historical individuals, heroes, older races, natural events, and occurrences concerning battles, wars, and other sorts of affairs. And just as the family and the difference of clans is the starting-point of the state, so the Greeks also had their family gods, Penates, tribal gods, and moreover the protective deities of single cities and states. But in connection with this pointing to history the thesis is advanced that the origin of the Greek gods in general is to be derived from such historical facts, heroes, or ancient kings. This is a plausible view, but a superficial one, even in the form in which Heyne has once again given it currency in recent times. In an analogous way, a Frenchman, Nicolas Fréret,[1] has adopted as a general principle underlying the war of the gods, e.g. the quarrels of different priesthoods. That such an historical factor plays its part here, that certain clans have made their views of the Divine prevail, that like-wise different localities have provided traits for the individualiza-tion of the gods, all this is of course to be granted; but the real origin of the gods lies not in this external historical material, but in the spiritual powers that govern life, and it is as such that the gods have been conceived. From this point of view a wider scope may be allowed to the positive, local, and historical factors only for the sake of making the presentation of single individuality more specific.

(γγ) Now further, since the god enters human ideas and, still more clearly, is portrayed by sculpture in a bodily and real shape to which man then relates himself afresh in religion and the acts of divine worship, this relationship provides a new material for portrayal within the sphere of the arbitrary and contingent. For example, what animals or fruits are sacrificed to each god, in what attire priests and people appear, in what sequence the particular actions proceed, all this piles up into single traits of the most various kinds. For each such action has an infinite mass of aspects and external features which, accidental in themselves, might be this or something else; but by belonging to a sacred action they are meant to be something fixed, not arbitrary, and to pass over

[1] 1688–1749.

into the sphere of the symbolic. In this context there falls, e.g., the colour of the clothing, in the case of Bacchus wine-colour, and also the deerskin in which those to be initiated into the Mysteries were veiled. The clothing and attributes of the gods, the bow of the Pythian Apollo, the whip, the staff, and innumerable other externals also have their place here. Yet such things gradually become just customary; in the practice of his religion no one thinks any longer of the ultimate origin of these things; and while by way of a little erudition we might exhibit their meaning, they still remain a mere external affair in which a man participates out of an immediate interest, a frolic, a pleasantry, a momentary pleasure, devotion, or because it is purely customary, immediately established thus, and participated in by others too. When in Germany, e.g., young people light St. John's fire[1] in the summer-time or gambol elsewhere or throw things at windows, this is a purely external usage in which the proper meaning has been relegated to the background, just as it has been too in the case of the festal dances of Greek youths and maidens where the interlacings of the dance and their figures imitate the criss-cross movements of the planets, as the twists and turns of a labyrinth do also. We do not dance in order to think about what we are doing; interest is restricted to the dance and the tasteful and charming solemnity of its beautiful movement. The whole meaning which was the original basis of the thing, and the portrayal of which for imagination and sense-perception was of a symbolic character, therefore becomes an imaginative idea in general, the details of which we can accept with pleasure as we accept a fairy-tale or as we accept in historiography a specific action in the external world of time and space; and in these cases we can only say 'It is said, so the tale goes' or 'It *is* so', etc. The interest of art can therefore only consist in picking out one aspect of this material which has become something positive and external, and making out of it something which sets the gods before our eyes as concrete living individuals and still carries no more than echoes of a deeper meaning.

This positive element, worked on anew by imagination, gives to the Greek gods precisely the attraction of living men, since thereby what is otherwise purely substantial and mighty is drawn into the individual present, a present compacted as such of what is absolutely true and what is external and accidental; and the indeterminate

[1] Fires lit on hill-tops to celebrate St. John the Baptist's Day, 24 June.

element, otherwise always implicit in the idea of the gods, is more closely defined and more richly filled. But no further value can be attributed to detailed stories and particular characteristics; for this material, which earlier on had a symbolic significance in its ultimate origin, is now only there for the purpose of perfecting the spiritual individuality of the gods in contrast to men by making it determinate for perception and adding to it through this element, undivine in content and appearance, the aspect of arbitrariness and contingency which belongs to the concrete individual. Since sculpture brings the ideal gods before our vision in their purity and has to portray character and expression in a living body alone, it is least able to make the final external individualization appear visibly, yet it does assert this even in its own sphere: as, e.g., the head-dress, the sort of coiffure and locks, are different for every god and are not there at all for symbolic purposes, but for more detailed individualization. So, e.g., Hercules has short locks, Zeus an abundant growth rising upwards, Diana a different curl of the hair from Venus; Pallas has the Gorgon on her helmet, and this sort of thing runs through weapons, girdles, scarves, bracelets, and the most varied externals in the same way.

(γ) Now finally, a *third* source of the closer determinacy [of their individuality] the gods acquire through their relation to the present concrete world and its varied natural phenomena and human deeds and events. For just as we have seen spiritual individuality, partly in its universal essence, partly in its particular singleness, emerging from earlier symbolically significant natural bases and human activities, so now, as a spiritually independent personality, it also remains in a steadily living relation to nature and human existence. Here, as has already been brought out above, the poet's imagination gushes forth as the steadily prolific source of particular stories, character traits, and deeds reported of the gods. The artistic aspect of this stage consists in vitally interweaving the individual gods with human actions and gathering up the individual aspects of events into the universality of the Divine; just as we too say, e.g., of course in a different sense: this or that fate comes from God. Already in everyday life the Greek in the complications of his existence, in his needs, his fears, and his hopes took refuge in his gods. Therefore it was in the first place external accidents which the priests regarded as omens and interpreted in their bearing on human purposes and situations. If distress and misfortune actually occur, the priest has to explain the reason for the affliction, recognize the wrath and will of the gods, and proclaim the means of meeting the misfortune. Now the poets go still further in their explanations, because what concerns the universal and essential 'pathos', the moving power in human decisions and actions, they ascribe for the most part to the gods and their deed, so that human activity appears at the same time as the deed of the gods who bring their decisions to execution through men. The material in the case of these poetic interpretations is drawn from everyday circumstances in respect of which the poet explains whether it is this or that god who is speaking in the event portrayed and showing himself active within it. In this way poetry especially enlarges the range of the many detailed stories told of the gods.

In this connection we may recall a few examples which in a different context[1] have already served as illustrations in our treatment of the relation between the universal powers and human individual agents. Homer represents Achilles as the bravest of the Greeks before Troy. This pre-eminence of the hero he expresses by saying that Achilles is invulnerable in every part of his body except the ankle by which his mother had to hold him when she dipped him in the Styx. This story belongs to the imagination of the poet who is interpreting external fact. But if we take it as if it was supposed to be the expression of an actual fact which the ancients would have believed in as we believe in a fact on the evidence of our senses, this is an entirely crude idea which makes Homer, as well as all the Greeks and Alexander (who admired Achilles [according to Plutarch] and praised his good fortune in having had Homer as his bard) into simpletons; as Adelung[2] does e.g. through his reflection that bravery was not difficult for Achilles because he knew of his invulnerability. But in this way the true bravery of Achilles is by no means lessened since he knew also of his early death and yet never evaded danger wherever it lay.

A like situation is sketched quite differently in the *Nibelungenlied*. There [§ 6] the horned Siegfried is likewise invulnerable but besides he has his cap which makes him invisible. When in this invisibility he helps King Gunther in his contest with Brunhilde [§ 7], this is only the work of a crude barbaric wizardry which does not enhance our idea of the bravery of either Siegfried or King Gunther.

Of course in Homer the gods often act for the safety of individual

[1] pp. 225–36.   [2] J. C., 1732–1806.

heroes, but the gods appear only as the universal element in what the man is and achieves as an individual when he has to act with the whole energy of his heroic character. Otherwise the gods need only have slaughtered the whole of the Trojans in the battle in order to give the maximum aid to the Greeks. Whereas, when Homer describes the chief battle, he sketches in full the fights of individuals; and it is only when the scuffle and confusion become general, when the whole masses, the collective courage of the hosts, rage against one another that Ares himself storms across the field and gods are fighting against gods [*Iliad*, xx. 51 ff.]. And this is fine and splendid, not, as might be supposed, a mere heightening of the effect in general; on the contrary there is implicit the deeper point that in what is individual and distinctive Homer recognizes the individual heroes, but in the ensemble and the universal the universal mights and powers.

In another connection (ibid., xvi. 783–849) Homer makes Apollo appear too when it comes to the killing of Patroclus who wears the invincible armour of Achilles. Comparable to Ares, Patroclus thrice rushed into the Trojan host and thrice nine men had he slain. Then as he stormed in a fourth time, the god [Apollo], veiled in thick mist, wanders through the mêlée to confront him and smites him on the back and shoulders, tears his helmet from him, so that it rolled on the ground and clearly re-echoed from the hooves of the horses, and the plumes were soiled with blood and dust, a thing unthinkable before at any time. The god also breaks the brazen lance in the hands of Patroclus, slips his shield from his shoulders, and even deprives him of his breastplate.—This intervention of Apollo we may take as a poetic explanation of the fact that it is exhaustion, as if it were a natural death, which seizes on Patroclus and overpowers him in the tumult and heat of the battle at his fourth onrush.—Only now can Euphorbus pierce Patroclus' back between the shoulders with a lance; Patroclus did once try to withdraw from the battle, but Hector overtook him and thrust his spear deep into the softness of his belly. Then Hector exults and mocks him as he is sinking; but Patroclus, with a weak voice, retorts to him: 'Zeus and Apollo have overcome me without trouble because they have taken the arms from my shoulders; twenty men such as thou art would I have laid low with my lance, but pernicious fate and Apollo killed me, Euphorbus a second time, and thou, Hector, a third.'

Here too the appearance of the gods is only the interpretation of the fact that, although Patroclus was protected by the arms of Achilles, he wearies, is stunned, and is killed. And this is not, as may be supposed, a superstition or idle play of fancy; indeed it is just chatter if it is held that Hector's fame is diminished by Apollo's entry on the ground that, since all that we can think of in the narrative is the god's power throughout the affair, Apollo does not exactly play the most honourable part—such reflections are only a tasteless and idle superstition of the prosaic intellect. For in every case where Homer explains special events by such theophanies, the gods are what is immanent in man himself, the power of his own passion and reflection, or the powers of his situation generally, the power and the ground of what meets him and happens to him as a result of this situation. If occasionally too there are quite external, purely positive, traits in the appearance of the gods, then they become assimilated to jokes as, e.g., when the limping Hephaestus goes round as cup-bearer at a feast of the gods. But in general Homer is not in the last resort serious with these theophanies; at one time the gods act, at another they remain quite inactive again. The Greeks knew perfectly well that it was the poets who created these appearances; and if they believed in them, their belief touched on the spiritual which even so dwells in man's own spirit and is the universal actually effective and moving in present events. For all these reasons we need not bring any superstition with us to the enjoyment of this poetic portrayal of the gods.

(b) *Preservation of the Moral Basis*

This is the general character of the classical Ideal; its further development we will have to consider in connection with the individual arts [in Part III]. At this point all that need be added is the remark that however much gods and men get involved in the external world and its detail, still in classical art the affirmative moral basis must appear maintained. The subject always remains in unity with the substantial content of his power. While in Greek art the natural preserves a harmony with the spiritual and likewise is subordinate to the inner life even when it is an existent adequate thereto, still the subjective inner life of man is always presented in solid identity with the genuine objectivity of spirit, i.e. with the essential content of the moral and the true. Viewed thus, the classical Ideal knows neither of a separation between inner life and external shape, nor of one between the subject distracted in his aims and passions and therefore at the mercy of abstract caprice, on the one hand, and the therefore abstract universal on the other. The basis of the characters must therefore always be what is substantial; and the bad, the sinful, and the evil of subjective self-centredness are excluded from the representations of classical art; but, above all, the harshness, wickedness, infamy, and hideousness which gain a place in romantic art remain altogether foreign to classical. We do see many instances of transgression, e.g. matricide, parricide, and other crimes against family love and piety, treated repeatedly as subjects in Greek art, yet not as mere horrors, or, as was the fashion with us recently, as caused by the irrationality of a so-called fate with the false appearance of necessity; on the contrary, when transgressions are committed by men and partly commanded and defended by the gods, such actions are every time represented one way or another as possessed of an actually immanent justification.

(c) *Advance to Grace and Attractiveness*

Despite this substantial basis, however, we have seen the general artistic development of the classical gods emerge more and more out of the tranquillity of the Ideal into the variety of individual and external appearance, into the detailing of events, happenings, and actions which become ever more and more human. Therefore classical art proceeds at last, in its *content* to completing the process of individualization and its contingency, in its *form* to the agreeable and the attractive. The agreeable, in other words, is the development of the individuality of the external appearance at its every point, whereby the work of art now no longer grips the spectator merely in respect of his own substantial inner life; but on the contrary it acquires a many-sided relation to him by addressing itself to the finitude of his own subjective character. For it is precisely in the existent work of art's involvement with the finite that there is implicit a closer connection with the spectator as such who is finite himself and who now without more ado finds himself again, and is satisfied, in the work of art. The seriousness of the gods becomes a gracefulness which does not agitate a man or lift him above his particular character but lets him remain at peace in it and claims only to please him. If, in general, imagination seizes upon religious ideas, and shapes them freely with beauty as its aim, it begins to make the seriousness of devotion disappear and to this extent damages religion as such. This is what happens at the stage we have reached here, mostly owing to the agreeable and the pleasant. For what is developed further through the agreeable is not the substantial at all, the meaning of the gods and their universal element; on the contrary, it is the finite aspect, sensuous existence and the subjective inner life, which are to arouse interest and give satisfaction. Therefore the more the charm of the thing portrayed preponderates in beauty, so much the more does the thing's gracefulness entice us away from the universal and alienate us from the content through which alone could satisfaction be given to the deeper immersion [of the soul in itself].

Now with this externality and the determinacy of individuality into which the shape of the gods is introduced, there is linked the transition to another sphere of the forms of art. For externality implies the variety produced by finitude which, if given free play, finally opposes the inner Idea and its universality and truth and begins to awaken thought's discontent with the reality which is given to it and which no longer corresponds with it.

Chapter III

THE DISSOLUTION OF THE CLASSICAL FORM OF ART

The germ of their decline the classical gods have in themselves, and when the deficiency implicit in them is revealed to our minds through the development of art itself they therefore bring in their train the dissolution of the classical Ideal. The principle of this Ideal, as it appears here, we have laid down as the spiritual individuality which finds its wholly adequate expression in an immediate corporeal and external existent. But this individuality broke up into a group of divine individuals whose determinate character is not absolutely necessary and therefore from the start is surrendered to the contingency in which the eternally powerful gods acquire alike for the Greek mind and for artistic representation the source of their dissolution.

1. *Fate*

Sculpture in its full excellence does adopt the gods as substantial powers and gives them a shape in the beauty of which they repose on themselves in security at first, because the last thing which comes into appearance there is the contingent character of their external embodiment. But their plurality and difference is their *contingency*, and thought dissolves this into the determinate conception of the *one* divinity under whose might and necessity they fight and degrade one another reciprocally. For however universally the power of each particular god may be conceived, this power, as particular individuality, is still always of only limited range. Apart from this, the gods do not persist in their eternal repose; they set themselves in motion with particular ends in view, because by the situations and collisions confronting them in concrete reality they are drawn hither and thither in order now to help here, now to hinder or destroy there. These separate relationships into which the gods enter as individual agents retain an aspect of contingency which obscures the substantiality of the Divine, however much that may remain also as the dominant basis, and lures the gods into the clashes and battles of the finite world and its restrictions. Through this finitude immanent in the gods themselves they become involved in a contradiction between their grandeur and dignity and the beauty of their existent embodiment, and this too brings them down into the field of caprice and contingency.

The complete emergence of this contradiction the Ideal proper only escapes because, as is the case with genuine sculpture and its separate statues in temples, the divine individuals are portrayed as solitary, alone with themselves in blessed repose, and yet they retain an air of lifelessness, an aloofness from feeling, and that tranquil trait of mourning which we have already touched on [on pp. 485–6]. It is this mourning which already constitutes their fate because it shows that something higher stands above them, and that a transition is necessary from their existence as particulars to their universal unity. But, looking around for the manner and shape of this higher unity, we find it, contrasted with the individuality and relative determinacy of the gods, in what is inherently abstract and shapeless, namely necessity, the fate which, in this abstraction, is just the higher in general that overpowers gods and men but remains in itself incomprehensible and inconceivable. Fate is not yet an absolute independent end and therefore at the same time a subjective, personal, divine decree, but only the one universal power which surpasses the particular character of the individual gods and therefore cannot itself be represented over again as an individual because otherwise it would only appear as one amongst many individuals and would descend to their level. Therefore it remains without configuration and individuality, and in this abstraction it is just necessity as such, the unalterable fate to which gods (and men too) must submit and which they must obey when, as particulars, they separate themselves from one another, contend with one another, assert their individual power one-sidedly, and seek to rise above their restricted sphere and authority.

2. Dissolution of the Gods through their Anthropomorphism

Now since absolute necessity is not an attribute of the individual gods, does not afford the content of their own self-determination, and only hovers over them as an indeterminate abstraction, the result is that the particular and individual side of them is at once given free play and it cannot evade the fate of running into the external characteristics involved in human life and the finitudes incidental to anthropomorphism; these pervert the gods into the reverse of what constitutes the essence of the substantial and Divine. The downfall of these beautiful gods of art is therefore necessitated purely by their own nature, since in the end the mind cannot any longer find rest in them and therefore turns back from them into itself. But, looked at more closely, the dissolution of the gods alike for religious and poetic faith is already implicit in the character of Greek anthropomorphism in general.

(a) *Deficiency in Inner Subjectivity*

For [in Greece the] spiritual individuality [of the gods] does enter, as Ideal, into the human shape, but into the immediate, i.e. corporeal, shape, not into humanity pure and simple [in our conception of it as that] which in its inner world of subjective consciousness does know itself as distinct from God, yet which all the same cancels this difference, and thereby, as one with God, is inherently infinite absolute subjectivity.

(α) Therefore the plastic Ideal lacks the aspect of being represented as inwardness knowing itself as infinite. The plastically beautiful shapes are not merely stone and bronze, but they lack in their content and expression the infinitely subjective element. While you may be as spiritually animated as you like by [Greek] beauty and art, this spiritual animation is and remains something subjective, not found in the object of your vision, i.e. in the [Greek] gods. But for true totality this aspect of subjective self-knowing unity and infinity is also required, because it alone constitutes the living and knowing God and man. If it is not also essentially given prominence as belonging to the content and nature of the Absolute, then the Absolute does not truly appear as a spiritual subject, but confronts our contemplation only in its objectivity without any conscious spirit of its own. Now it is true that the individuality of the gods does contain the element of subjectivity too, but as contingency and in a development explicitly actuated outside that substantial repose and blessedness of the gods.

(β) On the other side, the subjectivity which has the plastic gods as its opposite is also not the inherently infinite and true subjectivity. For this, as we shall see in more detail in the third form of art, the romantic, has confronting it as its corresponding object the inherently infinite self-knowing God. But since the subject at this present stage is not present to *itself* in the perfectly beautiful figures of the gods and, precisely on this account, does not in what it contemplates bring itself into consciousness as being objective too and as something confronting it, it is itself still only different and separate from its absolute object and therefore is just a contingent and finite subject.

(γ) The transition to a higher sphere, we might suppose, could possibly have been apprehended by imagination and art as a new war of the gods, like the original transition from the symbolism of nature gods to the spiritual Ideals of classical art. Yet the transition was by no means of this nature; on the contrary, it has been carried through on a totally different field as a conscious battle in the field of reality and the present. Consequently, in connection with the higher content which art has to embody in new forms, art acquires a totally different position. This new content is not validated as having been revealed by *art*, but is independently revealed without it; it enters subjective knowing, first on the prosaic ground of rational controversy, and then in the heart and its religious feelings, especially as a result of miracles, martyrdoms, etc.— together with a consciousness of the opposition of everything finite to the Absolute which is now revealed in actual history as a course of events leading to a present not merely imagined but factual. The Divine, God himself, has become flesh, was born, lived, suffered, died, and is risen. This is material which art did not invent; it was present outside art; consequently art did not derive it from its own resources but found it ready for configuration. That original transition and battle of the gods had its origin, on the contrary, in artistic intuition and imagination which drew its doctrines and shapes out of its own inner being and gave their new gods to astonished men. But, for this reason, the classical gods have acquired their existent embodiment only through human imagination and are there only in stone and bronze or in contemplation, but not in flesh and blood or actual spirit. Therefore the anthropomorphism of the Greek gods lacked actual human existence, whether corporeal or spiritual. Christianity alone introduces this actuality in flesh and spirit as the determinate existence, life, and effectiveness of God himself. Now therefore this body, this flesh, is brought into honour, however much the natural and sensuous is known as the negative, and anthropomorphism is sanctified. Just as man was originally the image of God [Gen. 1 : 26], God is the image of man, and who sees the Son sees the Father, who loves the

Son loves the Father also [John 14: 9, 21]; God is to be known in an actual human being. Thus this new material is not brought to our minds by the conceptions of art but is given to art from outside as an actual happening, as the history of God made flesh. This transition could not have taken its starting-point from art; the clash of old and new would have been too disparate. The God of revealed religion, both in content and form, is the truly actual God; precisely for this reason his opponents would be mere creatures of men's imagination and they could not be matched with him on any terrain. On the other hand, the old and new gods of classical art both belong explicitly to the ground of imagination; their only reality is to be apprehended and represented by the finite spirit as powers of nature and spirit, and their opposition and battle is a serious matter. But if the transition from the Greek gods to the God of Christianity had been brought about by art, there would immediately have been no true seriousness in the portrayal of a battle of the gods.

(b) *The Transition to Christianity is only a Topic of Modern Art*

Consequently, as it turns out, this strife and transition has only in more recent times become a casual and distinct topic for art, a topic which has been unable to mark an era or in this form to be a decisive feature in the entirety of the development of art. In this connection I will refer here by the way to a few publications that have become famous. In recent times a complaint about the downfall of classical art has often been heard, and the longing for the Greek gods and heroes has frequently provided a subject-matter for the poets too. This mourning is then expressed principally in opposition to Christianity; there was indeed a willingness to grant that Christianity contained a higher truth, but with the qualification that, so far as the standpoint of art went, the downfall of classical antiquity was only to be regretted. Schiller's *Götter Griechenlands* [Gods of Greece] contains this theme, and it is worth while here not only to consider this poem as a poem in its beautiful presentation, its resounding rhythm, its living pictures, or the beautiful mourning of the heart from which it proceeded, but to take up its contents also, because Schiller's 'pathos' is always both truly and deeply thought.

The Christian religion of course itself contains art as one of its features but in the course of its development up to the time of the

Enlightenment it also reached a point at which thinking, the intellect, suppressed the element that art certainly needs, namely God's actual human shape and appearance. For the human shape and what it expresses and says, whether human event, action, or feeling, is the form in which art must grasp and represent the content of the spirit. Now since the intellect made God into a mere *ens rationis*, believed no longer in the appearance of his spirit in concrete reality, and so exiled the God of thought from all actual existence, the result was that this sort of religious enlightenment necessarily arrived at ideas and demands incompatible with art. But when the Understanding rose out of these abstractions to Reason again, there at once entered the need for something concrete and also for that concrete thing which art is. The period of the enlightened intellect, it is true, did also practise art, but in a very prosaic way, as we can see in Schiller himself who took his departure from this period; but then, in the need for Reason, imagination, and passion which the Understanding no longer satisfied, he felt a vital longing for art in general and in particular for the classical art of the Greeks and their gods and world outlook. Out of this longing, pent up by the abstract thoughts of his day, there proceeded the poem I have mentioned.

In the original version of the poem, Schiller's attitude to Christianity is polemical throughout, but later he softened its severity because he was only opposed to the outlook of the intellect in the Enlightenment, and this at a later date began to lose its domination. He began by happily praising the Greek outlook for which the whole of nature was animated and full of gods; then he passes over to the present and its prosaic treatment of natural laws and man's position in relation to God, and says: 'This sad quiet, does it proclaim to me my creator? Dark like himself is his veil, the one thing that can glorify him is my renunciation.'[1]

Of course in Christianity renunciation is an essential feature, but only in monastic ideas does it require man to kill in himself his

---

[1] This quotation seems to be relevant only if Hegel took the 'veil' to be nature as no longer animated and full of gods but as governed by natural laws. This seems to be a misrepresentation, because the context is a contrast between the gay beauty of Greek temples and the gloom of Christian churches. Hegel omits part of the first line of the quotation; when it is included, the translation might be: 'What sort of place am I entering? Does this sad place announce the presence of my creator? Dark like himself is his habitation, and the only thing that can glorify him is my renunciation.'

mind, his feeling, the so-called natural impulses, and not to embody himself in the moral, rational, and real world, in family and state— just as the Enlightenment and its Deism gives out that God is unknowable and so lays on man the supreme renunciation, the renunciation of knowing nothing of God, of not comprehending him. Whereas, according to the truly Christian view, renunciation is only the factor of mediation, the point of transition in which the purely natural, the sensuous, and the finite in general sheds its inadequacy in order to enable the spirit to come to higher freedom and reconciliation with itself, a freedom and blessedness unknown to the Greeks. Of celebrating a solitary god, of his pure separation and detachment from the world emptied of gods there cannot in that case be any question in Christianity, for it is precisely in that freedom and reconciliation of spirit that God is immanent, and, looked at from this point of view, Schiller's famous saying: 'Since the gods were then more human, men were more godlike' is altogether false. Therefore we must emphasize as more important the later alteration of the ending, where it is said of the Greek gods: 'Torn from the flood of time they hover, saved, o'er Pindus height; what shall live undyingly in song must pass away in life.'

With these words there is wholly ratified what we have just mentioned: the Greek gods had their seat only in ideas and imagination; they could neither maintain their place in the reality of life nor give final satisfaction to the finite spirit.

In another way, Parny,[1] called the French Tibullus on the strength of his successful Elegies, turned against Christianity in a lengthy poem in ten books, a sort of epic, *La guerre des Dieux*, in order to make fun of Christian ideas by joking and jesting with an obvious frivolity of wit, yet with good humour and spirit. But these pleasantries went no further than frolicsome levity, and moral depravity was not made into something sacred and of the highest excellence as it was at the time of Friedrich von Schlegel's *Lucinde*.[2] Mary of course comes off very badly in Parny's poem; monks, Dominicans, Franciscans, etc. are seduced by wine and Bacchantes, and nuns by fauns, and thus it goes on perversely enough. But finally the gods of the Greek world are conquered and they withdraw from Olympus to Parnassus.

[1] E. D. D., Vicomte de, 1753–1814. His epic reached a second edition at Paris, 1799.
[2] Berlin, 1799. See Hegel's *Philosophy of Right*, Addition to § 164.

Lastly, in his *Braut von Korinth*[1] Goethe has sketched in a living picture the banning of love more deeply, according less to the true principle of Christianity than to the misunderstood demand for renunciation and sacrifice; what he does is to contrast natural human feelings with the false asceticism which proposes to condemn a woman's vocation for wedlock and regard compulsory celibacy as something more sacrosanct than marriage. Just as in Schiller's case we find the opposition between the Greek imagination and the modern Enlightenment's abstractions of the Understanding, so here we see, contrasted with the Greek moral and sensuous justification of love and marriage, ideas which have belonged only to a one-sided and untrue view of the Christian religion. With great art a terrifying tone is given to the whole work, especially because it remains uncertain whether the action concerns an actual maiden or a dead one, a living one or a ghost, and in an equally most masterly way the love-affair is metrically interwoven with a solemnity which thereby becomes all the more dreadful.

(c) Dissolution of Classical Art in its own Sphere

But before we endeavour to get to the bottom of the new art-form whose opposition to the old does not belong to the course of artistic development as we have to treat it here in its essential features, we must first bring to view in its clearest form that transition which falls within ancient art itself. The principle of this transition lies in the fact that, while the individuality of the spirit was hitherto visualized as in harmony with the true substances of nature and human existence, and while the spirit knew and found itself in this harmony throughout its own life, willing, and activity, now the spirit begins to withdraw into the infinity of its inner life, though instead of true infinity it wins only a formal, and indeed a still finite, return into itself.

If we cast a closer glance at the concrete circumstances corresponding to the principle mentioned, we saw already in the previous chapter that the Greek gods embodied the substances of actual human life and action. But man's highest vocation, and his universal interest and end, had now become present in the world outside religion, as something existent at the same time. Just as external and actual appearance was essential for the Greek spiritual art-form,

---

[1] Often translated as the *Bride of Corinth*, but *Braut* means fiancée.

so too the absolute spiritual destiny of man was accomplished in the phenomenal world as a real actuality [the state] with the substance and universality of which the individual demanded to be in harmony. This supreme end in Greece was the life of the state, the body of the citizens, and their ethical life and living patriotism. Beyond this interest there was none higher or truer. But political life as a mundane and external phenomenon, like the circumstances of mundane reality in general, falls a prey to transitoriness. It is not hard to show that a state with such a kind of freedom, so immediately identical with all the citizens who as such have in their hands the supreme agency in all public affairs, can only be small and weak and must either be destroyed by itself or demolished from without in the course of world history.

For in this immediate coalescence of the individual with the universality of politics (*a*) the subject's own character and his private individuality does not yet come into its rights and it cannot find room to develop in a way harmless to the whole. But by being distinct from the substantial organization into which it has not been incorporated, it remains the restricted natural self-interest which now goes its own way independently, pursues interests far removed from the true interest of the whole and therefore leads to the ruin of the state itself which in the end, after a struggle, it succeeds in opposing with its subjective power. (*b*) On the other hand, within this freedom itself there is awakened the need for a higher freedom of the subject in himself; he claims to be free not only in the state, as the substantial whole, not only in the accepted ethical and legal code, but in his own heart, because he wants to generate out of his own resources the good and the right in his subjective knowing and to bring it into recognition. The subject wants to have the consciousness of being substantial in himself as subject, and therefore there arises in this freedom a new conflict between an end for the state and one for himself as an inherently free individual. Such a clash had already begun at the time of Socrates, while on the other side vanity, self-interest, and the licentiousness of democracy and demagogy disrupted the actual state in such a way that men like Xenophon and Plato felt disgust at the condition of their native city in which the administration of public affairs lay in self-interested and frivolous hands.

The spirit of the transition rests primarily, therefore, on the general cleavage between the explicitly independent spiritual realm and external existence. In this severance from its reality in which it finds itself no longer, the spiritual is the abstractly spiritual; yet not, as might be thought, the one oriental god, but on the contrary the actual knowing subject who produces and retains every intellectual universal, the true, the good, the moral, in his subjective inner consciousness, where he has no knowledge of present reality but only of his own thoughts and convictions. This situation, in so far as it does not transcend opposition, but sets its two sides over against one another as simply opposed, is of a purely prosaic nature. Yet to this prose we have not yet come at this stage. On the one hand, in other words, there is present the consciousness of a subject who, as firm in himself, wills the good and envisages the fulfilment of his desires and the realization of his essential being in the virtue of his heart as well as in the old gods, the old moral and legal life; but at the same time he is irritated by the present as it exists, by the actual political life of his time and by the dissolution of the old dispensation, i.e. of the earlier patriotism and political wisdom, and therefore is caught of course in the opposition between his subjective inner life and external reality. For in his own inner life he does not enjoy full satisfaction in those mere ideas of true ethical life and therefore he turns outward against the external situation to which he relates himself negatively, with hostility, with the aim of altering it. Therefore, as was said just above, on the one hand there is of course present to his mind an inner content which is self-determined and, while he steadily expresses it, he has to do at the same time with a world confronting him, contradicting that content, and he has the task of sketching this reality in the traits of its corruption which is opposed to the good and the true; yet on the other hand this opposition still finds its resolution in art itself. In other words, a new art-form appears in which the struggle between the opposites is not conducted by thoughts which leave the opposition intact; on the contrary, what is brought into the artistic portrayal is reality itself in the madness of its ruin, destroying itself within, whereby, precisely in this self-destruction of the right, the true can display itself on this mirror as a fixed and abiding power, and madness and unreason are not left with the power of directly contradicting what is inherently true. Of this kind of art an example is comedy as Aristophanes among the Greeks has handled it without anger, in pure and serene joviality, in relation to the most essential spheres in the world of his time.

3. Satire

Yet this still artistically adequate resolution we see disappearing all the same, because the antithesis itself persists in the form of opposition and therefore presents, in place of the poetic reconciliation, a prosaic relation between the two sides; the result is that the classical art-form appears as superseded, since this relation leads to the downfall of the plastic gods and the beautiful world of men. Now here we have at once to look around for the art-form which can still be inserted in this transition to a higher mode of configuration and can actually make this transition. We found the culmination of symbolic art likewise in a variety of forms, in fable, comparison, parable, riddle, etc., all having in common the separation of the shape as such from its meaning. If at this point too the ground of dissolution is a similar cleavage, the question arises about the difference between the present sort of transition and the earlier one. The difference is as follows.

(a) Difference between the Dissolution of Classical Art and that of Symbolic Art

In the strictly symbolic and comparative art-form the shape and meaning are strange to one another from the start, despite their affinity and relationship; yet they stand in no negative relation but in a friendly one, for it is precisely the identity or similarity of the qualities and traits on both sides that proves to be the basis of their connection and comparison. Their persistent separation and strangeness within such a unification is not such as to be *hostility* between the separated sides, nor does it rend them apart and disrupt their absolutely close amalgamation. On the other hand, the Ideal of classical art proceeds from the perfect interfusion of meaning and shape, spiritual inner individuality and its corporeality; and if therefore the sides joined together in such a perfect unity are detached from one another, this only happens because they can no longer agree with one another and must desert their peaceful reconciliation for incompatibility and enmity.

(b) Satire

Furthermore, with this *form* of relation, in distinction from the symbolic, the *content* of the two sides which now stand in opposition to one another is altered too. In the symbolic form of art, it is abstractions, more or less, general thoughts, or even specific propositions in the form of general reflections which acquire through the symbolic art-form an allusive illustration; whereas, in the form asserting itself in this transition to romantic art, although the content does consist of similar abstractions of universal thoughts, sentiments, and intellectual propositions, it is not these abstractions as such but their existence in *subjective* consciousness and self-subsistent self-consciousness which affords the content for one side of the opposition. For the first demand of this intermediate stage is that the spiritual, attained by the Ideal, shall emerge independently on its own account. Already in classical art spiritual individuality was the chief thing although in respect of its reality it remained reconciled with its immediate existence. But now it is a matter of portraying a subjectivity which tries to gain dominion over its no longer adequate shape and over external reality in general. Thereby the spiritual world becomes explicitly free; it has liberated itself from the sensuous and therefore appears, through this withdrawal into itself, as a self-conscious subject, self-contented only in its inner life. But this subject which spurns externality is on its spiritual side not yet the true totality which has for its content the Absolute in the form of self-conscious spirit; on the contrary, as afflicted with opposition to the real, it is a purely abstract, finite, unsatisfied subject.

Contrasted with it there is an equally finite reality which now on its side also becomes free, yet just because the truly spiritual has reverted out of it into the inner life and no longer will or can find itself in it, this reality appears as a godless one and a corrupt existence. In this way, a thinking spirit, a subject reposing on himself as subject in abstract wisdom with a knowledge of the good and the virtuous and a will to achieve it, is brought by art into a hostile opposition to the corruption of the present. The unresolved nature of this opposition in which inner and outer remain in fixed disharmony constitutes the prosaic character of the relation between the two sides. A noble spirit, a virtuous heart always deprived of the actualization of its convictions in a world of vice and folly, turns with passionate indignation or keener wit and colder bitterness against the reality confronting it, and is enraged with or scoffs at the world which directly contradicts its abstract idea of virtue and truth.

This art-form which assumes this shape of the emerging opposition between finite subjectivity and degenerate externality is *Satire* to which common theories have been unable to do proper justice because they remain in perplexity about its classification. For Satire has nothing at all of Epic, and it does not properly belong to Lyric either, since in Satire what is expressed is not the feeling of the heart but the universality of the good and the inherently necessary which, interwoven indeed with the personality of the individual, appears as the virtuousness of this or that man; yet Satire does not enjoy the free unhindered beauty of imagination or pour forth this enjoyment; on the contrary, it clings discontentedly to the disharmony between its own subjectivity, with its abstract principles, and empirical reality, and to this extent produces neither true poetry nor true works of art. Therefore the satirical point of view is not to be understood by reference to one of those species of poetry but must be apprehended more generally as this transitional form of the classical Ideal.

(c) The Roman World as the Soil where Satire Flourishes

Now since what is disclosed in Satire is the dissolution of the Ideal, a dissolution prosaic in its inner content, we have not to look for its actual soil in Greece as the land of beauty. Satire in the form just described belongs properly to the Romans. The spirit of the Roman world is domination by abstraction (i.e. by dead law), the demolition of beauty and joyous customs, the suppression of the family *qua immediate* natural ethical life, in general the sacrifice of individuality which now surrenders itself to the state and finds its cold-blooded dignity and intellectual satisfaction in obedience to the abstract law. The principle of this political virtue is opposed to true art; abroad, its cold harshness subjugates all the individuality of nations, while, at home, formal law is developed to perfection in similar rigour. After all we find no beautiful, free, and great art in Rome. Sculpture and painting, lyric and dramatic poetry, the Romans took over from the Greeks and learnt their lesson from them. It is remarkable that what may be regarded as native in the case of the Romans is comic farces, Fescennine verses, and Atellan burlesques, whereas the more cultivated comedies of Plautus, and of Terence too, were borrowed from the Greeks and were more a matter of imitation than of independent production. Even Ennius drew on Greek sources and then made mythology prosaic.

What is peculiarly Rome's own is only that mode of art which is prosaic in principle, didactic poetry, e.g. (especially if it has a moral content and gives to its general reflections merely the external adornment of metre, images, similes, and a rhetorically fine diction), but above all Satire. Here it is the spirit of a virtuous ill-humour about the surrounding world which strives to give itself some relief in hollow declamations. This form of art, prosaic in itself, can become poetic only if it so brings the corrupt shape of reality before our eyes that this corruption collapses in itself by reason of its own folly; Horace, e.g., who, as a lyric poet worked his way entirely into the Greek form and manner of art, outlines in his *Satires* and *Epistles*, where he is more original, a living picture of the manners of his time by sketching for us follies which, unskilled in the means they use, are self-destructive. Yet this is only a joviality satisfied with making the bad laughable; it may be exquisite and cultivated, but it is certainly not poetic. In the case of other writers, on the other hand, the abstract idea of law and virtue is directly contrasted with vices; and here it is ill-humour, vexation, wrath, and hatred which expatiate in abstract rhetoric about virtue and wisdom, or, with the indignation of a nobler soul and with bitterness, launch out against the corruption and slavery of the times; or again, without any true hope or faith, they hold up before the vices of the day the picture of old manners, the old freedom, the virtues of a totally different world-situation in the past; yet they have nothing to set against the vacillation, the vicissitudes, the distress and danger of an ignominious present except stoic equanimity and the inner imperturbability of a virtuous disposition of heart. This dissatisfaction gives something of the same tone too to Roman historiography and philosophy. Sallust must declaim against the moral corruption to which he did not himself remain a stranger; in spite of his rhetorical elegance, Livy seeks consolation and satisfaction in sketching the olden days; and above all it is Tacitus who, with discontent as magnificent as profound, without cold declamation, indignantly and vividly discloses the evils of his time in sharp outlines. Among the satirists, Persius especially is full of harshness, more bitter than Juvenal. Later on, finally, we see Lucian, the Greek Syrian, turning with cheerful levity against everything, heroes, philosophers, and gods, and especially satirizing the old Greek gods on the score of their humanity and individuality, Yet he often fails to get beyond chatter about the externals of the shapes and actions of the gods and therefore becomes wearisome, especially for us. For, on the one hand, as a result of our faith we have already done with what he wanted to destroy, and on the other hand we know that these traits of the gods, considered in their beauty, have their eternal validity in spite of his jokes and ridicule.

Nowadays satires will not succeed any more. Cotta[1] and Goethe have arranged prize-competitions for satires; no poems of this sort have been forthcoming. Satire entails fixed principles with which the present world stands in contradiction; but while a wisdom that remains abstract, a virtue that with inflexible energy clings only to itself, may well contrast itself with reality, it cannot achieve either the genuine poetic dissolution of the false and the disagreeable or a genuine reconciliation in the truth.

But art cannot remain in this cleavage of the abstract inner disposition from external objectivity without abandoning its own principle. The subjective must be interpreted as what is inherently infinite and absolute which, even if it does not let finite reality subsist as the truth, yet does not relate itself to it negatively in bare opposition; on the contrary, it proceeds all the same to reconciliation and in this activity alone comes to be portrayed, contrasted with the ideal individuals of the classical art-form, as absolute subjectivity.

[1] J. F., 1764–1832, the publisher.

SECTION III

THE ROMANTIC FORM OF ART

Introduction—Of the Romantic in General

The form of romantic art is determined, as has been the case every time in our treatment hitherto, by the inner essence of the content which art is called upon to represent, and so we must in the first place endeavour to make clear the distinctive principle of the new content which now, as the absolute content of truth, comes into consciousness in the shape of a new vision of the world and a new artistic form.

At the stage of the *beginning* of art the urge of imagination consisted in striving out of nature into spirit. But this striving remained only a quest of the spirit, and therefore, not yet providing the proper content of art, the spirit could only assert itself as an external form for meanings drawn from nature or for impersonal abstract ideas drawn from the substantial inner life, and it was these which formed the real centre of this form of art.

The opposite, *secondly*, we found in classical art. Here although the spirit could only struggle on to independence by annulling the natural meanings, it is the basis and principle of the content, while the external form is the natural phenomenon in a corporeal and sensuous shape. Yet this form did not remain, as it did at the first stage, purely superficial, indeterminate, and not penetrated by its content; on the contrary, the perfection of art reached its peak here precisely because the spiritual was completely drawn through its external appearance; in this beautiful unification it idealized the natural and made it into an adequate embodiment of spirit's own substantial individuality. Therefore classical art became a conceptually adequate representation of the Ideal, the consummation of the realm of beauty. Nothing can be or become more beautiful.

Yet there is something higher than the beautiful appearance of spirit in its immediate sensuous shape, even if this shape be created by spirit as adequate to itself. For this unification, which is achieved in the medium of externality and therefore makes sensuous reality into an appropriate existence [of spirit], nevertheless is once more opposed to the true essence of spirit, with the result that spirit is pushed back into itself out of its reconciliation in the corporeal into a reconciliation of itself within itself. The simple solid totality of the Ideal is dissolved and it falls apart into the double totality of (a) subjective being in itself and (b) the external appearance, in order to enable the spirit to reach through this cleavage a deeper reconciliation in its own element of inwardness. The spirit, which has as its principle its accord with itself, the unity of its essence with its reality, can find its correspondent existence only in its own native spiritual world of feeling, the heart, and the inner life in general. Thereby the spirit comes to the consciousness of having its opposite, i.e. its *existence*, on and in itself as spirit and therewith alone of enjoying its infinity and freedom.

1. The Principle of Inner Subjectivity

By this elevation of the spirit *to itself* the spirit wins in itself its objectivity, which hitherto it had to seek in the external and sensuous character of existence, and in this unification with itself it senses and knows itself. This spiritual elevation is the fundamental principle of romantic art. Bound up with it at once is the essential point that at this final stage of art the beauty of the classical ideal, and therefore beauty in its very own shape and its most adequate content, is no longer the ultimate thing. For at the stage of romantic art the spirit knows that its truth does not consist in its immersion in corporeality; on the contrary, it only becomes sure of its truth by withdrawing from the external into its own intimacy with itself and positing external reality as an existence inadequate to itself. Even if, therefore this new content too comprises in itself the task of making itself *beautiful*, still beauty in the sense hitherto expounded remains for it something subordinate, and beauty becomes the *spiritual* beauty of the absolute inner life as inherently infinite spiritual subjectivity.

But therefore to attain its infinity the spirit must all the same lift itself out of purely formal and *finite* personality into the *Absolute*; i.e. the spiritual must bring itself into representation as the subject filled with what is purely substantial and, therein, as the willing and self-knowing subject. Conversely, the substantial and the true must not be apprehended as a mere 'beyond' of humanity, and the anthropomorphism of the Greek outlook must not be stripped away; but the human being, as actual subjectivity, must be made the principle, and thereby alone, as we already saw earlier [on pp. 435–6, 505–6], does the anthropomorphic reach its consummation.

2. The More Detailed Features of the Content and Form of the Romantic

Out of the more detailed features implicit in this fundamental definition we have now to develop in a general way the group of topics [in romantic art] and their form. This altered form is conditioned by the new content of romantic art.

The true content of romantic art is absolute inwardness, and its corresponding form is spiritual subjectivity with its grasp of its independence and freedom. This inherently infinite and absolutely universal content is the absolute negation of everything particular, the simple unity with itself which has dissipated all external relations, all processes of nature and their periodicity of birth, passing away, and rebirth, all the restrictedness in spiritual *existence*, and dissolved all particular gods into a pure and infinite self-identity. In this Pantheon all the gods are dethroned, the flame of subjectivity has destroyed them, and instead of plastic polytheism art knows now only *one* God, one spirit, one absolute independence which, as the absolute knowing and willing of itself, remains in free unity with itself and no longer falls apart into those particular characters and functions whose one and only cohesion was due to the compulsion of a dark necessity.[1]

Yet absolute subjectivity as such would elude art and be accessible to thinking alone if, in order to be *actual* subjectivity in correspondence with its essence, it did not also proceed into external existence and then withdraw out of this reality into itself again. This moment of actuality is inherent in the Absolute, because the Absolute, as infinite negativity, has for the result of its activity *itself*, as the simple unity of knowing with itself and therefore as *immediacy*. On account of this immediate existence which is grounded in the Absolute itself, the Absolute does not turn out to be the one jealous God who merely cancels nature and finite human existence without shaping himself there in appearance as actual

[1] See above, p. 503.

divine subjectivity; on the contrary, the true Absolute reveals itself and thereby gains an aspect in virtue of which it can be apprehended and represented by art.

But the determinate being of God is not the natural and sensuous as such but the sensuous elevated to non-sensuousness, to spiritual subjectivity which instead of losing in its external appearance the certainty of itself as the Absolute, only acquires precisely through its embodiment a present actual certainty of itself. God in his truth is therefore no bare ideal generated by imagination; on the contrary, he puts himself into the very heart of the finitude and external contingency of existence, and yet knows himself there as a divine subject who remains infinite in himself and makes this infinity explicit to himself. Since therefore the actual individual man is the appearance of God, art now wins for the first time the higher right of turning the human form, and the mode of externality in general, into an expression of the Absolute, although the new task of art can only consist in bringing before contemplation in this human form not the immersion of the inner in external corporeality but, conversely, the withdrawal of the inner into itself, the spiritual consciousness of God in the individual. The different moments which constitute the totality of this world view as the totality of truth itself now therefore find their appearance in man in such a way that content and form are not afforded either by the natural as such, as sun, sky, stars, etc., or by the beautiful group of the Greek gods, or by heroes and external deeds wrought on the ground of family obligations and political life; on the contrary, it is the actual individual person in his inner life who acquires infinite worth, since in him alone do the eternal moments of absolute truth, which is actual only as spirit, unfold into existence and collect together again.

If we compare this vocation of romantic art with the task of classical art, fulfilled in the most adequate way by Greek sculpture, the plastic shape of the gods does not express the movement and activity of the spirit which has retired into itself out of its corporeal reality and made its way to inner self-awareness. The mutability and contingency of empirical individuality is indeed expunged in those lofty figures of the gods, but what they lack is the actuality of self-aware subjectivity in the knowing and willing of itself. This defect is shown externally in the fact that the expression of the soul in its simplicity, namely the light of the eye, is absent from the sculptures.[1] The supreme works of beautiful sculpture are sightless, and their inner being does not look out of them as self-knowing inwardness in this spiritual concentration which the eye discloses. This light of the soul falls outside them and belongs to the spectator alone; when he looks at these shapes, soul cannot meet soul nor eye eye. But the God of romantic art appears seeing, self-knowing, inwardly subjective, and disclosing his inner being to man's inner being. For infinite negativity, the withdrawal of the spirit into itself, cancels effusion into the corporeal; subjectivity is the spiritual light which shines in itself, in its hitherto obscure place, and, while natural light can only illumine an object, the spiritual light is itself the ground and object on which it shines and which it knows as itself. But this absolute inner expresses itself at the same time in its actual determinate existence as an appearance in the human mode, and the human being stands in connection with the entire world, and this implies at the same time a wide variety in both the spiritually subjective sphere and also the external to which the spirit relates itself as something its own.

The shape that absolute subjectivity may thus take in reality has the following forms of content and appearance.

(a) The original starting-point we must take from the Absolute itself which as actual spirit gives itself an existence, knows itself and is active in reality. Here the human shape is so represented that it is immediately known as having the Divine in itself. The man [Jesus] appears not as man in a purely human character with restricted passions, finite ends and achievements, or as merely conscious *of* God, but as the self-knowing sole and universal God himself in whose life and suffering, birth, death, and resurrection there is now revealed even to man's finite consciousness what spirit, what the eternal and infinite, is in its truth. Romantic art presents this content in the story of Christ, his mother, his Disciples, and also of all others in whom the Holy Spirit is effective and the entire Godhead is present. For because it is God who appears in human existence, for all that he is universal in himself too, this reality is not restricted to individual immediate existence in the shape of Christ; it is unfolded into the whole of mankind in which the spirit of God makes itself present, and in this reality remains in unity with itself. The diffusion of this self-contemplation of spirit, of its inwardness and self-possession, is peace, the reconciliation of

[1] Cf. pp. 153–4, 433–4.

spirit with itself in its objectivity—a divine world, a Kingdom of God, in which the Divine (which from the beginning had reconciliation with its reality as its essence) is consummated in virtue of this reconciliation and thereby has true consciousness of itself.

(b) But however far this identification is grounded in the essence of the Absolute itself, still, as spiritual freedom and infinity, it is no immediate reconciliation present from the beginning in mundane, natural, and spiritual reality; on the contrary, it is brought about only by the elevation of the spirit out of the finitude of its immediate existence into its truth. This implies that the spirit, in order to win its totality and freedom, detaches itself from itself and opposes itself, as the finitude of nature and spirit, to itself as the inherently infinite. With this self-diremption there is bound up, conversely, the necessity of rising out of this state of scission (within which the finite and the natural, the immediacy of existence, the natural heart, are determined as the negative, the evil, and the bad) and of entering the realm of truth and satisfaction only through the overcoming of this negative sphere. Therefore the spiritual reconciliation is only to be apprehended and represented as an activity, a movement of the spirit, as a process in the course of which a struggle and a battle arises, and grief, death, the mournful sense of nullity, the torment of spirit and body enter as an essential feature. For just as God at first cuts himself off from finite reality, so finite man, who begins of himself outside the Kingdom of God, acquires the task of elevating himself to God, detaching himself from the finite, abolishing its nullity, and through this killing of his immediate reality becoming what God in his appearance as man has made objective as true reality. The infinite grief[1] of this sacrifice of subjectivity's very heart, as well as suffering and death, which were more or less excluded from the representations of classical art or rather appeared there as mere natural suffering, acquire their real necessity only in romantic art.

We cannot say that the Greeks interpreted death in its essential meaning. Neither the natural as such nor spirit's immediate unity with the body counted with them as something inherently negative, and therefore death for them was only an abstract passing, without terrors and formidability, a ceasing without further immeasurable consequences for the dying individual. But when subjectivity in its spiritual inwardness is of infinite importance, then the negative

---

[1] In these words, which he often uses, Hegel refers to the Crucifixion.

implicit in death is a negation of this loftiness and importance itself and is therefore frightening—an expiry of the soul which by death can find itself to be the absolutely negative itself, excluded from all happiness, absolutely unhappy and consigned to eternal damnation.

Greek individuality, on the other hand, regarded as spiritual subjectivity, does not ascribe this value to itself and may therefore surround death with cheerful images. For man is afraid only for what is of great value to him. But life has this infinite value for our minds only if the person as spiritual and self-conscious is the one and only actuality, and now in a justified fear must image himself as negatived by death. Yet on the other hand death does not gain for classical art the *affirmative* meaning which it acquires in romantic art. The Greeks did not take seriously what we call immortality. Only for the later reflection of subjective consciousness on itself, in the case of Socrates, has immortality had a deeper sense and satisfied a more far-reaching need. Odysseus, e.g. (*Odyssey*, xi. 465–91), congratulates Achilles in the underworld on the ground of his happiness, greater than that of all those before or after him, because, hitherto honoured as though he were a god, he is now a ruler among the dead. Achilles, as everyone knows, puts the minimum of value on this happiness and answers: 'Odysseus should speak me no word of consolation for death; rather would I be a serf, and, poor myself, serve a poor man for wages, than rule here below over all the shades of the dead.'

In romantic art, on the contrary, death is only a perishing of the *natural* soul and *finite* subjectivity, a perishing (related negatively only to the inherently negative) which cancels nullity and thereby is the means of liberating the spirit from its finitude and disunion as well as spiritually reconciling the individual person with the Absolute. For the Greeks what was affirmative was only the life united with natural, external, and mundane existence, and death therefore was just a negation, the dissolution of immediate reality. But in the romantic outlook death has the significance of negativity, in the sense of the negation of the negative, and therefore changes all the same into the affirmative as the resurrection of the spirit out of its mere natural embodiment and the finitude which is inadequate to it. The grief and death of the dying individual reverses into a return to self, into satisfaction, blessedness, and that reconciled affirmative existence which spirit can attain only through the killing of its negative existence in which it is barred from its proper truth and life. Therefore this fundamental principle does not merely affect the fact of death as it comes to man from the side of nature; on the contrary, death is a process through which the spirit, now independent of what negates it externally, must itself go in order truly to live.

(c) The *third* aspect of this absolute world of spirit is framed by man in so far as he neither brings immediately into appearance on himself the Absolute and Divine as *Divine*, nor presents the process of elevation to God and reconciliation with God, but remains within his own human sphere. Here, then, the subject-matter consists of the finite as such, both on the side of spiritual aims, mundane interests, passions, collisions, sorrows and joys, hopes and satisfactions, and also on the side of the external, i.e. nature and its kingdoms and most detailed phenomena. Yet for the mode of treating this matter a twofold position arises. On the one hand, namely, because spirit has won affirmation with itself, it issues on this ground as on an element justified and satisfying in itself, and of this element it presents only the purely positive character it has, out of which its own affirmative satisfaction and deep feeling are reflected; but, on the other hand, the same content is degraded to mere contingency which cannot claim any independent validity because in it the spirit does not find its true existence and therefore only comes into unity with itself by explicitly dissolving this finitude of spirit and nature as being something finite and negative.

3. *Relation of the Subject-matter to the Mode of Representation*

Now finally, with regard to the relation between this entire subject-matter and its mode of representation, it appears in the first place, in conformity with what we have seen just now, that

(a) the subject-matter of romantic art, at least in relation to the Divine, is very circumscribed. For, first, as we have already indicated above [on pp. 507, 520], nature is emptied of gods; the sea, mountains, valleys, rivers, springs, time and night, as well as the universal processes of nature, have lost their value so far as concerns the presentation and content of the Absolute. Natural formations are no longer augmented symbolically; they have been robbed of their characteristic of having forms and activities capable of being traits of a divinity. For all the great questions about the origin of the world, about the whence, wherefore, and whither of created nature and humanity, and all the symbolic and plastic attempts to solve and represent these problems, have disappeared owing to the revelation of God in the spirit; and even in the spiritual realm the variegated coloured world with its classically shaped characters, actions, and events is gathered up into *one* ray of the Absolute and its eternal history of redemption. The entire content [of romantic art] is therefore concentrated on the inner life of the spirit, on feeling, ideas, and the mind which strives after union with the truth, seeks and struggles to generate and preserve the Divine in the subject's consciousness, and now may not carry through aims and undertakings in the world for the sake of the world but rather has for its sole essential undertaking the inner battle of man in himself and his reconciliation with God; and it brings into representation only the personality and its preservation along with contrivances towards this end. The heroism which may enter here accordingly is no heroism which from its own resources gives laws, establishes organizations, creates and develops situations, but a heroism of submission. It submits to a determinate and cut and dried [system of divine truth] and no task is left to it but to regulate the temporal order by that, to apply what is higher and absolutely valid to the world confronting it, and to make it prevail in the temporal. But since this absolute content appears compressed into one point, i.e. into the *subjective* heart, so that all process is transported into the inner life of man, the scope of the subject-matter is therefore also infinitely *extended* again. It opens out into a multiplicity without bounds. For although that objective history constitutes the substantial basis of the heart, the artist yet runs through it in every direction, presents single points drawn from it or presents himself in steadily added new human traits; over and above this, he can draw into himself the whole breadth of nature as the surroundings and locality of spirit and devote it to the one great end.

In this way the history of mentality becomes infinitely rich and it can adapt its shape to ever-altered circumstances and situations in the most multifarious ways. And if a man once leaves this absolute circle [of mind] and concerns himself with mundane affairs, then the range of interests, aims, and feelings becomes all the further beyond computation, the deeper the spirit has become in itself in accordance with this whole principle. The spirit therefore unfolds itself in the course of its development into an infinitely

enhanced wealth of inner and outer collisions, distractions, gradations of passion, and into the most manifold degrees of satisfaction.
The purely inherently universal Absolute, in so far as it is conscious
of itself in man, constitutes the inner content of romantic art, and
so also the whole of mankind and its entire development is that
art's inexhaustible material.

(b) But it is not at all by being *art* that romantic art produces
this content, as was the case to a great extent in the symbolic and
above all from the classical form of art and its ideal gods. As
we saw earlier [on p. 505 above], romantic art as *art* is not the
didactic revelation which produces the content of truth for contemplation simply and solely in the form of art; on the contrary,
the content of romantic art is already present explicitly to mind
and feeling outside the sphere of art. *Religion*, as the universal
consciousness of the truth, constitutes here in a totally different
degree the essential *presupposition* for art, and, even regarded in its
manner of appearing externally to actual consciousness in the real
perceptible world, it confronts us as a prosaic phenomenon in the
present. Since, in other words, the content of the revelation to
spirit is the eternal absolute nature of the *spirit* itself which detaches
itself from the natural as such and devalues it, therefore the position acquired by spirit's manifestation in what is immediately
present is that this externality, so far as it subsists and has existence,
remains only a contingent world out of which the Absolute
gathers itself together into the inner world of the spirit and only so
comes to truth in its own eyes. Therewith externality is regarded
as an indifferent element in which spirit has no final trust or persistence. The less the spirit regards the shape of external reality as
worthy of it, the less can it seek its satisfaction therein and attain
reconciliation with itself through union with it.

(c) On this principle, therefore, the mode of actual configuration
in romantic art, in respect of external appearance, does not essentially get beyond ordinary reality proper, and it is by no means
averse from harbouring this real existence in its finite deficiency
and determinacy. Thus this means the disappearance of that ideal
beauty which lifts the contemplation of the external away above
time and the traces of evanescence in order to give to existence the
bloom of beauty instead of its otherwise stunted appearance.
Romantic art no longer has as its aim [the representation of]
the free vitality of existence with its infinite tranquillity and the

immersion of the soul in the corporeal, or *this life* as such in its very own essential nature; on the contrary, it turns its back on this summit of beauty; it intertwines its inner being with the contingency of the external world and gives unfettered play to the bold lines of the ugly.

Thus in romantic art we have two worlds: a spiritual realm, complete in itself, the heart which reconciles itself within and now bends back the otherwise rectilineal repetition of birth, death, and rebirth into the true rotation (i.e. return into self) and into the genuine phoenix-life of the spirit; on the other side, the realm of the external as such which, released from its fixedly secure unification with the spirit, now becomes a purely empirical reality by the shape of which the soul is untroubled. In classical art, spirit dominated empirical appearance and permeated it completely because it was in this that it was to acquire its complete reality. But now the inner life is indifferent to the way in which the immediate world is configurated, because immediacy is unworthy of the soul's inner bliss. External appearance cannot any longer express the inner life, and if it is still called to do so it merely has the task of proving that the external is an unsatisfying existence and must point back to the inner, to the mind and feeling as the essential element. But just for this reason romantic art leaves externality to go its own way again for its part freely and independently, and in this respect allows any and every material, down to flowers, trees, and the commonest household gear, to enter the representation without hindrance even in its contingent natural existence. Yet this subject-matter, by being purely external material, carries with it at the same time the character of being indifferent and vulgar, and only attaining worth of its own if the heart has put itself into it and if it is to express not merely something inner but the heart's *depth of feeling*, which instead of fusing with the external appears only as reconciled with itself in itself. In this relation, the inner, so pushed to the extreme, is an expression without any externality at all; it is invisible and is as it were a perception of itself alone, or a musical sound as such without objectivity and shape, or a hovering over the waters,[1] or a ringing tone over a world which in and on its heterogeneous phenomena can only accept and re-mirror a reflection of this inwardness of soul.

Therefore if we sum up in *one* word this relation of content and

[1] Gen. 1: 2 (in Luther's version).

form in romantic art wherever this relation is preserved in its own special character, we may say that, precisely because the ever expanded universality and the restlessly active depths of the heart are the principle here, the keynote of romantic art is *musical* and, if we make the content of this idea determinate, *lyrical*. For romantic art the lyric is as it were the elementary fundamental characteristic, a note which epic and drama strike too and which wafts even round works of visual art as a universal fragrance of soul, because here spirit and heart strive to speak, through every one of their productions, to the spirit and the heart.

4. *Division of the Subject*

Now lastly, for the more detailed development of our consideration of this third great sphere of art we must settle the division of the subject; and the fundamental essence of the romantic in its inner ramification breaks up into the following three phases.

The first sphere is formed by religion as such; its centre is supplied by the history of redemption, by the life of Christ, his death and Resurrection. The chief point to be made here is reversion, the fact that the spirit turns negatively against its immediacy and finitude, overcomes it, and through this liberation wins for itself its infinity and absolute independence in its own province.

Then, secondly, this independence passes out of the inherent divinity of the spirit, and out of the elevation of finite man to God, into mundane reality. Here it is primarily the subject as such who has become affirmative in his own eyes and has as the substance of his consciousness and as the interest of his existence the virtues of this affirmative subjectivity, namely honour, love, fidelity, and bravery, the aims and duties of romantic chivalry.

The content and form of the third chapter may be described in general as the formal independence of character. If, in other words, subjectivity has advanced to the point of having spiritual independence as the essential thing for it, so too the particular content, with which this subjectivity is linked as with what is its own, will share the like independence—which yet can only be of a formal kind because it is not implicit in the substantiality of the subjective life as it is in the sphere of absolute religious truth. Conversely, the shape of external circumstances, situations, and the complexity of events, also becomes explicitly free and therefore has its ups and downs in capricious adventures. Therefore we acquire as the culmination of the romantic in general the contingency of both outer and inner, and the separation of these two sides, whereby art annuls itself and brings home to our minds that we must acquire higher forms for the apprehension of truth than those which art is in a position to supply.

Chapter I

THE RELIGIOUS DOMAIN OF
ROMANTIC ART

In its representation of absolute subjectivity as the whole of truth, romantic art has for its substantial content the reconciliation of God with the world and therefore with himself, the unification of the spirit with its essence, the satisfaction of the heart, and therefore at this stage the Ideal seems at last to be completely at home. For it was blessedness and independence, satisfaction, tranquillity, and freedom which we named[1] as the chief characteristics of the Ideal. Of course we may not deny the Ideal to the essence and reality of romantic art, but in comparison with the classical Ideal it takes a quite different form there. Although this relation has already been indicated in general above [in the Introduction to this Section], we must here at the very beginning expound it in its more concrete meaning in order to make clear the fundamental type of the romantic way of portraying the Absolute.

In the classical Ideal the Divine is on the one hand restricted to individuality; on the other hand, the soul and blessedness of the particular gods are entirely transfused through their corporeal shape; and, thirdly, since the underlying principle is the unseparated unity of the individual in himself and in his external world, there cannot appear as an essential factor the negativity of diremption within the self, of bodily and spiritual grief, of sacrifice and renunciation. In classical art the Divine collapses indeed into a group of gods but it does not divide itself within itself as (*a*) universal essentiality and (*b*) individual subjective empirical appearance in the human form and the human spirit; and neither, as a non-appearing Absolute, has it confronting it a world of evil, sins, and error, and consequently with the task of reconciling these oppositions and being truly actual and divine only as this reconciliation.

On the other hand, [i] in the *Concept* of absolute subjectivity there is implicit the opposition between substantial universality and personality, an opposition whose completed reconciliation fills the subject with his substance and raises the substance into a knowing

[1] On p. 157 above.

and willing absolute subject. But, (ii) to the *actuality* of subjectivity as spirit there belongs the deeper opposition to a finite world; through that world's cancellation as finite and its reconciliation with the Absolute, the Infinite makes its own essence explicit to itself through its own absolute activity and only so is absolute spirit. The appearance of this actuality on the soil and in the shape of the human spirit therefore acquires in respect of its *beauty* a totally different relation from what it has in classical art. Greek beauty displays the inner life of spiritual individuality as entirely embodied in its corporeal shape, in actions and events, as expressed entirely in the outer, and living blissfully there. Whereas for romantic beauty it is absolutely necessary for the soul, although appearing in externality, to show itself at the same time as being brought back out of this corporeality into itself and as living in itself. Therefore at this stage the body can express the inwardness of the spirit only by revealing the fact that the soul has its congruent reality not in this real existence, but in itself. For this reason beauty will now reside, no longer in the idealization of the objective shape, but in the inner shape of the soul in itself; it becomes a beauty of deep feeling, as the manner in which every content in the subject's inner life is formed and developed, and without retaining the external shape penetrated by the spirit [as in Greece].

Now because in this way interest in clarifying real existence into this classical unity is lost and is concentrated instead on the opposite aim of breathing a new beauty into the inner shape of the spiritual itself, art now gives itself little trouble with the external; it takes it up immediately, as it finds it, letting it, as it were, shape itself at will. In romantic art, reconciliation with the Absolute is an act of the inner life, an act which does appear externally but does not have the external itself in its real shape for its essential content and aim. With this indifference to the idealizing unification of soul and body there enters essentially, for the more special individuality of the external side, *portraiture* which does not blot out either particular traits and forms as they actually exist,[1] or the poverty of nature and the deficiencies of temporality, in order to put something more appropriate in their place. In general, even in this matter a correspondence [between soul and body] must indeed

---

[1] Previously Hegel has said that some portraits are 'disgustingly like' (Introduction, p. 43) and that portraiture must 'flatter' (pp. 155, 165). Here the instructions to Lely seem to be approved.

be demanded; but the specific shape of it is indifferent and not purified from the contingencies of finite empirical existence.

The necessity for this sweeping characterization of romantic art can be equally justified from another point of view. When the classical ideal figure is at its true zenith, it is complete in itself, independent, reserved, unreceptive, a finished individual which rejects everything else. Its shape is its own; it lives entirely in it and in it alone and may not surrender any part of it to affinity with the purely empirical and contingent. Therefore, whoever approaches these ideal figures as a spectator cannot make their existence his own as something external related to his own external appearance; although the shapes of the eternal gods are human, they still do not belong to the mortal realm, for these gods have not themselves experienced the deficiency of finite existence but are directly raised above it. Community with the empirical and the relative is broken off. Whereas infinite subjectivity, the Absolute of romantic art, is not immersed in its appearance; it is in itself and just for this reason has its external expression not for [apprehension by] itself but by others as something external, set free, and surrendered to everyone. Further, this external side *must* enter the shape of common life, of empirical humanity, because here God himself descends into finite temporal existence in order to mediate and reconcile the absolute opposition inherent in the Concept of the Absolute. Owing to this [Incarnation] too, empirical man acquires an aspect from which a relationship and point of linkage [with God] opens up to him, so that in his immediate natural being he approaches himself with confidence because the external shape [i.e. the Incarnation] does not rebuff him with a classical rigorousness towards the particular and contingent, but offers to his sight what he himself has or what he knows and loves in others around him. It is the fact that it is so much at home in the commonplace that enables romantic art to attract us so familiarly by its external forms. But the externality which has been surrendered has the function, owing to this very surrender, of referring us back to beauty of soul, to the elevation of intimate feeling and the sanctity of the heart, and thus it encourages us at the same time to plunge into the inner life of the spirit and its absolute content and appropriate this inner life to ourselves.

Finally, in this self-surrender [of the Incarnation] there is implicit in general the universal Idea, namely that in romantic art infinite subjectivity is not lonely in itself like a Grecian god who lives in himself absolutely perfect in the blessedness of his isolation; on the contrary, it emerges from itself into a relation with something else which, however, is its own, and in which it finds itself again and remains communing and in unity with itself. This being at one with itself in its other is the really beautiful subject-matter of romantic art, its Ideal which has essentially for its form and appearance the inner life and subjectivity, mind and feeling. Therefore the romantic Ideal expresses a relation to another spiritual being which is so bound up with depth of feeling that only in this other does the soul achieve this intimacy with itself. This life in self in another is, as feeling, the spiritual depth of love.

We may therefore name *love* as the general content of the romantic in its religious domain. Yet its truly ideal configuration love only acquires if it expresses the *affirmative* immediate reconciliation of the spirit. But before we can consider this stage of the most beautiful ideal satisfaction, we have first, on the one hand, to run through the process of *negativity* which the absolute subject enters in the course of overcoming the finitude and immediacy of his human appearance—a process which is unfolded in the life and suffering of God and his death for the world and mankind whereby mankind's reconciliation with God was made possible. On the other hand, it is now humanity, conversely, which for its part has to go through the same process in order to make explicit in itself what was implicit in that reconciliation. Between these stages (the heart of which is the *negative* aspect—the sensuous and spiritual entry to death and the grave) there lies the expression of the *affirmative* bliss of satisfaction which in this sphere characterizes art's most beautiful creations.

For the more detailed division of our first chapter we have therefore to traverse three different spheres:

First, the redemptive history of Christ; i.e. the moments of the absolute Spirit, represented in God himself in so far as he becomes man, has an actual existence in the world of finitude and its concrete relationships, and in this existence, individual at first, brings the Absolute itself into appearance.

Secondly, love in its positive shape as the feeling of reconciliation between man and God: the Holy Family, Mary's maternal love, Christ's love, and the love of the Disciples.

Thirdly, the Community [the Church]: the spirit of God as present in humanity through the conversion of the heart and the annihilation of the natural and the finite, in short through the reversion of mankind to God—a conversion in which penances and tortures in the first place mediate the union of man with God.

1. *The Redemptive History of Christ*

The reconciliation of the spirit with itself, the absolute history, the process of the truth, is brought to our view and conviction by the appearance of God in the world. The simple heart of this reconciliation is the coalescence of absolute essentiality with the individual human subject; an individual man is God, and God an individual man. This implies that the human spirit, in its Concept and essence, is *implicitly* true spirit, and every individual subject, therefore, as man, has the infinite vocation and importance of being one of God's purposes and being in unity with God. But on this account man is all the same faced with the demand that he give actuality to this his Concept which at first is purely implicit, i.e. that he make union with God the goal of his being, and achieve it. If he has fulfilled this vocation, then in himself he is free infinite spirit. This is possible for him only because that unity is the original fact, the eternal basis of human and divine nature. [In the first place] this goal is at the same time the absolute beginning, the presupposition of the romantic religious consciousness that God himself is man, flesh, that he has become this individual person in whom therefore the reconciliation does not remain something implicit (in which case it would be known only in its *Concept*) but stands forth *objectively* existent for human senses and conscious contemplation as this individual actually existing man. It is on account of this moment of individuality that in Christ every individual has a vision of his own reconciliation with God which in its essence is no mere possibility; it is actual and therefore has to appear in this one man as really achieved. But, secondly, since this unity, as the spiritual reconciliation of opposed moments, is no mere *immediate* coalescence into one, it follows that in this *one* man the process of spirit too, through which alone consciousness is truly spirit, must attain existence as the history of this man. This history of the spirit, consummated in one individual, contains nothing except what we have already touched on above, namely that the individual man casts aside his individuality of body and spirit, i.e. that he suffers and dies, but conversely through the grief of death rises out of death, and ascends as God in his glory, as the actual spirit which now has indeed entered existence as an individual, as this subject, yet even so is essentially truly God only as Spirit in his Church.

(a) Apparent Superfluity of Art

This history provides the fundamental topic for religious romantic art, and yet for this topic art, taken purely as art, becomes to a certain extent something superfluous. For the chief thing lies here in the inner conviction, feeling, and conception of this eternal truth, in the *faith* which bears witness to itself of the absolute truth and thereby imparts it to the inner life of mind. A developed faith, in other words, consists in the immediate conviction that the conception of the factors in this history suffices to bring truth itself before consciousness. But if it is a matter of the consciousness of *truth*, then the *beauty* of the appearance, and the representation, is an accessory and rather indifferent, for the truth is present for consciousness independently of art.

(b) Necessary Emergence of Art

Yet, on the other hand, the religious material contains in itself at the same time a factor whereby it is not only made accessible to art but does in a certain respect actually *need* art. In the religious ideas of romantic art, as has been indicated more than once already, this material involves pushing anthropomorphism to an extreme, in that it is precisely this material (i) which has as its centre the coalescence of the Absolute and Divine with a human person as actually perceived and therefore as appearing externally and corporeally, and (ii) which must present the Divine in this its individuality, bound as it is to the deficiency of nature and the finite mode of appearance. In this respect, for the appearance of God art provides to the contemplative consciousness the special presence of an actual individual shape, a concrete picture too of the external features of the events in which Christ's birth, life and sufferings, death, Resurrection, and Ascension to the right hand of God are displayed, so that, in general, the actual appearance of God, which has passed away, is repeated and perpetually renewed in art alone.

(c) *The Details of the External Appearance are Accidental*

But in so far as in this appearance the accent is laid on the fact that God is essentially an individual person, exclusive of others, and displays the unity of divine and human subjectivity not simply in general but as *this* man, there enter here again, in art, on account of the subject-matter itself, all the aspects of the contingency and particularity of external finite existence from which beauty at the height of the classical Ideal had been purified. What the free Concept of the beautiful had discarded as inappropriate, i.e. the non-Ideal, is here necessarily adopted and brought before our vision as a factor emerging from the subject-matter itself.

(α) While therefore the Person of Christ as such is frequently chosen as a subject, every time those artists have proceeded in the worst possible way who have attempted to make out of Christ an ideal in the sense and in the manner of the classical ideal. For although such heads and figures of Christ do display seriousness, calm, and dignity, Christ should have on the one hand subjective personality and *individuality*, and, on the other, inwardness and purely *universal* spirituality; both these characteristics are inconsistent with the imprint of bliss on the visible aspect of the human form. To combine both these extremes in expression and form is of supreme difficulty, and painters especially found themselves in perplexity every time they departed from the traditional type.

Seriousness and depth of consciousness must be expressed in these heads, but the features and forms of the face and the figure must neither be of purely ideal beauty nor deviate into the commonplace and the ugly or rise to pure sublimity as such. The best thing in relation to the external form is the mean between natural detail and ideal beauty. To hit this due mean correctly is difficult, and so in this matter what may be especially conspicuous is the skill, sense, and spirit of the artist.

In general, in the case of representations throughout this whole sphere, we are referred, independently of the subject-matter, which belongs to faith, to the matter of the artist's subjective creation, more than is the case in the classical ideal. In classical art the artist aims at presenting the spiritual and the Divine directly in the forms of the body itself and in the organization of the human figure, and therefore the bodily forms in their modifications, when these diverge from the customary and the finite, afford

a principal part of the interest. In the sphere now under consideration the shape remains the customary and familiar one; its forms
are to a certain extent indifferent, something particular, which may
be thus or otherwise, and may in this respect be treated with great
freedom. Therefore the preponderating interest lies on the one
hand in the manner in which the artist still makes the spiritual and
the most inward content shine, as this spiritual element itself,
through this customary and familiar material; on the other hand, in
the artist's execution, in the technical means and skills whereby he
has been able to breathe spiritual vitality into his shapes and make
the most spiritual things perceptible and comprehensible.

(β) As for the further subject-matter, it lies, as we have seen
already, in the absolute history which springs from the Concept of
spirit itself and which makes objective the conversion of bodily and
spiritual individuality into its essence and universality. For the
reconciliation of the individual person with God does not enter as
a harmony directly, but as a harmony proceeding only from the
infinite grief, from surrender, sacrifice, and the death of what is
finite, sensuous, and subjective. Here finite and infinite are bound
together into one, and the reconciliation in its true profundity,
depth of feeling, and force of mediation is exhibited only through
the magnitude and harshness of the opposition which is to be
resolved. It follows that even the whole sharpness and dissonance
of the suffering, torture, and agony involved in such an opposition,
belong to the nature of spirit itself, whose absolute satisfaction is
the subject-matter here.

This process of the spirit, taken in and by itself, is the essence
and Concept of spirit in general, and therefore it entails the characteristic of being for consciousness the universal history which is
to be repeated in every individual consciousness. For consciousness, as a multiplicity of individuals, is precisely the reality and
existence of the universal spirit. At first, however, because the
Spirit has as its essential factor reality in the individual, that universal history itself proceeds only in the shape of *one* individual in
whom it happens as his, as the history of his birth, his suffering,
his death, and his return from death, though in this individual it
preserves at the same time the significance of being the history of
the universal absolute Spirit.

The real turning-point in this life of God is the termination of his
individual existence as *this* man, the story of the Passion, suffering

on the cross, the Golgotha of the Spirit, the pain of death. This sphere of portrayal is separated *toto caelo* from the classical plastic ideal because here the subject-matter itself implies that the external bodily appearance, immediate existence as an individual, is revealed in the grief of his negativity as the negative, and that therefore it is by sacrificing subjective individuality and the sensuous sphere that the Spirit attains its truth and its Heaven. On the one hand, in other words, the earthly body and the frailty of human nature in general is raised and honoured by the fact that it is God himself who appears in human nature, but on the other hand it is precisely this human and bodily existent which is negatived and comes into appearance in its grief, while in the classical ideal it does not lose undisturbed harmony with what is spiritual and substantial. Christ scourged, with the crown of thorns, carrying his cross to the place of execution, nailed to the cross, passing away in the agony of a torturing and slow death—this cannot be portrayed in the forms of Greek beauty; but the higher aspect in these situations is their inherent sanctity, the depth of the inner life, the infinity of grief, present as an eternal moment in the Spirit as sufferance and divine peace.

The wider group around this figure is formed partly of friends, partly of enemies. The friends are likewise no ideal figures but, in accordance with the Concept,[1] particular individuals, ordinary men whom the pull of the Spirit brings to Christ. But the enemies are presented to us as inwardly evil because they place themselves in opposition to God, condemn him, mock him, torture him, crucify him, and the idea of inner evil and enmity to God brings with it on the external side, ugliness, crudity, barbarity, rage, and distortion of their outward appearance. In connection with all these there enters here as a necessary feature what is unbeautiful in comparison with the beauty of Greek art.

(γ) But the process of death is to be treated in the divine nature only as a point of transition whereby the reconciliation of the Spirit with itself is brought about, and the divine and human sides, the sheerly universal and the subjective appearance, whose mediation is in question, close together affirmatively. This affirmation is in

---

[1] The moments or essential factors in the Concept are, as we have seen, the universal, the particular, and the individual. The universal remains abstract until it is actualized in particulars or individuals, and this actualization is a necessary movement of thought or spirit.

general the basis and the original foundation [of the divine history] and must therefore also be made evident in this positive way. For this purpose the most favourable events in the history of Christ are supplied especially by the Resurrection and the Ascension, apart from the scattered moments at which Christ appears as teacher. But here there arises, especially for the visual arts, a supreme difficulty. For (a) it is the spiritual as such which is to be portrayed in its inwardness, (b) it is the absolute Spirit which in its infinity and universality must be put affirmatively in unity with subjectivity [i.e. in Christ] and yet, raised above immediate existence, must in the bodily and external shape bring before contemplation and feeling the entire expression of its infinity and inwardness.

2. *Religious Love*

The absolute Spirit is, as spirit, not an immediate topic for art. Its supreme actual reconciliation within itself can only be a reconciliation and satisfaction in the spiritual as such; and this in its purely ideal element is not susceptible of expression in art, since absolute truth is on a higher level than the appearance of beauty which cannot be detached from the soil of the sensuous and apparent. But if the Spirit in its affirmative reconciliation is to acquire through art a *spiritual* existence in which it is not merely known as pure thought, as ideal, but can be *felt* and contemplated, then we have left as the sole form which fulfils the double demand (that of spirituality on the one hand and comprehensiblity and portrayability by art on the other) only the deep feeling of the spirit, or the soul and feeling. This depth of feeling, which alone corresponds to the essential nature of the spirit which is free and satisfied in itself, is *love*.

(a) *Concept of the Absolute as Love*

In love, in other words, those phases are present, in its *content*, which we cited as the fundamental essence of the absolute Spirit: the reconciled return out of another into self. By being the other in which the spirit remains communing with itself, this other can only be spiritual over again, a spiritual personality. The true essence of love consists in giving up the consciousness of oneself, forgetting oneself in another self, yet in this surrender and oblivion having and possessing oneself alone. This reconciliation of the spirit with itself and the completion of itself to a totality is the Absolute, yet not, as may be supposed, in the sense that the Absolute as a purely singular and therefore finite subject coincides with itself in another finite subject; on the contrary, the content of the subjectivity which reconciles itself with itself in another is here the Absolute itself: the Spirit which only in another spirit is the knowing and willing of itself as the Absolute and has the satisfaction of this knowledge.

(b) The Heart [or Soul]

Now, looked at more closely, this subject-matter, by being love, has the *form* of feeling, concentrated into itself, which, instead of revealing its content, bringing it into consciousness in its determinacy and universality, rather draws directly together into the simple depth of the heart that content's extent and boundlessness without unfolding for our apprehension all the ramifications which its wealth contains. Therefore the same content which in its purely spiritually stamped universality would be denied to art, in this subjective existence as feeling is again prehensible by art; this is because on the one hand in view of its still undisclosed depth, characteristic of the heart, it is not compelled to explain itself to the length of complete clarity, while on the other hand it acquires from this form at the same time an element suitable to art. For however inward the soul, emotion, and feeling remain, they still always have a connection with the sensuous and corporeal, so that they can now disclose the inmost life and existence of spirit outwardly through the body itself, through a look, facial expressions, or, more spiritually, through words and musical notes. But the external can enter here only as being called upon to express this inmost inner life itself in its inwardness of soul.

(c) Love as the Romantic Ideal

Since we defined the Concept of the Ideal as the reconciliation of the inner life with its reality, we may now describe love as the ideal of romantic art in its religious sphere. It is *spiritual* beauty as such. The classical Ideal too displayed the mediation and reconciliation of the spirit with its opposite. But there the opposite of spirit was the external permeated by spirit, spirit's bodily organism. In love, on the contrary, the spirit's opposite is not nature but itself a spiritual consciousness, another person, and the spirit is therefore realized for itself in what it itself owns, in its very own element. So in this affirmative satisfaction and blissful reality at rest in itself, love is the ideal but purely spiritual beauty which on account of its inwardness can also be expressed only in and as the deep feeling of the heart. For the spirit which is present to itself and immediately sure of itself in [another] spirit, and therefore has the spiritual itself as the material and ground of its *existence*, is in itself, is depth of feeling, and, more precisely, is the spiritual depth of love.

(α) God is love and therefore his deepest essence too is to be apprehended and represented in this form adequate to art in Christ. But Christ is *divine* love; as its object, what is manifest is on the one hand God himself in his invisible essence, and, on the other, mankind which is to be redeemed; and thus what then comes into appearance in Christ is less the absorption of one person in another limited person than the Idea of love in its universality, the Absolute, the spirit of truth in the element and form of feeling. With this universality of love's object, love's expression is also universalized, with the result that the subjective concentration of heart and soul does not become the chief thing in that expression—just as, even in the case of the Greeks, what is emphasized, although in a totally different context, in Venus Urania[1] and the old Titanic deity, Eros, is the universal Idea and not the subjective element, i.e. individual shape and feeling. Only when Christ is conceived in the portrayals of romantic art as more than an individual subject, immersed in himself, does the expression of love become conspicuous in the form of subjective deep feeling, always elevated and borne, however, by the universality of its content.

(β) But in this sphere the most accessible topic for art is Mary's love, *maternal love*, the most successful object of the religious imagination of romantic art. For the most part real and human, it is yet entirely spiritual, without the interest and exigency of desire, not sensuous and yet present: absolutely satisfied and blissful spiritual depth. It is a love without craving, but it is not friendship; for be friendship never so rich in emotion, it yet demands

[1] Originally the goddess of the sky, but later, as distinct from Aphrodite Pandemos, the goddess of higher and purer love.

a content, something essential, as a mutual end and aim. Whereas, without any reciprocity of aim and interests, maternal love has an immediate support in the natural bond of connection. But in this instance the mother's love is not at all restricted to the natural side. In the child which she conceived and then bore in travail, Mary has the complete knowledge and feeling of herself; and the same child, blood of her blood, stands all the same high above her, and nevertheless this higher being belongs to her and is the object in which she forgets and maintains herself. The natural depth of feeling in the mother's love is altogether spiritualized; it has the Divine as its proper content, but this spirituality remains lowly and unaware, marvellously penetrated by natural oneness and human feeling. It is the blissful maternal love, the love of the one mother alone who was the first recipient of this joy. Of course this love too is not without grief, but the grief is only the sorrow of loss, lamentation for her suffering, dying, and dead son, and does not, as we shall see at a later stage,[1] result from injustice and torment from without, or from the infinite battle against sins, or from the agony and pain brought about by the self. Such deep feeling is here spiritual beauty, the Ideal, human identification of man with God, with the spirit and with truth: a pure forgetfulness and complete self-surrender which still in this forgetfulness is from the beginning one with that into which it is merged and now with blissful satisfaction has a sense of this oneness.

In such a beautiful way maternal love, the picture as it were of the Spirit, enters romantic art in place of the Spirit itself because only in the form of feeling is the Spirit made prehensible by art, and the feeling of the unity between the individual and God is present in the most original, real, and living way only in the Madonna's maternal love. This love must enter art necessarily if, in the portrayal of this sphere, the Ideal, the affirmative satisfied reconciliation is not to be lacking. There was therefore a time when the maternal love of the blessed Virgin belonged in general to the highest and holiest [part of religion] and was worshipped and represented as this supreme fact. But when the Spirit brings itself into consciousness of itself in its own element, separated from the whole natural grounding which feeling supplies, then too it is only the spiritual mediation, free from such a grounding, that can be regarded as the free route to the truth; and so, after all, in Protes-

---

[1] See the following 3(a).

tantism, in contrast to mariolatry in art and in faith, the Holy Spirit and the inner mediation of the Spirit has become the higher truth.

(γ) Thirdly and lastly, the affirmative reconciliation of the spirit is displayed as feeling in Christ's Disciples and in the women and friends who follow him. These for the most part are characters who have experienced the austerity of the Idea of Christianity at the hand of their divine friend through the friendship, teaching, and preaching of Christ without going through the external and internal agony of conversion; they have perfected this Idea, mastered it and themselves, and they remain pensive and powerful in the same. True, they lack that immediate unity and deep feeling of the mother's love, but as their bond of union there is still left to them the presence of Christ, the habit of communal life, and the direct pull of the Spirit.

3. The Spirit of the Community

As for the transition into the last sphere of this topic, we may link it with what was already touched upon above in relation to the story of Christ. The immediate existence of Christ, as this one individual man who is God, is posited as superseded, i.e. what comes to light in the very appearance of God as man is the fact that the true reality of God is not immediate existence but spirit. The reality of the Absolute as infinite subjectivity is just the spirit itself; God exists only in knowing, in the element of the inner life. This absolute existence of God as pure universality, alike ideal and subjective, is therefore not restricted to this individual [Jesus] who in his history has made visible the reconciliation of human and divine personality, but is broadened into the human consciousness which is reconciled with God, in short into mankind which exists as a plurality of individuals. Yet taken by himself as an individual personality, the man [Jesus] is not divine *immediately* at all; on the contrary, he is the finite and human being who only attains reconciliation with God in so far as he actually posits himself as the negative which he is implicitly and so cancels his finitude. Only through this deliverance from the imperfection of finitude does humanity proclaim itself as the existence of the absolute Spirit, as the community's spirit in which the unification of the human spirit with the divine within human reality itself is completed as the mediation in reality of what implicitly, in the essential nature of spirit, is originally in unity.

The chief forms which are of importance in relation to this new content of romantic art may be specified as follows:

The individual person, separated from God, living in sin, in the battle of immediacy and in the poverty of finitude, has the infinite vocation of coming into reconciliation with himself and God. But since in the redemptive history of Christ the negativity of immediate individuality has appeared as the essential feature of the spirit, the individual person is able to rise to freedom and to peace in God as a result solely of the conversion of the natural element and finite personality.

This transcendence of finitude enters here in a threefold way:

First, as the external repetition of the Passion story; this becomes actual physical suffering—martyrdom.

Secondly, the conversion is transferred into the inner life of the mind as an inner mediation through repentance, penance, and the return of the soul to God.

Thirdly and lastly, the appearance of the Divine in mundane reality is so interpreted that the ordinary course of nature and the natural form of other happenings is superseded in order to make possible a revelation of the power and presence of the Divine: whereby miracle becomes the form in which this revelation is presented.

(a) Martyrs

The first phenomenon in which the spirit of the community is revealed as effective in the human person consists in man's mirroring in himself the reflection of the divine process and making himself a new determinate embodiment of the eternal history of God. Here the expression of that *immediately* affirmative reconciliation disappears again, because man has to secure it only through the cancellation of his finitude. What therefore was the centre at the first stage [i.e. the negative], returns here again in a thoroughly enhanced degree because the inadequacy and unworthiness of man is the presupposition, and to extinguish this counts as the supreme and sole task of man.

(α) The proper subject-matter of this sphere, therefore, is endurance of cruelties, and a man's own freely willed renunciation, sacrifice, and privation. These he imposes on himself for the sake of privation and for the sake of occasioning his suffering, torments, agonies of every kind by means of which the spirit may be transfigured within and feel itself at one, satisfied, and blissful in its Heaven. In martyrdom this negative—grief—is an end in itself, and the magnitude of the transfiguration is measured by the awfulness of what the man has suffered and the frightfulness to which he has submitted. Now given his still unfulfilled inner life, the first thing that can be negatived in the martyr, with a view to his sanctification and his release from the world, is his *natural* being, his life, and the satisfaction of the most elementary needs necessary for his existence. Thus the chief topic in this sphere is provided by physical tortures inflicted on the believer; they are partly perpetrated out of hatred and vindictiveness by enemies and persecutors of the faith, partly undergone, with complete renunciation and at his own instigation, as an expiation of sins. Both of these he accepts in a fanaticism of resignation, not as an injustice, but as a blessing through which alone the hardness of the heart, the flesh, and the mind conscious of original sin are to be broken and reconciliation with God achieved.

But since in such situations the conversion of the inner life can only be portrayed in dreadfulness and in the brutality of the tortures, the sense of beauty is easily damaged and the topics in this sphere constitute a very hazardous material for art. For on the one hand, in a much higher degree than what we required in the history of Christ's Passion, the individuals must be shown as actual single individuals stamped with the mark of temporal existence and caught in the deficiency of finitude and natural life; on the other hand, the agonies, the unheard-of frightfulnesses, the distortions and dislocations of limbs, the physical torments, the scaffolds, the beheadings, roastings, burning at the stake, boiling in oil, fastening to the wheel, etc.—all these are inherently hateful, repugnant, disgusting externals; their distance from beauty is too great to allow any healthy art to select them as its subject-matter. The artist's way of treating [these subjects] may indeed be excellent in its execution, but in that case the interest in this excellence always relates only to the artist's subjective activity which, even if it may seem to be in accord with art, yet labours in vain to create a perfect harmony between itself and this material.

(β) Therefore the portrayal of this negative process requires still another feature which overrides this agony of body and soul and leans towards the affirmative reconciliation. This is the reconciliation of the spirit in itself which is won as the aim and result of all the horror that has been suffered. From this point of view the martyrs are the preservers of the Divine against the crudity of external power and the barbarity of unbelief; for the sake of the Kingdom of Heaven they endure grief and death, and this courage, strength, endurance, and blessedness must therefore appear in them equally. Yet this deep feeling of faith and love in its spiritual beauty is not the spiritual health which permeates the body healthily; on the contrary, it is an inwardness which grief has wrought upon, or which is portrayed in suffering and even still contains in transfiguration the element of grief as the strictly essential thing. Painting especially has often made such piety its subject-matter. Having done so, it has as its chief task the expression of the *bliss* of torment, contrasted with the abominable lacerations of the flesh, simply in the lines of the face, the look, etc., as resignation, the overcoming of grief, and satisfaction in achieving the living presence of the divine spirit in the inner life of the martyr. If, on the other hand, sculpture proposes to bring the same material before our eyes, it is less capable of portraying concentrated deep feeling in this spiritualized way and therefore will have to emphasize what is grievous and distorted because this is manifested in a more developed form in the bodily organism.

(γ) But, thirdly, the aspect of self-denial and endurance is at this stage not concerned merely with natural existence and immediate finitude; on the contrary, it exaggerates the heart's bent towards heavenly things to such an extreme that the human and the mundane sphere, even if in itself it is of an ethical and rational kind, is thrust into the background and disdained. The spirit here, that is to say, vitalizes in itself the idea of its conversion; but the less the spirit is developed to begin with, all the more barbarically and abstractly does it turn with its concentrated force of piety against everything that, as the finite, stands contrasted with this inherently simple infinity of religious feeling: against all specific human feeling, against the many-sided moral inclinations, relations, circumstances, and duties of the heart. For ethical life in the family, the bonds of friendship, blood, love, the state, calling—all these belong to the mundane sphere; and in so far as here the mundane is not yet penetrated by the absolute ideas of faith, and developed into unity and reconciliation therewith, it is not adopted into the sphere of inner feeling and obligation, but instead appears to the abstract deep feeling of the believing heart as null in itself and therefore hostile and detrimental to piety. The ethical organization of the human world is therefore not yet respected, because its parts and duties are not yet recognized as necessary and justified links in the chain of an inherently rational actuality; in such an actual organization nothing one-sided may rise to an isolated independence, yet must all the same be retained as a valid factor and not sacrificed. In this respect the religious reconciliation itself remains here in an *abstract* form, and it is displayed in the inherently simple heart as an intensity of faith without extension, as the piety of a heart lonely with itself which has not yet framed itself into a universal and developed confidence and into a discerning comprehensive certainty of itself. Now if the force of such a heart clings to itself in itself against the actuality which it has treated purely negatively, and if it violently detaches itself from all human ties, even were they those originally most firm, then this is a crudity of spirit and a barbaric power of abstraction which must revolt us. Therefore, from the standpoint of our modern consciousness, we may be able to respect and value highly that germ of religious feeling in representations of such an attitude, but if piety goes so far that we see it exaggerated into violence against what is inherently rational and moral, not only can we not sympathize with such fanaticism of sanctity, but this sort of renunciation must appear to us as immoral and contrary to religious feeling because it rejects, demolishes, and tramples underfoot what is absolutely justified and sacrosanct.

Of this sort there are many legends, stories, and poems. For example, the story of the man full of love for his wife and family and loved by them in return who leaves his home and goes away on a pilgrimage, and when at last he comes back in the guise of a beggar, he does not reveal himself; alms are given him, and out of sympathy a little place is reserved for him to stay in under the stairs; in this way he lives in his house for twenty years long, looks on at his family's sorrow for him, and only on his deathbed does he make himself known. This is a horrible selfishness of fanaticism which we are supposed to reverence as sanctity. This persistence in renunciation may remind us of the profound penances which the Indians likewise impose on themselves of their own free will for

religious ends. Yet the sufferings of the Indians have a quite different character, because in *their* case the penitent transposes himself
into dullness and unconsciousness; whereas *here* grief and the
deliberate consciousness and feeling of grief is the real end which is
supposed to be attained all the more purely the more the suffering
is bound up with a consciousness of the value of the relationships
that have been surrendered and love for them, and also with a
continuous contemplation of renunciation. The richer the heart
that loads itself with such trials, the more it possesses a noble
treasure while yet believing itself forced to condemn this possession
as null and to stamp it as sin, all the harsher is the lack of reconciliation, a lack that can generate the most frightful hysteria and the
most raving disunion. Indeed such a heart which is at home only in
the intelligible and not in the mundane world as such, which therefore also feels itself just lost in the absolutely valid spheres and aims
of this specific reality, and which, although held and bound in it
with its whole soul, treats this moral order as negative in contrast to
its own absolute vocation—yes, indeed, such a heart must appear to
us according to our outlook as mad in its self-created suffering and
in its renunciation, so that we cannot feel pity for it or draw any
edification from it. Such actions lack a valid and solid end, for what
they achieve is only purely subjective, is an end of the individual
man himself alone, for the salvation of *his* soul and for *his* bliss. But
it matters very little whether a man just like this is blissful or not.

(b) *Repentance and Conversion*

In the same sphere, the opposite mode of representation disre-
gards the *external* torture of the body, on the one hand, and, on the
other, the negative bent against what is absolutely justified in
mundane reality, and thereby, both in content and form, wins
ground more adequate to ideal art. This ground is the conversion
of the *inner* life which expresses itself solely in its *spiritual* grief, in
its change of heart. Therefore here, for one thing, the ever-repeated
horrors and dreadfulnesses of bodily torture have no place; for
another thing, the barbaric religiosity of the heart is no longer kept
so rigidly in opposition to the ethical life of humanity that, in the
abstraction of its purely intellectual satisfaction, it can trample
violently under foot every other kind of enjoyment, satisfied as it is
in the grief of an absolute renunciation; now, on the contrary, it

turns only against what is in fact sinful, criminal, and evil in human nature. It is a lofty conviction that faith, this inner bent of the spirit towards God, is capable of making into something alien to the agent the deed that has been committed, even if it be sin and crime, of making it undone and washing it away. This retreat from evil, from the absolute negative, is actual in the person after his subjective will and spirit has scorned and extinguished the evil self that it has been. This return to the positive, which is now established as what is really actual in contrast with earlier existence in sin, is the truly infinite power of religious love, the presence and actuality of the absolute Spirit in the person himself. The sense of the strength and endurance of one's own spirit which, through God to whom it turns, conquers evil, and by harmonizing itself with him knows itself one with him, thus affords the satisfaction and bliss of seeing God as absolutely other than the sins of temporality, yet of knowing this infinite Being as at the same time identical with me as this person, and of carrying in me, with the same assurance as I have of my own being, this self-consciousness of God as my self, as my self-consciousness. It is true that such a revolution proceeds entirely in the inner life and therefore belongs rather to religion than to art; yet since it is the deep feeling of the heart which is principally the master of this act of conversion and which can also shine through the external, it follows that visual art itself, i.e. [here] painting, acquires the right of bringing before our eyes the history of such conversions. Yet if it portrays the entire course of such histories completely, then here again much that is not beautiful may creep in, because in this case after all the criminal and repugnant must be presented as, e.g., in the story of the prodigal son. Therefore things go most favourably for painting when it concentrates the conversion into *one* picture alone, without further detailing the crime. An example of this is Mary Magdalene, who is to be reckoned one of the most beautiful subjects in this sphere and is treated excellently, and consistently with art, especially by Italian painters. Here she appears both in soul and in presence as the *beautiful* sinner in whom the sin is as attractive as the conversion. Yet in this case neither the sin nor the sanctity is taken very seriously; much was forgiven her because she had loved much [Luke 7: 47]; because of her love and beauty she is forgiven, and the touching thing consists in the fact that she yet makes a conscience for herself out of her love, and in her beauty of soul and richness of feeling pours forth tears of grief. It is not that she loved so much that is her error; on the contrary, what is as it were her beautiful touching error is that she *believes* herself to be a sinner, for her deep feeling and her beauty give rise only to the impression that in her love she has been noble and moved profoundly.

(c) Miracles and Legends

The final aspect, which is associated with the two previous ones and which may be prevalent in both, concerns the miracles which in general play a leading role in this whole sphere. In this connection we may describe miracles as the history of the conversion of immediate natural existence. Reality confronts us as a common contingent fact; this finite existent is touched by the Divine which, by entering directly upon what is purely external and particular, breaks it up, inverts it, makes it into something sheerly different, and interrupts what we commonly call the natural course of things. Now it is a chief theme of many legends to represent the heart as having its ideas of the finite upset because it has been captivated by such unnatural phenomena in which it believes that it recognizes the presence of the Divine. In fact, however, the Divine can touch and rule nature only as reason, i.e. as the unchangeable laws of nature itself which God has implanted in it; and the Divine is not to be shown precisely as the Divine in individual circumstances and effects which are breaches of natural laws; for it is only the eternal laws and categories of reason that actually make their way into nature. This is why the legends often pass over without difficulty into what is abstruse, tasteless, senseless, and laughable, because spirit and heart are supposed to be moved towards faith in the presence and activity of God precisely by what is absolutely irrational, false, and non-divine. In these legends, emotion, piety, conversion may still be of interest, but these are only *one* aspect, the inner and subjective one; if these enter into relation with their opposite, i.e. with something external, and if this external thing is to bring about the conversion of the heart, then this external thing must not be in itself something senseless and irrational.

These we may take to be the chief elements in the substantial subject-matter which in this sphere amounts to God's explicit nature and the process through and in which he is Spirit. This is the absolute theme which art does not create and reveal from its own resources, but which it has received from religion and which it approaches, with the consciousness that it is the absolute truth, in order to express and display it. This is the content of the believing and yearning heart which in and for itself is the infinite totality, so that now the external sphere remains more or less external and contingent without coming into complete harmony with the inner sphere and therefore it often becomes a repellent material not thoroughly conquerable by art.

Chapter II

CHIVALRY

As we saw in Section III, 1, the principle of inherently infinite subjectivity has primarily as the content of faith and art the Absolute itself, the Spirit of God as it is mediated and reconciled with human consciousness, and thereby is truly explicit to itself. Since this romantic mysticism is restricted to the achievement of bliss in the Absolute, it remains an abstract depth of feeling because, instead of permeating the mundane and accepting it affirmatively, this feeling contrasts itself with it and spurns it. In this abstraction faith is separated from life, and removed from the concrete reality of human existence, from a positive relation of men to one another who only in faith and on account of faith know their identity with one another and love one another in a third thing, i.e. the spirit of the community. This third thing is alone the clear spring in which their picture is mirrored; at this stage men do not look one another in the face, enter into a direct relation with each other, and sense as something concrete and alive the unity of their love, trust, confidence, aims, and actions. What constitutes the hope and longing of the inner life, man finds in his abstract religious depth of feeling only in the form of life in the Kingdom of God, in community with the Church; he has not yet dismissed this identity in a third thing from his consciousness in order to have immediately before himself, in the knowing and willing of others too, what he is in his concrete self. The entire religious subject-matter therefore does assume the form of reality, but it still remains in the inwardness of ideas which consumes existence in its living expansion, and is far from satisfying in life itself the higher demand of its own life, even if that life be filled with the mundane and unfolded into reality.[1]

The heart which is only now perfected in its simple bliss has therefore to leave the heavenly kingdom of its substantive sphere, to look into itself, and attain a mundane content appropriate to the

[1] See the Introduction to ch. III below. Even though religion necessarily takes an external form, it knows itself to be too elevated ever to be satisfied in real life.

individual subject as such. Therefore the earlier *religious* inwardness now becomes one of a *worldly* kind. Christ did say: 'Ye must leave father and mother and follow me', and likewise 'Brother will hate brother; men will crucify you and persecute you',[1] etc. But when the Kingdom of God has won a place in the world and is active in penetrating worldly aims and interests and therefore in transfiguring them, when father, mother, brother, meet in the community, then the worldly realm too for its part begins to claim and assert its right to validity. If this right be upheld, the emotion which at first is exclusively religious loses its negative attitude to human affairs as such; the spirit is spread abroad, is on the lookout for itself in its present world, and widens its actual mundane heart. The fundamental principle itself is not altered; inherently infinite subjectivity only turns to another sphere of the subject-matter. We may indicate this transition by saying that subjective individuality now becomes explicitly free as individuality independently of reconciliation with God. For precisely in that reconciliation, in which individuality rid itself of its purely finite restriction and natural character, it has traversed the road of negativity, and now, after it has become affirmative in and for itself, it emerges freely as subject with the demand that, as subject in its infinity (even if here still primarily formal infinity), it shall secure complete reverence for itself and others. In this *its* subjectivity, therefore, it places the entire inwardness of the infinite heart which hitherto God alone had filled.

Yet if we ask what then at this new stage is the human breast in its inwardness full of, [we reply that] the content is concerned only with subjective infinite self-relation; the subject is only full of himself by being inherently infinite individuality; he does not need the importance or further concrete development of an inherently objective substantial content of interests, aims, and actions. But, in more detail, there are especially three feelings which in the person rise to this infinity: subjective honour, love, and fidelity. These are not strictly ethical qualities and virtues, but only forms of the romantic self-filled inwardness of the subject. For honour's fight for personal independence is not bravery defending the common weal and the call of justice in the same or of rectitude in the sphere of private life; on the contrary, honour's struggle is only for the recognition and the abstract inviolability of the individual person.

[1] Matt. 23: 34, 24: 10. Luke 14: 26. John 15: 20.

So too love, the centre of this sphere, is only the accidental passion of one person for another and, even if it be widened by imagination and deepened by spiritual profundity, is still not the ethical relation of marriage and the family. Fidelity indeed has more the look of an ethical character since it does not merely will something on its own behalf; on the contrary, it keeps in view something higher, something in common with others; it surrenders itself to another's will, to the wish or command of a master and therefore renounces the selfishness and independence of the agent's own particular will; but the feeling of fidelity does not touch the objective interest of the common weal explicitly developed in its freedom into the life of the state; it is linked, on the contrary, only with the person of the master who acts for himself in an individual way or keeps together more general relationships and is active on their behalf.

These three aspects taken together and interpenetrated by one another constitute—apart from the religious associations which may play their part here too—the chief content of *chivalry* and provide the necessary transition from the principle of religious inwardness to its entry into mundane spiritual life. In the sphere of these aspects romantic art now gains a position from which it can create independently from its own resources[1] and become as it were a freer beauty. For it stands here freely midway between the absolute content of explicitly fixed religious ideas and the varied particularity and restrictedness of finitude and the world. Amongst the particular arts it is especially poetry which has been able to master this material in the most appropriate way, because it is the one most competent to express both the inwardness which is concerned solely with itself, and also its aims and adventures.

Since we now have before us a material which man takes from his own heart, from the world of the purely human, it might seem that here romantic art stands on the same ground with the classical, and thus this is the best place to compare and contrast the two with one another. We have already earlier [in Part II, ch. II] described classical art as the ideal of objectively and inherently true humanity. Its imagination requires as its centre a subject-matter of a substantial kind with an ethical 'pathos'. In the Homeric poems and the tragedies of Aeschylus and Sophocles the treatment is concerned with the interests of something really solid, with a strict check on

---

[1] i.e. its content or material is not now given to it by religion, and so the beauty which it creates is freer.

CHIVALRY 555

the passions involved, and with a profound diction and execution adequate to the thought lying in the topic; and above the group of heroes and figures, who are individually independent only when animated by such a 'pathos', there stands a group of gods with still more greatly enhanced objectivity. Even where art becomes more subjective in the endless plays of sculpture, in bas-reliefs e.g., and in the later elegies, epigrams, and other elegances of lyric poetry, the manner of presenting the subject-matter is more or less given by that matter itself because it already has its objective form; imaginative pictures come on the scene, like Venus, Bacchus, the Muses, fixed and determinate in their character, and similarly the later epigrams contain descriptions of what is there, or familiar flowers are tied together, as by Meleager,[1] into a garland and, through feeling, the bond which they acquire becomes an exquisite sentiment. All this is a cheerful activity in a house richly furnished, filled with a store of resources, products, and utensils ready for any purpose; the poet and artist is only the magician who evokes them, collects and groups them.

In romantic poetry it is quite different. In so far as it is mundane and not directly rooted in sacred history, the virtues and aims of its heroic characters are not those of the Greek heroes whose moral actions early Christianity regarded as only splendid vices.[2] For Greek ethical life presupposes a fully formed present condition of human life; there the will is supposed to pursue its activity absolutely in accordance with its essential nature, and there it has attained a specific area for its exercise in which the actualized relationships are free and absolutely valid. These are the relations between parents and children, husband and wife, citizens and their city, and within the state in its realized freedom. Since this

[1] i.e. the *Garland*, forty-six poems in the Greek Anthology, collected by Meleager, poet and philosopher, c. 80 B.C.
[2] *virtutes gentium splendida vitia* is a phrase commonly ascribed to Augustine though it is apparently not in his works. In the following sentence Bassenge substitutes 'Christian' for 'Greek', the reading of both of Hotho's editions. The argument of the paragraph may not be wholly clear, but this emendation seems to me to be misconceived. Hegel is contrasting the 'objective' morality of Greece with the 'subjective' morality of the Christian conscience. The latter is found in chivalry, i.e. at a time when social institutions were undeveloped. A combination of the two sides is what Hegel discerns in the modern world (see part iii of the *Philosophy of Right*). For those who emphasize conscience or inner conviction alone, habitual instead of conscientious acceptance of the prevailing ethos is just a vice, however splendid.

objective content of action has been produced by the *development* of the human spirit on the positively recognized and assured basis of nature, it is now at variance with that concentrated inwardness of religion which strives to extinguish the natural side of man and must give way to the opposed virtue of humility, the sacrifice both of human freedom and the fixed resting of the self on itself. The virtues of Christian piety in their abstract attitude[1] kill the mundane and make the subject free only if he absolutely repudiates himself in his humanity. The subjective freedom of this present sphere [of chivalry] is indeed no longer conditioned by mere sufferance and sacrifice but is affirmative in itself and in the world, yet, as we saw, the infinity of the person has still once again as its content only inwardness as such, the subjective heart as inherently self-moving, as having its mundane ground in itself. In this respect poetry is not confronted here by any presupposed objectivity, any mythology, any imagery, any configurations lying there already cut and dried for it to express them. It rises entirely free, with no [given] material, purely creative and productive; it is like the bird which sings its song freely from its heart.

But even if here too the subject has a noble will and deep soul, still what enters into his actions and their relations and existence is only capriciousness and contingency, because freedom and its aims themselves originate from internal self-reflection which, so far as an ethical content goes, is still without substance. And so we find in these individuals not a particular 'pathos' in the Greek sense and, bound up therewith in the closest connection, a living independence of individuality, but rather only degrees of heroism in respect of love, honour, bravery, and fidelity, degrees the difference of which depends especially on iniquity or nobility of soul. Yet what the champions in the Middle Ages have in common with the heroes of antiquity is bravery, though even this acquires a quite different position here. It is less the natural courage which rests on healthy excellence and the force of the body and will which has not been weakened by civilization and serves to support the execution of objective interests; rather does it proceed from the inwardness of the spirit, from honour and chivalrousness, and is on the whole fantastic since it resigns itself to adventures of inner caprice and the contingencies of external entanglements, or to impulses of mystical

---

[1] i.e. the negative attitude of penance and martyrdom, or of conscience pursued *à outrance*.

piety, but in general to the subjective relation of the subject to himself.

Now this form of romantic art is at home in two hemispheres; in the West, in this decline of the spirit into its own subjective inner life, and, in the East, in this first expansion of consciousness unfolding itself into liberation from the finite. In the West, poetry rests on the heart that has withdrawn back into itself and has explicitly become the centre of its life, set midway between the two aspects of that life, the mundane world and the higher world of faith. In the East, it is especially the Arab who, as a single point which at first has nothing before itself but its dry deserts and its sky, emerges vigorously to the splendour and first extension of his world[1] and thereby still preserves his inner freedom at the same time. In the Orient it is in general the Mohammedan religion which has as it were cleared the ground by expelling all the idolatry of a finite and imaginative outlook, but has given to the heart the subjective freedom which entirely fills it. The result is that worldly things do not constitute a merely different province, but blossom into a realm of universal freedom where heart and spirit, without framing for themselves an objective embodiment of their god, live cheerfully at peace with themselves; they are like beggars, happy in eating and loving, satisfied and blissful in contemplating and glorifying their objects.

1. *Honour*

The motif of honour was unknown to ancient classical art. True, in the *Iliad* the wrath of Achilles constitutes its burden and moving principle, so that the whole further course of events is dependent on it; but what we understand by honour, in the modern sense, is not in view here at all. At bottom Achilles feels himself injured only because the actual share of the booty which belongs to him and is his reward of honour, his $\gamma\acute{\epsilon}\rho\alpha\varsigma$, has been taken from him by Agamemnon. The injury occurs here in respect of something real, a gift which of course implied a privilege, a recognition of fame and bravery, and Achilles is angry because Agamemnon treats him disgracefully and publicly deprives him of respect among the Greeks; but the injury does not pierce right to the very heart of personality as such, so that Achilles is now satisfied by the return of the share of which he had been deprived and by the addition of

[1] i.e. the spread of Mohammedanism.

more gifts and goods, and Agamemnon finally does not deny him this reparation, although according to our ideas both have insulted one another in the grossest possible way. Yet through the invective they have only made themselves angry, while the particular factual injury is cancelled in a way just as particular and factual.

(a) The Concept of Honour

Romantic honour, however, is of a different kind. In it the injury affects not the positive real value infringed, i.e. property, position, duty, etc., but the personality as such and its idea of itself, the value which the individual ascribes to himself on his own account. This value at this stage is just as infinite as the individual is infinite in his own eyes. In honour, therefore, the man has the first affirmative consciousness of his infinite subjectivity, no matter what the circumstances. Now in what the individual possesses, in what is only some *particular* aspect of himself and despite the loss of which he could subsist just as well as before, honour has placed the absolute validity of his whole subjective personality and in that possession has given him and others an idea of that personality. The measure of honour thus does not depend on what the man actually is but on what this idea of himself is. But this idea makes everything particular into the universal, so that my whole subjective personality lies in this particular possession of mine. Honour is only a show [*Schein*], it is often said. Of course this is the case; but, according to the view now under consideration, it is to be regarded, looked at more closely, as the shining [*Scheinen*] and reflection of subjectivity into itself, which, as the shining of something infinite, is infinite itself. Precisely owing to this infinity the show of honour becomes the real existence of the subject, his supreme actuality, and every particular quality which honour shines into, and which it makes its own, is through this shining itself already exalted to infinite worth. This kind of honour is a fundamental category in the romantic world and involves the presupposition that man has stepped out of purely religious ideas and the inner life and into living reality; and in the material of reality he now brings into existence only himself in his purely personal independence and absolute validity.

Now honour may have the most varied content. For everything that I am, that I do, that is done to me by others, belongs to my honour. Therefore I can make a point of honour of what is itself

purely substantive, fidelity to princes, to country, to calling, fulfilment of paternal duties, fidelity in marriage, honesty in buying and
selling, conscientiousness in scientific research, and so on. But from
the point of view of honour all these relationships, valid and true in
themselves, are not already sanctioned and recognized on their own
account, but only because I put my personality into them and
thereby make them a matter of honour. Therefore in every case the
man of honour always thinks first of himself; and the question is
not whether something is absolutely right or not, but whether it
suits *him*, whether it befits his honour to concern himself with it or
to stay aloof from it. And thus he may well do the worst of things
and still be a man of honour. Accordingly he fabricates capricious
aims for himself, presents himself in a certain [assumed] character,
and therefore binds himself in his own eyes and those of others to
something which has neither obligatoriness nor necessity in itself.
In that event it is not the thing itself but his subjective idea which
puts difficulties and complications in his way because it becomes
a point of honour to uphold the character he has assumed. So, for
example, Donna Diana regards it as contrary to her honour to
bestow on anyone the love that she feels, because she has once set
a great value on not giving ear to love.[1]

   In general, therefore, because the content of honour depends for
its worth only on the man and does not arise from his own immanent essence, it remains a victim of contingency. Therefore, in the
romantic plays, we see on the one hand what is absolutely justified
expressed as a law of honour, since the individual links with his
consciousness of the right the infinite self-consciousness of his
personality at the same time. In that case, the fact that honour
demands or forbids something expresses the insertion of the agent's
entire personality into the content of this demand or this prohibi-
tion, with the result that a transgression cannot be overlooked,
indemnified, or compensated through some sort of transaction,
and the man cannot now heed anything else. But, on the other hand
honour may also become something entirely formal and without
worth, when it contains nothing but the arid self which is infinite in its own eyes or even adopts an entirely bad action as obligatory. In this case, especially in dramatic works, honour remains
a thoroughly cold and dead topic, because its aims express not an

   [1] A Donna Diana appears in many Spanish plays but the reference here is
probably to the *El Desdén con el Desdén* of A. Moreto y Cabaña, 1618–69.

essential content but only an abstract subjectivity. But only an inherently substantial content has necessity and it alone can be developed, throughout its varied connections, in this necessity and brought into consciousness as necessary. This lack of a deeper content is especially in evidence when the subtlety of reflection also introduces into the scope of honour inherently contingent and meaningless matter which touches the man personally. For this purpose there is never any lack of material, for subtlety carries analysis on with the great ingenuity of its gift for making distinctions, and therefore many aspects are discovered and made points of honour though taken in themselves they are matters of complete indifference. The Spaniards especially have developed this casuistry of reflection on points of honour in their dramatic poetry and, as ratiocination, have put it into the mouths of their honour-conscious heroes. So, e.g., the fidelity of a married woman is investigated down to the most trivial possible details, and the mere suspicion of others, indeed the mere possibility of such suspicion—even when the husband knows that the suspicion is false—can become a matter of honour. If this leads to collisions, then their development involves no satisfaction for us because we have nothing substantial before us, and therefore instead of drawing from them the appeasement of a necessary antagonism, we have only a painfully straitened feeling. Even in French dramas it is often an arid honour, wholly abstract in itself, which is supposed to count as the essential interest. But still more in Friedrich von Schlegel's *Alarcos* [1802] we have this ice-cold and dead material: the hero murders his noble, loving wife—why?—to obtain honour, and this honour consists in his being able to marry the King's daughter, for whom he cherishes no passion at all, and thereby become the son-in-law of the King. This is a contemptible 'pathos' and a bad idea which prides itself on being something lofty and infinite.

(b) *Vulnerability of Honour*

Now since honour is not only a shining in *myself*, but must also be envisaged and recognized by *others* who again on their side may demand equal recognition for *their* honour, honour is something purely vulnerable. For how far I will extend my demand, and in relation to what, is something dependent entirely on my caprice. The tiniest offence may in this respect be of importance for me; and because a man stands within concrete reality in the most varied relations with a thousand things and may expand *ad infinitum* the range of what he reckons as his own and on which he stakes his honour, there is no end to strife and quarrelling owing to the independence of individuals and their inflexible singularity which likewise is implicit in the principle of honour. Even in the case of the injury, as of honour in general, the thing in which I must feel myself injured does not matter; for what is negated affects the personality which has made such a thing its own and now considers that what is attacked is *itself*, this ideal infinite point.

(c) Reconstitution of Honour

Therefore every injury to honour is regarded as something infinite in itself and can thus be indemnified only in an infinite way. True, once again there are many degrees of offence and just as many degrees of satisfaction; but what in general I regard in this sphere as an injury, how far I will feel myself offended and demand some satisfaction, this entirely depends here too once more on the subjective caprice which has the right to proceed to the utmost scrupulosity of reflection and the most irritable sensitivity. Thus in the case of such a demanded satisfaction both the man who has injured me and I myself must be recognized as men of honour. For I require him on his side to recognize *my* honour; but if he is to have honour in my eyes and through his action, he must count to me as a man of honour, i.e. he must count in my eyes as an infinite being in his personality, despite the injury he has done me and my subjective enmity towards him.

So then in the principle of honour in general it is a fundamental characteristic that no man in his actions may grant to any other a right over himself, and therefore whatever he may have done and perpetrated, he regards himself both before and afterwards as an unaltered infinite being, and in this capacity intends to be accepted and treated.

Now because in its quarrels and their satisfaction honour rests in this regard on personal independence which cannot be restricted by anything but which acts out of its own resources, we see here returning once again above all what was a fundamental characteristic of the Greek heroic-ideal figures, namely the independence of individuality. But in honour we have not only an adherence to self and an action from personal resources; on the contrary, independence is bound up here with the *idea* of itself; and this idea does precisely constitute the proper content of honour, so that in what is external and present honour perceives its own, and in its own it envisages itself in its entire subjectivity. Honour is thus that independence reflected into itself which has as its essence this reflection alone, and it leaves to pure contingency whether what is at stake is what is inherently ethical and necessary or contingent and meaningless.

2. *Love*

The second feeling which plays a preponderating role in the productions of romantic art is love.

(a) *Concept of Love*

While in honour the fundamental characteristic is personal subjectivity envisaged in its absolute independence, in love the supreme thing is rather the surrender of the person to an individual of the opposite sex, the sacrifice of one's independent consciousness and one's separate self-awareness; the sacrifice is made because one feels compelled to have one's knowledge of oneself solely in the consciousness of the other. In this respect love and honour are opposed to one another. But conversely we may regard love as also the realization of what was already implicit in honour, because honour needs to see itself recognized, and the infinity of the person accepted, in another person. This recognition is only genuine and total when my personality is not respected by others merely *in abstracto* or in a concrete separate and therefore restricted instance, but when with my whole subjective personality—with all that it is and contains—I penetrate the consciousness of another as this individual as I was, am, and will be, and constitute the other's real willing and knowing, striving and possessing. In that event this other lives only in me, just as I am present to myself only in her; in this accomplished unity both are self-aware for the first time and they place their whole soul and world in this identity. In this respect it is the same inner infinity of the person which gives love its importance for romantic art, an importance further enhanced by the higher wealth which the concept of love entails.

The next point is that love does not rest, as may so often be the case with honour, on intellectual reflections and casuistry; instead, it has its origin in feeling, and at the same time it has a foundation in spiritualized *nature*, because difference of sex plays its part in it.

Yet essentially this foundation is present here only because the person is absorbed in this sex-relation in accordance with his inner life, his infinity in himself. What constitutes the infinity of love is this losing, in the other, one's consciousness of self, this splendour of disinterestedness and selflessness through which alone the person finds himself again and becomes a self, this self-forgetfulness in which the lover does not exist, live, and care for himself, but finds the roots of his being in another, and yet in this other does entirely enjoy precisely himself; and beauty is chiefly to be sought in the fact that this emotion does not remain mere impulse and emotion but that imagination builds its whole world up into this relation; everything else which by way of interests, circumstances, and aims belongs otherwise to actual being and life, it elevates into an adornment of this emotion; it tugs everything into this sphere and assigns a value to it only in its relation thereto. It is especially in female characters that love is supremely beautiful, since for them this surrender, this sacrifice, is the acme of their life, because they draw and expand the whole of their actual and spiritual life into this feeling, find a support for their existence in it alone, and, if they are touched by a misfortune in connection with it, dwindle away like a candle put out by the first unkind breeze.

As this subjective spiritual depth of feeling, love does not occur in classical art, and when love does make its appearance there it is generally only a subordinate feature in the representation or only connected with sensuous enjoyment. In Homer either no great weight is laid on love or else it appears in its most dignified form: as marriage in the sphere of domesticity, e.g. in Penelope, or as the solicitude of wife and mother, e.g. in Andromache, or in other ethical relationships. On the other hand, the bond between Paris and Helen is recognized as unethical and the cause of the horrors and distress of the Trojan war; and the love of Achilles for Briseis has little depth and inwardness of feeling, for Briseis is a slave entirely at the hero's disposal. In the Odes of Sappho the language of love is indeed heightened to lyrical enthusiasm, yet it is the insidious and devouring flame of the blood which is expressed rather than the deep feeling of the subjective heart and mind. In the slight and graceful songs of Anacreon, love has a different aspect; it is a more cheerful and general enjoyment which, without endless sufferings, without this domination of the whole of existence or the pious devotion of an oppressed, silent, languishing heart, lets itself go cheerfully in immediate enjoyment as in something innocent with this or that character; and the endless importance of possessing *this* girl and no other remains just as unnoticed as the monk's notion of renouncing the sex-relationship altogether.

The high tragedy of the Greeks likewise knows nothing of the passion of love in the romantic sense. Especially in Aeschylus and Sophocles it lays claim to no essential interest in itself. For although Antigone is the intended bride of Haemon and he intercedes for her before his father, and even goes so far as to kill himself for her sake because he is in no position to save her, still before Creon [his father] he emphasizes objective ties only and not the subjective power of his passion, which also he does not feel in the sense that a modern heartfelt lover does. As a more essential 'pathos' love is treated by Euripides in the *Phaedra*, for example; yet even here it appears as a criminal aberration of the blood, a sensual passion, provoked by Venus who wants to destroy Hippolytus because he will not sacrifice to her. Similarly we have in the Medici Venus what is indeed a plastic picture of love, and nothing can be said against its elegance and the beautiful elaboration of its lines; but the expression of inwardness, as romantic art demands it, is altogether lacking. The same is the case in Roman poetry where, after the Republic and the strictness of ethical life had been destroyed, love appears as more or less a sensual enjoyment.

Whereas, even if Petrarch himself regarded his Sonnets as *jeux d'esprit*, and if it was on his Latin poems and works that he based his fame, what has made him immortal is just this imaginative love which, under the Italian sky and in the artistically developed ardour of the heart, formed a close union with religion. Dante's elation too emanated from his love for Beatrice which then was transfigured in him into religious love, while his courage and boldness were raised into an energy of religious and artistic vision in virtue of which he did what no one else would venture, for he made himself the judge of mankind and assigned men to Hell, Purgatory, and Paradise. As a contrast to this elation, Boccaccio displays love, sometimes in its vehemence of passion, sometimes quite lightheartedly regardless of morality, when he brings before us in his colourful tales the customs of his time and his country. In the German medieval love-poetry love is full of feeling, tender, without abundance of fancy, playful, melancholy, and monotonous. The Spanish love-poems are richly fanciful in expression, chevaleresque, subtle sometimes in searching out and defending love's rights and duties as a personal matter of honour, and ecstatic here too in expressing love's supreme splendour. Among the French, however, love becomes in later times more a matter of gallantry verging on emptiness, a feeling manufactured into poetry often with the aid of the maximum of *esprit* and also of ingenious sophistry, now a sensuous pleasure without passion, now a passion without pleasure, a sublimated feeling and sensitivity, full of reflection.—But I must break off these observations which this is not the place to pursue in detail.

(b) Love's Collisions

Next, mundane interests are divided into two spheres. On the one hand stands the objective world as such, family life, political ties, citizenship, laws, *droit*, ethics, etc., and [on the other hand], contrasted with this explicitly firm sphere, [subjective] love burgeons in noble and fiery hearts; this secular religion of the heart now unites itself with religion in every way, now subordinates it to itself and forgets it. Since it makes itself alone into the essential and even the sole or supreme business of life, not merely can it decide to sacrifice everything else and fly with the beloved into a desert, but in its extreme, where indeed it is unbeautiful, it proceeds to the unfree, slavish, and shameless sacrifice of the dignity of man, as, e.g., in *Kätchen von Heilbronn*.[1] Now owing to this diremption [of spheres] the aims of love cannot be achieved in concrete reality without collisions, because the other relations of life assert their demands and rights apart from love and may therefore impair the sole dominion of the passion of love.

(α) The *first* and commonest collision that we have to mention in this context is the conflict between love and honour. Honour, i.e., has on its side the same infinity as love, and some point of honour may stand in love's way as an absolute hindrance. The duty of honour may demand the sacrifice of love. From a certain point of view, for example, it would be contrary to the honour of a man in a higher class to love a girl of a lower class. The difference of classes is necessary and given in the nature of civil life. Now if mundane life has not yet been regenerated by the infinite concept of true freedom wherein class, calling, etc. are adopted by the person himself and his free choice, it is more or less always nature, i.e. birth,

[1] A drama (1807) by H. von Kleist, 1777–1811.

which assigns to man his fixed position, and the differences proceeding from birth, besides those proceeding from honour when it
makes its own class a point of honour, become fixed as absolute
and infinite.

(β) But apart from honour, *secondly*, the eternal substantial
powers themselves, the interests of the state, patriotism, family
duties, etc., may come into conflict with love and inhibit its realization. Especially in modern plays, in which the objective relations of
life have been brought out in their validity, this is a very popular
collision. In such a case, love as itself a vital right of subjective
emotion is either so opposed to other rights and duties that the
heart disembarrasses itself of these duties as being subordinate to
itself, or else it recognizes them and engages in a fight with itself
and the power of its own passion. [Schiller's] *Maid of Orleans*,
e.g., rests on this latter collision.

(γ) Yet, *thirdly*, there may in general be external circumstances
and hindrances which stem the flood of love: e.g. the usual course
of events, the prose of life, misfortunes, passion, prejudices, restrictions, stubbornness of others, and incidents of the most varied kind.
With these there is then often mixed much that is hateful, frightful,
and base, because it is the wickedness, barbarity, and savagery of
some other passion which opposes love's tender beauty of soul.
Especially in recent times we have often seen, in dramas, tales, and
novels, external collisions like these which are then supposed to
interest us especially by our participation in the sufferings, hopes,
and frustrated prospects of the unhappy lovers, and to touch and
satisfy us according as the denouement is bad or good, or in general
merely to entertain us. But this manner of conflicts rests on pure
accident and therefore is of a subordinate kind.

(c) Love's Contingency

In all these aspects love has of course a high quality in it in so far
as it does not remain in general a sexual attraction but is a sentiment in itself rich, beautiful, and noble which abandons itself and,
for the sake of unity with another, is living, active, bold, and
sacrificing, etc. But at the same time romantic love also has its
limitation. What its content lacks, that is to say, is absolute *universality*. It is only the *personal* feeling of the individual subject, and it
is obviously not filled with the eternal interests and objective content of human existence, with family, political ends, country,

duties arising from one's calling or class, with freedom and religious feeling, but only with its own self, the self that wishes to receive again the feeling that is reflected back from another self. This content of deep feeling, once more itself still formal, does not truly correspond with the totality which an inherently concrete individual must be. In the family, marriage, duty, and the state, it is not subjective feeling as such and the consequential unification with just *this* individual and no other, which should be the chief thing at issue. But in romantic love everything turns on the fact that *this* man loves precisely *this* woman, and she him. The sole reason why it is just this man or this individual woman alone is grounded in the person's own private character, in the contingency of caprice. Although they can very commonly find others, there is no man who does not regard his beloved as the most beautiful, no girl who does not regard her lover as the most magnificent, in all the world, beyond comparison with anyone else. But precisely because this exclusion is made by everyone, or at least by many people, and the object of a man's love is not the unique Aphrodite herself, for it is true rather that every man has an Aphrodite (or quite likely better than an Aphrodite) of his own, it is obvious that there are many women who count as the most beautiful; as, after all, everyone knows in fact that there are many pretty, or good and excellent girls in the world who all—or at least most of them—find their lovers, suitors, and husbands to whom they appear as beautiful, lovable, and paragons of virtue. To give absolute preference to one woman and precisely to this one alone is therefore in every case a private matter of the subjective heart and the particularity or peculiarity of the person, and the endless stubbornness of necessarily finding his life, his supreme consciousness, precisely in this woman alone is seen to be an endless caprice of fate. Of course in this situation the higher freedom of subjectivity and its absolute choice are recognized—the freedom of not being subjected, like the Phaedra of Euripides, to a 'pathos', to a divinity; but since the choice proceeds from a purely individual will, it appears at the same time as an idiosyncrasy and a pertinacity of personal caprice.

Therefore, especially when love is opposed and hostile to substantial interests, its collisions always retain an aspect of contingency and lack of justification, because it is subjective caprice as such which with its not absolutely valid demands opposes what has to claim recognition on the score of its own essential character. The individuals in the high tragedy of the Greeks, Agamemnon, Clytemnestra, Orestes, Oedipus, Antigone, Creon, etc., do likewise have an individual aim; but the substantial thing, the 'pathos' which, as the essence of their action, drives them on, has absolute justification and for that very reason is in itself of universal interest. What falls to their lot on account of their action is therefore not touching on the strength of its being an unfortunate fate but because it is a misfortune which at the same time does them absolute honour, since the 'pathos' which does not rest until it is satisfied has an explicitly necessary content. If the guilt of Clytemnestra in this concrete case is not punished, if the injury suffered by Antigone as a sister is not expunged, this is a wrong in itself. But those sufferings of love, those shattering hopes, that mere being in love, those endless griefs felt by a lover, that endless happiness and bliss which he foresees for himself, are in themselves of no universal interest but something affecting himself alone. Every man does have a heart for love and a right to become happy through it; but if here, precisely in this instance, under such and such circumstances, he does not achieve his end in relation to precisely this girl, then no wrong has occurred. For there is nothing inherently necessary in his taking a fancy for this girl alone, and we are therefore supposed to be interested in supreme contingency, in the man's caprice which has neither universality nor any scope beyond itself. This remains the aspect of coldness which freezes us despite all the heat of passion in its presentation.

3. Fidelity

The third feature which is of importance for romantic subjectivity within its mundane sphere is fidelity. Yet by 'fidelity' we have here to understand neither the consistent adherence to an avowal of love once given nor the firmness of friendship of which, amongst the Greeks, Achilles and Patroclus, and still more intimately, Orestes and Pylades counted as the finest model. Friendship in this sense of the word has youth especially for its basis and period. Every man has to make his way through life for himself and to gain and maintain an actual position for himself. Now when individuals still live in actual relationships which are indefinite on both sides, this is the period, i.e. youth, in which individuals become intimate and are so closely bound into one disposition, will, and activity that, as a result, every undertaking of the one becomes the undertaking of the other. In the friendship of adults this is no longer the case. A man's affairs go their own way independently and cannot be carried into effect in that firm community of mutual effort in which one man cannot achieve anything without someone else. Men find others and separate themselves from them again; their interests and occupations drift apart and are united again; friendship, spiritual depth of disposition, principles, and general trends of life remain, but this is not the friendship of youth, in the case of which no one decides anything or sets to work on anything without its immediately becoming the concern of his friend. It is inherent essentially in the principle of our deeper life that, on the whole, every man fends for himself, i.e. is himself competent to take his place in the world.

(a) Fidelity in Service

While fidelity in friendship and love subsists only between equals, fidelity as we have to consider it now affects a superior, someone higher in rank, or a master. Fidelity like this we find already among the Greeks in the fidelity of servants to the master's family and his house. The finest example of this is afforded by Odysseus's swineherd who sweats by night and in bad weather to tend the swine; he is full of concern for his master and in the end, as it turns out, lends him loyal aid against the suitors. The picture of similarly touching fidelity, though here it becomes a matter entirely of the mind alone, is sketched for us by Shakespeare, e.g. in *Lear* (I. iv) where Lear asks Kent, who wants to serve him, 'Dost thou know me, fellow?' 'No, sir', Kent replies, 'but you have that in your countenance which I would fain call master.' This gets very near to what we have defined here as romantic fidelity. For fidelity at the stage we have reached is not the fidelity of slaves and serfs, which may indeed be beautiful and touching, yet it lacks the free independence of the individual and his own aims and actions and therefore is of a subordinate kind.

What confronts us, on the contrary, is the vassal's fidelity in chivalry in which, despite his devotion to one of higher rank, whether Prince, King, or Emperor, he preserves his free self-dependence throughout as his preponderating characteristic. Yet this fidelity is so lofty a principle in chivalry because on it depends the chief bond of a community's connection and its social organization, at least when that is originating.

(b) Fidelity's Subjective Independence

But this new unification of individuals brings into appearance a more concrete end. This is not, as may be supposed, patriotism as an interest in something objective and universal; on the contrary it is bound up with only one person, the superior; and therefore once again it is conditioned by the vassal's own honour, particular advantage, and personal opinion. In its greatest splendour fidelity appears in an unformed, uncouth, external world where rights and laws have no dominion. Within such a lawless world the mightiest and most overpowering individuals get into the position of being fixed centres, i.e. leaders and princes, round which others group themselves of their own free will. Then, later on, such a relationship was itself developed into a legal bond of feudal overlordship where now each vassal claims rights and privileges for himself too. But the fundamental principle on which the whole rests, in its origin, is the vassal's free choice both of the superior on whom he is to depend and also of persistence in that dependence. Thus chivalry's *fidelity* can very well uphold property, law, the personal independence and honour of the individual, and therefore it is not recognized as a *duty* as such, which would have to be performed even against the arbitrary will of the vassal. On the contrary. Every individual takes it that the persistence of his obedience along with the persistence of the universal order is dependent on his pleasure, inclination, and private disposition.

(c) Fidelity's Collisions

Fidelity and obedience to the overlord may therefore very easily come into collision with subjective passion, the susceptibility of honour, the feeling of injury, love, and other inner and outer accidents and thereby become something extremely precarious. A knight, e.g., is true to his Prince, but his friend gets into a dispute with the Prince; therefore he has at once to choose between one loyalty and the other; and first of all he has to be faithful to himself, his honour, and his advantage. The finest example of such a collision we find in the Cid. He is true both to the King and to himself.

If the King acts rightly, he lends him his arm; but yet if his Prince acts wrongly or he, the Cid, is injured, he withdraws his powerful support.—The same relation appears in Charlemagne's Paladins.[1] There is a bond of obedience to an overlord, but it is rather like what we became acquainted with [above, on pp. 177, 187] in the relation between Zeus and the other gods. The overlord commands, blusters, and disputes, but the independent and powerful individuals oppose him how and when they like. But the truest and most graceful picture of the looseness and slackness of this association is in *Reynard the Fox*. Just as in this poem the magnates of the Kingdom really only served themselves and their independence, so the German Princes and knights in the Middle Ages were not at home when they were supposed to do something for the whole Empire and their Emperor; and perhaps the Middle Ages have been rated so highly precisely because in such a state of affairs everyone is justified, and is a man of honour, if he follows his own caprice—something that cannot be allowed him in a rationally organized political life!

At all these three stages, Honour, Love, and Fidelity, the basis is the independence of the subject in himself, the heart which yet always opens itself to wider and richer interests and in them remains reconciled with itself. It is here that romantic art comes into possession of the fairest part of the sphere lying outside religion as such. The aims here concern what is human; with this, in one of its aspects at least, namely the aspect of subjective freedom, we can sympathize, and, unlike what is now and again the case in the religious field, we do not find the material or the manner of presenting it in collision with our conceptions. But nevertheless this sphere may be brought into relation with religion in many ways, so that now religious interests are interwoven with those of worldly chivalry, as, e.g., the adventures of the Knights of the Round Table in connection with the search for the Holy Grail. Then in this interlacing of divine and secular there comes into the poetry of chivalry much that is mystical and fanciful, as well as much that is allegorical. But, even so, the mundane sphere of love, honour, and fidelity may also appear quite independently of absorption in religious aims and dispositions and bring before our eyes only the earliest movement of the heart in its inner mundane

[1] Hegel probably has the *Chanson de Roland* (*c.* 1170) in mind and perhaps Wieland's *Oberon* (1782) also.

subjective life. Yet what is still lacking at this present stage is the filling of this inwardness with the concrete content of human relations, characters, passions, and real existence in general. In contrast to this variety, the inherently infinite heart remains still abstract and formal, and therefore gets the task of adopting this wider material too into itself and presenting it transformed in an artistic way.

Chapter III

THE FORMAL INDEPENDENCE OF
INDIVIDUAL CHARACTERISTICS

To glance back over what lies behind us, we *first* considered subjectivity in its absolute sphere: consciousness in its reconciliation
with God, the universal process of the spirit reconciling itself
within. Here the abstraction consisted in the fact that the heart,
sacrificing the mundane, the natural and human as such (even
when this was moral and therefore justified), withdrew into itself
in order to find its satisfaction in the pure heaven of the spirit.
Secondly, human subjectivity did become affirmative for itself and
others, without displaying the negativity implicit in that reconciliation; yet the content of this mundane infinite as such was only the
personal independence of honour, the deep feeling of love, and the
vassalage of fidelity—a content which can come before our eyes in
many kinds of relationships, in a great variety and gradation of
feeling and passion amid a great change of external circumstances,
but which yet displays within these things only that same independence of the person and his inner life. The *third* point now
therefore remaining to us for consideration is the manner and way
in which there can enter into the form of romantic art the further
material of human existence, both outer and inner—nature and
its interpretation and significance for the heart. Thus here it
is the world of the particular, of the existent in general, which
becomes explicitly free and, because it does not appear permeated
by religion and compression into the unity of the Absolute,
stands on its own feet and treads independently in its own
domain.

In this third sphere of the romantic form of art, therefore, the
religious materials have vanished together with chivalry and the
lofty views and aims which it generated out of its inner being and
to which nothing in the present and in reality directly corresponds.
On the other hand, the thing which gives new satisfaction is the
thirst for this present and this reality itself, the delight of the self
in what is *there*, contentment with self, with the finitude of man

and, generally, with the finite, the particular, and with paintings like portraits.[1] In his present world man wants to see the present itself as it is—even at the cost of sacrificing beauty and ideality of content and appearance—as a live presence recreated by art, as his own human and spiritual work. As we saw at the outset, the Christian religion, unlike the oriental and Greek gods, has not grown up, either in content or form, on the ground of imagination. Now while imagination [in the East] creates the meaning from its own resources in order to [try, though in vain, to] bring about the unification of the true inner with its perfect shape, and while it does actually bring about this linkage in classical art, we find on the contrary in the Christian religion the mundane particularity of appearance, just as it is immediately from the start, accepted as one factor in the Ideal,[2] and the heart is satisfied in the familiarity and contingency of the external, without making any demand for beauty. But nevertheless man is at first only implicitly and potentially reconciled with God; all are indeed called to felicity, but few are chosen;[3] and the man to whose heart the kingdom alike of heaven and this world remains a 'beyond' must in the spirit renounce the world and his selfish presence therein. His point of departure is infinitely far away; and to make what is at first merely sacrificed into an affirmative 'here' for him, i.e. to bring about the positive discovery and willing of himself in his present world, which elsewhere is the *beginning*—this endeavour is but the *conclusion* of the development of romantic art and is the last thing which man reaches by plumbing his own depths and concentrating his whole experience into a single point.[4]

As for the form for this new content,[5] we found romantic art from its beginning onwards afflicted with the opposition that the inherently infinite subjective personality is in itself irreconcilable with the external material and is to remain unreconciled. This

---

[1] i.e. true to nature in detail, like the genre pictures discussed below in 3(*a*).

[2] i.e. Jesus is a particular individual in the world, but as the Second Person of the Trinity is one essential moment in the life of God. The religious consciousness is content to contemplate the individual without asking for beauty.

[3] Matt. 22: 14. But read 'many' for 'all' and omit 'to felicity'.

[4] i.e. only in religion, not in art, can this endeavour succeed. Man's inner self-concentration is ultimate in art; his reconciliation with the world, for which he strives in art, is achieved only in a higher sphere. In romantic art his thirst for presence in objective actuality is not quenched. Where art ends, religion begins.

[5] i.e. the development of the person's inner life.

independent confrontation of the two sides and the withdrawal of the inner into itself is what constitutes the subject-matter of romantic art. Developing themselves inwardly, these sides separate again ever anew until at the end they fall apart from one another altogether and therefore show that they have to seek their absolute unification in a field other than art. Owing to this falling apart from one another, the sides, in respect of art, become formal [i.e. abstract] since they cannot appear as one whole in that full unity which the classical ideal gives to them. Classical art stands in a circle of fixed shapes, in a mythology and its indissoluble products perfected by art; therefore, as we saw in the transition to the romantic form of art, the dissolution of classical art, apart from the, on the whole, more restricted sphere of comedy and satire, is a development towards something pleasing or an imitation which loses itself in pedantry, in death and frostiness, and finally degenerates into a perfunctory and bad technique. The topics, however, remain the same on the whole and only exchange the earlier spirited mode of production for an ever more spiritless presentation and a mechanical external tradition. Whereas the progress and end of romantic art is the inner dissolution of the artistic material itself which falls asunder into its elements; its parts become free and in this process, conversely, subjective skill and the art of portrayal are enhanced, and the more the substantial element is discarded, all the more are these perfected.

The more clear-cut division of this final chapter may now be made in the following way:

First of all, we have before us the independence of the character which yet is a particular character, a specific individual shut in upon himself with his world, his particular qualities and aims.

Secondly, contrasted with this formalism of the particularity of character there is the external shape of situations, events, and actions. Now since romantic inwardness as such is indifferent to the external environment, real phenomena enter here explicitly free, as neither penetrated by the inner significance of aims and actions nor shaped adequately thereto, and, in their unfettered, disconnected mode of appearance, they assert the contingency of complications, circumstances, sequence of events, mode of execution, etc., in the form of adventures.[1]

---

[1] The meaning of this term is explained and illustrated in 2 below. Since romantic art is concerned with inwardness, external events are for it devoid of

Thirdly and lastly, we see the severance of the sides, whose complete identity affords the proper essence of art, and therefore the decay and dissolution of art itself. On the one hand, art passes over to the presentation of common reality as such, to the presentation of objects as they exist in their contingent individuality with its particular characteristics, and it now has the interest of transforming this existence into a show by means of artistic skill; on the other hand, it turns vice versa into a mode of conception and portrayal completely contingent on the artist, i.e. into humour as the perversion and derangement of everything objective and real by means of wit and the play of a subjective outlook, and it ends with the artist's personal productive mastery over every content and form.

1. *The Independence of the Individual Character*

The subjective infinity of man in himself, from which we started in the romantic art-form, remains the fundamental characteristic in this present sphere too. What on the other hand enters this explicit independent infinity as something new is (*a*) the *particularity* of the material which constitutes the world of the individual subject; (*b*) the immediate coalescence of the subject with this his particularity and its wishes and aims; (*c*) the living individuality to which character in itself is confined. Therefore by the word 'character'[1] we must not mean here what, e.g., the Italians presented in their masques. For the Italian masqueraders, though indeed determinate characters too, display this determinacy only in its abstraction and universality, i.e. without subjective individuality. *Per contra* the characters at the present level of our discussion are each of them independently a special character, explicitly a whole, an individual person. If here, therefore, we nevertheless speak of formalism and abstraction of character, this is relevant only to the fact that the chief material, the world of such a character, appears on the one hand as restricted and therefore abstract, and on the other hand as accidental. What

---

spirit and are matters of chance, like episodes in a tale of adventure which might well occur in a different order. Hegel is using the word 'adventure' in the sense common in eighteenth-century English (if not more recently). In this sense 'adventure' has nothing to do with peril or risk, but means a chance occurrence, something happening without any design in unplanned circumstances.

[1] Cf. above, pp. 67-8, 236-44.

the individual is, is not carried and sustained by the substantial inherently justified element in his make-up, but by his character's mere subjectivity, which therefore instead of resting on something substantial and on an explicitly firm 'pathos' rests only formally on its own individual independence.

Within this formalism two chief differences may be distinguished.

On the one side there is the energetically self-sustaining firmness of character which limits itself to specific ends and puts the whole power of its one-sided individuality into the *realization* of these ends; on the other side, character appears as a *subjective* totality, but one which persists undeveloped in its inwardness and undisclosed depth of heart and cannot unbosom itself and completely express itself.

(a) Formal Firmness of Character

Thus what we have before us in the first place is the particular character who wishes to be simply what he immediately is. Just as animals are different and explicitly submit to this difference, the same is true here of different characters whose sphere and particularity remains contingent and cannot be firmly delimited through the Concept.

(α) Such a purely self-dependent individual has therefore no meditated intentions and ends which he has linked to some universal 'pathos'; on the contrary, what he has, does, and accomplishes, he draws immediately, without any further reflection, from his own specific nature which is just what it happens to be; he does not wish to base himself on something higher, to be lost in it, and to be justified in something substantive, but instead, unbending and unbent, he rests on himself and in this firmness either realizes himself or perishes. Such an independence of character can only occur when the fullest importance is given to what is external to the Divine, i.e. to the particular element in man. Shakespeare's characters especially are of this kind; in them it is precisely this taut firmness and one-sidedness that is supremely admirable. In them there is no question of religious feeling, of an action due to the man's own religious reconciliation, or of morality as such. On the contrary, we have individuals before us, resting independently on themselves alone, with particular ends which are their own, prescribed by their individuality alone, and which they now set themselves to execute with the unshakeable logic of passion, without any accompanying reflection or general principle, solely for their own satisfaction. The tragedies especially, like *Macbeth*, *Othello*, *Richard III*, and others, have as their chief topic one such character surrounded by others less prominent and energetic. So, for example, Macbeth's character is determined by his passion of ambition. At the start he hesitates, but then stretches out his hand to the crown, commits murder to get it, and, in order to maintain it, storms away through every atrocity. This reckless firmness, this identity of the man with himself and the end arising from his own decision, gives him an essential interest for us. Not respect for the majesty of the monarch, not the frenzy of his wife, not the defection of his vassals, not his impending destruction, nothing, neither divine nor human law, makes him falter or draw back; instead he persists in his course. Lady Macbeth is a similar character, and only the tasteless chatter of modern criticism has been able to regard her as affectionate. At her very first entrance (I. v), as she [reads] Macbeth's letter which tells of his meeting with the witches and their prophecy: 'Hail to thee, Thane of Cawdor, hail to thee, King thou shalt be', she exclaims, 'Glamis thou art and Cawdor; and shalt be what thou art promised. Yet do I fear thy nature. It is too full of the milk of human kindness to catch the nearest way.' In her no affectionate comfort appears, no joy for her husband's good fortune, no moral emotion, no co-operation, none of the pity that becomes a noble soul; she is merely frightened that her husband's character will stand in the way of his ambition; him she treats as a mere means, and in her there is no hesitation, no uncertainty, no reflection, no weakness like what even Macbeth had himself at first, no remorse, but only the pure abstraction and severity of character which carries out, without more ado, what is in line with it, until at last it breaks. What shatters Macbeth after he has done the deed is a storm from without, whereas his Lady is shattered by madness within her feminine soul. And the same is the case with Richard III, Othello, Queen Margaret, and so many others: the opposite of the miserableness of modern characters, Kotzebue's for example, which seem extremely noble, great, excellent, and yet within they are at the same time only trumpery. In a different way, others later who had a supreme contempt for Kotzebue have done no better, as, e.g., Heinrich von Kleist in his Käthchen and his Prince of Homburg: characters in whom, in contrast to a wideawake situation with fixed logical consequences, magnetism, somnambulism, and nightmares are presented as what is supreme and most excellent. The Prince of Homburg is the most contemptible General; distracted in making his military dispositions, he pens his orders badly, in the night before action he agitates himself with morbid stuff, and on the day of battle he acts like a bungler. Despite such duality, disruption, and inner dissonance in their characters, these authors suppose themselves to be disciples of Shakespeare. But they are far from being so, for his characters are self-consistent; they remain true to themselves and their passion, and in what they are and in what confronts them they beat about according only to their own fixed determinacy of character.

(β) Now the more idiosyncratic the character is which fixedly considers itself alone and which therefore is easily on the verge of evil, the more has the individual not only to maintain himself in concrete reality against the hindrances standing in his way and blocking the realization of himself, but the more he is also driven to his downfall through this very realization. In other words, because he succeeds, he is met by the fate proceeding from his own determinate character, i.e. by a self-prepared destruction. But the development of this fate is not merely a development out of the individual's *action*, but is at the same time an inner growth, a development of his *character* itself in its storming, brutishness, and violence, or in its fatigue. In the case of the Greeks, with whom the 'pathos', the substantial content of the action, and not the agent's personal character, is the important thing, fate is less inherent in this determinate character which is not further developed essentially within its action but at the end is what it was at the beginning. But at the stage we are now considering, the achievement of the action is *eo ipso* a further development of the individual in his subjective inner life and not merely the march of events. The action of Macbeth, e.g., appears at the same time as a demoralization of his heart with a consequence which, once indecision ceases and the die is cast, can no longer be averted. His spouse is decided from the start; in her the development is only an inner anguish which intensifies into physical and spiritual wreck, into the madness in which she perishes. And so it is with most of Shakespeare's characters, important and unimportant alike. The Greek characters are indeed shown as firm too, and so in their case there arise oppositions where no help is any longer possible, and a *deus ex machina* must come on the scene for their resolution; yet this firmness, like that of Philoctetes, for example, is fully concrete and on the whole penetrated by an ethically justified 'pathos'.

(γ) In the characters at this stage of our discussion, owing to the contingency of what they take as their end and the independence of their individuality, no reconciliation with objectivity is possible. The connection between what they are and what befalls them remains indefinite, and whence and whither is an unsolved riddle for them. Fate as the most abstract necessity comes back here once again, and the sole reconciliation for the individual is his infinite being in himself, his own firmness in which he surmounts his passion and its destiny. 'It is so', and what he meets, whether from the rule of fate, from necessity, or from chance, likewise just *is*, without his reflecting on whither or why; it happens, and the man makes himself inflexible and intends to remain inflexible in face of this rule.

(b) Character as Inner but Undeveloped Totality

But in a completely contrasted way, secondly, the formal character may be based in inwardness as such, in which the individual steadily remains without being able to expand and develop it in outward expression.

(α) This is the situation of the substantial hearts which incorporate a totality but in their simple compactness generate every deep feeling only in themselves without developing it outwardly and unbosoming themselves of it. The formalism which we have just considered was related to the determinacy of the object aimed at, the complete concentration of the individual on the one purpose which he made emerge completely in its firm severity, which he expressed and carried through, and therein, depending on the circumstances granted to him, perished or survived. The present second formalism consists conversely in undisclosedness, in absence of outward shape, in the lack of expression and development. Such a heart is like a costly precious stone which catches the light only on single facets and they then shine like a flash of lightning.

(β) If such a reserve is to be of worth and interest, there must be an inner richness of heart, but it lets us recognize its infinite depth and fullness only through precisely this stillness in a few, so to say dumb, expressions. Such simple, unselfconscious, and silent natures may exercise a supreme attraction. Yet, in that case, their silence must be the stillness of the unruffled surface of the sea, concealing unfathomable depths, not the silence of what is shallow, hollow, and pointless. For it may sometimes happen that a very common-place man, through a demeanour which expresses little but which here and there provides something half intelligible, arouses an impression of his great wisdom and inner resources, so that one thinks marvellous all that lies hidden in this heart and spirit, while at the end it is obvious that there is nothing behind his façade. Whereas the infinite content and depth of those still hearts is revealed (and this is something that demands great genius and skill on the part of the artist) through separate, scattered, naïve, and unpremeditated *spirituel* expressions which, without any eye on others who could understand them, show that such a heart grasps with deep feeling the substance of existing circumstances; yet that its reflection is not complicated by the whole concatenation of particular interests, concerns, and finite ends, and so is clear of them and unacquainted with them; and that such a heart cannot be distracted by ordinary emotions or by the seriousness and sympathies ordinarily involved.

(γ) But nevertheless for a heart so shut in upon itself a time must come when it is touched at one specific point of its inner life, when it throws its undivided force into one feeling determining its life, clings to it with undispersed strength, and is fortunate, or else, lacking support, perishes. For as a support man needs the de-veloped breadth of an ethical substance [like the state] which alone supplies objective firmness. Amongst characters of this sort are the most charming figures of romantic art, e.g. those created likewise by Shakespeare in the most beautiful perfection. Juliet in *Romeo and Juliet* is to be included in this class. You have seen the present performance of this play with Madame Crelinger as Juliet.[1] It is worth the trouble of seeing her. This is a production extremely moving, living, warm, glowing, intelligent, perfect, and noble. Yet Juliet can *not* otherwise be taken at the beginning than as a quite childlike simple girl, fourteen or fifteen years old; we perceive

---

[1] The text gives a reference to a 'Berlin performance in 1820'. The date is not impossible, because Hegel did lecture on Fine Art in Berlin in 1820-1. But Auguste Stich, whom Hegel knew personally, did not become, on her marriage, Madame Crelinger until later. In Hegel's letters she is Madame Stich until 1827.

that she still has no inner consciousness of herself and the world, no movement, no emotion, no wishes; on the contrary, in all naïveté she has peeped into her surroundings in the world, as into a magic-lantern show, without learning anything from them or coming to any reflection on them. Suddenly we see the development of the whole strength of this heart, of intrigue, circumspection, power to sacrifice everything and to submit to the harshest treatment; so that now the whole thing looks like the first blossoming of the whole rose at once in all its petals and folds, like an infinite outpouring of the inmost genuine basis of the soul in which previously there was no inner differentiation, formation, and development, but which now comes on the scene as an immediate product of an awakened single interest, unbeknown to itself, in its beautiful fullness and force, out of a hitherto self-enclosed spirit. It is a torch lit by a spark, a bud, only now just touched by love, which stands there unexpectedly in full bloom, but the quicker it unfolds, the quicker too does it droop, its petals gone. Miranda in *The Tempest* is a still better example; brought up in seclusion, she is shown to us by Shakespeare in her first knowledge of men; he sketches her in only a few scenes but in them he gives us a complete unrestricted idea of her. Although Schiller's Thekla[1] is a product of reflective poetry, she too can be reckoned a member of this class. In the midst of a life so great and rich she is untouched by it but remains without vanity, without reflection, in the naïveté of the one interest which alone engrosses her soul. In general it is beautiful and noble feminine characters especially for whom the world and their own inner being is first disclosed in love, so that now alone are they born spiritually.

In the same category of this inner depth of feeling which cannot be unfolded or completely unbosomed, there belong in the main also the folk-songs, especially Germanic ones, which show in their sterling compactness of heart how strongly the heart is gripped too by some one interest, yet can only bring itself to fragmentary expressions and reveal in them its depth of soul. This is a mode of presentation which in its taciturnity goes back again as it were into symbolism, since what it affords is not the open clear manifestation of the whole inner life but is only a sign and indication of it. Yet we get here not a symbol the meaning of which remains, as previously, something abstract and universal, but an expression

---

[1] In two plays, *Wallenstein*, parts ii and iii (1799).

of something inner, i.e. of precisely this subjective living actual heart itself. In more recent times, with our thoroughly reflective consciousness which is far removed from that self-absorbed naïveté, portrayals of such a heart have become of the greatest difficulty and provide proof of an originally poetic spirit. We have already seen earlier that Goethe, especially in his songs, is a master of symbolic depiction too, i.e. of laying open the whole fidelity and infinity of the heart in simple, apparently external, and indifferent traits. Of this kind, e.g., is *The King in Thule*, one of Goethe's most beautiful poems. The King discloses his love only through the drinking cup which this old man preserved as a gift from his beloved. In his death throes the old carouser stands in his lofty royal hall, surrounded by his knights; his kingdom, his treasures he bequeaths to his heir, but the drinking cup he flings into the waves; no one else is to have it. 'He saw it fall, fill, and sink to the bottom of the sea; then fell his eyelids and never a drop did he drink again.'[1]

But such a deep tranquil heart, which keeps its energy of soul pent up like the spark in the flint, which does not give itself outward form, and which does not develop its existence and reflection on it, has after all not freed itself through an imagery of this kind. When the discord of misfortune resounds through its life, it remains exposed to the grim contradiction of having no skill, no bridge to reconcile its heart with reality and so to ward off external circumstances, to be supported against them, and to be its own support. If it comes to a collision, it therefore knows of no help, it rushes rashly and thoughtlessly into activity or is passively involved in complications. So, e.g., Hamlet is a beautiful and noble heart; not inwardly weak at all, but, without a powerful feeling for life, in the feebleness of his melancholy he strays distressed into error; he has a keen sense of how the weather lies; no external sign, no ground for suspicion is there, but he feels uncanny, everything is not as it ought to be; he surmises the dreadul deed that has been done. His father's ghost gives him more details. Inwardly he is quickly ready for revenge; he steadily thinks of the duty prescribed to him by his own heart; but he is not carried away, like Macbeth; he does not kill, rage, or strike with the directness of

---

[1] This poem occurs in *Faust*, part I, scene viii. From this precious goblet, according to a previous stanza, the King always drank, and as he did so his eyes filled with tears.

Laertes; on the contrary, he persists in the inactivity of a beautiful inner soul which cannot make itself actual or engage in the relationships of his present world. He waits, looks in the beautiful uprightness of his heart for objective certainty, but, even after he has found it, he comes to no firm decision but lets himself be led by external circumstances. In this unreality he now makes a mistake, even in what confronts him, and kills old Polonius instead of the King; he acts too hastily when he should have investigated prudently, while when the right energy was needed he remains sunk into himself—until, without his action, in this developed course of circumstances and chances, the fate of the whole realm and of himself has steadily been developed in his own withdrawn inner life.

But in modern times this attitude appears especially in the case of men belonging to the lower classes who are without education enough to understand national purposes and without a variety of objective interests, and therefore when *one* purpose of their own fails, they cannot now find in another a stay for their inner life or a firm footing for their activity. The more rooted this lack of education is, the more stiffly and obstinately do self-enclosed minds cling to what, be it ever so one-sided, has made a claim on them involving their whole individuality. Such a monotony in buttoned-up, speechless men is principally characteristic of Germans who therefore in their reserve easily appear headstrong, stubborn, gnarled, unapproachable, and perfectly unreliable and contradictory in their actions and speech. As a master in depicting and representing such dumb minds in the lower orders of the people, I will mention here only Hippel, the author of *Lebensläufe in aufsteigender Linie*,[1] one of the few original German works of humour. It keeps far away throughout from Jean Paul's situations with their sentimentality and tastelessness, and has instead a wonderful individuality, freshness, and vitality. He can depict, extremely grippingly, repressed characters especially who cannot disburden themselves and, when it comes to action, act violently in a frightful way. In a dreadful way too they resolve the endless contradiction between their inner life and the unfortunate circum-

---

[1] i.e. *Careers in an ascending Line*, by T. G. Hippel, 1741–96. This book was a favourite of Hegel's from his university days. His judgement on it here has been found 'astounding' and even shocking (see, e.g., H. Glockner's *Hegel*, Stuttgart, 1929, vol. i, pp. 412 ff.).

stances in which they see themselves involved, and by this means bring about what elsewhere an external fate does—as, e.g., in *Romeo and Juliet* where external accidents frustrate the cleverness and artfulness of the go-between Friar and bring about the death of the lovers.

(c) *What the Substantial Interest is in the Presentation of Formal Character*

Thus, then, these formal characters either display generally only the endless will-power of the particular person who asserts himself just as he is and storms ahead at will, or alternatively, they present an inherently total and unrestricted heart which, touched on some specific side of its inner being, now concentrates the breadth and depth of its whole individuality on this one point, yet, by possessing no development into the external world, falls into a collision and cannot find itself and help itself prudently.

A third point which we now have to mention consists in this, that if these one-sided characters, restricted in their aims but developed in their consciousness, are to interest us not only superficially but profoundly, we must at the same time come to see in them that this restrictedness of their personality is itself only a fate, i.e. an entanglement of their peculiar restricted character with a deeper inner life. Now this depth and this wealth of spirit Shakespeare does in fact let us find in them. He exhibits them as men of free imaginative power and gifted spirit, since their reflection rises above and lifts them above what they are in their situation and specific ends, so that, as it were, it is only through the ill-luck of the circumstances, through the collision involved in their own situation, that they are impelled on to what they accomplish. Yet this is not to be taken as if in Macbeth's case, e.g., what he ventures were to be blamed only on the evil witches; rather are the witches only the poetic reflection of his own fixed will. What the Shakespearean figures carry out, their particular end, has its origin and the root of its force in their own individuality. But in one and the same individuality they preserve at the same time the loftiness which wipes away what they really are, i.e. in their aims, interests, and actions; it aggrandizes them and enhances them above themselves. Thus Shakespeare's vulgar characters, Stephano, Trinculo, Pistol, and the absolute hero of them all, Falstaff, remain sunk in their vulgarity, but at the same time they are shown to be men of intelligence with a genius fit for anything, enabling them to have an entirely free existence, and, in short, to be what great men are. Whereas in French tragedies even the greatest and best characters, closely examined, prove to be nothing but strutting evil brutes with only enough brains to justify themselves by sophistry. In Shakespeare we find no justification, no condemnation, but only an observation of the universal fate; individuals view its necessity without complaint or repentance, and from that standpoint they see everything perish, themselves included, as if they saw it all happening outside themselves.

In all these respects the sphere of such individual characters is an infinitely rich field but it is readily in danger of declining into emptiness and banality, so that there have been only a few masters with enough poetry and insight to apprehend its truth.

2. *Adventures*

Now after considering the inner side which can be portrayed at this stage, we must secondly turn our eyes also to the outer side, to the particular circumstances and situations which stir the character, to the collisions in which it is involved, and also to the whole form which the inner life assumes within concrete reality.

As we have seen several times already, a fundamental characteristic of romantic art is that spirituality, the mind as reflected into itself, constitutes a whole and therefore it is related to the external not as to its own reality permeated by itself, but as to something purely external separated from it, a place where everything goes on released from spirit into independence, and which is a scene of complications and the rough and tumble of an endlessly flowing, mutable, and confusing contingency. For the fixedly enclosed mind, it is just as much a matter of indifference to which circumstances it turns as it is a matter of accident which circumstances confront it. For, in the case of its action, to complete a work grounded in itself and persisting through itself matters less to it than asserting itself in general and getting something done.

(a) *The Contingency of Aims and Collisions*

Here we have before us what in another connection[1] may be called the rejection of God from nature. The spirit has withdrawn into itself out of the externality of appearances which now on

---

[1] See, e.g., pp. 374-5 above.

their side are shaped no matter how, for they are unconnected with the subject since his inner world no longer sees itself in them. In its truth, the spirit is in itself mediated and reconciled with the Absolute; since, however, as we stand here on the ground of independent individuality which has no point of departure but itself just as it directly is, and so clings to itself, the same rejection of the Divine affects the character of the agent in his action also; he, therefore, with his own contingent ends, comes out into a contingent world with which he does not set himself in one to form a consistent whole. Adventure, which provides for the form of events and actions the fundamental type of the romantic, is constituted by this relativity of ends in a relative environment, the specific character and complication of which do not lie in the individual person but are determined from without and accidentally, and so lead to accidental collisions as the extraordinarily intertwined ramifications of the situation.

Action and event, taken in the stricter sense of the Ideal and classical art, require an inherently true and absolutely necessary end; such an end includes in itself what determines both its external shape and also the manner of carrying it out in the real world. In the case of the deeds and events of romantic art this is not so. For if here too inherently universal and substantial ends are displayed in their realization, still these ends in themselves neither determine the action nor order and articulate its inner course; on the contrary, this aspect of actualization they must let go and therefore yield it to contingency and accident.

(α) The romantic world had only one absolute work to complete, the spread of Christianity and the continued activity of the spirit of the [Christian] community. Within a hostile world, first of unbelieving antiquity, later of barbarism with its crudity of mind, this work, when it left doctrines for deeds, became chiefly a passive work of enduring grief and martyrdom, the sacrifice of one's own temporal existence for the eternal salvation of the soul. The further act, related to the like end, is in the Middle Ages the work of Christian chivalry, the expulsion of the Moors, the Arabs, Mohammedans in general, from Christian countries, and then, above all, the conquest of the Holy Sepulchre in the Crusades. Yet this was not an end affecting men as human beings, but one which had to be achieved by a mere collection of single individuals who just streamed together at will as individuals. From this point of view, the Crusades may be called a collective adventure of the Christian Middle Ages, an adventure inherently broken in twain and fantastic: of a spiritual kind and yet without a truly spiritual aim and, in relation to actions and characters, a sham. For, considered from the religious point of view, the Crusades have an aim extremely external to religion. Christendom is supposed to have its salvation in the spirit alone, in Christ who, risen, has ascended to the right hand of God and has his living actuality, his abode, in the Spirit, not in his grave and in the visible immediately present places where once he had his temporal abode. But the incentive and the religious longing of the Middle Ages was concentrated only on the place, the external locality of the Passion and the Holy Sepulchre. Just as contradictorily there was immediately bound up with the religious aim the purely mundane aspect of conquest and gain, which in its externality bore a character quite different from the religious one. So men wanted to gain something spiritual and inward, and they made their aim the purely external locality from which the spirit had vanished; they strove for temporal gain and linked this mundane thing to religion as such. This discordance constitutes here the broken and fantastic situation in which externality perverts the inner, and *vice versa*, instead of both being brought into harmony. Therefore it turns out that in the execution of the enterprise opposites are linked together without any reconciliation. Piety turns into inhumanity and barbaric cruelty, and the same inhumanity which leads to the outbreaks of every selfishness and passion of which men are capable, turns round again into the eternal deep emotion and penitence of the spirit which was properly the thing at issue. In these opposed elements, deeds and events with one and the same end turn out after all to lack all unity and consistency of leadership: the whole collection of Crusaders was scattered, split away into adventures, victories, defeats, and various accidents, and the outcome does not correspond to the means used and the great preparations made. Indeed the aim itself is cancelled by its achievement. For the Crusades wished to make the word true again: 'Thou lettest him not rest in the grave, neither wilt thou suffer thine Holy One to see corruption.'[1] But precisely this longing to look for Christ, the living one, in such places and localities, even in the grave, the place of death, and to find satis-

---

[1] Hegel's adaptation of Ps. 16: 10.

faction for the spirit in this search, is itself, no matter what a substantial thing Chateaubriand makes of it, a corruption of the spirit
out of which Christendom was to arise in order to revert to the
fresh full life of concrete reality.

A similar aim, mystical on one side, fantastic on the other, and
adventurous in its accomplishment, is the search for the Holy Grail.

(β) A higher work is that which every man has to achieve in
himself, i.e. his life, whereby he settles for himself his eternal
fate. This topic Dante has taken up from a Catholic point of view
in his *Divine Comedy*, where he conducts us through Hell, Purgatory, and Paradise. But here, despite the strict organization of the
whole, there is no lack of fantastic ideas or adventures in so far
as this work of salvation and damnation comes before us not only
absolutely in its universality but as a list of practically innumerable
individuals brought forward in their particular characteristics—
and, besides this, the *poet* claims for himself the right of the
Church, holds the keys of the Kingdom of Heaven in his hands,
pronounces salvation and damnation, and so makes himself the
world's judge who removes into Hell, Purgatory, or Paradise the
best known individuals of the classical and the Christian world,
poets, citizens, warriors, Cardinals, and Popes.

(γ) Consequently, on mundane ground the other basic causes
of actions and events consist of the endlessly varied adventurousness of ideas and of the external and internal contingency of love,
honour, and fidelity; here we see men hitting around for the sake
of their own fame, there we see them leaping to the aid of perse-
cuted innocence, accomplishing the most astounding exploits for
their lady's honour, or restoring the rights of the oppressed by the
force of their fists or the skill of their arm, even if the 'innocence'
thus freed be only a gang of rascals.[1] In most of these things
there is no state of affairs, no situation, no conflict which would
make the action *necessary*; the heart just wants out and looks for
adventures deliberately. So here the actions on behalf of love,
e.g., in their more detailed character have in them, in great part,
no other determining factor save affording proofs of firmness,
fidelity, and constancy in love, and showing that the surrounding
reality with the whole complex of its relationships counts only as
material for the manifestation of love. Thereby the specific act of
this manifestation, since it is only the proof [of love] that matters,

---

[1] This is an allusion to *Don Quixote*, part i, ch. 22.

is not determined by itself but is left to the fancy or mood of the lady and to the caprice of external contingencies. Exactly the same is the case with the aims of honour and bravery. They belong for the most part to the individual who still keeps far aloof from all wider substantive content [for his action] and who can put his personality at stake in every matter casually confronting him and find himself injured as a result, or look in it for an opportunity to display his courage and adroitness. Just as here there is no measuring-rod for what must be made an object of the agent's action and what not, so there is missing also a criterion for what can actually be an injury to honour or be the true objective of bravery. With the administration of law, likewise an aim of chivalry, there is no difference. Here, in other words, right and law do not yet evince themselves as an absolutely fixed situation and end which is being steadily realized in accordance with law and its necessary provisions, but as only a purely subjective fancy, so that both judicial proceedings and the judgement of what in this or that case is right or wrong remains remitted to the person's purely capricious estimate.

(b) The Comic Treatment of Contingency

Thus what in general, especially on the field of the mundane, we have before us (i) in chivalry and (ii) in the formal independence of characters is more or less the contingency, both of the circumstances within which actions are done, and also of the mind that wills. For those one-sided individual figures may take as their aim something wholly contingent which is sustained only by the energy of their character and which is carried out, or results in failure, under the influence of collisions conditioned from without. The same is true of chivalry which nevertheless contains in honour, love, and fidelity a higher justification similar to that belonging to the truly ethical. On the one hand, owing to the individuality of the circumstances to which it reacts, chivalry directly becomes a matter of contingency because, instead of a universal work, only particular ends are to be accomplished, and absolutely necessary connections are missing; on the other hand, consequentially, on the side of the subjective spirit of the individuals, caprice or deception occurs in relation to projects, plans, and undertakings. Carried through consistently, this whole field of adventures proves in its actions and events, as well as in their outcome, to be an inherently self-dissolving and therefore comical world of incidents and fates.

This dissolution of (i) chivalry from within and of (ii) those individual characters in their singularity has come home to our minds and achieved its most appropriate portrayal above all, (i) in Ariosto and Cervantes, and (ii) in Shakespeare.

(α) In Ariosto we are amused in particular by the endless complications of fates and ends, the fictitious entanglement of fantastic relations and foolish situations with which the poet plays adventurously up to the point of frivolity. What the heroes are supposed to be serious with is pure downright folly and madness. Love especially is degraded from the divine love of Dante, and from the fanciful tenderness of Petrarch, down to sensual and obscene stories and ludicrous collisions, while heroism and bravery are screwed up to such a pitch that what is aroused is not so much a credulous astonishment as mere laughter at the fabulousness of the deeds. But along with indifference in regard to the manner in which situations are brought about, we find marvellous ramifications and conflicts introduced, begun, broken off, re-entangled, cross-cut, and finally resolved in a surprising way. In the comic treatment of chivalry, however, Ariosto can safeguard and emphasize what is noble and great in knighthood, courage, love, honour, and bravery just as well as he can depict other passions excellently, e.g. astuteness, cunning, presence of mind, and so much else.

(β) Now while Ariosto leans rather to the fairy-tale side of adventurousness, Cervantes develops the romance side. His Don Quixote is a noble nature in whom chivalry becomes lunacy, because we find his adventurousness inserted into the midst of the stable specific situation of a real world precisely depicted with its external relationships. This provides the comic contradiction between an intelligible self-ordered world and an isolated mind which proposes to create this order and stability solely by himself and by chivalry, whereby it could only be overturned. Despite this comic aberration, however, there is wholly contained in Don Quixote what we previously eulogized in Shakespeare. Cervantes too has made his hero into an originally noble nature, equipped with many-sided spiritual gifts which always truly interest us at the same time. In his lunacy Don Quixote is a heart completely sure of itself and its business, or rather this only is his lunacy that he is and remains so sure of himself and his business. Without this peaceful lack of reflection in regard to the object and outcome of his actions, he would not be genuinely romantic, and this self-assurance, if we look at the substance of his disposition, is throughout great and gifted, adorned with the finest traits of character. Even so, the whole work is on the one hand a mockery of romantic chivalry, genuinely ironical from beginning to end, while in the case of Ariosto the adventurousness remains as it were only a frivolous joke; on the other hand, the adventures of Don Quixote are only the thread on which a row of genuinely romantic tales is strung in the most charming way in order to exhibit as preserved in its true worth what the rest of the romance dissipates comically.

(γ) Just as here we see chivalry turning into the comic even in its most important interests, Shakespeare too either places comic figures and scenes alongside his firm individual characters and tragic situations and conflicts, or else by a profound humour lifts these characters away above themselves and their crude, restricted, and false aims. For example, Falstaff, the Fool in *Lear*, the Musicians' scene in *Romeo and Juliet* [IV, v] are examples of the first kind, Richard III of the second.

(c) Romantic Fiction

This dissolution of the romantic, in the form of the romantic hitherto considered, closes, thirdly and finally, with romance in the modern sense of the word which the knightly and pastoral romances precede in time. This romantic fiction is chivalry become serious again, with a real subject-matter. The contingency of external existence has been transformed into a firm and secure order of civil society and the state, so that police,[1] law-courts, the army, political government replace the chimerical ends which the knights errant set before themselves. Thereby the knight-errantry of the heroes as they act in more modern romances is also altered. As individuals with their subjective ends of love, honour, and ambition, or with their ideals of world-reform, they stand opposed to this substantial order and the prose of actuality which puts difficulties in their way on all sides. Therefore, in this opposition,

---

¹ In Hegel's day this word had a much wider sense than it has now. P. Colquhoun, *Treatise on the Police of the Metropolis* (1795), has virtually nothing to say about 'police' in the modern sense. At that date the word meant 'the whole system of public regulations and agencies for the preservation of the morals, order, and comfort of civil society' (N. Gash, *Mr. Secretary Peel*, London, 1961, p. 311).

subjective wishes and demands are screwed up to immeasurable heights; for each man finds before him an enchanted and quite alien world which he must fight because it obstructs him and in its inflexible firmness does not give way to his passions but interposes as a hindrance the will of a father or an aunt and civil relationships, etc. Young people especially are these modern knights who must force their way through the course of the world which realizes itself instead of their ideals, and they regard it as a misfortune that there is any family, civil society, state, laws, professional business, etc., because these substantive relations of life with their barriers cruelly oppose the ideals and the infinite rights of the heart. Now the thing is to breach this order of things, to change the world, to improve it, or at least in spite of it to carve out of it a heaven upon earth: to seek for the ideal girl, find her, win her away from her wicked relations or other discordant ties, and carry her off in defiance.[1] But in the modern world these fights are nothing more than 'apprenticeship', the education of the individual into the realities of the present, and thereby they acquire their true significance. For the end of such apprenticeship consists in this, that the subject sows his wild oats, builds himself with his wishes and opinions into harmony with subsisting relationships and their rationality, enters the concatenation of the world, and acquires for himself an appropriate attitude to it. However much he may have quarrelled with the world, or been pushed about in it, in most cases at last he gets his girl and some sort of position, marries her, and becomes as good a Philistine as others. The woman takes charge of household management, children arrive, the adored wife, at first unique, an angel, behaves pretty much as all other wives do; the man's profession provides work and vexations, marriage brings domestic affliction—so here we have all the headaches of the rest of married folk.—We see here the like character of adventurousness except that now it finds its right significance, wherein the fantastic element must experience the necessary corrective.

3. Dissolution of the Romantic Form of Art

The last matter with which we now still have to deal in more detail is the point at which romanticism, already *implicitly* the

---

[1] This passage elucidates Hegel's sarcastic remark above (p. 571) about the popularity of the Middle Ages in his day. 'Apprenticeship' is an obvious allusion to Goethe's *Wilhelm Meisters Lehrjahre*.

principle of the dissolution of the classical ideal, now makes this dissolution appear clearly in fact as dissolution.

Now here above all there at once comes into consideration the complete contingency and externality of the material which artistic activity grasps and shapes. In the plastic figures of classical art the subjective inner element is so related to the external one that this external is the very own shape of the inner itself and is not released therefrom into independence. In romantic art, on the contrary, where inwardness withdraws itself into itself, the entire material of the external world acquires freedom to go its own way and maintain itself according to its own special and particular character. Conversely, if subjective inwardness of heart becomes the essential feature to be represented, the question of which specific material of external actuality and the spiritual world is to be an embodiment of the heart is equally a matter of accident. For this reason the romantic inwardness can display itself in *all* circumstances, and move relentlessly from one thing to another in innumerable situations, states of affairs, relations, errors, and confusions, conflicts and satisfactions, for what is sought and is to count is only its own inner subjective formation, the spirit's expression and mode of receptivity, and not an objective and absolutely valid subject-matter. In the presentations of romantic art, therefore, everything has a place, every sphere of life, all phenomena, the greatest and the least, the supreme and the trivial, the moral, immoral, and evil; and, in particular, the more art becomes secular, the more it makes itself at home in the finite things of the world, is satisfied with them, and grants them complete validity, and the artist does well when he portrays them as they are. So, for example, because in Shakespeare's plays actions as a rule run their course in the most limited connection with others, for they are isolated and broken up into a series of accidents and every situation has its own importance, we see alongside the loftiest regions and most important interests the most insignificant and incidental ones: as, in *Hamlet*, the sentries alongside the King's Court; in *Romeo and Juliet*, the domestics; apart from this, in other pieces there are fools, louts, all sorts of everyday vulgarities, taverns, carters, chamber-pots, and fleas, just precisely, as in the religious sphere of romantic art, in the case of the birth of Christ and the Adoration of the Kings, oxen and asses, the manger and straw must not be left out. And it is the same throughout, so that even in art the saying is fulfilled that 'They that humble themselves, the same shall be exalted'.[1]

Within this contingency of the objects which come to be portrayed partly as a mere environment for an inherently more important subject-matter, but partly also as independent on their own account, there is presented the collapse of romantic art, which we have already touched on above. On one side, in other words, there stands the real world in, from the point of view of the ideal, its prosaic *objectivity*: the contents of ordinary daily life which is not apprehended in its substance (in which it has an element of the ethical and divine), but in its mutability and finite transitoriness. On the other side, it is the *subjectivity* of the artist which, with its feeling and insight, with the right and power of its wit, can rise to mastery of the whole of reality; it leaves nothing in its usual context and in the validity which it has for our usual way of looking at things; and it is satisfied only because everything drawn into this sphere proves to be inherently dissoluble owing to the shape and standing given to it by its subjective opinion, mood, and originality; and for contemplation and feeling it *is* dissolved.

We have therefore in this connection to speak *first* of the principle of those numerous works of art whose mode of portraying common life and external reality approaches what we are accustomed to call the imitation of nature;

secondly, of the subjective humour which plays a great role in modern art and provides, especially for many poets, the fundamental type of their works;

thirdly, in conclusion, what still remains to us is only to indicate the standpoint from which art can pursue its activity even in these days.

(a) The Subjective Artistic Imitation of the Existent Present

The group of topics which this sphere can comprise widens indefinitely because art takes for its subject-matter not the inherently necessary, the province of which is complete in itself, but contingent reality in its boundless modification of shapes and relationships, i.e. nature and its variegated play of separate products, man's daily active pursuits in his natural necessities and comfortable satisfaction, in his casual habits and situations, in the activities of family life and civil society business, but, in

[1] Hegel's memory of Matt. 23: 12.

short, the incalculable mutability of the external objective world. Thereby art becomes not only what romantic art is more or less throughout, i.e. portrait-like, but it completely dissolves into the presentation of a portrait, whether in plastic art, painting, or descriptive poetry; and it reverts to the imitation of nature, i.e. to an intentional approach to the contingency of immediate existence which, taken by itself, is unbeautiful and prosaic.

Therefore the question soon arises whether such productions in general are still to be called works of art. If in considering them we keep before our eyes the essential nature of works of art proper (i.e. of the Ideal), where the important thing is both a subject-matter not inherently arbitrary and transient and also a mode of portrayal fully in correspondence with such a subject-matter, then in the face of works of that kind the art-products of the stage we are now considering must undoubtedly fall far short. On the other hand, art has still another feature which is here essentially of special importance: the artist's subjective conception and execution of the work of art, the aspect of the individual talent which can remain faithful both to the manifestations of spirit and also to the inherently substantial life of nature, even in the extreme limits of the contingency which that life reaches, and can make significant even what is in itself without significance, and this it does through this fidelity and through the most marvellous skill of the portrayal. Then in addition there is the subjective vivacity with which the artist with his spirit and heart breathes life entirely into the existence of such topics according to their whole inner and outer shape and appearance, and presents them to our vision in this animation. In view of these aspects we may not deny the name of works of art to the creations of this sphere.

In more detail, amongst the particular arts it is poetry and painting especially which have applied themselves to such topics. For on the one hand it is what is essentially a particular emotion that provides the content; on the other hand, the form of the presentation is to be external appearance in its own character, contingent but in its own sphere genuine. Neither architecture nor sculpture nor music is qualified to fulfil such a task.

(α) In poetry, common domestic life, which has the honesty, worldly wisdom, and morality of its day as its substance, is portrayed in the complications of ordinary civil life, in scenes and figures drawn from the middle and lower classes. In the case of the

French, it is Diderot[1] especially who has insisted in this sense on naturalness and the imitation of the present. Amongst our Germans, on the contrary, it was Goethe and Schiller who, in a higher sense, took a similar road in their youth, but within this living naturalness with its particular details they sought a deeper content and essential conflicts full of interest; while at that time Kotzebue and Iffland,[2] the one with superficial swiftness of conception and production, the other with more serious precision and commonplace bourgeois morality, counterfeited the daily life of their time in prosaic rather narrow respects with little sense for true poetry. But in general our art has adopted this tone as its greatest favourite, even if most recently, and reached a measure of virtuosity in it. For art, long since until now, was something more or less strange to us, borrowed and not our own creation. Now this turning to the reality confronting the artist implies that the material for art requires to be immanent, indigenous, the national life of the poet and the public. When art began to appropriate this material and when purely in subject-matter and presentation it was to be our own and at home with us even at the sacrifice of beauty and the ideal, the urge which led to such representations was let loose. Other nations have rather despised such things or are only now coming to a livelier interest in such materials drawn from what exists today and every day.

(β) Yet if we wish to bring to our notice the most marvellous thing that can be achieved in this connection, we must look at the genre painting of the later Dutch painters. What, in its general spirit, is the substantial basis out of which it issued, is a matter on which I touched above in the consideration of the Ideal as such [on pp. 168–9]. Satisfaction in present-day life, even in the commonest and smallest things, flows in the Dutch from the fact that what nature affords directly to other nations, they have had to acquire by hard struggles and bitter industry, and, circumscribed in their locality, they have become great in their care and esteem of the most insignificant things. On the other hand, they are a nation of fishermen, sailors, burghers, and peasants and therefore from the start they have attended to the value of what is necessary and useful in the greatest and smallest things, and this

---

[1] See his *Essay on Painting* (1765, published 1796). It was translated by Goethe, but with severe critical comments.
[2] A. W., 1759–1814.

they can procure with the most assiduous industry. In religion the Dutch were Protestants, an important matter, and to Protestantism alone the important thing is to get a sure footing in the prose of life, to make it absolutely valid in itself independently of religious associations, and to let it develop in unrestricted freedom. To no other people, under its different circumstances, would it occur to make into the principal burden of its works of art subjects like those confronting us in Dutch painting. But in all their interests the Dutch have not lived at all in the distress and poverty of existence and oppression of spirit; on the contrary, they have reformed their Church themselves, conquered religious despotism as well as the Spanish temporal power and its grandeur, and through their activity, industry, bravery, and frugality they have attained, in their sense of a self-wrought freedom, a well-being, comfort, honesty, spirit, gaiety, and even a pride in a cheerful daily life. This is the justification for their choice of subjects to paint.

A deeper sense arising from an inherently true subject-matter cannot be satisfied by subjects like these; but if heart and thought remain dissatisfied, closer inspection reconciles us to them. For the art of painting and of the painter is what we should be delighted and carried away by. And in fact if we want to know what painting is we must examine these little pictures in order to say of this or that master: *He* can paint. Therefore it is not at all the painter's business, as may be supposed, to give us through his work of art an idea of the subject that he brings before us. Of grapes, flowers, stags, trees, sandhills, the sea, the sun, the sky, the finery and decoration of the furnishings of daily life, of horses, warriors, peasants, smoking, teeth-extraction, domestic scenes of the most varied kind, of all these we have the most complete vision in advance; the world provides us with plenty of things like this. What should enchant us is not the subject of the painting and its lifelikeness, but the pure appearance which is wholly without the sort of interest that the subject has. The one thing certain about beauty is, as it were, appearance for its own sake, and art is mastery in the portrayal of all the secrets of this ever profounder pure appearance of external realities. Especially does art consist in heeding with a sharp eye the momentary and ever changing traits of the present world in the details of its life, which yet harmonize with the universal laws of aesthetic appearance, and always faithfully and truly keeping hold of what is most fleeting. A tree, or a landscape, is something already fixed, independent and permanent. But the lustre of metal, the shimmer of a bunch of grapes by candlelight, a vanishing glimpse of the moon or the sun, a smile, the expression of a swiftly passing emotion, ludicrous movements, postures, facial expressions—to grasp this most transitory and fugitive material, and to give it permanence for our contemplation in the fulness of its life, is the hard task of art at this stage. While classical art essentially gave shape in its ideal figures only to what is substantial, here we have, riveted and brought before our eyes, changing nature in its fleeting expressions, a burn, a waterfall, the foaming waves of the ocean, still-life with casual flashes of glass, cutlery, etc., the external shape of spiritual reality in the most detailed situations, a woman threading a needle by candlelight, a halt of robbers in a casual foray, the most momentary aspect of a look which quickly changes again, the laughing and jeering of a peasant; in all this Ostade, Teniers, and Steen are masters.[1] It is a triumph of art over the transitory, a triumph in which the substantial is as it were cheated of its power over the contingent and the fleeting.

While here it is just the pure appearance of the things depicted that provides the true subject of the picture, art goes still further by making the fugitive appearance stationary. In other words, apart from the things depicted, the means of the portrayal also becomes an end in itself, so that the artist's subjective skill and his application of the means of artistic production are raised to the status of an objective matter in works of art. The older Dutch painters made a most thorough study of the physical effects of colour; van Eyck, Hemling, and Scorel[2] could imitate in a most deceptive way the sheen of gold and silver, the lustre of jewels, silk, velvet, furs, etc. This mastery in the production of the most striking effects through the magic of colour and the secrets of its spell has now an independent justification. While the spirit reproduces itself in thinking, in comprehending the world in ideas and thoughts, the chief thing now—independently of the topic itself— is the subjective re-creation of the external world in the visible element of colours and lighting. This is as it were an objective

[1] A. van Ostade, 1610–85. D. Teniers, 1610–90. J. Steen, 1626–79.
[2] For 'Hemling' read Memling'. J. van Eyck, 1370–1441. H. Memling, 1433–94. J. van Scorel, 1495–1562.

music, a peal in colour. In other words, just as in music the single note is nothing by itself but produces its effect only in its relation to another, in its counterpoint, concord, modulation, and harmony, so here it is just the same with colour. If we look closely at the play of colour, which glints like gold and glitters like braid under the light, we see perhaps only white or yellow strokes, points of colour, coloured surfaces; the single colour as such does not have this gleam which it produces; it is the juxtaposition *alone* which makes this glistening and gleaming. If we take, e.g., Terburg's[1] satin, each spot of colour by itself is a subdued gray, more or less whitish, bluish, yellowish, but when it is looked at from a certain distance there comes out through its position beside another colour the beautiful soft sheen proper to actual satin. And so it is with velvet, the play of light, cloud vapour, and, in general, with everything depicted. It is not the reflex of the heart which wishes to display itself in subjects such as these, as it often does in the case of a landscape, for example; on the contrary, it is the entire subjective skill of the artist which, as skill in using the means of production vividly and effectively in this objective way, displays its ability by its own efforts to generate an objective world.

(γ) But therefore interest in the objects depicted is inverted, so that it is the stark subjectivity of the artist himself which intends to display itself and to which what matters is not the forming of a finished and self-subsistent work, but a production in which the productive artist himself lets us see himself alone. When this subjectivity of the artist no longer infects the external means of representation only, but the subject-matter itself, art thereby becomes the art of caprice and humour.

(b) *Subjective Humour*

In humour it is the person of the artist which comes on the scene in both its superficial and deeper aspects, so that what is at issue there is essentially the spiritual worth of his personality.

(α) Now humour is not set the task of developing and shaping a topic objectively and in a way appropriate to the essential nature of the topic, and, in this development, using its own means to articulate the topic and round it off artistically; on the contrary, it is the artist himself who enters the material, with the result that his chief activity, by the power of subjective notions, flashes

---

[1] G. Terborch, 1617–81. Not his 'Atlas', as Osmaston has it.

of thought, striking modes of interpretation, consists in destroying and dissolving everything that proposes to make itself objective and win a firm shape for itself in reality, or that seems to have such a shape already in the external world. Therefore every independence of an objective *content* along with the inherently fixed connection of the *form* (given as that is by the subject-matter) is annihilated in itself, and the presentation is only a sporting with the topics, a derangement and perversion of the material, and a rambling to and fro, a criss-cross movement of subjective expressions, views, and attitudes whereby the author sacrifices himself and his topics alike.

(β) The natural error in this connection is to suppose that it is very easy to make jests and to be funny about oneself and everything available, and that this is why the form of the humorous is commonly snatched at; but it happens equally commonly that the humour becomes flat if the author lets himself go in the field of the contingency of his notions and pleasantries which, strung loosely together, deviate into indefiniteness, and, often with deliberate bizarrerie, conjoin the most heterogeneous things. Some nations are more indulgent to this sort of humour, others are more severe. In the case of the French, the humorous in general meets with little success, in our case with more, and we are more tolerant of aberrations. So with us Jean Paul, e.g., is a favourite humourist, and yet he is astonishing, beyond everyone else, precisely in the baroque mustering of things objectively furthest removed from one another and in the most confused disorderly jumbling of topics related only in his own subjective imagination. The story, the subject-matter and course of events in his novels, is what is of the least interest. The main thing remains the hither and thither course of the humour which uses every topic only to emphasize the subjective wit of the author. In thus drawing together and concatenating material raked up from the four corners of the earth and every sphere of reality, humour turns back, as it were, to symbolism where meaning and shape likewise lie apart from one another, except that now it is the mere subjective activity of the poet which commands material and meaning alike and strings them together in an order alien to them. But such a string of notions soon wearies us, especially if we are expected to acclimatize ourselves and our ideas to the often scarcely guessable combinations which have casually floated before the poet's mind. Especially in the case of

Jean Paul one metaphor, one witticism, one joke, one simile, kills the other; we see nothing develop, everything just explodes. But what is to be resolved in a denouement must previously have been unfolded in a plot and prepared in advance. On the other side, if the artist himself is devoid of the core and support of a mind filled with genuine objectivity, humour readily slips into what is namby-pamby and sentimental, and of this too Jean Paul provides an example.

(γ) True humour which wishes to hold aloof from these outgrowths therefore requires great depth and wealth of spirit in order to raise the purely subjective appearance into what is actually expressive, and to make what is substantial emerge out of contingency, out of mere notions. The self-pursuit of the author in the course of his expressions must, as is the case with Sterne and Hippel, be an entirely naïve, light, unostentatious jogging along which in its triviality affords precisely the supreme idea of depth; and since here there are just individual details which gush forth without any order, their inner connection must lie all the deeper and send forth the ray of the spirit in their disconnectedness as such.

Herewith we have arrived at the end of romantic art, at the standpoint of most recent times, the peculiarity of which we may find in the fact that the artist's subjective skill surmounts his material and its production because he is no longer dominated by the given conditions of a range of content and form already inherently determined in advance, but retains entirely within his own power and choice both the subject-matter and the way of presenting it.

(c) The End of the Romantic Form of Art

Art, as it has been under our consideration hitherto, had as its basis the unity of meaning and shape and so the unity of the artist's subjective activity with his topic and work. Looked at more closely, it was the specific kind of this unification [at each stage] which provided, for the content and its corresponding portrayal, the substantial norm penetrating all artistic productions.

In this matter we found at the beginning of art, in the East, that the spirit was not yet itself explicitly free; it still sought for its Absolute in nature and therefore interpreted nature as in itself divine. Later on, the vision of classical art represented the Greek gods as naïve and inspired, yet even so essentially as individuals burdened with the natural human form as with an *affirmative* feature. Romantic art for the first time deepened the spirit in its own inwardness, in contrast to which the flesh, external reality, and the world in general was at first posited as *negative*, even though the spirit and the Absolute had to appear in this element alone; yet at last this element could be given validity for itself again in a more and more positive way.

(α) These ways of viewing the world constitute religion, the substantial spirit of peoples and ages, and are woven into, not art alone, but all the other spheres of the living present at all periods. Now just as every man is a child of his time in every activity, whether political, religious, or scientific, and just as he has the task of bringing out the essential content and the therefore necessary form of that time, so it is the vocation of art to find for the spirit of a people the artistic expression corresponding to it. Now so long as the artist is bound up with the specific character of such a world-view and religion, in immediate identity with it and with firm faith in it, so long is he genuinely in earnest with this material and its representation; i.e. this material remains for him the infinite and true element in his own consciousness—a material with which he lives in an original unity as part of his inmost self, while the form in which he exhibits it is for him as artist the final, necessary, and supreme manner of bringing before our contemplation the Absolute and the soul of objects in general. By the substance of his material, a substance immanent in himself, he is tied down to the specific mode of its exposition. For in that case the material, and therefore the form belonging to it, the artist carries immediately in himself as the proper essence of his existence which he does not imagine for himself but which he *is*; and therefore he only has the task of making this truly essential element objective to himself, to present and develop it in a living way out of his own resources. Only in that event is the artist completely inspired by his material and its presentation; and his inventions are no product of caprice, they originate in him, out of him, out of this substantial ground, this stock, the content of which is not at rest until through the artist it acquires an individual shape adequate to its inner essence. If, on the other hand, we nowadays propose to make the subject of a statue or a painting a Greek god, or, Protestants as we are today, the Virgin Mary, we are not seriously in earnest with this material.

It is the innermost faith which we lack here, even if the artist in days when faith was still unimpaired did not exactly need to be what is generally called a pious man, for after all in every age artists have not as a rule been the most pious of men! The requirement is only this, that for the artist the content [of his work] shall constitute the substance, the inmost truth, of his consciousness and make his chosen mode of presentation necessary. For the artist in his production is at the same time a creature of nature, his skill is a *natural* talent; his work is not the pure activity of comprehension which confronts its material entirely and unites itself with it in free thoughts, in pure thinking; on the contrary, the artist, not yet released from his *natural* side, is united *directly* with the subject-matter, believes in it, and is identical with it in accordance with his very own self. The result is then that the artist is entirely absorbed in the object; the work of art proceeds entirely out of the undivided inwardness and force of genius; the production is firm and unwavering, and in it the full intensity [of creation] is preserved. This is the fundamental condition of art's being present in its integrity.

(β) On the other hand, in the position we have been forced to assign to art in the course of its development, the whole situation has altogether altered. This, however, we must not regard as a mere accidental misfortune suffered by art from without owing to the distress of the times, the sense for the prosaic, lack of interest, etc.; on the contrary, it is the effect and the progress of art itself which, by bringing before our vision as an object its own indwelling material, at every step along this road makes its own contribution to freeing art from the content represented. What through art or thinking we have before our physical or spiritual eye as an object has lost all absolute interest for us if it has been put before us so completely that the content is exhausted, that everything is revealed, and nothing obscure or inward is left over any more. For interest is to be found only in the case of lively activity [of mind]. The spirit only occupies itself with objects so long as there is something secret, not revealed, in them. This is the case so long as the material is identical with the substance of our own being. But if the essential world-views implicit in the concept of art, and the range of the content belonging to these, are in every respect revealed by art, then art has got rid of this content which on every occasion was determinate for a particular people, a particular age, and the true need to resume it again is awakened only with the need to turn *against* the content that was alone valid hitherto; thus in Greece Aristophanes rose up against his present world, and Lucian against the whole of the Greek past, and in Italy and Spain, when the Middle Ages were closing, Ariosto and Cervantes began to turn against chivalry.

Now contrasted with the time in which the artist owing to his nationality and his period stands with the substance of his being within a specific world-view and its content and forms of portrayal, we find an altogether opposed view which in its complete development is of importance only in most recent times. In our day, in the case of almost all peoples, criticism, the cultivation of reflection, and, in our German case, freedom of thought have mastered the artists too, and have made them, so to say, a *tabula rasa* in respect of the material and the form of their productions, after the necessary particular stages of the romantic art-form have been traversed. Bondage to a particular subject-matter and a mode of portrayal suitable for this material alone are for artists today something past, and art therefore has become a free instrument which the artist can wield in proportion to his subjective skill in relation to any material of whatever kind. The artist thus stands above specific consecrated forms and configurations and moves freely on his own account, independent of the subject-matter and mode of conception in which the holy and eternal was previously made visible to human apprehension. No content, no form, is any longer immediately identical with the inwardness, the nature, the unconscious substantial essence of the artist; every material may be indifferent to him if only it does not contradict the formal law of being simply beautiful and capable of artistic treatment. Today there is no material which stands in and for itself above this relativity, and even if one matter be raised above it, still there is at least no absolute need for its representation by *art*. Therefore the artist's attitude to his topic is on the whole much the same as the dramatist's who brings on the scene and delineates different characters who are strangers to him. The artist does still put his genius into them, he weaves his web out of his own resources but only out of what is purely universal or quite accidental there, whereas its more detailed individualization is not his. For this purpose he needs his supply of pictures, modes of configuration, earlier forms of art which, taken in themselves, are indifferent to him and only become important if they seem to him to be those most suitable for precisely this or that material. Moreover, in most arts, especially the visual arts, the topic comes to the artist from the outside; he works to a commission, and in the case of sacred or profane stories, or scenes, portraits, ecclesiastical buildings, etc., he has only to see what he can make of his commission. For, however much he puts his heart into the given topic, that topic yet always remains to him a material which is not in itself directly the substance of his own consciousness. It is therefore no help to him to adopt again, as that substance, so to say, past world-views, i.e. to propose to root himself firmly in one of these ways of looking at things, e.g. to turn Roman Catholic as in recent times many have done for art's sake in order to give stability to their mind and to give the character of something absolute to the specifically limited character of their artistic product in itself. The artist need not be forced first to settle his accounts with his mind or to worry about the salvation of his own soul. From the very beginning, before he embarks on production, his great and free soul must know and possess its own ground, must be sure of itself and confident in itself. The great artist today needs in particular the free development of the spirit; in that development all superstition, and all faith which remains restricted to determinate forms of vision and presentation, is degraded into mere aspects and features. These the free spirit has mastered because he sees in them no absolutely sacrosanct conditions for his exposition and mode of configuration, but ascribes value to them only on the strength of the higher content which in the course of his re-creation he puts into them as adequate to them.

In this way every form and every material is now at the service and command of the artist whose talent and genius is explicitly freed from the earlier limitation to one specific art-form.

(γ) But if in conclusion we ask about the content and the forms which can be considered as *peculiar* to this stage of our inquiry in virtue of its general standpoint, the answer is as follows.

The universal forms of art had a bearing above all on the absolute truth which art attains, and they had the origin of their particular differences in the specific interpretation of what counted for consciousness as absolute and carried in itself the principle for its mode of configuration. In this matter we have seen in symbolic art natural meanings appearing as the *content*, natural things and human personifications as the *form* of the representation; in classical art spiritual individuality, but as a corporeal, not inwardized, present over which there stood the abstract necessity of fate; in romantic art spirituality with the subjectivity immanent therein, for the inwardness of which the external shape remained accidental. In this final art-form too, as in the earlier ones, the Divine is the absolute subject-matter of art. But the Divine had to objectify itself, determine itself, and therefore proceed out of itself into the secular content of subjective personality. At first the infinity of personality lay in honour, love, and fidelity, and then later in particular individuality, in the specific character which coalesced with the particular content of human existence. Finally this cohesion with such a specific limitation of subject-matter was cancelled by humour which could make every determinacy waver and dissolve and therefore made it possible for art to transcend itself. Yet in this self-transcendence art is nevertheless a withdrawal of man into himself, a descent into his own breast, whereby art strips away from itself all fixed restriction to a specific range of content and treatment, and makes *Humanus* its new holy of holies: i.e. the depths and heights of the human heart as such, mankind in its joys and sorrows, its strivings, deeds, and fates. Herewith the artist acquires his subject-matter in himself and is the human spirit actually self-determining and considering, meditating, and expressing the infinity of its feelings and situations: nothing that can be living in the human breast is alien to that spirit any more.[1] This is a subject-matter which does not remain determined artistically in itself and on its own account; on the contrary, the specific character of the topic and its outward formation is left to capricious invention, yet no interest is excluded— for art does not need any longer to represent only what is absolutely at home at one of its specific stages, but everything in which man as such is capable of being at home.

In face of this breadth and variety of material we must above all make the demand that the actual presence of the spirit today shall be displayed at the same time throughout the mode of treating this material. The modern artist, it is true, may associate himself with the classical age and with still more ancient times; to be a follower of Homer, even if the last one, is fine, and productions reflecting

[1] Hegel is obviously alluding to the familiar line of Terence. See p. 46, note.

the medieval veering to romantic art will have their merits too; but the universal validity, depth, and special idiom of some material is one thing, its mode of treatment another. No Homer, Sophocles, etc., no Dante, Ariosto, or Shakespeare can appear in our day; what was so magnificently sung, what so freely expressed, has been expressed; these are materials, ways of looking at them and treating them which have been sung once and for all. Only the present is fresh, the rest is paler and paler.

The French must be reproached on historical grounds, and criticized on the score of beauty, for presenting Greek and Roman heroes, Chinese, and Peruvians, as French princes and princesses and for ascribing to them the motives and views of the time of Louis XIV and XV; yet, if only these motives and views had been deeper and finer in themselves, drawing them into present-day works of art would not be exactly bad. On the contrary, all materials, whatever they be and from whatever period and nation they come, acquire their artistic truth only when imbued with living and contemporary interest. It is in this interest that artistic truth fills man's breast, provides his own mirror-image, and brings truth home to our feelings and imagination. It is the appearance and activity of imperishable humanity in its many-sided significance and endless all-round development which in this reservoir of human situations and feelings can now constitute the absolute content of our art.

If after thus determining in a general way the subject-matter peculiar to this stage, we now look back at what we have considered in conclusion as the forms of the dissolution of romantic art, we have stressed principally how art falls to pieces, on the one hand, into the imitation of external objectivity in all its contingent shapes; on the other hand, however, into the liberation of subjectivity, in accordance with its inner contingency, in humour. Now, finally, still within the material indicated above, we may draw attention to a coalescence of these extremes of romantic art. In other words, just as in the advance from symbolic to classical art we considered the transitional forms of image, simile, epigram, etc., so here in romantic art we have to make mention of a similar transitional form. In those earlier modes of treatment the chief thing was that inner meaning and external shape fell apart from one another, a cleavage partly superseded by the subjective activity of the artist and converted, particularly in epigram, so far as possible into an identification.

Now romantic art was from the beginning the deeper disunion of the inwardness which was finding its satisfaction in itself and which, since objectivity does not completely correspond with the spirit's inward being, remained broken or indifferent to the objective world. In the course of romantic art this opposition developed up to the point at which we had to arrive at an exclusive interest, either in contingent externality or in equally contingent subjectivity. But if this satisfaction in externality or in the subjective portrayal is intensified, according to the principle of romantic art, into the heart's deeper immersion in the object, and if, on the other hand, what matters to humour is the object and its configuration within its subjective reflex, then we acquire thereby a growing intimacy with the object, a sort of *objective* humour. Yet such an intimacy can only be partial and can perhaps be expressed only within the compass of a song or only as part of a greater whole. For if it were extended and carried through within objectivity, it would necessarily become action and event and an objective presentation of these. But what we may regard as necessary here is rather a sensitive abandonment of the heart in the object, which is indeed unfolded but remains a *subjective* spirited movement of imagination and the heart—a fugitive notion, but one which is not purely accidental and capricious but an inner movement of the spirit devoted entirely to its object and retaining it as its content and interest.

In this connection we may contrast such final blossomings of art with the old Greek epigram in which this form appeared in its first and simplest shape. The form meant here displays itself only when to talk of the object is not just to name it, not an inscription or epigraph which merely says in general terms what the object is, but only when there are added a deep feeling, a felicitous witticism, an ingenious reflection, and an intelligent movement of imagination which vivify and expand the smallest detail through the way that poetry treats it. But such poems to or about something, a tree, a mill-lade, the spring, etc., about things animate or inanimate, may be of quite endless variety and arise in any nation, yet they remain of a subordinate kind and, in general, readily become lame. For especially when reflection and speech have been developed, anyone may be struck in connection with most objects and circumstances by some fancy or other which he now has skill enough to express, just as anyone is good at writing a letter. With such a general sing-song, often repeated even if with new nuances, we soon become bored. Therefore at this stage what is especially at stake is that the heart, with its depth of feeling, and the spirit and a rich consciousness shall be entirely absorbed in the circumstances, situation, etc., tarry there, and so make out of the object something new, beautiful, and intrinsically valuable.

A brilliant example of this, even for the present and for the subjective spiritual depth of today, is afforded especially by the Persians and Arabs in the eastern splendour of their images, in the free bliss of their imagination which deals with its objects entirely contemplatively. The Spaniards and Italians too have done excellent work of this kind. Klopstock does say[1] of Petrarch: 'Petrarch sang songs of his Laura, beautiful to their admirer, but to the lover—nothing.' Yet Klopstock's love-poems are full only of moral reflections, pitiable longing, and strained passion for the happiness of immortality—whereas in Petrarch we admire the freedom of the inherently ennobled feeling which, however much it expresses desire for the beloved, is still satisfied in itself. For the desire, the passion, cannot be missing in the sphere of these subjects, provided it be confined to wine and love, the tavern and the glass, just as, after all, the Persian pictures are of extreme voluptuousness. But in its subjective interest imagination here removes the object altogether from the scope of practical desire; it has an interest only in this imaginative occupation, which is satisfied in the freest way with its hundreds of changing turns of phrase and conceits, and plays in the most ingenious manner with joy and sorrow alike. Amongst modern poets those chiefly possessed of this equally ingenious freedom of imagination, but also of its subjectively more heartfelt depth, are Rückert, and Goethe in his *West-östliche Divan*. Goethe's poems in the *Divan* are particularly and essentially different from his earlier ones. In *Willkommen und Abschied* [Welcome and Farewell], e.g., the language and the depiction are beautiful indeed, and the feeling is heartfelt, but otherwise the situation is quite ordinary, the conclusion trivial, and imagination and its freedom has added nothing further. Totally different is the poem called *Wiederfinden* [Meeting again] in the *Divan*. Here love is transferred wholly into the imagination, its movement, happiness, and bliss. In general, in similar productions of this kind we have before us no subjective

[1] In *Die künftige Geliebte* (The Future Sweetheart), 1747.

longing, no being in love, no desire, but a pure delight in the topics, an inexhaustible self-yielding of imagination, a harmless play, a freedom in toying alike with rhyme and ingenious metres— and, with all this, a depth of feeling and a cheerfulness of the inwardly self-moving heart which through the serenity of the outward shape lift the soul high above all painful entanglement in the restrictions of the real world.

With this we may close our consideration of the particular forms into which the ideal of art has been spread in the course of its development. I have made these forms the subject of a rather extensive investigation in order to exhibit the content out of which too their mode of portrayal has been derived. For it is the content which, as in all human work, so also in art is decisive. In accordance with its essential nature, art has nothing else for its function but to set forth in an adequate sensuous present what is itself inherently rich in content, and the philosophy of art must make it its chief task to comprehend in thought what this fullness of content and its beautiful mode of appearance are.